THE LOEB CLASSICAL LIBRARY

4

THE LOEB CLASSICAL LIBRARY

OVID: THE ART OF LOVE AND OTHER POEMS. J. H. Mozley.

OVID: FASTI. Sir James G. Frazer.

OVID: HEROIDES AND AMORES. Grant Showerman.

OVID: METAMORPHOSES. F. J. Miller. 2 Vols.

OVID: TRISTIA AND EX PONTO. A. L. Wheeler.

PETRONIUS. M. Heseltine; SENECA: APOCOLOCYNTOSIS. W. H. D. Rouse.

PHAEDRUS AND BABRIUS (Greek). B. E. Perry.

PLAUTUS. Paul Nixon. 5 Vols.

PLINY: LETTERS, PANEGYRICUS. B. Radice. 2 Vols.

PLINY: NATURAL HISTORY. 10 Vols. Vols. I-V and IX. H. Rackham. Vols. VI-VIII. W. H. S. Jones. Vol. X. D. E. Eichholz.

PROPERTIUS. H. E. Butler.

PRUDENTIUS. H. J. Thomson. 2 Vols.

QUINTILIAN. H. E. Butler. 4 Vols.

REMAINS OF OLD LATIN. E. H. Warmington. 4 Vols. Vol. I (Ennius and Caecilius). Vol. II (Livius, Naevius, Pacuvius, Accius). Vol. III (Lucilius, Laws of the XII Tables). Vol. IV (Archaic Inscriptions).

SALLUST. J. C. Rolfe.

SCRIPTORES HISTORIAE AUGUSTAE. D. Magie. 3 Vols.

SENECA: APOCOLOCYNTOSIS. *Cf.* PETRONIUS.

SENECA: EPISTULAE MORALES. R. M. Gummere. 3 Vols.

SENECA: MORAL ESSAYS. J. W. Basore. 3 Vols.

SENECA: TRAGEDIES. F. J. Miller. 2 Vols.

SIDONIUS: POEMS AND LETTERS. W. B. Anderson. 2 Vols.

SILIUS ITALICUS. J. D. Duff. 2 Vols.

STATIUS. J. H. Mozley. 2 Vols.

SUETONIUS. J. C. Rolfe. 2 Vols.

TACITUS: AGRICOLA AND GERMANIA. Maurice Hutton; DIALOGUS. Sir Wm. Peterson.

TACITUS: HISTORIES AND ANNALS. C. H. Moore and J. Jackson. 4 Vols.

TERENCE. John Sargeaunt. 2 Vols.

TERTULLIAN: APOLOGIA AND DE SPECTACULIS. T. R. Glover; MINUCIUS FELIX. G. H. Rendall.

VALERIUS FLACCUS. J. H. Mozley.

VARRO: DE LINGUA LATINA. R. G. Kent. 2 Vols.

VELLEIUS PATERCULUS AND RES GESTAE DIVI AUGUSTI. F. W. Shipley.

VIRGIL. H. R. Fairclough. 2 Vols.

VITRUVIUS: DE ARCHITECTURA. F. Granger. 2 Vols.

THE LOEB CLASSICAL LIBRARY

CICERO : DE SENECTUTE, DE AMICITIA, DE DIVINATIONE. W. A. Falconer.
CICERO : IN CATILINAM, PRO MURENA, PRO SULLA, PRO FLACCO. Louis E. Lord.
CICERO : LETTERS TO ATTICUS. E. O. Winstedt. 3 Vols.
CICERO : LETTERS TO HIS FRIENDS. W. Glynn Williams. 3 Vols.
CICERO : PHILIPPICS. W. C. A. Ker.
CICERO : PRO ARCHIA, POST REDITUM, DE DOMO, DE HARUSPICUM RESPONSIS, PRO PLANCIO. N. H. Watts.
CICERO : PRO CAECINA, PRO LEGE MANILIA, PRO CLUENTIO, PRO RABIRIO. H. Grose Hodge.
CICERO : PRO CAELIO, DE PROVINCIIS CONSULARIBUS, PRO BALBO. R. Gardner.
CICERO : PRO MILONE, IN PISONEM, PRO SCAURO, PRO FONTEIO, PRO RABIRIO POSTUMO, PRO MARCELLO, PRO LIGARIO, PRO REGE DEIOTARO. N. H. Watts.
CICERO : PRO QUINCTIO, PRO ROSCIO AMERINO, PRO ROSCIO COMOEDO, CONTRA RULLUM. J. H. Freese.
CICERO : PRO SESTIO, IN VATINIUM. R. Gardner.
[CICERO] : RHETORICA AD HERENNIUM. H. Caplan.
CICERO : TUSCULAN DISPUTATIONS. J. E. King.
CICERO : VERRINE ORATIONS. L. H. G. Greenwood. 2 Vols.
CLAUDIAN. M. Platnauer. 2 Vols.
COLUMELLA : DE RE RUSTICA, DE ARBORIBUS. H. B. Ash, E. S. Forster, E. Heffner. 3 Vols.
CURTIUS, Q.: HISTORY OF ALEXANDER. J. C. Rolfe. 2 Vols.
FLORUS. E. S. Forster ; and CORNELIUS NEPOS. J. C. Rolfe.
FRONTINUS : STRATAGEMS AND AQUEDUCTS. C. E. Bennett and M. B. McElwain.
FRONTO : CORRESPONDENCE. C. R. Haines. 2 Vols.
GELLIUS. J. C. Rolfe. 3 Vols.
HORACE : ODES AND EPODES. C. E. Bennett.
HORACE : SATIRES, EPISTLES, ARS POETICA. H. R. Fairclough.
JEROME : SELECT LETTERS. F. A. Wright.
JUVENAL AND PERSIUS. G. G. Ramsay.
LIVY. B. O. Foster, F. G. Moore, Evan T. Sage, A. C. Schlesinger and R. M. Geer (General Index). 14 Vols.
LUCAN. J. D. Duff.
LUCRETIUS. W. H. D. Rouse.
MARTIAL. W. C. A. Ker. 2 Vols.
MINOR LATIN POETS : from PUBLILIUS SYRUS to RUTILIUS NAMATIANUS, including GRATTIUS, CALPURNIUS SICULUS, NEMESIANUS, AVIANUS, with " Aetna," " Phoenix " and other poems. J. Wight Duff and Arnold M. Duff.

THE LOEB CLASSICAL LIBRARY

VOLUMES ALREADY PUBLISHED

1

THE LOEB CLASSICAL LIBRARY

PROCOPIUS: HISTORY OF THE WARS. H. B. Dewing. 7 Vols.
PTOLEMY: TETRABIBLOS. *Cf.* MANETHO.
QUINTUS SMYRAENUS. A. S. Way. Verse trans.
SEXTUS EMPIRICUS. Rev. R. G. Bury. 4 Vols.
SOPHOCLES. F. Storr. 2 Vols. Verse trans.
STRABO: GEOGRAPHY. Horace L. Jones. 8 Vols.
THEOPHRASTUS: CHARACTERS. J. M. Edmonds; HERODES, etc. A. D. Knox.
THEOPHRASTUS: ENQUIRY INTO PLANTS. Sir Arthur Hort. 2 Vols.
THUCYDIDES. C. F. Smith. 4 Vols.
TRYPHIODORUS. *Cf.* OPPIAN.
XENOPHON: ANABASIS. C. L. Brownson.
XENOPHON: CYROPAEDIA. Walter Miller. 2 Vols.
XENOPHON: HELLENICA. C. L. Brownson.
XENOPHON: MEMORABILIA AND OECONOMICUS. E. C. Marchant. SYMPOSIUM AND APOLOGY. O. J. Todd.
XENOPHON: SCRIPTA MINORA. E. C. Marchant and G. W. Bowersock.

VOLUMES IN PREPARATION

GREEK AUTHORS

ARISTIDES: ORATIONS. C. A. Behr.
MUSAEUS: HERO AND LEANDER. T. Gelzer and C. H. Whitman.
THEOPHRASTUS: DE CAUSIS PLANTARUM. G. K. K. Link and B. Einarson.

LATIN AUTHORS

ASCONIUS: COMMENTARIES ON CICERO'S ORATIONS. G. W. Bowersock.
BENEDICT: THE RULE. P. Meyvaert.
JUSTIN-TROGUS. R. Moss.
MANILIUS. G. P. Goold.

DESCRIPTIVE PROSPECTUS ON APPLICATION

CAMBRIDGE, MASS.   LONDON
HARVARD UNIV. PRESS   WILLIAM HEINEMANN LTD

THE LOEB CLASSICAL LIBRARY

Edgar. 2 Vols. LITERARY SELECTIONS (Poetry). D. L. Page.

PARTHENIUS. *Cf.* LONGUS.

PAUSANIAS: DESCRIPTION OF GREECE. W. H. S. Jones. 5 Vols. and Companion Vol. arranged by R. E. Wycherley.

PHILO. 10 Vols. Vols. I-V. F. H. Colson and Rev. G. H. Whitaker. Vols. VI-X. F. H. Colson. General Index. Rev. J. W. Earp.

Two Supplementary Vols. Translation only from an Armenian Text. Ralph Marcus.

PHILOSTRATUS: THE LIFE OF APOLLONIUS OF TYANA. F. C. Conybeare. 2 Vols.

PHILOSTRATUS: IMAGINES; CALLISTRATUS: DESCRIPTIONS. A. Fairbanks.

PHILOSTRATUS AND EUNAPIUS: LIVES OF THE SOPHISTS. Wilmer Cave Wright.

PINDAR. Sir J. E. Sandys.

PLATO: CHARMIDES, ALCIBIADES, HIPPARCHUS, THE LOVERS, THEAGES, MINOS AND EPINOMIS. W. R. M. Lamb.

PLATO: CRATYLUS, PARMENIDES, GREATER HIPPIAS, LESSER HIPPIAS. H. N. Fowler.

PLATO: EUTHYPHRO, APOLOGY, CRITO, PHAEDO, PHAEDRUS. H. N. Fowler.

PLATO: LACHES, PROTAGORAS, MENO, EUTHYDEMUS. W. R. M. Lamb.

PLATO: LAWS. Rev. R. G. Bury. 2 Vols.

PLATO: LYSIS, SYMPOSIUM, GORGIAS. W. R. M. Lamb.

PLATO: REPUBLIC. Paul Shorey. 2 Vols.

PLATO: STATESMAN, PHILEBUS. H. N. Fowler; ION. W. R. M. Lamb.

PLATO: THEAETETUS AND SOPHIST. H. N. Fowler.

PLATO: TIMAEUS, CRITIAS, CLITOPHO, MENEXENUS, EPISTULAE. Rev. R. G. Bury.

PLOTINUS. A. H. Armstrong. 6 Vols. Vols. I-III.

PLUTARCH: MORALIA. 16 Vols. Vols. I-V. F. C. Babbitt. Vol. VI. W. C. Helmbold. Vol. VII. P. H. De Lacy and B. Einarson. Vol. VIII. P. A. Clement, H. B. Hoffleit. Vol. IX. E. L. Minar, Jr., F. H. Sandbach, W. C. Helmbold. Vol. X. H. N. Fowler. Vol. XI. L. Pearson, F. H. Sandbach. Vol. XII. H. Cherniss, W. C. Helmbold. Vol. XIV. P. H. De Lacy and B. Einarson. Vol. XV. F. H. Sandbach.

PLUTARCH: THE PARALLEL LIVES. B. Perrin. 11 Vols.

POLYBIUS. W. R. Paton. 6 Vols.

THE LOEB CLASSICAL LIBRARY

EURIPIDES. A. S. Way. 4 Vols. Verse trans.
EUSEBIUS : ECCLESIASTICAL HISTORY. Kirsopp Lake and
J. E. L. Oulton. 2 Vols.
GALEN : ON THE NATURAL FACULTIES. A. J. Brock.
THE GREEK ANTHOLOGY. W. R. Paton. 5 Vols.
THE GREEK BUCOLIC POETS (THEOCRITUS, BION, MOSCHUS).
J. M. Edmonds.
GREEK ELEGY AND IAMBUS WITH THE ANACREONTEA. J. M.
Edmonds. 2 Vols.
GREEK MATHEMATICAL WORKS. Ivor Thomas. 2 Vols.
HERODES. Cf. THEOPHRASTUS : CHARACTERS.
HERODIAN : C. R. Whittaker. 2 Vols. Vol. I.
HERODOTUS. A. D. Godley. 4 Vols.
HESIOD AND THE HOMERIC HYMNS. H. G. Evelyn White.
HIPPOCRATES AND THE FRAGMENTS OF HERACLEITUS. W. H. S.
Jones and E. T. Withington. 4 Vols.
HOMER : ILIAD. A. T. Murray. 2 Vols.
HOMER : ODYSSEY. A. T. Murray. 2 Vols.
ISAEUS. E. S. Forster.
ISOCRATES. George Norlin and LaRue Van Hook. 3 Vols.
[ST. JOHN DAMASCENE]: BARLAAM AND IOASAPH. Rev. G. R.
Woodward, Harold Mattingly and D. M. Lang.
JOSEPHUS. 9 Vols. Vols. I-IV. H. St. J. Thackeray. Vol.
V. H. St. J. Thackeray and Ralph Marcus. Vols. VI
and VII. Ralph Marcus. Vol. VIII. Ralph Marcus and
Allen Wikgren. Vol. IX. L. H. Feldman.
JULIAN. Wilmer Cave Wright. 3 Vols.
LIBANIUS : SELECTED WORKS. A. F. Norman. 3Vols. Vol.I.
LONGUS : DAPHNIS AND CHLOE. Thornley's translation re-
vised by J. M. Edmonds ; and PARTHENIUS. S. Gaselee.
LUCIAN. 8 Vols. Vols. I-V. A. M. Harmon. Vol. VI. K.
Kilburn. Vols. VII and VIII. M. D. Macleod.
LYCOPHRON. Cf. CALLIMACHUS.
LYRA GRAECA. J. M. Edmonds. 3 Vols.
LYSIAS. W. R. M. Lamb.
MANETHO. W. G. Waddell ; PTOLEMY : TETRABIBLOS. F. E.
Robbins.
MARCUS AURELIUS. C. R. Haines.
MENANDER. F. G. Allinson.
MINOR ATTIC ORATORS. 2 Vols. K. J. Maidment and
J. O. Burtt.
NONNOS : DIONYSIACA. W. H. D. Rouse. 3 Vols.
OPPIAN, COLLUTHUS, TRYPHIODORUS. A. W. Mair.
PAPYRI. NON-LITERARY SELECTIONS. A. S. Hunt and C. C.

THE LOEB CLASSICAL LIBRARY

ARISTOTLE: POETICS; LONGINUS ON THE SUBLIME. W. Hamilton Fyfe; DEMETRIUS ON STYLE. W. Rhys Roberts.

ARISTOTLE: POLITICS. H. Rackham.

ARISTOTLE: POSTERIOR ANALYTICS. H. Tredennick; TOPICS. E. S. Forster.

ARISTOTLE: PROBLEMS. W. S. Hett. 2 Vols.

ARISTOTLE: RHETORICA AD ALEXANDRUM. H. Rackham. (With PROBLEMS, Vol. II.)

ARISTOTLE: SOPHISTICAL REFUTATIONS. COMING-TO-BE AND PASSING-AWAY. E. S. Forster; ON THE COSMOS. D. J. Furley.

ARRIAN: HISTORY OF ALEXANDER AND INDICA. Rev. E. Iliffe Robson. 2 Vols.

ATHENAEUS: DEIPNOSOPHISTAE. C. B. Gulick. 7 Vols.

BABRIUS AND PHAEDRUS (Latin). B. E. Perry.

ST. BASIL: LETTERS. R. J. Deferrari. 4 Vols.

CALLIMACHUS: FRAGMENTS. C. A. Trypanis.

CALLIMACHUS: HYMNS AND EPIGRAMS, AND LYCOPHRON. A. W. Mair; ARATUS. G. R. Mair.

CLEMENT OF ALEXANDRIA. Rev. G. W. Butterworth.

COLLUTHUS. *Cf.* OPPIAN.

DAPHNIS AND CHLOE. *Cf.* LONGUS.

DEMOSTHENES I: OLYNTHIACS, PHILIPPICS AND MINOR ORATIONS: I-XVII AND XX. J. H. Vince.

DEMOSTHENES II: DE CORONA AND DE FALSA LEGATIONE. C. A. Vince and J. H. Vince.

DEMOSTHENES III: MEIDIAS, ANDROTION, ARISTOCRATES, TIMOCRATES, ARISTOGEITON. J. H. Vince.

DEMOSTHENES IV-VI: PRIVATE ORATIONS AND IN NEAERAM. A. T. Murray.

DEMOSTHENES VII: FUNERAL SPEECH, EROTIC ESSAY, EXORDIA AND LETTERS. N. W. and N. J. DeWitt.

DIO CASSIUS: ROMAN HISTORY. E. Cary. 9 Vols.

DIO CHRYSOSTOM. 5 Vols. Vols. I and II. J. W. Cohoon. Vol. III. J. W. Cohoon and H. Lamar Crosby. Vols. IV and V. H. Lamar Crosby.

DIODORUS SICULUS. 12 Vols. Vols. I-VI. C. H. Oldfather. Vol. VII. C. L. Sherman. Vol. VIII. C. B. Welles. Vols. IX and X. Russel M. Geer. Vols. XI and XII. F. R. Walton. General Index. Russel M. Geer.

DIOGENES LAERTIUS. R. D. Hicks. 2 Vols.

DIONYSIUS OF HALICARNASSUS: ROMAN ANTIQUITIES. Spelman's translation revised by E. Cary. 7 Vols.

EPICTETUS. W. A. Oldfather. 2 Vols.

PLUTARCH'S
MORALIA

VIII

Plutarchus.

PLUTARCH'S
MORALIA

IN SIXTEEN VOLUMES

VIII

612 B—697 C

WITH AN ENGLISH TRANSLATION BY

PAUL A. CLEMENT

UNIVERSITY OF CALIFORNIA

HERBERT B. HOFFLEIT

UNIVERSITY OF CALIFORNIA

CAMBRIDGE, MASSACHUSETTS
HARVARD UNIVERSITY PRESS
LONDON
WILLIAM HEINEMANN LTD
MCMLXIX

Printed in Great Britain

CONTENTS OF VOLUME VIII

PREFATORY NOTE

Books I-III of the *Quaestiones Convivales* are the work of Paul A. Clement and Books IV-VI are the work of Herbert B. Hoffleit. There is no joint responsibility.

THE TRADITIONAL ORDER of the Books of the *Moralia* as they appear since the edition of Stephanus (1572), and their division into volumes in this edition.

THE TRADITIONAL ORDER

THE TRADITIONAL ORDER

* To be added to this edition later.

THE TRADITIONAL ORDER

INTRODUCTION TO BOOKS I-III

THE text for Books I-III is based on C. Hubert's Teubner text of 1938. Notes to text and notes to translation are in great part excerpted from Hubert's critical apparatus and testimonia and, for Books I-II, also from the commentary in H. Bolkestein's *Adversaria critica et exegetica ad Plutarchi Quaestionum Convivalium librum primum et secundum*. In these works there is information not to be found here; conversely, there is here matter not to be found there. The archetype of all extant MSS. of the *Quaestiones Convivales* is *Codex Vindobonensis Graecus* 148 (T) of the 10th or early 11th century, purchased in Constantinople about 1562 (Hubert, *Plutarchi Moralia*, IV, pp. xi-xiv). I have worked with photostats of this manuscript before me, and, where I have checked Hubert's reports of its readings, I have generally found them accurate. I have also had before me the editions of Bernardakis (Teubner, 1892), Hutten (Tübingen, 1798), and, more important, Wyttenbach (Oxford, 1797). For emendations by other and older scholars I have generally depended upon these editors or upon Hubert or upon Bolkestein—to all of whom my gratitude is due. Most that one may wish to know either about Plutarch or about the *Quaestiones Convivales* is now readily available in the monograph printed by K. Ziegler as " Plutarchos "

PLUTARCH'S MORALIA

in Pauly-Wissowa, *Realencyclopädie*, xxi. 1 (1951), cols. 636-962. To this work must be added, and not alone for the *De facie,* Harold Cherniss's introduction to that dialogue in *Moralia,* xii (LCL, 1957), pp. 2-33.

PAUL A. CLEMENT

UNIVERSITY OF CALIFORNIA
LOS ANGELES

TABLE-TALK
(QUAESTIONES CONVIVALES)
BOOK I

ΒΙΒΛΙΟΝ ΠΡΩΤΟΝ[1]

Τὸ " μισέω μνάμονα συμπόταν," ὦ Σόσσιε
Σενεκίων, ἔνιοι πρὸς τοὺς ἐπιστάθμους εἰρῆσθαι
λέγουσιν, φορτικοὺς ἐπιεικῶς καὶ ἀναγώγους ἐν
τῷ πίνειν ὄντας· οἱ γὰρ ἐν Σικελίᾳ Δωριεῖς ὡς
ἔοικε τὸν ἐπίσταθμον " μνάμονα " προσηγόρευον.
D ἔνιοι δὲ τὴν παροιμίαν οἴονται τοῖς παρὰ πότον
λεγομένοις καὶ πραττομένοις ἀμνηστίαν ἐπάγειν·
διὸ τήν τε λήθην οἱ πάτριοι λόγοι καὶ τὸν νάρθηκα
τῷ θεῷ συγκαθιεροῦσιν, ὡς ἢ μηδενὸς δέον μνημονεύειν τῶν ἐν οἴνῳ πλημμεληθέντων ἢ παντελῶς

---

[1] T begins: Βιβλίον Α .: . (line 1) Πλουτάρχου συμποσιακῶν
βιβλία Θ : ἐν τῷ Α (line 2), after which come the titles of the
ten essays which constitute Book I, arranged in tabular form
and each title numbered (lines 3-19). Line 20 is blank except
for a row of decorative sigla. Line 21 repeats the title of the
first essay : εἰ δεῖ φιλοσοφεῖν παρὰ πότον, with Α in the right
margin. Line 22 begins the preface Τὸ μισέω μνάμονα συμπόταν, ὦ Σόσσιε, the initial capital somewhat elaborated.

---

[a] Bergk, *Poetae Lyrici Graeci*, Adespoton 141 ; Diehl,
Anthologia Lyrica Graeca, ii (1942), p. 205. 6 ; H. Bolkestein, *Adversaria Critica et Exegetica* (Amsterdam, 1946), pp.
47-49, has a slightly different interpretation for ἐπίσταθμος :
" magistratus cuiusdam esse appellationem conicio."

[b] See below on 697 c (LCL *Mor.* ix, p. 4). His greatgrand-
daughter Sosia Flaconilla is known from two honorary inscriptions, one from the Athenian Agora (*Hesperia*, x [1941], pp.

NINE BOOKS OF TABLE-TALK

BOOK ONE

The saying " I dislike a drinking-companion with a good memory " [a] some say, my dear Sossius Senecio,[b] was meant by its author to refer to masters of ceremonies who are rather tiresome men and wanting in taste when the drinking is on. For it seems that the Dorians in Sicily called a master of ceremonies " remembrancer." On the other hand, some think that the proverb recommends amnesty for all that is said and done during the drinking; it is for this reason that in our traditional legends forgetfulness [c] and the wand [d] are together consecrated to the god, the implication being that one should remember either none of the improprieties committed over cups or only those which call for an altogether light and

---

255-258, no. 61) and one from Cirta in Numidia (*C.I.L.* viii. 7066).

[c] For Mneia and Lethê in Bacchic Mysteries at Ephesus in Hadrian's time see *Ancient Greek Inscriptions in the British Museum*, iii. 600. 28-29 (*cf.* Kroll, *RE*, *s.v.* " Lethê," col. 2142. 47-51).

[d] *Cf. Mor.* 462 b. The narthex (fennel-stalk) served the Greeks for many purposes. Prometheus in its pithy stalk brought fire to earth, schoolmasters used it for canes, doctors for splints, and the religious and convivial for their ritual wands or thyrsoi : *RE*, *s.v.*, and Sir John Beazley, *Am. Jour. Arch.* xxxvii (1933), pp. 400 ff. The " god " here is Dionysus.

(612) ἐλαφρᾶς καὶ παιδικῆς νουθεσίας δεομένων. ἐπεὶ
δὲ καὶ σοὶ δοκεῖ τῶν μὲν ἀτόπων ἡ λήθη τῷ ὄντι
σοφὴ κατ' Εὐριπίδην εἶναι, τὸ δ' ὅλως ἀμνημονεῖν
τῶν ἐν οἴνῳ μὴ μόνον τῷ φιλοποιῷ λεγομένῳ
μάχεσθαι τῆς τραπέζης, ἀλλὰ καὶ τῶν φιλοσόφων
τοὺς ἐλλογιμωτάτους ἀντιμαρτυροῦντας ἔχειν, Πλάτωνα καὶ Ξενοφῶντα καὶ Ἀριστοτέλη[1] καὶ Σπεύ-
σιππον Ἐπίκουρόν τε καὶ Πρύτανιν καὶ Ἱερώνυ-
E μον καὶ Δίωνα τὸν ἐξ Ἀκαδημίας, ὡς ἄξιόν τινος
σπουδῆς πεποιημένους ἔργον ἀναγράψασθαι λόγους
παρὰ πότον γενομένους, ᾠήθης τε δεῖν ἡμᾶς τῶν
σποράδην πολλάκις ἔν τε Ῥώμῃ μεθ' ὑμῶν καὶ
παρ' ἡμῖν ἐν τῇ Ἑλλάδι παρούσης ἅμα τραπέζης
καὶ κύλικος φιλολογηθέντων συναγαγεῖν τὰ ἐπι-
τήδεια, πρὸς τοῦτο γενόμενος τρία μὲν ἤδη σοι
πέπομφα τῶν βιβλίων, ἑκάστου δέκα προβλήματα
περιέχοντος, πέμψω δὲ καὶ τὰ λοιπὰ ταχέως, ἂν
ταῦτα δόξῃ μὴ παντελῶς ἄμουσα μηδ' ἀπροσδιόνυσ'
εἶναι.[2]

[1] So T, which Bolkestein (*Adv. Crit.* p. 51) defends against
its copies and Hubert.
[2] In T (folio 2 *r*, line 18) πρῶτον δὲ πάντων τέτακται immediately follows εἶναι. The style and location of the heading
here printed are an editorial convention which, with minor
variations, is of long standing.

***

[a] *Orestes*, 213.
[b] Cato called the dining-table " highly friend-making " ;
so Plutarch, *Life of Cato*, xxv (351 F).
[c] The *Symposium* of Plato and that of Xenophon are preserved.
[d] V. Rose, *Aristotelis Fragmenta* (Leipzig, 1886), pp. 97
ff., for the fragments of Aristotle's Συμπόσιον ἢ περὶ μέθης ;
see also Sir David Ross, *Select Fragments* in *The Works of
Aristotle Translated*, xii (Oxford, 1952), pp. 8-15.
[e] Plato's successor as head of the Academy. His *Sym-*

6

playful reproof. Since you too, Senecio, believe that
forgetfulness of folly is in truth " wise," as Euripides
says,[a] yet to consign to utter oblivion all that occurs
at a drinking-party is not only opposed to what we
call the friend-making character of the dining-table,[b]
but also has the most famous of the philosophers to
bear witness against it,—Plato, Xenophon,[c] Aristotle,[d] Speusippus,[e] Epicurus,[f] Prytanis,[g] Hieronymus,[h] and Dio of the Academy,[i] who all considered
the recording of conversations held at table a task
worth some effort,—and since, moreover, you thought
that I ought to collect such talk as suits our purpose
from among the learned discussions in which I have
often participated in various places both at Rome in
your company and among us in Greece, with table
and goblet before us, I have applied myself to the
task and now send you three of the books, each
containing ten questions which we have discussed,
and I mean to send you the rest very soon if these
seem to you not altogether lacking in charm nor yet
irrelevant to Dionysus.[j]

posium is known only from this passage ; cf. Lang, De Speu-
sippi Academici Scriptis (Bonn diss., 1911), pp. 34, 85.

[f] On the Symposium of Epicurus see Hirzel, Der Dialog, i,
p. 363. Usener, Epicurea, pp. 115-119, gives the fragments
and testimonia.

[g] Peripatetic philosopher, beginning of third century B.C. :
cf. Athenaeus, xi, 477 e ; Hirzel, op. cit. i, p. 361 ; RE, s.v.,
no. 5.

[h] Also a Peripatetic philosopher of the beginning of the
third century B.C. : Diogenes Laertius, iv. 41 ; Hirzel, op.
cit. i, pp. 345, note 3, and 361 ; RE, s.v., no. 12, cols. 1561 ff.

[i] This Dio is quoted on the subject of wine and " beer "
among the Egyptians in Athenaeus, i, 34 b ; RE, s.v. " Dion,"
no. 14.

[j] Cf. infra 615 A, 671 E ; Athenaeus, 494 b with Gulick's
note ; Pohlenz, Nachr. Ges. Wiss. Göttingen, 1926, p. 302.

PLUTARCH'S MORALIA

ΠΡΟΒΛΗΜΑ Α

Εἰ δεῖ φιλοσοφεῖν παρὰ πότον

Collocuntur Aristo, Plutarchus, Crato, Sossius Senecio

1. Πρῶτον δὲ πάντων τέτακται τὸ περὶ τοῦ φιλοσοφεῖν παρὰ πότον. μέμνησαι γὰρ ὅτι, ζητήσεως Ἀθήνησι μετὰ δεῖπνον γενομένης εἰ F χρηστέον ἐν οἴνῳ φιλοσόφοις λόγοις καὶ τί μέτρον ἔστι χρωμένοις, Ἀρίστων παρών, " εἰσὶν γάρ," ἔφησε, " πρὸς τῶν θεῶν οἱ φιλοσόφοις χώραν ἐπ' οἴνῳ μὴ διδόντες; "

Ἐγὼ δ' εἶπον, " ἀλλὰ γὰρ εἰσίν, ὦ ἑταῖρε, καὶ πάνυ γε σεμνῶς κατειρωνευόμενοι λέγουσι μὴ δεῖν ὥσπερ οἰκοδέσποιναν ἐν οἴνῳ φθέγγεσθαι 613 φιλοσοφίαν, καὶ τοὺς Πέρσας ὀρθῶς φασι μὴ ταῖς γαμεταῖς ἀλλὰ ταῖς παλλακίσι συμμεθύσκεσθαι καὶ συνορχεῖσθαι· ταὐτὸ δὴ καὶ ἡμᾶς ἀξιοῦσι ποιεῖν εἰς τὰ συμπόσια τὴν μουσικὴν καὶ τὴν ὑποκριτικὴν ἐπεισάγοντας φιλοσοφίαν δὲ μὴ κινοῦντας, ὡς οὔτε συμπαίζειν ἐκείνην ἐπιτήδειον οὖσαν οὔθ' ἡμᾶς τηνικαῦτα σπουδαστικῶς ἔχοντας· οὐδὲ γὰρ Ἰσοκράτη τὸν σοφιστὴν ὑπομεῖναι δεομένων εἰπεῖν τι παρ' οἶνον ἀλλ' ἢ τοσοῦτον· ' ἐν οἷς μὲν ἐγὼ δεινός, οὐχ ὁ νῦν καιρός· ἐν οἷς δ' ὁ νῦν καιρός, οὐκ ἐγὼ δεινός.' "

2. Καὶ ὁ Κράτων ἀνακραγών, " εὖ γ'," εἶπεν,

---

[a] Imitated by Macrobius, *Saturnalia*, vii. 1; *cf. Mor.* 133 B.

[b] This practice is attributed to Parthians by Macrobius, *Saturnalia*, vii. 1. 3 ; however Bolkestein notes (*Adv. Crit.* p. 53) that Macrobius is merely adapting Plutarch. In Herodotus, v. 18, Persians claim the custom of dining with mistresses and wives together.

QUESTION 1[a]

Whether philosophy is a fitting topic for conversation
at a drinking-party

Speakers : Ariston, Plutarch, Crato, and Sossius Senecio

1. THE question of philosophical talk over the cups I
have placed first of all, Senecio ; for surely you recall
that after a dinner at Athens, when the question
arose whether one should engage in philosophical
talk while drinking and what limit those who do so
should observe, Ariston, who was present, said :
" By the gods, are there really men who do not offer
philosophers a place at their parties ? "

And I replied, " Certainly there are, my friend,
and the pretext they very solemnly employ is that
philosophy should no more have a part in conversation
over wine than should the matron of the house. They
commend the Persians for doing their drinking and
dancing with their mistresses rather than with their
wives [b] ; this they think we ought to imitate by
introducing music and theatricals into our drinking-
parties, and not disturb philosophy. For they hold
that philosophy is not a suitable thing to make sport
with and that we are not on these occasions inclined
to seriousness. Indeed they claim that not even
Isocrates the sophist yielded to requests to speak at
a drinking-party, except only to say : ' What I excel
in suits not the present occasion ; in what suits the
present occasion I do not excel.' "

2. Then Crato,[c] raising his voice, " By Dionysus,"

[c] A relative of Plutarch (*RE*, s.v., col. 651. 26-43 [see below,
p. 48, note a], and col. 668. 55-68) ; though presumably a
physician (*cf.* 669 c), there is no reason to identify him with
the physician Crato of Gargettos whose tombstone is preserved (*I.G.* II². 5395, end of second century A.D.). In the

(613)
B

" νὴ τὸν Διόνυσον ἐξώμνυτο τὸν λόγον, εἰ τοιαύτας
ἔμελλε περαίνειν περιόδους αἷς ἔμελλεν Χαρίτων
ἀνάστατον γενέσθαι συμπόσιον. οὐχ ὅμοιον δ᾽
οἶμαι ῥητορικὸν ἐξαιρεῖν συμποσίου λόγον καὶ
φιλόσοφον, ἀλλ᾽ ἕτερόν ἐστι τὸ τῆς[1] φιλοσοφίας,
ἣν τέχνην περὶ βίον οὖσαν οὔτε τινὸς παιδιᾶς οὔτε
τινὸς ἡδονῆς διαγωγὴν ἐχούσης ἀποστατεῖν εἰκὸς
ἀλλὰ πᾶσι παρεῖναι τὸ μέτρον καὶ τὸν καιρὸν ἐπι-
φέρουσαν· ἢ μηδὲ σωφροσύνην μηδὲ δικαιοσύνην
οἰώμεθα δεῖν εἰς τοὺς πότους δέχεσθαι, κατειρωνευόμενοι τὸ σεμνὸν αὐτῶν. εἰ μὲν οὖν, ὥσπερ
οἱ τὸν Ὀρέστην ἑστιῶντες, ἐν Θεσμοθετείῳ σιωπῇ
τρώγειν καὶ πίνειν ἐμέλλομεν, ἦν τι τοῦτο τῆς
C ἀμαθίας οὐκ ἀτυχὲς παραμύθιον· εἰ δὲ πάντων μὲν
ὁ Διόνυσος Λύσιός ἐστι καὶ Λυαῖος, μάλιστα δὲ
τῆς γλώττης ἀφαιρεῖται τὰ χαλινὰ καὶ πλείστην
ἐλευθερίαν τῇ φωνῇ δίδωσιν, ἀβέλτερον οἶμαι καὶ
ἀνόητον ἐν λόγοις πλεονάζοντα καιρὸν ἀποστερεῖν
τῶν ἀρίστων λόγων, καὶ ζητεῖν μὲν ἐν ταῖς διατριβαῖς περὶ συμποτικῶν καθηκόντων καὶ τίς ἀρετὴ
συμπότου καὶ πῶς οἴνῳ χρηστέον, ἐξ αὐτῶν δὲ τῶν

---

[1] τῆς added by Reiske; cf. Bolkestein, Adv. Crit. p. 54.

conversation reported in Quaest. Conviv. ii. 6, Plutarch's
kinsman contributed to the talk on a problem of grafting.

[a] Bolkestein, op. cit. pp. 53 f., and Bases, Ἀθηνᾶ, xi (1889),
pp. 220 f. (which Bolkestein cites), understand " break up a
party of the Graces."

[b] Cf. Cicero, Acad. ii. 8. 23 with Reid's note; O. Stählin,
Clemens Alexandrinus, i, p. 171, on Paedagogus, ii. 25. 3;
P. Wendland, Quaestiones Musonianae (Berlin diss., 1866), p.
12 : a definition established among the early Stoics.

[c] Cf. Mor. 643 A-B ; Athenaeus, x, 437 c-d. The legend of
Orestes' reception at Athens provided an aetiology for the
section of the Anthesteria called Choes (L. Deubner, Attische

he said, " it's well he refused to speak if he meant to
finish off such periods as would cause the Graces to
abandon the company.[a] However, I think that excluding an orator's talk from a drinking-party is not
the same thing as excluding a philosopher's. No,
the nature of philosophy is different. It is the art of
life,[b] and therefore it is not reasonably excluded from
any amusement or from any pleasure that diverts the
mind, but takes part in all, bringing to them the
qualities of proportion and fitness. Otherwise we
must consider it our duty to refuse even temperance
and justice admission to our drinking-parties, alleging
their solemnity as excuse. The matter comes to this :
if, like Orestes and his hosts, we were about to eat
and drink in silence at the Thesmotheteum,[c] this
circumstance would be a rather happy remedy for
stupidity ; but if Dionysus is the Looser and the
Liberator of all things, and if especially he unbridles
the tongue and grants the utmost freedom to speech,
it is silly and foolish, I think, to deprive ourselves of
the best conversations at a time when talk abounds,
to debate in our schools about what is appropriate
for drinking-parties, what makes a good drinking-
companion, and how wine ought to be used, but to

Feste, pp. 96 and 98 ; Jane E. Harrison, Prolegomena to the
Study of Greek Religion, p. 41). The Thesmotheteum was an
official building of the archons, or of the six specifically known
as thesmothetai (Aristotle, Ath. Pol. 3. 5). Form and location of the building are uncertain. Pollux, iv. 122 (Hyperei-
des, frag. 139 Blass[3]) does not explicitly equate στοά with
Thesmotheteum, though scholars sometimes assume that he
does (K. Latte in RE, s.v. Θεσμοθετεῖον, col. 33. 18 ; Mar-
garet Crosby, Hesperia, vi [1937], p. 447). Against Judeich's
location on the northwest slope of the Acropolis (Topographie
von Athen[2], p. 303) see Miss Crosby's argument in Hesperia,
loc. cit.

11

(613) συμποσίων ἀναιρεῖν φιλοσοφίαν ὡς ἔργῳ βεβαιοῦν
ἃ διδάσκει λόγῳ μὴ δυναμένην.''

3. Σοῦ δ' εἰπόντος οὐκ ἄξιον εἶναι Κράτωνι περὶ
τούτων ἀντιλέγειν, ὅρον δέ τινα καὶ χαρακτῆρα
τῶν παρὰ πότον φιλοσοφουμένων ζητεῖν ἐκφεύ-
γοντα τοῦτο δὴ τὸ παιζόμενον οὐκ ἀηδῶς πρὸς
τοὺς ἐρίζοντας καὶ σοφιστιῶντας

D νῦν δ' ἔρχεσθ' ἐπὶ δεῖπνον ἵνα ξυνάγωμεν Ἄρηα,

καὶ παρακαλοῦντος ἡμᾶς ἐπὶ τὸν λόγον, ἔφην ἐγὼ
πρῶτον ὅτι μοι δοκεῖ σκεπτέον εἶναι τὸ τῶν
παρόντων. '' ἂν μὲν γὰρ πλείονας ἔχῃ φιλολόγους
τὸ συμπόσιον, ὡς τὸ Ἀγάθωνος Σωκράτας Φαί-
δρους Παυσανίας Ἐρυξιμάχους καὶ τὸ Καλλίου
Χαρμίδας Ἀντισθένας Ἑρμογένας ἑτέρους τούτοις
παραπλησίους, ἀφήσομεν αὐτοὺς [μύθῳ]¹ φιλοσοφεῖν, οὐχ ἧττον ταῖς Μούσαις τὸν Διόνυσον ἢ ταῖς
Νύμφαις κεραννύντας· ἐκεῖναι μὲν γὰρ αὐτὸν τοῖς
σώμασιν ἵλεω καὶ πρᾶον, αὗται δὲ ταῖς ψυχαῖς
E μειλίχιον ὄντως καὶ χαριδότην ἐπεισάγουσι. καὶ
γὰρ ἂν ὀλίγοι τινὲς ἰδιῶται παρῶσιν, ὥσπερ
ἄφωνα γράμματα φωνηέντων ἐν μέσῳ πολλῶν τῶν
πεπαιδευμένων ἐμπεριλαμβανόμενοι φθογγῆς τινος
οὐ παντελῶς ἀνάρθρου καὶ συνέσεως κοινωνήσουσιν.
ἂν δὲ πλῆθος ᾖ τοιούτων ἀνθρώπων, οἳ παντὸς μὲν

---

¹ μύθῳ φιλοσοφεῖν Τ; μύθῳ καὶ λόγῳ φ. Hubert (Bolkestein approving, op. cit. pp. 55-56).

---

[a] Iliad, ii. 381.
[b] Tragic poet who, to celebrate his victory at the Lenaea in
February, 416 B.C., gave the dinner described in Plato's Symposium.
[c] Wealthy Athenian who entertained the sophists in Plato's

remove philosophy from the parties themselves, as though it were unable to make good in practice what it teaches in theory."

3. Then you, Senecio, said that, rather than argue with Crato about this, it was worth while to make some inquiry into the province and nature of philosophical talk at parties in order that we might avoid that pleasant jibe reserved for disputatious wranglers

Now come ye in to dinner, battle must be joined.[a]

And when you invited us to discuss the matter, I said that it seemed to me necessary to consider first the character of the guests. " For if the majority of the guests at a party are learned men, like Socrates, Phaedrus, Pausanias, and Eryximachus at the dinner of Agathon,[b] and Charmides, Antisthenes, Hermogenes, and others like them at the dinner of Callias,[c] we shall let them talk philosophy, blending Dionysus not less with the Muses than with the Nymphs ; for, while it is the Nymphs who introduce him as a kind and gentle god to our bodies, it is the Muses who present him as one really gracious and a giver of joy to our souls.[d] In fact, if some few men without erudition are present, included in a large company of learned men like mute consonants among sonant vowels, they will take no wholly inarticulate part in talk and ideas.[e] But if the company consists mainly of the kind of men who pay more attention to the note of

Protagoras and the guests here mentioned at the party which gave Xenophon the subject for his *Symposium*.

[d] In simpler terms : mix wine (Dionysus) with wit (the Muses) as well as water (the Nymphs). Dionysus the Gracious (Meilichios) reputedly gave the Naxians the fig : Athenaeus, 78 c ; Farnell, *Cults of the Greek States*, v, p. 119.

[e] Cf. *Mor.* 710 B ; Plato, *Protagoras*, 347 c, and *Symposium*, 176 E.

(613) ὀρνέου παντὸς δὲ νεύρου καὶ ξύλου μᾶλλον ἢ
φιλοσόφου φωνὴν ὑπομένουσιν, τὸ τοῦ Πεισι-
στράτου χρήσιμον· ἐκεῖνος γὰρ ἐν διαφορᾷ τινι
πρὸς τοὺς υἱοὺς γενόμενος, ὡς ᾔσθετο τοὺς ἐχθροὺς
χαίροντας, ἐκκλησίαν συναγαγὼν ἔφη βούλεσθαι
μὲν αὐτὸς πεῖσαι τοὺς παῖδας, ἐπεὶ δὲ δυσκόλως
ἔχουσιν, αὐτὸς ἐκείνοις πείσεσθαι καὶ ἀκολου-
F θήσειν. οὕτω δὴ καὶ φιλόσοφος ἀνὴρ ἐν συμπόταις
μὴ δεχομένοις τοὺς λόγους αὐτοῦ μεταθέμενος
ἕψεται καὶ ἀγαπήσει τὴν ἐκείνων διατριβήν, ἐφ'
ὅσον μὴ ἐκβαίνει τὸ εὔσχημον, εἰδὼς ὅτι ῥητο-
ρεύουσι μὲν ἄνθρωποι διὰ λόγου, φιλοσοφοῦσι δὲ
καὶ σιωπῶντες καὶ παίζοντες καὶ νὴ Δία σκωπτόμενοι καὶ σκώπτοντες. οὐ γὰρ μόνον ' ἀδικίας
614 ἐσχάτης ἐστίν,' ὥς φησι Πλάτων, ' μὴ ὄντα
δίκαιον εἶναι δοκεῖν,' ἀλλὰ καὶ συνέσεως ἄκρας
φιλοσοφοῦντα μὴ δοκεῖν φιλοσοφεῖν καὶ παίζοντα
διαπράττεσθαι τὰ τῶν σπουδαζόντων. ὡς γὰρ αἱ
παρ' Εὐριπίδῃ μαινάδες ἄνοπλοι καὶ ἀσίδηροι τοῖς
θυρσαρίοις παίουσαι τοὺς ἐπιτιθεμένους τραυματί-
ζουσιν, οὕτω τῶν ἀληθινῶν φιλοσόφων καὶ τὰ
σκώμματα καὶ οἱ γέλωτες τοὺς μὴ παντελῶς
ἀτρώτους κινοῦσιν ἁμωσγέπως καὶ συνεπιστρέ-
φουσιν.

4. " Οἶμαι δὲ καὶ[1] διηγήσεων εἶναί τι συμποτικὸν
γένος, ὧν τὰς μὲν ἱστορία δίδωσι, τὰς δ' ἐκ τῶν
B ἀνὰ χεῖρα πραγμάτων λαβεῖν ἔστι, πολλὰ μὲν εἰς

---

[1] καὶ added by Reiske.

[a] The same sort of story is told of Pisistratus and certain

14

every bird, of every cithara-string and sounding-board than to the voice of a philosopher, then it is useful to recall the story and example of Pisistratus. For when some quarrel arose between Pisistratus and his sons, and he saw the pleasure it gave his enemies, he summoned the assembly into session and announced that, though he wished to persuade his sons, since they were stubborn, he would be persuaded by them and follow them.[a] In just such a manner a philosopher too, when with drinking-companions who are unwilling to listen to his homilies, will change his role, fall in with their mood, and not object to their activity so long as it does not transgress propriety. For he knows that, while men practise oratory only when they talk, they practise philosophy when they are silent, when they jest, even, by Zeus, when they are the butt of jokes and when they make fun of others. Indeed, not only is it true that ' the worst injustice is to seem just when one is not,' as Plato says,[b] but also the height of sagacity is to talk philosophy without seeming to do so, and in jesting to accomplish all that those in earnest could. Just as the Maenads in Euripides,[c] without shield and without sword, strike their attackers and wound them with their little thyrsoi, so true philosophers with their jokes and laughter somehow arouse men who are not altogether invulnerable and make them attentive.

4. " Then, too, there are, I think, topics of discussion that are particularly suitable for a drinking-party. Some are supplied by history ; others it is possible to take from current events ; some contain

of his friends who had revolted against his rule and established themselves in Phylê: *Mor.* 189 B. Both are doubtless apocryphal (*RE, s.v.* "Peisistratos," col. 158).

   [b] *Republic,* 361 A, freely quoted.   [c] *Bacchae,* 734 ff.

(614) φιλοσοφίαν παραδείγματα πολλὰ δ' εἰς εὐσέβειαν
ἐχούσας, ἀνδρικῶν τε πράξεων καὶ μεγαλοθύμων
ἐνίας δὲ χρηστῶν καὶ φιλανθρώπων ζῆλον ἐπαγού-
σας· αἷς ἦν τις ἀνυπόπτως χρώμενος διαπαιδαγωγῇ
τοὺς πίνοντας, οὐ τὰ ἐλάχιστα τῶν κακῶν ἀφαι-
ρήσει τῆς μέθης.

" Οἱ μὲν οὖν τὰ βούγλωσσα καταμιγνύντες εἰς
τὸν οἶνον καὶ τοῖς ἀποβρέγμασι τῶν ἀριστερεώνων[1] καὶ ἀδιάντων τὰ ἐδάφη ῥαίνοντες, ὡς
τούτων τινὰ τοῖς ἑστιωμένοις εὐθυμίαν καὶ φιλοφροσύνην ἐνδιδόντων, ἀπομιμούμενοι τὴν Ὁμηρι-
κὴν Ἑλένην ὑποφαρμάττουσαν τὸν ἄκρατον, οὐ
C συνορῶσιν ὅτι κἀκεῖνος ὁ μῦθος ἐκπεριελθὼν ἀπ'
Αἰγύπτου μακρὰν ὁδὸν εἰς λόγους ἐπιεικεῖς καὶ
πρέποντας ἐτελεύτησεν· ἡ γὰρ Ἑλένη πίνουσιν
αὐτοῖς διηγεῖται περὶ τοῦ Ὀδυσσέως, ' οἷον ἔρεξε
καὶ ἔτλη καρτερὸς ἀνήρ, αὐτόν μιν πληγῇσιν
ἀεικελίῃσι δαμάσσας '· τοῦτο γὰρ ἦν ὡς ἔοικε τὸ
' νηπενθὲς ' φάρμακον καὶ ἀνώδυνον, λόγος ἔχων
καιρὸν ἁρμόζοντα τοῖς ὑποκειμένοις πάθεσι καὶ
πράγμασιν. οἱ δὲ χαρίεντες, κἂν ἀπ' εὐθείας
φιλοσοφῶσιν, τηνικαῦτα διὰ τοῦ πιθανοῦ μᾶλλον ἢ
βιαστικοῦ τῶν ἀποδείξεων ἄγουσι τὸν λόγον. ὁρᾷς
γὰρ ὅτι καὶ Πλάτων ἐν τῷ Συμποσίῳ περὶ τέλους
D διαλεγόμενος καὶ τοῦ πρώτου ἀγαθοῦ καὶ ὅλως
θεολογῶν οὐκ ἐντείνει τὴν ἀπόδειξιν οὐδ' ὑποκο-

---

[1] ἀριστερεώνων (ἀριστερέων T) Bolkestein (*Adv. Crit.* p. 58 ;
cf. Chantraine, *Rev. de Phil.* xxii [1948], p. 97); περιστερεώνων
Junius.

---

[a] This property of alkanet and vervain is noted by the
medical writer Dioscorides Pedanius (*De Materia Medica*, iv.

many lessons bearing on philosophy, many on piety ; some induce an emulous enthusiasm for courageous and great-hearted deeds, and some for charitable and humane deeds. If one makes unobtrusive use of them to entertain and instruct his companions as they drink, not the least of the evils of intemperance will be taken away.

" Now those who mix alkanet in their wine and sprinkle their floors with infusions of vervain and maidenhair because, as they believe, these things to some extent contribute to the cheerfulness and gaiety of their guests,[a] do so in imitation of Homer's Helen, who secretly added a drug to the undiluted wine[b] ; but they do not see that that legend too, having fetched a long course from Egypt, has its end in the telling of appropriate and suitable stories. For as they drink, Helen tells her guests a tale about Odysseus,

> What deed he dared to do, that hero strong,
> His body with unseemly stripes o'ercome.[c]

This, I take it, was the ' assuaging ' and pain-allaying drug, a story with a timeliness appropriate to the experiences and circumstances of the moment. Men of breeding, then, even if they talk straightforward philosophy, manage the conversation at such times by the persuasiveness rather than the compulsion of their arguments. Indeed, you see that Plato in his *Symposium*, even when he talks about the final cause and the primary good,—in short, when he discourses upon divine matters,—does not labour his proof nor

60 and 127) and by his contemporary the elder Pliny (*Nat. Hist.* xxv. 81 and 107).

[b] *Odyssey*, iv. 220.
[c] *Odyssey*, iv. 242 and 244.

17

(614) νίεται, τὴν λαβὴν ὥσπερ εἴωθεν εὔτονον ποιῶν καὶ
ἄφυκτον, ἀλλ' ὑγροτέροις λήμμασι καὶ παρα-
δείγμασι καὶ μυθολογίαις προσάγεται τοὺς ἄνδρας.

5. " Εἶναι δὲ δεῖ καὶ αὐτὰς τὰς ζητήσεις ὑγρο-
τέρας καὶ γνώριμα τὰ προβλήματα καὶ τὰς πεύσεις
ἐπιεικεῖς καὶ μὴ γλίσχρας, ἵνα μὴ πνίγωσι τοὺς
ἀνοητοτέρους μηδ' ἀποτρέπωσιν. ὥσπερ γὰρ τὰ
σώματα¹ πινόντων δι' ὀρχήσεως καὶ χορείας νενό-
μισται σαλεύειν, ἂν δ' ὁπλομαχεῖν ἀναστάντας ἢ
δισκεύειν ἀναγκάζωμεν αὐτούς, οὐ μόνον ἀτερπὲς
Ε ἀλλὰ καὶ βλαβερὸν ἔσται τὸ συμπόσιον, οὕτω τὰς
ψυχὰς αἱ μὲν ἐλαφραὶ ζητήσεις ἐμμελῶς καὶ
ὠφελίμως κινοῦσιν, ' ἐριδαντέων ' δὲ κατὰ Δημόκριτον καὶ ' ἱμαντελικτέων ' λόγους ἀφετέον, οἳ αὑτούς τε κατατείνουσιν ἐν πράγμασι γλίσχροις καὶ
δυσθεωρήτοις τούς τε παρατυγχάνοντας ἀνιῶσιν·
δεῖ γὰρ ὡς τὸν οἶνον κοινὸν εἶναι καὶ τὸν λόγον, οὗ
πάντες μεθέξουσιν. οἱ δὲ τοιαῦτα προβλήματα
καθιέντες οὐδὲν ἂν τῆς Αἰσωπείου γεράνου καὶ
ἀλώπεκος ἐπιεικέστεροι πρὸς κοινωνίαν φανεῖεν·
ὧν ἡ μὲν ἔτνος τι λιπαρὸν κατὰ λίθου πλατείας
καταχεαμένη ⟨τὴν γέρανον εἱστίασεν, οὐκ εὐωχου-

---

¹ Meziriacus (cf. Bolkestein, Adv. Crit. pp. 59-60) ; συμπόσια.

ᵃ The observation is copied by Macrobius, Saturnalia, i.
1. 3.

gird himself for a fight and get his customary tight and unbreakable hold, but with simple and easy premises, with examples, and with mythical legends he brings the company into agreement with him.[a]

5. " The matters of inquiry must be in themselves rather simple and easy, the topics familiar, the subjects for investigation suitably uncomplicated, so that the less intellectual guests may neither be stifled nor turned away. For just as the bodies of men who are drinking are accustomed to sway in time with pantomimic and choral dancing, but if we compel them to get up and exercise in heavy armour or throw the discus, they will find the party not only unpleasant but even harmful, just so their spirits are harmoniously and profitably stirred by subjects of inquiry that are easy to handle ; but one must banish the talk of ' wranglers,' as Democritus calls them,[b] and of ' phrase-twisting ' sophists, talk which involves them in strenuous argument about complex and abstruse subjects and irritates those who happen to be present. Indeed, just as the wine must be common to all, so too the conversation must be one in which all will share, and those who propose complex and abstruse topics for discussion would manifestly be no more fit for society than the crane and the fox of Aesop.[c] The fox entertained the crane at dinner, serving her a clear broth poured out upon a flat stone. The crane not only went without her dinner, but in

---

[b] Diels and Kranz, *Die Fragmente der Vorsokratiker*, ii[10] (1960), p. 172, frag. 150. On the trickster's game of ἱμαντελιγμός, literally " thong-twisting," see Pollux, ix. 118.

[c] The fable is included in the Aesopic corpus on the testimony of this passage ; it is also found in Phaedrus, i. 26 ; in La Fontaine, i. 18 ; and in numerous Latin versions (see *A.J.P.* lxvi [1945], pp. 195 ff.).

(614) μένη⟩ν,[1] ἀλλὰ γέλωτα πάσχουσαν,[2] ἐξέφευγε γὰρ
ὑγρότητι τὸ ἔτνος τὴν λεπτότητα τοῦ στόματος
αὐτῆς· ἐν μέρει τοίνυν ἡ γέρανος αὐτῇ καταγ-
F γείλασα δεῖπνον ἐν λαγυνίδι προὔθηκε λεπτὸν
ἐχούσῃ καὶ μακρὸν τράχηλον, ὥστ' αὐτὴν μὲν
καθιέναι τὸ στόμα ῥᾳδίως καὶ ἀπολαύειν, τὴν δ'
ἀλώπεκα μὴ δυναμένην κομίζεσθαι συμβολὰς πρε-
πούσας. οὕτω τοίνυν, ὅταν οἱ φιλόσοφοι παρὰ
πότον εἰς λεπτὰ καὶ διαλεκτικὰ προβλήματα
καταδύντες ἐνοχλῶσι τοῖς πολλοῖς ἕπεσθαι μὴ
615 δυναμένοις, ἐκεῖνοι δὲ πάλιν ἐπ' ᾠδάς τινας καὶ
διηγήματα φλυαρώδη καὶ λόγους βαναύσους καὶ
ἀγοραίους ἐμβάλωσιν[3] ἑαυτούς, οἴχεται τῆς συμπο-
τικῆς κοινωνίας τὸ τέλος καὶ καθύβρισται ὁ
Διόνυσος. ὥσπερ οὖν, Φρυνίχου καὶ Αἰσχύλου τὴν
τραγῳδίαν[4] εἰς μύθους καὶ πάθη προαγόντων,
ἐλέχθη τὸ ' τί ταῦτα πρὸς τὸν Διόνυσον; ', οὕτως
ἔμοιγε πολλάκις εἰπεῖν παρέστη πρὸς τοὺς ἕλκοντας
εἰς τὰ συμπόσια τὸν Κυριεύοντα ' ὦ ἄνθρωπε, τί
ταῦτα πρὸς τὸν Διόνυσον; ' ᾄδειν μὲν γὰρ ἴσως
τὰ καλούμενα σκόλια, κρατῆρος ἐν μέσῳ προ-
B κειμένου καὶ στεφάνων διανεμομένων, οὓς ὁ θεὸς
ὡς ἐλευθερῶν ἡμᾶς ἐπιτίθησιν, ⟨εὔλογον· λόγοις

---

[1] καταχεαμένη . . . εὐωχουμένην Bolkestein, *Mnemosynê*, iv
(1951), pp. 304-307, οὐκ εὐωχουμένην from a glossator's note
in the margin of T ; see further *A.J.P.* lxvi (1945), pp. 192-
196 : καταχεαμένην T, the final *nu* erased by a later hand.
[2] The reading of T is defended by Bolkestein, *loc. cit.* p.
307 ; παρέχουσαν Wyttenbach.
[3] Defended by Bolkestein, *Adv. Crit.* p. 60 ; ἐμβάλλωσιν
Bernardakis.   [4] So Stephanus : τὴν before Φρυνίχου.

addition was made ridiculous because the broth, being liquid, always slipped out of her bill, which was so thin. In turn, then, the crane invited the fox and served up the dinner in a jar with a long and narrow neck ; into this she easily inserted her bill and enjoyed the food, while the fox, unable to put his mouth inside, got for himself the portion he deserved. And so philosophers, whenever they plunge into subtle and disputatious arguments at a drinking-party, are always irksome to most of the guests, who cannot follow ; and these in turn throw themselves into the singing of any kind of song, the telling of foolish stories, and talk of shop and market-place. Gone then is the aim and end of the good fellowship of the party, and Dionysus is outraged. Accordingly, just as people said when Phrynichus and Aeschylus introduced old legends and tales of suffering into tragedy, ' What has all this to do with Dionysus ? ',[a] just so it has often occurred to me to say to those who drag ' The Master ' [b] into table-talk, ' Sir, what has this to do with Dionysus ? ' Indeed, when the great bowl is placed in our midst and the crowns are distributed which the god gives as token of our freedom, I dare say it is a reasonable thing to sing those songs called scolia, but to engage in pedan-

---

[a] Cf. supra, 612 E, with note j ; further, Pickard-Cambridge, *Dithyramb, Tragedy, and Comedy*, pp. 117 and 166-168 (=pp. 85 and 124-126 of the 2nd edition revised by T. B. L. Webster). Plutarch's statement suggested to Grace H. Macurdy, *Class. Weekly*, xxxvii (1943-44), pp. 239-240, that Phrynichus was first to present women characters in situations of terror.

[b] A name given to a particular kind of syllogism (*cf. Mor.* 1070 c and 133 c with Wyttenbach's note on the latter and Babbitt's note b, LCL *Mor.* ii, p. 270 ; Aulus Gellius, i. 2. 4 ; Epictetus, ii. 19).

21

(615) δὲ γλίσχροις παρὰ πότον κεχρῆσθαι σοφιστικὸν
μέν,⟩¹ οὐ καλὸν δ' οὐδὲ συμποτικόν.

"Ἐπεί τοι καὶ τὰ σκολιά φασιν οὐ γένος
ᾀσμάτων εἶναι πεποιημένων ἀσαφῶς, ἀλλ' ὅτι
πρῶτον μὲν ᾖδον ᾠδὴν τοῦ θεοῦ κοινῶς ἅπαντες
μιᾷ φωνῇ παιανίζοντες, δεύτερον δ' ἐφεξῆς ἑκάστῳ
μυρσίνης παραδιδομένης, ἣν αἴσακον οἶμαι διὰ
τὸ ᾄδειν τὸν δεξάμενον ἐκάλουν, ἐπὶ δὲ τούτῳ
λύρας περιφερομένης ὁ μὲν πεπαιδευμένος ἐλάμ-
βανε καὶ ᾖδεν ἁρμοζόμενος, τῶν δ' ἀμούσων οὐ
προσιεμένων σκολιὸν ὠνομάσθη τὸ μὴ κοινὸν αὐτοῦ μηδὲ ῥᾴδιον. ἄλλοι δέ φασι τὴν μυρσίνην οὐ
καθεξῆς βαδίζειν, ἀλλὰ καθ' ἕκαστον ἀπὸ κλίνης ἐπὶ
C κλίνην διαφέρεσθαι· τὸν γὰρ πρῶτον ᾄσαντα τῷ
πρώτῳ τῆς δευτέρας κλίνης ἀποστέλλειν, ἐκεῖνον
δὲ τῷ πρώτῳ τῆς τρίτης, εἶτα τὸν δεύτερον ὁμοίως
τῷ δευτέρῳ, καὶ τὸ ποικίλον καὶ πολυκαμπὲς ὡς
ἔοικε τῆς περιόδου σκολιὸν ὠνομάσθη."

¹ εὔλογον . . . κεχρῆσθαι added in the margin by the
glossator of 614 ε (Hubert, *Moralia*, iv, p. xiii) who also
deleted δ' after οὐ καλὸν; σοφιστικὸν μὲν added by P. A. C.

ᵃ As if αἴσακος were derived from ᾄδειν, " to sing."

ᵇ From the secondary meaning of σκολιός, " puzzling,"
" obscure."

ᶜ Correctly, no doubt, from the primary meaning
" curved," " winding." On these etymological speculations

tic argumentation over one's wine is a sophistical thing to do, and it is not seemly nor is it suitable to a party.

" As for the scolia, some say that they do not belong to a type of obscurely constructed songs, but that first the guests would sing the god's song together, all raising their hymn with one voice, and next when to each in turn was given the myrtle spray (which they called aisakos, I think, because the man to receive it sings) [a] and too the lyre was passed around, the guest who could play the instrument would take it and tune it and sing, while the unmusical would refuse, and thus the scolium owes its name to the fact that it is not sung by all and is not easy.[b] But others say that the myrtle spray did not proceed from each guest to his neighbour in orderly sequence, but was passed across from couch to couch each time, that the first man to sing sent it over to the first man on the second couch, and the latter to the first man on the third couch, then the second man to the second on the neighbouring couch, and so on ; so, they say, it seems the song was named scolium because of the intricate and twisted character of its path." [c]

cf. Dicaearchus, frags. 88-89 with Wehrli's commentary, *Die Schule des Aristoteles*, i, pp. 69-71 ; see also Bolkestein, *Adv. Crit.* p. 9 and particularly note 8.

ΠΡΟΒΛΗΜΑ Β[1]

Πότερον αὐτὸν δεῖ κατακλίνειν τοὺς ἑστιωμένους τὸν
ὑποδεχόμενον ἢ ἐπ' αὐτοῖς ἐκείνοις ποιεῖσθαι

Collocuntur Timo, pater Plutarchi, Plutarchus, Lamprias, alii

1. Τίμων ὁ ἀδελφὸς ἑστιῶν πλείονας ἕκαστον
ἐκέλευε τῶν εἰσιόντων ὅποι βούλεται παρεμβάλλειν
D καὶ κατακλίνεσθαι, διὰ τὸ καὶ ξένους καὶ πολίτας
καὶ συνήθεις[2] καὶ οἰκείους καὶ ὅλως παντοδαποὺς
τοὺς κεκλημένους εἶναι. πολλῶν οὖν ἤδη παρόντων
ξένος τις ὥσπερ εὐπάρυφος ἐκ κωμῳδίας, ἐσθῆτί
τε περιττῇ καὶ ἀκολουθίᾳ παίδων ὑποσολοικότερος,
ἧκεν ἄχρι τῶν θυρῶν τοῦ ἀνδρῶνος, καὶ κύκλῳ
ταῖς ὄψεσιν ἐπελθὼν τοὺς κατακειμένους οὐκ
ἠθέλησεν εἰσελθεῖν ἀλλ' ᾤχετ' ἀπιών· καὶ πολλῶν
μεταθεόντων οὐκ ἔφη τὸν ἄξιον ἑαυτοῦ τόπον ὁρᾶν
λειπόμενον. ἐκεῖνον μὲν οὖν πολλῷ γέλωτι

χαίροντας εὐφημοῦντας ἐκπέμπειν δόμων

E ἐκέλευον οἱ κατακείμενοι· καὶ γὰρ ἦσαν πολλοὶ
μετρίως ὑποπεπωκότες.

2. Ἐπεὶ δὲ τὰ περὶ τὸ δεῖπνον τέλος εἶχεν, ὁ
πατὴρ ἐμὲ πορρωτέρω κατακείμενον προσειπών,
" Τίμων," ἔφη, " κἀγὼ κριτήν σε πεποιήμεθα
διαφερόμενοι· πάλαι γὰρ ἀκούει κακῶς ὑπ' ἐμοῦ

---

[1] The heading in T omits πρόβλημα, and B stands in the
right margin,—the normal arrangement in T.

[2] ἀσυνήθεις Reiske (cf. Chantraine, Rev. de Phil. xxii,
[1948], p. 97).

---

[a] The situation here described is used again by Plutarch in
Septem Sapientium Convivium where Alexidemus takes
offence and leaves the party of Periander (Mor. 148 E ff.).
The word here translated " grandee " (cf. also Mor. 57 A) is

QUESTION 2

Whether the host should arrange the placing of his guests or
leave it to the guests themselves

Speakers : Timon, Plutarch, the father of Plutarch, Lamprias, and others

1. My brother Timon, upon an occasion when he was
host to a considerable number of guests, bade them
each as they entered take whatever place they wished
and there recline, for among those who had been
invited were foreigners as well as citizens, friends as
well as kinsmen, and, in a word, all sorts of people.
Now when many guests were already assembled, a
foreigner came up to the door of the banquet room,
like a grandee out of a comedy,[a] rather absurd with
his extravagant clothes and train of servants ; and,
when he had run his eyes round the guests who
had settled in their places, he refused to enter, but
withdrew and was on his way out when a number of
the guests ran to fetch him back, but he said that he
saw no place left worthy of him. Thereupon the
guests at table with much laughter urged them

> With joy and blessings send him from the house,[b]

for the fact is there were many who had had a little
something to drink.

2. When the dinner had come to an end, my father,
whose place was rather far from mine, spoke to me
and said, " Timon and I have made you judge of our
dispute, for I have long been scolding him now on

used of a luxurious garment connected with New Comedy
(Pollux, vii. 46 ; *cf.* Kock, *Com. Att. Frag.* ii, p. 222. 9) and
then of the men who wore them.

[b] Euripides, frag. 449, line 4 (Nauck, *Trag. Gr. Frag.* p.
498).

(615) διὰ τὸν ξένον· εἰ γὰρ διετάττετ᾽ ἀπ᾽ ἀρχῆς, ὥσπερ
ἐκέλευον ἐγώ, τὰς κλίσεις, οὐκ ἂν εὐθύνας ὑπείχο-
μεν ἀταξίας ἀνδρὶ δεινῷ

κοσμῆσαι ἵππους τε καὶ ἀνέρας ἀσπιδιώτας.

καὶ γὰρ δὴ Παῦλον Αἰμίλιον στρατηγὸν λέγουσιν,
ὅτε Περσέα καταπολεμήσας ἐν Μακεδονίᾳ πότους
συνεκρότει, κόσμῳ τε θαυμαστῷ περὶ πάντα καὶ
F περιττῇ[1] τάξει χρώμενον εἰπεῖν ὅτι τοῦ αὐτοῦ
ἀνδρός ἐστι καὶ φάλαγγα συστῆσαι φοβερωτάτην
καὶ συμπόσιον ἥδιστον, ἀμφότερα γὰρ εὐταξίας
εἶναι. καὶ τοὺς ἀρίστους καὶ βασιλικωτάτους ὁ
ποιητὴς εἴωθε ‘ κοσμήτορας λαῶν ’ προσαγορεύειν.
καὶ τὸν μέγαν θεὸν ὑμεῖς πού φατε τὴν ἀκοσμίαν
616 εὐταξίᾳ μεταβαλεῖν εἰς κόσμον οὔτ᾽ ἀφελόντα τῶν
ὄντων οὐδὲν οὔτε προσθέντα, τῷ δ᾽ ἕκαστον ἐπὶ
τὴν προσήκουσαν χώραν καταστῆσαι τὸ κάλλιστον
ἐξ ἀμορφοτάτου σχῆμα περὶ τὴν φύσιν ἀπεργα-
σάμενον.

‘‘ Ἀλλὰ ταῦτα μὲν τὰ σεμνότερα καὶ μείζονα
παρ᾽ ὑμῶν μανθάνομεν· αὐτοὶ δὲ καὶ τὴν περὶ τὰ
δεῖπνα δαπάνην ὁρῶμεν οὐδὲν ἔχουσαν ἐπιτερπὲς
οὐδ᾽ ἐλευθέριον, εἰ μὴ τάξεως μετάσχοι. διὸ καὶ
γελοῖόν ἐστι τοῖς μὲν ὀψοποιοῖς καὶ τραπεζοκόμοις
σφόδρα μέλειν τί πρῶτον ἢ τί δεύτερον ἢ μέσον ἢ
τελευταῖον ἐπάξουσιν, καὶ νὴ Δία μύρου τινὰ καὶ
στεφάνων καὶ ψαλτρίας, ἂν τύχῃ παροῦσα, χώραν
B καὶ τάξιν εἶναι, τοὺς δ᾽ ἐπὶ ταῦτα καλουμένους

---

[1] Hubert : τῇ λοιπῇ (defended by Bolkestein).

[a] *Iliad*, ii. 554.
[b] In 168 B.C. See *Life of Aemilius Paulus*, xxviii. 5 ; *Mor.*
198 B.   [c] *e.g. Iliad*, i. 16.

account of the foreigner. If he had arranged the placing of his guests at the beginning, as I told him to do, we would not be under suspicion of disorderliness and liable to public audit under the rule of a man skilful

in marshalling horses and shield-bearing men.[a]

Indeed, the story is told of the general Aemilius Paullus that, when he had conquered Perseus in Macedonia,[b] he gave drinking-parties which were characterized by wonderfully good order and remarkable organization in all their details, holding it to be the same man's duty to organize infantry divisions to be as terrifying and dinner-parties to be as agreeable as possible, for he claimed that both were the result of good organization. And the Poet is accustomed to call the bravest and most kingly men

marshallers of the people.[c]

Moreover, you philosophers, I suppose, admit that it was by good organization that the great god changed chaos into order,[d] neither taking anything from what existed nor adding anything, but working the fairest form in nature out of the most shapeless by settling each element into its fitting place.

" However, in these very solemn and important matters we are your pupils, but we see for ourselves that extravagant dinners are not pleasant or munificent without organization. Thus it is ridiculous for our cooks and waiters to be greatly concerned about what they shall bring in first, or what second or middle or last,—also, by Zeus, for some place to be found and arrangement made for perfume and crowns and a harp-girl, if there is a girl,—yet for those invited to

---

[d] Plato, *Timaeus*, 30 A ; *infra*, 719 C-D.

(616) εἰκῆ καὶ ὡς ἔτυχεν κατακλίναντα χορτάζειν, μήθ᾽
ἡλικίᾳ μήτ᾽ ἀρχῇ μήτ᾽ ἄλλῳ τινὶ τῶν ὁμοίων τὴν
ἁρμόττουσαν ἀποδιδόντα τάξιν, ἐν ᾗ τιμᾶται μὲν ὁ
προέχων ἐθίζεται δ᾽ ὁ δευτερεύων γυμνάζεται δ᾽
ὁ τάττων πρὸς διάκρισιν καὶ στοχασμὸν τοῦ
πρέποντος. οὐ γὰρ ἕδρα μὲν ἔστι καὶ στάσις τοῦ
κρείττονος, κατάκλισις δ᾽ οὐκ ἔστιν· οὐδὲ προ-
πίεται μὲν[1] ἑτέρῳ πρὸ ἑτέρου μᾶλλον ὁ ἑστιῶν,
περὶ δὲ τὰς κατακλίσεις παρόψεται τὰς διαφοράς,
εὐθὺς ἐν ἀρχῇ τὴν λεγομένην ' μίαν Μύκονον '
ἀποφήνας τὸ συμπόσιον." ἡ μὲν οὖν τοῦ πατρὸς
δικαιολογία τοιαύτη τις ἦν.

C   3. Ὁ δ᾽ ἀδελφὸς εἶπεν ὅτι τοῦ Βίαντος οὐκ εἴη
σοφώτερος ὥστ᾽ ἐκείνου δυεῖν φίλων ἀπειπαμένου
δίαιταν αὐτὸς ὁμοῦ τοσούτων μὲν οἰκείων τοσούτων
δ᾽ ἑταίρων γίνεσθαι κριτής, οὐ περὶ χρημάτων
ἀλλὰ περὶ πρωτείων ἀποφαινόμενος, ὥσπερ οὐ
φιλοφρονήσασθαι παρακεκληκὼς ἀλλ᾽ ἀνιᾶσαι τοὺς
ἐπιτηδείους. " ἄτοπος μὲν οὖν," ἔφη, " καὶ παροιμιώδης Μενέλαος, εἴ γε σύμβουλος ἐγένετο μὴ
παρακεκλημένος· ἀτοπώτερος δ᾽ ὁ ποιῶν ἑαυτὸν
ἀνθ᾽ ἑστιάτορος δικαστὴν καὶ κριτὴν τῶν οὐκ
ἐπιτρεπόντων οὐδὲ κρινομένων, τίς ἐστι βελτίων
τίνος ἢ χείρων· οὐ γὰρ εἰς ἀγῶνα καθείκασιν[2]
D ἀλλ᾽ ἐπὶ δεῖπνον ἥκουσιν. ἀλλ᾽ οὐδ᾽ εὐχερὴς ἡ

---

[1] Added by Benseler.   [2] Aldine edition : καθήκασιν.

---

[a] Strabo explains (x. 5. 9, p. 487) that the proverb derives
from the myth that giants slain by Heracles were buried
under Myconos and " is applied to those who bring under
one title even those things which are by nature separate "

this entertainment to be fed at places selected haphazardly and by chance, which give neither to age nor to rank nor to any other distinction the position that suits it, one which does honour to the outstanding man, leaves the next best at ease, and exercises the judgement and sense of propriety of the host. For the man of quality does not have his honour and his station in the world, yet fail to receive recognition in the place he occupies at dinner ; nor will a host drink to one of his guests before another, yet overlook their distinctions in placing them at table, and immediately at the beginning declare the dinner subject to the proverbial ' Myconos Equality.' " [a] Some such as this was my father's plea.

3. My brother, however, replied that he for his part was not wiser than Bias that he should become a judge over so many comrades and so many relatives too when Bias had refused to arbitrate between two of his friends, and should hand out decisions, not about property indeed, but about precedence, as though he had invited his friends not to entertain them, but to annoy them. " Certainly," he continued, " it was inept of Menelaüs, proverbially so, to become an adviser without being asked [b] ; more inept is the man who, instead of playing the host, makes himself a juryman and a judge over people who do not call upon him to decide an issue and are not on trial as to who is better than who, or worse; for they have not entered a contest, but have come for dinner.

(trans. H. L. Jones, LCL Strabo, v, p. 171) ; Strabo further notes that bald men are called Myconians because baldness is prevalent on the island. Further : Leutsch and Schneidewin, *Corpus Paroemiographorum Graecorum*, i, p. 445 ; Kock, *Com. Att. Frag.* iii, Adespoton 515.

[b] *Iliad*, ii. 408.

(616) διάκρισίς ἐστι, τῶν μὲν ἡλικίᾳ τῶν δὲ δυνάμει
τῶν δὲ χρείᾳ τῶν δ' οἰκειότητι διαφερόντων, ἀλλὰ
δεῖ καθάπερ ὑπόθεσιν μελετῶντα συγκριτικὴν τοὺς
Ἀριστοτέλους Τόπους ἢ τοὺς Θρασυμάχου Ὑπερ-
βάλλοντας ἔχειν προχείρους οὐδὲν τῶν χρησίμων
διαπραττόμενον ἀλλὰ τὴν κενὴν δόξαν ἐκ τῆς
ἀγορᾶς καὶ τῶν θεάτρων εἰς τὰ συμπόσια μετ-
άγοντα, καὶ τὰ μὲν ἄλλα πάθη πειρώμενον ἀνιέναι[1]
συνουσίᾳ, τὸν δ' ἐκ τύχης[2] ἐπισκευάζοντα τῦφον
ὃν[3] πολὺ μᾶλλον οἶμαι προσήκει τῆς ψυχῆς ἢ[4] τὸν
πηλὸν ἀπονιψαμένους τῶν ποδῶν ἐλαφρῶς καὶ
E ἀφελῶς παρὰ πότον ἀλλήλοις συμφέρεσθαι. νῦν
δὲ τὴν μὲν ἐξ ὀργῆς τινος ἢ πραγμάτων ἔχθραν
πειρώμεθα τῶν κεκλημένων ἀφαιρεῖν, τῇ δὲ φιλο-
τιμίᾳ πάλιν ὑπεκκάομεν καὶ ἀναζωπυροῦμεν, τοὺς
μὲν ταπεινοῦντες τοὺς δ' ὀγκοῦντες. καίτοι γ',
εἰ μὲν ἀκολουθήσουσι τῇ κατακλίσει προπόσεις τε
συνεχέστεραι καὶ παραθέσεις ἔτι δ' ὁμιλίαι καὶ
προσαγορεύσεις, παντάπασι γενήσεται σατραπικὸν
ἡμῖν ἀντὶ φιλικοῦ τὸ συμπόσιον· εἰ δὲ περὶ τἆλλα
τὴν ἰσότητα τοῖς ἀνδράσι φυλάξομεν, τί οὐκ ἐντεῦθεν ἀρξάμενοι πρῶτον ἐθίζομεν ἀτύφως καὶ ἀφελῶς
κατακλίνεσθαι μετ' ἀλλήλων, εὐθὺς ἀπὸ τῶν
F θυρῶν ὁρῶντας, ὅτι δημοκρατικόν ἐστι τὸ δεῖπνον[5]

[1] Schott : ἄ (not ἅ) before an erasure of 5-6 letters in which
a later hand has written φαιρεῖν τῆς and then added ς to
συνουσία.

[2] δ' ἐκ τύχης Hubert : δὲ τύχῃ, the last changed by a later
hand to τῦφον.

[3] τῦφον ὅν Turnebus : lac. 5 ον T, later corrected to ὅν
presumably by the hand which changed τύχῃ to τῦφον.

30

Moreover the decision is not easy, differing as the guests do in age, in influence, in intimacy, and in kinship ; on the contrary, one must have at hand, like the student of a principle of comparison, the *Methodology* of Aristotle [a] or the *Dominants* of Thrasymachus,[b] even though he accomplishes nothing useful, but rather transfers empty fame from market-place and theatre to social gatherings, and, in his attempt to relax by fellowship the other passions, accidentally refurbishes a vanity which I think much more fitting for men to have washed from their soul than the mud from their feet, if they are to meet at drink with each other easily and without affectation. As things are now, we try to remove our guests' hostility, no matter what angry passion or troubles it comes from ; but if we humble some of them and exalt others, we shall rekindle their hostility and set it aflame again through ambitious rivalry. And indeed, if the continuous toasts and the serving of food, and the conversation and discourse as well, shall be in strict conformity with the order of the guests' seating, our party will become in all respects a completely viceregal affair instead of a friendly gathering. If in other matters we are to preserve equality among men, why not begin with this first and accustom them to take their places with each other without vanity and ostentation, because they understand as soon as they enter the door

---

[a] *Topics*, 116 ff. The title Τόποι used by Plutarch is appropriate for the content of this section of the Τοπικά ; it also gives him a pun on τόποι, " places at table."

[b] Diels-Kranz, *Frag. d. Vorsokratiker*, ii¹⁰, p. 325, frag. 7.

---

[4] Added by presumably the same later hand in T.

[5] δημοτικόν (δημοκρατικόν Pohlenz) ἐστι τὸ δεῖπνον Kronenberg : δημόκριτος ἐπὶ τὸ δεῖπνον.

(616) καὶ οὐκ ἔχει τόπον[1] ἐξαίρετον ὥσπερ ἀκρόπολιν,[2]
ἐφ᾽ οὗ κατακλιθεὶς ὁ πλούσιος ἐντρυφήσει τοῖς εὐτελεστέροις; "[3]

4. Ἐπεὶ δὲ καὶ ταῦτ᾽ ἐρρήθη καὶ τὴν κρίσιν ἀπ-
ῄτουν οἱ παρόντες, ἔφην ἐγὼ διαιτητὴς ᾑρημένος
οὐ κριτὴς βαδιεῖσθαι διὰ μέσου. " νέους μὲν
γάρ," εἶπον, " ἑστιῶντας καὶ πολίτας καὶ συνήθεις
617 ἐθιστέον, ὥς φησι Τίμων, ἀφελῶς καὶ ἀτύφως
κατανέμειν αὐτοὺς εἰς ἣν ἂν τύχωσι χώραν, καλὸν
εἰς φιλίαν ἐφόδιον τὴν εὐκολίαν λαμβάνοντας· ἐν
δὲ ξένοις ἢ ἄρχουσιν ἢ πρεσβυτέροις φιλοσοφοῦντες
δέδια μὴ δοκῶμεν τῇ αὐλείῳ τὸν τῦφον ἀπο-
κλείοντες εἰσάγειν τῇ παραθύρῳ μετὰ πολλῆς
ἀδιαφορίας. ἐν ᾧ καὶ συνηθείᾳ τι καὶ νόμῳ
δοτέον· ἢ καὶ προπόσεις καὶ προσαγορεύσεις ἀν-
έλωμεν, αἷσπερ οὐ[4] τοὺς ἐπιτυγχάνοντας οὐδ᾽ ἀκρί-
τως ἀλλ᾽ ὡς ἐνδέχεται μάλιστ᾽ εὐλαβῶς[5] χρώμενοι
τιμῶμεν

B ἕδρῃ τε κρέασίν τ᾽ ἠδὲ πλείοις δεπάεσσιν

ὥς φησιν ὁ τῶν Ἑλλήνων βασιλεύς, τὴν τάξιν ἐν
πρώτῃ τιμῇ τιθέμενος. ἐπαινοῦμεν δὲ καὶ τὸν
Ἀλκίνουν, ὅτι τὸν ξένον ἱδρύει παρ᾽ αὐτὸν

---

[1] ἔχει τόπον added by Kronenberg : lac. 3-4.
[2] ωσ lac. 5-6 πολιν as restored by a later hand in T.
[3] ἐντρυφήσει τοῖς εὐτελεστέροις Hubert : ἐν τῆι κατακλίσει
τοῖς εὐτελεστάτοις.
[4] αἷσπερ οὐ Bases : αἷς πρός.

that the dinner is a democratic affair and has no outstanding place like an acropolis where the rich man is
to recline and lord it over meaner folk ?"

4. When these arguments had been delivered and
those present were demanding the decision, I said
that, since I had been chosen arbitrator, not judge, I
would take a middle course. " Now if," I said, " we
are entertaining young men, fellow citizens and intimates, we must accustom them, as Timon says, to
take for themselves without ostentation and vanity
whatever places they happen to find, taking good
humour as a fine viaticum to friendship ; but when
we are occupied with learned talk in the company of
foreigners or magistrates or older men, I am afraid
that, if we shut vanity out at the court-yard gate, we
may seem to be letting it in by the side gate, and
with plenty of non-distinctions. In this we must
yield something to custom and usage; otherwise, let
us do away with the drinking of toasts and with
familiar greetings, of which we make use when we
are doing honour not just to anyone nor carelessly,
but as carefully as possible

> With place at table, meat, and many a cup,

as the king of the Greeks says,[a] putting order in
highest honour. And we praise Alcinoüs too because
he seats the stranger beside himself :

[a] The verse stands in a speech of Hector's at *Iliad*, viii.
162, in a speech of Sarpedon's at *Iliad*, xii. 311. Like mis-
takes are made by Plutarch elsewhere (for example, 630 E and
741 F). As Hubert notes, the error at 617 A may indeed be
due to the confused recollection of Agamemnon's remarks
about dinners in honour of the Elders (*Iliad*, iv. 343 ff.).

---

[5] μάλιστ᾽ εὐλαβῶς Capps, μάλιστα πεφυλαγμένως Reiske :
μάλιστα.

(617)   υἱὸν ἀναστήσας, ἀγαπήνορα Λαομέδοντα,
          ὅς οἱ πλησίον ἷζε, μάλιστα δέ μιν φιλέεσκεν.

τὸ γὰρ εἰς τὴν τοῦ φιλουμένου χώραν καθίσαι τὸν
ἱκέτην ἐπιδέξιον ἐμμελῶς καὶ φιλάνθρωπον. ἔστι
δὲ καὶ παρὰ τοῖς θεοῖς διάκρισις τῶν τοιούτων· ὁ
μὲν γὰρ Ποσειδῶν καίπερ ὕστατος εἰς τὴν ἐκκλησίαν παραγενόμενος ' ἷζεν ἄρ' ἐν μέσσοισιν,'
ὡς ταύτης αὐτῷ τῆς χώρας προσηκούσης. ἡ δ'
Ἀθηνᾶ φαίνεται τὸν πλησίον ἀεὶ τοῦ Διὸς τόπον
ἐξαίρετον ἔχουσα· καὶ τοῦτο παρεμφαίνει μὲν ὁ
ποιητὴς δι' ὧν ἐπὶ τῆς Θέτιδός φησιν

C   ἡ δ' ἄρα πὰρ Διὶ πατρὶ καθέζετο, εἶξε δ'
    Ἀθήνη,

διαρρήδην δ' ὁ Πίνδαρος λέγει

        πῦρ πνέοντος ἅ τε κεραυνοῦ
        ἄγχιστα ἡμένη.

καίτοι φήσει Τίμων οὐ δεῖν ἀφαιρεῖσθαι τῶν
ἄλλων ἑνὶ προσνέμοντα τὴν τιμήν. ὅπερ αὐτὸς
ἔοικε ποιεῖν μᾶλλον· ἀφαιρεῖται γὰρ ὁ κοινὸν
ποιῶν τὸ ἴδιον (ἴδιον δὲ τὸ κατ' ἀξίαν ἑκάστου)
καὶ ποιεῖ δρόμου καὶ σπουδῆς τὸ πρωτεῖον ἀρετῇ
καὶ συγγενείᾳ[1] καὶ ἀρχῇ καὶ τοῖς τοιούτοις ὀφειλό-
μενον. καὶ τὸ λυπηρὸς εἶναι τοῖς κεκλημένοις
φεύγειν δοκῶν μᾶλλον ἐφέλκεται καθ' αὑτοῦ· λυπεῖ
γὰρ ἀποστερῶν τῆς συνήθους τιμῆς ἕκαστον.

---

[1] εὐγενείᾳ Herwerden.

[a] *Odyssey*, vii. 170 f.   Plutarch's Laomedon is a variant
(found also in some mss. of Homer) on Laodamas.
[b] *Iliad*, xx. 15.   [c] *Iliad*, xxiv. 100.

> His manly son Laomedon, who sat
> Beside him, dearest of his sons, he caused
> To rise and gave the guest his place.[a]

For it is exquisitely courteous and considerate to seat a suppliant in the place of a loved one. Furthermore, among the gods too a distinction prevails in such matters. Poseidon, for instance, even though he came last into the assembly,

> Took his seat in the middle,[b]

implying that this place belonged to him. And Athena is always seen to occupy the place of honour beside Zeus; this the Poet shows incidentally by what he says of Thetis,

> She then sat down next Father Zeus,
> Athena giving place to her[c];

and Pindar expressly says of Athena,

> She sat beside the thunderbolt
> That breathes out fire.[d]

Nevertheless Timon will say that one ought not to rob the other guests of the honour due to position by granting the position of honour to one of them. Yet this is just what he himself seems to do by preference; for the man who turns an individual's prerogative (each man's according to his worth) into common property is committing a theft, and the recognition due to virtue, kinship, public service, and such things he is giving to the foot-race and to speed. Though he thinks that he avoids being offensive to his guests, he draws it down all the more upon himself to be so, for he offends each one of them by depriving him of his accustomed honour.

---

[d] Frag. 146 (Snell) with omissions.

(617) " Ἐμοὶ δ' οὐ λίαν χαλεπὸν εἶναι δοκεῖ τὸ περὶ
D τὴν διάκρισιν· πρῶτον μὲν γὰρ ἐφάμιλλοι τοῖς
ἀξιώμασι πολλοὶ πρὸς μίαν κλῆσιν οὐ ῥᾳδίως
ἀπαντῶσιν· ἔπειτα πλειόνων τόπων ἐν δόξῃ γεγονότων ἀφθονία τῆς διανομῆς ἔστιν, ἄν τις εὐστοχεῖν
δύνηται, τὸν μὲν ὅτι πρῶτος, τὸν δ' ὅτι μέσος,
τὸν δ' ὅτι παρ' αὐτὸν ἢ μετὰ φίλου τινὸς ἢ
συνήθους ἢ καθηγητοῦ, διδοὺς ἑκάστῳ τῶν ἀξιω-
ματικῶν λεγομένων, τοῖς δ' ἄλλοις δωρεὰς καὶ
φιλοφροσύνην, ἄλυπον[1] ἀνάπαυλαν μᾶλλον τῆς
τιμῆς. ἂν δ' ἄκριτοι[2] μὲν αἱ ἀξίαι δύσκολοι δ'
οἱ ἄνδρες ὦσιν, ὅρα τίνα μηχανὴν ἐπάγω· κατα-
κλίνω γὰρ εἰς τὸν ἔνδοξον μάλιστα τόπον, ἂν μὲν
ᾖ πατήρ, τοῦτον ἀράμενος, εἰ δὲ μή, πάππον ἢ
E πενθερὸν ἢ πατρὸς ἀδελφὸν ἤ τινα τῶν ὁμολο-
γουμένην καὶ ἰδίαν ἐχόντων παρὰ τῷ δεχομένῳ τιμῆς ὑπεροχήν, ἐκ τῶν Ὁμήρου τὸ θεώρημα τοῦτο
λαμβάνων καθηκόντων. καὶ γὰρ ἐκεῖ δήπουθεν ὁ
Ἀχιλλεὺς τὸν Μενέλεων καὶ τὸν Ἀντίλοχον περὶ
τῶν δευτερείων τῆς ἱπποδρομίας ὁρῶν διαφερο-
μένους καὶ δεδοικὼς μὴ πορρωτέρω προέλθωσιν
ὀργῆς καὶ φιλονεικίας ἑτέρῳ βούλεται τὸ ἔπαθλον
ἀποδιδόναι, λόγῳ μὲν Εὔμηλον οἰκτίρων καὶ τι-
μῶν, ἔργῳ δὲ τῆς ἐκείνων διαφορᾶς τὴν αἰτίαν
ἀφαιρῶν.''

5. Ἐμοῦ δὲ τοιαῦτα λέγοντος ὁ Λαμπρίας ἐκ
παραβύστου καθήμενος καθάπερ εἰώθει μέγα
F φθεγξάμενος ἠρώτα τοὺς παρόντας, εἰ διδόασιν

---

[1] Wyttenbach : ἔλιπον.
[2] δ' ἄκριτοι Capps, Helmbold, Bolkestein : δὲ lac. 3-4 τοι.

" To me, however, the matter of making distinctions among one's guests does not seem very hard. In the first place it does not easily happen that many men who are rivals in honour meet at one party. Next, inasmuch as there are a number of places which have come to be held in honour, their distribution does not arouse jealousy if the host is able to guess rightly and give to each of the so-called dignitaries the place he likes,—because it is the first, or in the middle, or beside the host himself, or some friend of the guest, or intimate, or teacher,—and receive the other guests with gifts and friendly courtesies, an undisturbed tranquillity rather than honour of place. But if the honours are hard to decide, and the guests are touchy, then see what device I apply. If my father is present, I do him the honour of putting him in the most distinguished place ; if he is not present, I honour my grandfather, or my father-in-law, or my father's brother, or any one among those guests who admittedly have a particular claim to precedence at the hands of the host, and it is from the poems of Homer that I get this rule of propriety. There, you may recall, when Achilles sees Menelaüs and Antilochus disputing about the second prize in a horse-race,[a] he is afraid that they may become too angry and quarrelsome and so proposes to give the prize to another, ostensibly because he feels sorry for Eumelus, whom he thus honours, but actually in order to remove the cause of the quarrel between Menelaüs and Antilochus."

5. As I was speaking in this fashion, Lamprias from a small couch which he occupied asked the assembled company in his customary loud voice if

---

[a] *Iliad*, xxiii. 534 ff.

(617) αὐτῷ νουθετῆσαι ληροῦντα δικαστήν· κελευόντων
δὲ πάντων χρῆσθαι παρρησίᾳ καὶ μὴ φείδεσθαι,
" τίς δ᾽ ἄν," ἔφη, " φείσαιτο φιλοσόφου γένεσι καὶ
618 πλούτοις καὶ ἀρχαῖς ὥσπερ θέαν ἐν συμποσίῳ
κατανέμοντος ἢ προεδρίας ψηφισμάτων ἀμφι-
κτυονικῶν διδόντος, ὅπως μηδ᾽ ἐν οἴνῳ τὸν τῦφον
ἀποφύγωμεν; οὔτε γὰρ πρὸς τὸ ἔνδοξον ἀλλὰ
πρὸς τὸ ἡδὺ δεῖ ποιεῖσθαι τὰς κατακλίσεις, οὔτε
τὴν ἑνὸς ἑκάστου σκοπεῖν ἀξίαν ἀλλὰ τὴν ἑτέρου
πρὸς ἕτερον σχέσιν καὶ ἁρμονίαν, ὥσπερ ἄλλων[1]
τινῶν εἰς μίαν κοινωνίαν παραλαμβανομένων. οὐδὲ
γὰρ ὁ οἰκοδόμος τὸν Ἀττικὸν λίθον ἢ τὸν Λακωνι-
κὸν πρὸ τοῦ βαρβαρικοῦ διὰ[2] τὴν εὐγένειαν τίθησιν
οὐδ᾽ ὁ ζωγράφος τῷ πολυτελεστάτῳ χρώματι τὴν
ἡγουμένην ἀποδίδωσι χώραν οὐδ᾽ ὁ ναυπηγὸς
B προτάττει τὴν Ἰσθμικὴν πίτυν ἢ τὴν Κρητικὴν
κυπάριττον, ἀλλ᾽ ὡς ἂν ἀλλήλοις ἕκαστα συντεθέντα καὶ συναρμοσθέντα μέλλῃ τὸ κοινὸν ἔργον
ἰσχυρὸν καὶ καλὸν καὶ χρήσιμον παρέχειν, οὕτω
κατανέμουσιν. καὶ τὸν θεὸν ὁρᾷς, ὃν ' ἀριστο-
τέχναν ' ἡμῖν[3] ὁ Πίνδαρος προσεῖπεν, οὐ πανταχοῦ
τὸ πῦρ ἄνω τάττοντα καὶ κάτω τὴν γῆν, ἀλλ᾽ ὡς
ἂν αἱ χρεῖαι τῶν σωμάτων ἀπαιτῶσιν·

τοῦτο μὲν ἐν κόγχαισι θαλασσονόμοις βαρυνώ-
τοις,

ναὶ μὴν κηρύκων τε λιθορρίνων χελύων τε,

φησὶν Ἐμπεδοκλῆς,

ἔνθ᾽ ὄψει χθόνα χρωτὸς ὑπέρτατα ναιετάουσαν,

---

[1] ὑλῶν Kronenberg.
[2] Added by Vulcobius.

they gave him leave to reprove a judge who was talking nonsense. When all urged him to speak his mind freely and show no mercy, " But who could," he said, " show mercy to a philosopher who assigns places at a dinner-party to family, wealth, and official position as one would assign seats at a show, a philosopher who grants honours of precedence after the fashion of amphictyonic decrees, so that not even when we sit over wine may we flee conceit ? For it is not prestige, but pleasure which must determine the placing of guests ; it is not the rank of each which must be considered, but the affinity and suitability of each to each, as is done when other things are associated for a common purpose. The builder does not value Attic or Laconian stone more highly because of its noble origin than he does foreign stone, nor does the painter give foremost place to the most expensive pigment, nor the shipwright prefer Isthmian pine or Cretan cypress, but they select such materials as may be likely, when combined and joined with each other, to render the finished product strong, beautiful, and useful. And you yourself see that god, whom Pindar named the ' master artisan,' [a] does not in all cases place fire above and earth below, but disposes them as the needs of bodies require. Empedocles says :

> In heavy-backed sea-mussels this is found
> And turtles stony skinned and herald-fish,
> Where you will see the earth-material
> At rest upon the highest parts of flesh,[b]

[a] Frag. 57, line 2 (Snell). The god is Zeus of Dodona.
[b] Diels-Kranz, *Frag. d. Vorsokratiker*, i[10], p. 339, frag. 76. " Herald-fish," the purple mollusc.

---

[3] Bolkestein : ἡμῶν, with a superfluous acute accent to the left of the circumflex, but no separation between μ and ω.

(618) οὐχ ἦν ἡ φύσις δίδωσι χώραν, ἀλλ᾽ ἦν ἡ πρὸς τὸ
C κοινὸν ἔργον ποθεῖ σύνταξις, ταύτην ἔχουσαν.
πανταχοῦ μὲν οὖν ἀταξία πονηρόν, ἐν δ᾽ ἀνθρώποις,
καὶ ταῦτα πίνουσιν, ἐγγινομένη μάλιστα τὴν αὑτῆς
ἀναδείκνυσι μοχθηρίαν ὕβρει καὶ κακοῖς ἄλλοις
ἀμυθήτοις, ἃ προϊδέσθαι καὶ φυλάξασθαι τακτικοῦ
καὶ ἁρμονικοῦ ἀνδρός ἐστιν."

6. Ὀρθῶς οὖν ἔφαμεν λέγειν αὐτὸν ἡμεῖς, καί,
"τί δὴ φθονεῖς τῶν τακτικῶν ἡμῖν καὶ ἁρμονι-
κῶν;" [ὧν]¹ ἐλέγομεν.

"Οὐδείς," ἔφη, "φθόνος, ἂν μέλλητε πείθεσθαι
μετακινοῦντί μοι καὶ μετακοσμοῦντι τὸ συμπόσιον,
ὥσπερ τῷ Ἐπαμεινώνδᾳ τὴν φάλαγγα." συνε-
D χωροῦμεν οὖν οὕτω ποιεῖν ἅπαντες. ὁ δὲ τοὺς
παῖδας ἐκ μέσου κελεύσας γενέσθαι, καταβλέψας
ἕκαστον, "ἀκούσατ᾽," εἶπεν, "ὡς μέλλω συντάτ-
τειν ὑμᾶς ἀλλήλοις· βούλομαι γὰρ προειπεῖν.
δοκεῖ γάρ μοι καὶ τὸν Ὅμηρον οὐκ ἀδίκως ὁ
Θηβαῖος αἰτιάσασθαι Παμμένης ὡς τῶν ἐρωτικῶν
ἄπειρον, ὅτι φῦλα φύλοις συνέταξεν καὶ φρατρίας
φρατρίαις συνέμιξεν, δέον ἐραστὴν μετ᾽ ἐρωμένου
παρεμβάλλειν ἵν᾽ ᾖ σύμπνους ἡ φάλαγξ δι᾽ ὅλης
ἔμψυχον ἔχουσα δεσμόν. τοιοῦτο κἀγὼ βούλομαι
ποιῆσαι τὸ συμπόσιον ἡμῶν, οὐ πλουσίῳ πλούσιον
οὐδὲ νέῳ νέον οὐδ᾽ ἄρχοντι συγκατακλίνων ἄρχοντα
E καὶ φίλῳ φίλον· ἀκίνητος γὰρ αὕτη καὶ ἀργὴ πρὸς
εὐνοίας ἐπίδοσιν ἢ γένεσιν ἡ τάξις· ἀλλὰ τῷ

---

¹ ὧν deleted by Xylander (translation); ὧν ἐλέγομεν deleted by Bolkestein.

that is, not occupying the position which nature allots, but the position which the functional order of the organism demands. Now disorder is everywhere a mischievous thing, but when it occurs among men, and that too when they are drinking, then especially it reveals its viciousness by the insolence and other unspeakable evils it engenders ; to foresee these and guard against them is the duty of a man with any pretension to being an organizer and an arranger."

6. "So why grudge us our organizers and arrangers ? " I said, admitting the truth of his statement. "There is no grudging," he replied, "if you will allow me to change and rearrange our party as Epaminondas changed infantry formations." We all agreed to do so. He then ordered the servants to leave the room and with a glance of appraisal at each of us continued : "Hear, then, how I intend to array you with each other,—for I want to tell you beforehand. The fact is I think that Pammenes [a] the Theban was not unfair in accusing Homer of being a man without skill in the ways of love because he arrayed clans with clans and joined brotherhoods with brotherhoods,[b] when he ought to have brigaded lover with beloved in order that throughout its whole the army might possess a living bond and be animated by one spirit. Such a company I wish to make our dinner-party, not seating rich men with rich man, nor young man with young man, nor official with official and friend with friend, for this arrangement is static and inefficient in the promotion and creation of good-fellowship ; but I supply what suits him to the man

---

[a] *Pelopidas*, xviii ; *Amatorius*, 761 B. For Epaminondas' revolutionary tactic at Leuctra see *Kl. P.* ii. 281.

[b] *Iliad*, ii. 363.

(618) δεομένῳ τὸ οἰκεῖον προσαρμόττων κελεύω φιλο-
λόγῳ μὲν ὑποκατακλίνεσθαι φιλομαθῆ δυσκόλῳ
δὲ πρᾶον ἀδολέσχῳ δὲ πρεσβύτῃ φιλήκοον νεα-
νίσκον τῷ δ' ἀλαζόνι τὸν εἴρωνα τῷ δ' ὀργίλῳ τὸν
σιωπηλόν· ἐὰν δέ που κατίδω πλούσιον μεγα-
λόδωρον, ἄξω πρὸς αὐτὸν ἐκ γωνίας τινὸς ἀναστήσας πένητα χρηστόν, ἵν' ὥσπερ ἐκ πλήρους
κύλικος εἰς κενὴν ἀπορροή τις γένηται. σοφιστὴν
δὲ κωλύω συγκατακλίνεσθαι σοφιστῇ καὶ ποιητὴν
ποιητῇ·

F   πτωχὸς γὰρ πτωχῷ φθονέει[1] καὶ ἀοιδὸς ἀοιδῷ·

καίτοι Σωσικλῆς οὗτος καὶ Μόδεστος ἐνταῦθα
συνερείδοντες ἔπος παρ' ἔπος[2] ἀναζωπυρεῖν[3] φλόγα
μεγάλην[4] κινδυνεύουσιν τὰ κάλλιστα. διίστημι δὲ
καὶ στραγγαλιῶντας καὶ φιλολοιδόρους καὶ ὀξυ-
θύμους πρᾶον[5] τινα παρεντιθεὶς μέσον ὥσπερ
619 μάλαγμα τῆς ἀντιτυπίας, ἀλειπτικοὺς δὲ καὶ
κυνηγετικοὺς καὶ γεωργικοὺς συνάγω· τῶν γὰρ
ὁμοιοτήτων ἡ μὲν μάχιμος ὥσπερ ἀλεκτρυόνων,
ἡ δ' ἐπιεικὴς ὥσπερεὶ[6] τῶν κολοιῶν. συνάγω δὲ
καὶ ποτικοὺς εἰς ταὐτὸ καὶ ἐρωτικούς, οὐ μόνον
' ὅσοις ἔρωτος δῆγμα παιδικῶν[7] πρόσεστιν,' ὥς
φησι Σοφοκλῆς, ἀλλὰ καὶ τοὺς ἐπὶ γυναιξὶ καὶ
τοὺς ἐπὶ παρθένοις δακνομένους· τῷ γὰρ αὐτῷ
θαλπόμενοι πυρὶ μᾶλλον ἀλλήλων ἀντιλήψονται,

---

[1] φθονέει added by Xylander.
[2] παρ' ἔπος Stephanus : παρὰ lac. 6-8.
[3] Bernardakis : ζωπυρίων.
[4] Bernardakis : μὲν ἀλλά.
[5] Bernardakis : lac. 3-4.
[6] Doehner : ὥσπερ οἱ (sic).
[7] παιδικῶν added by Bernardakis from Mor. 77 B, which

who lacks it and invite him who is eager to learn to
sit with a learned man, the gentle with the peevish,
the young who like to listen with the old who like to
talk, the reticent with the braggart, the calm with the
irascible. And if by chance I see a guest who is rich
and munificent, I shall rout out from some corner an
honest poor man and introduce him, so that an out-
pouring from a full into an empty goblet may take
place. But sophist I shall forbid to sit with sophist
and poet with poet,

> For beggar is jealous of beggar and bard of bard.[a]

Indeed, Sosicles and Modestus here, as they set verse
against verse,[b] run a very fair risk of kindling a great
flame. My way is to separate contentious, abusive,
and quick-tempered men by placing between them
some easy-going man as a cushion to soften their
clashing ; and athletes, hunters, and farmers I intend
to bring together ; for the characteristic which unites
the former group is a contentiousness like that of
cocks, while the latter group have the gentleness of
daws. And I shall put together men who like to
drink,—and lovers too, not only those

> Who feel the bite of love for lads,

as Sophocles says,[c] but also those bitten by love for
women and for girls. For they will cleave to each
other all the more for being heated by the same fire,

---

[a] Hesiod, *Works and Days*, 26.

[b] *Cf.* Aristophanes, *Clouds*, 1375.

[c] Nauck, *Trag. Gr. Frag.*[2], p. 309, frag. 757 ; Pearson,
The Fragments of Sophocles, iii, p. 55, frag. 841. Quoted also
at *Mor.* 77 B.

Pearson misjudges (Sophocles, frag. 841) and Babbitt mis-
translates (LCL *Mor.* i, p. 413).

(619) καθάπερ ὁ κολλώμενος σίδηρος, ἂν μὴ νὴ Δία τοῦ
αὐτοῦ τύχωσιν ἢ τῆς αὐτῆς ἐρῶντες.''

ΠΡΟΒΛΗΜΑ Γ

B   Διὰ τί τῶν τόπων ὁ καλούμενος ὑπατικὸς ἔσχε τιμήν

Collocuntur iidem qui in qu. II

Ἐκ¹ τούτου περὶ τῶν τόπων ἐνέπεσε ζήτησις.
ἄλλοι γὰρ ἄλλοις ἔντιμοι, Πέρσαις μὲν ὁ μεσαίτατος
ἐφ' οὗ κατακλίνεται βασιλεύς, Ἕλλησι δ' ὁ πρῶτος,
Ῥωμαίοις δ' ὁ τῆς μέσης κλίνης τελευταῖος ὃν
ὑπατικὸν προσαγορεύουσιν, τῶν δὲ περὶ τὸν Πόντον
Ἑλλήνων ἐνίοις, ὥσπερ Ἡρακλεώταις, ἔμπαλιν ὁ
τῆς μέσης πρῶτος. ἀλλὰ περὶ τοῦ γ' ὑπατικοῦ
λεγομένου μάλιστα διηποροῦμεν. οὗτος γὰρ ἐπρώ-
τευε τῇ τιμῇ καθ' ἡμᾶς, καὶ τὴν αἰτίαν οὔθ' ὡς
C ὁ πρῶτος οὔθ' ὡς ὁ μέσος εἶχεν νενομισμένην
ἔτι, καὶ τῶν συμβεβηκότων αὐτῷ τὰ μὲν οὐκ ἦν
ἴδια τούτου μόνου τὰ δ' οὐδεμιᾶς ἄξια σπουδῆς
ἐφαίνετο. πλὴν τρία γε τῶν λεχθέντων ἐκίνει,
πρῶτον μὲν ὅτι τοὺς βασιλεῖς καταλύσαντες οἱ
ὕπατοι καὶ πρὸς τὸ δημοτικώτερον ἅπαντα μετακο-
σμήσαντες ἐκ τῆς μέσης καὶ βασιλικῆς χώρας
ὑπῆγον αὐτοὺς κάτω συγχωροῦντες, ὡς μηδὲ
τοῦτο τῆς ἀρχῆς αὐτῶν καὶ ἐξουσίας ἐπαχθὲς εἴη

¹ ἐκ added by Reiske, ἐκ δὲ by Xylander (see Bolkestein,
Adv. Crit. p. 70).

ᵃ I accept Bolkestein's interpretation of καθ' ἡμᾶς (Adv.
Crit. p. 70). For the imperfects of the Greek in this sentence
see Kühner-Gerth, Ausfüh. Gr. Gram. i, p. 145. 5 ; Smyth,
Gr. Gram. 1901.

like welded iron,—unless, by Zeus, they happen to be
in love with the same lad or the same girl."

QUESTION 3

Why the place at banquets called the consul's acquired honour

The speakers are the same as in the preceding conversation

NEXT our inquiry fell upon the subject of the places
at a banquet. It did so because different peoples hold
different places in honour : the Persians the most
central place, occupied by the king ; the Greeks the
first place ; the Romans the last place on the middle
couch, called the consul's place ; and some of the
Greeks who dwell around the Pontus (the people of
Heraclea, for example) contrariwise the first place of
the middle couch. However, it was about the so-
called consul's place that we were particularly puzzled.
For in our time [a] this place is held first in honour, and
yet the reason is no longer recognized as it is in the
case of the first or the middle place ; and of the
characteristics of the consul's place some do not belong to it alone and the rest seem worthy of no serious
consideration. Yet three of the explanations advanced made an impression upon us.[b] The first was
that the consuls, when they had put down the
monarchy and rearranged everything in a more democratic fashion, by way of concession demoted themselves from the royal central place, in order that not
even this mark of their office and their power should

[b] For the interpretation of the following passage see
Becker and Göll, *Gallus*, iii (Berlin, 1882), pp. 380 ff. ; *cf.*
RE, *s.v.* " Triclinium," col. 95.

(619) τοῖς συνοῦσιν· δεύτερον δ' ὅτι, τῶν δυεῖν κλινῶν
ἀποδεδομένων τοῖς παρακεκλημένοις, ἡ τρίτη καὶ
D ταύτης ὁ πρῶτος τόπος μάλιστα τοῦ ἑστιῶντός
ἐστιν· ἐνταῦθα γὰρ ὥσπερ ἡνίοχος ἢ κυβερνήτης
ἐπὶ δεξιὰ πρὸς τὴν ἐπίβλεψιν ἐξικνεῖται τῆς
ὑπηρεσίας καὶ τοῦ φιλοφρονεῖσθαι καὶ διαλέγεσθαι
τοῖς παροῦσιν οὐκ ἀπήρτηται· τῶν δὲ[1] συνέγγιστα
τόπων ὁ μὲν[2] ὑπ' αὐτὸν ἢ γυναικὸς ἢ παίδων ἐστίν,
ὁ δ' ὑπὲρ αὐτὸν εἰκότως τῷ μάλιστα τιμωμένῳ
τῶν κεκλημένων ἀπεδόθη, ἵν' ἐγγὺς ᾖ τοῦ ἑστιῶντος. τρίτον δ' ἔχειν ἴδιον οὗτος ὁ τόπος ἐδόκει
τὸ πρὸς τὴν πρᾶξιν εὐφυές· οὐ γάρ ἐστιν ὁ τῶν
Ῥωμαίων ὕπατος οἷος Ἀρχίας ὁ Θηβαίων πολέ-
μαρχος, ὥστε, γραμμάτων ἢ λόγων αὐτῷ μεταξὺ
E δειπνοῦντι φροντίδος ἀξίων προσπεσόντων, ἐπι-
φθεγξάμενος, " εἰς ἕω τὰ σπουδαῖα," τὴν μὲν
ἐπιστολὴν παρῶσαι λαβεῖν δὲ τὴν Θηρίκλειον,

ἀλλὰ μάλ' ἐμμεμαὼς

καὶ περιεσκεμμένος ἐν τοῖς τοιούτοις καιροῖς. οὐ
γὰρ μόνον

ὠδῖνα τίκτει νὺξ κυβερνήτῃ σοφῷ[3]

κατὰ τὸν Αἰσχύλον,[4] ἀλλὰ καὶ πότου πᾶσα καὶ
ἀνέσεως ὥρα στρατηγῷ[5] καὶ ἄρχοντι φροντίδος
ἄξιον ἔργον.[6] ἵνα τοίνυν[7] ἀκοῦσαί θ' ἃ δεῖ καὶ

---

[1] Added by Vulcobius.
[2] γὰρ after μὲν deleted by Vulcobius.
[3] So Xylander from Aeschylus : τίκτει κυβ lac. 6-8.
[4] τὸν Αἰσχύλον Emperius (so Bolkestein, op. cit. p. 71) : τὸ
lac. 5-7.
[5] ἀνέσεως ἡδονὴ στρατη>γῷ Stephanus, ὥρα for ἡδονὴ
Pohlenz : lac. 5-8.

46

remain to offend their associates. The second explanation was that, inasmuch as two of the couches are given over to the guests, the third couch and the first place on it certainly belongs to the host,—for here, like a charioteer or a pilot, he is favourably placed to watch over the service and is not prevented from entertaining and conversing with those who are present,—and of the places nearest him the one which is below him belongs either to his wife or his children, while the one above him was given properly enough to the guest of honour in order that he might be near his host. Thirdly, this place seemed to have peculiar advantages for the transaction of business ; for the consul of the Romans is not like the Theban polemarch Archias,[a] and, when letters or messages deserving notice are brought to his attention in the midst of a dinner, does not push the letter aside with the remark " serious things tomorrow ! " and take up his Thericlean goblet [b] ; on the contrary the consul " is very stern " and prudent at such times. For not only does

> Night bring a skilful pilot
> The misery of fear,

as Aeschylus [c] says, but also every hour spent in drinking and in relaxation brings to a general or governor some business worthy of close attention. In order, then, that he may be able to hear about all

[a] See *Mor.* 596 E-F, and *Life of Pelopidas*, x, for more details and some variants of this anecdote ; *cf.* Nepos, *Pelopidas*, 3.
[b] For the Thericlean cylix see Athenaeus, 470 e, and *RE*, *s.v.* " Therikles," no. 2.
[c] *Suppliants*, 770 ; *cf. Mor.* 1090 A.

---

[6] ἔργον or τι (*sc.* τίκτει) Pohlenz ; ἐστιν. "Ita vero longius a traditione aberrabimus" : Bolkestein, *loc. cit.*
[7] Added by Bernardakis : lac. 3-4.

(619) προστάξαι καὶ ὑπογράψαι δύνηται, τοῦτον ἐξαίρε
τον ἔχει τὸν τόπον· ἐν ᾧ τῆς δευτέρας κλίνης τῇ
τρίτῃ[1] συναπτούσης, ἡ γωνία διάλειμμα ποιοῦσα
τῇ καμπῇ δίδωσιν καὶ γραμματεῖ καὶ ὑπηρέτῃ καὶ
F φύλακι σώματος καὶ ἀγγέλῳ τῶν ἀπὸ στρατο
πέδου προσελθεῖν διαλεχθῆναι πυθέσθαι, μήτε τινὸς
ἐνοχλοῦντος αὐτῷ μήτε τινὸς ἐνοχλουμένου τῶν
συμποτῶν, ἀλλὰ καὶ χεῖρα καὶ φωνὴν ὑπερδέξιον
ἔχοντι καὶ ἀκώλυτον.

620 ΠΡΟΒΛΗΜΑ Δ

Ποῖόν τινα δεῖ τὸν συμποσίαρχον εἶναι

Collocuntur Plutarchus, Crato, Theo

1. Κράτων ὁ γαμβρὸς ἡμῶν καὶ Θέων ὁ ἑταῖρος
ἔν τινι πότῳ παροινίας ἀρχὴν λαβούσης εἶτα
παυσαμένης λόγον ἐποιήσαντο περὶ τῆς συμποσιαρ
χίας, οἰόμενοί με δεῖν στεφανηφοροῦντα μὴ περι
ιδεῖν παλαιὸν[2] ἔθος ἐκλειφθὲν παντάπασιν, ἀλλ'
ἀνακαλεῖν καὶ καταστῆσαι πάλιν τῆς ἀρχῆς τὴν
νενομισμένην ἐπιστασίαν περὶ τὰ συμπόσια καὶ
διακόσμησιν. ἐδόκει δὲ ταῦτα καὶ τοῖς ἄλλοις,
B ὥστε θόρυβον ἐκ πάντων καὶ παράκλησιν γενέσθαι.
" Ἐπεὶ τοίνυν," ἔφην ἐγώ, " δοκεῖ ταῦτα πᾶσιν,

[1] Meziriacus : πρώτῃ.
[2] Added by Bernardakis : lac. 5.

---

[a] Presumably the husband of a niece (so Ziegler, after
Wilamowitz, *RE*, *s.v.* " Plutarchos," col. 651. 26-43). Further, see above, p. 9, note *c*.
[b] Cherniss (LCL *Mor.* xii, p. 7) believes that Θέων ὁ ἑταῖρος
here and in *De E*, 386 D, is probably the Theon of *De Pythiae
Oraculis, Non Posse Suaviter Vivi*, and *Quaest. Conviv.* iv. 3
(667 A) and viii. 6 (726 A ff.) ; further, that the Theon of *De*

urgent matters, give orders, and sign instructions, the consul occupies this special place at the banquet; there the space made at the corner where the line of couches turns between the second and third enables secretary, servant, bodyguard, or messenger reporting conditions at camp to approach the consul, speak with him, and learn his will without any of the guests annoying the consul or being annoyed by him,—on the contrary, the consul can write and speak under favourable conditions and without hindrance.

QUESTION 4

What sort of man the symposiarch must be

Speakers: Plutarch, Crato, Theon

1. CRATO, my relative by marriage,[a] and my friend Theon,[b] at a drinking-party at which tipsy fun had begun and then quieted down, got into a discussion about the office of symposiarch, being of the opinion that I ought to assume the chaplet and not allow an old custom to be altogether abandoned, but should revive and establish again the traditional authority of the office in regard to drinking-parties and their regulation. The other guests were of the same opinion, so that a great clamour arose from all sides and insistence that I should serve.

" Since, then," I said, "you are all of one opinion, I

Facie, whose home was in Egypt (939 c-d), is probably the Θέων ὁ γραμματικός of Quaest. Conviv. i. 9 (626 E) and viii. 8 (728 F); and finally, that certainly Θέων ὁ ἑταῖρος is not the same as the Theon of De Facie. Others have other solutions (Flacelière, Sur l'E de Delphes, p. 11; Ziegler, RE, s.v. " Plutarchos," col. 686, and s.v. " Theon," no. 10),—much less reasonable in my opinion.

(620) ἐμαυτὸν αἱροῦμαι συμποσίαρχον ὑμῶν καὶ κελεύω
τοὺς μὲν ἄλλους ὡς βούλονται πίνειν ἐν τῷ
παρόντι, Κράτωνα δὲ καὶ Θέωνα, τοὺς εἰσηγητὰς
καὶ νομοθέτας τοῦ δόγματος, ἔν τινι τύπῳ βραχέως
διελθεῖν, ὁποῖον ὄντα δεῖ τὸν συμποσίαρχον αἱρεῖ-
σθαι καὶ τί ποιούμενος τέλος ὁ αἱρεθεὶς ἄρξει καὶ
πῶς χρήσεται¹ τοῖς κατὰ τὸ² συμπόσιον· διελέσθαι
δὲ³ τὸν λόγον ἐφεξῆς⁴ αὐτοῖς ἐπιτρέπω.''⁵

2. Μικρὰ μὲν οὖν ἠκκίσαντο παραιτούμενοι·
κελευόντων δὲ πάντων πείθεσθαι τῷ ἄρχοντι καὶ
C ποιεῖν τὸ προσταττόμενον, ἔφη πρότερος ὁ Κράτων
ὅτι δεῖ τὸν μὲν φυλάκων ἄρχοντα φυλακικώτατον,
ὥς φησιν ὁ Πλάτων, εἶναι, τὸν δὲ συμποτῶν
συμποτικώτατον. '' ἔστι δὲ τοιοῦτος ἂν μήτε τῷ
μεθύειν εὐάλωτος ᾖ μήτε πρὸς τὸ πίνειν ἀπρό-
θυμος, ἀλλ' ὡς ὁ Κῦρος ἔλεγεν πρὸς Λακεδαι-
μονίους γράφων ὅτι τά τ' ἄλλα τοῦ ἀδελφοῦ
βασιλικώτερος εἴη καὶ φέροι καλῶς πολὺν ἄκρα-
τον· ὅ τε γὰρ παροινῶν ὑβριστὴς καὶ ἀσχήμων, ὅ
τ' αὖ παντάπασι νήφων ἀηδὴς καὶ παιδαγωγεῖν
μᾶλλον ἢ συμποσιαρχεῖν⁶ ἐπιτήδειος. ὁ μὲν οὖν
Περικλῆς, ὁσάκις ἡρημένος στρατηγὸς ἀναλαμ-

---

¹ Amyot: χρῆσθαι.

appoint myself your symposiarch, and I bid the rest
of you drink as you like for the present, but Crato and
Theon, the instigators and authors of this resolution,
I order to sketch in brief outline the qualities a man
ought to have to be chosen symposiarch, the objec-
tives the man selected will keep in view in the ad-
ministration of his office, and the manner in which he
will make use of drinking-party customs. I leave to
their discretion to determine between themselves the
order of their speaking."

2. Thus summoned to speak, with some small
degree of affected diffidence they tried to beg off, but
when all commanded them to obey the leader and do
his bidding, Crato began by saying that the com-
mander of guardsmen must be the quintessence of a
guardsman, to use Plato's phrase,[a] and the leader of
a company of drinkers must be the quintessence of a
convivial man. " And he is such if he is neither easily
overcome by drunkenness nor reluctant to drink,[b] but
like Cyrus,[c] who said in a letter to the Lacedaemonians that he was in general more kingly than his
brother and besides found no difficulty in carrying a
great deal of undiluted wine,—for the drunkard is
insolent and rude and, on the other hand, the complete teetotaler is disagreeable and more fit for tending children than for presiding over a drinking-party.
Now Pericles, after he had been elected head of

[a] *Republic*, 412 c.
[b] *Cf.* 645 A and 715 D.
[c] The Younger : *cf. Mor.* 173 E ; *Life of Artaxerxes*, vi.

---

2 Added by Wilamowitz.
3 Amyot : δεῖ.
4 Hubert, ἐκείνοις Bolkestein : ἐ lac. 3-5.
5 Amyot : ἐπιτρέπων.
6 Basel edition : ποσιαρχεῖν.

(620)

D βάνοι τὴν χλαμύδα, πρῶτον¹ εἰώθει διαλέγεσθαι
πρὸς αὐτὸν ὥσπερ ὑπομιμνήσκων, ' ὅρα, Περί-
κλεις· ἐλευθέρων ἄρχεις, Ἑλλήνων ἄρχεις, Ἀθηναίων ἄρχεις'· ὁ δὲ συμποσίαρχος ἡμῶν ἐκεῖνος²
λεγέτω πρὸς αὐτόν, ' φίλων ἄρχεις,' ἵνα μήτ'
ἀσχημονεῖν ἐπιτρέπῃ μήτε τὰς ἡδονὰς ἀφαιρῇ.
δεῖ δὲ καὶ σπουδῆς τὸν ἄρχοντα πινόντων οἰκεῖον
εἶναι καὶ παιδιᾶς μὴ ἀλλότριον, ἀλλ' εὖ πως
συγκεκραμένον πρὸς ἀμφότερα, σμικρῷ δὲ μᾶλλον,
ὥσπερ οἶνον ἀστεῖον, ἀπονεύοντα τῇ φύσει πρὸς τὸ
αὐστηρόν· ὁ γὰρ οἶνος ἄξει τὸ ἦθος εἰς τὸ μέτριον μαλακώτερον ποιῶν καὶ ἀνυγραίνων. ὥσπερ
γὰρ ὁ Ξενοφῶν ἔλεγεν τοῦ Κλεάρχου τὸ σκυθρωπὸν
E καὶ ἄγροικον ἄλλως ἐν ταῖς μάχαις ἡδὺ καὶ
φαιδρὸν ἐπιφαίνεσθαι διὰ τὸ θαρραλέον, οὕτως ὁ
μὴ φύσει πικρὸς ἀλλὰ σεμνὸς καὶ αὐστηρὸς ἐν τῷ
πίνειν ἀνιέμενος ἡδίων γίγνεται καὶ προσφιλέστε-
ρος. ἔτι τοίνυν αὐτῷ δεῖ προσεῖναι τὸ μάλιστα
μὲν ἑκάστου τῶν συμποτῶν ἐμπείρως ἔχειν, τίνα
λαμβάνει μεταβολὴν ἐν οἴνῳ καὶ πρὸς τί πάθος
ἀκροσφαλής ἐστι καὶ πῶς φέρει τὸν ἄκρατον (οὐ γὰρ
οἴνου μὲν ἔστι πρὸς ὕδωρ ἕτερον ἑτέρα μῖξις, ἣν
οἱ βασιλικοὶ γιγνώσκοντες οἰνοχόοι νῦν μὲν πλέον

---

¹ Franke : πρῶτος. ² Hubert : ἐκεῖνα.

ᵃ The anecdote is repeated in *Regum et Imperatorum
Apophthegmata* (*Mor.* 186 c), where it is applied to military
command (*cf.* Babbitt, LCL *Mor.* iii, p. 97). It is also repeated in *Praecepta Gerendae Reipublicae* (*Mor.* 813 E).
Gomme conflates 186 c and 813 E and applies both to military
command (*Commentary on Thucydides*, i, pp. 23-24), but the
context at 813 E and here at 620 c suggests to me not so much

state,[a] every time he took up his cloak, would first say
to himself, as though reminding himself, ' Keep in
mind, Pericles, you govern free men, you govern
Greeks, you govern Athenians ' ; so let that symposiarch of ours say to himself, ' You govern friends,'
in order that he may neither allow them to misbehave
nor deprive them of their pleasures. Further, one
who governs drinkers must be congenial to seriousness and no stranger to play, must have both qualities
properly blended, and yet, like a choice wine, incline
a little towards austerity, for the wine he drinks will
bring his character to a happy mean, making it softer
and more pliant. Clearchus's sullen and churlish
aspect, according to Xenophon,[b] appeared in combat paradoxically pleasant and cheerful because of
the man's courage ; just so one who is not naturally
bitter, but dignified and austere, becomes pleasanter
and more lovable when he is relaxed in drinking.
Moreover the symposiarch must have a very good
understanding of each of the drinkers, knowing what
change drinking produces in each, into what emotional
state he is apt to fall, and how he carries strong drink
—for just as mixtures of wine and water vary with
different waters, which the royal wine-stewards know
and so pour into the wine now more water and now

the specifically military as the general political aspect of the
strategia, an office to which Pericles was elected year after
year and which did in fact provide him the basis of his political control of Athens (cf. Life of Pericles, xvi. 3). I therefore paraphrase στρατηγός, literally " general " (there were
ten such elected each year), with " head of state," though the
Athenian constitution made no provision for an office legally
so called. For the strategia see C. Hignett, A History of the
Athenian Constitution, pp. 244-251 and 347-356 ; A. H. M.
Jones, Athenian Democracy, pp. 124-127.

[b] Anabasis, ii. 6. 11 f.

(620) νῦν δ' ἔλαττον ὑποχέουσιν, ἀνθρώπου δὲ πρὸς
F οἶνον οὐκ ἔστ' ἰδία κρᾶσις, ἣν τῷ συμποσιάρχῳ
γιγνώσκειν προσήκει καὶ γιγνώσκοντι φυλάττειν,
ἵν' ὥσπερ ἁρμονικὸς τὸν μὲν ἐπιτείνων τῇ πόσει
τὸν δ' ἀνιεὶς καὶ ὑποφειδόμενος εἰς ὁμαλότητα καὶ
συμφωνίαν ἐκ διαφορᾶς καταστήσῃ τὰς φύσεις),
ὅπως μὴ κοτύλῃ μηδὲ κυάθοις τὸ ἴσον, ἀλλὰ
καιροῦ τινι μέτρῳ καὶ σώματος δυνάμει τὸ οἰκεῖον
621 ἑκάστῳ καὶ πρόσφορον ἀπονέμηται. εἰ δὲ τοῦτό
γε δύσκολον, ἐκεῖνα δὲ[1] πάντως ἐξειδέναι τῷ
συμοσιάρχῳ προσήκει, τὰ κοινὰ περὶ τὰς φύσεις
καὶ τὰς ἡλικίας· οἷον πρεσβῦται τάχιον μεθύσκονται νέων, σαλευόμενοι δ' ἠρεμούντων, ἔλλυποι[2] δὲ
καὶ πεφροντικότες εὐθύμων καὶ ἱλαρῶν, οἱ δὲ
μὴ[3] ἀνέδην καὶ κατακόρως[4] διάγοντες[5] τῶν ἀσελ-
γαινόντων. κἄλλα τοιαῦθ' ἃ[6] γιγνώσκων ἄν[7] τις
μᾶλλον τοῦ ἀγνοοῦντος εὐσχημοσύνην καὶ ὁμό-
νοιαν συμποσίου πρυτανεύσειεν. καὶ μὴν ὅτι γε
δεῖ τὸν συμποσίαρχον οἰκείως ἔχειν καὶ φιλικῶς
πρὸς ἅπαντας ὕπουλον δὲ μηδενὶ μηδ' ἀπεχθῆ τῶν
ἑστιωμένων εἶναι παντί που δῆλον· οὔτε γὰρ
ἐπιτάττων ἀνεκτὸς οὔτ' ἀπονέμων ἴσος οὔτε προσ-
B παίζων ὅμως ἀνέγκλητος ἔσται. τοιοῦτον," ἔφη,
" σοι, Θέων, ἐγὼ τὸν ἄρχοντα συμποσίου πλάσας
ὥσπερ ἐκ κηροῦ τοῦ λόγου παραδίδωμι."

3. Καὶ ὁ Θέων, " ἀλλὰ δέχομαι μέν," εἶπεν,

---

[1] δὴ Pohlenz.
[2] Stephanus : ἄλυποι lac. 4-6.
[3] οἱ δὲ μὴ Hubert, οἱ μὴ Doehner : lac. 4-6.
[4] Stephanus : κατα lac. 6-8.
[5] Doehner : ἀπάγοντες.
[6] Hubert : καὶ τοιαῦτα.
[7] Emperius : μὲν partially erased.

less, so does toleration for wine vary from person to person, which it is the duty of the symposiarch to know and, knowing, to watch over, that, like a musician, keying one up to drinking and relaxing another and scanting him a little, he may bring the natural dispositions of the guests from diversity into smooth and harmonious accord,—the symposiarch, I say, must know how each guest carries his wine so that he may serve to each not an equal amount kotylê by kotylê or kyathos by kyathos but the amount which is a proper and suitable measure for each man's temporary condition or permanent capacity. If this is difficult, then it is the symposiarch's business by all means to know the characteristics common to men of the same temperament or to men of the same age: namely, that old men get drunk more quickly than young men, tempestuous men more quickly than calm men, gloomy and apprehensive men more quickly than happy and cheerful men, and those who are not immoderate and intemperate in their living than those whose life is dissipated. With knowledge of these and like characteristics he can regulate the decorum and harmony of a party better than the man who knows them not. And certainly it is obvious to everyone, I imagine, that the symposiarch must be intimate and friendly with all of the guests, and cankerous and hateful to none,—for he will be unbearable when imposing his orders upon them, inequitable when serving them, and, though he joke with them, yet will he not avoid giving offence. Such," Crato concluded, "is the leader of the dinner-party that I turn over to you, Theon, fashioned out of the wax of talk, as it were."

3. And Theon replied, "Well, I accept the man

(621) " οὕτως ὁμαλὸν[1] ἀπειργασμένον τὸν ἄνδρα καὶ
συμποτικόν· εἰ δὲ χρήσομαι κατὰ τρόπον[2] αὐτῷ
καὶ μὴ καταισχυνῶ τὸ ἔργον, οὐκ οἶδα· εὔκρατον[3]
δέ μοι δοκεῖ τοιοῦτος[4] ὢν τὸ συμπόσιον διαφυλά-
ξειν[5] ἡμῖν καὶ μὴ περιόψεσθαι[6] νῦν μὲν ἐκκλησίαν
δημοκρατικὴν νῦν δὲ σχολὴν σοφιστοῦ γιγνομένην
αὖθις δὲ κυβευτήριον εἶτά που σκηνὴν καὶ θυμέλην.
ἢ[7] γὰρ οὐχ ὁρᾶτε τοὺς μὲν δημαγωγοῦντας καὶ
δικαζομένους παρὰ δεῖπνον, τοὺς δὲ μελετῶντας
C καὶ ἀναγιγνώσκοντας αὑτῶν τινα συγγράμματα,
τοὺς δὲ μίμοις καὶ ὀρχησταῖς ἀγωνοθετοῦντας;
Ἀλκιβιάδης δὲ καὶ Θεόδωρος τελεστήριον ἐποίησαν
τὸ Πουλυτίωνος[8] συμπόσιον ἀπομιμούμενοι δᾳδου-
χίας καὶ ἱεροφαντίας. ὧν οὐδὲν οἶμαι τῷ ἄρχοντι
περιοπτέον· ἀλλὰ καὶ λόγοις καὶ θεάμασι καὶ
παιδιαῖς δώσει τόπον ἐκείνοις μόνοις, ὅσα πρὸς τὸ
συμποτικὸν τέλος ἐξικνεῖται· τοῦτο δ' ἦν φιλίας
ἐπίτασιν ἢ γένεσιν δι' ἡδονῆς ἐνεργάσασθαι τοῖς
παροῦσιν· διαγωγὴ γάρ ἐστιν ἐν οἴνῳ τὸ συμπόσιον εἰς φιλίαν ὑπὸ χάριτος τελευτῶσα.

" Ἐπεὶ δὲ πανταχοῦ πλήσμιον καὶ πολλαχοῦ
D βλαβερὸν τὸ ἄκρατον, ἡ δὲ μῖξις, οἷς ἂν ἐν καιρῷ
καὶ μετὰ μέτρου παραγένηται πράγμασιν, ἀφαιρεῖ
τἄγαν, ᾧ[9] καὶ βλάπτει τὰ ἡδέα καὶ λυπεῖ τὰ

---

[1] οὕτως ὁμαλὸν Hubert : οὕτω μᾶλλον.
[2] κατὰ τρόπον Hubert : κατὰ πᾶν.
[3] Paton : lac. 6 τον.
[4] Stephanus : τοι lac. 1-2 σων (sic).
[5] Wyttenbach : lac. 5-7 άξειν.
[6] Reiske : ὄψεσθαι.   [7] P. A. C. : ἢ.
[8] Bolkestein : Πολυτίωνος.

56

fashioned to be so equable and convivial. But
whether I shall make fitting use of him and not bring
dishonour upon your work of art, I do not know ; yet
it seems to me that such a man will keep our party
temperate and will not allow it to become now a
rabble-ruled congress, now a sophist's school, and
again a gaming-establishment, and then perhaps a
stage and a dancing-floor. For do you not see men
who play the politician and harangue a jury at dinner,
others who declaim and read selections from their
own writings, and others who put on shows with
mummers and dancers ? Alcibiades and Theodorus
made Poulytion's party a Telesterion with their
mimicry of the torch ceremony and the initiation
ritual.[a] None of this, I think, must our leader allow ;
rather he will only give a place to that talk, that
spectacle, that amusement which accomplishes a
party's aim, and this aim is through pleasure to produce among those who are present the heightening
of friendship or to bring it into existence ; for the
drinking-party is a passing of time over wine which,
guided by gracious behaviour, ends in friendship.

"What is undiluted is everywhere surfeiting and
often harmful, but dilution, on those occasions when
timely and measured use is made of it, takes away the
excess which makes pleasure harmful and profit dis-

---

[a] The notorious profanation of the Mysteries just before
the Sicilian expedition of 415 B.C. : Plutarch, *Alcibiades*, xix ;
Andocides, i. 11 ff. ; [Plato], *Eryxias*, 394 B. The record of
the sale of property confiscated by the Athenian state from
these two and from their friends is in part preserved : W. K.
Pritchett and D. A. Amyx, "The Attic Stelai," *Hesperia*,
xxii (1953), pp. 225-299 ; xxv (1956), pp. 178-328 ; xxvii
(1958), pp. 163-310 ; xxx (1961), pp. 23-29.

---

[9] ἀφαιρεῖ τἄγαν ᾧ Bernardakis : ἀφαιρεῖται ἄνω.

(621) ὠφέλιμα, δῆλον ὅτι καὶ τοῖς πίνουσιν ὁ ἐπιστάτης
μεμιγμένην τινὰ παρέξει διαγωγήν. ἀκούων οὖν
πολλῶν λεγόντων, ὅτι πλοῦς μὲν ὁ παρὰ γῆν
περίπατος δ' ὁ παρὰ θάλατταν ἥδιστός ἐστιν,
οὕτως παραβαλεῖ[1] τῇ σπουδῇ τὴν παιδιάν, ὅπως
οἵ τε παίζοντες ἀμωσγέπως σπουδῆς τινος ἔχωνται
καὶ πάλιν οἱ σπουδάζοντες ἀναθαρρῶσιν, ὥσπερ οἱ
ναυτιῶντες ἐγγύθεν εἰς γῆν[2] τὴν παιδιὰν ἀπο-
βλέποντες. ἔστι γὰρ καὶ γέλωτι χρῆσθαι πρὸς
πολλὰ τῶν ὠφελίμων καὶ σπουδὴν ἡδεῖαν παρα-
E σχεῖν,

> ὡς ἂν' ἐχινόποδας καὶ ἀνὰ τρηχεῖαν ὄνωνιν
> φύονται μαλακῶν ἄνθεα λευκοΐων.

ὅσαι δ' ἄνευ σπουδῆς ἐπεισκωμάζουσιν τοῖς συμποσίοις παιδιαί, ταύτας ἐπιμελῶς διακελεύσεται τοῖς
συμπόταις εὐλαβεῖσθαι, μὴ λάθωσιν ὕβριν πικρὰν[3]
καθάπερ ὑοσκύαμον ἐμβαλόντες[4] οἴνῳ, ὡς[5] τοῖς
λεγομένοις προστάγμασιν ἐξυβρίζουσιν, προστάτ-
τοντες ᾄδειν ψελλοῖς ἢ κτενίζεσθαι φαλακροῖς ἢ
ἀσκωλιάζειν χωλοῖς. ὥσπερ Ἀγαμήστορι[6] τῷ
Ἀκαδημαϊκῷ λεπτὸν ἔχοντι καὶ κετεφθινηκὸς τὸ
F σκέλος ἐπηρεάζοντες οἱ ξυμπόται πάντας ἐκέλευσαν
ἐπὶ τοῦ δεξιοῦ ποδὸς ἑστῶτας ἐκπιεῖν τὸ ποτήριον
ἢ ζημίαν καταβαλεῖν· τοῦ δὲ προστάσσειν περιελ-

---

[1] Stephanus : παραβάλλει.
[2] Added by Doehner.
[3] Pohlenz : lac. 4-6.
[4] Salmasius : λαβόντες.
[5] ὡς Bernardakis, οἶον Hubert, καὶ (which avoids hiatus) ...
ἐξυβρίζωσιν (but ἐξυβρίζουσιν T) Wyttenbach.
[6] Basel edition : Ἀγαπήστορι.

---

[a] Diehl, *Anth. Lyr. Gr.* i, p. 111, no. 1 ; quoted also at

tressful ; therefore, it is clear that the gentleman who presides will provide for the drinkers a mixed programme of entertainment. And so, giving heed to the testimony of many that the pleasantest sailing is along the coast, while the pleasantest walk is by the sea, he will accordingly throw in something playful alongside the serious in order that men of playful dispositions may in some fashion make contact with a certain degree of seriousness and again that serious men, like seasick voyagers catching sight of land near by, may cheer up as they catch sight of something playful. For laughter serves for many useful purposes and seriousness can be pleasant,

> As flowering soft white violets grow
> Mid urchin's-foot and rough restharrow.[a]

He will take care to bid the drinkers beware of all those games that, with no intent of seriousness, come roistering into parties like a drunken crowd, lest unawares the members of the party introduce an insolent violence bitter as henbane in their wine as they run riot with their so-called commands, ordering stammerers to sing, or bald men to comb their hair, or the lame to dance on a greased wine-skin. Thus, by way of rudely mocking Agamestor the Academician,[b] who had a weak and withered leg, his fellow-banqueters proposed that each man of them all drain off his cup while standing on his right foot, or pay a penalty. But when it came the turn of Agamestor

[a] *Mor.* 44 E and 485 A and at Athenaeus, 97 d. In the Index of Plants in vol. vii of Pliny, *Nat. Hist.* (LCL) ἐχινόπους is identified as the broom *Genista acanthoclada.*

[b] According to Apollodorus (frag. 47, Jacoby, *Frag. Griech. Historiker,* ii, p. 1033) the philosopher Agamestor died in the archonship of Xenocles, 168/7 B.C. (Meritt, *Ath. Year,* p. 236.)

(621) θόντος εἰς αὑτόν, ἐκέλευσε πάντας οὕτως πιεῖν,
ὡς ἂν αὐτὸν ἴδωσιν· καὶ κεραμίου στενοῦ[1] κομι-
σθέντος εἰς τοῦτο τὸν ἀσθενῆ πόδα καθεὶς ἐξέπιε τὸ
ποτήριον, οἱ δ' ἄλλοι πάντες, ὡς ἐφαίνετο πει-
622 ρωμένοις ἀδύνατον, ἀπέτισαν τὴν ζημίαν. χαρίεις
οὖν Ἀγαμήστωρ,[2] καὶ ποιητέον εὐκόλους οὕτω
καὶ ἱλαρὰς τὰς ἀμύνας· τοῖς δὲ[3] προστάγμασιν
ἐθιστέον χρῆσθαι πρὸς ἡδονὴν καὶ ὠφέλειαν, τὰ
οἰκεῖα καὶ δυνατὰ καὶ κοσμοῦντα τὸν δρῶντα
προστάσσοντας, ᾠδικοῖς ᾆσαι ῥητορικοῖς εἰπεῖν
φιλοσόφοις λῦσαί τι τῶν ἀπορουμένων ποιηταῖς
προενέγκασθαι[4] στίχους. ἡδέως γὰρ εἰς τοῦθ'
ἕκαστος ἄγεται καὶ προθύμως,

   ἵν' αὐτὸς αὑτοῦ τυγχάνῃ[5] κράτιστος ὤν.

" Ὁ μὲν οὖν τῶν Ἀσσυρίων βασιλεὺς ἆθλον
ὑπὸ κήρυκος κατήγγειλεν τῷ καινὴν ἡδονὴν ἐξ-
ευρόντι· συμποσίου δὲ βασιλεὺς ἀστεῖον ἆθλον
B ἂν καὶ γέρας προθείη[6] τῷ παιδιὰν ἀνύβριστον
εἰσηγησαμένῳ καὶ τέρψιν ὠφέλιμον καὶ γέλωτα μὴ
μώμου μηδ' ὕβρεων ἀλλὰ χάριτος καὶ φιλοφροσύνης ἑταῖρον· ἐν οἷς τὰ πλεῖστα ναυαγεῖ συμπόσια
μὴ τυχόντα παιδαγωγίας ὀρθῆς. ἔστι δὲ σώφρονος
ἀνδρὸς ἔχθραν φυλάττεσθαι καὶ ὀργήν, ἐν ἀγορᾷ

---

[1] Amyot : κενοῦ, defended by Paton, perhaps rightly.

[2] Basel edition : Ἀγαπήστωρ.

[3] τοῖς δὲ P. A. C., εἶτα Capps, ἀλλὰ καὶ Vulcobius : lac.
5-7.   [4] Stephanus : προσενέγκασθαι.

[5] τυγχάνει Bernardakis : τυγχάνῃ (sic). E. R. Dodds denies that the generic subjunctive can properly omit ἄν with
ἵνα (Plato, Gorgias, note on 484 E 7).

[6] Vulcobius : προσθείη.

---

[a] Euripides, frag. 183, line 3 (Nauck, Trag. Gr. Frag.², p.
413). Cf. Moralia, 43 B, 514 A, 630 B.

to give the order, he commanded them all to drink as they saw him drink. Then he had a narrow jar brought to him, put his defective foot inside it, and drained off his cup ; but all the others, since it was manifestly impossible for them to do so, though they tried, paid the penalty. Thus Agamestor showed himself an urbane gentleman ; and, following his example, one should make his ripostes good-natured and merry. As for the hazards, one must accustom the banqueters to use those conducive to pleasure and profit, setting commands that are suitable, possible, and such as display the talents of the performer, as, for example, for the musical to sing, orators to declaim, philosophers to resolve some crux, poets to recite their verses. For gladly is each man led, and willingly, to that activity

> Where the best of his abilities
> Chance to lie. . . .ᵃ

" The king of the Assyrians ᵇ proclaimed by herald a prize for the man who discovered a new pleasure ; and the king of a drinking-party could offer a charming prize and reward to the man introducing a game free from offence, a delight that has usefulness in it, and a laughter that is the companion not of ridicule and insolence, but of goodwill and friendliness. It is in these respects that most drinking-parties, without proper guidance, suffer shipwreck. The sensible man will guard against the hatred and anger which

---

ᵇ The extravagance is also credited to the Persians, Cicero, *Tusc.* 5. 20, and Valerius Maximus, 9. 1, Ext. 3 (Xerxes), testimonia to which Bolkestein (*Adv. Crit.* p. 81) has added Athenaeus, 144 e (Theophrastus, frag. 125 Wimmer), 514 e (Clearchus of Soli, *F.H.G.* ii. 304), 529 d, and 539 b (the Darius who lost to Alexander).

(622) τὴν ἐκ πλεονεξίας, ἐν γυμνασίοις καὶ παλαίστραις
ἐκ φιλονικίας, ἐν δ' ἀρχαῖς καὶ φιλοτιμίαις ἐκ
φιλοδοξίας, ἐν δὲ δείπνῳ καὶ παρὰ πότον ἐκ παιδιᾶς ἐπιτιθεμένην.''

C   ΠΡΟΒΛΗΜΑ Ε

Πῶς εἴρηται τὸ '' ποιητὴν[1] δ' ἄρα Ἔρως διδάσκει''

Collocuntur Sossius Senecio et alii

1. Πῶς εἴρηται τὸ

                ποιητὴν[2] δ' ἄρα
Ἔρως διδάσκει, κἂν ἄμουσος ᾖ τὸ πρίν

ἐζητεῖτο παρὰ Σοσσίῳ Σαπφικῶν τινων ᾀσθέντων,
ὅπου καὶ τὸν Κύκλωπα '' μούσαις εὐφώνοις
ἰᾶσθαι '' φησὶ '' τὸν ἔρωτα '' Φιλόξενος. ἐλέχθη
μὲν οὖν ὅτι πρὸς πάντα τόλμαν ὁ ἔρως καὶ καινο-
τομίαν συγχορηγῆσαι[3] δεινός ἐστι, ὥσπερ καὶ
Πλάτων '' ἴτην ''[4] αὐτὸν καὶ '' παντὸς ἐπιχειρητὴν ''
D ὠνόμασεν· καὶ γὰρ λάλον ποιεῖ τὸν σιωπηλὸν καὶ
θεραπευτικὸν τὸν αἰσχυντηλόν, ἐπιμελῆ δὲ καὶ
φιλόπονον τὸν ἀμελῆ καὶ ῥᾴθυμον· ὃ δ' ἄν τις
μάλιστα θαυμάσειεν, φειδωλὸς ἀνήρ τε καὶ μικρο-
λόγος ἐμπεσὼν εἰς ἔρωτα καθάπερ εἰς πῦρ σίδηρος

---

[1] ποιητὴν T in table of contents fol. 1 r, here μουσικ written
by a later hand above an erasure of 5 (?) letters before ην.
[2] Cobet from 405 f and 762 b : μουσικήν.
[3] Madvig (cf. Helmbold, C.P. xxxvi, 1941, p. 85 ; Bolkestein, Adv. Crit. p. 82) : συγχωρῆσαι.
[4] Wyttenbach : τὸν.

---

[a] Euripides, frag. 663 Nauck, quoted also at 405 f and at
762 b. The verse is borrowed by Aristophanes (Wasps, 1074),
by Plato (Symposium, 196 e), by Theocritus's friend the
physician Nicias of Miletus (in the scholia on Idyll xi : see

in the market-place is imposed by covetousness, in the gymnasia and the palaestrae by rivalry, in politics and public munificences by eagerness for glory, at dinner and in drinking by frivolity."

QUESTION 5

Why it is held that " love teaches a poet "

Speakers : Sossius Senecio and others

1. At one of Sossius's dinners, after the singing of some Sapphic verses, a discussion arose on why it is held that

> Love instructs a poet then,
> Though he before was songless,[a]

whereas Philoxenus claims that actually

> Cyclops cured his love with fair-voiced song.[b]

It was said, then, that love is skilful at supplying boldness and initiative for all situations ; Plato, for example, called it " dashing " and " ready for any undertaking." [c] And in fact, love makes the silent man talkative, the bashful man attentive, the careless and easy-going man careful and industrious, and— most amazing—the man who is penurious and penny-pinching, when he falls in love, melted and softened

---

Gow, *Theocritus*, ii, p. 209), by Aristides (i, pp. 51 and 322), and by the author of the Περὶ ὕψους (39. 2). The passages are conveniently collected by Nauck, *loc. cit.*

[b] Philoxenus's poem on Cyclops and Galatea preceded Theocritus's *Idyll* xi. For the extant fragments of the poem, and an account of Philoxenus as good as it is convenient, see Pickard-Cambridge, *Dithyramb, Tragedy and Comedy*, pp. 61-64 ; *cf.* Gow, *op. cit.* ii, p. 210, note on line 7.

[c] *Symposium*, 203 d ; *Timaeus*, 69 d.

(622) ἀνεθεὶς καὶ μαλαχθεὶς ἁπαλὸς καὶ ὑγρὸς καὶ
ἡδίων, ὥστε τουτὶ τὸ παιζόμενον μὴ πάνυ φαίνεσθαι γελοῖον ὅτι " πράσου φύλλῳ τὸ τῶν ἐρώντων¹
δέδεται βαλλάντιον."

Ἐλέχθη δὲ καὶ ὅτι τῷ μεθύειν τὸ ἐρᾶν ὅμοιόν
ἐστιν· ποιεῖ γὰρ θερμοὺς καὶ ἱλαροὺς καὶ διακε-
χυμένους, γενόμενοι δὲ τοιοῦτοι πρὸς τὰς ἐπῳδοὺς
E καὶ ἐμμέτρους² μάλιστα φωνὰς ἐκφέρονται· καὶ
τὸν Αἰσχύλον φασὶ τὰς τραγῳδίας πίνοντα ποιεῖν
καὶ διαθερμαινόμενον. ἦν δὲ Λαμπρίας ὁ ἡμέτερος
πάππος ἐν τῷ πίνειν εὑρετικώτατος αὐτὸς αὑτοῦ
καὶ λογιώτατος· εἰώθει δὲ λέγειν ὅτι τῷ λιβανωτῷ
παραπλησίως ὑπὸ θερμότητος ἀναθυμιᾶται. καὶ
μὴν ἥδιστα τοὺς ἐρωμένους ὁρῶντες οὐχ ἧττον
ἡδέως ἐγκωμιάζουσιν ἢ ὁρῶσιν, καὶ πρὸς πάντα
λάλος ὢν ἔρως λαλίστατός ἐστιν ἐν τοῖς ἐπαίνοις.
αὐτοί τε γὰρ οὕτως πεπεισμένοι τυγχάνουσιν καὶ
F βούλονται πεπεῖσθαι πάντας ὡς καλῶν καὶ ἀγαθῶν
ἐρῶντες. τοῦτο καὶ τὸν Λυδὸν ἐπῆρεν Κανδαύλην³
τῆς ἑαυτοῦ γυναικὸς ἐπισπᾶσθαι θεατὴν εἰς τὸ
δωμάτιον τὸν οἰκέτην⁴· βούλονται γὰρ ὑπ' ἄλλων
μαρτυρεῖσθαι· διὸ καὶ γράφοντες ἐγκώμια τῶν
καλῶν ἐπικοσμοῦσιν αὐτὰ μέλεσι καὶ μέτροις καὶ
ᾠδαῖς, ὥσπερ εἰκόνας χρυσῷ καλλωπίζοντες,
ὅπως ἀκούηταί τε μᾶλλον ὑπὸ πολλῶν καὶ μνημο-
νεύηται· καὶ γὰρ ἂν ἵππον καὶ ἀλεκτρυόνα κἂν

---

¹ Turnebus : ἐρώτων.   ² Reiske : συμμέτρους.
³ Stephanus : lac. 4-6.
⁴ Xylander, οἰκέτην οὐ βουλόμενον Capps : lac. 3 τὴν · οὐ.

like iron in fire, he is malleable, pliant, and more agreeable, so that the proverb " the purse of lovers is fastened with a leek's leaf," [a] though meant as a jest, does not seem altogether a joke.

Furthermore, it was said that love is like drunkenness, for it makes men hot, gay, and distraught, and when they get in that condition, they are carried away into song-like and quite metrical speech : Aeschylus allegedly wrote his tragedies while drinking, indeed thoroughly heated with wine. My grandfather Lamprias was his most ingenious and eloquent self when drinking, and it was his habit to say that, much as incense is volatilized by heat, so was he by wine. Furthermore, men find their greatest pleasure in seeing those whom they love and are not less glad to sing their praises than to see them ; it is in praise that love, loquacious in everything, is most loquacious. For inasmuch as lovers have persuaded themselves that the objects of their affections are fair and noble, they want everybody to be persuaded. This desire incited the Lydian Candaules [b] to drag his servant into his own wife's bedroom to gaze upon her : for lovers want others to bear them witness. Thus, when they write eulogies of their fair beloved, they adorn their eulogies with melody and rhythm and song, as men beautify statues with gold, so that the praise of their beloved may be more likely to come to the ears of many people and be remembered. And indeed, if they give their beloved a horse, a cock,

---

[a] Leutsch and Schneidewin, *Paroemiogr. Graec.* i, p. 447, and ii, p. 47. By transposing the first two words and expanding the verb to its compound συνδέδεται Cobet obtained an incomplete and a complete iambic trimeter (Kock, *Com. Att. Frag.* iii, p. 446, no. 197).

[b] Herodotus, i. 8 f.

623 ἄλλο τι τοῖς ἐρωμένοις διδῶσι, καλὸν εἶναι καὶ
κεκοσμημένον ἐκπρεπῶς βούλονται καὶ περιττῶς
τὸ δῶρον, μάλιστα δὲ λόγον κόλακα προσφέροντες
ἡδὺν ἐθέλουσι φαίνεσθαι καὶ γαῦρον καὶ περιττόν,
οἷος ὁ ποιητικός ἐστιν.

2. Ὁ μέντοι Σόσσιος ἐπαινέσας ἐκείνους εἶπεν
ὡς οὐ χεῖρον ἄν τις[1] ἐπιχειρήσειεν ὁρμηθεὶς ἀφ'
ὧν Θεόφραστος εἴρηκεν περὶ μουσικῆς· "καὶ γὰρ
ἔναγχος," ἔφη, "τὸ βιβλίον ἀνέγνων. λέγει δὲ
μουσικῆς ἀρχὰς τρεῖς εἶναι, λύπην, ἡδονήν, ἐνθουσιασμόν, ὡς ἑκάστου τῶν παθῶν τούτων[2] παρατρέ-
ποντος[3] ἐκ τοῦ συνήθους καὶ παρεγκλίνοντος[4] τὴν
φωνήν. αἵ τε γὰρ λῦπαι[5] τὸ γοερὸν καὶ θρηνη-
B τικὸν ὀλισθηρὸν εἰς ᾠδὴν ἔχουσιν, διὸ καὶ τοὺς
ῥήτορας ἐν τοῖς ἐπιλόγοις καὶ τοὺς ὑποκριτὰς ἐν
τοῖς ὀδυρμοῖς ἀτρέμα τῷ μελῳδεῖν προσάγοντας
ὁρῶμεν καὶ παρεντείνοντας τὴν φωνήν.. αἵ τε
σφοδραὶ περιχάρειαι τῆς ψυχῆς τῶν μὲν ἐλαφρο-
τέρων τῷ ἤθει καὶ τὸ σῶμα συνεπαίρουσιν[6] καὶ
παρακαλοῦσιν εἰς ἔνρυθμον κίνησιν, ἐξαλλομένων
καὶ κροτούντων εἴπερ ὀρχεῖσθαι μὴ δύνανται[7]·

μανίαι τ' ἀλαλαί[8] τ' ὀρινομένων ῥιψαύχενι[9] σὺν
    κλόνῳ

κατὰ Πίνδαρον· οἱ δὲ χαρίεντες ἐν τῷ πάθει τούτῳ
γενόμενοι τὴν φωνὴν μόνην εἰς τὸ ᾄδειν καὶ φθέγγεσθαι μέτρα[10] καὶ μέλη προΐενται. μάλιστα δ' ὁ

---

[1] χεῖρον ἄν τις Xylander: χειρόμαντις with the beginning of
an erasure at μ.
[2] παθῶν τούτων Bernardakis : lac. 3-4 αὐτῶν.
[3] Xylander : παρατρε lac. 4.
[4] καὶ παρεγκλίνοντος Bernardakis : lac. 4-5 ἐγκλίναντος.
[5] So a later hand in T and the Basel edition : λύσσαι.

or anything else, they want the gift to be beautiful
and splendidly, exquisitely groomed ; if it is a flatter-
ing address they offer, they particularly want it to
appear agreeable, elegant, and exquisite, qualities
which are characteristic of poetry.

2. Sossius, however, after praising them, said that
one would not make a bad attempt at a solution by
beginning with what Theophrastus has to say about
music. " For I have recently read the book," he
continued, " and Theophrastus [a] holds that music has
three sources, sorrow, joy, and religious ecstasy ; for
each of these emotions diverts and deflects the voice
from its customary range. Sorrows, as we know,
involve weeping and wailing that naturally slips into
song ; this is why we find that our orators in their
perorations and our actors in their laments by degrees
raise the pitch of their speaking voice and approach
song. And the soul's intense joys stir men of light
character to bodily activity and invite them to
rhythmic movement,—they jump up and clap their
hands if they can't dance,

> The madness and shrieking of men
> Excited by neck-breaking clash
> Of the fight,

as Pindar [b] has it,—but men of wit and taste who experience these emotions raise their voice alone to
sing and recite verses and lyrics. Ecstasy, especially,

[a] Frag. 90 Wimmer.
[b] Frag. 208 Dithyramb ii, lines 13 f. (Snell), quoted also
with slight variation at 417 c, 706 E.

---

[6] Reiske : πᾶν ἐπαίρουσιν.   [7] Bernardakis : δύνωνται.
  [8] Xylander (cf. 706 E) : ἄλλαι.
    [9] Turnebus (cf. 706 E, 417 c) : ἐριαύχενι.
[10] Faehse (cf. Bolkestein, Adv. Crit. p. 77) : μέγα.

(623)
C θουσιασμὸς ἐξίστησι καὶ παρατρέπει τό τε σῶμα
καὶ τὴν φωνὴν τοῦ συνήθους καὶ καθεστηκότος.
ὅθεν αἵ τε βακχεῖαι ῥυθμοῖς χρῶνται καὶ τὸ χρη-
σμῳδεῖν ἐμμέτρως παρέχεται τοῖς ἐνθεαζομένοις,
τῶν τε μαινομένων ὀλίγους ἰδεῖν ἔστιν ἄνευ μέτρου καὶ ᾠδῆς ληροῦντας. οὕτω δὲ τούτων ἐχόντων εἰ βούλοιο καθορᾶν ὑπ᾿ αὐγὰς διαπτύξας τὸν
ἔρωτα καὶ καταμανθάνειν, οὐκ ἂν ἄλλο πάθος εὕροις οὔτε λύπας δριμυτέρας ἔχον οὔτε σφοδροτέρας
περιχαρείας οὔτε μείζονας ἐκστάσεις καὶ παραφρο-
σύνας, ἀλλ᾿ ὥσπερ τὴν Σοφόκλειον[1] πόλιν ἀνδρὸς
ἐρωτικοῦ ψυχὴν

ὁμοῦ μὲν θυμιαμάτων
γέμουσαν,

D   ὁμοῦ δὲ παιάνων τε καὶ στεναγμάτων.

οὐδὲν οὖν ἄτοπον οὐδὲ θαυμαστόν, εἰ πάσας, ὅσαι
μουσικῆς εἰσιν ἀρχαί, περιέχων ὁ ἔρως ἐν αὑτῷ
καὶ συνειληφώς, λύπην ἡδονὴν ἐνθουσιασμόν, τά τ᾿
ἄλλα φιλόφωνός[2] ἐστι καὶ λάλος εἴς τε ποίησιν
μελῶν καὶ μέτρων ὡς οὐδὲν ἄλλο πάθος ἐπίφορος
καὶ κατάντης.''

ΠΡΟΒΛΗΜΑ ϛ

Περὶ τῆς Ἀλεξάνδρου πολυποσίας

Collocuntur Philinus, Plutarchus, alii

1. Λόγος ἦν περὶ Ἀλεξάνδρου τοῦ βασιλέως ὡς
οὐ πολὺ πίνοντος ἀλλὰ πολὺν χρόνον ἐν τῷ πίνειν
E καὶ[3] διαλέγεσθαι τοῖς φίλοις ἕλκοντος. ἀπε-

---

[1] Bolkestein, citing Life of Antony, xxiv. 3, ἡ Σοφόκλειος
ἐκείνη πόλις ; τὴν Σοφοκλέους Xylander : τὸν Σοφοκλέα.

changes and diverts both body and voice from their
usual habits. Hence the Bacchic celebrations make
use of rhythmic movements, to the god-inspired it is
given to chant oracles in metre, and few madmen can
one find whose ravings are not in verse and song. In
view of these facts, if you should care to spread love
out beneath the rays of the sun, to examine it and
understand it, you would find that there is no other
emotion which contains more bitter sorrows, more
violent joy, or greater ecstasy and delirium ; the soul
of a man in love, like Sophocles' city, is full

> Of incense-smoke and simultaneously
> Of hymns triumphant and of lamentation.[a]

It is neither strange nor remarkable, then, if love,
containing and comprehending within itself all the
sources of music,—namely, sorrow, joy, and ecstasy,—
is itself a noisy and talkative emotion in general and
also one more conducive and inclined to the making
of songs and verses than any other."

QUESTION 6

Concerning Alexander's excessive drinking [b]

Speakers : Philinus, Plutarch, others

1. THE conversation was about Alexander the king,
and the consensus was that he did not drink excessively, but did spend much time in drinking and con-

---

[a] *Oedipus Tyrannus*, 4 ; cited also at *Mor.* 95 c, 169 D,
445 D, and *Life of Antony*, xxiv. 3. Here Plutarch adapts the
γέμει of Sophocles.
[b] The title is only partially descriptive of the content.

---

[2] Faehse (*cf.* Bolkestein, *Adv. Crit.* p. 77) : Φιλόπονος.
[3] Added by Stephanus.

(623) δείκνυεν δ' αὐτοὺς φλυαροῦντας Φιλῖνος ἐκ τῶν
βασιλικῶν ἐφημερίδων, ἐν αἷς συνεχέστατα γέγρα-
πται καὶ πλειστάκις ὅτι '' τήνδε τὴν ἡμέραν ἐκ τοῦ
πότου καθεύδων '' ἔστι δ' ὅτε '' καὶ τὴν ἐφεξῆς '' · διὸ
καὶ πρὸς τὰς συνουσίας ἀργότερος ἦν, ὀξὺς δὲ καὶ
θυμοειδὴς ἅπερ ἐστὶ σωματικῆς θερμότητος. λέγεται δὲ καὶ τοῦ χρωτὸς ἥδιστον ἀποπνεῖν ὥστε
καταπιμπλάναι τοὺς χιτωνίσκους εὐωδίας ἀρωματι-
ζούσης, ὃ δοκεῖ καὶ αὐτὸ θερμότητος εἶναι· διὸ
καὶ τῆς οἰκουμένης οἱ ξηρότατοι καὶ θερμότατοι
τόποι τήν τε κασίαν καὶ τὸν λιβανωτὸν ἐκφέρουσιν·
F πέψει γάρ τινι τῶν ὑγρῶν ὁ Θεόφραστός φησιν
ἐπιγίγνεσθαι τὴν εὐωδίαν, ὅταν ἐξαιρεθῇ τὸ
βλαβερὸν περισσὸν[1] ὑπὸ θερμότητος. δοκεῖ δὲ
καὶ Καλλισθένης[2] ἐν διαβολῇ γενέσθαι πρὸς αὐτόν,[3]
ὡς δυσχεραίνων[4] τὸ συνδειπνεῖν[5] διὰ τὸν ἄκρατον[6]·
ἐπεὶ καὶ κύλικα λεγομένην Ἀλεξάνδρου μεγάλην
624 ἐλθοῦσαν ἐπ' αὐτὸν ἀπεώσατο φήσας οὐκ ἐθέλειν
Ἀλεξάνδρου πιὼν Ἀσκληπιοῦ δεῖσθαι. ταῦτα μὲν
οὖν περὶ τῆς Ἀλεξάνδρου πολυποσίας.

---

[1] Hubert : ρισσὸν.
[2] Turnebus : lac. 4.
[3] γενέσθαι πρὸς αὐτόν Turnebus : γε lac. 3-5 τόν.
[4] Turnebus : δυσχεραι lac. 3 δειπνεῖν.
[5] τὸ συνδειπνεῖν Bolkestein, συνδειπνεῖν Faehse.
[6] Bolkestein from Athenaeus, 434 d : lac. 3-4.

---

[a] See *Life of Alexander*, xxiii ; Athenaeus, 434 b, f.
[b] A friend and fellow townsman of Plutarch (*RE, s.v.*
'' Plutarchos,'' col. 681). J. H. Oliver offers to identify an
Athenian branch of the family in an ephebe inscription of the
latter part of the 3rd century after Christ (*Hesperia*, ii [1933],
p. 510, and, for a more complete text, xi [1942], p. 71, no. 37).
[c] See note a and *cf. RE, s.v.* '' Ephemerides.''

versing with his friends.[a] Philinus,[b] however, showed their talk nonsense, taking his proof from the royal *Journal*[c] where, with repetitious frequency, it is written, " after a bout of drinking Alexander slept this day through," sometimes with the addition of " and the following day also." [d] Accordingly he was very lazy about love-making, though his bold and choleric temperament indicated a hot-natured body. Furthermore a very pleasant odour is said to have emanated from his skin ; and his clothing, as a result, was filled with a fragrant aroma,—which too seems indicative of heat. Thus cassia and frankincense are produced in the driest and hottest parts of our world, for fragrance, according to Theophrastus, comes from a sort of distillation of moistures when their harmful excess is removed by heat.[e] It seems, moreover, that Callisthenes [f] incurred the enmity of Alexander because, so the story goes, he could not endure to dine with the king on account of the strong drink. Indeed, even the great loving-cup called Alexander's, when once it was passed to him, he thrust aside with the remark that he did not wish to drink from Alexander's cup and so stand in need of Asclepius's.[g] This, then, was the conversation about Alexander's excessive drinking.

[d] *Cf.* Aelian, *Varia Hist.* iii. 23.

[e] The characteristics of Alexander are also reported in the *Life* (ch. iv), there on the authority of Aristoxenus, and their explanation is again found in Theophrastus's hypothesis concerning fragrance : *cf.* Wehrli, *Aristoxenus*, frag. 132 with commentary (*Die Schule des Aristoteles*, ii, pp. 40 and 87-88).

[f] An Olynthian, Aristotle's nephew, and an Alexander historian executed for participation in the Pages' Conspiracy (Jacoby, *Frag. Griech. Historiker*, no. 124).

[g] This anecdote is found again at 454 D and at Athenaeus, 434 d.

71

(624)   2. Μιθριδάτην δὲ τὸν πολεμήσαντα Ῥωμαίοις ἐν
τοῖς ἀγῶσιν, οὓς ἐπετέλει πολυφαγίας ἆθλα θεῖναι
καὶ πολυποσίας φασίν, νικῆσαι δ' αὐτὸν ἀμφότερα,
καὶ ὅλως πιεῖν πλεῖστον τῶν[1] καθ' αὐτὸν ἀνθρώπων,
διὸ καὶ Διόνυσον ἐπικληθῆναι. τοῦθ' ἡμεῖς εἴπομεν
ἕν τι τῶν εἰκῆ πεπιστευμένων εἶναι, τὸ περὶ τὴν
αἰτίαν τῆς ἐπικλήσεως· νηπίου γὰρ ὄντος αὐτοῦ
κεραυνὸς ἐπέφλεξε τὰ σπάργανα, τοῦ δὲ σώματος
οὐχ ἥψατο, πλὴν ὅσον ἴχνος τι τοῦ πυρὸς ἐν τῷ
B μετώπῳ κρυπτόμενον[2] ὑπὸ τῆς κόμης ⟨διαμέν⟩ειν[3]
αὐτῷ παιδί· γεγονότος δ'[4] ἀνδρὸς ἤδη πάλιν ἐπὶ
τὸ δωμάτιον ἐμπεσὼν κεραυνὸς αὐτοῦ μὲν παρέ-
πεσεν[5] καθεύδοντος, τῆς δὲ φαρέτρας ὑπερκρε-
μαμένης[6] διεξῆλθε τὰ βέλη πυρακτώσας. οἱ μὲν
οὖν μάντεις ἀπεφήναντο πλεῖστον αὐτὸν ἰσχύσειν
ἀπὸ τῆς τοξικῆς καὶ κούφης στρατιᾶς, οἱ δὲ
πολλοὶ Διόνυσον αὐτὸν ἀπὸ τῶν κεραυνοβολιῶν
ὁμοιότητι τοῦ πάθους προσηγόρευσαν.

   3. Ἐκ τούτου πάλιν[7] περὶ τῶν πολὺ πιόντων ἦν
λόγος· ἐν οἷς καὶ τὸν πύκτην Ἡρακλείδην ἐτίθεσαν,

---

[1] Added by Turnebus.
[2] Bernardakis, κρατούμενον Bolkestein : κρατουμένῳ.
[3] Bernardakis, μένειν exemplum Turnebi : lac. 5-6 ειν.
[4] παιδί· γεγονότος δ' Ziegler ; παιδί· καὶ exemplum Turnebi,
Amyot (cf. Wyttenbach ad loc.) : παι lac. 4-6.
[5] Emperius : κατέπεσεν.
[6] Reiske : ὑποκρεμαμένης.
[7] Added by Hubert.

---

[a] Mithridates the Great of Pontus, who fought Sulla, Lu-
cullus, and Pompey.   For the anecdote cf. Athenaeus, 415 e,

2. According to report, the Mithridates [a] who made war against the Romans put up prizes for the greatest eater and the greatest drinker in the contests he sponsored, himself won the prizes for both, was by far the greatest drinker among his contemporaries, and so was nicknamed Dionysus.[b] In my opinion that account of the reason for his nickname was one of those stories that gain credence without good grounds. Actually, when he was a baby, a bolt of lightning burned his swaddling-clothes, but did not touch his body, except for a trace of the fire which remained upon his forehead as a youth and was concealed by his hair. When he became a man, a bolt of lightning again fell near him, striking his house as he slept, passing through the quiver which hung above his head, and charring the arrows in it.[c] His prophets thereupon declared that he would derive his greatest strength from archers and light-armed troops, but the multitude called him Dionysus because of the similarity of his experience with bolts of lightning.[d]

3. From this the conversation returned to the subject of those who drink excessively. Among them was placed the boxer Heraclides,[e] who lived in the time

from Nicolaüs of Damascus, frag. 73 (Jacoby, *Frag. Griech. Historiker*, ii, p. 377).

[b] *Cf.* Poseidonius, frag. 36 (Jacoby) in Athenaeus, v, 212 d.   [c] *Cf. infra*, 665 B-E.

[d] An allusion to the story that Dionysus's mother Semelê was struck and killed by Zeus's lightning when she was pregnant with the god to be (*cf.* H. J. Rose in *O.C.D., s.v.* " Semelê ") ; the lightning that killed Semelê made Dionysus immortal and the implication is not without flattery to Mithridates.

[e] Included in a short list of heavy drinkers by Aelian, *Varia Hist.* xii. 26. The nickname, as Bolkestein notes (*Adv. Crit.* p. 90), apparently occurs as an ordinary name in *I.G.* xii. 3. 21 (Symê).

(624) ὃν Ἡρακλῶν Ἀλεξανδρεῖς ὑπεκορίζοντο, κατὰ
τοὺς πατέρας ἡμῶν γενόμενον. οὗτος ἀπορῶν
C συμπότου παραμένοντος ἐκάλει τοὺς μὲν ἐπὶ πρό-
πομα τοὺς δ᾽ ἐπ᾽ ἄριστον ἄλλους δ᾽ ἐπὶ δεῖπνον,
ἐσχάτους δέ τινας ἐπὶ κῶμον· ἀπαλλαττομένων
δὲ τῶν πρώτων οἱ[1] δεύτεροι συνῆπτον εἶτ᾽ ἐφεξῆς
οἱ τρίτοι καὶ τέταρτοι· κἀκεῖνος οὐθὲν διάλειμμα
ποιῶν ἅπασιν ἐξήρκει καὶ τοὺς τέσσαρας πότους
συνδιέφερεν.

4. Τῶν δὲ Δρούσῳ τῷ Τιβερίου Καίσαρος υἱῷ
συμβιούντων ὁ πάντας ἐν τῷ πίνειν προτρεπόμενος[2]
ἰατρὸς ἑάλω τῶν πικρῶν ἀμυγδαλῶν πέντ᾽ ἢ ἓξ
ἑκάστοτε προλαμβάνων ἕνεκα τοῦ μὴ μεθύσκεσθαι·
κωλυθεὶς δὲ καὶ παραφυλαχθεὶς οὐδ᾽ ἐπὶ μικρὸν
D ἀντέσχεν. ἔνιοι μὲν οὖν ᾤοντο τὰς ἀμυγδαλίδας
δηκτικόν τι καὶ ῥυπτικὸν ἔχειν τῆς σαρκός, ὥστε
καὶ τῶν προσώπων τὰς ἐφηλίδας ἐξαιρεῖν· ὅταν
οὖν προληφθῶσι, τῇ πικρότητι τοὺς πόρους ἀμύσ-
σειν καὶ δηγμὸν ἐμποιεῖν, ὑφ᾽ οὗ τὸ ὑγρὸν κατα-
σπῶσιν ἀπὸ τῆς κεφαλῆς διατμιζόμενον. ἡμῖν δὲ
μᾶλλον ἡ τῆς πικρότητος ἐδόκει δύναμις ἀνα-
ξηραντικὴ καὶ δάπανος ὑγρῶν εἶναι· διὸ τῇ τε
γεύσει πάντων ἐστὶ τῶν χυλῶν ὁ πικρὸς ἀηδέστατος
(τὰ γὰρ φλέβια τῆς γλώττης, ὡς ὁ Πλάτων φησίν,
μαλακὰ καὶ μανότερ᾽ ὄντα συντείνεται[3] παρὰ φύ-

---

[1] Added by Franke.
[2] προτρεχόμενος Xylander (citing Athenaeus, 52 d); παρ-
ερχόμενος Bernardakis (which Gulick prefers, also citing ὑπερ-
βάντα at Athenaeus, 52 d : A.J.P. lx [1939], p. 493).
[3] Hubert : συντείνει.

---

[a] Athenaeus at 52 d quotes this passage from Plutarch,
whom he names (cf. Gulick, A.J.P. lx [1939], p. 493). Pliny

of our fathers and was affectionately called Heraclous by the Alexandrians. Unable to find a drinking-companion to stay with him, he was in the habit of inviting people in for a round of drinks before luncheon, others for luncheon itself, still others for dinner, and finally new people again for an after-dinner bout of drinking. As the first group departed, the second arrived, then the third in their turn, and the fourth. Heraclides, without any let-up, was a match for them all and fully carried his part of the four sessions of drinking.

4. Among the companions of Drusus, the son of Tiberius Caesar, a doctor outstripped them all in drinking, and it was proved on him that before each party he took five or six bitter almonds to avoid getting drunk.[a] When he was stopped from doing so and closely watched, he did not hold out against the power of the wine even for a short time. Some were of the opinion that the almonds had an irritant, cathartic property affecting the flesh, so that they even removed pimples [b] from the face ; thus, when taken before drinking, they were thought by reason of their bitterness to excite and irritate the pores and by this action to draw moisture from the head in the form of vapour. To me, however, the action of bitterness seemed to be desiccant and moisture-dissipating ; for this reason a bitter flavour is the most unpleasant of all to the taste (for, as Plato says,[c] the small veins of the tongue, which are soft and widely spaced, are unnaturally contracted by dryness

[a] (*Nat. Hist.* xxiii. 145) claims the same property for almonds (*cf.* Dioscorides, i. 123. 2).

[b] Perhaps " freckles."

[c] The allusion rather garbles *Timaeus*, 65 c ff., on which see A. E. Taylor, *Commentary*, pp. 465 f.

(624) σιν ὑπὸ τῆς ξηρότητος, ἐκτηκομένων τῶν ὑγρῶν)
καὶ τὰ ἕλκη τοῖς πικροῖς ἀπισχναίνουσι φαρμάκοις,
ὡς ὁ ποιητής φησιν

E   ἐπὶ δὲ ῥίζαν βάλε πικρὴν
χερσὶ διατρίψας ὀδυνήφατον, ἥ οἱ ἁπάσας
ἔσχ᾽ ὀδύνας· τὸ μὲν ἕλκος ἐτέρσετο,[1] παύσατο
δ᾽ αἷμα.

τὸ γὰρ τῇ γεύσει πικρὸν τῇ δυνάμει ξηραντικὸν
ὀρθῶς προσηγόρευσεν. φαίνεται δὲ καὶ τὰ δια-
πάσματα τῶν γυναικῶν, οἷς ἀναρπάζουσι τοὺς
ἱδρῶτας, πικρὰ τῇ γεύσει[2] καὶ στυπτικὰ ὄντα,
σφοδρότητι τοῦ στρυφνοῦ ξηραίνειν.[3] '' οὕτως
οὖν,'' ἔφην, '' τούτων ἐχόντων, εἰκότως ἡ τῶν
ἀμυγδαλῶν πικρότης βοηθεῖ πρὸς τὸν ἄκρατον,
ἀναξηραίνουσα τοῦ σώματος τὰ ἐντὸς καὶ οὐκ
F ἐῶσα πίμπλασθαι τὰς φλέβας, ὧν διατάσει φασὶ καὶ
ταραχῇ συμβαίνει τὸ μεθύειν. τεκμήριον δὲ τοῦ
625 λόγου μέγα τὸ συμβαῖνον περὶ τὰς ἀλώπεκας· ἂν
γὰρ ἀμυγδάλας πικρὰς φαγοῦσαι μὴ[4] ἐπιπίωσιν,
ἀποθνήσκουσι[5] τῶν ὑγρῶν ἀθρόως ἐκλειπόντων.''[6]

ΠΡΟΒΛΗΜΑ Ζ

Διὰ τί μᾶλλον ἀκράτῳ χαίρουσιν οἱ γέροντες

Collocuntur Plutarchus et alii

Ἐζητεῖτο περὶ τῶν γερόντων, διὰ τί μᾶλλον
ἀκρατοτέρῳ τῷ ποτῷ χαίρουσιν. οἱ μὲν οὖν
κατεψυγμένην τὴν ἕξιν αὐτῶν καὶ δυσεκθέρμαντον

---

[1] ἁπάσας ... ἐτέρσετο added by Xylander from *Iliad*, xi.
847-848.
[2] Hubert : φύσει.

as moisture is dissipated), and this is why festering wounds are dried up by the use of bitter drugs, as the Poet says,[a]

> Thereon he placed a bitter drug,
> One crushed by hand, a killer of pain,
> Which checked that warrior's suffering;
> It dried the wound and staunched the blood.

He rightly called desiccant in action what is bitter in taste. Moreover, the dusting-powders which women use to dry perspiration have a bitter, puckery taste and seem to act as desiccants because of their vigorous astringency. "Since this is so," I concluded, "the bitterness of almonds is naturally helpful against wine, for it dries up the inside of the body and does not let the veins become full; and drunkenness, in common opinion, is due to the dilation and disturbance of the veins. A great proof of this opinion is what happens to foxes: if they eat bitter almonds and drink nothing afterwards, they die of complete desiccation."

QUESTION 7

Why old men are very fond of strong wine

Speakers: Plutarch and others

UNDER discussion was the question why old men are very fond of drink that is rather strong. Some thought the constitution of old men, being chill and hard to

[a] *Iliad*, xi. 846 ff.

---

[3] ξηραίνειν Reiske: τὸ πικρόν.
[4] Exemplum Turnebi: lac. 3.
[5] ἐπιπίωσι⟨ν ἀποθνήσκουσι⟩ exemplum Turnebi: lac. 5-7.
[6] ἀθρό⟨ως ἐκλει⟩πόντων exemplum Turnebi: lac. 9.

(625) οὖσαν οἰόμενοι διὰ τοῦτο τῇ σφοδρότητι τῆς
κράσεως ἐναρμόττειν ἐφαίνοντο κοινόν τι καὶ
πρόχειρον οὐχ ἱκανὸν δὲ πρὸς τὴν αἰτίαν οὐδ᾽
ἀληθὲς λέγοντες· καὶ γὰρ ἐπὶ τῶν ἄλλων αἰσθήσεων
τὸ αὐτὸ συμβέβηκεν· δυσκίνητοι γάρ εἰσι καὶ
B δυσμετάβλητοι πρὸς τὰς ἀντιλήψεις τῶν ποιοτήτων,
ἂν μὴ κατάκοροι καὶ σφοδραί[1] προσπέσωσιν.
αἰτία δ᾽ ἡ τῆς ἕξεως ἄνεσις· ἐκλυομένη γὰρ καὶ
ἀτονοῦσα πλήττεσθαι φιλεῖ. διὸ τῇ τε γεύσει
μάλιστα τοὺς δηκτικοὺς προσίενται χυμούς, ᾗ τ᾽
ὄσφρησις αὐτῶν ὅμοια πέπονθε πρὸς τὰς ὀσμάς,
κινεῖται γὰρ ὑπὸ τῶν ἀκράτων καὶ σφοδρῶν[2]
ἥδιον· ἡ δ᾽ ἁφὴ πρὸς[3] τὰ ἕλκη δυσπαθής,[4] τραύματα
γὰρ ἐνίοτε[5] λαμβάνοντες οὐ μάλα[6] πονοῦσιν·
ὁμοιότατον[7] δὲ γίγνεται τὸ[8] τῆς ἀκοῆς, οἱ γὰρ
μουσικοὶ γηρῶντες ὀξύτερον ἁρμόζονται καὶ σκλη-
ρότερον οἷον ὑπὸ πληγῆς[9] τῆς συντόνου φωνῆς
C ἐγείροντες τὸ αἰσθητήριον. ὅ τι γὰρ σιδήρῳ πρὸς
ἀκμὴν στόμωμα, τοῦτο σώματι πνεῦμα παρέχει
πρὸς αἴσθησιν· ἐνδόντος δὲ τούτου καὶ χαλάσαντος,
ἀργὸν ἀπολείπεται καὶ γεῶδες τὸ αἰσθητήριον καὶ
σφοδροῦ τοῦ νύττοντος, οἷον ὁ ἄκρατός ἐστι
δεόμενον.

---

[1] Reiske : σφόδρα.
[2] καὶ σφοδρῶν exemplum Turnebi : lac. 4-6.
[3] Exemplum Turnebi : lac. 5-7.
[4] Exemplum Turnebi : δυσπα lac. 4-6.

warm, was on this account compatible with a strong
mixture of wine and water ; obviously their argument was platitudinous and facile, and neither an
adequate nor an accurate analysis of the causation.
For the same thing occurs in regard to an old man's
perception of other stimuli ; in apprehending sensations he is hard to stir and hard to rouse, unless they
strike him with excessive strength. The cause is the
decline of his physical vigour ; enfeebled and ex-
hausted, his system likes shock. Thus an old man
likes flavours very pungent to his taste ; and odours
affect in like manner his sense of smell, for it is
pleasantly stimulated by scents which are unadulterate and strong. His tactile sense is dulled to
wounds, for, though he is sometimes hurt, he does
not feel much pain. And his sense of hearing is much
the same, for a musician, as he grows old, tunes
more sharply and harshly, as though to waken his
hearing by the whip-lashes of high-pitched sound.
What tempering gives the steel's edge, is given the
body's perception by the breath of life [a] ; when this
gives in and grows weak, the senses are left blunted
and clod-like and in need of a vigorous stimulant,
which strong wine is.

[a] Cf. 666 A, below.

---

[5] Exemplum Turnebi : lac. 6-8.
[6] οὐ μάλα exemplum Turnebi : lac. 4-6 ἅ.
[7] Exemplum Turnebi : ἐ lac. 3-5 τατον.
[8] Added by Bernardakis.
[9] καὶ after πληγῆς deleted by Reiske.

(625)

ΠΡΟΒΛΗΜΑ Η

Διὰ τί τὰ γράμματα πόρρωθεν οἱ πρεσβύτεροι μᾶλλον
ἀναγιγνώσκουσιν

Collocuntur Lamprias, Plutarchus, alii

1. Ταῦτα δ' ἡμῶν εἰς τὸ προκείμενον εὑρησι-
λογούντων ἐδόκει τὸ τῆς ὄψεως ἀντιπίπτειν. οἱ
D γὰρ πρεσβύτεροι πόρρω τὰ γράμματα τῶν ὀμμάτων
ἀπάγοντες ἀναγιγνώσκουσιν, ἐγγύθεν δ' οὐ δύνανται·
καὶ τοῦτο παραδηλῶν ὁ Αἰσχύλος φησίν·

σὺ δ' ἐξ ἀπόπτου[1] αὐτόν, οὐ γὰρ ἐγγύθεν
δύναιό γ' ἄν[2]· γέρων δὲ γραμματεὺς γενοῦ
σαφής.

ἐνδηλότερον δὲ Σοφοκλῆς τὸ αὐτὸ περὶ τῶν γε-
ρόντων·

βραδεῖα μὲν γὰρ ἐν λόγοισι προσβολὴ
μόλις δι' ὠτὸς ἔρχεται ῥυπωμένου[3]·
πρόσω[4] δὲ λεύσσων, ἐγγύθεν δὲ πᾶς τυφλός.

εἴπερ οὖν πρὸς τὴν ἐπίτασιν καὶ σφοδρότητα
μᾶλλον ὑπακούει τὰ[5] τῶν γερόντων αἰσθητήρια,
E πῶς ἐν τῷ ἀναγιγνώσκειν τὸν ἐγγύθεν ἀντιφωτι-
σμὸν οὐ φέρουσιν, ἀλλὰ προάγοντες[6] ἀπωτέρω τὸ
βιβλίον ἐκλύουσι τὴν λαμπρότητα τῷ ἀέρι καθάπερ
οἶνον ὕδατι κατακεραννυμένην;

---

[1] σὺ δ' ἐξ ἀπόπτου Headlam (*Journal of Philology*, xxiii,
1895, p. 271 ; for the hiatus *cf.* Sophocles, *Philoctetes*, 446,
and *Oedipus Tyrannus*, 332 : οὐδὲ ἀπὸ lac. 3.
[2] δύναιό γ' ἄν P. A. C. : lac. 6.
[3] Meineke : τρυπωμένου.
[4] Dindorf : πόρρω.

QUESTION 8

Why old men hold writing at a greater distance for reading

Speakers : Lamprias, Plutarch, others

1. THE phenomena of sight seemed to oppose the solution I devised for the preceding problem, for old men place writing far from their eyes to read it, and when the writing is near, they are unable to decipher it. Aeschylus intimates this when he says [a] :

> But you must read it far away,
> For close up you could surely not,
> And you must be a lucid scribe,
> Though old.

And Sophocles more clearly says the same thing about old men [b] :

> The sound of talking falls with slow impress,
> And hardly penetrates the stopped-up ear ;
> But each man sees afar, is blind when close.

If, then, the senses of old men respond better to intensity and strength, why is it that in reading they do not endure the impact of light from near by, but destroy its brightness by moving the book farther away and so diluting that brightness with air as wine is diluted with water?

---

[a] Frag. 358 Nauck (*Trag. Gr. Frag.* p. 107), 196 Smyth (LCL *Aeschylus*, ii, p. 493).

[b] Frag. 774 Nauck (*op. cit.* pp. 312 f.), 858 Pearson (*Fragments of Sophocles*, iii, p. 64). The translation here printed for lines 1-2 is Headlam's except for one word (*cf.* Pearson's note, *loc. cit.*).

---

5 Added by Meziriacus.
6 Hubert : παράγοντες.

(625)   2. Ἦσαν μὲν οὖν οἱ πρὸς τοῦτο λέγοντες,[1] ὡς
ἀπάγουσι τῶν ὄψεων τὸ βιβλίον οὐ μαλακώτερον
τὸ φῶς ποιοῦντες, ἀλλ' οἷον ἐπιδραττόμενοι καὶ
περιλαμβάνοντες αὐγὴν πλείονα καὶ πληροῦντες
ἀέρος λαμπροῦ τὴν μεταξὺ τῶν ὀμμάτων καὶ τῶν
γραμμάτων χώραν. ἕτεροι δὲ τοῖς συμβάλλουσι
τὰς αὐγὰς μετεῖχον· ἐπεὶ γὰρ ἀποτείνεται τῶν
ὀφθαλμῶν ἑκατέρου κῶνος, πρὸς τῷ ὄμματι τὴν
F κορυφὴν ἔχων, ἕδραν δὲ καὶ βάσιν ἢ περιλαμβάνει
τὸ ὁρώμενον, ἄχρι μέν τινος εἰκός ἐστιν ἰδίᾳ τῶν
κώνων ἑκάτερον φέρεσθαι· γενόμενοι δ' ἀπωτέρω
καὶ συμπεσόντες ἀλλήλοις ἕν τὸ φῶς ποιοῦσι· διὸ
καὶ τῶν ὁρωμένων ἕκαστον ἓν οὐ δύο φαίνεται,
καίπερ ἀμφοτέροις ἅμα τοῖς ὄμμασι καταφαινό-
μενον· αἰτία γὰρ ἡ τῶν κώνων σύναψις εἰς ταὐτὸ
καὶ σύλλαμψις ἐκ δυεῖν μίαν ὄψιν ἀπειργασμένη.
τούτων δ' οὕτως ἐχόντων οἱ μὲν ἐγγὺς προσ-
626 άγοντες τὰ γράμματα πρεσβῦται, μηδέπω τῶν
αὐγῶν[2] συγκεχυμένων ἀλλ' ἑκατέρα[3] χωρὶς ἐπιθιγ-
γάνοντες, ἀσθενέστερον ἐπιλαμβάνονται· οἱ δ'
ἀπωτέρω[4] προθέμενοι, μεμιγμένου τοῦ φωτὸς ἤδη
καὶ πολλοῦ γεγονότος, μᾶλλον ἐξακριβοῦσιν, ὥσπερ
οἱ ταῖς δυσὶν ὁμοῦ χερσὶ κατέχοντες ὃ τῇ ἑτέρᾳ μὴ
δύνανται.

3. Λαμπρίας δ' ὁ ἀδελφὸς[5] τὴν Ἱερωνύμου δόξαν[6]
οὐκ ἀνεγνωκὼς μέν,[7] αὐτὸς δὲ δι'[8] εὐφυΐαν ἐμπεσὼν
εἶπεν[9] ὅτι τοῖς προσπίπτουσιν ἀπὸ τῶν ὁρατῶν

---

[1] οἱ . . . λέγοντες Hubert : οἳ . . . λέγουσιν.
[2] Stephanus : αὐτῶν.
Xylander (translation) : ἑκάτερα (sic).
[4] Stephanus : ἀνωτέρω.
[5] Stephanus : lac. 5-6.
[6] Pohlenz : lac. 4-5.

82

2. Now there were some who replied to this that old men hold the book away from their eyes not to soften the light, but, as it were, to lay hold of and encompass more light and fill with bright air the space between their eyes and the writing. And others agreed with the joined-rays school of thought[a] : inasmuch as a cone of rays extends from each of the eyes, its apex at the eye, its base and foundation encompassing the object viewed, it is probable that each of the cones proceeds separately up to a certain point, but when they have attained a greater distance and merged with each other, they unite their light, and consequently each object viewed appears as one, not two, even though it appears to both eyes at the same time ; the reason for this is the simultaneous contact of the cones on the same object, and a union of light which produces single rather than dual vision. Since this is so, the elderly gentlemen who bring writing near their eyes, the rays of vision being not yet fused, contact the writing with each cone separately and lay weaker hold upon it ; but those who place the writing farther away, the light now fused and intensified, apprehend the writing with greater exactness, like men who master with both hands together what they can not with either alone.

3. My brother Lamprias expressed the opinion that we see by means of the forms which fall upon the vision from the objects viewed, the hypothesis of

[a] This concept is attributed to Hipparchus in *De Placitis*, 901 B. Further, see Bolkestein, *Adv. Crit.* pp. 93-94, and Hubert, *ad loc.*

---

[7] ἀνεγνωκὼς μέν Pohlenz : ἀνέγνωκεν.

[8] αὐτὸς δὲ δι' Pohlenz : lac. 4-5.

[9] εἶπεν Paton : lac. 2.

(626) εἴδεσιν[1] πρὸς τὴν ὄψιν ὁρῶμεν, ἃ πρῶτον μὲν
ἀπέρχεται μεγάλα καὶ παχυμερῆ, διὸ τοὺς γέρον-
τας ἐγγύθεν ἐπιταράττει βραδυπόρον καὶ σκληρὰν
B ἔχοντας τὴν ὅρασιν· ἀνενεχθέντων δ' εἰς τὸν ἀέρα
καὶ λαβόντων διάστημα, τὰ μὲν γεώδη περιθραύ-
εται καὶ ἀποπίπτει, τὰ δὲ λεπτὰ προσπελάζοντα
ταῖς ὄψεσιν ἀλύπως καὶ ὁμαλῶς ἐναρμόττει τοῖς
πόροις, ὥσθ' ἧττον ταραττομένους μᾶλλον ἀντιλαμβάνεσθαι. καὶ γὰρ αἱ τῶν ἀνθῶν ὀσμαὶ πόρρωθεν εὐωδέστεραι προσπίπτουσιν, ἂν δ' ἐγγύθεν
ἄγαν προσάγῃς, οὐχ οὕτω καθαρὸν οὐδ' ἄκρατον
ὀδώδασιν· αἴτιον δ' ὅτι πολλὰ τῶν γεωδῶν καὶ
θολερῶν συναποφέρεται τῇ ὀσμῇ καὶ διαφθείρει
τὴν εὐωδίαν ἐγγύθεν λαμβανομένης,[2] ἂν δ' ἄπωθεν,
τὰ μὲν[3] θολερὰ καὶ γεώδη περιρρεῖ καὶ ὑποπίπτει,
τὸ δ' εἰλικρινὲς καὶ θερμὸν αὐτῆς[4] ὑπὸ λεπτότητος
C διασῴζεται πρὸς τὴν αἴσθησιν.
    4. Ἡμεῖς δὲ τὴν Πλατωνικὴν φυλάττοντες ἀρχὴν
ἐλέγομεν ὅτι πνεῦμα τῶν ὀμμάτων αὐγοειδὲς
ἐκπῖπτον ἀνακίρναται τῷ περὶ τὰ σώματα φωτὶ
καὶ λαμβάνει σύμπηξιν, ὥσθ' ἓν ἐξ ἀμφοῖν σῶμα
δι' ὅλου συμπαθὲς γενέσθαι. κεράννυται δ' ἕτερον
ἑτέρῳ συμμετρίας λόγῳ τε καὶ ποσότητος· οὐ γὰρ
ἀναιρεθῆναι δεῖ θάτερον ὑπὸ θατέρου κρατηθέν,
ἀλλ' ἀπ' ἀμφοῖν εἴς τι μέσον ἁρμονίᾳ καὶ κοινωνίᾳ
συναχθέντων μίαν δύναμιν ἀποτελεσθῆναι. ὄντος
οὖν τοῦ τῶν παρηλίκων, εἴτε ῥεῦμα χρὴ προσαγο-

----

[1] Stephanus : lac. 2-3 συν.
[2] Hubert : λαμβανομένην.
[3] ἄπωθεν, τὰ μὲν Stephanus : ἀπὸ μὲν.
[4] Hubert : αὐτοῦ.

----

[a] The peripatetic from Rhodes mentioned *supra*, 612 D;

Hieronymus,[a] which Lamprias had not read, but had hit upon by his own cleverness. These forms, when they first come off, are large and coarse, and so at close quarters they disturb old men whose vision is slow and stiff; but where they rise into the air and gain distance, their earthy parts are broken and fall away, while the light parts, as they approach the eyes, painlessly and evenly fit into the passageways, and thus old men are less disturbed and more readily apprehend the forms. The scent of flowers, too, is sweeter when it reaches you from a distance, but if you bring them too close, their odour is not so pure and unadulterated. The reason is that much that is earthy and coarse accompanies the scent and destroys its pleasant odour when received near by, but if from a distance, the coarse and earthy parts slip off all round and fall, while the pure and fresh part of the scent by its lightness is brought intact to the sense of smell.

4. But I took my stand on the Platonic principle [b] and argued that a bright emanation which flows out from the eyes mixes with the light which surrounds objects and undergoes a fusion with it, so that from the two one body is formed compatible through its entirety. Each mingles with the other in proportion to their commensurability and quantity; for one must not be overwhelmed and destroyed by the other, but a single power must be created from both brought together on common ground in concord and partnership. Now inasmuch as the stream—whether

cf. RE, s.v. no. 12, where (col. 1562) it is suggested that the present theory was put forward in the On Suspension of Judgement.

[b] Timaeus, 45 B f.; cf. Republic, 507 D-E, 508 D, and Mor. 390 B, 433 D, 436 D, 921 D-E.

(626) ῥεύειν τὸ διὰ τῆς κόρης φερόμενον εἴτε πνεῦμα
D φωτοειδὲς εἴτ' αὐγήν, ἀσθενοῦς καὶ ἀδρανοῦς, οὐκ[1]
ἐγγίγνεται κρᾶσις πρὸς τὸ φῶς[2] τὸ ἐκτὸς οὐδὲ
μῖξις ἀλλὰ φθορὰ καὶ σύγχυσις,[3] ἂν μὴ μακρὰν τὰ
γράμματα τῶν ὀμμάτων ἀπάγοντες ἐκλύωσι τὴν
ἄγαν λαμπρότητα τοῦ φωτός, ὥστε μὴ πολλὴν
μηδ' ἄκρατον ἀλλ' ὁμοιοπαθῆ[4] καὶ σύμμετρον ἀπ-
αντῆσαι πρὸς τὴν ὄψιν. ὃ δὴ καὶ τοῦ περὶ τὰ νυ-
κτίνομα τῶν ζῴων παθήματος αἴτιόν ἐστιν· ἡ γὰρ
ὄψις αὐτῶν ὑπὸ τοῦ μεθημερινοῦ φωτὸς ἀδρανὴς
οὖσα κατακλύζεται καὶ κρατεῖται, μὴ δυναμένη πρὸς
πολὺ καὶ ἰσχυρὸν ἀπ'[5] ἀσθενοῦς καὶ ὀλίγης ἀρχῆς
κεράννυσθαι· πρὸς δὲ τὸ ἀμαυρὸν καὶ λεπτὸν οἷον
E ἀστέρος φῶς αὐγὴν διαρκῆ καὶ σύμμετρον ἐξίησιν,
ὥστε κοινωνεῖν καὶ συνεργεῖσθαι τὴν αἴσθησιν.

ΠΡΟΒΛΗΜΑ Θ

Διὰ τί τῷ ποτίμῳ μᾶλλον ἢ τῷ θαλαττίῳ πλύνεται τὰ ἱμάτια

Collocuntur Theo, Themistocles, Plutarchus

1. Θέων ὁ γραμματικὸς ἑστιωμένων ἡμῶν παρὰ
Μεστρίῳ Φλώρῳ πρὸς Θεμιστοκλέα τὸν Στωικὸν

---

[1] Added by Xylander.
[2] πρὸς τὸ φῶς P. A. C. (T. C., " with the Light about the
Object " : Morals, Translated . . . by Several Hands, vol. ii,
London [1691], p. 442), cf. Mor. 433 D and Plato, Timaeus,
45 c ; προσπίπτοντι πρὸς Hubert : προσ lac. 5-6.
[3] Meziriacus : σύγκρισις.
[4] Bernardakis (cf. Cherniss, De Facie, 921 E [LCL Mor.
xii, p. 44, note 6]) : ὁμοπαθῆ.
[5] Added by Reiske.

one ought to apply this term to what passes through the pupil of the eye, or call it "luminous emanation," or " ray "—is weak and powerless in men past their prime, no mixing and mingling is effected with the light outside, but only the extinction and disintegration of vision, unless by removing the writing to a distance from their eyes old men destroy the excessive brilliance of the outside light, so that a sympathetic and commensurate rather than a large and unadulterate amount of it meets the vision. It is this phenomenon too which is responsible for the behaviour of night-ranging animals ; for their vision, without strength, is overwhelmed and mastered by the mid-day light because it is unable, by reason of its weak and small beginning, to mix with the great, strong light of mid-day ; but with light that is dim and faint, such as that of a star, their vision sends forth a ray that is sufficient and commensurate, so that ray and outside light join and produce sight.

QUESTION 9

Why fresh water instead of sea water is used to wash clothes [a]

Speakers : Theon, Themistocles, Plutarch

1. WHEN we were being entertained at the house of Mestrius Florus,[b] Theon the critic [c] raised the ques-

[a] Imitated by Macrobius, *Saturnalia*, vii. 13, 17-27.
[b] *RE*, *s.v.* " Plutarchos," col. 687 : prominent Roman, consul under Vespasian, later proconsul of Asia, close friend of Plutarch, his guide to the battle-field of Betriacum, where Florus had fought (*Life of Otho*, xiv), participant in no less than ten of the Dinner Conversations, *e.g.* iii. 3 ff., v. 7, vii. 1 (where see note on 698 E).
[c] See p. 48, note *b* above.

(626) διηπόρησεν, τί δήποτε Χρύσιππος ἐν πολλοῖς τῶν
παραλόγων καὶ ἀτόπων ἐπιμνησθείς, οἷόν ἐστι τὸ
" τάριχος, ἂν ἅλμῃ βρέχηται, γλυκύτερον γίνεσθαι " καὶ τὸ " τῶν ἐρίων τοὺς πόκους ἧττον
ὑπακούειν τοῖς βίᾳ διασπῶσιν ἢ τοῖς ἀτρέμα
F διαλύουσιν " καὶ τὸ " νηστεύσαντας ἀργότερον
ἐσθίειν ἢ προφαγόντας," οὐδενὸς αὐτῶν αἰτίαν
ἀπέδωκεν. ὁ δὲ Θεμιστοκλῆς εἰπὼν ὅτι ταῦτα
Χρύσιππος ἄλλως ἐν παραδείγματος λόγῳ πρού-
θετο, ῥᾳδίως ἡμῶν καὶ ἀλόγως ὑπὸ τοῦ εἰκότος
ἁλισκομένων καὶ πάλιν ἀπιστούντων τῷ παρὰ τὸ
εἰκός, ἐπιστρέφων, " σοὶ δ'," ἔφη, " βέλτιστε, τί
627 πρᾶγμα περὶ τούτων διαπορεῖν; εἰ γὰρ ἡμῖν αἰτίων
ζητητικὸς καὶ θεωρητικὸς γέγονας, μὴ μακρὰν
οὕτως ἀποσκήνου τῶν ἰδίων, ἀλλ' εἰπὲ δι' ἣν
αἰτίαν Ὅμηρος ἐν τῷ ποταμῷ πλύνουσαν οὐκ ἐν
τῇ θαλάττῃ, καίπερ ἐγγὺς οὔσῃ, τὴν Ναυσικάαν
πεποίηκεν. καίτοι θερμοτέραν γε καὶ διαφανεστέ-
ραν εἰκὸς καὶ ῥυπτικωτέραν εἶναι."

2. Καὶ ὁ Θέων, " ἀλλὰ τοῦτό γ'," εἶπε, " διὰ[1]
τῶν γεωδῶν Ἀριστοτέλης πάλαι διαλέλυκεν, ὃ
προβέβληκας[2] ἡμῖν. πολὺ γὰρ[3] τῇ θαλάττῃ τὸ
τραχὺ καὶ γεῶδες ἐνδιέσπαρται καὶ τοῦτο ποιεῖ
B τὴν ἁλυκότητα μεμιγμένον· ᾗ καὶ μᾶλλον ἡ θάλαττα τούς τε νηχομένους ἐξαναφέρει καὶ στέγει
τὰ βάρη, τοῦ γλυκέος ἐνδιδόντος διὰ κουφότητα

[1] Added by Hubert.   [2] ὃ προβέβληκας Xylander : βέβληκας.
[3] πολὺ γὰρ Hubert : lac. 6-8.

_____

[a] The great Themistocles's descendant, whom Plutarch
knew as a fellow student under Ammonius (_Life of Themi-
stocles_, xxxii. 6).
[b] Head of the Stoics from 232 B.C. to his death in 207

tion with Themistocles the Stoic [a] why Chrysippus [b]
never gave an explanation for any of the strange and
extraordinary things he frequently mentions : for
example, " salted fish are fresher [c] if wetted with
brine " ; " fleeces of wool yield less easily if one
tears them apart violently than if one parts them
gently " ; and " people who have fasted eat more
deliberately than those who have taken food beforehand." Themistocles answered that Chrysippus mentioned such things incidentally, by way of example,
because we are easily and irrationally trapped by
what appears likely, and contrariwise disbelieve what
appears unlikely, and turning to Theon, he continued : " But what business have you, sir, to raise
a question about these matters ? For if you have
become inquisitive and speculative in the matter of
explanations, do not camp so far away from your own
province, but tell us for what reason Homer has made
Nausicaä do her washing in the river instead of the
sea,[d] though the latter was near by and quite likely
was warmer, clearer, and more cleansing."

2. " But," said Theon, " this problem you propose
to us Aristotle [e] long ago solved by considering the
earthy matter in sea-water. Much coarse, earthy
matter is scattered in the sea ; being mixed with the
water, this matter is responsible for the saltness, and
because of it sea-water also supports swimmers better
and floats heavy objects, while fresh water lets them

(fragments : von Arnim, *Stoic. Vet. Frag.* ii and iii [p. 146,
frag. 546 for this passage]).

[c] The Greek says " sweeter " ; the meaning is " less
salty " ; *cf. infra*, 627 в, where " sweet water " is non-salt
water.

[d] *Odyssey*, vi. 59.

[e] Frag. 217 Rose.

(627) καὶ ἀσθένειαν· ἔστι γὰρ ἄμικτον καὶ καθαρόν· ὅ-
θεν ἐνδύεται διὰ λεπτότητα καὶ διεξιὸν τοῦ θαλατ-
τίου μᾶλλον ἐκτήκει τὰς κηλῖδας. ἢ οὐ δοκεῖ σοι
τοῦτο πιθανῶς λέγειν Ἀριστοτέλης; "

3. " Πιθανῶς," ἔφην ἐγώ, " οὐ μὴν ἀληθῶς·
ὁρῶ γὰρ ὅτι καὶ τέφρα καὶ λίτρῳ,[1] κἂν μὴ παρῇ
δὲ ταῦτα, κονιορτῷ πολλάκις παχύνουσι τὸ ὕδωρ,
ὡς μᾶλλον τῶν γεωδῶν τῇ τραχύτητι καταπλύνειν
δυναμένων τὸν ῥύπον, αὐτοῦ δὲ τοῦ ὕδατος διὰ
C λεπτότητα καὶ ἀσθένειαν οὐχ ὁμοίως τοῦτο δρῶν-
τος. τὸ μὲν οὖν παχυμερὲς τῆς θαλάττης οὐδὲν
κωλύει γε τοῦτο ποιεῖν οὐδ' ἧττον πρὸς τὴν
κάθαρσιν συνεργεῖ διὰ[2] τὴν δριμύτητα· καὶ γὰρ
αὕτη τοὺς πόρους[3] ἀναστομοῦσα καὶ ἀνοίγουσα[4]
κατασύρει τὸν ῥύπον. ἐπεὶ δὲ πᾶν τὸ λιπαρὸν
δυσέκπλυτόν ἐστι καὶ κηλῖδα ποιεῖ, λιπαρὰ δ' ἡ
θάλασσα, τοῦτ' ἂν αἴτιον εἴη μάλιστα τοῦ μὴ
καλῶς πλύνειν. ὅτι δ' ἐστὶ λιπαρά, καὶ αὐτὸς
εἴρηκεν Ἀριστοτέλης· οἵ τε γὰρ ἅλες λίπος ἔχουσιν
καὶ τοὺς λύχνους βέλτιον παρέχουσι καομένους,
αὐτή θ' ἡ θάλαττα προσραινομένη ταῖς φλοξὶ συν-
εκλάμπει, καὶ κάεται μάλιστα τῶν ὑδάτων τὸ θα-
D λάττιον· ὡς δ' ἐγῷμαι, διὰ τοῦτο καὶ θερμότατόν
ἐστιν.

" Οὐ μὴν ἀλλὰ καὶ κατ' ἄλλον τρόπον· ἐπεὶ τῆς
πλύσεως τέλος ἡ ῥύψις[5] ἐστὶν καὶ μάλιστα φαίνεται
καθαρὸν τὸ τάχιστα[6] ξηρὸν γιγνόμενον, δεῖ δὴ τὸ
πλῦνον ὑγρὸν τῷ ῥύπῳ[7] συνεξελθεῖν, ὥσπερ τῷ

---

[1] Doehner : λίθοι.
[2] οὐδὲν . . . διὰ Bernardakis from Macrobius, Saturnalia,
vii. 13. 22 : οὐ lac. 5-6 πετουτόποτε lac. 5-6 πρὸς τὴν κα lac.
6 δὲ.
[3] Stephanus : lac. 3-4.   [4] Stephanus : lac. 4-5.

sink since it is light and unsubstantial. For the latter
is unmixed and pure, and so because of its light consistency it soaks into cloth and, as it passes through,
dissolves out stains more readily than sea-water.[a]
Don't you think what Aristotle says is plausible ? "

3. "Plausible," I said, "but not true. For I
observe that people frequently thicken their water
with ash, or soda, or, if these are not at hand, with a
powdery solid ; the earthy matter, it would seem, is
more easily able by its roughness to wash out dirt,
while the water alone because of its lightness and
weakness does not do this with equal facility. It is
not, therefore, the coarseness of sea-water that prevents this action, nor is sea-water a less efficient
cleanser because of its acridness, for this quality
cleans out and opens up the mesh of the cloth and
sweeps away the dirt.[b] But since everything oily is
hard to wash and makes a stain, and the sea is oily,
this would surely be the reason for its not cleaning
efficiently. That the sea is oily Aristotle himself has
said.[c] For salt contains fat, so making lamps burn
better ; and sea-water itself, when it is sprinkled into
flames, flashes up with them. Indeed among waters
it is particularly sea-water that is flammable, and, in
my view, this is the reason why it is also the warmest.

"What is more, the phenomenon can also be explained in another manner. Since cleansing is the
aim of washing, and what dries quickest appears
cleanest, the washing liquid must depart with the

[a] Cf. 696 d, below.
[b] Cf. 684 b-c, below.
[c] [Aristotle], *Problems*, 933 a 18 ff. ; cf. *Mor.* 911 e.

---

[5] ῥύψις P. Maas : ψῦξις.   [6] Doehner : μάλιστα.
[7] Stephanus : lac. 4-5 ὤ.

91

(627) νοσήματι τὸν ἐλλέβορον. τὸ μὲν οὖν γλυκὺ ῥᾳδίως ὁ ἥλιος ἐξάγει διὰ κουφότητα, τὸ δ' ἁλμυρὸν ἐνισχόμενον τοῖς πόροις διὰ τραχύτητα δυσξήραντόν ἐστιν."

4. Καὶ ὁ Θέων ὑπολαβών, " οὐδέν," ἔφη, " λέγεις· Ἀριστοτέλης γὰρ ἐν τῷ αὐτῷ βυβλίῳ φησὶν τοὺς ἐν θαλάττῃ λουσαμένους τάχιον ἀποξηραίνεσθαι τῶν γλυκεῖ χρησαμένων, ἂν ἐν ἡλίῳ στῶσιν."

E " Λέγει γάρ," εἶπον· " ἀλλ' ᾤμην σε μᾶλλον Ὁμήρῳ τἀναντία λέγοντι πιστεύσειν. ὁ γὰρ Ὀδυσσεὺς μετὰ τὸ ναυάγιον ἐντυγχάνει τῇ Ναυσικάᾳ 'σμερδαλέος' ὀφθῆναι 'κεκακωμένος ἅλμῃ,' καὶ πρὸς τὰς θεραπαινίδας φησίν·

> ἀμφίπολοι, στῆθ' οὕτω[1] ἀπόπροθεν, ὄφρ' [ἂν][2]
> ἐγὼ αὐτὸς
> ἅλμην ὤμοιιν ἀπολούσομαι,[3]

καταβὰς δ' εἰς τὸν ποταμὸν ' ἐκ κεφαλῆς ἔσμηχεν ἁλὸς χνόον,' ὑπερφυῶς τοῦ ποιητοῦ τὸ γιγνόμενον συνεωρακότος· ὅταν γὰρ ἐκ τῆς θαλάττης ἀναδύντες ἐν τῷ ἡλίῳ στῶσιν, τὸ λεπτότατον καὶ F κουφότατον τῆς ὑγρασίας ἡ θερμότης διεφόρησεν, τὸ δ' ἁλμυρὸν αὐτὸ καὶ τραχὺ καταλειφθὲν ἐφίσταται καὶ παραμένει τοῖς σώμασιν ἁλώδης ἐπίπαγος, μέχρι ἂν αὐτὸ ποτίμῳ καὶ γλυκεῖ κατακλύσωσιν."

---

[1] Xylander from Homer : οὕτως.
[2] Deleted by Xylander, omitted in text of Homer and at Macrobius, *Saturnalia*, vii. 13. 26.
[3] Xylander from Homer (aor. subj.) : ἀπολούσωμαι.

dirt, as hellebore does with the sickness it purges. The sun easily evaporates fresh water because of its lightness, but salt water dries up with difficulty since its coarseness holds it in the mesh of the cloth."

4. Theon interrupted and said, " You are talking nonsense, for Aristotle in the same book says [a] that those who wash themselves in the sea, if they stand in the sun, dry off faster than those who use fresh water."

" He does say so," I replied, " but I thought you would put your confidence rather in Homer, who implies the opposite. For it chanced that Odysseus, after his shipwreck, was seen by Nausicaä

> terribly dirtied with brine. [b]

And to her maidservants he says,

> Girls, stay away, while I wash from my shoulders the brine of the sea. [c]

And going down to the river, he

> washed from his head all the foam of the sea, [d]

the poet understanding very well what happens. For when men come out of the sea and stand in the sun, the heat evaporates the finest and lightest part of the moisture, [e] and the salty, coarse residue itself remains coated upon their bodies, a briny scum, until they wash it away with fresh drinking water."

[a] [Aristotle], *Problems*, 932 b 25.
[b] *Odyssey*, vi. 137.
[c] *Odyssey*, vi. 218 f.
[d] *Odyssey*, vi. 226.
[e] Cf. *infra*, 697 B.

628 ΠΡΟΒΛΗΜΑ Ι

Διὰ τί τῆς Αἰαντίδος φυλῆς Ἀθήνησιν οὐδέποτε τὸν χορὸν
ἔκρινον ὕστατον

Collocuntur Marcus, Milo, Philopappus, Glaucias,
Plutarchus, alii

1. Ἐν δὲ τοῖς Σαραπίωνος ἐπινικίοις, ὅτε τῇ
Λεοντίδι φυλῇ τὸν χορὸν διατάξας ἐνίκησεν, ἑστιωμένοις ἡμῖν ἅτε δὴ καὶ φυλέταις οὖσι δημοποιή-
τοις οἰκεῖοι λόγοι τῆς ἐν χειρὶ φιλοτιμίας παρῆσαν.
ἔσχε γὰρ ὁ ἀγὼν ἐντονωτάτην ἅμιλλαν, ἀγωνο-
θετοῦντος ἐνδόξως καὶ μεγαλοπρεπῶς Φιλοπάππου

---

[a] To Sarapion is dedicated *De E apud Delphos* (384 D)
and he is a member of the company in *De Pythiae Oraculis*
(396 D), where it appears that he is both a poet and a Stoic
philosopher (*cf. RE, s.v.* " Plutarchos," cols. 683-684). Two
rather bitter iambic trimeters perhaps by this Sarapion are
preserved in Stobaeus (iii. 10. 2 Hense). Presumably also
by this Sarapion are the dactylic hexameters on the duties of
a physician published on the " Sarapion Monument " apparently erected in the Asclepieum on the south slope of the
Athenian Acropolis by Q. Statius Sarapion, who would then
be the grandson of Plutarch's friend Sarapion ; several
generations later a paean of Sophocles and the names of the
paeanistae who recited it were added to the monument (see
Paul Maas and James H. Oliver, " An Ancient Poem on the
Duties of a Physician," *Bulletin of the History of Medicine*,
vii [1939], pp. 315-323, particularly pp. 321-323 ; *cf.* also R.
Flacelière, *Rev. Ét. Grec.* lxiv [1951], pp. 323-327 ; and further, James H. Oliver, *Hesperia*, Suppl. viii [1949], pp. 243-
248, where, too, necessary references to the earlier literature
can be found).

[b] Syrian prince, Roman consul, Athenian archon, and
demesman of Besa. His grave monument (A.D. 114–116) still
stands, in part, on the summit of the hill Mouseion across
from the south-west corner of the Acropolis (Judeich, *Topographie von Athen*[2], pp. 100 and 388-389 ; the inscriptions,
I.G. ii[2]. 3451 ; *cf.* Kirchner, *RE, s.v.* " Philopappos "). To him

QUESTION 10

Why the chorus of the phylê Aiantis at Athens is never
judged last

Speakers: Marcus, Milo, Philopappus, Glaucias,
Plutarch, and others

1. WHEN Sarapion [a] won the prize with the chorus he
directed for the phylê Leontis, he entertained at a
victory celebration at which I was present,—for I was
an adopted member of the phylê,—and suitably
enough our talk was concerned with the recent competition. For the contest had produced intense
rivalry since King Philopappus [b] had presided in a

Plutarch dedicated the *De Adulatore et Amico*. In *I.G.* ii².
3112 (A.D. 75/6–87/8) the phylê Oeneïs, which had contes-
ted with a dithyramb, honoured Philopappus as agono-
thetes of the Dionysia in the year of his archonship. Pickard-
Cambridge's text of this document reads ἡ Οἰνηὶς φυλὴ διὰ
τῶν εὖ ἀγωνισαμένων . . ., and ". . . the inscription," he writes,
" suggests that the Oeneïd tribe had just won a victory . . ."
(*Dramatic Festivals of Athens*, p. 74 and note 6). But
actually the εὖ, though cut on the stone, was erased and so
must be deleted from the text (see P. Graindor, *Album d'inscriptions attiques*, p. 23, no. 26, and pl. XIX). Presumably
Oeneïs honoured Philopappus for his munificence rather
than for their victory, a victory which, if indeed the document
of Oeneïs and Plutarch's essay both refer to the same occasion,
had actually been won by Leontis. Boulon, the choregus for
Oeneïs, and Sarapion, presumably the like for Leontis, would
be only nominally so, for Philopappus was, as well as agono-
thetes, the *de facto* choregus who defrayed the expenses of
choruses for all the phylae together. The inscription of
Oeneïs would also be evidence that the subject matter of the
Quaestiones Convivales ranged through some twenty to
thirty years, more or less, of Plutarch's life, if the Favorinus
of viii. 10 is indeed Favorinus of Arles (the same, Ziegler,
RE, *s.v.* " Plutarchos," col. 713 ; " probably the same . . ."
Sandbach on 734 F [LCL *Mor.* ix, p. 205, note *c*] *infra*).

(628)

B τοῦ βασιλέως ταῖς φυλαῖς ὁμοῦ πάσαις χορηγοῦν-
τος. ἐτύγχανε δὲ συνεστιώμενος ἡμῖν καὶ τῶν
παλαιῶν τὰ μὲν λέγων τὰ δ᾽ ἀκούων διὰ φιλανθρωπίαν οὐχ ἧττον ἢ φιλομάθειαν.

2. Προεβλήθη δέ τι τοιοῦτον ὑπὸ Μάρκου τοῦ
γραμματικοῦ. Νεάνθη τὸν Κυζικηνὸν ἔφη λέγειν
ἐν τοῖς κατὰ πόλιν μυθικοῖς, ὅτι τῇ Αἰαντίδι φυλῇ
γέρας ὑπῆρχεν τὸ μὴ κρίνεσθαι τὸν ταύτης[1] χορὸν
ἔσχατον· '' εὐχερὴς[2] μὲν οὖν,'' ἔφη, '' πρὸς ἀπόδειξιν[3] ἱστορίας ὁ ἀναγράψας,[4] εἰ δὲ τοῦτό γ᾽ οὐ[5]
νοθεύει, προκείσθω τῆς αἰτίας ἐν κοινῷ πᾶσιν ἡ
ζήτησις.''

Εἰπόντος δὲ τοῦ ἑταίρου Μίλωνος, '' ἂν οὖν
ψεῦδος ᾖ τὸ λεγόμενον;'', '' οὐδέν,'' ἔφη, '' δεινόν,''
ὁ Φιλόπαππος, '' εἰ ταὐτὸ πεισόμεθα Δημοκρίτῳ
C τῷ[6] σοφῷ διὰ φιλολογίαν. καὶ γὰρ ἐκεῖνος ὡς
ἔοικε τρώγων σίκυον, ὡς ἐφάνη μελιτώδης ὁ
χυμός, ἠρώτησε τὴν διακονοῦσαν, ὁπόθεν πρίαιτο·
τῆς δὲ κῆπόν τινα φραζούσης, ἐκέλευσεν ἐξαναστὰς
ἡγεῖσθαι καὶ δεικνύναι τὸν τόπον· θαυμάζοντος δὲ
τοῦ γυναίου καὶ πυνθανομένου τί βούλεται, ' τὴν
αἰτίαν,' ἔφη, ' δεῖ με τῆς γλυκύτητος εὑρεῖν, εὑρήσω
δὲ τοῦ χωρίου γενόμενος θεατής.'

[1] Hubert : lac. 3-4.   [2] Pohlenz : lac. 5-7.
[3] πρὸς ἀπόδειξιν Wyttenbach : προ lac. 5-6 ξιν.
[4] Mueller : ἀνα lac. 4-6.
[5] γ᾽ οὐ Vulcobius : γοῦν.   [6] Added by Stephanus.

[a] Who is a member of the company also at ix. 5 (740 E).
[b] There are two writers of Cyzicus so named. One
flourished at the beginning of the third century, the other at

96

notable manner and, with great munificence, had furnished choruses for all the phylae together. It happened that he was one of the guests with us and spoke of antiquarian matters and listened to antiquarian talk because of his courtesy not less than his eagerness to learn.

2. One such subject was introduced by the critic Marcus.[a] He remarked that Neanthes of Cyzicus [b] said in his *Legends of the States* that the phylê Aiantis had the honour of not having its chorus judged last. " So," he continued, " in spite of the fact that this writer is reckless in the history he publishes, if in this matter at least he does not falsify, let us all join in seeking out the reason."

His companion Milo [c] said, " What if actually the information is false ? "

" No matter ! " said Philopappus. " It's not bad if the same thing does happen to us that happened to the wise Democritus because of love for learning.[d] It seems that the juice of a cucumber he was eating appeared to have a honeylike taste, and he questioned his serving-woman about where she had bought it. When she indicated a certain garden, he got up and told her to take him and show him the place. The woman was astonished and asked what he had in mind. ' I must find,' he replied, ' the explanation for the sweetness, and I shall find it if I see the place.'

the end ; and most references cannot with certainty be assigned to one or to the other : Jacoby, *Frag. Griech. Historiker*, no. 84 (Neanthes) with Commentary II C, pp. 144 ff. (who assigns this passage to the earlier man, as indeed he does all but one) ; *cf.* Richard Laqueur, *RE, s.v.* " Neanthes."

[c] Milo appears only here (*RE, s.v.* " Plutarchos," col. 668).
[d] Diels-Kranz, *Frag. d. Vorsokratiker*, ii[10], p. 87, 17 a.

(628)   "' Κατάκεισο δή,' τὸ γύναιον εἶπε μειδιῶν, ' ἐγὼ
γὰρ ἀγνοήσασα τὸ σίκυον εἰς ἀγγεῖον ἐθέμην μεμε-
λιτωμένον.'

"' Ὁ δ' ὥσπερ ἀχθεσθείς, ' ἀπέκναισας,' εἶπεν,
D ' καὶ οὐδὲν ἧττον ἐπιθήσομαι τῷ λόγῳ καὶ ζητήσω
τὴν αἰτίαν, ὡς ἂν οἰκείου καὶ συγγενοῦς οὔσης τῷ
σικύῳ τῆς γλυκύτητος.'

"Οὐκοῦν μηδ' ἡμεῖς τὴν Νεάνθους ἐν ἐνίοις εὐχέ-
ρειαν ἀποδράσεως ποιησώμεθα[1] πρόφασιν· ἐγγυ-
μνάσασθαι γάρ, εἰ μηδὲν ἄλλο χρήσιμον, ὁ λόγος
παρέξει."

3. Πάντες οὖν ὁμαλῶς ἐρρύησαν πρὸς τὸ τὴν
φυλὴν ἐγκωμιάζειν, εἴ τι καλὸν πρὸς δόξαν αὐτῇ
ὑπῆρχεν ἀναλεγόμενοι. καὶ γὰρ ὁ Μαραθὼν εἰς
μέσον εἵλκετο, δῆμος ὢν ἐκείνης τῆς φυλῆς· καὶ
τοὺς περὶ Ἁρμόδιον Αἰαντίδας ἀπέφαινον, Ἀφι-
δναίους γε δὴ τῶν δήμων γεγονότας. Γλαυκίας
E δ' ὁ ῥήτωρ[2] καὶ τὸ δεξιὸν κέρας Αἰαντίδαις τῆς
ἐν Μαραθῶνι παρατάξεως ἀποδοθῆναι, ταῖς Αἰσχύ-

---

[1] Bernardakis : ποιησόμεθα.
[2] εἶπε added by Bernardakis (cf. 698 d where ἔφη was
added by Turnebus).

---

[a] Presumably an empty honey-jar not yet cleaned. Bolkestein suggested a jar the interior of which had been smeared
with honey to preserve the food stored in it, and he cited three
passages (Adv. Crit. p. 97) ; of these one refers to the em-
balmer's art (Pliny, Nat. Hist. xxii. 108) and the other two
have nothing to do with the case (Columella, ix. xvi. 13 ;
Horace, Epodes, ii. 15).

[b] RE, s.v. " Marathon," col. 1427.

[c] The younger of the " Tyrannicides " who paradoxically
became " Heroes of the Revolution " in the literature concerned with the fall of the Pisistratids towards the end of the
6th century B.C. (cf. RE, s.v. " Aristogeiton " and s.v.
" Harmodios ").

" ' Sit down,' said the woman with a smile, ' the fact is I accidentally put the cucumber in a honey-jar.' *a*

" ' That was very annoying of you,' said Democritus with pretended anger, ' and I shall apply myself not the less to the problem and seek the explanation as if sweetness were proper and natural to this cucumber.'

" Let us not, then, make Neanthes's recklessness in some items a pretext for running away, for this discussion will be a good exercise, if nothing else useful."

3. Thereupon all together proceeded to praise the phylê, taking for their theme any claim to distinction it possessed. Marathon was drawn into the talk, it being a deme of that phylê *b* ; and Harmodius *c* and his coterie, it was pointed out, belonged to Aiantis, for they were from Aphidna, also a deme of the phylê. The orator Glaucias *d* said that the right flank of the battle line at Marathon was given to men of Aiantis ; this he based on the elegiac poem of Aeschylus *e* . . .

---

d A member of the company at vii. 9 and 10 (714 A ff.) and at ix. 12 and 13 (741 c ff.).

e This passage may be added to the convenient collection of testimonia and elegiac fragments in the second edition of Professor Gilbert Murray's *Aeschyli . . . Tragoediae* (Oxford, 1955), p. 371 (lines 2-4, 15-18) and pp. 373-374. The present passage ". . . attests an elegiac poem precisely about the battle of Marathon, though the corruption of its title is not healed and seems to be incurable " (Jacoby, *Hesperia*, xiv [1945], p. 182, note 101). But the Marathon epigram, Murray, *op. cit.* p. 374, no. 5 should be deleted from the collection (*cf.* Jacoby, *ibid.* pp. 179-185). For the Marathon epigrams see now (in addition to Jacoby, *ibid.* pp. 161-185) B. D. Meritt, *The Aegean and the Near East : Studies Presented to Hetty Goldman* (1956), pp. 268-280 ; *A.J.P.* lxxxiii (1962), pp. 294-298, and lxxxv (1964), p. 417 ; and *cf.* W. K. Pritchett, *University of California Publications in Classical Archaeology*, iv. 2 (1960), pp. 160-168, and *A.J.P.* lxxxv (1964), pp. 50-55.

(628) λου †τὴν μεθορίαν†¹ ἐλεγείαις πιστούμενος, ἠγωνι-
σμένου τὴν μάχην ἐκείνην ἐπιφανῶς· ἔτι δὲ καὶ
Καλλίμαχον ἀπεδείκνυεν τὸν πολέμαρχον ἐξ ἐκείνης
ὄντα τῆς φυλῆς, ὃς αὐτόν τε παρέσχεν ἄριστον ἄνδρα καὶ τῆς μάχης μετά γε Μιλτιάδην αἰτιώτατος
κατέστη σύμψηφος ἐκείνῳ γενόμενος. ἐγὼ δὲ τῷ
Γλαυκίᾳ προσετίθην, ὅτι καὶ τὸ ψήφισμα, καθ' ὃ
τοὺς Ἀθηναίους ἐξήγαγεν, τῆς Αἰαντίδος φυλῆς
πρυτανευούσης γραφείη, καὶ ὅτι περὶ τὴν ἐν Πλα-
ταιαῖς μάχην εὐδοκιμήσειεν ἡ φυλὴ μάλιστα· διὸ
καὶ ταῖς Σφραγίτισι Νύμφαις τὴν ἐπινίκιον καὶ
F πυθόχρηστον ἀπῆγον Αἰαντίδαι θυσίαν εἰς Κιθαι-
ρῶνα, τῆς πόλεως τὸ ἱερεῖον καὶ τὰ ἄλλα παρεχού-
σης αὐτοῖς. " ἀλλ' ὁρᾷς," ἔφην, " ὅτι πολλὰ καὶ
ταῖς ἄλλαις φυλαῖς ὑπάρχει, καὶ πρώτην γε τὴν
629 ἐμὴν ἴστε δὴ τὴν Λεοντίδα μηδεμιᾷ δόξης² ὑφ-
ιεμένην. σκοπεῖτε δή, μὴ πιθανώτερον λέγεται τὸ³
παραμύθιον τοῦ ἐπωνύμου τῆς φυλῆς καὶ παραίτη-
σιν εἶναι τὸ γιγνόμενον· οὐ γὰρ εὔκολος ἐνεγκεῖν

---

¹ τὴν μεθορίαν presumably an " incurable " corruption of
the title of Aeschylus's poem on Marathon (Jacoby).
² Turnebus : δόξῃι.
³ τι Bolkestein.

ᵃ The reference is to Herodotus, vi. 109-110. Callimachus,
who perished in the battle (id. vi. 114), was by virtue of his
office commander-in-chief at Marathon ; Miltiades was one
of the commander-in-chief's ten generals (id. vi. 103). For
the problem of the relationship between polemarch and
generals see C. Hignett, A History of the Athenian Constitution, pp. 166-173. For fragments of the dedication made by
Callimachus before the battle and a supplement added after

who had fought brilliantly in that battle. Furthermore, Glaucias pointed out that the polemarch Callimachus was of that phylê, a man who proved himself very brave and by casting his vote with Miltiades was most responsible, at least next to Miltiades, for the decision to commit the Athenians to battle.[a] I added to the remarks of Glaucias the fact that the decree by the stipulations of which the polemarch led the Athenians out to battle was passed during the prytany of the phylê Aiantis, furthermore that the phylê distinguished itself in the highest degree at the battle of Plataea. It was because of this that men of Aiantis conducted to Cithaeron the victory sacrifice ordained by the Pythian oracle in honour of the Sphragitid Nymphs, and the state supplied them the sacrificial victim and other things needful.[b] "However," I continued, " you are to take cognizance of the fact that the other phylae, too, possess many honours, and you all know well enough that my own phylê Leontis is among the foremost and inferior to none in distinction. Now consider, is it not more plausible to say that the preference shown Aiantis in never judging its chorus last is for the purpose of appeasing and mollifying the eponym of the phylê ? For the son of Telamon is not good natured about en-

---

the battle see *I.G.* i². 609 = Tod, *Gr. Hist. Inscr.* no. 13, with Jacoby's interpretation in *Hesperia*, xiv (1945), p. 158, note 8 ; and *cf.* Shefton, *B.S.A.* xlv (1950), pp. 140-164.

[b] This account of the rôle of Aiantis at Plataea is repeated with greater detail in the *Life of Aristeides*, xix. 6, where Kleidemos is cited for " an enlargement " of the record of Herodotus, ix. 70. The Sphragitid Nymphs reappear at *Arist.* xi. 3-4, and at Pausanias, ix. 3. 9. The evidence is collected and discussed by Jacoby, *Frag. Griech. Historiker*, no. 323 (Kleidemos), frag. 22, and 3 b Suppl., vol. i, pp. 82-83, with notes in vol. ii, p. 76.

(629) ἧτταν ὁ Τελαμώνιος, ἀλλ' οἷος ἀφειδεῖν πάντων
ὑπ' ὀργῆς καὶ φιλονεικίας· ἵν' οὖν μὴ χαλεπὸς ᾖ
μηδ' ἀπαραμύθητος, ἔδοξε τῆς ἥττης ἀφελεῖν τὸ
δυσχερέστατον, εἰς τὴν ἐσχάτην χώραν μηδέποτε
τὴν φυλὴν αὐτοῦ καταβαλόντας."[1]

[1] In T καταβαλόντας ends line 14, fol. 35 r; line 15,
Πλουτάρχου συμποσιακῶν ᾶ; line 16, a decorative row of
sigla; line 17, the heading for Book II.

---

[a] W. K. Pritchett noted that the discussion reaches no
satisfactory conclusion (*U.C. Pub. Class. Arch.* iv. 2 [1960],
p. 148, note 76). W. S. Ferguson suggested the possibility of
finding other " privileges " for Aiantis in the operation of the

during a position of inferiority ; on the contrary, when driven by passion and envy, he is the sort who is reckless of everything. Therefore, to keep him from being harsh and implacable, it was decided to remove the worst feature of inferiority by never putting his phylê down in last place." [a]

tribal cycles (*Athenian Tribal Cycles* [1932], pp. 78-80). It may be that Plutarch's own solution and indeed the subject of the problem are a *jeu de littérature* based on the fact that Aiantis in the official order for listing the Athenian phylae (A. G. Woodhead, *The Study of Greek Inscriptions*, pp. 112-114) occupied the penultimate or at times the antepenultimate position in the order—always close to last, but never last.

TABLE-TALK
(QUAESTIONES CONVIVALES)
BOOK II

ΣΥΜΠΟΣΙΑΚΩΝ

ΒΙΒΛΙΟΝ ΔΕΥΤΕΡΟΝ[1]

C Τῶν εἰς τὰ δεῖπνα καὶ τὰ συμπόσια παρασκευαζο-
μένων, ὦ Σόσσιε Σενεκίων, τὰ μὲν ἀναγκαίων[2]
ἔχει τάξιν, ὥσπερ οἶνος καὶ σιτία καὶ στρωμναὶ
δηλαδὴ καὶ τράπεζαι· τὰ δ' ἐπεισόδια γέγονεν
ἡδονῆς ἕνεκεν, χρείας μὴ συναγομένης,[3] ὥσπερ
ἀκροάματα καὶ θεάματα καὶ γελωτοποιός τις ἐν
Καλλίου Φίλιππος, οἷς παροῦσι μὲν ἥδονται, μὴ
παρόντα δ' οὐ πάνυ ποθοῦσιν οὐδ' αἰτιῶνται τὴν
συνουσίαν ὡς ἐνδεέστερον ἔχουσαν. οὕτω δὴ καὶ
τῶν λόγων τοὺς μὲν ἐπὶ χρείᾳ τῇ περὶ τὰ συμπόσια
παραλαμβάνουσιν οἱ μέτριοι, τοὺς δ' ἄλλους δέχον-
D ται θεωρίαν πιθανὴν καὶ τῷ καιρῷ μᾶλλον αὐλοῦ
καὶ βαρβίτου πρέπουσαν ἔχοντας. ὧν καὶ τὸ
πρῶτον ἡμῖν βιβλίον εἶχε μεμιγμένα δείγματα,
τοῦ μὲν προτέρου γένους τὸ περὶ τοῦ φιλοσοφεῖν
παρὰ πότον καὶ περὶ τοῦ διανέμειν αὐτὸν ἢ τοῖς
δειπνοῦσιν ἐφιέναι τὰς κλίσεις καὶ τὰ τοιαῦτα[4]·
τοῦ δὲ δευτέρου περὶ τοῦ τοὺς ἐρῶντας ποιητικοὺς

---

[1] In T, folio 35 r, the heading συμποσιακῶν β′ is followed by
a tabulation of the " questions " as in Book I. On folio 35 v,
after a row of decorative sigla, the proem of Book II begins at
line 15.

[2] Kronenberg : ἀναγκαίαν.

[3] Bolkestein, *Adv. Crit.* pp. 101 f., defends the text.

TABLE-TALK

BOOK TWO

Some of the preparations which are made for dinners and drinking-parties rank as necessities, my dear Sossius Senecio ; such are the wine, the food, the cuisine, and of course the couches and tables. Others are diversions introduced for pleasure's sake, and no essential function attaches to them ; such are music, spectacles, and any buffooning Philip-at-Callias's.[a] With these latter, if they are present, the guests are pleased, but if they are absent, the guests do not very much desire them or criticize the party as being very deficient. So it is with the conversation ; some topics are accepted by the average run of men as the proper business of drinking-parties, while other topics are entertained because they possess an attractive theme more suitable to the moment than pipe and lyre. Examples of these were mixed together in my first book. To the first category belong the conversation on philosophical talk at drinking-parties, that on the subject whether the host himself assigns places or allows the guests to take their own, and such matters ; to the second category belong the conversation on the

[a] Philip is the buffoon at Callias's party in Xenophon's *Symposium*, i. 11 ff.

---

[4] καὶ τὰ τοιαῦτα Salmasius : lac. 4-6 αὗτα.

(629) εἶναι καὶ περὶ τῆς Αἰαντίδος φυλῆς. ὧν τὰ μὲν[1]
καλῶ δῆτα καὶ αὐτὸς[2] ἰδίᾳ[3] συμποτικά· τὰ δὲ
συναμφότερα[4] κοινῶς συμποσιακά.

Σποράδην δ' ἀναγέγραπται καὶ οὐ διακεκριμένως
ἀλλ' ὡς ἕκαστον εἰς μνήμην ἦλθεν. οὐ δεῖ δὲ
θαυμάζειν τοὺς ἀναγιγνώσκοντας, εἰ σοὶ προσ-
E φωνοῦντές τινα τῶν ποτε ῥηθέντων[5] καὶ[6] ὑπὸ σοῦ
συνηγάγομεν· καὶ γὰρ ἂν αἱ μαθήσεις ἀναμνήσεις
μὴ ποιῶσιν, πολλάκις εἰς ταὐτὸ τῷ μανθάνειν τὸ
ἀναμιμνήσκεσθαι καθίστησιν.

ΠΡΟΒΛΗΜΑ Α[7]

Τίν' ἐστὶν ἃ Ξενοφῶν παρὰ πότον ἥδιον ἐρωτᾶσθαί φησι καὶ
σκώπτεσθαι ἢ μή

Collocuntur Sossius Senecio et Plutarchus

1. Δέκα δὲ προβλημάτων εἰς ἕκαστον νενεμη-
μένων βιβλίον, ἐν τούτῳ πρῶτόν ἐστιν ὃ τρόπον
τινὰ Ξενοφῶν ὁ Σωκρατικὸς ἡμῖν προβέβληκεν.[8]
τὸν γὰρ Γωβρύαν φησὶ συνδειπνοῦντα τῷ Κύρῳ
τά τ' ἄλλα θαυμάζειν τῶν Περσῶν καὶ ὅτι τοιαῦτα

---

[1] ὧν τὰ μὲν Hubert : lac. 2.
[2] αὐτὸς Stephanus : lac. 4.
[3] ἰδίᾳ Bernardakis : τά.
[4] δὲ συναμφότερα Bolkestein : δ lac. 3-4 τερα.
[5] ποτε ῥηθέντων Wilamowitz : προρρηθέντων.
[6] καὶ Bolkestein : ἤ.
[7] The text of Question 1 follows the proem without caption or break, but with α΄ in the margin. The title comes from the index prefixed to the proem in T.
[8] προβέβληκεν Meziriacus : παραβέβληκεν.

poetical disposition of lovers and the one concerned with the phylê Aiantis. The first group indeed I also call specifically drinking-party topics, but both together generally suitable table-talk.

The conversations which follow have been written in a haphazard manner, not systematically but as each came to mind. Nor must my readers be surprised if, though addressing myself to you, I have introduced some of your own past conversation also ; for indeed, if the getting of knowledge does not insure that one remembers it,[a] frequently the same end is attained by recollection as by learning.

QUESTION 1

What the subjects are about which Xenophon says people, when they are drinking, are more pleased to be questioned and teased than not [b]

Speakers : Sossius Senecio and Plutarch

1. THE first of the ten questions allocated to each book is here one which Xenophon the Socratic has in a manner of speaking placed before us. He tells us that Gobryas,[c] when dining with Cyrus, admired the qualities of the Persians, in particular the fact that

---

[a] Bolkestein, *Adv. Crit.* pp. 103 f., follows Vollgraff in transposing αἱ to ἀναμνήσεις and translating " etsi enim recordationes nullas efficiunt novarum rerum cognitiones," etc. : " if memory does not actually produce new knowledge, yet to be reminded of certain things often amounts to the same thing as learning." *Cf. infra*, 686 B.

[b] Imitated in Macrobius, *Saturnalia*, vii. 2 f. ; *cf.* Aristotle, *Eth. Nic.* iv. 8.

[c] Friend and relative by marriage to Cyrus the Elder. The present anecdote is from Xenophon, *Cyropaedia*, v. 2. 18.

(629) μὲν ἀλλήλους ἠρώτων ἃ ἥδιον ἦν ἐρωτηθῆναι ἢ μή,
ἔσκωπτον δ' ἃ¹ σκωφθῆναι ἥδιον ἢ μή²· εἰ γὰρ
ἐπαινοῦντες ἕτεροι πολλάκις λυποῦσι³ καὶ προσ-
F ίστανται, πῶς οὐκ ἄξιον ἦν ἄγασθαι τὴν εὐτρα-
πελίαν ἐκείνων καὶ τὴν σύνεσιν, ὧν καὶ τὰ σκώμματα τοῖς σκωπτομένοις ἡδονὴν καὶ χάριν παρεῖχεν;
δεχόμενος οὖν ἡμᾶς ἐν Πάτραις ἡδέως ἂν ἔφης⁴
πυθέσθαι τὰ τοιαῦτ' ἐρωτήματα ποίου γένους εἴη
καὶ τίς αὐτῶν τύπος· "οὐ γάρ τι μικρόν," ἔφης,⁵
" τῆς ὁμιλητικῆς μόριον ἡ περὶ τὰς ἐρωτήσεις καὶ
τὰς παιδιὰς τοῦ ἐμμελοῦς ἐπιστήμη καὶ τήρησις."

630   2. " Μέγα μὲν οὖν," ἔφην ἐγώ, " ἀλλ' ὅρα μὴ
καὶ αὐτὸς ὁ Ξενοφῶν ἔν τε τῷ Σωκρατικῷ καὶ
τοῖς Περσικοῖς ἐπιδείκνυσι συμποσίοις τὸ γένος.
εἰ δὲ δοκεῖ καὶ ἡμᾶς ἐπιθέσθαι τῷ⁶ λόγῳ, πρῶτον
ἡδέως ἐρωτᾶσθαί μοι δοκοῦσιν ἃ ῥᾳδίως ἀποκρί-
νασθαι δύνανται· ταῦτα δ' ἐστὶν ὧν ἐμπειρίαν
ἔχουσιν. ἃ γὰρ ἀγνοοῦσιν, ἢ⁷ μὴ λέγοντες ἄχθονται
καθάπερ αἰτηθέντες ὃ δοῦναι μὴ δύνανται ἢ λέγοντες ἀπὸ δόξης καὶ εἰκασίας οὐ βεβαίου δια-
ταράσσονται καὶ κινδυνεύουσιν. ἂν δὲ μὴ μόνον
ἔχῃ τὸ ῥᾴδιον ἀλλὰ καί τι⁸ περιττὸν ἡ ἀπόκρισις,
B ἡδίων ἐστὶ τῷ ἀποκρινομένῳ· περιτταὶ δ' εἰσὶν αἱ
τῶν ἐπισταμένων ἃ μὴ πολλοὶ γιγνώσκουσι μηδ'
ἀκηκόασιν, οἷον ἀστρολογικῶν, διαλεκτικῶν, ἅπερ

---

¹ ἔσκωπτον δ' ἃ Bernardakis, καὶ ὡς ἔσκωπτον οἷα Xylander; lac. 8.
² ἥδιον ἢ μή Xylander: σκωφθῆναι καὶ lac. 4.
³ Bernardakis: lac. 6.
⁴ Wyttenbach: ἔφη E, ἔφυ T.   ⁵ Wyttenbach: ἔφησε.

they asked each other such questions as it is more agreeable to be asked than not and joked each other on matters about which it was more agreeable to be teased than not; for if other men often vex and annoy by their praise, as they do, surely it was right for Gobryas to admire the urbanity and understanding of men whose very jokes offered pleasure and gratification to those who were the butts? And so, when you were entertaining me at Patras, you said you would be glad to learn what kind such questions were and what their general character. " For no small portion of the art of conversation," you said, " is the knowledge and observance of good taste in question-posing and fun-making."

2. " Certainly, a great portion," I replied; " but surely Xenophon himself, in the Socratic *Symposium* as well as in his writing about Persian drinking-parties, shows what kind such questions are. And yet if it is decided that we too apply ourselves to the problem, it seems to me, in the first place, that men are glad to be asked what they are able to answer easily, that is, questions about matters in which they have experience; for about what they do not know, either they say nothing and are chagrined as though asked for what they cannot give or they reply with a guess and an uncertain conjecture and so find themselves in a distressing and dangerous situation. However, if the answer is not only easy but somehow striking, it is more agreeable to the answerer. Striking are the answers of those who have knowledge of matters which many neither understand nor have heard about: for example, astronomy or dialectics, if it is in these

---

6 Hubert: τινί.　　　　　7 Jannot: οἱ.
8 τι added by Hubert, τὸ Reiske.

(630) ἕξιν ἐν αὐτοῖς ἔχωσιν. οὐ γὰρ πράττων μόνον ἕκαστος οὐδὲ διημερεύων, ὡς Εὐριπίδης φησίν, ἀλλὰ
καὶ διαλεγόμενος

ἵν' αὐτὸς αὑτοῦ τυγχάνῃ κράτιστος ὢν

ἡδέως διατίθεται.

"Καὶ χαίρουσι τοῖς ἐρωτῶσιν ἃ γιγνώσκοντες ἀγ-
νοεῖσθαι καὶ λανθάνειν οὐ θέλουσιν. διὸ καὶ περὶ
χώρας ἀποίκου καὶ ξένης θαλάττης ἐθῶν τε βαρ-
βαρικῶν καὶ νόμων οἱ πεπλανημένοι καὶ πεπλευ-
κότες ἥδιον ἐρωτῶνται καὶ προθύμως διηγοῦνται
καὶ διαγράφουσι κόλπους καὶ τόπους, οἰόμενοι
C καὶ χάριν τινὰ τῶν πόνων ταύτην καὶ παραμυθίαν
κομίζεσθαι. καθόλου δ' ὅσα μηδενὸς ἐρωτῶντος
αὐτοὶ διηγεῖσθαι καὶ λέγειν ἀφ' ἑαυτῶν εἰώθαμεν,
ἥδιον ἐρωτώμεθα, χαρίζεσθαι τούτοις δοκοῦντες,
ὧν ἔργον ἦν ἐνοχλουμένων ἀποσχέσθαι. καὶ τοῦτο
μὲν ἐν τοῖς πλωτικοῖς μάλιστα φύεται τὸ γένος τοῦ
νοσήματος· οἱ δὲ κομψότεροι ταῦτ' ἐρωτᾶσθαι
θέλουσιν ἃ βουλόμενοι λέγειν αἰδοῦνται καὶ φείδονται τῶν παρόντων· οἷον ὅσα τυγχάνουσιν αὐτοὶ
διαπεπραγμένοι καὶ κατωρθωκότες. ὀρθῶς γοῦν
ὁ Νέστωρ τὴν φιλοτιμίαν τοῦ Ὀδυσσέως ἐπιστά-
μενος

εἴπ' ἄγε μ', ὦ πολύαιν' Ὀδυσεῦ,—φησί,—μέγα
κῦδος Ἀχαιῶν,

D   ὅππως[1] τούσδ' ἵππους λάβετον.

—————
[1] ὅππως Xylander from Homer : ὅπως δή.

subjects that the answerers have skill. For not only in the activity in which he passes his days but also in his conversation each man is agreeably occupied

> Where the best of his abilities
> Chance to lie,

as Euripides has it.[a]

" People are pleased with those who ask them questions on subjects which, because they themselves have knowledge of them, they are unwilling to let go unknown and lie hidden. Thus travellers and sailors are very glad to be questioned about a far-away place and a foreign sea and about the customs and laws of alien men, and they willingly describe and delineate gulfs and localities with the notion that thus they obtain for themselves a kind of reward and a consolation for their labours. In general we are glad to be questioned on matters which we are in the habit of describing and talking about of our own accord even when no one asks us, for so we think we give pleasure to those whose business it was to refrain from putting questions to us if our conversation annoyed them. This kind of disease is rampant among seafaring men, and the more courteous prefer to be questioned about what, in spite of their desire, they hesitate to speak because of modesty and their consideration for the company, as, for example, all that they themselves have accomplished and achieved. And so it was right for Nestor, knowing Odysseus's love for fame, to say

> Come tell me, famed Odysseus, glorious
> And great Achaean, how you both did take
> These horses.[b]

---

[a] Frag. 183 Nauck, line 3. *Cf. Moralia*, 622 A, 514 A, 43 B.   [b] *Iliad*, x. 544 f.

(630) ἄχθονται γὰρ τοῖς αὐτοὺς ἐπαινοῦσιν καὶ τὰς ἑαυτῶν εὐτυχίας διεξιοῦσιν, ἂν μὴ κελεύσῃ ἄλλος τις τῶν παρόντων καὶ οἷον βιαζόμενοι[1] λέγωσιν.

" Ἡδέως[2] γοῦν ἐρωτῶνται περὶ[3] πρεσβειῶν καὶ περὶ[4] πολιτειῶν ὅσοι[5] μέγα τι καὶ λαμπρὸν εἰργασμένοι τυγχάνουσιν. ὅθεν ἥκιστα περὶ τούτων οἱ[6] φθονεροὶ καὶ κακοήθεις ἐρωτῶσι, κἂν ἄλλος τις ἔρηται[7] τὰ τοιαῦτα, διακρούονται καὶ παρατρέπουσιν, χώραν τῇ διηγήσει μὴ διδόντες μηδὲ βουλόμενοι λόγου τὸν λέγοντα κοσμοῦντος ἀφορμὰς προέσθαι. καὶ ταῦτ᾽ οὖν ἐρωτῶντες χαρίζονται[8] τοῖς ἀποκρινομένοις, ἃ τοὺς ἐχθροὺς καὶ δυσμενεῖς αἰσθάνονται μὴ βουλομένους ἀκούειν.

E   3. " Καὶ μὴν ὅ γ᾽ Ὀδυσσεὺς τῷ Ἀλκινόῳ

σοὶ δ᾽ ἐμὰ κήδεα θυμὸς ἐπετράπετο στονόεντα
εἴρεσθ᾽, ὄφρ᾽ ἔτι μᾶλλον ὀδυρόμενος στεναχίζω.

καὶ πρὸς τὸν χορὸν ὁ Οἰδίπους

δεινὸν μὲν τὸ πάλαι κείμενον ἤδη κακόν, ὦ
ξεῖν᾽, ἐπεγείρειν[9]·

ὁ δ᾽ Εὐριπίδης τοὐναντίον

ὡς ἡδύ τοι σωθέντα μεμνῆσθαι πόνων,[10]

⟨καίτοι καὶ αὐτὸς δηλῶν ὡς ἡδὺ μόνοις τοῖς ἤδη

---

[1] καὶ οἷον βιαζόμενοι Bernardakis : lac. 6-9 ζόμενοι.
[2] ἡδέως Turnebus : lac. 5-7.
[3] περὶ Turnebus : lac. 4-5.
[4] περὶ Turnebus : lac. 3-5.
[5] ὅσοι Hubert : εἰ Turnebus : lac. 4.
[6] οἱ Stephanus : ὡς.
[7] ἄλλος τις ἔρηται Cobet, ἄλλος αὐτοὺς ἐρωτᾷ Bollaan (Helmbold, Class. Phil. xxxvi [1941], p. 87) : ἄλλο lac. 6-7 ται.

114

For people are irritated by those who praise themselves and recount at length their own successes, unless some other member of the company bid them do so, and they are, as it were, compelled to speak.

" At any rate everybody who happens to have achieved some great and brilliant success on foreign mission or in political office at home is glad to be asked about it. That is why spiteful and malicious people are in the habit of asking about such matters least of all and resist and turn aside such questions if asked by some one else, granting the story no place, nor willing to countenance the first words of a tale reflecting credit upon the teller. Accordingly, those who ask about matters they know the disaffected enemies of the questioned do not wish to hear, are the men who please their interlocutors.

3. " To proceed : Odysseus said to Alcinoüs,

> Thy heart inclined to ask about my mournful
> fate, that I might cry and moan still more.[a]

And Oedipus said to the chorus,

> It is dreadful, O Stranger, to stir
> Such an evil, long dormant till now.[b]

But the opposite we find in Euripides,

> To remember toil, how sweet—when one is safe.[c]

Yet he himself makes plain how sweet to those alone

---

[a] *Odyssey*, ix. 12 f.
[b] Sophocles, *Oedipus at Colonus*, 510; see *supra*, p. 33, note *a*.   [c] Frag. 133 Nauck.

---

[8] χαρίζονται Meziriacus : χαρίζεσθαι.
[9] ξεῖν', ἐπεγείρειν Xylander from Sophocles : ξεῖνε lac. 4-5 γειρεν.
[10] τοι σωθέντα μεμνῆσθαι added by Turnebus from Macrobius, *Saturnalia*, vii. 2. 9 : lac. 4-5.

(630) σωθεῖσιν⟩[1] οὐ τοῖς ἔτι πλανωμένοις καὶ κακὰ[2]
φέρουσιν. τῶν οὖν κακῶν φυλακτέον ἐστὶ τὰς
ἐρωτήσεις· ἀνιῶνται γὰρ διηγούμενοι καταδίκας

F αὐτῶν ἢ ταφὰς παίδων ἤ τινας κατὰ γῆν οὐκ
εὐτυχεῖς ἢ κατὰ θάλατταν ἐμπορίας. τὸ δὲ πῶς
εὐημέρησαν ἐπὶ βήματος ἢ προσηγορεύθησαν ὑπὸ
τοῦ βασιλέως ἢ τῶν ἄλλων περιπεσόντων χειμῶσιν
ἢ λῃσταῖς αὐτοὶ διέφυγον τὸν κίνδυνον, ἡδέως
ἐρωτῶνται πολλάκις καὶ τρόπον τινὰ τῷ λόγῳ τοῦ
πράγματος ἀπολαύοντες ἀπλήστως ἔχουσι τοῦ δι-

631 ηγεῖσθαι καὶ μνημονεύειν. χαίρουσι δὲ καὶ περὶ
φίλων εὐτυχούντων ἐρωτώμενοι καὶ περὶ παίδων
προκοπτόντων ἐν μαθήμασιν ἢ[3] συνηγορίαις ἢ
φιλίαις βασιλέων.

'' Ἐχθρῶν δὲ καὶ δυσμενῶν ὀνείδη καὶ βλάβας
καὶ καταδίκας ἐξελεγχθέντων καὶ σφαλέντων ἥδιον
ἐρωτώμενοι καὶ προθυμότερον ἐξαγγέλλουσιν· αὐτοὶ δ' ἀφ' αὑτῶν ὀκνοῦσι φυλαττόμενοι δόξαν
ἐπιχαιρεκακίας. ἥδιον δὲ καὶ περὶ κυνῶν ἄνδρα
θηρευτικὸν ἐρωτᾶν καὶ φιλαθλητὴν περὶ γυμνικῶν
ἀγώνων καὶ περὶ καλῶν ἐρωτικόν. ὁ δ' εὐσεβὴς
καὶ φιλοθύτης, διηγηματικὸς ὀνείρων καὶ ὅσα
χρησάμενος ἢ φήμαις ἢ ἱεροῖς[4] θεῶν εὐμενείᾳ

B κατώρθωσεν, ἡδέως ἂν καὶ περὶ τούτων ἐρωτῷτο.[5]
τοῖς δὲ πρεσβύταις, κἂν μηδὲν ἡ διήγησις ᾖ

---

[1] Text in brackets added by Hubert : lac. 25-28   -οῖς
οὐκέτι for οὐ τοῖς ἔτι Helmbold, *loc. cit.*

who have now been saved, not to those who still endure misfortunes in their wanderings. It is therefore
necessary to keep one's questions away from the subject of misfortunes, for it distresses people to speak
of lawsuits lost, of children buried, of any unsuccessful
business-deals on land or sea. But they are glad to be
asked over and over how they met with success in the
Assembly, or were addressed by the king, or, when
others fell in with storms or pirates, they themselves
avoided the danger ; and they are insatiable in recalling and relating their experience because their
talk in a sense enables them to continue their pleasure
in it. And they are happy to be asked about friends
who are successful and about children who are making
progress in studies or in lawsuits or in the friendship
of kings.

"They are even more delighted to be asked about
the disgraces, the injuries, and the unsuccessful lawsuits of enemies and adversaries who have been convicted and ruined ; about such matters they are very
willing to report in detail, but of their own accord
they hesitate to do so, bewaring of a reputation for
spite. It is also very agreeable to ask a huntsman
questions about dogs, a keen athlete about games,
and an amorist about his handsome loves. The pious
ritualist, fond of recounting dreams and all that he
by the gods' goodwill has brought to success through
use of omens or of sacrifices, would very gladly be
asked about these matters. Those who address
questions to elderly men please them very much and

---

² καὶ κακὰ Stephanus, κἀνίας Bernardakis : καινὰς.
³ ἡ added by Bernardakis.
⁴ ἡ after ἱεροῖς deleted by Hubert.
⁵ Duebner : ἐρωτῶνται.

(631) προσήκουσα, πάντως οἱ ἐρωτῶντες χαρίζονται καὶ
κινοῦσι βουλομένους.

> ὦ Νέστορ Νηληιάδη, σὺ δ' ἀληθὲς ἐνίσπες,
> πῶς ἔθαν' Ἀτρείδης;
> ποῦ Μενέλαος ἔην;
> ἦ οὐκ Ἄργεος ἦεν Ἀχαιικοῦ;

πόλλ' ἐρωτῶν ἅμα καὶ πολλῶν λόγων ἀφορμὰς
προϊέμενος,[1] οὐχ ὥσπερ ἔνιοι συστέλλοντες εἰς τὸ
ἀναγκαῖον αὐτὸ καὶ συνελαύνοντες τὰς ἀποκρίσεις
ἀφαιροῦνται τῆς γεροντικῆς διατριβῆς τὸ ἥδιστον.
ὅλως δ' οἱ θέλοντες εὐφραίνειν μᾶλλον ἢ λυπεῖν
τοιαύτας ἐρωτήσεις προφέρουσιν, ὧν ταῖς ἀποκρί-
C σεσιν οὐ ψόγος ἀλλ' ἔπαινος, οὐδὲ μῖσος ἢ νέμεσις
ἀλλ' εὔνοια καὶ χάρις ἔπεται παρὰ τῶν ἀκου-
σάντων. ταῦτα μὲν οὖν τὰ περὶ τὰς ἐρωτήσεις.

4. " Σκώμματος δὲ τῷ μὴ δυναμένῳ μετ' εὐλαβείας καὶ τέχνης κατὰ καιρὸν ἅπτεσθαι παντάπασιν ἀφεκτέον· ὥσπερ γὰρ τοὺς[2] ἐν ὀλισθηρῷ τόπῳ,
κἂν θίγωσιν ἐκ παραδρομῆς μόνον, ἀνατρέπουσιν,
οὕτως ἐν οἴνῳ πρὸς πᾶσαν ἀφορμὴν λόγου μὴ
κατὰ σχῆμα γιγνομένην ἐπισφαλῶς ἔχομεν. τοῖς
δὲ σκώμμασιν ἔστιν ὅτε μᾶλλον ἢ ταῖς λοιδορίαις
ἐκκινούμεθα, τὸ μὲν ὑπ' ὀργῆς πολλάκις ἀβουλ-
ήτως ὁρῶντες γιγνόμενον, τὸ δ' ὡς οὐκ ἀναγκαῖον
ἀλλ' ἔργον ὕβρεως καὶ κακοηθείας προβαλλόμενοι·
D καὶ καθόλου τῷ[3] διαλέγεσθαι τοῖς ἀστεϊζομένοις[4]
μᾶλλον ἢ τοῖς εἰκῆ[5] φλυαροῦσι χαλεπαίνομεν·

---

[1] Anonymous note in the margin of a copy of the Basel
edition preserved at Leyden, Reiske : προσιέμενος (προσ-
ιεμένους wrongly Hubert).
[2] γὰρ τοὺς added by Stephanus. γὰρ Xylander.
[3] τῷ added by Paton.

stir up willing talkers, even if the subject matter in no way relates to the speaker :

> O Nestor, son of Neleus, speak the truth.
> How perished the son of Atreus . . . ?
> And where was Menelaüs . . . ?
> In Achaean Argos was he not, for sure ? [a]

Many were the questions he [Telemachus] put at one and the same time and many were the stories for which he offered the occasion, not like some men, who take away the most pleasant pastime of old age by causing the answers they receive to be contracted and compressed to bare essentials. To sum up : those who wish to give happiness rather than distress put questions of such sort that the answers are attended not by blame from the audience but by praise, not by hatred and anger but friendliness and goodwill. This, then, is what I have to say upon the subject of questions.

4. " The man who cannot engage in joking at a suitable time, discreetly and skilfully,[b] must avoid jokes altogether ; for just as men in a slippery place are upset however lightly brushed, so in drinking we are apt to be overthrown at every unseemly outburst of talk that arises. And there are times when we are more roused by jokes than by insults, for we may frequently see that insults are the unintended result of anger, while we may suppose that jokes are the gratuitous result of insolence and bad character. Further, we are generally more offended when the talk is with clever men than when it is with heedless

---

[a] *Odyssey*, iii. 247 ff.
[b] *Cf. Precepts of Statecraft*, vii, 803 b ff.

---

⁴ Paton : lac. 6-7 νοις.   ⁵ Pohlenz : lac. 4.

(631) εἰδότες¹ ὅτι δόλος τῷ² ὑβρίσματι³ πρόσεστιν.⁴
δοκεῖ γὰρ⁵ τὸ σκῶμμα λοιδόρημα δεδογμένον⁶
εἶναι καὶ πεποιημένον ἐκ παρασκευῆς. ὁ γὰρ
εἰπὼν ταριχοπώλην αὐτόθεν ἐλοιδόρησεν, ὁ δὲ
φήσας, '' μεμνήμεθά σε τῷ βραχίονι ἀπομυτ-
τόμενον,'' ἔσκωψεν. καὶ Κικέρων πρὸς 'Οκτα-
ούιον, ἐκ Λιβύης εἶναι δοκοῦντα λέγοντος δ' αὐτοῦ
φάσκοντα μὴ ἀκούειν, '' καὶ μὴν τετρυπημένον,''
ἔφη, '' ἔχεις⁷ τὸ οὖς.'' καὶ Μελάνθιος ὑπὸ τοῦ
κωμῳδιοποιοῦ καταγελώμενος ἔφη, '' οὐκ ὀφειλό-
μενόν μοι ἀποδίδως ἔρανον.''

'' Μᾶλλον οὖν τὰ σκώμματα δάκνει, καθάπερ τὰ
E παρηγκιστρωμένα βέλη πλείονα χρόνον ἐμμένοντα.
καὶ λυπεῖ τοὺς σκωφθέντας ἡ τέρψις τῇ κομψότητι
καθ' ὅσον⁸ ἡδύνει τοὺς παρόντας· ἡδόμενοι γὰρ
ἐπὶ τῷ λεγομένῳ, πιστεύειν δοκοῦσι καὶ συν-
διασύρειν⁹ τῷ λέγοντι. ὀνειδισμὸς¹⁰ γάρ ἐστιν
τῆς¹¹ ἁμαρτίας παρεσχηματισμένος τὸ¹² σκῶμμα
κατὰ τὸν Θεόφραστον· ὅθεν ἐξ αὐτοῦ τῇ ὑπονοίᾳ
προστίθησιν ὁ ἀκούσας τὸ ἐλλεῖπον ὡς εἰδὼς καὶ
πιστεύων. ὁ γὰρ γελάσας καὶ ἡσθείς, τοῦ Θεοκρί-
του πρὸς τὸν δοκοῦντα λωποδυτεῖν ἐρωτῶντα δ'

---

¹ Paton : lac. 2-3.
² δόλος τῷ Paton : δ' ὅλως τό.
³ ὑβρίσματι Paton : lac. 2-4 ματι.
⁴ πρόσεστι Reiske : προσέσται.
⁵ δοκεῖ γὰρ Paton : lac. 4-5.
⁶ δεδογμένον Paton : δὲ lac. 4-5.
⁷ Xylander : ἔχει.   ⁸ καθ' ὅσον Post : καὶ.
⁹ δοκοῦσι καὶ συν- Duebner : lac. 3-4.
¹⁰ Turnebus : lac. 2 σμος.
¹¹ Turnebus, τινος Bolkestein : lac. 2.
¹² παρεσχηματισμένος τὸ Turnebus : παρε lac. 5.

ᵃ Literally, '' on your arm.'' Bion of Borysthenes attri-

120

fools, for in the case of the clever man we know that cunning is compounded with his offensiveness,—indeed his joke seems to be deliberate abuse purposely delivered. The man who calls you ' fishmonger ' is obviously being insulting, but it's *joking* when someone says, ' I remember when you used to wipe your nose on your sleeve.' [a] And when a man named Octavius, who was supposed to be from Libya, said to Cicero that he did not hear what Cicero was saying, the latter's answer was, ' And yet you have holes in your ears ! ' [b] Again, when Melanthius [c] was ridiculed by the comic poet, he said, ' It's not the coin you owe me that you pay me back.'

" Thus jokes are more biting, for like barbed arrows they lie longer embedded. The delight in their cleverness distresses the victims in the degree it gives pleasure to the company, for by taking pleasure in what is said the company seem to believe the speaker and join in with his ridicule. The joke, as Theophrastus has it, is a disguised reproach for error [d]; accordingly the listener of his own accord supplies in thought what is missing as though he knew it and believed it. For example, Theocritus,[e] in reply to the question of a man reputed to be a robber, who

butes both the habit and the occupation to his father : Diogenes Laertius, *Lives of Philosphers*, iv. 46.

[b] *Life of Cicero*, xxvi. 4 ; *Mor.* 205 b. In Xenophon, *Anabasis*, iii. 1. 31, pierced ears are given as proof of non-Hellenic origin, as here of non-Roman ; see further John E. B. Mayor, *Juvenal*, i. 104, with note ; Macrobius's version of this passage is explicit in citing this as a Libyan practice.

[c] Aristophanes, *Peace*, 804, *Birds*, 151 ; a tragic poet ridiculed also by Eupolis, Plato comicus, Pherecrates, etc.

[d] *Cf. Tract. Coisl.* 4 f. in Kaibel, *Com. Gr. Frag.* I. i, p. 50 ; Lane Cooper, *Aristotelian Theory of Comedy*, pp. 259 ff.

[e] Of Chios, *F.H.G.* ii. 87, *cf. infra*, 633 c ; *RE*, *s.v.*, no. 2.

(631) αὐτὸν εἰ ἐπὶ δεῖπνον βαδίζει φήσαντος βαδίζειν,
ἐκεῖ μέντοι καθεύδειν, βεβαιοῦντι τὴν διαβολὴν
F ὅμοιός ἐστιν. διὸ καὶ προσαναπίμπλησι τοὺς
παρόντας ὁ σκώπτων παρὰ μέλος κακοηθείας, ὡς
ἐφηδομένους καὶ συνυβρίζοντας.[1] ἐν δὲ τῇ καλῇ
Λακεδαίμονι τῶν μαθημάτων ἐδόκει τὸ σκώπτειν
ἀλύπως καὶ σκωπτόμενον φέρειν· εἰ δέ τις ἀπείποι
σκωπτόμενος, εὐθὺς ὁ σκώπτων ἐπέπαυτο. πῶς
οὖν οὐ χαλεπὸν εὑρεῖν σκῶμμα τῷ σκωπτομένῳ
632 κεχαρισμένον, ὅπου καὶ τὸ μὴ λυποῦν[2] τοῦ σκώμματος οὐ τῆς τυχούσης ἐμπειρίας καὶ δεξιότητός
ἐστιν;
    5. " Οὐ μὴν ἀλλὰ πρῶτά μοι δοκεῖ τὰ λυποῦντα
τοὺς ἐνόχους σκώμματα τοῖς μακρὰν οὖσι τῆς
διαβολῆς ἡδονήν τινα καὶ χάριν ποιεῖν. οἷον ὁ
Ξενοφῶν τὸν ὑπέραισχρον καὶ ὑπέρδασυν ἐκεῖνον
ὡς παιδικὰ τοῦ Σαμβαύλα σκωπτόμενον εἰσάγει
μετὰ παιδιᾶς. καὶ Κυήτου τοῦ ἡμετέρου, μέμνησαι
γάρ, ἐν ἀσθενείᾳ τὰς χεῖρας ἔχειν ψυχρὰς λέγοντος,
Αὐφίδιος Μόδεστος, ' ἀλλὰ μήν,' ἔφη, ' θερμὰς
ἀπὸ τῆς ἐπαρχίας κεκόμικας αὐτάς '· τοῦτο γὰρ
ἐκείνῳ μὲν γέλωτα καὶ διάχυσιν παρέσχεν, κλέπτῃ
B δ' ἀνθυπάτῳ λοιδόρημα καὶ ὄνειδος ἦν. διὸ καὶ
Κριτόβουλον ὁ Σωκράτης εὐπροσωπότατον ὄντα
προκαλούμενος εἰς σύγκρισιν εὐμορφίας ἔπαιζεν

---

[1] Reiske : συνυβριζομένους.
[2] Stephanus, λυπεῖν διὰ Ziegler : λυπεῖν.

[a] In Xenophon, *Cyropaedia*, ii. 2. 28 f.
[b] To whom, if the emendation at these places is correct, are

was asking whether Theocritus was going out to
dinner, said that he was indeed going out to dinner,
but was passing the night there ; whoever laughs at
the remark and takes pleasure in it is in the position
of one who confirms the slander. Thus the ill-bred
joker infects the company with his bad manners,
since they too are delighted and join in his malice.
In fair Lacedaemon it was thought that one of the
things a man must learn was to tease without giving
offence and to endure being teased ; and if anyone
should ever succumb under teasing, the teaser always
stopped at once. How then can it fail to be hard to
find a joke agreeable to the man at whom it is
directed when joking without offending is a matter
of no ordinary skill and cleverness ?

5. " Nevertheless, it seems to me that jokes which
distress the guilty are foremost in causing a certain
pleasure and mirth in men of unimpeachable reputation. An example is Xenophon's playful introduction
of that exceedingly ugly and shaggy individual who
is teased as the ' darling ' of Sambaulas.[a] When our
own Quietus [b] during his illness remarked that his
hands were cold,—surely you remember,—Aufidius
Modestus [c] said, ' But you have brought them back
hot from your province.' This made Quietus laugh
merrily, though for a thieving proconsul it would
have been an insulting rebuke. So too Socrates,
when he challenged the very handsome Critobulus [d]
to a beauty-contest, was teasing him amiably, not

dedicated *De Fraterno Amore* (with Nigrinus; see 478 B with
note [LCL]) and *De Sera Numinis Vindicta* (548 A).

[c] *RE, s.v.* " Aufidius," no. 30 ; above, 618 F.

[d] Xenophon, *Symposium*, iv. 19 ; rather, it is Critobulus
who is ironic at Socrates's expense, but Socrates lightly
returns the irony.

(632) οὐκ ἐχλεύαζεν. καὶ Σωκράτην πάλιν Ἀλκιβιάδης
ἔσκωπτεν εἰς ζηλοτυπίαν τὴν περὶ Ἀγάθωνος.

"Ἥδονται δὲ καὶ βασιλεῖς τοῖς λεγομένοις ὡς εἰς
πένητας αὐτοὺς καὶ ἰδιώτας, ὥσπερ ὑπὸ Φιλίππου
σκωφθεὶς ὁ παράσιτος εἶπεν· ' οὐκ ἐγώ σε τρέφω; '
τὰ γὰρ οὐ προσόντα φαῦλα λέγοντες ἐμφαίνουσι
τὰ προσόντα χρηστά. δεῖ δ' ὁμολογουμένως καὶ
βεβαίως προσεῖναί τι χρηστόν· εἰ δὲ μή, τὸ
C λεγόμενον τοὐναντίον¹ ἀμφισβητήσιμον ἔχει τὴν
ὑπόνοιαν. ὁ γὰρ τῷ πάνυ πλουσίῳ τοὺς δανειστὰς
ἐπάξειν λέγων ἢ τὸν ὑδροπότην καὶ σώφρονα
παροινεῖν καὶ μεθύειν ἢ τὸν εὐδάπανον καὶ μεγα-
λοπρεπῆ καὶ χαριστικὸν κίμβικα καὶ κυμινοπρί-
στην² προσαγορεύων ἢ τὸν ἐν συνηγορίαις καὶ
πολιτείαις μέγαν ἀπειλῶν ἐν ἀγορᾷ λήψεσθαι
διάχυσιν καὶ μειδίαμα παρέσχεν. οὕτως ὁ Κῦρος
ἐν οἷς ἐλείπετο τῶν ἑταίρων εἰς ταῦτα προκαλούμενος ἐγίγνετο προσηνὴς καὶ κεχαρισμένος. καὶ
τοῦ Ἰσμηνίου τῇ θυσίᾳ προσαυλοῦντος, ὡς οὐκ
ἐκαλλιέρει, παρελόμενος τοὺς αὐλοὺς ὁ μισθωτὸς
ηὔλησε γελοίως· αἰτιωμένων³ δὲ τῶν παρόντων,
D ' ἔστιν,' ἔφη, ' τὸ κεχαρισμένως αὐλεῖν θεόθεν '·
ὁ δ' Ἰσμηνίας γελάσας, ' ἀλλ' ἐμοῦ μὲν αὐλοῦντος
ἡδόμενοι διέτριβον οἱ θεοί, σοῦ δ' ἀπαλλαγῆναι
σπεύδοντες ἐδέξαντο τὴν θυσίαν.'

6. "Ἔτι τοίνυν οἱ τὰ χρηστὰ τῶν πραγμάτων

¹ Pohlenz deletes τὸ before λεγόμενον, Hartman deletes τὸ
from ἐναντίον.
² Xylander : κύμινον.
³ ἀνιωμένων Naber (Helmbold, *Class. Phil.* xxxvi [1941], p.
87).

mocking him. And it was again Socrates whom Alcibiades teased for his jealousy over Agathon.[a]

" Kings are pleased to be addressed like mere labourers and common men : for example, the parasite's reply to Philip's teasing, ' Do I not feed you ? ' For by referring to a disability which does not exist one emphasizes the merit which does. The presence of merit of some sort, certain and generally recognized, is essential ; otherwise the real meaning of the statement of the contrary is ambiguous. Mirth and laughter are the result when someone says that he will introduce money-lenders to the very wealthy so-and-so, or asserts that a sober water-drinker gets riotously drunk, or calls the free-spending, magnificent, bounteous man a niggardly skinflint, or threatens the man prominent at the bar and in government that he will catch him in the Agora.[b] So it was a kind and agreeable act for Cyrus [c] to challenge his companions to contests in which his skill was inferior to theirs. And when Ismenias [d] was playing the pipe at a sacrifice, was not obtaining favourable omens, and the professional took the pipe, played in a ridiculous manner, and answered the reproaches of the bystanders with ' To play the pipe agreeably is a gift of the god,' Ismenias laughed and said, ' With my playing the gods were pleased and protracted the ceremony ; but in their eagerness to get rid of you they accepted the sacrifice.'

6. " Furthermore, those who jokingly apply abusive

[a] Plato, *Symposium*, 213 c.
[b] The implication is that the Agora is the centre of judicial and political activity, as indeed it was at Athens.
[c] Xenophon, *Cyropaedia*, i. 4. 4 ; *cf. Mor.* 514 B.
[d] Presumably a member of the Theban family : *RE, s.v.*, no. 6 ; *cf. Life of Pericles*, i. 5.

(632) τοῖς λοιδορουμένοις ὀνόμασι μετὰ παιδιᾶς καλοῦντες, ἂν ἐμμελῶς ποιῶσιν, αὐτῶν μᾶλλον εὐφραί-
νουσι τῶν ἀπ᾽ εὐθείας ἐπαινούντων. καὶ γὰρ
δάκνουσι μᾶλλον οἱ διὰ τῶν εὐφήμων ὀνειδίζοντες,
ὡς οἱ τοὺς πονηροὺς Ἀριστείδας καὶ τοὺς δειλοὺς
Ἀχιλλεῖς καλοῦντες καὶ ὁ¹ τοῦ Σοφοκλέους
Οἰδίπους . . .

　　　ταύτης Κρέων ὁ πιστὸς οὐξ ἀρχῆς φίλος.²

ἀντίστροφον οὖν ἔοικε γένος εἰρωνείας εἶναι³ τὸ
E περὶ τοὺς ἐπαίνους· ᾧ καὶ Σωκράτης ἐχρήσατο, τοῦ
Ἀντισθένους τὸ φιλοποιὸν καὶ συναγωγὸν ἀνθρώπων εἰς εὔνοιαν μαστροπείαν καὶ⁴ προαγωγείαν⁵
ὀνομάσας . . .⁶ Κράτητα δὲ τὸν φιλόσοφον, εἰς
πᾶσαν οἰκίαν εἰσιόντα μετὰ τιμῆς καὶ φιλοφροσύνης δεχομένων, ‘ θυρεπανοίκτην ’ ἐκάλουν.
　　7. ‘‘ Ποιεῖ δ᾽ εὔχαρι σκῶμμα καὶ μέμψις ἐμφαί-
νουσα χάριν· ὡς Διογένης περὶ Ἀντισθένους ἔλεγεν

　　　ὅς με ῥάκη⁷ τ᾽ ἤμπισχε κἀξηνάγκασεν
　　　πτωχὸν γενέσθαι κἀκ δόμων ἀνάστατον·

οὐ γὰρ ἂν ὁμοίως πιθανὸς ἦν λέγων· ‘ ὅς με σοφὸν καὶ αὐτάρκη καὶ μακάριον ἐποίησεν.’ καὶ ὁ
F Λάκων ἄκαπνα ξύλα τῷ γυμνασιάρχῳ παρασχόντι
προσποιούμενος ἐγκαλεῖν ἔλεγεν, ‘ δι᾽ ὃν οὐδ᾽

---

¹ καὶ ὁ Stephanus : ὁ καί.
² ταύτης and ἀρχῆς Xylander from Sophocles : lac. 6 της
and a lac. 5-6 χῆς; after Οἰδίπους perhaps no omission except
ταν, Hubert.
³ Bernardakis : εἶναι εἰρωνείας.
⁴ καὶ συναγωγίαν deleted by Wyttenbach before καί.

words to anything praiseworthy, if they do so with
tact, give more pleasure than even men straightforward in their praise. And those who are fairspoken
in their censure are actually more bitingly effective,
like one who calls a rascal an Aristides and a coward
an Achilles, and like Sophocles's Oedipus,[a]

> For this the trusted Creon, long my friend . . . [sc. desires
> to cast me out, has caught me with his tricks].

Now it seems that for praise there is a corresponding
kind of irony. Socrates [b] used it when he applied
the terms 'pandering' and 'pimping' to Antisthenes's
habit of bringing men together in fellowship and goodwill . . . a lacuna of c. 45 letters . . . And Crates the
philosopher,[c] who had entry to every house and the
friendly esteem of his hosts, was called ' Gate-
crasher.'

7. " Censure too, provided it shows gratification,
makes an agreeable pleasantry. As Diogenes said of
Antisthenes :

> In rags he clothed me and compelled that I
> Be poor and from my home outcast.[d]

He would not be equally effective if he said, ' He
made me wise, independent, and happy.' And there
is the Laconian who pretended to bring suit against
the gymnasium-master who furnished smokeless
faggots : ' Because of him,' said the Laconian, ' even

---

[a] *Oedipus Tyrannus*, 385 ; " For this "=to obtain my
position for himself, *sc.* τῆσδε σ' ἀρχῆς οὕνεκα from two lines
before.　　[b] Xenophon, *Symposium*, iv. 61 ff.

[c] Diogenes Laertius, vi. 86.

[d] Nauck, *Trag. Gr. Frag.*, Adespoton 394.

---

[5] προαγωγείαν Wyttenbach from Xenophon : ἀγωγίαν.
　　[6] Lac. 45.　　　　[7] Stephanus : κάρη.

(632) ἀποδακρῦσαι γέγονεν[1] ἡμῖν.' καὶ ὁ[2] τὸν δειπνίζοντα καθ' ἡμέραν ἀνδραποδιστὴν καλῶν καὶ
τύραννον, δι' ὃν ἐτῶν τοσούτων οὐχ ἑώρακεν τὴν
ἑαυτοῦ τράπεζαν. καὶ ὁ λέγων ὑπὸ τοῦ βασιλέως
ἐπιβεβουλευμένος ἀφηρῆσθαι τὴν σχολὴν καὶ τὸν
ὕπνον, πλούσιος γεγονὼς ἐκ πένητος. καὶ εἴ τις
ἀντιστρέψας αἰτιῷτο τοὺς Αἰσχύλου Καβείρους
633 ' ὄξους σπανίζειν δῶμα ' ποιήσαντας, ὥσπερ αὐτοὶ
παίζοντες ἠπείλησαν. ἅπτεται γὰρ ταῦτα μᾶλλον
ἔχοντα δριμυτέραν χάριν, ὥστε μὴ προσίστασθαι
μηδὲ λυπεῖν τοὺς ἐπαινουμένους.

8. " Δεῖ δὲ τὸν ἐμμελῶς σκώμματι χρησόμενον
εἰδέναι καὶ νοσήματος διαφορὰν πρὸς ἐπιτήδευμα,
λέγω δὲ φιλαργυρίας καὶ φιλοινίας πρὸς φιλομου-
σίαν καὶ φιλοθηρίαν· ἐπ' ἐκείνοις μὲν γὰρ ἄχθονται
σκωπτόμενοι, πρὸς ταῦτα δ' ἡδέως ἔχουσιν. οὐκ
ἀηδῶς γοῦν Δημοσθένης ὁ Μιτυληναῖος, φιλῳδοῦ
τινος καὶ φιλοκιθαριστοῦ θύραν κόψας, ὑπακούσαν-
τος αὐτοῦ καὶ κελεύσαντος εἰσελθεῖν, ' ἂν πρῶ-
B τον,' ἔφη, ' τὴν κιθάραν δήσῃς.'· ἀηδῶς δ' ὁ τοῦ
Λυσιμάχου[3] παράσιτος, ἐμβαλόντος αὐτοῦ σκορπίον
ξύλινον εἰς τὸ ἱμάτιον ἐκταραχθεὶς καὶ ἀναπηδήσας,
ὡς ᾔσθετο τὴν παιδιάν, ' κἀγώ σε,' φησίν, ' ἐκφο-
βῆσαι βούλομαι, ὦ βασιλεῦ· δός μοι τάλαντον.'

9. " Εἰσὶ δὲ καὶ περὶ τὰ σωματικὰ τοιαῦται
διαφοραὶ τῶν ποιοτήτων.[4] οἷον εἰς γρυπότητα

---

[1] ἐν after γέγονεν deleted by Stephanus.
[2] ὁ added by Franke.
[3] Basel edition, cf. Athenaeus, vi, 246 e : λυσίου.
[4] Helmbold (*Class. Phil.* xxxvi [1941], p. 87), Bolkestein, τῶν ποιῶν Madvig (Bolkestein) : τῶν πολλῶν.

tears are denied us.' A dinner-guest called the host who dined him day after day ' slave-dealer ' and ' tyrant ' on whose account he had not seen his own table these many years. And the man who rose from poverty to riches complained that he was now being deprived of leisure and sleep by the plotting of the king. Again, one might reverse the rôles and scold the Cabiri in Aeschylus [a] for ' emptying the house of vinegar,' as they themselves playfully threatened to do. The gratification these remarks express is the more telling because they are a bit tart and accordingly do not vex and annoy those who are praised.

8. " The man who would make tactful use of joking must know the difference between a diseased and a normal habit (for example, between miserliness or drunkenness and love of music or hunting). Teased about the former, men are annoyed ; about the latter, they are pleased. At any rate, when Demosthenes of Mitylenê [b] knocked on the door of a man who was devoted to song and the cithara, and his friend answered and invited him to enter, it was not offensive for Demosthenes to reply, ' If first you will lock up your cithara.' But when Lysimachus tossed a wooden scorpion into the cloak of his parasite,[c] and the parasite jumped up in terror, it was offensive for the parasite to say, after he saw it was a joke, ' Now I will frighten you, Sire : Give me a talent ! '

9. " Many such differences exist, too, where physical characteristics are concerned. For example,

---

[a] Frag. 97 Nauck, 49 Smyth (LCL). By guaranteeing abundant good wine the divinities will drive out the sour stuff.   [b] *RE, s.v.,* no. 8 ; only here.

[c] Athenaeus, vi, 246 e, gives his name as Bithys ; *RE, s.v.* " Bithys," no. 6.

(633) καὶ σιμότητα σκωπτόμενοι γελῶσιν, ὡς ὁ Κασάν-
δρου φίλος οὐκ ἠχθέσθη τοῦ Θεοφράστου πρὸς
αὐτὸν εἰπόντος, ' θαυμάζω σου τοὺς ὀφθαλμοὺς
ὅτι οὐκ ᾄδουσιν, τοῦ μυκτῆρος αὐτοῖς ἐνδεδωκό-
C τος '· καὶ ὁ Κῦρος ἐκέλευσε τὸν γρυπὸν σιμὸν
ἀγαγέσθαι γύναιον,[1] οὕτω γὰρ ἐφαρμόσειν· εἰς δὲ
δυσωδίαν μυκτῆρος ἢ στόματος ἄχθονται σκωπτόμενοι. καὶ πάλιν εἰς φαλακρότητα πράως φέρουσιν, εἰς δὲ πήρωσιν ὀφθαλμῶν ἀηδῶς. καὶ γὰρ
Ἀντίγονος αὐτὸς μὲν ἑαυτὸν εἰς τὸν ὀφθαλμὸν
ἔσκωπτεν, καί ποτε λαβὼν ἀξίωμα μεγάλοις
γράμμασι γεγραμμένον, ' ταυτὶ μέν,' ἔφη, ' καὶ
τυφλῷ δῆλα '· Θεόκριτον δὲ τὸν Χῖον ἀπέκτεινεν,
ὅτι φήσαντός τινος, ' εἰς[2] ὀφθαλμοὺς ἂν βασιλέως
παραγένῃ,[3] σωθήσῃ,'[4] ' ἀλλά μοι,'[5] εἶπεν, ' ἀδύνα-
τόν τιν' ὑποφαίνεις τὴν σωτηρίαν.'[6]

" Λέων[7] ὁ Βυζάντιος, εἰπόντος Πασιάδου πρὸς
D αὐτὸν ὀφθαλμισθῆναι δι' αὐτοῦ τοὺς ὀφθαλμούς,
' ἀσθένειαν,' ἔφη, ' σώματος ὀνειδίζεις, νέμεσιν
οὐχ ὁρῶν ἐπὶ τῶν ὤμων βαστάζοντά σου τὸν
υἱόν '· εἶχε δὲ κυρτὸν ὁ Πασιάδης υἱόν. ἠγανάκτησε
δὲ καὶ Ἄρχιππος ὁ δημαγωγὸς τῶν Ἀθηναίων

---

[1] σιμὸν ἀγαγέσθαι γύναιον added by Bernardakis; σιμὴν ἀγαγέσθαι γυναῖκα Turnebus; cf. Xenophon, Cyropaedia, viii.
4. 21.

[2] τινὸς εἰς Turnebus (adding τοὺς from the Aldine edition):
τῇ.

[3] βασιλέως παραγένηται Turnebus, παραγένῃ Bernardakis:
lac. 5-6 ραγενῃ.

[4] σωθήσῃ Bernardakis, σωθῆναι Turnebus: σωθῇ.

[5] ἀλλά μοι Bernardakis, ἀλλ' ἐμοὶ Turnebus, ἀλλὰ μὰ Δι'
Castiglioni: ἀλλ' ἅμα.

[6] Pohlenz: ἀδυνάτου τὰ ὑπὸ τὴν σ.

men laugh when they are teased about a hooked nose
or a snub nose. Cassander's friend was not angry
with Theophrastus who said to him, ' I am amazed
that your eyes don't sing, for your nose gives them
the pitch.' [a] Cyrus [b] advised a hooked-nose officer of
his to marry a snub-nosed woman, for thus they would
fit each other. But men get angry when they are
teased about a bad-smelling nose or mouth. Again,
people support with equanimity being teased about
baldness, but with asperity about impairment of sight.
Indeed, Antigonus,[c] though it was his habit to make
fun of himself about his one eye and once, when he
received a petition written in big letters, he said,
' This is clear even to a blind man,'—the same Antigonus nevertheless put to death Theocritus of Chios [d]
because, when someone said, ' Stand before the eyes
of the king, and you will be saved,' Theocritus replied,
' The salvation you recommend me is impossible.'

" Leon of Byzantium [e] said to Pasiades, when that
gentleman remarked that the very sight of Leon
sickened his eyes, ' You reproach me for a bodily in-
firmity and you do not see that your son carries
heaven's wrath upon his shoulders.' Pasiades had a
hunchback son. Archippus,[f] the Athenian politician,

[a] Apparently a far-fetched pun, the Greek verb having
various meanings, from " set in " to " set the tune."
[b] Xenophon, *Cyropaedia*, viii. 4. 21.
[c] Antigonus I, called the One-eyed or the Cyclops, *RE*,
s.v., no. 3 ; *Mor.* 11 B-C.   [d] See above, p. 121, note e.
[e] Defender of his city against Philip of Macedon ; for the
anecdote, which is found slightly altered in *Mor.* 88 F, see
RE, xii. 2010 f., xviii. 2057.
[f] Unknown otherwise. On Melanthius, if the same one,
see above, p. 121, note c.

[7] Λέων added by the Basel edition ; *cf. Mor.* 88 F.

(633) ὑπὸ Μελανθίου σκωφθεὶς εἰς τὸ κυρτόν· ἔφη γὰρ
αὐτὸν ὁ Μελάνθιος οὐ προεστάναι τῆς πόλεως
ἀλλὰ προκεκυφέναι.[1] τινὲς δὲ ταῦτα πράως καὶ
μετρίως φέρουσιν, ὥσπερ ὁ φίλος τοῦ Ἀντιγόνου
τάλαντον αἰτήσας καὶ μὴ λαβὼν ᾔτησε προπομποὺς
καὶ φύλακας, ' ὅπως,' ἔφη, ' μὴ ἐπιβουλευθῶ,'
προσπαίξαντος[2] κατ' ὤμου τὸ τάλαντον φέρειν.
E οὕτω μὲν περὶ τὰ ἐκτὸς ἔχουσι διὰ τὴν ἀνωμαλίαν·
ἄλλοι γὰρ ἐπ' ἄλλοις ἄχθονται.[3] [Ἐπαμεινώνδας
μετὰ τῶς συναρχόντων ἑστιώμενος ἐπέπινεν ὄξος,
καὶ πυνθανομένων εἰ πρὸς ὑγίειαν ἀγαθόν, ' οὐκ
οἶδ',' εἶπεν, ' ὅτι μέντοι πρὸς τὸ μεμνῆσθαι τῆς
οἴκοι διαίτης ἀγαθόν, ἐπίσταμαι.']⁴ διὸ δεῖ καὶ
πρὸς τὰς φύσεις καὶ τὰ ἤθη σκοποῦντα ταῖς
παιδιαῖς χρῆσθαι, πειρώμενον ἀλύπως καὶ κεχαρισμένως ἑκάστοις ὁμιλεῖν.

10. '' Ὁ δ' ἔρως τά τ' ἄλλα ποικιλώτατός ἐστι
καὶ τοῖς σκώμμασιν οἱ μὲν ἄχθονται καὶ ἀγανα-
κτοῦσιν οἱ δὲ χαίρουσιν. δεῖ δ' εἰδέναι τὸν καιρόν·
ὡς γὰρ τὸ πῦρ ἐν ἀρχῇ μὲν ἀποσβέννυσι τὸ
F πνεῦμα διὰ τὴν ἀσθένειαν, αὐξηθέντι δὲ τροφὴν
παρέχει καὶ ῥώμην, οὕτως φυόμενος ὁ ἔρως ἔτι
καὶ λανθάνων δυσκολαίνει καὶ ἀγανακτεῖ πρὸς
τοὺς ἀποκαλύπτοντας,[5] ἐκλάμψας δὲ καὶ διαφανεὶς
τρέφεται καὶ προσγελᾷ τοῖς σκώμμασι φυσώμενος.
ἥδιστα δὲ σκώπτονται παρόντων τῶν ἐρωμένων

---

[1] Basel edition : κεκυφέναι.
[2] Kronenberg : προστάξας.
[3] ἄχθονται added by Stephanus.
[4] This sentence is deleted by Hubert as wrongly inserted
here, perhaps from Plutarch's notes.
[5] ἀποσκώπτοντας Blümner, Helmbold (*Class. Phil.* xxxvi
[1941], p. 87).

got mad at Melanthius for teasing him about the hump on his back, for Melanthius said that Archippus did not stand as leader over the city, but stooped before it. Some men endure this affliction with gentle equanimity, as did the friend of Antigonus who asked for a talent and did not get it and then, in reply to the teasing of Antigonus that he was carrying the talent upon his shoulders,[a] asked for an escort and guards, ' in order that no one,' he said, ' will waylay me.' This is the way men, in their diversity, are about physical appearance : some get mad at one thing, others at another. [Epaminondas, when dining with his fellow officers, was in the habit of drinking a vinegary wine ; when they inquired if it was good for the health, he replied, ' I don't know, but I am certain that it is good for keeping me in mind of the fare at home.'] Accordingly the man who would indulge in teasing must have an eye to the natures and dispositions of the company, trying to converse with all in a pleasant and agreeable manner.

10. " Love is a very complex emotion, in regard to jokes as to everything else : some lovers are distressed and annoyed by jokes ; others are pleased. One must know the right time. For just as a fire [b] in its early stages is extinguished, weak as it is, by a breath of air, but when it has grown larger, it is nourished and strengthened ; so love, while still nascent and hidden, is irritated and distressed by detection, but when it has blazed out and become visible, it smiles upon the wind of ridicule that nourishes it. In the presence of those they love, men

---

[a] Or " shoulder," if we may perhaps assume that the deformity of Antigonus's friend resembled a money-box (or the like) carried on one shoulder.

[b] Cf. Ennius in Cicero, De Oratore, ii. 54. 222.

(633) εἰς αὐτὸ τὸ ἐρᾶν εἰς ἄλλο δ' οὐδέν. ἐὰν δὲ καὶ
γυναικῶν ἐρῶντες ἰδίων τύχωσιν ἢ νεανίσκων
634 φιλοκάλων ἔρωτα γενναῖον, παντάπασι γάνυνται
καὶ καλλωπίζονται τῷ σκώπτεσθαι πρὸς αὐτούς.
διὸ καὶ Ἀρκεσίλαος, ἐν τῇ σχολῇ τοιαύτης μετα-
δόσεως αὐτῷ γενομένης ὑπό τινος τῶν ἐρωτικῶν·
' δοκεῖ μοι μηδὲν ἅπτεσθαι μηδενός,' ' οὐδὲ[1] σὺ
τοίνυν,' ἔφη, ' τοῦδ' ἅπτῃ; ' δείξας τινὰ τῶν
καλῶν καὶ ὡραίων παρακαθήμενον.

11. " Ἤδη δὲ καὶ τὸ τῶν παρόντων σκεπτέον·
ἃ γὰρ ἐν φίλοις καὶ συνήθεσιν ἀκούοντες γελῶσι,
ταῦτα δυσχεραίνουσιν, ἂν λέγηται πρὸς αὐτοὺς τῆς
γαμετῆς παρούσης ἢ τοῦ πατρὸς ἢ τοῦ καθηγητοῦ, πλὴν ἂν μή τι κεχαρισμένον ᾖ τῶν λεγομένων
ἐκείνοις· οἷον ἄν τις[2] σκώπτηται τοῦ φιλοσόφου
παρόντος εἰς ἀνυποδησίαν ἢ νυκτογραφίαν ἢ τοῦ
B πατρὸς ἀκούοντος εἰς[3] μικρολογίαν ἢ τῆς γυναικὸς
εἰς τὸ ἀνέραστον ἑτέρων ἐκείνης δὲ δοῦλον καὶ
θεραπευτικόν, ὡς ὁ Τιγράνης ὑπὸ τοῦ Κύρου, ' τί δ',
ἄν σ' ἡ γυνὴ σκευοφοροῦντ' ἀκούσῃ; ', ' ἀλλ' οὐκ
ἀκούσεται,' εἶπεν, ' ὄψεται δ' αὐτὴ παροῦσα.'

12. " Ποιεῖ δ' ἀλυπότερα τὰ σκώμματα καὶ τὸ
κοινωνεῖν ἁμωσγέπως τοὺς λέγοντας· οἷον ἂν[4] εἰς
πενίαν λέγῃ πένης ἢ δυσγενὴς εἰς δυσγένειαν ἢ

---

[1] οὐδὲ Turnebus : ὁ δὲ.
[2] Added by Xylander : erasure in T.
[3] Added by Stephanus.
[4] οἷον ἂν Hubert, οἷον ὅταν Reiske : ὅ τ' ἂν (sic) T.

---

[a] Of the Middle Academy. Hubert discovers the geometrical problem here proposed in Sextus Empiricus, *Adversus Mathematicos*, iii. 79 : it is not things themselves that
are contiguous, but their peripheries.

find it very agreeable to be teased about love itself, but about nothing else. And if they happen to be in love with their own wives or to have a generous love for elegant young men, they are perfectly delighted and proud to be teased about them. Accordingly, when at one of the lectures of Arcesilaüs [a] an auditor at the moment engaged in a love-affair advanced the following proposition, ' In my opinion nothing touches anything else,' Arcesilaüs pointed to a youth who was sitting beside the gentleman—a fine handsome young man—and said, ' Am I to infer that you in particular are not touching this lad ? '

11. " Now we must turn to consideration of the type of guest present at the party. Among friends and comrades men laugh at remarks they take amiss if made to them in the presence of wife, father, or teacher unless what is said is in some way pleasing to these latter. I mean if one, when a philosopher is among the company, is teased about going barefoot or writing into the late hours of the night ; or about his thriftiness, when his father is listening to the conversation ; or, in the hearing of his wife, how he is no lover of other women, but her slave and servant—like Tigranes,[b] who, asked by Cyrus, ' But what if your wife hears that you are carrying baggage ? ', replied, ' She will not hear about it ; she will be there to see it herself.'

12. " It makes teasing less distressing, too, for those who tease to share in some way or other the condition ridiculed : for example, if a pauper speaks of poverty, or a low-born man of mean birth, or a

[b] Tigranes in Xenophon, *Cyropaedia*, iii. 1. 36 and 41, says in the hearing of his wife that he would give his life to prevent her enslavement, and *ibid.* 43 utters in different words the sentiment quoted here at the end of the sentence.

(634) ἐρῶν εἰς ἔρωτα[1]· δοκεῖ δ' οὐχ ὕβρει παιδιᾷ δέ τινι
γίγνεσθαι μᾶλλον ὑπὸ τῶν ὁμοίων· εἰ δὲ μή, παροξύνει καὶ λυπεῖ. τὸν γοῦν ἀπελεύθερον τοῦ βασι-
C λέως νεόπλουτον ὄντα φορτικῶς δὲ καὶ σοβαρῶς
ἐπιπολάζοντα τοῖς συνδειπνοῦσι φιλοσόφοις καὶ
τέλος ἐρωτῶντα πῶς ἔκ τε τῶν λευκῶν καὶ τῶν
μελάνων κυάμων ὁμοίως χλωρὸν γίγνεται τὸ ἔτνος,
ἀντερωτήσας ὁ Ἀριδίκης πῶς ἐκ τῶν λευκῶν καὶ
μελάνων ἱμάντων φοινικοῖ γίγνονται μώλωπες,
ἐποίησεν ἀναστῆναι περίλυπον γενόμενον. ὁ δὲ
Ταρσεὺς Ἀμφίας ἐκ κηπουροῦ δοκῶν γεγονέναι,
σκώψας δὲ τὸν φίλον τοῦ ἡγεμόνος εἰς δυσγένειαν,
εἶθ' ὑπολαβὼν εὐθύς, ' ἀλλὰ καὶ ἡμεῖς ἐκ τῶν
αὐτῶν σπερμάτων γεγόναμεν,' γέλωτ' ἐποίησεν.
κομψῶς δὲ καὶ τοῦ Φιλίππου τὴν ὀψιμαθίαν ἅμα
καὶ περιεργίαν ὁ ψάλτης ἐπέσχεν· οἰομένου γὰρ
αὐτὸν ἐξελέγχειν τοῦ Φιλίππου περὶ κρουμάτων
D καὶ ἁρμονιῶν, ' μὴ γένοιτό σοι,' εἶπεν, ' ὦ βασιλεῦ,
κακῶς οὕτως, ἵν' ἐμοῦ σὺ ταῦτ' εἰδῇς βέλτιον.'
σκώπτειν γὰρ ἑαυτὸν δοκῶν, ἐκεῖνον ἀλύπως ἐνου-
θέτησεν. διὸ καὶ τῶν κωμικῶν ἔνιοι τὴν πι-
κρίαν ἀφαιρεῖν δοκοῦσι τῷ σκώπτειν ἑαυτούς, ὡς
Ἀριστοφάνης εἰς τὴν φαλακρότητα καὶ τὴν Ἀγάθωνος ἀπόλειψιν[2]· Κρατῖνος δὲ τὴν Πυτίνην . . .[3]
ἐδίδαξεν.

13. " Οὐχ ἥκιστα δὲ δεῖ[4] προσέχειν καὶ φυλάττειν, ὅπως ἐκ τοῦ παρατυχόντος ἔσται τὸ σκῶμμα

---

[1] Reiske, Xylander : ἐρῶντα.
[2] Bernardakis : lac. 5 λυμιν.
[3] αὐτὸς φιλοποτῶν added by Hubert, ὡς ἐραστὴς αὐτῆς Pohlenz, εἰς αὐτόν Bolkestein : lac. 4-5.
[4] Added by Stephanus.

lover of love. For, if it is done by similar people, the teasing seems to spring not from insolence but rather from a kind of playfulness ; otherwise it is irritating and distressful. Take the case of the king's new-rich freedman : he was behaving in a vulgar and pompous manner towards the philosophers who were his companions at dinner and ended by asking how it is that white beans and black alike make yellow soup, and Aridices [a] caused him to get up and leave the party mortally offended by asking in turn how it is that white and black lashes make red stripes. But when Amphias of Tarsus was teasing the governor's friend about his mean birth and immediately interrupted himself to say, ' But I too have sprung from the same seed,' he got a laugh, for he himself was reputed to be a gardener's son. And a harper delightfully rebuked Philip's late-won knowledge and officiousness : when Philip thought to dispute with him on a question of notes and scales, the harper said, ' May you never fare so ill, Sire, that you have better knowledge of these matters than I.' [b] By seeming to ridicule himself he reproved Philip without offence. So some of the comic poets seem to take away bitterness by ridiculing themselves, as Aristophanes [c] on the subject of baldness and Agathon's departure,[d] and Cratinus brought out the *Wine-Flask*. . . .

13. " Not least is it necessary to watch out and see to it that a joke occasioned by any question or amuse-

---

[a] Pupil of Arcesilaüs, Athenaeus, x, 420 d ; *cf. RE, s.v.*, no. 2 ; Bolkestein, *Adv. Crit.* p. 114 : *Bull. Corr. Hell.* xxvi (1912), pp. 230 ff.

[b] *Cf. Mor.* 67 F, 179 B, 334 c—of Philip II, the father of Alexander.

[c] Aristophanes, *Peace*, 767, 771.

[d] *Frogs*, 83 : Agathon had gone to Macedon.

(634) πρός τινας ἐρωτήσεις αὐτόθεν ἢ παιδιὰς γιγνόμενον,
ἀλλὰ μὴ πόρρωθεν οἷον ἐκ παρασκευῆς ἐπεισόδιον.
E ὡς γὰρ ὀργὰς καὶ μάχας τὰς ἐκ τῶν συμποσίων
πραότερον φέρουσιν, ἐὰν δ' ἐπελθών τις ἔξωθεν
λοιδορῆται καὶ ταράττῃ τοῦτον ἐχθρὸν ἡγοῦνται
καὶ μισοῦσιν, οὕτως μέτεστι συγγνώμης σκώμματι
καὶ παρρησίας, ἂν ἐκ τῶν παρόντων ἔχῃ τὴν
γένεσιν ἀφελῶς καὶ ἀπλάστως φυόμενον, ἂν δ'
ᾖ μὴ πρὸς λόγον ἀλλ' ἔξωθεν,[1] ἐπιβουλῇ καὶ ὕβρει
προσέοικεν· οἷον τὸ Τιμαγένους πρὸς τὸν ἄνδρα
τῆς ἐμετικῆς[2]

κακῶν γὰρ ἄρχεις τήνδε μοῦσαν εἰσάγων[3]·

καὶ πρὸς Ἀθηνόδωρον τὸν φιλόσοφον, ' εἰ φυσικὴ[4]
ἡ πρὸς τὰ ἔκγονα[5] φιλοστοργία.' ἡ γὰρ ἀκαιρία
καὶ τὸ μὴ πρὸς λόγον ὕβριν ἐμφαίνει καὶ δυσ-
F μένειαν. οὗτοι μὲν οὖν κατὰ Πλάτωνα κουφοτά-
του πράγματος, λόγων, βαρυτάτην ζημίαν ἔτισαν·

---

[1] ἔξωθεν Bernardakis, ἔξω Stephanus : ἐξ ὧν.
[2] ἐμετικῆς Jannot : γαμετικῆς T, the first two letters according to Hubert in a later hand.
[3] Athenaeus, xiv, 616 c, quotes this line with a different
text : κακῶν κατάρχεις τήνδ' ἐμοῦσαν εἰσάγων.
[4] φυσικὴ Amyot : μουσική.
[5] ἔκγονα added by Turnebus, τέκνα Franke ; cf. Diogenes
Laertius, vii. 120.

---

[a] According to Athenaeus, xiv, 616 c, Telesphorus (RE,
s.v., no. 2) misquoted this line (Nauck, Trag. Gr. Frag.,
Adespoton 395 ; Müller, F.H.G. iii, p. 319) with the slight
change of τήνδε Μοῦσαν to τήνδ' ἐμοῦσαν="this retching
woman " for " this Muse " in allusion to Arsinoë, wife of his
king, Lysimachus. Telesphorus's punishment is described

ment be casual and spontaneous, not brought in from a distance like previously prepared entertainment. For just as we easily endure the flarings of temper and the discord which arise within the circle of a drinking-party, but if anyone comes in from outside with insults and disturbance, he is considered an enemy and hateful; so do we pardon and license a joke that springs simply and unfeignedly from the immediate circumstances, while it seems a planned insult if it is foreign to the context of the talk. Examples are the remark of Timagenes [a] to the husband of the women given to vomiting,

> The first of wrongs you sure commit
> When you this retching muse admit
> Into your house

and his question to the philosopher Athenodorus [b] ' Is love for one's children a natural thing? ' [c] For inopportuneness and irrelevancy to the conversation emphasize an ill-natured insult. Men who joke thus pay the heaviest penalty for their words, the lightest

in *Mor.* 606 B. Timagenes, if the historian (*RE, s.v.,* no. 2), is later, his name here presumably the result of confusion: cf. Bolkestein, *Adv. Crit., ad loc.*

[b] *RE, s.v.,* no. 18 and 19: either Athenodorus Cordylion, friend of the younger Cato, or the son of Sandon, one of the teachers of Augustus in philosophy; Müller, *F.H.G.* iii, p. 486.

[c] A question affirmatively answered by the Stoics (von Arnim, *Stoic. Vet. Frag.* iii. 731 from Diog. Laert. vii. 120). Note the possibility of a pun like the preceding, ἔκγον' ἀφιλοστοργία = " absence of love for one's children." The meaning of the passage is not clear. Bolkestein, *loc. cit.,* suggests that it may refer to Athenodorus Cordylion and his practice, while librarian at Pergamon, of cutting from Stoic books passages objectionable to him (Diog. Laert. vii. 34; cf. *RE, s.v.* " Athenodorus," no. 18).

(634) οἱ δὲ τὸν καιρὸν εἰδότες καὶ φυλάττοντες αὐτῷ
τῷ Πλάτωνι μαρτυροῦσιν, ὅτι τοῦ πεπαιδευμένου
καλῶς ἔργον ἐστὶ τὸ παίζειν ἐμμελῶς καὶ κεχαρισμένως."

635   ΠΡΟΒΛΗΜΑ Β

Διὰ τί βρωτικώτεροι γίγνονται περὶ τὸ μετόπωρον

Collocuntur Xenocles, Plutarchus, Glaucias, Lamprias

Ἐν Ἐλευσῖνι μετὰ τὰ μυστήρια τῆς πανηγύρεως ἀκμαζούσης εἰστιώμεθα παρὰ Γλαυκίᾳ τῷ
ῥήτορι. πεπαυμένων δὲ δειπνεῖν τῶν ἄλλων, Ξενοκλῆς ὁ Δελφὸς[1] ὥσπερ εἰώθει τὸν ἀδελφὸν ἡμῶν
Λαμπρίαν εἰς ἀδηφαγίαν Βοιώτιον ἐπέσκωπτεν.
ἐγὼ δ' ἀμυνόμενος ὑπὲρ[2] αὐτοῦ τὸν Ξενοκλέα τοῖς
Ἐπικούρου λόγοις χρώμενον, " οὐ γὰρ ἅπαντες,"
εἶπον, " ὦ βέλτιστε, ποιοῦνται τὴν τοῦ ἀλγοῦντος
ὑπεξαίρεσιν ὅρον ἡδονῆς καὶ πέρας· Λαμπρίᾳ δὲ
B καὶ ἀνάγκη, πρὸ τοῦ κήπου κυδαίνοντι τὸν περίπατον καὶ τὸ Λύκειον, ἔργῳ μαρτυρεῖν Ἀριστοτέλει·
φησὶ γὰρ ὁ ἀνὴρ βρωτικώτατον ἕκαστον αὐτὸν
αὐτοῦ περὶ τὸ φθινόπωρον εἶναι, καὶ τὴν αἰτίαν
ἐπείρηκεν· ἐγὼ δ' οὐ μνημονεύω."

" Βέλτιον," εἶπεν ὁ Γλαυκίας· " αὐτοὶ γὰρ ἐπιχειρήσομεν ζητεῖν, ὅταν παυσώμεθα δειπνοῦντες."

Ὡς οὖν ἀφῃρέθησαν αἱ τράπεζαι, Γλαυκίας μὲν
καὶ Ξενοκλῆς ᾐτιάσαντο τὴν ὀπώραν διαφόρως,
ὁ μὲν ὡς[3] τὴν κοιλίαν ὑπεξάγουσαν καὶ τῷ κενοῦ-

────────
[1] Wyttenbach : ἀδελφὸς.   [2] Added by Stephanus.
[3] Leonicus : εἰς.

────────
[a] Laws, 717 c-d, 935 a.   [b] Cf. Laws, 654 b.
[c] RE, s.v. " Plutarchos," col. 668. Glaucias appears infra,
vii. 9 and ix. 12, 13. Xenocles only here.

of things, as Plato [a] says ; but those who understand
what is appropriate and observe it bear witness to
Plato himself that to joke with grace and good taste
is a task for the well-educated man." [b]

QUESTION 2

Why men become hungrier in autumn

Speakers : Xenocles, Plutarch, Glaucias, and Lamprias

At Eleusis after the mysteries, the climax of the
festival, we were dining at the house of Glaucias [c] the
professor of Public-Speaking. After the others had
finished dinner, Xenocles of Delphi, as usual, began
to tease my brother Lamprias about his " Boeotian
gluttony." In defence of my brother I launched an
attack upon Xenocles, follower of the teachings of
Epicurus, by saying, " Not all men, Sir, make the
removal of the painful the limit and perfection of
pleasure.[d] Lamprias honours The Walk and The
Lyceum before The Garden and so must bear active
witness to Aristotle, for this gentleman says that
each man is hungriest in the fall of the year.[e] And
he has given the reason, but I do not remember it."

" It is better so," said Glaucias, " for we ourselves
shall undertake the search for it when we finish
dining."

After the tables were taken away, then, Glaucias
and Xenocles both attributed the cause to the
autumn's fruit, but each for a different reason. The
former held that it cleaned out the bowels and by

[d] Epicurus, *Kyriai Doxai*, 3 ; *cf.* Cicero, *De Finibus*, i. 11
37, etc., in Usener, *Epicurea*, p. 397.
[e] Frag. 222 in the Prussian Academy's edition of Aristotle,
vol. v.

(635) σθαι τὸ σῶμα νεαρὰς ὀρέξεις ἀεὶ παρασκευάζουσαν·
ὁ δὲ Ξενοκλῆς ἔλεγεν εὔστομόν τι καὶ δηκτικὸν
C ἔχοντα τῶν ὡραίων τὰ πλεῖστα τὸν στόμαχον ἐπὶ
τὴν βρῶσιν ἐκκαλεῖσθαι παντὸς μᾶλλον ὄψου καὶ
ἡδύσματος· καὶ γὰρ τοῖς ἀποσίτοις τῶν ἀρρώστων
ὀπώρας τι προσενεχθὲν ἀναλαμβάνει τὴν ὄρεξιν.
ὁ δὲ Λαμπρίας εἶπεν, ὅτι τὸ οἰκεῖον καὶ¹ σύμφυτον
θερμὸν ἡμῶν, ᾧ τρέφεσθαι πεφύκαμεν, ἐν μὲν τῷ
θέρει διέσπαρται καὶ γέγονεν ἀσθενέστερον καὶ
μανόν, ἐν δὲ τῷ φθίνοντι καιρῷ συναγείρεται
πάλιν καὶ ἰσχύει, κατακρυπτόμενον ἐντὸς διὰ τὴν
περίψυξιν καὶ τὴν πύκνωσιν τοῦ σώματος.

Ἐγὼ δ' ὑπὲρ τοῦ μὴ δοκεῖν ἀσύμβολος τοῦ
λόγου μετασχεῖν εἶπον, ὅτι τοῦ θέρους διψητι-
κώτεροι γιγνόμεθα καὶ πλείονι χρώμεθα τῷ ὑγρῷ
D διὰ τὸ καῦμα· νῦν οὖν ἡ φύσις ἐν τῇ μεταβολῇ
ζητοῦσα τοὐναντίον, ὥσπερ εἴωθεν, πεινητικωτέ-
ρους ποιεῖ, καὶ τὴν ξηρὰν τροφὴν τῇ κράσει τοῦ
σώματος ἀνταποδίδωσιν. οὐ μὴν οὐδὲ τὰ σιτία
φήσαι τις ἂν αἰτίας ἀμοιρεῖν παντάπασιν, ἀλλ' ἐκ
νέων καὶ προσφάτων γενόμενα καρπῶν, οὐ μόνον
μάζας καὶ ὄσπρια καὶ ἄρτους καὶ πυροὺς ἀλλὰ²
καὶ κρέα ζῴων εὐωχουμένων τὰ ἐπέτεια, τοῖς τε
χυμοῖς διαφέρειν³ τῶν παλαιῶν καὶ μᾶλλον ἐπ-
άγεσθαι τοὺς χρωμένους καὶ ἀπολαύοντας.

---

¹ τὸ after καὶ deleted by Hubert.

emptying the body was always re-creating appetite. And Xenocles said that the pleasant, piquant quality of most fruits invited hunger in the belly more efficiently than any dainty dish and sauce. Indeed a bit of fruit offered the sick who have lost their taste for food, restores their appetite. It was the opinion of Lamprias that our own innate heat, by the activity of which we are naturally nourished, is dispersed, rather weak, and of little consequence in summer, but in autumn collects again and grows strong, hidden within us by the cooling and solidification of our bodies.[a]

And I, to avoid the appearance of sharing in the conversation without paying my contribution,[b] said that in summer we become thirstier and because of the heat use more liquid[c]; so now nature, in the process of change seeking the other extreme, as her custom is, makes us hungrier and replenishes the solid food in the body's mixture. Yet one cannot say that food itself has absolutely nothing to do with the causation; on the contrary, food prepared from new or freshly slaughtered produce—not only barley-cakes, legumes, bread, and wheat but also flesh of animals fattened on this year's fodder does differ in flavour from the old and is more inviting to those who experience it and partake of it.

---

[a] *Cf. supra*, 623 E f., *infra*, vi. i, 686 E ff., *Mor.* 123 A. For strange theories as to " heat " or " innate heat " in animals, plants, or substances, *cf.* 642 C, 647 C, E, 648 A, C-E, 649 B., 650 F ff., 652 A ff., 676 A, 681 A, 685 A f., 695 D, 697 A, and Bury, *Philebus of Plato*, p. 190, with Aristotle, *De Partibus Animal*, there cited. [b] *Cf.* iv. 3. 2, 666 F.

[c] Bolkestein makes the rest of the section a direct quotation.

---

[2] Added by Xylander. [3] Basel edition : διαφέρει.

(635)

ΠΡΟΒΛΗΜΑ Γ

Πότερον ἡ ὄρνις πρότερον[1] ἢ τὸ ᾠὸν ἐγένετο

Collocuntur Alexander, Plutarchus, Sulla, Firmus, Sossius
Senecio

E   1. Ἐξ ἐνυπνίου[2] τινὸς ἀπειχόμην[3] ᾠῶν πολὺν
ἤδη χρόνον[4] παρὰ τοῦτο ποιούμενος,[5] ἐν ᾧ καθάπερ ἐν Καρὶ διάπειραν[6] λαβεῖν τῆς ὄψεως ἐναργῶς
μοι πολλάκις γενομένης· ὑπόνοιαν μέντοι παρέσχον,
ἑστιῶντος ἡμᾶς Σοσσίου Σενεκίωνος, ἐνέχεσθαι
δόγμασιν Ὀρφικοῖς ἢ Πυθαγορικοῖς καὶ τὸ ᾠόν,
ὥσπερ ἔνιοι καρδίαν καὶ ἐγκέφαλον, ἀρχὴν ἡγού-
μενος γενέσεως ἀφοσιοῦσθαι· καὶ προὔφερεν Ἀλέξ-
ανδρος ὁ Ἐπικούρειος ἐπὶ γέλωτι τὸ

ἶσόν τοι κυάμους ἔσθειν[7] κεφαλάς τε τοκήων,

ὡς δὴ κυάμους τὰ ᾠὰ διὰ τὴν κύησιν αἰνιττομένων
F τῶν ἀνδρῶν, διαφέρειν δὲ μηδὲν οἰομένων τὸ
ἐσθίειν ᾠὰ τοῦ χρῆσθαι τοῖς τίκτουσι τὰ ᾠὰ ζῴοις.
ἐγίγνετο δὴ τὸ τῆς αἰτίας ἀπολόγημα τῆς αἰτίας
αὐτῆς ἀλογώτερον, Ἐπικουρείῳ λέγειν ἐνύπνιον.
ὅθεν οὐ παρῃτούμην τὴν δόξαν ἅμα προσπαίζων τι
τῷ Ἀλεξάνδρῳ· καὶ γὰρ ἦν χαρίεις καὶ φιλόλογος
ἐπιεικῶς.

---

[1] πρότερον omitted here in T, but included in the index to
Book II, folio 35 r.
[2] ἐξ ἐνυπνίου Xylander : ἐξυπνίου.
[3] Turnebus : ἀπε lac. 4-5 μην.
[4] ἤδη χρόνον Turnebus : ἤδο lac. 2-3.
[5] Reiske : ποιούμενοι.
[6] Καρὶ διάπειραν Wyttenbach, Καρὶ πεῖραν Reiske : καρδίαι
πεῖραν.   [7] Xylander : ἐσθίειν.

---

[a] Imitated by Macrobius, *Saturnalia*, vii. 16. 1-14.

QUESTION 3

Whether the hen or the egg came first [a]

Speakers: Alexander, Plutarch, Sulla, Firmus, Sossius Senecio

1. BECAUSE of a dream, I had for a long time now been avoiding eggs, and I was acting so for this reason, that I might test by an egg, as by a Carian,[b] the vision which came to me clearly and frequently. But my companions at one of Sossius Senecio's dinners suspected me of being committed to beliefs of the Orphics or the Pythagoreans and holding the egg taboo, as some hold the heart and brain, because I thought it to be the first principle of creation. And Alexander the Epicurean [c] teasingly recited:

Now eating beans is much like eating parents' heads.[d]

For these people call eggs " beans " (kuamoi), punning on the word conception (kuesis), and they think that eating eggs in no way differs from using the creatures which produce the eggs. To explain to an Epicurean with talk of dreams the reason for my avoidance was surely more unreasonable than the reason itself. So I said nothing to deny their opinion, though I did tease Alexander a little, for he was a man of parts and considerable learning.

[b] In corpore vili, cf. Cratinus, Herdsmen, frag. 16 (Edmonds or Kock with Edmonds's note), Leutsch and Schneidewin, Paroemiogr. Graec. i, pp. 70 f. Slaves were often from Caria, so that the ethnic was used to refer to any slave.

[c] An Epicurean Alexander appears in I.G. ii². 3793 and 3819, discussed by A. E. Raubitschek in Hesperia, xviii (1949), pp. 99 f.

[d] Kern, Orph. 291. See Athenaeus, ii, 65 f, with τρώγειν for ἐσθειν, and Gulick's note, LCL Athen. i, p. 286.

636   2. Ἐκ δὲ τούτου τὸ ἄπορον καὶ πολλὰ πράγματα τοῖς ζητητικοῖς παρέχον εἰς μέσον εἵλκετο[1]
πρόβλημα περὶ τοῦ ᾠοῦ καὶ τῆς ὄρνιθος, ὁπότερον
γένοιτο πρότερον αὐτῶν. καὶ Σύλλας μὲν ὁ ἑ-
ταῖρος εἰπὼν ὅτι μικρῷ προβλήματι καθάπερ ὀργάνῳ μέγα καὶ βαρὺ σαλεύομεν τὸ περὶ τοῦ κόσμου
τῆς γενέσεως ἀπηγόρευσεν· τοῦ δ' Ἀλεξάνδρου
τῆς ζητήσεως ὡς μηδὲν προσφυὲς φερούσης κατα-
γελάσαντος ὁ γαμβρὸς ἡμῶν Φίρμος, '' ἐμοὶ τοίνυν,'' ἔφη, '' χρῆσον ἐν τῷ παρόντι τὰς ἀτόμους.[2]
εἰ γὰρ τὰ μικρὰ δεῖ στοιχεῖα τῶν μεγάλων καὶ[3]
ἀρχὰς ὑποτίθεσθαι, πρῶτον[4] εἰκός ἐστιν τὸ ᾠὸν
B γεγονέναι τῆς ὄρνιθος· ἔστι γὰρ καὶ ἁπλοῦν, ὡς
ἐν αἰσθητοῖς, ποικίλον δὲ καὶ μεμιγμένον μᾶλλον
ἡ ὄρνις. καθόλου δ' ἡ μὲν ἀρχὴ πρῶτον ἀρχὴ δὲ
τὸ σπέρμα, τὸ δ' ᾠὸν σπέρματος μὲν πλέον ζῴου
δὲ μικρότερον· ὡς γὰρ ἡ προκοπὴ μέσον εὐφυΐας
εἶναι δοκεῖ καὶ ἀρετῆς, οὕτω τὸ ᾠὸν προκοπή τίς
ἐστι τῆς φύσεως ἐπὶ τὸ ἔμψυχον ἀπὸ τοῦ σπέρματος πορευομένης. ἔτι δ', ὥσπερ ἐν τῷ ζῴῳ
πρῶτα γίγνεσθαι λέγουσιν ἀρτηρίας καὶ φλέβας,
οὕτω λόγον ἔχει καὶ τοῦ ζῴου τὸ ᾠὸν γεγονέναι
πρῶτον, ὡς περιέχον ἐμπεριεχομένου.[5] καὶ γὰρ
αἱ τέχναι πρῶτον ἀτύπωτα καὶ ἄμορφα πλάτ-
C τουσιν, εἶθ' ὕστερον ἕκαστα τοῖς εἴδεσι διαρθροῦ-

---

[1] Hubert : εἵλκεν.
[2] Reiske : τοῖς ἀτόμοις.
[3] Added by Hubert.
[4] πρότερον Reiske.
[5] Turnebus : ἐν περιεχομένῳ.

2. From this context the problem about the egg and the hen, which of them came first, was dragged into our talk, a difficult problem which gives investigators much trouble. And Sulla [a] my comrade said that with a small problem, as with a tool, we were rocking loose a great and heavy one, that of the creation of the world, and he declined to take part. And after Alexander had ridiculed the inquiry on the ground that it yielded no firm solution, my relative Firmus [b] said : " Well then lend me your atoms for the moment, for if small things must be assumed to be the elements and the beginnings of large, it is likely that the egg existed first before the hen, for among sensible things the egg is indeed simple while the hen is a more intricate and complex organism. And, speaking generally, the initial cause comes first, and the seed is an initial cause ; the egg is greater than the seed on the one hand, on the other less than the creature. Indeed, as development admittedly exists between innate merit and perfected virtue, so the intermediate development in nature's passage from the seed to the living creature is the egg. Furthermore, just as in the creature the first parts to be formed, they say, are the arteries and veins, so too, it stands to reason, the egg is formed before the hen just as that which contains is formed before that which is contained. And in the arts, formless and shapeless parts are first fashioned, then afterwards all details in the figures are correctly articulated ;

[a] On Sulla see Cherniss in LCL *Mor.* xii, p. 3.

[b] *RE*, *s.v.* " Plutarchos," col. 651 : since Plutarch's daughter died in infancy and Plutarch speaks of at least three γαμβροί, Wilamowitz suggested (*Comment. grammat.* iii, Göttingen, 1889, p. 23) that the term refers to the husbands of nieces. Firmus only here.

(636) σιν· ἢ Πολύκλειτος ὁ πλάστης εἶπεν χαλεπώτατον
εἶναι τὸ ἔργον, ὅταν ἐν ὄνυχι ὁ πηλὸς γένηται.

"Διὸ καὶ τῇ φύσει τὸ πρῶτον εἰκός ἐστιν
ἀτρέμα κινούσῃ τὴν ὕλην ἀργοτέραν ὑπακούειν,
τύπους[1] ἀμόρφους καὶ ἀορίστους ἐκφέρουσαν ὥσπερ
τὰ ᾠά, μορφουμένων δὲ τούτων καὶ διαχαρασ-
σομένων ὕστερον ἐνδημιουργεῖσθαι τὸ ζῷον. ὡς
δὲ κάμπη γίγνεται τὸ πρῶτον, εἶτ' ἐκπαγεῖσα διὰ
ξηρότητα καὶ περιρραγεῖσ' ἕτερον[2] πτερωθὲν δι'
αὑτῆς τὴν καλουμένην ψυχὴν μεθίησιν, τὸν αὐτὸν
τρόπον ἐνταῦθα προϋφίσταται τὸ ᾠὸν οἷον ὕλη τῆς
D γενέσεως. ἀνάγκη γὰρ ἐν πάσῃ μεταβολῇ πρότερον εἶναι τοῦ μεταβάλλοντος τὸ[3] ἐξ οὗ μετέβαλε.
σκόπει δ' ὅτι σκνῖπες ἐν δένδρῳ καὶ τερηδόνες
ἐμφύονται ξύλῳ κατὰ σῆψιν ὑγρότητος ἢ πέψιν·
ὧν οὐδεὶς ἂν ἀξιώσειεν μὴ προϋποκεῖσθαι μηδὲ
πρεσβύτερον εἶναι φύσει τὸ γεννῶν. ἡ γὰρ ὕλη
λόγον ἔχει πρὸς τὰ γιγνόμενα μητρὸς ὥς φησι
Πλάτων καὶ τιθήνης· ὕλη δὲ πᾶν ἐξ οὗ σύστασιν
ἔχει τὸ γεννώμενον.

"Τὸ δ' ἐπὶ τούτοις," ἔφη γελάσας, "'ἀείσω
ξυνετοῖσι' τὸν Ὀρφικὸν καὶ ἱερὸν λόγον, ὃς οὐκ
ὄρνιθος μόνον τὸ ᾠὸν ἀποφαίνει πρεσβύτερον,
ἀλλὰ καὶ συλλαβὼν ἅπασαν αὐτῷ τὴν ἁπάντων
E ὁμοῦ πρεσβυγένειαν ἀνατίθησιν. καὶ τἆλλα μὲν

---

[1] τύπους corrected from τόπους E, τόπους T.
[2] ἕτερόν τι Doehner, ἑρπετὸν Damsté in Bolkestein, Adv.
Crit. p. 121, ἔντομον or ἔντερον Wyttenbach.

it is for this reason that the sculptor Polyclitus said that the work is hardest when the clay is at the nail.[a]

"And so it is likely that matter at first yields slowly to the gentle stirring of nature and produces forms that are shapeless and undefined, like eggs ; later, when these forms receive shape and configuration, the living creature is produced. And just as the caterpillar exists first, then, made brittle by dryness, it bursts asunder and itself releases another creature, winged, the so-called *psyche* (butterfly) ; so in like manner the egg here exists first, as material of generation. For, in every process of change, the form from which a change is made necessarily precedes the form which results from change. Consider bark-beetles in a tree and woodworms how they grow in the wood in proportion to the decay and disintegration which moisture causes. No one could rightly claim that the thing which produced them did not exist before them and was not naturally older than they. For matter has the relation of mother or nurse to things which exist, as Plato says [b] ; and matter is all from which whatever is created has its substance.

"What is more," he added with a laugh, "' I shall recite for men of understanding ' the sacred Orphic tenet which not only declares the egg older than the hen, but also attributes to it the absolute primordiality over all things together without exception.[c] As

---

[a] *i.e.*, close to the finishing touches : Polyclitus in Diels, *Frag. d. Vorsokratiker*, frag. 1 (Diels-Kranz[3] 40 B 1) ; *cf.* Plut. *Mor.* 86 A with Babbitt's note (LCL).

[b] *Timaeus*, 49 A, 50 D, 52 D.

[c] *Mor.* 391 D, O. Kern, *Orph.*, p. 143 and p. 334, no. 334.

---

[3] Added by Meziriacus.

(636) ' εὔστομα κείσθω ' καθ' Ἡρόδοτον, ἔστι γὰρ
μυστικώτερα· ζῴων δὲ πολλὰς φύσεις τοῦ κόσμου
περιέχοντος, οὐδὲν ὡς εἰπεῖν γένος ἄμοιρόν ἐστι
τῆς ἐξ ᾠοῦ γενέσεως, ἀλλὰ καὶ πτηνὰ γεννᾷ καὶ
νηκτὰ μυρία καὶ χερσαῖα, σαύρας, καὶ ἀμφίβια,[1]
κροκοδείλους, καὶ δίποδα, τὸν ὄρνιν, καὶ ἄποδα,
τὸν ὄφιν, καὶ πολύποδα, τὸν ἀττέλεβον· ὅθεν οὐκ
ἀπὸ τρόπου τοῖς περὶ τὸν Διόνυσον ὀργιασμοῖς ὡς
μίμημα τοῦ τὰ πάντα γεννῶντος καὶ περιέχοντος
ἐν ἑαυτῷ συγκαθωσίωται."

3. Ταῦτα τοῦ Φίρμου διεξιόντος, ὁ Σενεκίων
ἔφη τὴν τελευταίαν τῶν εἰκόνων αὐτῷ πρώτην
F ἀντιπίπτειν. " ἔλαθες γάρ," εἶπεν, " ὦ Φίρμε,
τὸν κόσμον ἀντὶ τῆς παροιμιακῆς θύρας ' ἐπὶ
σεαυτὸν ἀνοίξας.' ὁ γὰρ κόσμος προϋφέστηκε
πάντων τελειότατος ὤν· καὶ λόγον ἔχει τοῦ ἀτελοῦς
φύσει πρότερον εἶναι τὸ τέλειον, ὡς τοῦ πεπηρω-
μένου τὸ ὁλόκληρον καὶ τοῦ μέρους τὸ ὅλον· οὐδὲ[2]
γὰρ ἔχει λόγον εἶναι μέρος οὗ μέρος ἐστὶ μὴ
γεγονότος. ὅθεν οὐδεὶς λέγει τοῦ σπέρματος
εἶναι τὸν ἄνθρωπον οὐδὲ τοῦ ᾠοῦ τὴν ἀλεκτορίδα,
637 τῆς δ' ἀλεκτορίδος τὸ ᾠὸν εἶναι καὶ τὸ σπέρμα τοῦ
ἀνθρώπου λέγομεν, ὡς τούτων ἐπιγιγνομένων ἐκείνοις καὶ τὴν γένεσιν ἐν ἐκείνοις λαμβανόντων εἶθ'
ὥσπερ ὄφλημα τῇ φύσει τὴν γένεσιν ἀποδιδόντων.
ἐνδεᾶ γάρ ἐστι τοῦ οἰκείου· διὸ καὶ βούλεσθαι

---

[1] καὶ after ἀμφίβια deleted in Basel edition.
[2] Stephanus, οὐδένα Hubert : οὐδέν.

---

[a] ii. 171 on the Egyptian mysteries at Saïs and the Greek
Thesmophoria in honour of Demeter.
[b] *Mor.* 1108 D ; *Paroemiogr. Graec.* i, p. 114 (Zenobius,

for the rest of the doctrine, ' let reverent silence
prevail,' as Herodotus [a] says ; for it is very much of
a mystical secret. Though the world contains many
kinds of creatures, there is no race, one might say, in
which birth from the egg is absent. On the contrary,
the egg produces countless creatures of air and sea ;
and land creatures, as lizards ; amphibious creatures,
as crocodiles ; two-legged creatures, as the bird ;
legless, as the snake ; many-legged, as the locust. It
is therefore not inappropriate that in the rites of
Dionysus the egg is consecrated as a symbol of that
which produces everything and contains everything
within itself."

3. When Firmus finished what he had to say,
Senecio pointed out that the last item of his imagery
was first to tell against him. " For you fail to notice,
Firmus," he continued, " that instead of the proverbial door [b] you have opened up the world, to your
own despite. The world in fact pre-exists everything,
for it is the most complete of all things, and it stands
to reason that the complete is naturally earlier than
the incomplete, as the perfect pre-exists the defective
and the whole the part. For it is not reasonable to
hold that the part exists if that of which it is a part
does not. Thus nobody says that the man is a part
of the seed or that the hen is a part of the egg ; rather
we say that the egg is a part of the hen and the seed
a part of the man, for egg and seed come into being
after hen and man respectively and have their birth
in them, then pay back their genesis as a debt to
nature. For things are in need of their own kind,
and therefore it is natural for them to wish to make

Century, iv. 98) has Lydus (the Lydian ?) closing, not opening, the door as a proverb applied to a stupid thief.

(637) ποιεῖν πέφυκεν ἄλλο τοιοῦτον, οἷον ἦν ἐξ οὗ
ἀπεκρίθη.[1] καὶ τὸν σπερματικὸν λόγον ὁρίζονται
γόνον ἐνδεᾶ γενέσεως· ἐνδεὲς δ' οὐδέν ἐστι τοῦ
μὴ γενομένου μηδ' ὄντος.

" Τὰ δ' ᾠὰ καὶ παντάπασι βλέπεται τὴν φύσιν
ἔχοντα τῆς ἔν τινι ζῴῳ πήξεως καὶ συστάσεως
ὀργάνων τε τοιούτων καὶ ἀγγείων δεομένην· ὅθεν
B οὐδ' ἱστόρηται γηγενὲς ᾠόν, ἀλλὰ καὶ τὸ Τυνδά-
ρειον οἱ ποιηταὶ λέγουσιν οὐρανοπετὲς ἀναφανῆναι.[2]
ζῷα δ' αὐτοτελῆ καὶ ὁλόκληρα μέχρι νῦν ἀναδίδωσιν ἡ γῆ, μῦς ἐν Αἰγύπτῳ πολλαχοῦ δ' ὄφεις καὶ
βατράχους καὶ τέττιγας, ἀρχῆς ἔξωθεν ἑτέρας καὶ
δυνάμεως ἐγγενομένης· ἐν δὲ Σικελίᾳ περὶ τὸν
δουλικὸν πόλεμον, αἵματος πολλοῦ καὶ νεκρῶν ἀτά-
φων ἐπὶ[3] τῇ γῇ κατασαπέντων, πλῆθος ἀττελέβων
ἐξήνθησεν καὶ τὸν σῖτον ἔφθειρον πανταχοῦ σκεδα-
σθέντες ἐπὶ τὴν νῆσον. ταῦτα τοίνυν ἐκ γῆς φύεται
καὶ τρέφεται καὶ τροφῆς περίσσωμα[4] ποιεῖ γόνιμον,
ᾧ καθ' ἡδονὰς πρὸς ἄλληλα τρέπεται, καὶ συν-
C δυαζόμενα τῇ μίξει τὰ μὲν ᾠοτοκεῖν τὰ δὲ ζῳοτο-
κεῖν πέφυκε. καὶ τούτῳ μάλιστα δῆλόν ἐστιν,
ὅτι τὴν πρώτην γένεσιν ἐκ γῆς λαβόντα καθ'

---

[1] συνεκρίθη Bolkestein.
[2] Vulcobius : ἀναφῆναι.
[3] Hubert : ἐν.   [4] Basel edition : περὶ σῶμα.

---

[a] A Stoic term, see von Arnim, *Stoic. Vet. Frag.* ii. 717 and
739.
[b] The Dioscuri ; Helen's birth from an egg is earlier
attested : *cf. RE, s.v.* " Dioskuren," col. 1113. *Cf.* also
Athenaeus, ii, 57 f : " the egg from which Helen sprang fell
from the moon " (Gulick, LCL).

such another as was that from which they have been separated. Indeed, the seminal principle [a] is defined as product in need of production of its own kind, and nothing is in need of what has not come into being and is not.

" It is undoubtedly to be seen that eggs have a natural constitution which lacks the frame and structure possessed by animals, as well as such organs and vessels as these possess. Hence an earth-born egg is not on record, but the poets say even of the egg whence came the sons of Tyndareüs [b] that it appeared as fallen from heaven. Yet the earth in our own time produces creatures complete in themselves and perfect,—mice in Egypt [c] and everywhere snakes and frogs and cicadas,—as the result of the presence of a foreign and extrinsic initial cause and power. In Sicily in the time of the Slave War,[d] when a quantity of blood and unburied corpses had rotted on the ground, a multitude of locusts burst forth, scattered abroad everywhere on the island, and destroyed the grain. These creatures, then, grow from the earth, and take their nourishment, and from nourishment create a seminal residue [e] which causes them to turn to each other for pleasure, and coupled in intercourse some, in producing offspring, are naturally oviparous, some naturally viviparous. And in this it is very clear that, though they take their own first origin

[c] Diodorus Siculus, i. 10. 2 ; Ovid, *Metamorph.* i. 422 ff. ; further, Diodorus Siculus, i. 6. 2 ff., and Lucretius, v. 772-877, with Cyril Bailey's commentary (vol. III, pp. 1450 ff.).

[d] Either 135–132 B.C. or 104–100. In 125 Africa suffered a plague of locusts before they vanished in the sea : *RE*, s.v. " Heuschrecke," *cf.* Pliny, *Nat. Hist.* xi. 105 and Julius Obsequens, *Prodigies*, 30 (in LCL Livy xiv, p. 264).

[e] See *infra*, D and note *a* on 641 A, p. 173.

(637) ἕτερον τρόπον ἤδη καὶ δι᾽ ἀλλήλων ποιεῖται τὰς
τεκνώσεις.

" Καθόλου δ᾽ ὅμοιόν ἐστι τῷ λέγειν, ᾽ πρὸ τῆς
γυναικὸς ἡ μήτρα γέγονεν ᾽· ὡς γὰρ ἡ μήτρα πρὸς
τὸν ἄνθρωπον,[1] οὕτω πάλιν τὸ ᾠὸν πρὸς τὸν νεοσ-
σὸν πέφυκε, κυόμενον ἐν αὐτῷ καὶ λοχευόμενον·
ὥστε μηδὲν διαφέρειν τὸν διαποροῦντα, πῶς ὄρνιθες ἐγένοντο μὴ γενομένων ᾠῶν, τοῦ πυνθανομένου,
πῶς ἄνδρες ἐγένοντο καὶ γυναῖκες πρὶν αἰδοῖα γενέσθαι καὶ μήτρας. καίτοι τῶν μερῶν τὰ πλεῖστα
συνυφίσταται τοῖς ὅλοις, αἱ δὲ δυνάμεις ἐπιγίγνον-
D ται τοῖς μέρεσιν αἱ δ᾽ ἐνέργειαι ταῖς δυνάμεσιν
τὰ δ᾽ ἀποτελέσματα ταῖς ἐνεργείαις· ἀποτέλεσμα
δὲ τῆς γεννητικῆς τῶν μορίων δυνάμεως τὸ σπέρμα
καὶ τὸ ᾠόν· ὥστε τῆς τῶν ὅλων καθυστερεῖν
γενέσεως. σκόπει δὲ μή, καθάπερ οὐ δυνατόν
ἐστι πέψιν τροφῆς εἶναι πρὶν ἢ γενέσθαι ζῷον,
οὕτως οὐδ᾽ ᾠὸν οὐδὲ σπέρμα· καὶ γὰρ ταῦτα
πέψεσί τισι καὶ μεταβολαῖς ἔοικεν ἐπιγενέσθαι[2]·
καὶ οὐχ οἷόν τε, πρὶν ἢ γενέσθαι ζῷον, ἔχειν ζῴου
τροφῆς περίττωμα τὴν φύσιν. οὐ μὴν ἀλλὰ τὸ
σπέρμα μὲν ἀμωσγέπως[3] ἀρχῆς τινος ἀντιποιεῖται,
τὸ δ᾽ ᾠὸν οὔτ᾽ ἀρχῆς ἔχει λόγον, οὐ γὰρ ὑφίσταται
πρῶτον, οὔθ᾽ ὅλου φύσιν, ἀτελὲς γάρ ἐστιν.

E " Ὅθεν ἀρχῆς μὲν ἄνευ γεγονέναι ζῷον οὐ
λέγομεν, ἀρχὴν δ᾽ εἶναι ζωογονίας ὑφ᾽ ἧς πρῶτον
ἡ ὕλη μετέβαλε δυνάμεως, κρᾶσίν τινα καὶ μῖξιν
ἐνεργασαμένης γόνιμον· τὸ δ᾽ ᾠὸν ἐπιγέννημ᾽
εἶναι, καθάπερ τὸ αἷμα καὶ τὸ γάλα, τοῦ ζῴου
μετὰ τροφὴν καὶ πέψιν. οὐ γὰρ ὦπται συνιστά-

---

[1] τὸν ἄνθρωπον Hubert : τὸ ᾠόν.

from the earth, they then perform their own acts of procreation in a different manner and with each other.

"In general it is like saying 'the womb existed before the woman.' For as womb to child so in turn is the egg to the chick that is conceived in it and brought to birth. Accordingly he who raises the question how fowl came into being when the egg did not exist is in no way different from him who asks how men and women came into being before genitals and womb existed. Indeed most parts co-exist with wholes, and powers follow upon the existence of parts, activities upon powers, results upon activities. The seed and the egg are the result of the generative power of parts ; accordingly they are subsequent to the creation of wholes. And consider this : just as it is impossible to have digestion of food before an animal exists, so it is impossible to have either seed or egg ; for these, I suppose, are incident to certain processes of digestion and transformation, and nature cannot possess a residue of an animal's food before the animal itself exists. Nevertheless the seed has a sort of claim to be a first principle, but the egg does not satisfy the definition of a first principle (for it does not exist first) nor does it possess the nature of a whole (for it is incomplete).

"Thus we do not say that there is no elementary principle connected with the birth of a creature, but we do say the principle of generation is that power which caused the first change in matter, the power which made union and intercourse fruitful. And we say that the egg, like blood and milk, is a product of the animal's digestion of its nourishment, for no

---

[2] Hubert : ἐπιγενέσθαι ἔοικεν.
[3] Xylander : ἄλλως γέ πως.

(637) μενον ᾠὸν ἐκ τῆς[1] ἰλύος, ἀλλ' ἐν μόνῳ ζῴῳ τοῦτο
τὴν σύστασιν ἔχει καὶ γένεσιν· ζῷα δὲ καθ' αὑτὰ
μυρία συνίσταται. καὶ τί δεῖ λέγειν τἆλλα; πολλῶν γὰρ ἐγχέλεων ἁλισκομένων οὐδεὶς ἑώρακεν
οὔτε θορὸν οὔτ' ᾠὸν ἔγχελυν ἔχουσαν, ἀλλὰ κἂν
τὸ ὕδωρ τις ἐξαρύσῃ καὶ τὴν ἰλὺν ἀναξύσῃ πᾶσαν,
F εἰς τὸν τόπον ὕδατος συρρυέντος ἐγχέλεις ζῳογο-
νοῦνται. δεῖ οὖν ὕστερον ἀνάγκῃ γεγονέναι τὸ
θατέρου δεόμενον πρὸς γένεσιν, ᾧ δὲ καὶ νῦν
θατέρου χωρὶς ἄλλως ὑπάρχει συνίστασθαι, τοῦτο
προτερεῖν τῇ ἀρχῇ τῆς γενέσεως. περὶ ἐκείνης
γὰρ ἔστι τῆς πρώτης ὁ λόγος· ἐπεὶ νῦν γε καὶ
νεοττιὰς συντίθησι τὰ πτηνὰ πρὸ τῆς ᾠοτοκίας
καὶ σπάργανα παρασκευάζουσιν αἱ γυναῖκες· ἀλλ'
638 οὐκ ἂν εἴποις καὶ νεοττιὰν ᾠοῦ γεγονέναι πρότερον
καὶ σπάργανα παίδων. 'οὐ γὰρ γῆ,' φησὶν ὁ
Πλάτων, 'γυναῖκα, γῆν δὲ γυνὴ μιμεῖται' καὶ
τῶν ἄλλων θηλέων ἕκαστον. διὸ πρώτην γένεσιν
εἰκός ἐστιν ἐκ γῆς τελειότητι καὶ ῥώμῃ τοῦ γεννῶντος αὐτοτελῆ καὶ ἀπροσδεῆ γενέσθαι, τοιούτων
ὀργάνων καὶ στεγασμάτων καὶ ἀγγείων μὴ δεο-
μένην, ἃ νῦν ἡ φύσις ἐν τοῖς τίκτουσιν ἐργάζεται
καὶ μηχανᾶται δι' ἀσθένειαν.''

[1] τῆς E, and according to Hubert the other Planudean
mss.: γῆς T. Bolkestein approves Hubert's suggestion γῆς
ἢ ἰλύος.

egg has ever been seen to form out of mud, but its formation and production take place in a living creature alone. Yet countless are the living creatures which are self-produced. One need cite only the eel. For many eels have been caught, yet nobody has ever seen one with either seed or egg [a] ; but even if one draws off the water in a place and scrapes up all the mud, eels are produced alive when water collects again.[b] Whatever, then, is in need of another for birth, must necessarily have come into being later ; and what even now can be formed otherwise apart from another, this must have priority in the origin of creation. For our discussion is concerned with that first creation. Birds now prepare nests before they lay their eggs and women make ready baby-garments before the birth of their children, but you would not say that nest existed before egg and garments before children. ' For earth does not imitate woman,' says Plato,[c] ' but woman earth,' as indeed does each of the other females. So it is likely that the first creature was born from earth, fully grown and self-sufficient in the perfection and strength of its parent, the process of birth requiring no such organs, sheaths, and vessels as nature because of weakness now contrives and devises in the parent."

    [a] Aristotle, *Historia Animal.* vi. 14. 14 ; 16. 1.
        [b] Aristotle, *ibid.* vi. 16. 2.
            [c] *Menexenus,* 238 A.

ΠΡΟΒΛΗΜΑ Δ

Εἰ πρεσβύτατον ἡ πάλη τῶν ἀγωνισμάτων

Collocuntur Lysimachus, Plutarchus, Sosicles, Philinus

B   Σωσικλέα τὸν Κορωνῆθεν, Πυθίοις[1] νενικηκότα
ποιητάς, εἰστιῶμεν τὰ ἐπινίκια. τοῦ δὲ γυμνικοῦ
ἀγῶνος ἐγγὺς ὄντος, ὁ πλεῖστος ἦν λόγος περὶ τῶν
παλαιστῶν· πολλοὶ γὰρ ἐτύγχανον ἀφιγμένοι καὶ
ἔνδοξοι. παρὼν οὖν Λυσίμαχος, εἷς τῶν Ἀμφι-
κτυόνων ἐπιμελητής, ἔναγχος ἔφη γραμματικοῦ
τινος ἀκοῦσαι τὴν πάλην ἀρχαιότατον[2] ἀθλημάτων
πάντων ἀποφαίνοντος, ὡς καὶ τοὔνομα μαρτυρεῖν·
ἐπιεικῶς γὰρ ἀπολαύειν τὰ νεώτερα πράγματα κει-
μένων ἐν τοῖς παλαιοτέροις ὀνομάτων· ὥς που καὶ
C τὸν αὐλὸν " ἡρμόσθαι " λέγουσιν καὶ " κρούματα "
τὰ[3] αὐλήματα καλοῦσιν, ἀπὸ τῆς λύρας λαμβάνοντες τὰς προσηγορίας. τὸν οὖν τόπον, ἐν ᾧ γυμνά-
ζονται πάντες οἱ ἀθληταί, παλαίστραν καλοῦσι, τῆς
πάλης[4] κτησαμένης τὸ πρῶτον, εἶτα καὶ τοῖς αὖθις
ἐφευρεθεῖσιν ἐμπαρασχούσης.[5]

Τοῦτ᾽ ἔφην ἐγὼ τὸ μαρτύριον οὐκ ἰσχυρὸν
εἶναι· κεκλῆσθαι γὰρ ἀπὸ τῆς πάλης τὴν παλαίστραν[6] οὐχ ὅτι πρεσβύτατόν ἐστι τῶν ἄλλων, ἀλλ᾽
ὅτι μόνον τῶν τῆς ἀγωνίας εἰδῶν πηλοῦ καὶ
κονίστρας καὶ κηρώματος τυγχάνει δεόμενον· οὔτε
D γὰρ δρόμον οὔτε πυγμὴν ἐν παλαίστραις διαπο-

[1] ἐν Πυθίοις Faehse, Bolkestein.
[2] Bollaan : ἀρχαιοτέραν T, defended by Bolkestein.
[3] Added by Wyttenbach.
[4] τοὔνομα after πάλης deleted by Bases, Paton ; Bolkestein
transposes to next phrase as object of ἐμπαρασχεῖν.
[5] Anonymous : ἐμπαρασχεῖν, defended by Bolkestein.
[6] Basel edition : τῆς παλαίστρας.

158

QUESTION 4

Whether wrestling is the oldest of the sports [a]

Speakers : Lysimachus, Plutarch, Sosicles, Philinus

WE were celebrating the victory of Sosicles of Co-
ronê,[b] who had won the prize over all the poets at the
Pythia. The gymnastic contests being near, most
of the conversation concerned the wrestlers, for it so
happened that many famous ones had come. And
Lysimachus,[c] an epimeletes of the Amphictyons who
was present, said that he had recently heard a gram-
marian show that wrestling, on the evidence even of
the word, was the oldest of all sports, for it is reasonable to assume (he said) that the more recent insti-
tutions make use of terms established for the older.
For example, one says that the pipe is " tuned ' and
the notes of the pipe one calls by the term signifying
" strokes," these locutions being taken from the lyre.
And so one calls " palaestra " the place in which all
athletes exercise, the inference being that wrestling
(palê) occupied it first before sharing it with sports
subsequently invented.

I said that this was not strong evidence ; for the
palaestra (I continued) is not named for wrestling
because this is the oldest of the sports, but because
it alone of the forms of gymnastic contests happens
to require clay, dusting-pit, and ring ; for it is not at
running nor at boxing that one toils away in the

---

[a] Cf. 675 c infra. On the order of institution of the various
games see W. Jaeger, Paedeia (Engl. ed.), i, pp. 206 ff., p. 464,
note 71 ; cf. H. A. Harris, Greek Athletes and Athletics,
particularly p. 24 with note 2.

[b] See i. 2, 618 F supra, and infra, v. 4, 677 D.

[c] Lysimachus only here and in the next Question.

(638) νοῦσιν, ἀλλὰ πάλην[1] καὶ παγκρατίου τὸ περὶ τὰς
κυλίσεις· ὅτι γὰρ μέμικται τὸ παγκράτιον ἔκ τε
πυγμῆς καὶ πάλης, δῆλόν ἐστιν. '' ἄλλως δὲ
πῶς,'' ἔφην, '' λόγον ἔχει τεχνικώτατον καὶ
πανουργότατον τῶν ἀθλημάτων τὴν πάλην οὖσαν
ἅμα καὶ πρεσβύτατον εἶναι; τὸ γὰρ ἁπλοῦν καὶ
ἄτεχνον καὶ βίᾳ μᾶλλον ἢ μεθόδῳ περαινόμενον
αἱ χρεῖαι πρῶτον ἐκφέρουσιν.'' ἐμοῦ δὲ ταῦτ'
εἰπόντος, ὁ Σωσικλῆς, '' ὀρθῶς,'' ἔφη, '' λέγεις,
καὶ συμβάλλομαί σοι πίστιν ἀπὸ τοῦ ὀνόματος·
ἡ γὰρ πάλη μοι δοκεῖ τῷ παλεύειν,[2] ὅπερ ἐστὶ
δολοῦν[3] καὶ καταβάλλειν δι' ἀπάτης, κεκλῆσθαι.''

E   Καὶ ὁ Φιλῖνος, '' ἐμοὶ δ','' εἶπεν, '' ἀπὸ τῆς πα-
λαιστῆς[4]· τούτῳ γὰρ μάλιστα τῷ μέρει τοῖν χεροῖν
ἐνεργοῦσιν οἱ παλαίοντες, ὥσπερ οἱ πυκτεύοντες
αὖ πάλιν τῇ πυγμῇ· διὸ κἀκεῖνο πυγμὴ καὶ τοῦτο
πάλη προσηγόρευται τὸ ἔργον. οὐ μὴν ἀλλὰ καὶ τὸ
συμπᾶσαι τῶν ποιητῶν καὶ καταπᾶσαι ' παλῦναι '
λεγόντων, ᾧ μάλιστα χρωμένους τοὺς παλαιστὰς
ὁρῶμεν, ἔστι καὶ ταύτῃ προσάγειν τὴν ἐτυμότητα
τοῦ ὀνόματος. σκόπει δ' ἔτι,'' εἶπεν, '' μὴ τοῖς
μὲν δρομεῦσιν ἔργον ἐστὶν ὅτι πλεῖστον ἀπολιπεῖν
καὶ πορρωτάτω διαστῆναι, τοὺς δὲ πύκτας οὐδὲ πάνυ
βουλομένους ἐῶσιν οἱ βραβευταὶ συμπλέκεσθαι· μό-
F νους δὲ τοὺς παλαιστὰς ὁρῶμεν ἀλλήλους ἀγκαλιζο-
μένους καὶ περιλαμβάνοντας· καὶ τὰ πλεῖστα τῶν
ἀγωνισμάτων, ἐμβολαί, παρεμβολαί, συστάσεις,
παραθέσεις, συνάγουσιν αὐτοὺς καὶ ἀναμιγνύουσιν

---

[1] Wyttenbach : πάλης, defended by Jüthner, Bolkestein.
[2] Basel edition : παλαίειν.   [3] Bernardakis: δόλου.

palaestra, but at wrestling and at the roll-and-tumble
of the pancratium, which is indeed a clear mixture of
boxing and wrestling. " And besides," I said, " how
does it make sense that wrestling, which is the most
skilful and cunning of sports, is at the same time the
oldest too ? For necessity produces first what is
simple, artless, and accomplished by force rather than
systematic skill." When I had spoken, Sosicles said,
" You are right, and I'll offer you confirmation with
an etymology, for ' wrestling ' (palê) seems to me to
be derived from *paleuein*, which means ' to trick,' ' to
overthrow by deceit.' "

And Philinus said, " It seems to me to be derived
from *palaistê*, ' palm,' for it is principally with this part
of the hand that wrestlers operate, as, on the contrary, boxers do with the fist (*pugmê*) ; so the one
activity is called ' boxing' (*pugmê*), the other ' wrestling ' (palê). And there is another possibility : since
the poets say ' besprinkle ' (*palunai*) for ' dusting '
and ' powdering,' of which we see wrestlers (*palaistai*)
make much use, it is possible also in this way to derive the true meaning of the word. Consider again,"
he said, " is it not the task of runners to distance
each other as much as possible, to put the maximum
amount of space between each other ? And boxers [a]
are not allowed by referees to clinch, however eager
they may be ; it is only the wrestlers we see laying
hold of each other and embracing each other,—most
parts of the contest, frontal and lateral attacks, frontal
and lateral stances, bring them together and mix
them up with each other. Clearly the inference is that

---

[a] *Cf.* Harris, *op. cit.* pp. 97 f. and p. 103 with note 59.

[4] Turnebus : τοῦ παλαιστοῦ.

(638) ἀλλήλοις. διὸ τῷ πλησιάζειν μάλιστα καὶ γίγνεσθαι
πέλας οὐκ ἄδηλόν ἐστι τὴν πάλην ὠνομάσθαι.''

639   ΠΡΟΒΛΗΜΑ Ε

Διὰ τί τῶν ἀθλημάτων Ὅμηρος πρῶτον ἀεὶ τάττει τὴν πυγμὴν
εἶτα τὴν πάλην καὶ τελευταῖον τὸν δρόμον

Collocuntur Lysimachus, Timo, Menecrates, Plutarchus,
alii

1. Ῥηθέντων δὲ τούτων καὶ τὸν Φιλῖνον ἡμῶν
ἐπαινεσάντων, αὖθις ὁ Λυσίμαχος ἔφη, '' ποῖον οὖν
φαίη τις ἂν τῶν ἀγωνισμάτων γεγονέναι πρῶτον;
ἢ τὸ στάδιον, ὥσπερ Ὀλυμπίασιν; . . .''[1] '' . . .
ἐνταῦθα δὲ παρ' ἡμῖν καθ' ἕκαστον ἄθλημα τοὺς
ἀγωνιζομένους εἰσάγουσιν, ἐπὶ παισὶ παλαισταῖς
ἄνδρας παλαιστὰς καὶ πύκτας ἐπὶ πύκταις ὁμοίως
καὶ παγκρατιαστάς· ἐκεῖ δ', ὅταν οἱ παῖδες δι-
B αγωνίσωνται, τότε τοὺς ἄνδρας καλοῦσιν. σκόπει
δὲ μὴ μᾶλλον,'' ἔφη, '' τὴν κατὰ χρόνον τάξιν
Ὅμηρος ἀποδείκνυσιν· πρῶτον γὰρ ἀεὶ πυγμὴ
παρ' αὐτῷ, δεύτερον πάλη, καὶ τελευταῖον ὁ δρόμος τῶν γυμνικῶν ἀεὶ τέτακται.'' θαυμάσας οὖν
Μενεκράτης ὁ Θεσσαλός, '' ὦ Ἡράκλεις,'' εἶπεν,
'' ὅσα λανθάνει ἡμᾶς· εἰ δέ τινα τῶν ἐπῶν ἐστί
σοι πρόχειρα, μὴ φθονήσῃς ἀναμνῆσαι.''

Καὶ ὁ Τίμων, '' ἀλλ' ὅτι μέν,'' εἶπεν, '' αἱ Πατρόκλου ταφαὶ ταύτην ἔχουσι τῶν ἀγωνισμάτων
τὴν τάξιν, ἅπασιν ὡς ἔπος εἰπεῖν ἔναυλόν ἐστιν·
διατηρῶν δὲ τὴν τάξιν ὁμαλῶς ὁ ποιητὴς τὸν μὲν

---

[1] Xylander detected a lacuna here ; Reiske places it before
ἢ τὸ στάδιον.

wrestling (*palê*) got its name from ‘ draw near ’ (*plêsiazein*) and ‘ be close ’ (*pelas*).” [a]

QUESTION 5

Why Homer always arranges a series of athletic sports with boxing first, then wrestling, and last racing

Speakers: Lysimachus, Timon, Menecrates,
Plutarch, others

1. WHEN these words had been spoken and we had praised Philinus, Lysimachus again said, “ What could one say was the first athletic contest, then ? Was it the foot-race, as at Olympia ? . . . . .” [a lacuna of uncertain length] “ . . . here among us they introduce the contestants sport by sport, men wrestlers after boy wrestlers, and likewise for boxers and pancratiasts ; but there the men are called in only when the boys are through. But consider whether it is not rather Homer who displays the temporal order ; for always in his works boxing is listed first among the gymnastic sports, wrestling second, and racing last.” Then Menecrates [b] of Thessaly said in astonishment, “ Heracles, how much escapes us ! If you have any of his verses at hand, do not grudge us the recollection of them.”

“ Well,” said Timon, “ it rings in everyone’s ears, if I may say so, that the athletic contests at the funeral games of Patroclus follow this order. The Poet has made Achilles say to Nestor, consistently

[a] The true etymology is unknown ; see Boisacq, *s.v.* πα-
λαίω.
[b] Otherwise unknown.

(639) Ἀχιλλέα λέγοντα τῷ Νέστορι πεποίηκεν
C   δίδωμι δέ σοι τόδ' ἄεθλον
αὔτως· οὐ γὰρ πύξ γε μαχήσεαι οὐδὲ παλαίσεις,
οὐδέ τ' ἀκοντιστὺν ἐνδύσεαι οὐδὲ πόδεσσι
θεύσεαι·

τὸν δὲ πρεσβύτην ἐν τῷ ἀποκρίνεσθαι παραδολε-
σχοῦντα γεροντικῶς ὅτι
πὺξ μὲν ἐνίκησα Κλυτομήδεα, Οἴνοπος υἱόν,
Ἀγκαῖον δὲ¹ πάλῃ Πλευρώνιον,
Ἴφικλον δὲ πόδεσσι παρέδραμον·

αὖθις δὲ τὸν μὲν Ὀδυσσέα τοὺς Φαίακας προκα-
λούμενον
ἢ πὺξ ἠὲ πάλῃ ἢ καὶ ποσίν,
τὸν δ' Ἀλκίνουν ὑποτιμώμενον
D οὐ γὰρ πυγμάχοι εἰμὲν ἀμύμονες οὐδὲ παλαισταί,
ἀλλὰ ποσὶ κραιπνοῖς θέομεν·

ὡς οὐ κατὰ τύχην ἐκ τοῦ παρισταμένου τῇ τάξει
χρώμενος ἄλλοτ' ἄλλως, ἀλλὰ τοῖς εἰθισμένοις τότε
καὶ δρωμένοις κατὰ νόμον ἐπακολουθῶν· ἑδρᾶτο
δ' οὕτως τὴν παλαιὰν ἔτι τάξιν αὐτῶν διαφυλατ-
τόντων."

2. Παυσαμένου δὲ τοῦ ἀδελφοῦ, τἆλλα μὲν ἔφην
ἀληθῶς λέγεσθαι, τὴν δ' αἰτίαν τῆς τάξεως οὐκ
ἐπήνουν. ἐδόκει δὲ καὶ τῶν ἄλλων τισὶ μὴ πιθανὸν
εἶναι γεγονέναι² τὸ πυκτεύειν καὶ παλαίειν πρότερον
ἐν ἀγῶνι καὶ ἁμίλλῃ τοῦ τροχάζειν, καὶ παρεκά-
λουν ἐξάγειν εἰς τὸ ἀνώτερον. ἔφην δ' ἐκ τοῦ

¹ Added by Xylander.
² γεγονέναι added by Bernardakis here, but after ἀγῶνι by
Wyttenbach. Faehse (and Wilamowitz) proposed προτερεῖν
for πρότερον, omitting γεγονέναι.

preserving the order,

> And so I give this prize to you, for not
> At boxing will you fight, nor will you wrestle,
> Nor enter for the javelin throw, nor run
> A foot-race.[a]

And he made the old gentleman answer garrulously, as old gentlemen will,

> I knocked out Clytomedeus, Oenops's son[b]; and in wrest-
> ling I worsted Ancaeus, son of Pleuron, and Iphicles
> I outran in the foot-race.

Again, he has Odysseus challenge the Phaeacians

> To box, to wrestle, or to race,[c]

and Alcinoüs propose the lesser trial,

> For we are not good boxers, wrestlers we
> Are not, but races swift we run.[d]

He does not make haphazard use of any chance order, now one way and now another, but he follows the customs of that time and the things habitually done. And so it was done, so long as they still preserved the old order."

2. When my brother had finished, I said that the rest of his remarks were true, but I could not commend his explanation of the order. Furthermore, it seemed improbable to some of the others that boxing and wrestling existed earlier than racing in competitive sports, and they invited me to explore the matter further. And I said, extemporizing, that all

---

[a] *Iliad*, xxiii. 620 ff.
[b] *Ibid.* 634 (here and at *Odyssey*, xxi. 144, mss. of Homer vary between Οἴνοπος and Ἥνοπος).   [c] *Odyssey*, viii. 20.
[d] *Ibid.* 246 f.

(639) παραστάντος, ὅτι ταῦτά μοι πάντα μιμήματα
E δοκεῖ καὶ γυμνάσματα τῶν πολεμικῶν εἶναι· καὶ
γὰρ ὁπλίτης ἐπὶ πᾶσιν εἰσάγεται, μαρτυρούμενος
ὅτι τοῦτο τὸ τέλος ἐστὶ τῆς σωμασκίας καὶ¹ τῆς
ἁμίλλης· καὶ τὸ τοῖς νικηφόροις εἰσελαύνουσιν² τῶν
τειχῶν ἐφίεσθαι μέρος διελεῖν καὶ καταβαλεῖν τοιαύτην ἔχει διάνοιαν, ὡς οὐ μέγα πόλει τειχῶν
ὄφελος ἄνδρας ἐχούσῃ μάχεσθαι δυναμένους καὶ
νικᾶν. ἐν δὲ Λακεδαίμονι τοῖς νενικηκόσι στεφα-
νίτας ἀγῶνας ἐξαίρετος ἦν ἐν ταῖς παρατάξεσι
χώρα, περὶ αὐτὸν τὸν βασιλέα τεταγμένους μάχε-
σθαι· καὶ τῶν ζῴων μόνῳ τῷ ἵππῳ μετουσία
στεφάνου καὶ ἀγῶνός ἐστιν, ὅτι μόνος καὶ πέφυκε
καὶ ἤσκηται μαχομένοις παρεῖναι καὶ συμπολεμεῖν.

F   "Εἰ δὲ δὴ ταῦτα λέγεται μὴ κακῶς, ἤδη σκοπῶμεν," ἔφην, " ὅτι τῶν μαχομένων πρῶτον ἔργον
ἐστὶ τὸ πατάξαι καὶ φυλάξασθαι, δεύτερον δὲ
συμπεσόντας ἤδη καὶ γενομένους ἐν χερσὶν ὠθι-
σμοῖς τε χρῆσθαι καὶ περιτροπαῖς ἀλλήλων, ᾧ δὴ
μάλιστά φασιν ἐν Λεύκτροις τοὺς Σπαρτιάτας ὑπὸ
640 τῶν ἡμετέρων, παλαιστρικῶν ὄντων, καταβιασθη-
ναι³· διὸ καὶ παρ' Αἰσχύλῳ τις τῶν πολεμικῶν
ὀνομάζεται ' βριθὺς ὁπλιτοπάλας ' καὶ Σοφοκλῆς
εἴρηκέ που περὶ τῶν Τρώων ὡς

  ' φίλιπποι καὶ κερουλκοί,
  σὺν σάκει ' δὲ ' κωδωνοκρότῳ παλαισταί '.

---

¹ τὸ after καὶ deleted by Stephanus.
² Salmasius : ἐλαύνουσιν.   ³ Wyttenbach : καταβιβασθῆναι.

ᵃ See Jüthner in *RE*, *s.v.* " Hoplites," 3.
ᵇ Cf. *Life of Lycurgus*, xxii. 4.
ᶜ As the Spartans, deliberately, were not ; *cf. Mor.* 233 E,
no. 27.

these sports seemed to me to mimic warfare and to train for battle ; indeed, the race in armour is presented after all the rest,[a] so testifying that military fitness is the aim of athletics and competition. Also the fact that victorious athletes, as they enter the city, are permitted to destroy and throw down a part of the walls, has some such meaning : a city which possesses men able to fight and conquer has no great need of walls. In Lacedaemon there was a specially chosen place in the battle-line for those who had won the victor's wreath in the Games, namely, to fight stationed beside the king himself[b] ; and among animals the horse alone participates in crown and contest because it alone is fitted by nature and training to accompany fighters and to go to war together with them.

" If my statement of the analogy is right so far," I continued, " let us consider the matter further. The first task of fighters is to strike out and to defend themselves. And their next task, when they are now met in hand-to-hand conflict, is to strain body against body and overthrow each other. By this especially, it is reported, the Spartans at Leuctra were overpowered by our men who were practised wrestlers[c] ; and so it is that in Aeschylus one of the men-of-arms is called ' a weighty wrestler-in-armour '[d] and Sophocles somewhere said of the Trojans that they are ' lovers of the horse, drawers of the bow,' and ' wrestlers with a clanging shield.'[e] And finally the

---

[d] Aeschylus in Hiller-Crusius, *Anth. Lyr.* p. 124, no. 4 ; Bergk, *Poet. Lyr. Graec.* ii, p. 242, frag. 5 ; Diehl[2] i, p. 79, no. 4 ; LCL Aeschylus, frag. 270, more fully quoted at *Mor.* 317 E, 334 D, and *Compar. of Demosth. and Cicero.*

[e] Frag. 775 Nauck, 859 Pearson.

(640) καὶ μὴν ἐπὶ πᾶσί γε τὸ τρίτον ἐστὶν νικωμένους
φεύγειν ἢ διώκειν νικῶντας. εἰκότως οὖν ἡ πυγμὴ
προεισῆγε,[1] δευτέραν δ᾽ εἶχεν ἡ πάλη τάξιν, καὶ
τελευταίαν ὁ δρόμος· ὅτι πυγμὴ μέν ἐστι μίμημα
πληγῆς καὶ φυλακῆς, πάλη δὲ συμπλοκῆς καὶ ὠθι-
σμοῦ, δρόμῳ δὲ μελετῶσι φεύγειν καὶ διώκειν.''

ΠΡΟΒΛΗΜΑ ϛʹ

Διὰ τί πεύκη καὶ πίτυς καὶ τὰ ὅμοια τούτοις οὐκ
ἐνοφθαλμίζεται[2]

Collocuntur Crato, Philo, Soclarus

B   1. Σώκλαρος ἑστιῶν ἡμᾶς ἐν κήποις ὑπὸ τοῦ
Κηφισοῦ ποταμοῦ περιρρεομένοις ἐπεδείκνυτο δένδρα παντοδαπῶς πεποικιλμένα τοῖς λεγομένοις
ἐνοφθαλμισμοῖς[3]· καὶ γὰρ ἐκ σχίνων ἐλαίας ἀνα-
βλαστανούσας ἑωρῶμεν καὶ ῥοιὰς ἐκ μυρρίνης·
ἦσαν δὲ καὶ δρύες ἀπίους ἀγαθὰς ἐκφέρουσαι καὶ
πλάτανοι μηλεῶν δεδεγμέναι καὶ συκαῖ μορεῶν
ἐμβολάδας, ἄλλαι τε μίξεις φυτῶν κεκρατημένων
ἄχρι καρπογονίας. οἱ μὲν οὖν ἄλλοι πρὸς τὸν
C Σώκλαρον ἔπαιζον, ὡς τῶν ποιητικῶν σφιγγῶν
καὶ χιμαιρῶν τερατωδέστερα γένη καὶ θρέμματα
βόσκοντα· Κράτων δὲ προὔβαλεν ἡμῖν διαπορῆσαι
περὶ τῆς αἰτίας, δι᾽ ἣν μόνα τῶν φυτῶν τὰ ἐλα-
τώδη[4] δέχεσθαι τὰς τοιαύτας ἐπιμιξίας οὐ πέφυκεν·

---

[1] Hubert, προῆγε Wyttenbach : πρόεισί γε.
[2] Bernardakis : ἐνοφθαλμιάζεται.
[3] Stephanus : ἐνόφθαλμις T, ἐν ὀφθαλμοῖς E.

soldier's third task is to run away when beaten and to pursue when winning. It is reasonable, therefore, for boxing to lead off the list, for wrestling to have second place, and for racing the last, because boxing mimics attack and defence, wrestling the twisting and struggling of close-quarter combat, and in the foot-race one practises the art of fleeing the battle-field and of pursuing those who do so."

QUESTION 6

Why the fir and the pine and trees like them are not grafted [a]

Speakers : Crato, Philo, Soclarus

1. SOCLARUS,[b] while entertaining us in his gardens bordered by the Cephissus River, showed us trees which had been fancified in all sorts of ways by what is called grafting; we saw olives growing upon mastic trees and pomegranates upon the myrtle; and there were oaks which bore good pears, plane trees which had received grafts of apples, and figs grafts of mulberries, and other mixtures of trees mastered to the point of producing fruit. Then the rest of the company began to tease Soclarus for raising, as they said, classes and specimens more marvellous than the sphinxes and chimaeras of the poets ; but Crato [c] proposed that we discuss the question of the cause why the evergreens alone of plants do not naturally

---

[a] On grafting see A. S. Pease in *Trans. Amer. Philol. Assoc.* lxiv (1933), pp. 66 ff., esp. pp. 69 f.

[b] For Soclarus see Bolkestein, *Adv. Crit.* p. 128.

[c] See note c, p. 9, above.

---

[4] Pohlenz : ἐλαιώδη.

(640) οὔτε γὰρ κῶνον οὔτε κυπάριττον ἢ πίτυν ἢ πεύκην
ἐκτρέφουσάν τι τῶν ἑτερογενῶν ὁρᾶσθαι.

2. Ὑπολαβὼν δὲ Φίλων ἔφη, '' λόγος τις ἔστιν,
ὦ Κράτων, παρὰ τοῖς σοφοῖς, βεβαιούμενος ὑπὸ
τῶν γεωργικῶν. τὸ γὰρ ἔλαιον εἶναί φασι τοῖς
φυτοῖς πολέμιον καὶ τάχιστ' ἂν ἀπολέσθαι φυτὸν
ὃ βούλοιο χριόμενον ἐλαίῳ, καθάπερ τὰς μελίττας.
τὰ δ' εἰρημένα δένδρα πίονα καὶ πέπειραν ἔχει
D τὴν φύσιν, ὥστε πίσσαν ἀποδακρύειν καὶ ῥητίνην·
ὅταν δὲ πληγῇ, ταῖς διακοπαῖς οἴκοθεν ὥσπερ[1]
ἰχῶρας συνάγει· ἥ τε δὰς αὐτῶν ἐλαιηρὰν ἀφίησιν
ἰκμάδα καὶ περιστίλβει τὸ λιπαρὸν αὐτῇ· διὸ καὶ
πρὸς τὰ ἄλλα γένη δυσμίκτως ἔχει, καθάπερ αὐτὸ
τὸ ἔλαιον.'' παυσαμένου δὲ τοῦ Φίλωνος, ὁ μὲν
Κράτων ᾤετο καὶ τὴν τοῦ φλοιοῦ φύσιν πρὸς τοῦτο
συνεργεῖν· λεπτὸν γὰρ ὄντα καὶ ξηρὸν οὐ παρέχειν
ἕδραν οὐδ' ἐμβίωσιν τοῖς ἐντιθεμένοις, οὐδ',[2] ὥσπερ τὰ φλοιώδη καὶ νοτερὰ καὶ[3] μαλακά, τοῖς ὑπὸ
τὸν φλοιὸν[4] μέρεσι προσδεχομένοις περιπτύσσεσθαι
κολλώμενον.

3. Αὐτὸς δὲ Σώκλαρος ἔφη καὶ τὸν[5] ταῦτα
E λέγοντα μὴ κακῶς προσεννοεῖν, ὅτι δεῖ τὸ δεχό-
μενον ἑτέραν φύσιν εὔτρεπτον εἶναι, ἵνα κρατηθὲν
ἐξομοιωθῇ καὶ μεταβάλῃ τὴν ἐν ἑαυτῷ τροφὴν
πρὸς τὸ ἐμφυτευόμενον. '' καὶ γὰρ τὴν γῆν

---

[1] Wilamowitz : ὥσπερ οἴκοθεν.
[2] οὐδ', ὥσπερ P. A. C., οὐχ ὥσπερ Hubert : ὥσπερ.
[3] τὰ after καὶ omitted by Reiske, Hubert.
[4] ὄντα after φλοιὸν omitted by Reiske.
[5] τὸν added by Reiske ; Bolkestein prefers either to omit
τὸν or to insert it after ταῦτα.

---

[a] The conifer (presumably) that Plutarch meant by kônos

accept such mixtures, for (he said) neither *konos* [a] nor cypress, pine or fir, does one see supporting a scion of another species.

2. Philo said in answer, " The learned have an account of the matter, Crato, and farmers confirm it. For they say that oil is inimical to plants, and what plant you like, touched with oil, would very quickly perish [b]—just like bees. The trees mentioned are naturally fat and full of sap, so that they ooze pitch and resin ; when they are struck, they collect in the cuts a juice, as it were from within themselves ; the kindling-wood split from them emits an oily liquid, and the fatty substance in it glitters ; and so it is that they are bad mixers with other woods, like oil itself." When Philo finished, Crato advanced his notion that the nature of the bark also contributed to this end ; for (he said) since the bark is thin and dry, it does not offer the scion an environment maintaining life, nor does it cleave to the scion, as do moist and soft bark-like substances, bedding it in the parts beneath the bark that receive it."

3. Soclarus himself said that one who spoke thus possessed no mediocre power of observation, seeing that it is necessary for the plant used as stock for another kind to be easily changed so that it may be dominated [c] and assimilated and transform for the scion the nourishment in itself. " Indeed, we first

is obscure. In elegiacs attributed to Plato the tree is part of an idyllic setting (if Scaliger rightly emended κῶμον to κῶνον): *Anth. Plan.* 13 = Diehl, *Anth. Lyr. Graec.* i³ (1949), p. 108, 27 (Bergk 25), with notes. See Hort's Theophrastus, *Enquiry into Plants* (LCL), ii, Index *s.vv.* πίτυς, πεύκη.

[b] *Cf.* Plato, *Protagoras*, 334 в : olive oil is highly injurious to all plants and to the hair of animals.

[c] *Cf.* the theory of digestion at iii. 6. 2, 654 в, and iv. 1. 2, 661 в *infra.*

(640) προδιαλύομεν καὶ μαλάσσομεν, ἵνα κοπεῖσα μεταβάλῃ δι᾽ εὐπάθειαν καὶ ἅψηται τῶν ἐμφυτευο-
μένων· ἡ γὰρ ἀτενὴς καὶ σκληρὰ δυσμετάβλητος.
ταῦτα δὲ τὰ δένδρα κοῦφα¹ τοῖς ξύλοις ὄντα
κρᾶσιν οὐ ποιεῖ διὰ τὸ μὴ κρατεῖσθαι μηδὲ μεταβάλλειν. ἔτι δ᾽,'' εἶπεν, '' οὐκ ἄδηλον ὅτι δεῖ
πρὸς τὸ ἐμφυτευόμενον χώρας λόγον ἔχειν τὸ
δεξόμενον· τὴν δὲ χώραν δεῖ θήλειαν ἔχειν καὶ
γόνιμον· ὅθεν τὰ πολυκαρπότατα τῶν φυτῶν . . .²
F ἐκλεγόμενοι παραπηγνύουσιν, ὥσπερ γυναιξὶν πολυ-
γαλακτούσαις³ ἕτερα βρέφη⁴ προσβάλλοντες. πεύκην δὲ καὶ κυπάριττον καὶ τὰ τοιαῦτα πάντα
641 γλίσχρα καὶ ἀγεννῆ τοῖς καρποῖς ὁρῶμεν. ὥσπερ
γὰρ οἱ πολυσαρκίᾳ κεχρημένοι καὶ ὄγκῳ ὡς ἐπὶ
τὸ πλεῖστον ἄτεκνοι (τὴν γὰρ τροφὴν εἰς τὸ σῶμα
καταναλίσκοντες οὐ ποιοῦσιν ἐξ αὐτῆς περίττωμα
σπερματικόν), οὕτω τὰ τοιαῦτα δένδρα τῆς τροφῆς
ἀπολαύοντα, πάσης εἰς αὐτὰ δαπανωμένης, εὐσω-
ματεῖ τοῖς μεγέθεσι καὶ αὐξάνεται, καρπὸν δὲ τὰ
μὲν οὐ φέρει τὰ δὲ φέρει μικρὸν καὶ συντελούμενον
βραδέως· ὥστ᾽ οὐ δεῖ θαυμάζειν, εἰ μὴ φύεται
τἀλλότριον, ἐν ᾧ κακῶς τρέφεται καὶ τὸ οἰκεῖον.''

¹ κωφὰ Herwerden, Hubert, '' insensitive.''
² Lac. 4-7 T: ἐμβολάσιν Hubert, '' for grafts,'' or the like,
προσεκλεγόμενοι Bernardakis.

break up the earth and soften it so that, having been tilled, it may undergo a transformation by reason of its adaptability and cling to what we plant, for tight, hard earth undergoes transformation with difficulty. But these trees, their wood being light, do not make combinations because they are not dominated nor do they undergo transformation. Further," he continued, " it is quite clear that the stock to be grafted fulfils the function of soil for the scion ; soil and stock must be fertile and productive, and so they select the most fruitful of plants and insert the scions in them, much like putting infants out to nurse with women who have abundant milk. But fir and cypress and all such trees are niggardly and ungenerous with their fruit, as we see. For just as those who are fleshy and heavy are for the most part childless (because they use up their nourishment on their bodies and do not create from it a surplus for seed),[a] so such trees, having the enjoyment of their nourishment all spent on themselves, thrive and increase in size, but some bear no fruit and others bear fruit that is small and slow to ripen. Accordingly, one must not be amazed if another's does not grow in what nourishes poorly even its own."

[a] *Supra*, 637 B, D ; *infra*, 724 E ; *Mor.* 919 c ; Aristotle, *De Gen. Animal.* i. 18. 57-59.

---

[3] Cobet : lac. 5-6 γαλακτούσαις.
[4] Xylander : lac. 7-8.

(641)

ΠΡΟΒΛΗΜΑ Ζ

Περὶ τῆς ἐχενηίδος

Collocuntur Chaeremonianus, Plutarchus, alii

B 1. Χαιρημονιανὸς[1] ὁ Τραλλιανὸς ἰχθυδίων ποτὲ
παντοδαπῶν παρατεθέντων ἐν ἐπιδείξας ἡμῖν ὀξὺ
τῷ κεφαλίῳ καὶ πρόμηκες ἔλεγε τούτῳ προσεοι-
κέναι τὴν ἐχενηίδα· θεάσασθαι γὰρ πλέων ἐν τῷ
Σικελικῷ καὶ θαυμάσαι τὴν δύναμιν, οὐκ ὀλίγην
βραδυτῆτα καὶ διατριβὴν παρὰ τὸν πλοῦν ἀπερ-
γασαμένης τῆς ἐχενηίδος, ἕως ὑπὸ τοῦ πρῳρέως
ἑάλω προσεχομένη τῷ τοίχῳ τῆς νεὼς ἔξωθεν.
ἦσαν μὲν οὖν οἱ καταγελῶντες τοῦ Χαιρημονιανοῦ
ὡς πλάσμα μυθῶδες παραδεδεγμένου καὶ ἄπιστον,
ἦσαν δὲ καὶ οἱ τὰς ἀντιπαθείας θρυλοῦντες, καὶ
ἄλλα πολλὰ ⟨καὶ δὴ καὶ ταῦτα περὶ τῶν ἀντι-⟩
παθόντων[2] ἦν ἀκούειν, ὅτι μαινόμενον ἐλέφαντα
C καταπαύει κριὸς ὀφθείς, ἔχιδναν δὲ φηγοῦ κλωνίον
ἐὰν προσαγάγῃς καὶ θίγῃς ἵστησιν· ἄγριος δὲ
ταῦρος ἀτρεμεῖ καὶ πραΰνεται συκῇ προσδεθείς·
τὸ δ' ἤλεκτρον πάντα κινεῖ καὶ προσάγεται τὰ
κοῦφα πλὴν ὠκίμου καὶ τῶν ἐλαίῳ βρεχομένων·
ἡ δὲ σιδηρῖτις λίθος οὐκ ἄγει τὸν σίδηρον, ἂν
σκόρδῳ χρισθῇ. τούτων γὰρ ἐμφανῆ τὴν πεῖραν
ἐχόντων, χαλεπὸν εἶναι τὴν αἰτίαν, εἰ μὴ καὶ
παντελῶς ἀδύνατον, καταμαθεῖν.

---

[1] Χαιρήμων Reiske ; cf. RE, s.v. " Plutarchos," col. 671.
[2] Added by Diels.

---

[a] A sucking-fish (remora), Pliny, Nat. Hist. ix. 79 ; D'Arcy
Thompson, Glossary of Greek Fishes, pp. 68-70, where the
evidence is summarized.

[b] Only here, but the commoner name Chaeremon (cf.

QUESTION 7

Concerning the echeneïs [a]

Speakers : Chaeremonianus, Plutarch, others

1. Once, when small fish of all sorts were served to us, Chaeremonianus [b] of Tralles pointed out one with a sharp, elongated head and said that the echeneïs resembled it ; he had seen (he said) the echeneïs while sailing off Sicily and had been amazed at its power, for during the course of the voyage it had been responsible for no little loss of speed and delay until the look-out had caught it sticking to the outer face of the vessel's hull. At this, some laughed at Chaeremonianus for accepting a mythical and unbelievable fabrication ; others chatted about the " antipathies " [c] ; and one could hear much else and also the following about things antipathetic : the sight of a ram stops a mad elephant ; if you point an oak twig at a viper and touch it, the viper is brought to a standstill ; a wild bull is quieted and made gentle if bound to a fig-tree [d] ; amber moves and attracts all light things, except basil and whatever is wet with oil ; the loadstone does not attract iron rubbed with garlic. Indeed these things are subject to a clear test, but it is hard (they said) to determine the cause, if not altogether impossible.

critical note) may be the right reading ; a man of this name is honoured for restoring (ὤρθωσε) Tralles after an earthquake (Appendix to *Palatine Anthology*, Tauchnitz, 1829, no. 222, p. 381).

   [c] Bolus of Mendes, the forger of Democritus exposed by Callimachus, wrote a *Sympathies and Antipathies* (in nature) ; see Diels, *Frag. d. Vorsokratiker*, Demokritos 300. 1-5 ; *cf. infra*, iv. 2, 664 c.

   [d] *Cf. infra*, 696 f, where the theory is different.

(641)   2. Ἐγὼ δὲ τοῦτο μὲν ἔφην ἀπόδρασιν εἶναι τῆς
ἐρωτήσεως μᾶλλον ἢ τῆς αἰτίας ἀπόδοσιν. '' σκοπῶμεν δ','' εἶπον, '' ὅτι πολλὰ συμπτώματος[1]
ἔχοντα φύσιν[2] αἰτιῶν λαμβάνει δόξαν οὐκ ὀρθῶς·
D ὅμοιον ὡς εἴ τις οἴοιτο τῇ ἀνθήσει τοῦ ἄγνου
πεπαίνεσθαι τὸν τῆς ἀμπέλου καρπόν, ὅτι δή,[3]
τοῦτο τὸ λεγόμενον,

ἤ τ'[4] ἄγνος ἀνθεῖ χὡ[5] βότρυς πεπαίνεται,

ἢ τοῖς ἐπὶ τῶν λύχνων φαινομένοις μύκησι συγ-
χεῖσθαι καὶ συννεφεῖν τὸ περιέχον, ἢ[6] τὴν γρυπότητα τῶν ὀνύχων αἴτιον ἀλλὰ μὴ συμβεβηκὸς
εἶναι τοῦ περὶ σπλάγχνον ἕλκους. ὥσπερ οὖν
τούτων ἕκαστον ἐπακολούθημα τοῦ πάθους ἐστὶν
ἐκ τῶν αὐτῶν γεννώμενον αἰτιῶν, οὕτως ἔφην ἐγὼ
μίαν αἰτίαν εἶναι δι' ἣν βραδέως τε πλεῖ καὶ
προσάγεται τὴν ἐχενηίδα τὸ πλοῖον· ξηρᾶς μὲν
γὰρ οὔσης καὶ μὴ[7] σφόδρα βαρείας ὑγρότητι τῆς
νεώς, εἰκὸς ἐπολισθάνουσαν[8] ὑπὸ κουφότητος τῇ θα-
E λάττῃ τὴν τρόπιν διαλαβεῖν[9] τὸ κῦμα ξύλῳ[10] καθαρῷ
διαιρούμενον καὶ[11] ἀφιστάμενον εὐπετῶς· ὅταν δὲ
νοτερὰ σφόδρα καὶ διάβροχος οὖσα φυκία τε πολλὰ
καὶ βρυώδεις ἐπιπάγους προσάγηται, τοῦ τε ξύλου
τὸν τόμον ἀμβλύτερον ἴσχει τό τε κῦμα τῇ γλι-
σχρότητι προσπῖπτον οὐ ῥᾳδίως ἀπολύεται. διὸ
καὶ παραψήχουσι τοὺς τοίχους, τὰ βρύα καὶ τὰ
φυκία τῶν ξύλων ἀποκαθαίροντες, οἷς εἰκός ἐστι

---

[1] Wilamowitz, συμπτωμάτων Madvig, Paton : συμπτώματα.
[2] φύσιν Wilamowitz, Paton, τάξιν Madvig : lac. 4 σιν.
[3] Basel edition : δεῖ.
[4] Added by Emperius.
[5] Xylander : καὶ ὁ.
[6] Added by the Basel edition.

2. I remarked that all this avoided the question rather than explained the cause. " Let us reflect," I continued, " that many things essentially accidental wrongly get the reputation of being causes,—as if, for example, one should think that the vine's crop is ripened by the flowering of the chaste tree [*Agnus castus*] because, as they say,

The chaste tree flowers and the grapes get ripe, [a]

or that the snuff which appears on lamps makes the atmosphere muggy and cloudy, or that crookedness of the nails is the cause rather than a symptom of internal ulcer. As each of these, then, accompanies the condition and is produced by the same causes, so there is one cause, I said, both for the ship's sailing slowly and for attracting to itself the echeneïs ; for when a ship is sound and not exceedingly water-logged, its keel naturally glides lightly through the sea, cleaving the wave which easily parts and makes way for the clean wood; but when a ship is thoroughly soaked with water and accumulates much seaweed and encrustation of laver, its hull offers greater resistance, and the sea, meeting the impediment of the encrustation, does not let the ship pass easily. And so it is that hulls are scraped to clean laver and seaweed off the wood, and it is likely enough

---

[a] *Trag. Graec. Frag.* Nauck, Adespoton 396 ; Diehl, *Anth. Lyr. Graec.* i, fasc. 3, p. 69, no. 7.

[7] Added by Stephanus.
[8] Reiske : ὑπολισθάινουσαν (*sic*).
[9] καὶ after διαλαβεῖν deleted by Wyttenbach, διαβάλλειν καὶ σχίζειν Reiske, διαλαβεῖν καὶ σχίσαι Bolkestein.
[10] Stephanus : lac. 4-5 λῶ.
[11] διαιρούμενον καὶ Stephanus : διαι lac. 7.

(641) τὴν ἐχενηίδα προσισχομένην ὑπὸ τῆς γλισχρότητος
αἴτιον τῆς βραδυτῆτος ἀλλ᾽ οὐκ ἐπακολούθημα τοῦ
τὴν βραδυτῆτα ποιοῦντος αἰτίου νομισθῆναι.''

ΠΡΟΒΛΗΜΑ Η

F   Διὰ τί τοὺς λυκοσπάδας ἵππους θυμοειδεῖς εἶναι λέγουσιν

Collocuntur Plutarchi pater, Plutarchus, alii

Ἵππους λυκοσπάδας οἱ μὲν ἀπὸ τῶν χαλινῶν
τῶν λύκων ἔφασαν ὠνομάσθαι, διὰ τὸ θυμοειδὲς
καὶ δυσκάθεκτον οὕτω σωφρονιζομένους· ὁ δὲ πα-
642 τὴρ ἡμῶν ἥκιστα περὶ τὰς εὑρησιλογίας[1] αὐτο-
σχέδιος ὢν καὶ κεχρημένος ἀεὶ κρατιστεύουσιν
ἵπποις ἔλεγε τοὺς ὑπὸ λύκων ἐπιχειρηθέντας ἐν
πώλοις, ἄνπερ ἐκφύγωσιν, ἀγαθοὺς μὲν ἀποβαίνειν
καὶ ποδώκεις, καλεῖσθαι δὲ λυκοσπάδας. ταῦτα
δὲ πλειόνων αὐτῷ μαρτυρούντων ἀπορίαν αἰτίας
παρεῖχεν, δι᾽ ἣν τὸ σύμπτωμα τοῦτο θυμικωτέρους
καὶ γοργοτέρους ποιεῖ τοὺς ἵππους. καὶ ὁ μὲν
πλεῖστος ἦν λόγος τῶν παρόντων, ὅτι φόβον τὸ
πάθος οὐ θυμὸν ἐνεργάζεται τοῖς ἵπποις, καὶ
γιγνόμενοι ψοφοδεεῖς καὶ πρὸς ἅπαν εὐπτόητοι τὰς
ὁρμὰς ὀξυρρόπους καὶ ταχείας ἴσχουσιν, ὥσπερ
τὰ λινόπληκτα[2] τῶν θηρίων. ἐγὼ δὲ σκοπεῖν
B ἔφην χρῆναι, μὴ τοὐναντίον ἐστὶ τοῦ δοκοῦντος·
οὐ γὰρ[3] γίγνεσθαι δρομικωτέρους τοὺς πώλους,
ὅταν ἐκφύγωσι τὰς βλάβας τῶν θηρίων ἐπιχειρη-
θέντες, ἀλλ᾽ οὐκ ἂν ἐκφυγεῖν, εἰ μὴ φύσει θυμικοὶ

---

[1] εὑρησιλογίας Paton (also a reviewer in *Class. Rev.* xxxii
[1918], pp. 150-153) : ἰσηγορίας.

that the echeneïs, attached to this sticky material, has come to be considered the cause of the vessel's slowness rather than a consequence of the actual factor responsible for the slowness."

QUESTION 8

Why horses bitten by wolves are said to be mettlesome

Speakers : Plutarch's father, Plutarch, others

SEVERAL gentlemen said that the term *lycospades* applied to horses is derived from " wolf-bit," for this is the type of bit used to control horses that are mettlesome and hard to hold ; but father, a skilful man indeed at finding an argument and one who always possessed the very best horses, said that colts attacked by wolves, if they escape, turn out to be fine, swift horses and are called *lycospades* (" wolf-bitten "). When many of the company testified to the truth of his statement of the matter, he proposed the question of the reason why this mischance makes horses more mettlesome and spirited. Most of the talk of the company was to the effect that the experience engenders in the horses fear, not spirit ; they become timid and skittish at everything, and so are sudden and quick in their movements, like net-shy wild animals. For my part, I said that one must consider whether the fact is not the opposite of what is thought to be the case. Actually colts do not become faster runners by escaping harm when attacked by wild animals, but they would not have escaped unless they had been

---

² λινόληπτα Naber (Helmbold, *Class. Phil.* xxxvi [1941], p. 87).　　³ οὐ γὰρ Stephanus : ὅτι.

(612) καὶ ταχεῖς ἦσαν· οὐδὲ¹ γὰρ τὸν Ὀδυσσέα γενέσθαι
φρόνιμον ὑπεκδράντα τοῦ Κύκλωπος, ἀλλ' ὅτι
τοιοῦτος ἦν ὑπεκδρᾶναι.

ΠΡΟΒΛΗΜΑ Θ

Διὰ τί τὰ λυκόβρωτα τῶν προβάτων τὸ κρέας μὲν γλυκύτερον
τὸ δ' ἔριον φθειροποιὸν ἴσχει

Collocuntur Patrocleas, Plutarchus, alii

Μετὰ τοῦτο περὶ τῶν λυκοβρώτων ἐζητεῖτο²
προβάτων, ἃ λέγεται τὸ μὲν κρέας γλυκύτατον
C παρέχειν τὸ δ' ἔριον φθειροποιόν. οὐ φαύλως οὖν
ἐδόκει Πατροκλέας ὁ γαμβρὸς ἐπιχειρεῖν περὶ
τῆς γλυκύτητος, ὡς τοῦ θηρίου τῷ δήγματι τὴν
σάρκα τακερὰν ποιοῦντος· καὶ γὰρ εἶναι τὸ πνεῦμα
τοῦ λύκου περίθερμον οὕτω καὶ πυρῶδες, ὥστε τὰ
σκληρότατα τῶν ὀστῶν ἐν τῇ κοιλίᾳ τήκειν καὶ
καθυγραίνειν· διὸ καὶ σήπεσθαι τὰ λυκόβρωτα τῶν
ἄλλων τάχιον. περὶ δὲ τῶν ἐρίων διηπορούμεν,
μήποτ' οὐ γεννᾷ τοὺς φθεῖρας ἀλλ' ἐκκαλεῖται,
τραχύτητός τινος ἀμυκτικῆς ἢ θερμότητος ἰδιότητι
διακρίνοντα τὴν σάρκα· ταύτην δὲ τοῖς ἐρίοις τὴν
D δύναμιν ἐγγίγνεσθαι³ πρὸς τὸ τοῦ λύκου δῆγμα καὶ
τὸ πνεῦμα μεταβάλλοντος ἄχρι τῶν τριχῶν τοῦ
σφαττομένου.

Καὶ συνεβάλλετο τῷ λόγῳ πίστιν ἡ ἱστορία·
τῶν γὰρ κυνηγῶν καὶ τῶν μαγείρων ἐπιστάμεθα

¹ Stegmann : οὔτε.   ² Xylander : ἐξηγεῖτο.
³ Stephanus : οὐ γινεσθαι.

naturally spirited and fast. It was not his escape from Cyclops that made Odysseus clever, but because he was so, he did escape.

QUESTION 9

Why sheep bitten by wolves have a sweeter
flesh, but a wool which breeds lice

Speakers : Patrocleas, Plutarch, others

AFTER the preceding conversation, our inquiry turned to sheep which have been bitten by wolves ; these are said to supply the sweetest flesh, but a wool which breeds lice. And Patrocleas, a relative of mine, offered what seemed a not bad explanation of the sweetness, namely, that the bite of the animal makes the flesh tender. The fact is (he continued) the wolf's temper is so very hot and fiery that the hardest of bones melt and dissolve in its belly and so the flesh of sheep bitten by wolves decomposes more quickly than that of others. About the wool we were in doubt : perhaps the wool does not breed the lice but evokes them out of the animal, separating the flesh by means of a kind of lacerating roughness or characteristic heat ; and this power is generated in the wool (we reasoned) because even the hair of the slaughtered sheep is changed by the bite and temper [a] of the wolf.

And observation supported theory ; for we know that some hunters and cooks fell animals with one

---

[a] According to the Stoics, see G. Soury in *Rev. Ét. Anc.* xlii (1949), pp. 322 f. ; *cf. infra*, iv. 1. 3, 663 A on "heat in the vital spirit" and *De Tuenda Sanitate*, 130 B, on the relation of breath to body heat.

(642) τοὺς μὲν μιᾷ πληγῇ καταβάλλοντας, ὥστ' ἀπνευστὶ
τὰ πληγέντα[1] κεῖσθαι, τοὺς δὲ πολλαῖς μόγις καὶ
χαλεπῶς ἀναιροῦντας· ὃ δὲ τούτου θαυμασιώτερόν
ἐστι, τοὺς μὲν τοιαύτην ἐνιέντας μετὰ τοῦ σιδήρου
τῷ τιτρωσκομένῳ δύναμιν, ὥστε ταχὺ σήπεσθαι
καὶ μηδὲ πρὸς μίαν ἡμέραν ἀντέχειν, τοὺς δ'
ἀποκτείνοντας μὲν οὐ βράδιον ἐκείνων, οὐδὲν δὲ
τοιοῦτο γιγνόμενον περὶ τὴν σάρκα τῶν σφαγέντων
E ἀλλ' ἐπὶ χρόνον διαμένουσαν. ὅτι δ' αἱ κατὰ τὰς
σφαγὰς καὶ τοὺς θανάτους τῶν ζῴων μεταβολαὶ
μέχρι δερμάτων καὶ τριχῶν καὶ ὀνύχων διατείνου-
σιν, ὑποδηλοῦν[2] καὶ Ὅμηρον εἰωθότα λέγειν[3] ἐπὶ
τῶν δερμάτων καὶ τῶν ἱμάντων,[4] '' ἱμὰς[5] βοὸς
ἶφι κταμένοιο ''· τῶν γὰρ μὴ νόσῳ μηδὲ γήρᾳ
διαλυομένων ἀλλ' ὑπὸ σφαγῆς εὔτονον τὸ δέρμα
καὶ στιφρὸν[6] γίγνεσθαι· τὰ δ' ὑπὸ θηρίων δηχθέντα
καὶ τοὺς ὄνυχας μελαίνεσθαι καὶ τριχορροεῖν καὶ
τοῖς δέρμασι φλιδᾶν καὶ ῥακοῦσθαι.

ΠΡΟΒΛΗΜΑ Ι

Πότερον οἱ παλαιοὶ βέλτιον ἐποίουν πρὸς μερίδας ἢ οἱ νῦν ἐκ
κοινοῦ δειπνοῦντες

Collocuntur Hagias, Lamprias, alii

F 1. Ὅτε τὴν ἐπώνυμον ἀρχὴν ἦρχον οἴκοι, τὰ
πλεῖστα τῶν δείπνων δαῖτες ἦσαν, ἐν ταῖς θυσίαις

[1] So g, Stephanus : πνιγέντα.
[2] Stephanus : ἀποδηλοῦν.
[3] καὶ Ὅμηρον εἰωθότα λέγειν Wilamowitz: εἰωθότα λέγειν καὶ Ὅμηρος.
[4] ὅτι φησὶν after ἱμάντων deleted by Bernardakis.
[5] ἱμὰς deleted by Bernardakis. Homer : ῥῆξεν ἱμάντα.
[6] στιφρὸν Anonymous, Turnebus : στριφνόν.

blow, so that the victims lie lifeless, while others scarcely succeed in killing them with many blows ; and some, more amazingly still, with their knife inject into their victim the quality of quick decomposition, so that the meat is not preserved even for one day [a] ; but others kill not less quickly than these, yet no such thing happens to the flesh of the slaughtered animals, which continues for a time in a good state of preservation. And we know that Homer implies that changes conditioned by the manner of the killing and death of animals extend to their skins, their hair, and their claws or hooves, for in regard to skins and hides he has the habit of saying

hide of an ox who was felled with a powerful blow [b] ;

for strong and hard is the skin of those who die not of disease or age but by slaughter ; and when they are bitten by wild beasts, their hooves turn black, their hair falls out, and their skin becomes swollen with moisture and wrinkled.

QUESTION 10

Whether people of old did better with portions served to each, or people of to-day, who dine from a common supply

Speakers : Hagias, Lamprias, others

1. WHEN I was holding the eponymous archonship [c] at home, most of the dinners were portion-banquets,

---

[a] Cf. infra, vi. 10.
[b] Iliad, iii. 375. Cf. the Proclan scholium on Hesiod, Works and Days, 541-542 (Pertusi, p. 178).
[c] Volkmann i, p. 53 ; RE, s.v. " Plutarchos," col. 657 ; infra, vi. 8. 1, 693 F.

(642) ἑκάστῳ μερίδος ἀποκληρουμένης· ὅ τισι μὲν ἤρεσκε
θαυμαστῶς, οἱ δ' ὡς ἀκοινώνητον καὶ ἀνελεύθερον
ψέγοντες ᾤοντο δεῖν ἅμα τῷ καταθέσθαι τὸν
στέφανον ἐπὶ τὴν συνήθη δίαιταν αὖθις μεθαρμό-
σασθαι τὰς τραπέζας. "οὐ γὰρ τοῦ φαγεῖν," ὁ
643 Ἁγίας ἔφη, " χάριν οὐδὲ τοῦ πιεῖν, ἀλλὰ τοῦ
συμπιεῖν καὶ συμφαγεῖν ὡς ἐγᾦμαι καλοῦμεν
ἀλλήλους, ἡ δ' εἰς μερίδας αὕτη κρεωδαισία τὴν
κοινωνίαν ἀναιροῦσα πολλὰ δεῖπνα ποιεῖ καὶ πολλοὺς δειπνοῦντας, οὐδένα δὲ σύνδειπνον οὐδενός,
ὅταν ὥσπερ ἀπὸ κρεωπωλικῆς τραπέζης σταθμῷ
λαβὼν ἕκαστος μοῖραν ἑαυτῷ πρόθηται. καίτοι
τίν' ἔχει διαφορὰν[1] κύλικα καταθέντα τῶν κεκλημένων ἑκάστῳ καὶ χοῦν, ἐμπλησάμενον[2] οἴνου,
καὶ τράπεζαν ἰδίαν, ὥσπερ οἱ Δημοφωντίδαι τῷ
Ὀρέστῃ λέγονται, πίνειν κελεῦσαι μὴ προσέχοντα
B τοῖς ἄλλοις, ἢ τοῦθ' ὅπερ νῦν γίγνεται, κρέας προ-
θέμενον καὶ ἄρτον ὥσπερ ἐκ φάτνης ἰδίας ἕκαστον
εὐωχεῖσθαι, πλὴν ὅτι μὴ πρόσκειται σιωπῆς[3] ἡμῖν
ἀνάγκη, καθάπερ τοῖς τὸν Ὀρέστην ξενίζουσιν;

" Ἀλλὰ καὶ τοῦτ' ἴσως αὐτὸ πρὸς τὴν ἁπάντων
κοινωνίαν ἐκκαλεῖται τοὺς συνόντας, ὅτι καὶ λόγῳ
κοινῷ πρὸς ἀλλήλους χρώμεθα καὶ ᾠδῇ ψαλτρίας
τε τερπούσης καὶ αὐλητρίδος ὁμοίως μετέχομεν·
καὶ ὁ κρατὴρ οὗτος ὅρον οὐκ ἔχων ἐν μέσῳ
πρόκειται, πηγὴ φιλοφροσύνης ἄφθονος καὶ μέτρον

---

[1] ἢ after διαφορὰν deleted by Reiske.
[2] Stephanus : ἐπικλησάμενον.   [3] Meziriacus : σιωπὴ.

---

[a] Hagias, not otherwise identified, takes part also in iii. 7.

and each man at the sacrifices was allotted his share of the meal. This was wonderfully pleasing to some, but others blamed the practice as unsociable and vulgar and thought the dinners ought to be restored again to the customary style when my term as archon was over. " For in my opinion," said Hagias,[a] " we invite each other not for the sake of eating and drinking, but for drinking together and eating together, and this division of meat into shares kills sociability and makes many dinners and many diners with nobody anybody's dinner-companion when each takes his share by weight as from a butcher's counter and puts it before himself. Again how does placing a cup before each guest and a pitcher full of wine and his own table (as the Demophontidae [b] are said to have done for Orestes) and bidding him drink without heed to the others, differ from entertaining him in the manner which now prevails, serving him meat and bread as though from his individual manger, except that no compulsion to silence lies upon us as upon those who entertained Orestes ?

" Now the fact that we do engage in conversation with each other and enjoy alike the song of a delightful harp-girl or pipe-girl is perhaps the very thing that invites the company to general fellowship ; and the mixing-bowl here, limitless, is set in our midst an ever-flowing spring of delight, and its

---

[b] Demophon was the son of Celeus whom Demeter would have immortalized by fire ; either he (Athenaeus, x, 437 c-d) or his sons wished to keep Orestes before his trial from participating with others in the rites and libations of the Choes at the Anthesteria ; thus was explained the custom of all drinking from separate vessels at this festival. See Euripides, *Iphigenia in Tauris*, 947 ff. and *cf.* Schmid-Stählin, *Gesch. Gr. Lit.*, III, p. 527, note 4 ; see also above, p. 10, note *c*.

(643) ἔχουσα τῆς ἀπολαύσεως τὴν ὄρεξιν· οὐχ ὥσπερ
ἡ τοῦ κρέως καὶ τοῦ ἄρτου μερὶς ἀδικωτάτῳ[1]
μέτρῳ καλλωπίζεται τῷ ἴσῳ πρὸς ἀνίσους· τὸ
C γὰρ αὐτὸ τῷ μικροῦ[2] δεομένῳ πλέον ἐστὶν τῷ δὲ
μείζονος ἔλαττον. ὥσπερ οὖν, ὦ ἑταῖρ᾽, ὁ[3] κάμ-
νουσι πολλοῖς ἴσα φάρμακα μέτροις ἀκριβέσι καὶ
σταθμοῖς διανέμων παγγέλοιος, οὕτω τοιοῦτος
ἑστιάτωρ οἷος ἀνθρώπους οὔτε διψῶντας ὡσαύτως
οὔτε πεινῶντας εἰς ταὐτὸ συναγαγὼν ἀπὸ τῶν
ἴσων θεραπεύειν ἅπαντας, ἀριθμητικῶς οὐ γεωμε-
τρικῶς ὁρίζων τὸ δίκαιον. εἰς καπήλου μὲν οὖν
φοιτῶμεν ἑνὶ χρώμενοι μέτρῳ τῷ δημοσίῳ πάντες·
ἐπὶ δεῖπνον[4] δ᾽ ἕκαστος ἰδίαν ἥκει γαστέρα κομίζων,
ἣν οὐ τὸ ἴσον ἀλλὰ τὸ ἀρκοῦν ἐμπίπλησι.

" Τὰς δ᾽ Ὁμηρικὰς[5] ἐκείνας δαῖτας οὐ χρὴ μετα-
D φέρειν ἐκ τῶν στρατιωτικῶν καὶ παρεμβολικῶν
ἐνταῦθα δείπνων, ἀλλὰ μᾶλλον τὴν τῶν παλαιῶν
φιλανθρωπίαν ζηλοῦν, οὐ μόνον ὁμεστίους οὐδ᾽
ὁμωροφίους ἀλλὰ καὶ ὁμοχοίνικας καὶ ὁμοσιπύους[6]
τῷ πᾶσαν σέβεσθαι κοινωνίαν ἐν τιμῇ τιθεμένων.[7]
τὰ μὲν οὖν Ὁμήρου δεῖπνα χαίρειν ἐῶμεν· ὑπο-
λιμώδη γάρ ἐστι καὶ διψαλέα καὶ τοὺς ἑστιάρχας
βασιλεῖς ἔχοντα τῶν Ἰταλικῶν δεινοτέρους καπή-

---

[1] Hubert, Wilamowitz : ἀδικωτάτη.
[2] Basel edition : μικρῷ.
[3] Added by Stephanus.
[4] Vulcobius : δείπνῳ.
[5] Leonicus : ὀμβρικὰς.
[6] ὁμοσιπύους Scaliger (cf. Bolkestein, Adv. Crit. p. 136) :
ὁμοσίτους.
[7] Hubert, Hartman : τιθεμένους.

---

[a] See Plato, Republic, viii, 558 c, with Adam's note : Laws,
757 A.

measure of enjoyment is one's appetite; it does not,
like the division of meat and bread, pride itself upon
what is in fact a most unjust measure, the distribution
of equal portions to men who are actually unequal in
their capacities [a]; for the same amount is too much
for a man who requires little, too little for one who
requires more. It follows, friend,[b] that, just as one
is ridiculous who prescribes with precise weights and
measures an equal amount of drugs for many sick
men, so is the sort of host who brings to the same fare
men neither thirsty nor hungry in the same degree
and serves all alike, with an arithmetical instead of
geometrical determination of what suits them.[c] When
we go to the grocery, we all use the same official
measure, but to a dinner-party each man brings his
own stomach, and it is filled quite full not by the portion equal to that of others, but by the portion which
suffices it.

" Those portion-banquets of Homer we must not
introduce here from the military messes of the camps,
but rather emulate the kindliness of the men of long
ago, who, because they respected all companionship
with one's fellows, held in honour not only those who
shared their hearth and roof but also those who
shared their ration-measure and their meal-tub. Let
us then renounce Homer's dinners; for they are
dinners to leave one a bit hungry and thirsty, and
the kings who preside over them are more dreadful

[b] Friend = Plutarch himself, likely enough. See Cherniss
in LCL *Mor.* xii, p. 48, note *a*.
[c] See Adam on *Republic*, 558 c, *supra*, note *a*; Plato,
Laws, 757 c, and especially *Gorgias*, 508 A, with now E. R.
Dodds's note, which cites *inter alia* Aristotle, *Eth. Nic.* 1131
b 13 and Plutarch, *infra*, viii. 2. 2, 719 B, and *De Fraterno
Amore*, 484 B. See LCL *Mor.* ix, p. 123, note *e*.

(643) λων, ὥστε παρὰ τὰς μάχας, ἐν χερσὶ τῶν πολεμίων
ὄντων, ἀπομνημονεύειν ἀκριβῶς, πόσον ἕκαστος
τῶν δεδειπνηκότων παρ' αὐτοῖς πέπωκε· τὰ δὲ
Πινδαρικὰ βελτίω δήπουθεν, ἐν οἷς

E   ἥρωες αἰδοίαν ἐμίγνυντ' ἀμφὶ τράπεζαν θαμὰ[1]

τῷ κοινωνεῖν ἁπάντων ἀλλήλοις. ἐκεῖνο γὰρ ἦν
οἷον ἀνάμιξις καὶ σύγκρασις ἀληθῶς, τοῦτο δὲ
διαίρεσις καὶ διαβολὴ τῶν φιλτάτων εἶναι δοκούντων, ὡς μηδ' ὄψου κοινωνεῖν δυναμένων."
     2. Ἐπὶ τούτοις εὐδοκιμήσαντι τῷ Ἁγίᾳ Λαμ-
πρίαν[2] παρωξύναμεν ἐπιθέσθαι. ἔλεγεν οὖν οὐ[3]
ξένον τι πεπονθέναι πάθος Ἁγίαν, εἰ τὴν ἴσην
μερίδα λαμβάνων δυσκολαίνει, γαστέρα φορῶν
τηλικαύτην· καὶ γὰρ αὐτὸς εἶναι τῶν ἀδηφαγίᾳ
χαιρόντων· " ἐν γὰρ ξυνῷ ἰχθύι ἄκανθαι οὐκ
ἔνεισιν " ὥς φησιν ὁ Δημόκριτος. " ἀλλὰ τοῦτ'
αὐτό," ἔφη, " καὶ μάλιστα τὴν μοῖραν ὑπὲρ
F εἱμαρμένην ἡμῖν ἐπήγαγεν. ἰσότητος γάρ, ἣν

πόλεις τε πόλεσι συμμάχοις τε συμμάχους

ἡ Εὐριπίδειος γραῦς φησι συνδεῖν, οὐδὲν[4] οὕτως
ὡς ἡ περὶ τράπεζαν κοινωνία δεῖται, φύσει κοὐ[5]
νόμῳ καὶ ἀναγκαίαν οὐ καινὴν οὐδ' ἐπείσακτον

---

[1] Stephanus : ἥρως αἰδοῖ ἀνεμίγνυτο ἀμφὶ τράπεζαν θ' ἅμα.
[2] Λαμπρίαν added by Hubert from 635 A.
[3] Added by Meziriacus.
[4] οὖν after οὐδὲν deleted by Reiske, Wyttenbach.
[5] Bernardakis, καὶ οὐ Xylander : καὶ.

---

[a] Bolkestein, *Adv. Crit.* p. 136, cites a scholium (Σ A) on

than Italian inn-keepers: in battle, in hand-to-hand
combat with the enemy, they remember accurately
how much each man who dined with them drank.[a]
Clearly the banquets of Pindar are better where

About the noble table heroes often met [b]

all sharing everything with each other. That was
really like fellowship and communion ; but this is to
divide and put at enmity men held to be great friends,
on the ground that they are not able to share even in
meat."

2. We praised Hagias for his remarks, then urged
Lamprias to attack him. He began by remarking
that it was not strange for Hagias to experience some
irritation at receiving portions equal to those of the
rest, for the belly he carried around was so big; and
indeed he numbered himself (he added) among those
who like to eat their fill, " for there are no bones in a
fish shared with another," as Democritus says.[c] " But
this liking is the very thing," he continued, " which
has brought us to the custom of serving people more
than their share. Euripides's old woman says that
equal treatment

City with city entwines and ally with ally,[d]

and nothing is so in need of that quality as company at table ; their need is natural and not facti-
tious, fundamental and not a novelty introduced by

Iliad, iv. 345, which may be the basis for Plutarch's treatment
of Homer's Agamemnon here. In Homer (*Iliad*, iv. 343 ff.)
Agamemnon does not actually count the glasses or the viands
consumed.   [b] Frag. 187 (p. 277 Snell).
  [c] Frag. 151 Diels. No offence where the observer shares
the fault, as Bolkestein, *Adv. Crit.* pp. 136 f., argues.
  [d] *Phoenissae*, 537, quoted also at *Mor.* 481 A.

(643) ὑπὸ δόξης ἔχουσα χρείαν· τῷ πλέονα δ' ἐκ τῶν
κοινῶν ἐσθίοντι ' πολέμιον καθίσταται ' τὸ καθ-
644 υστεροῦν καὶ ἀπολειπόμενον, ὥσπερ ἐν ῥοθίῳ
ταχυναυτούσης τριήρους. οὐ γὰρ φιλικὸν οὐδὲ
συμποτικὸν οἶμαι προοίμιον εὐωχίας ὑφόρασις καὶ
ἁρπασμὸς καὶ χειρῶν ἅμιλλα καὶ διαγκωνισμός,
ἀλλ' ἄτοπα καὶ κυνικὰ καὶ τελευτῶντα πολλάκις
εἰς λοιδορίας καὶ ὀργὰς οὐ κατ' ἀλλήλων μόνον
ἀλλὰ καὶ κατὰ τῶν τραπεζοκόμων καὶ κατὰ τῶν
ἑστιώντων.

" Ὅσον δὲ χρόνον ἡ Μοῖρα καὶ ἡ Λάχεσις
ἰσότητι τὴν περὶ τὰ δεῖπνα καὶ συμπόσια κοινωνίαν
ἐβράβευον, οὐθὲν ἰδεῖν ἄκοσμον ἦν οὐδ' ἀνελεύ-
θερον· ἀλλὰ καὶ τὰ δεῖπνα ' δαῖτας ' ἐκάλουν καὶ
τοὺς ἑστιωμένους ' δαιτυμόνας,' ' δαιτροὺς ' δὲ τοὺς
B τραπεζοκόμους ἀπὸ τοῦ διαιρεῖν καὶ διανέμειν.
Λακεδαιμόνιοι δὲ κρεωδαίτας εἶχον οὐ τοὺς τυχόν-
τας ἀλλὰ τοὺς πρώτους ἄνδρας, ὥστε καὶ Λύσαν-
δρον ὑπ' Ἀγησιλάου τοῦ βασιλέως ἐν Ἀσίᾳ
κρεωδαίτην ἀποδειχθῆναι. τότ' οὖν αἱ νεμήσεις
ἐξέπεσον, ὅτ' ἐπεισῆλθον αἱ πολυτέλειαι τοῖς
δείπνοις· οὐ γὰρ ἦν οἶμαι πέμματα καὶ κανδύλους
καὶ καρυκείας ἄλλας τε παντοδαπὰς ὑποτριμμάτων
καὶ ὄψων παραθέσεις διαιρεῖν, ἀλλ' ἐξηττώμενοι
τῆς περὶ ταῦτα λιχνείας καὶ ἡδυπαθείας προήκαντο
τὴν ἰσομοιρίαν. τεκμήριον δὲ τοῦ λόγου τὸ[1] καὶ

_____
[1] Added by Hubert.

_____
[a] Euripides, *Phoenissae*, 539.

fashion. Those who eat too much from the dishes that belong to all antagonize [a] those who are slow and are left behind as it were in the wake of a swift-sailing ship. For suspicion, grabbing, snatching, and elbowing among the guests do not, I think, make a friendly and convivial prelude to a banquet ; such behaviour is boorish and crude and often ends in insults and angry outbursts aimed not only at fellow-guests, but at waiters and at hosts.

" However, nothing unseemly or unbecoming a gentleman could be seen so long as the goddesses Portion and Lot presided with equity over dinners and drinking-parties. Moreover, dinners were called ' distributions,' [b] the guests ' those to whom distribution is made,' and waiters ' distributors ' because they tend to the division and distribution of the food. And the Lacedaemonians had ' distributors of meat ' ; the incumbents of this office were not nobodies but the foremost men ; even Lysander [c] during the Asia campaign accepted from King Agesilaüs appointment as ' distributor of meat.' The custom of distributing portions of the meat was abandoned when dinners became extravagant ; for it was not possible, I suppose, to divide fancy cakes and Lydian puddings and rich sauces and all sorts of other dishes made of ground and grated delicacies [d] ; these luxurious dainties got the better of men and the custom of an equal share for all was abandoned. And the proof of my asserta-

[b] *Cf.* Athenaeus, i, 12 c, *Odyssey*, viii. 98, and *Iliad*, ix. 225. δαιτρός and δαιτυμών *passim* in *Odyssey*, *e.g.* i. 141, iv. 621. See G. Thompson, *Ancient Greek Society*, p. 330.

[c] *Life of Lysander*, xxiii ; *Life of Agesilaüs*, viii. 1 ; but in these accounts Agesilaüs did so in despite. The Asia campaign in question is that of 396–394 B.C.

[d] See *infra* on iv. 1, 664 A.

(644) νῦν ἔτι τὰς θυσίας καὶ τὰ δημόσια δεῖπνα πρὸς
μερίδα γίγνεσθαι διὰ τὴν ἀφέλειαν καὶ καθαριότητα
τῆς διαίτης· ὥσθ' ὁ τὴν νέμησιν[1] ἀναλαμβάνων
C ἅμα συνανασῴζει τὴν εὐτέλειαν.

" ' Ἀλλ' ὅπου τὸ ἴδιον ἔστιν, ἀπόλλυται τὸ
κοινόν '· ὅπου μὲν οὖν μὴ ἴσον ἔστιν· οὐ γὰρ
οἰκείου κτῆσις ἀλλ' ἀφαίρεσις ἀλλοτρίου καὶ
πλεονεξία περὶ τὸ κοινὸν ἀδικίας ἦρξε καὶ διαφορᾶς, ἣν ὅρῳ καὶ μέτρῳ τοῦ ἰδίου καταπαύοντες
οἱ νόμοι τῆς ἴσα νεμούσης εἰς τὸ κοινὸν ἀρχῆς καὶ
δυνάμεως ἐπώνυμοι γεγόνασιν. ἐπεὶ μηδὲ στέφανον ἀξίου διανέμειν ἡμῖν ἑκάστῳ τὸν ἑστιῶντα
μηδὲ κλισίας καὶ χώρας, ἀλλὰ κἂν ἐρωμένην τις
ἢ ψάλτριαν ἤκῃ κομίζων, ' κοινὰ τὰ φίλων,' ἵν'
D ' ὁμοῦ[2] πάντα χρήματα ' γίγνηται κατὰ τὸν Ἀνα-
ξαγόραν. εἰ δ' οὐδὲν ἡ τούτων ἰδίωσις ἐπιταράττει τὴν κοινωνίαν τῷ τὰ μέγιστα καὶ πλείστης
ἄξια σπουδῆς εἶναι κοινά, λόγους, προπόσεις,
φιλοφροσύνας, παυσώμεθα τὰς Μοίρας ἀτιμάζοντες
καὶ ' τὸν τῆς τύχης παῖδα κλῆρον ' ὡς Εὐριπίδης
φησίν, ὃς οὔτε πλούτῳ νέμων οὔτε δόξῃ τὸ
πρωτεῖον, ἀλλ' ὅπως ἔτυχεν ἄλλως ἄλλοτε συμ-
φερόμενος τὸν μὲν πένητα καὶ ταπεινὸν ἐπιγαυροῖ

---

[1] So γ: νέμεσιν.
[2] Wilamowitz: τά.

---

[a] Cf. Hesiod, Works and Days, 722 f.
[b] See supra, 642 F.
[c] Cf. 743 E, 767 D.

tion is the fact that even now at sacrifices and public banquets, because of the simplicity and frugality of the fare, each guest is still served his equal portion of the meal ; accordingly, whoever restores the custom of serving equal portions is at the same time recovering thrift.[a]

" ' But where each guest has his own private portion, companionship perishes.'[b] This is true where there is not an equitable distribution ; for not the possession of one's own, but the taking of another's and greed for what is common to all began injustice and strife ; this the laws hold in check by limiting and moderating private rights, and their very name they owe to their office and power of equitable distribution in regard to what is common to all. Otherwise, don't count it right for the host to assign us each a crown, couches, and places; but, if someone come bringing his mistress or a harp-girl to the party, don't think it proper for ' all possessions of friends to be common,' [c] in order that 'community of everything' may prevail, as Anaxagoras [d] had it. Private possession in such matters does not disturb the general fellowship, and this is due to the fact that the most important characteristics of a gathering and those worth most serious attention are in fact common, namely, conversation, toasts, and good fellowship ; and so let us stop dishonouring the goddesses of Portion, and ' Lot, child of Luck ' as Euripides calls him,[e] for he gives pre-eminence neither to wealth nor to glory, but, as he chances to fall, now this way, now that, he makes proud the poor and humble man,

[a] Frag. 1, cf. 679 A, infra. Cf. Kirk and Raven's interpretation in Presocratic Philosophers, pp. 368 f.
[e] Frag. 989 Nauck, cf. Mor. 965 E.

(644) καὶ συνεξαίρει[1] γενόμενόν[2] τινος αὐτονομίας, τὸν
δὲ πλούσιον καὶ μέγαν ἐθίζων ἰσότητι μὴ δυσκολαίνειν ἀλύπως σωφρονίζει."[3]

[1] Bernardakis, συνεπαίρει Emperius : οὐκ ἐξαίρει.
[2] Doehner : γενόμενόν.
[3] In T σωφρονίζει and decorative sigla end line 15, fol. 68 r;

exciting him with a taste of independence, while the rich and great he accustoms to bearing equal treatment without ill-temper and so teaches them self-control without giving offence."

---

the latter are repeated in line 16; the heading for Book III occupies line 17.

TABLE-TALK
(QUAESTIONES CONVIVALES)
BOOK III

ΣΥΜΠΟΣΙΑΚΩΝ

ΒΙΒΛΙΟΝ ΤΡΙΤΟΝ[1]

F   Σιμωνίδης ὁ ποιητής, ὦ Σόσσιε Σενεκίων, ἔν
τινι πότῳ ξένον ἰδὼν κατακείμενον σιωπῇ καὶ
μηδενὶ διαλεγόμενον, '' ὦ ἄνθρωπ᾽,'' εἶπεν, '' εἰ
μὲν ἠλίθιος εἶ, σοφὸν πρᾶγμα ποιεῖς· εἰ δὲ σοφός,
ἠλίθιον.'' '' ἀμαθίην γὰρ ἄμεινον,'' ὥς φησιν
Ἡράκλειτος, '' κρύπτειν,'' ἔργον δ᾽ ἐν ἀνέσει καὶ
παρ᾽ οἶνον

645   ὅστ᾽ ἐφέηκε πολύφρονά περ μάλ᾽ ἀεῖσαι,
  καί θ᾽ ἁπαλὸν γελάσαι καί τ᾽ ὀρχήσασθαι ἀνῆκεν,
  καί τι ἔπος προέηκεν, ὅπερ τ᾽ ἄρρητον ἄμεινον·

οἰνώσεως ἐνταῦθα τοῦ ποιητοῦ καὶ μέθης, ὡς ἐμοὶ
δοκεῖ, διαφορὰν ὑποδεικνύντος. ᾠδὴ μὲν γὰρ καὶ
γέλως καὶ ὄρχησις οἰνουμένοις μετρίως ἔπεισι· τὸ
δὲ λαλεῖν καὶ λέγειν,[2] ἃ βέλτιον[3] ἦν[4] σιωπᾶν,
παροινίας ἤδη καὶ μέθης ἔργον ἐστίν. διὸ καὶ
Πλάτων ἐν οἴνῳ μάλιστα καθορᾶσθαι τὰ ἤθη[5] τῶν

---

[1] The heading πλουτάρχου Συμποσιακῶν Γ′ is followed as
usual in T by the table of contents.
[2] λέγειν Xylander ; βλέπειν καὶ λαλεῖν, comparing '' kiss
and tell,'' Helmbold, *Class. Philol.* xxxvi (1941), p. 87 :
βλέπειν.   [3] ἃ βέλτιον Xylander : ἀβέλτερον.

TABLE-TALK

BOOK THREE

WHEN the poet Simonides at some drinking-party, my dear Sossius Senecio, saw a guest sitting in silence and holding no conversation with anyone, he said, " Sir, if you are a fool, you are doing a wise thing ; but if wise, a foolish thing." As Heraclitus [a] remarks, " it is certainly better to conceal ignorance,"— and it's a task to do so in the relaxation of drinking,

> Which sets a man to sing, though he be wise
> Indeed ; and starts him dancing, softly laughing ;
> And saying words that better were unsaid— [b]

where the poet shows, I think, the difference between exhilaration and drunkenness.[c] For song, laughter, and dancing are characteristic of men who drink wine in moderation ; but babbling and talking about what is better left in silence is at once the work of actual intoxication and drunkenness. Hence Plato,[d] too, holds that most men show their real natures most

---

[a] Frag. 95 Diels, cited also in *Mor.* 43 D, 439 D, and with κρέσσον for ἄμεινον and other slight modifications in Stobaeus, *Florilegium*, iii. 82.
[b] *Odyssey*, xiv. 464 ff., quoted also *Mor.* 503 E.
[c] *Cf.* von Arnim, *Stoic. Vet. Frag.* iii. 712.
[d] *Laws*, i, 649 D f. ; *cf. infra*, 715 F.

---

4 Xylander : ἤ.   5 Bernardakis : πάθη.

(645) πολλῶν νομίζει, καὶ Ὅμηρος εἰπὼν

οὐδὲ τραπέζῃ

γνώτην ἀλλήλων

δῆλός ἐστιν εἰδὼς τὸ πολύφωνον[1] τοῦ οἴνου καὶ
B λόγων[2] πολλῶν γόνιμον. οὐ γὰρ ἔστι τρωγόντων
σιωπῇ καὶ πινόντων γνῶσις· ἀλλ' ὅτι τὸ πίνειν εἰς
τὸ λαλεῖν προάγεται, τῷ δὲ λαλεῖν ἐμφαίνεται[3] καὶ
τὸ ἀπογυμνοῦσθαι πολλὰ τῶν ἄλλως λανθανόντων,
παρέχει τινὰ τὸ συμπίνειν κατανόησιν ἀλλήλων·
ὥστε μὴ φαύλως ἂν ἐπιτιμῆσαι τῷ Αἰσώπῳ· '' τί
τὰς θυρίδας, ὦ μακάριε, ζητεῖς ἐκείνας, δι' ὧν
ἄλλος ἄλλου κατόψεται τὴν διάνοιαν; ὁ γὰρ οἶνος
ἡμᾶς ἀνοίγει καὶ δείκνυσιν οὐκ ἐῶν ἡσυχίαν ἄγειν,
ἀλλ' ἀφαιρῶν τὸ πλάσμα καὶ τὸν σχηματισμόν,
ἀπωτάτω τοῦ νόμου καθάπερ παιδαγωγοῦ γεγονότων.'' Αἰσώπῳ μὲν οὖν καὶ Πλάτωνι, καὶ εἴ
C τις ἄλλος ἐξετάσεως τρόπου δεῖται, πρὸς τοῦτο
χρήσιμον ὁ ἄκρατος· οἱ δὲ μηδὲν ἀλλήλους βασανί-
ζειν δεόμενοι μηδὲ καταφωρᾶν ἀλλ' ἢ χρῆσθαι
φιλοφρόνως, τὰ τοιαῦτα προβλήματα καὶ τοὺς
τοιούτους[4] λόγους ἄγουσι[5] συνιόντες,[6] οἷς ἀπο-
κρύπτεται τὰ φαῦλα τῆς ψυχῆς,[7] τὸ δὲ βέλτιστον
ἀναθαρρεῖ καὶ τὸ[8] μουσικώτατον, ὥσπερ ἐπὶ λει-
μῶνας οἰκείους καὶ νομάς, ὑπὸ φιλολογίας προ-
ερχόμενον. ὅθεν καὶ ἡμεῖς τρίτην δεκάδα ταύτην

---

[1] Hutten : lac. 4 *νον*.
[2] Wyttenbach, omitting πολλῶν : lac. 5.
[3] ἐμφέρεται Ziegler, ἐμφύεται Reiske.
[4] Added by Reiske.
[5] εἰσάγουσι Faehse according to Bolkestein, *Adv. Crit.* p.
79.
[6] Basel edition : συνιόντας.

clearly when they drink, and Homer [a] by saying

> Not even at table came those two
> To knowledge of each other

shows that he understands wine's loquacity and its
engendering of much talk. The fact is there is no
way of getting to know a man who eats and drinks in
silence ; but, since drinking leads to talk, and talking
involves further the laying bare of much that is otherwise hidden, drinking together does give men a
chance to get some understanding of each other. It
follows that one can reproach Aesop [b] rather severely :
" Why, sir, are you looking for those windows through
which one man will discern another's mind ? For wine
reveals us and displays us by not allowing us to keep
quiet ; on the contrary, it destroys our artificial pat-
terns of behaviour, taking us completely away from
convention's tutorship, so to speak." Aesop and
Plato, then,—and any other in need of a method of
examination,—find wine useful for this purpose ; but
those who are under no compulsion to cross-question
each other or to catch each other out, but merely
want friendly entertainment, bring to their meetings
such topics of conversation and such talk as conceal
the mean parts of the soul ; the best and most
civilized part renews its courage, going onward, as it
were, to its proper meadows and pastures shepherded
by literature and learning.[c] And so I have produced for you this third collection of ten topics of

[a] *Odyssey*, xxi. 35 f.

[b] See B. E. Perry, *Aesopica*, i. 100, p. 360 ; Babrius, 59.
11 f. ; Lucian, *Hermotimus*, 20.

[c] *Cf.* Plato, *Phaedrus*, 248 в ; see G. Soury in *Rev. Ét.
Grec.* lxii (1949), p. 326.

<hr>

[7] Turnebus : τύχης.   [8] Basel edition : τὸν.

(645) σοι πεποιήμεθα συμποτικῶν ζητημάτων, τὸ περὶ
τῶν στεφάνων πρῶτον ἔχουσαν.

ΠΡΟΒΛΗΜΑ Α

D

Εἰ χρηστέον ἀνθίνοις στεφάνοις παρὰ πότον[1]

Collocuntur Ammonius, Plutarchus, Erato, Trypho

1. Ἐγένοντο γάρ ποτε καὶ περὶ στεφάνων λόγοι·
τὸ δὲ συμπόσιον ἦν Ἀθήνησιν, Ἐράτωνος τοῦ
ἁρμονικοῦ ταῖς Μούσαις τεθυκότος καὶ πλείονας
ἑστιῶντος. παντοδαπῶν γὰρ μετὰ τὸ δειπνῆσαι
στεφάνων περιφερομένων, ὁ Ἀμμώνιος ἐπέσκωψέ
πως ἡμᾶς ἀντὶ τοῦ δαφνίνου τοῖς ῥοδίνοις
ἀναδησαμένους· ὅλως γὰρ εἶναι τοὺς ἀνθίνους
κορασιώδεις καὶ παιζούσαις μᾶλλον ἐπιτηδείους
παρθένοις καὶ γυναιξὶν ἢ συνουσίαις φιλοσόφων
καὶ μουσικῶν ἀνδρῶν. " θαυμάζω δὲ καὶ Ἐρά-
τωνα τουτονὶ τὰς μὲν ἐν τοῖς μέλεσι παραχρώσεις
E βδελυττόμενον καὶ κατηγοροῦντα τοῦ καλοῦ Ἀγάθωνος, ὃν πρῶτον εἰς τραγῳδίαν φασὶν ἐμβαλεῖν
καὶ ὑπομῖξαι τὸ χρωματικόν, ὅτε τοὺς Μυσοὺς
ἐδίδασκεν, αὐτὸς δ' ἡμῖν ὡς ὁρᾶτε[2] ποικίλων
χρωμάτων καὶ ἀνθηρῶν τὸ συμπόσιον ἐμπέπληκεν,
καὶ τὴν διὰ τῶν ὤτων ἀποκλείει τρυφὴν καὶ
ἡδυπάθειαν, ταύτην τὴν κατὰ τὰ ὄμματα καὶ κατὰ

---

[1] No heading or caption in T, an α´ in the margin.
[2] ὁρᾶθ' ὡς Bernardakis, Hubert.

---

[a] Athenaeus, xv, 669 e ff., has a long, richly illustrated
disquisition on garlands, with several points of contact with
Plutarch.
[b] Erato the musician is present also in *Table-Talk*, ix. 14,
infra, 743 c, with Ammonius, Trypho, Plutarch, and others.

drinking-party inquiries, a collection which has for its first subject the inquiry into garlands.

QUESTION 1

Whether flower-garlands should be used at drinking-parties

Speakers: Ammonius, Plutarch, Erato, Trypho

1. For garlands [a] also were once the subject of our conversation. The party was at Athens where the musician Erato,[b] after a sacrifice to the Muses, was entertaining rather a large number of guests. Now when garlands of all kinds were offered us after dinner, and we put garlands of roses round our heads instead of laurel, Ammonius [c] teased us a bit for doing so, saying that garlands of flowers were quite girlish and more suitable for maids and women at play than for companies of learned and cultivated gentlemen. "And I am astonished at Erato here for hating the use of the chromatic scale in songs and censuring our fine Agathon,[d] the first (so people say) to introduce and blend chromatic music into tragedy when he produced the Mysoi, and yet Erato himself, as you see, has filled our party full of different kinds of flowery colours; and the extravagance and luxury he shuts out when experienced through our ears he

[c] Plutarch's teacher at Athens, Academic philosopher, frequent interlocutor in Plutarch's works, see particularly viii. 3. 1 and Book IX passim; RE, s.v. "Plutarchos," coll. 651 ff.

[d] See supra on 613 D, 632 B, 634 D, infra, 686 D. The tragic poet whose victory is celebrated in Plato's Symposium. The present passage is the only reference to his Mysians known to Nauck, Trag. Gr. Frag. p. 763. He is ridiculed in Aristophanes's Thesmophoriazusae (e.g. 101 ff., 130) for his musical style.

(645) τὰς ῥῖνας ὥσπερ καθ' ἑτέρας θύρας ἐπεισάγων τῇ
ψυχῇ καὶ τὸν στέφανον ἡδονῆς ποιῶν οὐκ εὐ-
σεβείας. καίτοι τό γε μύρον τοῦτο τῆς ἀνθίνης
ταύτης καὶ μαραινομένης ἐν ταῖς χερσὶ τῶν στε-
φανηπλόκων σπουδαιοτέραν ἀναδίδωσιν εὐωδίαν·

F ἀλλ' οὐκ ἔχει χώραν ἐν συμποσίῳ φιλοσόφων ἀνδρῶν ἡδονὴ πρὸς μηδεμίαν συμπεπλεγμένη χρείαν
μηδ' ἀκολουθοῦσα φυσικῆς ὀρέξεως ἀρχῇ. καθάπερ
γὰρ[1] οἱ μὲν ὑπὸ τῶν κεκλημένων ἀγόμενοι φίλων ἐπὶ τὸ δεῖπνον ἔθει φιλανθρώπῳ τυγχάνουσιν
τῶν αὐτῶν, ὥσπερ Ἀριστόδημος ὑπὸ Σωκράτους
εἰς[2] Ἀγάθωνος ἀχθεὶς ἑστιῶντος, εἰ δέ τις ἀφ'
646 αὑτοῦ βαδίζοι, τούτῳ δεῖ τὴν θύραν κεκλεῖσθαι,
οὕτως αἱ μὲν περὶ τὴν ἐδωδὴν καὶ πόσιν ἡδοναὶ
κεκλημέναι ὑπὸ τῆς φύσεως ταῖς ὀρέξεσιν ἑπόμεναι
τόπον ἔχουσιν, ταῖς δ' ἄλλαις ἀκλήτοις καὶ σὺν
οὐδενὶ λόγῳ φιληδονίαις[3] ἀπήλλακται.''[4]

2. Πρὸς ταῦθ' οἱ μὲν ἀήθεις τοῦ Ἀμμωνίου
νεανίσκοι διαταραχθέντες ἡσυχῇ παρελύοντο τοὺς
στεφάνους· ἐγὼ δ' εἰδὼς ὅτι γυμνασίας ἕνεκα καὶ
ζητήσεως καταβέβληκεν ἐν μέσῳ τὸν λόγον ὁ
Ἀμμώνιος, προσαγορεύσας Τρύφωνα τὸν ἰατρόν,
'' ὦ τᾶν, ἢ καταθέσθαι δίκαιος εἶ μεθ' ἡμῶν
τουτονὶ ' τὸν καλύκεσσι[5] φλέγοντα τοῖς ῥοδίνοις
B στέφανον,' ἢ λέγειν, ὥσπερ εἴωθας ἑκάστοτε πρὸς

---

[1] Added by Meziriacus.   [2] Basel edition : καί.
[3] φιληδονίαις Reiske : φιληδονίας.
[4] ἀποκέκλεισται or ἀπαλλακτέον Wyttenbach (the latter with accusative).
[5] Wilamowitz, cf. Clement of Alexandria, *Paedagogus*, ii. 70. 2 ; καλόν τε φλέγονθ' οἷς Helmbold (*loc. cit.*): καὶ lac. 5 T.

introduces into our soul by way of our eyes and noses, as by other doors, and makes our garland a thing for pleasure, not for piety.[a] Yet the perfume of piety yields a more excellent fragrance than this scent of flowers which perishes between the hands of the garland-weavers; besides, at a dinner party of learned men there is no place for pleasure not interwoven with usefulness, not conforming to the rule of natural appetite. For, as guests whom friends, themselves invited, bring along with them to a dinner-party receive by the usage of polite society the same welcome as the invited (for example, Aristodemus whom Socrates brought to Agathon's party),[b] but if a man comes quite on his own, the door must be shut against him, just so the pleasures concerned with food and drink, made welcome by nature because they follow the natural appetites, have a place at our dinner-parties, but for the rest, uninvited and unreasonable luxuries, there is no place left."

2. At this the young men, who were unused to Ammonius, were much embarrassed and quietly began to take off their garlands, but because I knew that Ammonius had tossed the topic into our midst for an exercise in discussion, I turned to Trypho,[c] the physician, and said, "Either it is right for you, Sir, to lay aside, along with us,

> the garland that blazes with rose-buds,

or tell us, as you are accustomed to do on every oc-

---

[a] Cf. F. Bacon, Of Praise: "A good name is like a precious ointment . . . for the odours of ointments are more durable than those of flowers."

[b] Plato, Symposium, 173 B and 174 A ff.

[c] See infra on v. 8. 1, 683 c and ix. 14. 4; RE, s.v. "Plutarchos," col. 668.

(646) ἡμᾶς, ὅσας ἔχουσιν οἱ ἄνθινοι στέφανοι πρὸς τὸ
πίνειν βοηθείας.'' ὑπολαβὼν δ' ὁ Ἐράτων, '' οὕτω
γάρ,'' εἶπεν, '' δέδοκται μηδεμίαν ἡδονὴν ἀσύμ-
βολον δέχεσθαι, ἀλλ' εὐφραινομένους δυσκολαίνειν,
ἂν μὴ μετά τινος μισθοῦ τοῦτο πάσχωμεν; ἢ τὸ
μὲν μύρον εἰκότως ὑποδυσωπούμεθα καὶ τὴν
πορφύραν διὰ τὴν ἐπίθετον πολυτέλειαν ὡς δολερὰ
εἵματα καὶ χρίματα[1] κατὰ τὴν τοῦ βαρβάρου
φωνήν, αἱ δ' αὐτοφυεῖς χρόαι καὶ ὀσμαὶ[2] τὸ ἀφελὲς οὐκ[3] ἔχουσι καὶ καθαρὸν καὶ οὐδὲν ὀπώρας
διαφέρουσιν; μὴ γὰρ εὔηθες ἦ τοὺς μὲν χυμοὺς
δρέπεσθαι καὶ ἀπολαύειν τῆς φύσεως διδούσης,
C ὀσμὰς δὲ καὶ χρόας ἃς αἱ[4] ὧραι[5] φέρουσι, διὰ τὴν
ἐπανθοῦσαν ἡδονὴν ταύταις[6] καὶ χάριν ἀτιμάζειν,
ἂν μή τι χρειῶδες ἔξωθεν ἄλλο συνεπιφέρωσιν.
ἐμοὶ μὲν[7] γὰρ αὐτὸ δοκεῖ τοὐναντίον, εἰ μηδὲν ἡ
φύσις, ὡς ὑμεῖς φατε δήπου,[8] μάτην πεποίηκε,
ταῦτα τῆς ἡδονῆς πεποιῆσθαι χάριν, ἃ μηδὲν
ἄλλο χρήσιμον ἔχοντα μόνον εὐφραίνειν πέφυκεν.
σκόπει δ' ὅτι τοῖς φυομένοις καὶ βλαστάνουσι τὰ
μὲν φύλλα σωτηρίας ἕνεκα τοῦ καρποῦ καὶ ὅπως
ὑπ' αὐτῶν[9] θαλπόμενα καὶ ψυχόμενα μετρίως φέρῃ
τὰς μεταβολὰς γέγονεν, τοῦ δ' ἄνθους ὄφελος
οὐδὲν ἐπιμένοντος, πλὴν εἴ τι χρωμένοις ἡμῖν

---

[1] Cobet, χρίσματα Stephanus : χρώματα.
[2] οὐ after ὀσμαὶ omitted in Basel edition.
[3] οὐκ added by P. A. C.
[4] Hubert, χρόας ἃς Stephanus : χρόας αἷ (not αἱ, as Hubert reports).
[5] Stephanus : ὧραν.
[6] ταύταις Herwerden, Hubert : ταῦτα.
[7] ἐμοὶ μὲν Wilamowitz : lac. 4–5 ἔν.
[8] δήπου Bernardakis : lac. 3-4.
[9] τὰ δένδρα omitted after αὐτῶν by Paton.

casion, in how many ways garlands of flowers benefit us in drinking." Erato interrupted, saying, " Are we indeed decided to receive no pleasure which fails to bring a useful contribution, but even in our merry-making fret about what we experience without profit ? At perfume and purple clothing, because of their excessive costliness, we quite properly look askance as deceitful garments and unguents (to use the foreigner's [a] phrase) ; but do not natural colours and scents have a simplicity and purity exactly like that of fruit ? The fact is, I am afraid it's rather silly to cull and enjoy the condiments nature provides and yet scorn the scents and colours which the seasons bring if they do not contribute something needful, scorning them simply because pleasure and delight flower in them. For I think, on the contrary, that if nature has made nothing without purpose [b] (as you claim, I believe), it is for pleasure's sake that she has made what by their nature only serve to delight us and possess no other useful quality. Consider how growing plants have leaves for the protection of their fruit [c] and for supporting within limits the changes of heat and cold ; but there is no use for the flower while it lasts, except that it offers us, if we avail our-

[a] The king of the Ethiopians in Herodotus, iii. 22. The saying is adapted to Plutarch's purpose here and somewhat differently, if the emendation here is right, in *Mor.* 270 E-F (χρώματα "colours" instead of χρίματα "unguents "). Clement of Alexandria, who has only χρίσματα, attributes the saying to the ancient Lacedaemonians : *Stromateis*, i. 48. 5 (Stählin and Früchtel) and *Paedagogus*, ii. 65. 1 (Stählin).

[b] Aristotle, *Politics*, 1253 a 9 ; Theophrastus, *De Causis Plant.* i. 1. 1. *Cf. infra*, 698 B, 960 E ; Aristotle, *Physics*, ii. 8, 198 b 35 ff. ; and other passages cited by C. J. de Vogel, *Greek Philosophy*, ii, p. 499 ; Ross on *Physics*, 198 b 14 (10) ff.

[c] *Cf.* Aristotle, *Physics*, 199 a 25.

(646)
D ἐπιτερπὲς ὀσφρέσθαι καὶ ἰδεῖν ἡδὺ παρέχει, θαυ-
μαστὰς μὲν ὀσμὰς ἀφιέντα, ποικιλίαν δ' ἀμιμήτοις
χρώμασι καὶ βαφαῖς ἀνοίγοντα.[1] διὸ τῶν μὲν
φύλλων ἀποσπωμένων οἷον ἀλγεῖ καὶ δάκνεται τὰ
φυτὰ καὶ γίγνεται περὶ αὐτὰ βλάβη τις ἑλκώδης
καὶ ψίλωσις ἀπρεπής, καὶ οὐ μόνης ὡς ἔοικε κατ'
Ἐμπεδοκλέα τῆς ' δάφνης τῶν φύλλων ἀπὸ πάμπαν ἔχεσθαι ' χρή, ἀλλὰ καὶ τῶν ἄλλων φείδεσθαι
δένδρων ἁπάντων καὶ μὴ κοσμεῖν ἑαυτοὺς ταῖς
ἐκείνων ἀκοσμίαις, βίᾳ καὶ παρὰ φύσιν τὰ φύλλα
συλῶντας αὐτῶν· αἱ δὲ τῶν ἀνθῶν ἀφαιρέσεις
τρυγήσεσιν ἐοίκασιν καὶ βλάπτουσιν οὐδέν, ἀλλὰ
E κἂν μὴ λάβῃ τις ἐν ὥρᾳ, περιερρύη μαρανθέντα.
καθάπερ οὖν οἱ βάρβαροι τῶν θρεμμάτων τοῖς
δέρμασιν ἀντὶ τῶν ἐρίων ἀμφιέννυνται,[2] οὕτω μοι
δοκοῦσιν οἱ μᾶλλον ἐκ τῶν φύλλων ἢ τῶν ἀνθῶν
ὑφαίνοντες τοὺς στεφάνους οὐ κατὰ λόγον χρῆσθαι
τοῖς φυτοῖς. ἐγὼ μὲν οὖν ταῦτα συμβάλλομαι
ταῖς στεφανοπώλισιν· οὐ γάρ εἰμι γραμματικός,
ὥστ' ἀπομνημονεύειν ποιημάτων, ἐν οἷς τοὺς πα-
λαιοὺς ἱερονίκας ἀναγιγνώσκομεν ἀνθίνοις ἀνα-
δουμένους[3] στεφάνοις· πλὴν ὅτι γε ταῖς Μούσαις ὁ
τῶν ῥόδων στέφανος ἐπιπεφήμισται, μεμνῆσθαί
μοι δοκῶ Σαπφοῦς λεγούσης πρός τινα τῶν
ἀμούσων καὶ ἀμαθῶν γυναικῶν

F
κατθάνοισα δὲ κείσεαι·
οὐ γὰρ πεδέχεις[4] ῥόδων
τῶν ἐκ Πιερίας.[5]

[1] ἀνοίγοντα Turnebus : ἀνοιγόμενα.
[2] Aldine edition : ἀμφιέννυται.
[3] Basel edition : ἀναδουμενοις (sic).
[4] Wyttenbach : πεδέχης.

selves of it, a delightful scent to smell and a sweet sight to see, for flowers emit wonderful scents and open up a tapestry of inimitable colours and hues. But when leaves are plucked, how the plants suffer and are distressed ; a kind of ulcerlike blight comes upon them and an ugly bareness ; and we must, it seems, not only ' rigorously refrain from using the leaves of the laurel ' (to borrow Empedocles's words),[a] but also must spare all other trees and not array ourselves by disarraying them, violently stripping their leaves contrary to nature. But picking flowers is like harvesting grapes, it harms nothing—on the contrary, if one does not gather them when they bloom, they wither and drop off. Those who weave garlands of leaves rather than flowers seem to me to use plants as illogically as outlanders use their domestic animals when they employ their hides for clothing rather than their wool. This, then, is my contribution to the garland trade. I am no literary man to be expected to remember poems where we read of old-time victors in the games wearing crowns of flowers, except that I do seem to recollect that the garland of roses is dedicated to the Muses, for Sappho spoke to some uncultivated and ignorant woman thus :

> Dead shall you lie, for you have no share
> Of the roses that come from Pieria.[b]

[a] Frag. 140 Diels. *Cf.* Kirk and Raven, *Presocratic Philosophers*, p. 224.

[b] Frag. 58 Diehl, i, p. 354 ; frag. 55 Lobel and Page, *Poet. Lesb. Frag.*, p. 40 : a longer excerpt by Plutarch at 146 A, the most extensive by Stobaeus, *Florilegium*, iv. 12 (i. 96 Meineke ; iii. 221 Hense).

---

[5] Πιερίης T. Hubert and Bernardakis adopt Πιερίας from *Mor.* 146 A and Stobaeus, iv. 12.

(646) εἰ δέ τινα καὶ Τρύφων ἀπὸ τῆς ἰατρικῆς δίδωσι
μαρτυρίαν, ἀκουστέον.''

3. Ἐκ τούτου δεξάμενος ὁ Τρύφων τὸν λόγον
οὐδενὸς ἔφη τούτων ἀσκέπτους γεγονέναι τοὺς
παλαιούς, ἅτε δὴ πλείστῃ κεχρημένους ἀπὸ φυτῶν
647 ἰατρικῇ· '' τεκμήρια δ' ἔσθ' ἅτιν'[1] ἔτι νῦν Τύριοι
μὲν Ἀγηνορίδῃ Μάγνητες δὲ Χείρωνι, τοῖς πρώτοις
ἰατρεῦσαι λεγομένοις, ἀπαρχὰς κομίζουσιν· ῥίζαι
γάρ εἰσι καὶ βοτάναι, δι' ὧν ἰῶντο τοὺς κάμνοντας.
ὁ δὲ Διόνυσος οὐ μόνον τῷ τὸν οἶνον εὑρεῖν,
ἰσχυρότατον φάρμακον καὶ ἥδιστον, ἰατρὸς ἐνομίσθη
μέτριος, ἀλλὰ καὶ τῷ τὸν κιττὸν ἀντιταττόμενον
μάλιστα τῇ δυνάμει πρὸς τὸν οἶνον εἰς τιμὴν
προαγαγεῖν καὶ στεφανοῦσθαι διδάξαι τοὺς βακχεύοντας ὡς ἧττον[2] ἀνιῶντο, τοῦ κιττοῦ κατα-
σβεννύντος τὴν μέθην τῇ ψυχρότητι. δηλοῖ δὲ
καὶ τῶν ὀνομάτων ἔνια τὴν περὶ ταῦτα πολυπραγ-
B μοσύνην τῶν παλαιῶν· τήν τε γὰρ καρύαν οὕτως
ὠνόμασαν, ὅτι πνεῦμα βαρὺ καὶ καρωτικὸν ἀφιεῖσα
λυπεῖ τοὺς ὑπ' αὐτῆς παρακεκλιμένους· καὶ τὸν
νάρκισσον ὡς ἀμβλύνοντα τὰ νεῦρα καὶ βαρύτητας
ἐμποιοῦντα ναρκώδεις· διὸ καὶ Σοφοκλῆς αὐτὸν
'' ἀρχαῖον μεγάλων θεῶν στεφάνωμα,'[3] τουτέστι
τῶν χθονίων, προσηγόρευκεν. φασὶ δὲ καὶ τὸ πήγανον ἀπὸ τῆς δυνάμεως ὠνομάσθαι· πήγνυσι γὰρ

---

[1] Wilamowitz : ἔστι τινά.
[2] ὑπὸ τοῦ οἴνου omitted after ἧττον by Wilamowitz and
Castiglioni, transposed after ἀνιῶντο by Doehner.
[3] μεγάλαιν θεαῖν ἀρχαῖον στ. mss. of Sophocles.

---

[a] Agenorides and Cheiron : E. and L. Edelstein, *Asclepius*, ii, p. 96, and i, T 50-T 62 (Cheiron).

But if Trypho, out of his knowledge of medicine, has any testimony to give us, he must be heard."

3. Then Trypho took up the conversation and said that the ancients neglected none of these matters, because, of course, much of their art of medicine depended upon the medicinal properties of plants. " Proof of this are the firstfruits which even now the Tyrians still bring to Agenorides and the Magnetes to Cheiron,[a] said to be the first two practitioners of medicine,—for the gifts are roots and plants with which these two used to treat the sick. And Dionysus was considered a pretty good physician not only for his discovery of wine, a very powerful and very pleasant medicine, but also for bringing into good repute ivy, which is quite opposed to wine in its action, and for teaching his celebrants to wear crowns of ivy that they might suffer less distress, since ivy by its coldness checks intoxication.[b] Some plant names also document the ancients' search for knowledge about these matters. The hazel (karua) they so named because it gives off a heavy and soporific (karôtikon) exhalation harmful to those who lie beneath it, and the narcissus they called by this name because it dulls the nerves and induces a narcotic heaviness,[c] —which is the reason why Sophocles has called it

ancient crown of great divinities,[d]

by which he means the Chthonic Goddesses. Rue (pêganon), too, is said to have been named from its

[b] The same properties were claimed for ivy by Philonides, a physician, and by Apollodorus: Athenaeus, xv, 675 a ff.

[c] This etymology is sound: Boisacq, Dict. étymol., s.v. νάρκισσος. E. H. Warmington notes that the property given for karua suggests walnut.

[d] Oedipus at Colonus, 683 f.

(647) ξηρότητι διὰ θερμότητα τὸ σπέρμα καὶ ὅλως πολέμιόν ἐστι ταῖς κυούσαις. οἱ δὲ καὶ τὴν ἀμέθυ-
στον οἰόμενοι τῷ πρὸς τὰς οἰνώσεις βοηθεῖν αὐτήν
τε καὶ τὴν ἐπώνυμον αὐτῆς λίθον οὕτω κεκλῆσθαι
διαμαρτάνουσιν. κέκληται γὰρ ἀπὸ τῆς χρόας ἑκα-
C τέρα· οὐ γὰρ[1] ἐστιν αὐτῆς τὸ φύλλον ἀκράτῳ[2] ἀλλ'
ἀναίμῳ[3] καὶ ὑδαρεῖ τὴν κρᾶσιν οἴνῳ προσεοικός.[4]
ἀλλὰ μέντοι πάμπολλα λαβεῖν ἔστιν, οἷς παρέσχον
τὰς κλήσεις αἱ δυνάμεις· ἀρκεῖ δὲ κἀκεῖνα τὴν
τῶν παλαιῶν ἐπιμέλειαν ὑποδηλῶσαι καὶ πολυ-
πειρίαν, ἀφ' ἧς ἐχρήσαντο τοῖς παροίνοις στεφάνοις.
μάλιστα μὲν γὰρ ὁ ἄκρατος, ὅταν τῆς κεφαλῆς
καθάψηται καὶ τομεύσῃ[5] τὰ σώματα πρὸς τὰς τῶν
αἰσθήσεων ἀρχάς, ἐπιταράσσει τὸν ἄνθρωπον· αἱ
δὲ τῶν ἀνθῶν ἀπόρροιαι πρὸς τοῦτο θαυμασίως
βοηθοῦσι καὶ ἀποτειχίζουσι τὴν κεφαλὴν ἀπὸ τῆς
D μέθης ὡς ἀκρόπολιν, τῶν μὲν θερμῶν μαλακῶς
ἀναχαλώντων τοὺς πόρους καὶ ἀναπνοὴν τῷ οἴνῳ
διδόντων, ὅσα δ' ἡσυχῇ ψυχρὰ τῷ μετρίως ἐπι-
ψαύειν ἀνακρουομένων τὰς ἀναθυμιάσεις, ὥσπερ ὁ
τῶν ἴων καὶ ῥόδων στέφανος· στύφει γὰρ ἀμφότερα καὶ συστέλλει[6] τῇ ὀσμῇ τὰς καρηβαρίας.
τὸ δὲ τῆς κύπρου ἄνθος καὶ ὁ κρόκος καὶ ἡ βάκκα-
ρις εἰς ὕπνον ἄλυπον ὑπάγει τοὺς πεπωκότας· ἔχει
γὰρ ἀπορροὴν λείαν καὶ προσηνῆ καὶ τὰς περὶ

---

[1] οὐ γάρ Turnebus : lac. 4-5.
[2] Wyttenbach : ἄκρατον.
[3] Hubert : ανινω. [4] Wyttenbach : προσέοικεν.
[5] P. A. C. (Hesychius τομεύουσι· τέμνουσι) ; διετονήσῃ
McDiarmid, comparing Theophrastus, de Sensibus, 7 : το-
νώσῃ.
[6] Xylander, cf. Clement of Alexandria, Paedagogus, ii. 71.
4 : στέλλει.

ability to stiffen (*pégnunai*) [a] the seminal fluid by the desiccating action of heat, and it is altogether harmful to pregnant women.[b] Those who imagine that the herb amethyst and the stone named from it are so called because they are helpful against intoxication [c] are mistaken ; each gets its name from the colour, for the leaf of the herb is not like pure wine in colour, but like a weak and dilute mixture of wine and water. Now one can find very many other things which owe their names to their properties, but even those I have mentioned suffice to document the study and experience upon which the ancients based their use of drinking-party garlands. For pure wine, when it attacks the head and severs body from mind's control, distresses a man ; and the exhalations of flowers are a wonderful help against this and protect the head against drunkenness as walls protect a citadel against attack—for warm flowers by their gentle relaxing action open the body's ducts (*poroi*) [d] and give the wine a vent ; and those which are soothingly cool check the fumes by their temperate touch, as for example the garland made of violets and roses, for the scent of both flowers diminishes and restrains headaches. The flower of henna, the saffron, and the hazelwort lull drinkers into an untroubled sleep, for they have a mild and gentle effluence [e] which quietly

---

[a] Doubtless connected (Boisacq, *s.v.* πήγανον), but not because of the alleged property of the plant.

[b] *Cf.* Pliny, *Nat. Hist.* xx. 143.

[c] Among them Boisacq, at least for the stone (*s.v.* ἀμέθυστος).

[d] On theories concerning *poroi* see *infra*, vi. 2 and 3.

[e] *Cf.* v. 7. 2, 681 A ff. (*aporrhoiai* and *rheumata*) and *cf. pneuma* in vi. 10, 697 B ; on the specific point Clement of Alexandria, *Paedag.* ii. 71, and Pliny, *Nat. Hist.* xxi. 130 ; in relation to heat Aristotle, *De Gen. Animal.* ii. 3. 11 f.

(647) τὸ σῶμα τῶν μεθυσκομένων ἀνωμαλίας καὶ τρα
χύτητας ἡσυχῇ διαχέουσαν, ὥστε γιγνομένης γα
λήνης ἀμβλύνεσθαι καὶ συνεκπέττεσθαι τὸ κραιπα
λῶδες. ἐνίων δ' ἀνθῶν ὀσμαῖς ἄνω σκιδναμέναις
E περὶ τὸν ἐγκέφαλον οἵ τε πόροι τῶν αἰσθητηρίων
ἐκκαθαίρονται καὶ λεπτύνεται τὰ ὑγρὰ πράως
ἄνευ πληγῆς καὶ σάλου τῇ θερμότητι διακρινόμενα,
καὶ φύσει ψυχρὸς ὢν ὁ ἐγκέφαλος ἀναθάλπεται.
διὸ μάλιστα τοὺς ἀνθίνους ἐκ τῶν τραχήλων
καθάπτοντες ' ὑποθυμίδας ' ἐκάλουν, καὶ τοῖς ἀπὸ
τούτων μύροις ἔκριον τὰ στήθη· μαρτυρεῖ δ'
Ἀλκαῖος κελεύων ' καταχέαι τὸ μύρον αὐτοῦ
κατὰ[1] τᾶς πόλλα παθοίσας κεφάλας καὶ[2] τῷ πολίῳ
στήθεος.' οὕτω καὶ ἐντεῦθεν αἱ ὀσμαὶ τοξεύουσιν
ὑπὸ θερμότητος εἰς τὸν ἐγκέφαλον ἁρπαζόμεναι
ταῖς ὀσφρήσεσιν. οὐ γάρ, ὅτι τῇ καρδίᾳ τὸν θυ
F μὸν ἐνστρατοπεδεύειν ᾤοντο, τοὺς περιδεραίους τῶν
στεφάνων ὑποθυμίδας ἐκάλουν (ἐπιθυμίδας γὰρ αὐ
τοῖς διά γε τοῦτο μᾶλλον ἦν καλεῖσθαι προσ
ῆκον[3]), ἀλλ' ὡς λέγω διὰ τὴν ἀποφορὰν καὶ
ὑποθυμίασιν. μὴ θαυμάζωμεν δ' εἰ τοσαύτην αἱ
τῶν στεφάνων ἀποφοραὶ δύναμιν ἔχουσιν· ἱστοροῦσι
γάρ, ὅτι καὶ σκιὰ σμίλακος ἀποκτείνυσιν ἀνθρώ
πους ἐγκαταδαρθόντας, ὅταν ὀργᾷ μάλιστα πρὸς
648 τὴν ἄνθησιν[4]· καὶ τὸ τῆς μήκωνος ἀπορρέον
πνεῦμα μὴ φυλαξαμένοις τοῖς τὸν ὀπὸν τρυγῶσιν

---

[1] κὰτ P. Oxy. 1233, frag. 32, l. 2 (Hunt, *Oxy. Papyri*, x
[1914], p. 65). [2] καὶ κὰτ *ibid.*, l. 3.
[3] Stephanus : προσὸν. [4] Basel edition : αἴσθησιν.

---

[a] *Cf.* Athenaeus, xv, 674 c-d, 678 d ; Alcaeus, Z 39 Lobel
and Page (*Poet. Lesb. Frag.* p. 275).
[b] Frag. 42 Bergk, 86 Diehl, 50 (B 18) Lobel and Page (*op.
cit.* p. 135). Two phrases of this quotation stand in frag. 32

disperses the distempers and exasperations of those who drink freely, with the result that they become calm and the effects of intoxication are blunted and assimilated. The scents of some flowers, as they disperse upward about the brain, clean out the conduits (*poroi*) of the organs of sense, and by their warmth thin and easily separate the humours without violence and shock, and warm the brain, which is cold by nature. That is certainly why men called the wreaths of flowers they hung around their necks " fumigators " (*hypothymides*) [a] and anointed their breasts with the perfumes from them. Alcaeus [b] witnesses to the practice when he utters the command :

> Pour its perfume down upon my head,
> Which has suffered much, and on my greying
> Breast.

Thus even from there scents are caught up by the nostrils and by the influence of heat shoot up into the brain. Now garlands which hang around the neck were not called *hypothymides* because men thought the spirit had its billet in the heart,—for in that event they ought rather to have been called *epithymides*,— but, as I say, their name is due to the fumigating property of the effluence from their flowers. We must not be astonished that the effluences of garlands have such great power ; indeed, it is a matter of record that even the shade of a yew kills men who sleep in it, especially when the tree is bursting into flower ; and it has happened to men engaged in gathering the poppy's juice that they fell into a faint if they did not protect themselves against the exhala-

of No. 1233 of the Oxyrhynchus Papyri, 2nd cent. A.D., and provide evidence that the papyrus is a collection of the poems of Alcaeus.

(648) συνέβη καταπεσεῖν. τὴν δ' ἄλυσσον καλουμένην
βοτάνην καὶ λαβόντες εἰς τὴν χεῖρα μόνον, οἱ δὲ
καὶ προσβλέψαντες, ἀπαλλάττονται λυγμοῦ· λέγεται
δὲ καὶ ποιμνίοις ἀγαθὴ καὶ αἰπολίοις, παραφυτευο-
μένη ταῖς μάνδραις. τὸ δὲ ῥόδον ὠνόμασται
δήπουθεν, ὅτι ῥεῦμα πολὺ τῆς ὀδωδῆς ἀφίησι· διὸ
καὶ τάχιστα μαραίνεται. ψυκτικὸν δ' ἐστὶ δυνάμει
τῇ δ' ὄψει πυρωπόν, οὐκ ἀλόγως· λεπτὸν γὰρ
αὐτῷ περιανθεῖ τὸ θερμὸν ἐπιπολῆς ἐξωθούμενον
ὑπὸ τῆς ψυχρότητος."[1]

B

ΠΡΟΒΛΗΜΑ Β

Περὶ τοῦ κιττοῦ πότερον τῇ φύσει θερμὸς ἢ ψυχρός ἐστιν

Collocuntur Plutarchus, Ammonius, Erato, Trypho

1. Ἐπαινεσάντων δ' ἡμῶν τὸν Τρύφωνα μειδιῶν
ὁ Ἀμμώνιος οὐκ ἄξιον ἔφη ποικίλον οὕτω καὶ
ἀνθηρὸν λόγον ὥσπερ στέφανον ἀντιλέγοντα δια-
λακτίζειν· '' πλὴν ὅ γε κιττὸς οὐκ οἶδ' ὅπως
συγκαταπέπλεκται ψυχρότητι συγκατασβεννύναι[2]
λεγόμενος τὸν ἄκρατον· ἔστι γὰρ ἔμπυρος καὶ
θερμότερος, καὶ ὅ γε καρπὸς αὐτοῦ μιγνύμενος
εἰς τὸν οἶνον μεθυστικὸν ποιεῖ καὶ ταρακτικὸν τῷ
πυροῦσθαι. τὸ δὲ κλῆμα λέγουσιν αὐτοῦ σπώμενον
C ὥσπερ τἀν[3] πυρὶ ξύλα συνδιαστρέφεσθαι. χιὼν δὲ
πολλάκις ἡμέρας συχνὰς ἐπιμένουσα τοῖς ἄλλοις
φυτοῖς φεύγει τάχιστα τὸν κιττόν, μᾶλλον δ'

---

[1] Junius, Xylander : θερμότητος.
[2] κατασβεννύναι Hubert in app. crit.
[3] Doehner : τὰ.

[a] Cf. note e on 647 D.

tion streaming from the poppy. And those who only take into their hands the herb called madwort—and some simply by looking at it—are relieved of hiccupping ; the herb is said also to be good for flocks of sheep and goats when planted beside their folds. And the rose has been so named, I suppose, because it gives off a great stream (*rheuma*) [a] of scent ; this too is the reason why it withers very quickly. In its action the rose is cooling, but in appearance fiery—which is not unreasonable, for its heat glows faintly round the surface of the rose, pushed outward by the cold of its interior."

QUESTION 2

Concerning ivy, whether its nature is hot or cold [b]

Speakers : Plutarch, Ammonius, Erato, Trypho

1. WE praised Trypho, and Ammonius remarked with a smile that it was improper for him by counterargument to kick aside so rich and flowery a speech as if it were a garland. "Except," he continued, " that I do not understand how ivy has come to be connected with coldness and acquire the reputation of mitigating the effect of strong wine. For it is a rather hot plant and a fiery one ; its berries, mixed with wine, inflame the wine and make it intoxicating and deleterious. And people say that a twig of it, when pulled, becomes warped like wood in fire. And snow, which so frequently stays for many days on other plants, very quickly vanishes from ivy ; what

[b] The heat or cold of a plant as " not perceptual, but rational " (R. E. Dengler), is discussed by Theophrastus, *De Causis Plant.* i. 21. 4 ff. *Cf. supra*, 623 E, and note a at 635 c.

(648) ὅλως εὐθὺς ἀπόλλυται καὶ περιτήκεται περὶ αὐτὸν
ὑπὸ θερμότητος.

" Ὁ δὲ μέγιστόν ἐστιν ὑπὸ Θεοφράστου δ'
ἱστόρηται, Ἀλεξάνδρου κελεύσαντος Ἑλληνικὰ
δένδρα τοῖς ἐν Βαβυλῶνι παραδείσοις ἐμβαλεῖν
Ἅρπαλον, μάλιστα δέ, τῶν τόπων ἐμπύρων ὄντων
καὶ περιφλεγόντων, τὰ ἀλσώδη καὶ εὐπέταλα καὶ
σκιερὰ καταμῖξαι τοῖς φυτοῖς, μόνον οὐκ ἐδέξατο
τὸν κιττὸν ἡ χώρα, καίτοι πολλὰ τοῦ Ἁρπάλου
πραγματευομένου καὶ προσφιλονεικοῦντος, ἀλλ' ἀπ-
D ώλλυτο καὶ κατεξηραίνετο, τῷ πυρώδης μὲν αὐτὸς
εἶναι πρὸς πυρώδη δὲ μίγνυσθαι γῆν οὐ λαμβάνων κρᾶσιν ἀλλ' ἐξιστάμενος. αἱ γὰρ ὑπερβολαὶ
φθείρουσι τὰς δυνάμεις· διὸ τῶν ἐναντίων μᾶλλον
ὀρέγονται, καὶ φιλόθερμόν ἐστι τὸ ψυχρὸν καὶ φιλό-
ψυχρον τὸ θερμόν· ὅθεν οἱ ὄρειοι καὶ πνευματώδεις
καὶ νιφόμενοι τόποι τὰ δαδώδη καὶ πισσοτρόφα
τῶν φυτῶν, μάλιστα πεύκας καὶ στροβίλους, ἐκφέρουσιν.

" Ἄνευ δὲ τούτων, ὦ φίλε Τρύφων, τὰ δύσριγα
καὶ ψυχρὰ φυλλορροεῖ, μικρότητι τοῦ θερμοῦ καὶ
ἀσθενείᾳ συστελλομένου καὶ προλείποντος τὸ φυ-
τόν· ἐλαίαν δὲ καὶ δάφνην καὶ κυπάριττον ἀειθαλῆ
E διαφυλάσσει τὸ λιπαρὸν καὶ τὸ θερμὸν ὥσπερ τὸν
κιττόν.[1] ὅθεν ὁ φίλτατος Διόνυσος οὐχ ὡς βοηθὸν
ἐπὶ τὴν μέθην οὐδ' ὡς πολέμιον τῷ οἴνῳ τὸν κιττὸν
ἐπήγαγεν, ὅς γε τὸν ἄκρατον ἄντικρυς ' μέθυ '
καὶ ' μεθυμναῖον ' αὐτὸς αὐτὸν ὠνόμασεν· ἀλλά
μοι δοκεῖ, καθάπερ οἱ φίλοινοι μὴ παρόντος ἀμπε-

---

[1] Turnebus : ὁ κιττός.

is more, in the vicinity of ivy snow is quite swiftly destroyed and melted by the plant's heat.

" The best evidence in support of my opinion is to be found in a story reported by Theophrastus.[a] When Alexander ordered Harpalus to plant Greek trees in the parks in Babylon and to be sure to combine leafy woodland shade-trees among the planted specimens, —for those places are blazing hot,—it was the ivy alone which the soil refused to accept, though Harpalus took much trouble and was persistent in his effort. But the ivy withered and died, for, being itself hot and being combined with a hot soil, it did not accept acclimatization, but rejected it. Indeed, excessive amounts of a given property destroy it utterly ; that is why opposites are more attracted to each other, and cold is heat-loving, heat cold-loving. This explains the fact that resinous, pitch-yielding trees, particularly pine and fir, grow in mountainous terrain exposed to wind and snow.

" Apart from this, my dear Trypho, frost-sensitive, cold-natured trees shed their leaves because they have a small amount of weak heat, which diminishes and forsakes the tree ; the olive, the laurel, and the cypress are kept evergreen by their oil and their heat, as is the ivy. And so our beloved Dionysus, who frankly named unmixed wine 'intoxicant' and himself 'Intoxicator,'[b] did not introduce ivy as a specific against drunkenness or as something inimical to wine. Rather it seems to me that, just as lovers

---

[a] *Hist. Plant.* iv. 4. 1 ; Pliny, xvi. 144, notes that ivy is native to Asia; *cf.* Strabo, xv. 1. 58. 711 f., and *RE*, v. 2830.

[b] *Cf.* Athenaeus, viii, 363 b, where *methy* and the epithet of the god, *Methymnaios*, are explained as " relaxing, letting oneself go." Plutarch has the right of the matter (*cf.* Boisacq, *s.v.* μέθυ).

(648) λίνου κριθίνῳ χρῶνται πόματι, καὶ μηλίτας τινάς,
οἱ δὲ φοινικίνους οἴνους ποιοῦσιν, οὕτω καὶ ὁ[1]
ποθῶν χειμῶνος ὥρᾳ[2] τὸν ἀπὸ τῆς ἀμπέλου
στέφανον, ὡς ἐκείνην ἑώρα γυμνὴν καὶ ἄφυλλον,
ἀγαπῆσαι τὴν ὁμοιότητα τοῦ κιττοῦ. καὶ γὰρ τοῦ
κλήματος τὸ ἑλικῶδες τοῦτο καὶ σφαλλόμενον ἐν
F τῇ πορείᾳ καὶ τοῦ πετάλου τὸ ὑγρὸν καὶ περι-
κεχυμένον ἀτάκτως, μάλιστα δ' αὐτὸς ὁ κόρυμβος
ὄμφακι πυκνῷ καὶ περκάζοντι προσεοικώς, ἐκμε-
μίμηται τὴν τῆς ἀμπέλου διάθεσιν. οὐ μὴν ἀλλὰ
κἂν βοηθῇ τι πρὸς μέθην ὁ κιττός, θερμότητι
τοῦτο ποιεῖν φήσομεν αὐτὸν ἀνοίγοντα τοὺς πόρους
ἢ συνεκπέττοντα μᾶλλον τὸν ἄκρατον, ἵνα καὶ μένῃ
σὴν χάριν, ὦ Τρύφων, ἰατρὸς ὁ Διόνυσος."
2. Πρὸς ταῦθ' ὁ μὲν Τρύφων ἄφωνος ἦν, ὅπως
649 ἀντείποι σκεπτόμενος· ὁ δ' Ἐράτων ἕκαστον ἡμῶν
τῶν νέων ἀνακαλούμενος ἐκέλευε βοηθεῖν τῷ
Τρύφωνι[3] ἢ τοὺς στεφάνους ἀποτίθεσθαι· καὶ Ἀμμώνιος ἔφη παρέχειν ἄδειαν, οὐ γὰρ ἀντερεῖν οἷς
ἂν ἡμεῖς εἴπωμεν. οὕτω δὴ καὶ τοῦ Τρύφωνος
ἐπικελεύοντος εἰπεῖν ἔφην ὅτι[4] τὸ μὲν ἀποδεῖξαι[5]
ψυχρὸν εἶναι τὸν κιττὸν οὐκ ἐμὸν ἦν ἔργον, ἀλλὰ
Τρύφωνος· οὗτος[6] γὰρ αὐτῷ ψύχοντι καὶ στύφοντι
πολλὰ χρῆται· "τῶν δ' εἰρημένων," ἔφην, "τὸ
μὲν μεθύσκειν κιττὸν οἴνῳ μιγνύμενον οὐκ ἀληθές
ἐστιν· ὃ γὰρ ἐμποιεῖ[7] τοῖς πιοῦσι πάθος οὐ μέθη
ἄν τις εἴποι, ταραχὴν δὲ καὶ παραφροσύνην, οἷον

---

[1] ὁδὶ Reiske, ὁ θεὸς Pohlenz.
[2] χειμῶνος ὥρᾳ Basel edition : μιμούμενος ὥρας.
[3] τῶν στεφάνων omitted after Τρύφωνι by the Anonymous
(so Wyttenbach) and by Hubert.
[4] ἔφην ὅτι Bernardakis : lac. 4 τί.
[5] τὸ μὲν ἀποδεῖξαι Bernardakis : τὰς μὲν ἀποδείξεις.

of wine, if the grape is not available, use beer [a] or a cider, and others make date-palm wine, so too Dionysus, when in wintertime he wanted a garland made from the vine and saw the vines stripped and leafless, welcomed the very similar ivy. And to be sure, it imitates the characteristics of the vine : its stem which twists and falls in its course, the freshness and disorderly profusion of its foliage, and especially its berry clusters which resemble a heavy setting of ripening grapes. Furthermore, even if ivy is in some degree a specific for drunkenness, I shall claim that its heat makes it so by causing the conduits (*poroi*) of the body to open or rather by aiding in the assimilation of the wine—and this I grant in order that Dionysus may remain a physician [b] for your sake, Trypho."

2. Trypho remained silent considering how he might answer this. Erato, however, appealed to each of us young men, urging us to help Trypho out or to put aside our garlands ; and Ammonius assured us a safe-conduct, for he would not argue against whatever we might say. Thus, when Trypho too requested us to take up the argument, it was I who replied, saying that it was not my task to show that ivy is cold, but Trypho's, for he made much use of it as a cooler and an astringent. " And what has been said," I continued, " about ivy mixed with wine causing intoxication is not true, for one cannot call the condition it induces in drinkers intoxication, but a disorder and

---

[a] Like the Spanish king in Polybius, xxxiv. 9. 15, quoted by Athenaeus, i, 16 c.

[b] For Dionysus as physician *cf.* Oracle 414 in Parke-Wormell, *The Delphic Oracle*, ii (1956), p. 167.

---

[6] Stephanus : οὕτως. [7] Basel edition : τὸ γὰρ ἐμποιεῖν.

(649)

B ὑοσκύαμος[1] ἐμποιεῖ καὶ πολλὰ τοιαῦτα κινοῦντα
μανικῶς τὴν διάνοιαν. ὁ δὲ τοῦ κλήματος σπα-
σμὸς ἄλογός ἐστιν· τοιαῦτα[2] γὰρ παρὰ φύσιν ἔργα
τῶν κατὰ φύσιν δυνάμεων[3] οὐκ ἔστιν· ἀλλὰ καὶ
τὰ ξύλα διαστρέφεται τοῦ πυρὸς τὸ ὑγρὸν ἕλκοντος ἐξ αὐτῶν βίᾳ κυρτότητας ἴσχοντα καὶ παρα-
βάσεις· τὸ δὲ συγγενὲς θερμὸν αὔξειν καὶ τρέφειν
πέφυκεν. σκόπει δὲ μὴ μᾶλλον ἀρρωστίᾳ τις καὶ
ψυχρότης σώματος τὸ πολυκαμπὲς καὶ χαμαιπετὲς
πέφυκε, προσκρούσεις[4] πυκνὰς καὶ[5] ἀντικοπὰς
λαμβάνοντος, ὥσπερ ὁδοιπόρου δι' ἀσθένειαν πολ-
C λάκις ἀποκαθίζοντος εἶτα πάλιν ἐρχομένου· διὸ
καὶ περιπλοκῆς δεῖται καὶ στηρίγματος, αὐτὸς
ἑαυτὸν ἀνέχειν καὶ ποδηγεῖν ἀδυνατῶν δι' ἔνδειαν
θερμότητος, ἧς τὸ ἀνωφερὲς[6] δύναμίς ἐστιν. ἡ
δὲ χιὼν ἀπορρεῖ καὶ περιτήκεται δι' ὑγρότητα τοῦ
φύλλου· τὸ γὰρ ὕδωρ σβέννυσιν αὐτῆς καὶ κόπτει
τὴν χαυνότητα διὰ τὸ[7] μικρῶν εἶναι καὶ πυκνῶν
ἄθροισμα πομφολύγων· ὅθεν οὐχ ἧττον[8] ἐν τοῖς
περιψύκτοις σφόδρα καὶ νοτεροῖς τόποις ἢ τοῖς
προσείλοις αἱ χιόνες ῥέουσιν. τὸ δ' ἀειθαλὲς τοῦτο
καὶ ὥς φησιν Ἐμπεδοκλῆς ' ἐμπεδόφυλλον ' οὐκ
ἔστι θερμότητος· οὐδὲ γὰρ ψυχρότητος τὸ φυλ-
D λορροεῖν· ἡ γοῦν[9] μυρρίνη καὶ τὸ ἀδίαντον[10] οὐκ
ὄντα τῶν θερμῶν ἀλλὰ τῶν ψυχρῶν ἀεὶ τέθηλεν.
ἔνιοι μὲν οὖν ὁμαλότητι κράσεως οἴονται παρα-

---

[1] Junius : lac. 2 κύαμος.   [2] Bernardakis : ταῦτα.
[3] Xylander : δυναμένων.
[4] Bernardakis, cf. Mor. 77 A : lac. 4-6 σεις.
[5] καὶ added by Stephanus.
[6] Turnebus : ἀνωφελὲς.

a derangement like that induced by henbane and
many similar things which excite the intellect to
madness. The pulling-of-the-twig argument is unreasonable too, for such unnatural effects are no part
of natural powers. Actually, wood is twisted, bent,
and warped by fire violently drawing water out of it.
It is the nature of innate heat, on the contrary, to
strengthen and to sustain. Consider whether the
convolutions of the ivy and its clinging to the ground
are not rather produced by a certain weakness and
coldness of body as the plant meets a succession of
curbs and checks—like a traveller weak with fatigue
who often sits down to rest, then continues on his
way. And so ivy needs a support to twine about,
being unable to hold itself up and guide itself because
it lacks heat, one property of which is upward motion.
Snow melts and flows off the plant because of the
moisture of its leaf, for snow is a collection of many
small globules, is therefore porous, and water cuts
through it and destroys it. This is why snow melts
away not less in very cold and wet places than in
places exposed to the sun. That ivy is an evergreen
with ' never-failing leaves,' as Empedocles says,[a] is
not a sign of heat, nor indeed is loss of foliage a sign
of coldness—at least myrtle and maidenhair, which
are not reckoned among hot plants, but among cold,
are evergreens. Now some think that plants retain
their foliage because they have an even mixture of

---

[a] Frags. 77-78 Diels and Kranz, *Frag. d. Vorsokratiker*,
i[10] (1961), p. 339.

---

[7] διὰ τὸ Bernardakis : ἅτε.
[8] οὐχ ἧττον added by Xylander, Stephanus.
[9] Reiske : οὖν.
[10] Junius : ἀδιάλειπτον.

(649) μένειν τὸ φύλλον· Ἐμπεδοκλῆς δὲ πρὸς τούτῳ
καὶ πόρων τινὰ συμμετρίαν αἰτιᾶται, τεταγμένως
καὶ ὁμαλῶς τὴν τροφὴν διιέντων, ὥστ᾽ ἀρκούντως[1]
ἐπιρρεῖν. τοῖς δὲ φυλλορροοῦσιν οὐκ ἔστι διὰ
μανότητα τῶν ἄνω καὶ στενότητα τῶν κάτω
πόρων, ὅταν οἱ μὲν μὴ ἐπιπέμπωσιν οἱ δὲ μὴ[2]
φυλάττωσιν ἀλλ᾽ ὀλίγον λαβόντες ἄθρουν ἐκχέωσιν,
ὥσπερ ἐν ἀνδήροις τισὶν οὐχ ὁμαλοῖς· τὰ δ᾽
ὑδρευόμεν᾽ ἀεὶ τὴν τροφὴν διαρκῆ[3] καὶ σύμμετρον
ἀντέχει καὶ παραμένει ἀγήρω καὶ χλοερά.

E   " ' Ἀλλ᾽ ἐν Βαβυλῶνι φυτευόμενος ἐξίστατο καὶ
ἀπηγόρευεν᾽· εὖ γε ποιῶν ὁ γενναῖος οὗτος ὅτι
Βοιωτίου θεοῦ πελάτης καὶ παράσιτος ὢν οὐκ
ἐβούλετο μετοικεῖν ἐν βαρβάροις οὐδ᾽ Ἀλέξανδρον
ἐζήλωσεν ἐξοικειούμενον ἐκείνοις τοῖς ἔθνεσιν,
ἀλλ᾽ ἔφευγε καὶ διεμάχετο πρὸς τὴν ἀποξένωσιν.
αἰτία δ᾽ οὐχ ἡ θερμότης ἦν, ἀλλὰ μᾶλλον ἡ ψυχρότης,
οὐχ ὑποφέρουσα τὴν ἐναντίαν κρᾶσιν· οὐ γὰρ
φθείρει τὸ οἰκεῖον, ἀλλὰ προσίεται καὶ τρέφει,[4]
καθάπερ τὸ θύμον ἡ ξηρὰ γῆ, καίτοι θερμὸν ὄν.
τὴν δὲ Βαβυλωνίαν οὕτω φασὶν ἀέρα πνιγώδη καὶ
βαρὺν περιέχειν, ὥστε πολλοὺς τῶν εὐπόρων, ὅταν
F ἐμπλήσωσιν ἀσκοὺς ὕδατος, ἐπὶ τούτων καθεύδειν
ἀναψυχομένους."

---

[1] Xylander : ὥστε σαρκούντων.
[2] μὴ added by Vulcobius.
[3] g γ according to Wyttenbach : διαρκεῖ.
[4] Bernardakis (Xylander *alitur*) : φθείρει.

heat and cold; but Empedocles claims for a cause, in addition to this, also a certain symmetry of the vessels (*poroi*) of their vascular system, which accordingly admit nourishment in an orderly and even manner, so that a sufficient amount is assimilated. This is not true of deciduous plants because of the openness of the vessels (*porci*) in the upper part of their vascular system and the narrowness of the vessels in the lower part, for the latter do not transmit sufficient nourishment and the former do not retain the little they have received but pour it out all at once, like water in unevenly diked irrigation-ditches; but plants which drink in sufficient and suitable nourishment resist leaf-fall and remain vigorous and green.

" ' Ivy planted in Babylon rejected and refused acclimitization,' you say. Well done by this noble plant, to be unwilling to live among barbarians, seeing that it was a neighbour and a companion of the Boeotian god! And well done not to emulate Alexander in becoming a renegade among those races, but to fight against expatriation and flee! And the reason was not heat in the ivy, but rather its coldness, which does not endure the opposite temperature; for the quality peculiar to a given property is not destructive, but receptive and nourishing—as, for example, dry soil nourishes thyme, though the plant is hot. And the air in Babylonia, people say, is so stifling and heavy that many of the well-to-do fill wineskins full of water and sleep on them to keep cool."

650   ΠΡΟΒΛΗΜΑ Γ

Διὰ τί γυναῖκες ἥκιστα μεθύσκονται τάχιστα δ' οἱ γέροντες

Collocuntur Florus et Sulla

Ἐθαύμαζε Φλῶρος, εἰ γεγραφὼς Ἀριστοτέλης
ἐν τῷ Περὶ μέθης, ὅτι μάλιστα μὲν οἱ γέροντες
ἥκιστα δ' αἱ γυναῖκες ὑπὸ μέθης ἁλίσκονται, τὴν
αἰτίαν οὐκ ἐξειργάσατο μηδὲν εἰωθὼς προΐεσθαι
τῶν τοιούτων· εἶτα μέντοι προῢβαλεν ἐν μέσῳ σκοπεῖν τοῖς παροῦσιν. ἦν δὲ τῶν συνήθων τὸ δεῖπνον.
ἔφη τοίνυν ὁ Σύλλας θατέρῳ θάτερον ἐμφαίνε-
σθαι· κἂν εἰ περὶ τῶν γυναικῶν ὀρθῶς τὴν αἰτίαν
λάβοιμεν, οὐκ ἔτι πολλοῦ λόγου δεήσεσθαι περὶ
τῶν γερόντων· ἐναντίας γὰρ εἶναι μάλιστα τὰς φύ-
B σεις τῇ θ' ὑγρότητι καὶ ξηρότητι καὶ λειότητι[1]
καὶ τραχύτητι καὶ μαλακότητι καὶ σκληρότητι.
" καὶ τοῦτ'," ἔφη, " λαμβάνω[2] κατὰ τῶν γυναικῶν
πρῶτον, ὅτι τὴν κρᾶσιν ὑγρὰν ἔχουσιν, ἣ καὶ τὴν
ἁπαλότητα τῆς σαρκὸς ἐμμεμιγμένη παρέχει καὶ
τὸ στίλβον ἐπὶ λειότητι καὶ τὰς καθάρσεις· ὅταν οὖν
ὁ οἶνος εἰς ὑγρότητα πολλὴν ἐμπέσῃ, κρατούμενος
ἀποβάλλει τὴν βαφὴν καὶ γίγνεται παντάπασιν
ἀναφὴς καὶ ὑδατώδης. ἔστι δέ τι καὶ παρ' αὐτοῦ
λαβεῖν Ἀριστοτέλους· τοὺς γὰρ ἄθρουν καὶ ἀ-
πνευστὶ πίνοντας, ὅπερ ʼ ἀμυστίζειν ʼ ὠνόμαζον οἱ
παλαιοί, φησὶν ἥκιστα περιπίπτειν μέθαις· οὐ γὰρ

---

[1] καὶ λειότητι added by Xylander (translation), Stephanus.
[2] Meziriacus : λαμβάνει.

---

[a] Imitated by Macrobius, Saturnalia, vii. 6. 14-21.
[b] Frag. 108 Rose (1886) ; in frag. 107 Rose Aristotle as-

QUESTION 3 [a]

Why women are least liable to intoxication and old men most quickly liable

Speakers : Florus, Sulla

FLORUS expressed amazement that Aristotle in his *Concerning Drunkenness* did not work out the element of causation when he wrote that old men were especially susceptible to drunkenness and women least susceptible, though it was not his habit to neglect such a matter.[b] Florus then proposed that the company consider the question—the occasion was a dinner of his friends. Sulla replied that one part of the problem threw light upon the other. If we should rightly determine the cause where women are concerned, there would be no further need of much speculation where old men are concerned, for their natures are very emphatically opposites : moist and dry, smooth and rough, soft and hard. " The first thing about women," he continued, " I take to be this, that they possess a moist temperament which, being a component of the female, is responsible for her delicate, sleek, smooth flesh, and for her menses ; wine, therefore, when it falls into a great amount of liquid, is overcome, loses its edge, and becomes completely insipid and watery. Furthermore, one can get some hint of the causation even from Aristotle himself ; for he says that people who drink all in one gulp, without drawing a breath,—a manner of drinking the ancients called ' tossing it off,'—are the people least apt to fall into a state of intoxication, since the

serts that susceptibility to intoxication in old men is due to their lack of heat and in the very young to their superabundance of heat.

(650)
C ἐνδιατρίβειν τὸν ἄκρατον αὐτοῖς,[1] ἀλλ' ἐξωθούμενον
ῥύμῃ διαπορεύεσθαι διὰ τοῦ σώματος· ἐπιεικῶς δὲ
τὰς γυναῖκας ὁρῶμεν οὕτω πινούσας. εἰκὸς δ'
αὐτῶν καὶ τὸ σῶμα διὰ τὸν ἐνδελεχῆ τῶν ὑγρῶν
κατασπασμὸν ἐπὶ τὰς ἀποκαθάρσεις[2] πολύπορον
γεγονέναι καὶ τετμῆσθαι καθάπερ ἀνδήροις καὶ
ὀχετοῖς· εἰς οὓς ἐμπίπτοντα τὸν ἄκρατον ὑπάγειν
ταχέως καὶ μὴ προσίστασθαι τοῖς κυρίοις μέρεσιν,
ὧν διαταραττομένων συμβαίνει τὸ μεθύειν.

" Οἱ δὲ γέροντες ὅτι μέν εἰσιν ἐνδεεῖς ἰκμάδος
οἰκείας, τοὔνομά μοι δοκεῖ φράζειν πρῶτον· οὐ γὰρ
ὡς ῥέοντες εἰς γῆν, ἀλλ' ὡς γεώδεις καὶ γεηροί
τινες ἤδη γιγνόμενοι τὴν ἕξιν οὕτω προσαγορεύ-
D ονται· δηλοῖ δὲ καὶ τὸ δυσκαμπὲς αὐτῶν καὶ
σκληρὸν ἔτι δ' ἡ τραχύτης τὴν ξηρότητα τῆς φύ-
σεως· ὅταν οὖν ἐμπίνωσιν, εἰκὸς ἀναλαμβάνεσθαι
τὸν οἶνον, τοῦ σώματος σφογγώδους διὰ τὸν αὐχ-
μὸν ὄντος, εἶτ' ἐμμένοντα πληγὰς καὶ βαρύτητας
ἐμποιεῖν· ὡς γὰρ τὰ ῥεύματα τῶν μὲν πυκνῶν
ἀποκλύζεται χωρίων καὶ πηλὸν οὐ ποιεῖ τοῖς δ'
ἀραιοῖς ἀναμίγνυται μᾶλλον, οὕτως ὁ οἶνος ἐν τοῖς
τῶν γερόντων σώμασιν ἔχει διατριβὴν ἑλκόμενος
ὑπὸ τῆς ξηρότητος. ἄνευ δὲ τούτων ἰδεῖν ἔστι τὰ
E συμπτώματα τῆς μέθης τὴν τῶν γερόντων φύσιν
ἐξ ἑαυτῆς ἔχουσαν· ἔστι γὰρ συμπτώματα μέθης
ἐπιφανέστατα, τρόμοι μὲν ἄρθρων ψελλισμοὶ δὲ
γλώσσης, πλεονασμοὶ δὲ λαλιᾶς ὀξύτητες δ' ὀργῆς,
λῆθαί τε καὶ παραφοραὶ διανοίας· ὧν τὰ πολλὰ καὶ

[1] Turnebus : αὐτόν.   [2] Stephanus : ἀπο lac. 6-8.

wine does not linger in them, but proceeds through the body and is pushed out by the force of the draught.[a] And we usually see women drinking in this fashion. Again, it is likely that the female body, on account of the constant drawing down of fluids for menstruation, has come to be provided with many passages and cut up as if by dikes and channels; and the wine doubtless falls into these, is quickly eliminated, and does not attack the body's sovereign parts, from the disturbance of which drunkenness results.

" As for ' old men ' the word itself (*gerontes*) seems to me to be the first thing to indicate that they are in need of proper moisture, for ' old men ' are so called, not as ' flowing into earth ' (*rheontes eis gên*), but as individuals now become ' soil-like ' and ' earthy ' (*geôdeis, geêroi*) in their condition ; their stiffness and hardness, and their roughness besides, show the dryness of their substance. Therefore, when they drink, it is likely that the wine is soaked up, for their bodies because of dryness are like sponges ; and then the wine lies there and afflicts them with its heaviness. For just as flood-waters run off from compact soils and do not make mud, but are soaked up in greater degree by soils of loose texture, so in the bodies of old men wine lingers on, attracted by the dryness there. Apart from these considerations, one can observe that the characteristics of intoxication are those peculiar to the nature of old men, for the characteristics of intoxication are very clear : trembling limbs and stammering tongue, excessive talkativeness, irascible temper, forgetfulness, wandering mind. Most of these exist even in healthy old men

----

[a] *Cf. infra*, vii. 1. 1, 698 c f. Apparently not Aristotle (*cf.* Hubert, who cites Rose, *Arist. Pseudepigr.*, p. 119).

(650) περὶ τοὺς ὑγιαίνοντας ὄντα πρεσβύτας ὀλίγης
ῥοπῆς δεῖται καὶ σάλου τοῦ τυχόντος· ὥστε μὴ
γένεσιν ἰδίων ἀλλὰ κοινῶν ἐπίτασιν συμπτωμάτων
γίνεσθαι τὴν μέθην τῷ γέροντι· τεκμήριον δὲ
τούτου τὸ[1] μηδὲν εἶναι γέροντι νέου μεθυσθέντος
ὁμοιότερον."

ΠΡΟΒΛΗΜΑ Δ

Πότερον ψυχρότεραι τῇ κράσει τῶν ἀνδρῶν ἢ θερμότεραί
εἰσιν αἱ γυναῖκες

Collocuntur Apollonides, Athryitus, Florus

F 1. Ὁ μὲν οὖν Σύλλας ταῦτ᾽ εἶπεν. ὁ δὲ τακτι-
κὸς Ἀπολλωνίδης ἔφη τὸν μὲν περὶ τῶν γερόντων
ἀποδέχεσθαι λόγον· ἐν δὲ ταῖς γυναιξὶν αὐτῷ δοκεῖν παραλελεῖφθαι τὸ τῆς ψυχρότητος, ᾗ θερμό-
τατον ἄκρατον ἀποσβέννυσθαι καὶ ἀποβάλλειν τὸ
πλῆττον καὶ πυρῶδες. πιθανοῦ δὲ καὶ τούτου
651 δοκοῦντος, Ἀθρύιτος ὁ Θάσιος ἰατρὸς ἐμβαλών
τινα τῇ ζητήσει διατριβὴν εἶναί τινας ἔφησεν, οἳ
τὰς γυναῖκας οὐ ψυχρὰς ἀλλὰ θερμοτέρας τῶν
ἀνδρῶν ὑπολαμβάνουσιν, ἑτέρους δὲ πάλιν[2] οἳ τὸν
οἶνον οὐ θερμὸν ἀλλὰ καὶ ψυχρὸν ἡγοῦνται.

2. Θαυμάσαντος δὲ τοῦ Φλώρου, "τὸν μὲν περὶ
τοῦ οἴνου λόγον," εἶπεν, "ἀφίημι τούτῳ," δείξας
ἐμέ· καὶ γὰρ ἐτυγχάνομεν ὀλίγαις ἡμέραις πρότερον εἰς τοῦτο διειλεγμένοι· "τῶν δὲ γυναι-

---

[1] Stephanus : τοῦ.
[2] Emperius : μᾶλλον.

---

[a] Imitated by Macrobius, *Saturnalia*, vii. 7. 1 ff. *Cf.* Aristotle, *De Part. Animal.* ii. 2. 10, citing Parmenides (Diels-
Kranz, *op. cit.* i, p. 227, 28 A 52). On natural heat see p. 143,
note *a*.

and need but a slight turn of the scale, an accidental disturbance, to bring them out. Consequently, intoxication in an old man does not produce symptomatic characteristics peculiar to the individual, but simply intensifies characteristics common to all old men. A proof of this is the fact that nothing is more like an old man than a young man drunk."

QUESTION 4 [a]

Whether women are colder in temperament than men or hotter

Speakers : Apollonides, Athryïtus, Florus

1. That, then, was what Sulla had to say. And Apollonides,[b] the tactician, remarked that he accepted the statement about old men ; but in regard to women, it seemed to him that we had failed to take account of the quality of coldness in their constitution and that by means of this they nullify the effect of the hottest wine and remove its kick and fire. When the likelihood of this was agreed upon, Athryïtus of Thasos, a physician, induced us to linger on the inquiry by saying that there are people who assume that women are not cold, but hotter than men ; and there are others in turn who consider wine not hot, but actually cold.

2. Florus expressed astonishment, and Athryïtus replied, " The question of wine I yield to this gentleman," pointing to me (and actually we happened to have been talking about this subject a few days earlier), " but with regard to women," he continued,

[b] Doubtless not the Apollonides of the *De Facie* : see Cherniss, LCL *Mor.* xii, p. 5.

(651) κῶν,'' ἔφη, '' τὴν θερμότητα πρῶτον ἀπὸ τῆς
ψιλότητος οἴονται δεικνύναι, καταναλισκομένου
τοῦ περιττώματος ὑπὸ τῆς θερμότητος, ὃ πλεονάζον εἰς τρίχας τρέπεται· δεύτερον δὲ τῷ πλήθει
B τοῦ αἵματος, ὃ πηγὴ μὲν εἶναι δοκεῖ τῆς ἐν τῷ
σώματι θερμότητος, ἔστι δὲ τοσοῦτον ταῖς γυναιξίν,
ὥστ'[1] αὐτὰς καταπιμπράναι καὶ περιφλέγειν, εἰ μὴ
πολλαὶ καὶ ταχεῖαι συμβαίνοιεν καθάρσεις. τρίτον τοῦτο τὸ περὶ τὰς ταφὰς αἱ⟨ρεῖ θερμότε⟩ρα[2]
τὰ θήλεα τῶν ἀρρένων εἶναι· λέγεται γὰρ ὑπὸ τῶν
σκευωρουμένων τὰ νομιζόμενα[3] συντίθεσθαι παρὰ
δέκα νεκροὺς ἀνδρῶν ἕνα γυναικὸς καὶ συνεξάπτειν,
δαδῶδές τι καὶ λιπαρὸν αὐτῶν τῆς σαρκὸς ἐχούσης,
ὥσθ' ὑπέκκαυμα γίγνεσθαι τῶν ἄλλων. ἔτι δ',
εἰ θερμότερον τὸ γονιμώτερον αἱ δὲ παρθένοι τῶν
παίδων ὀργῶσι πρότερον καὶ σαλεύονται πρὸς τὸ
γεννᾶν, οὐδ' αὕτη τις ἀσθενὴς ἀπόδειξις ἂν εἴη
C τῆς θερμότητος. ἔτι δὲ μείζων καὶ πιθανωτέρα τὸ
πρὸς τὰ κρύη καὶ τοὺς χειμῶνας εὐφόρως ἔχειν·
ἧττον γὰρ αἱ πλεῖσται ῥιγοῦσι τῶν ἀνδρῶν καὶ
παντάπασιν ἱματίων ὀλίγων δέονται.''

3. '' Ἀλλ' ἀπ' αὐτῶν οἶμαι τούτων,'' ὁ Φλῶρος
ἔφη, '' τῶν ἐπιχειρημάτων ἐλέγχεσθαι τὸ δόγμα.
πρῶτον μὲν γὰρ ἀντέχουσι τῷ ψύχει μᾶλλον, ὅτι
πολλάκις τὸ ὅμοιον ὑπὸ τοῦ ὁμοίου δυσπαθέστερόν
ἐστιν. ἔπειτα μέντοι καὶ τὸ σπέρμα μὴ προγε-
γονέναι τὸ παράπαν αὐταῖς φαίνεται γόνιμον[4] διὰ
κατάψυξιν, ἀλλ' ὕλην μόνον καὶ τροφὴν παρέχειν

---

[1] ὥστ'⟨ἂν⟩ αὐτὰς Vulcobius (according to Hutten), Hubert.
[2] Stephanus : αι lac. 6-7 ρα.
[3] Hubert : μὲν.

" their heat is thought to be proved, in the first place, by the lack of hair on their bodies, for it is heat which consumes the excess of nourishment which, when it is present in abundance, is converted into hair ; and secondly by their great amount of blood, which, it seems, is a source of the heat in the body— women have so much of it that it would burn them up and utterly consume them except for the quick recurrence of their periods of menstruation. Thirdly, the following practice at burials proves that females are hotter than males : those who tend to the customary procedures for disposal of the dead, it is said, place with every ten male corpses one female and set it on fire, for the flesh of women possesses a kind of resinous and oily quality, so that the female corpse becomes kindling-wood for the others. Again, if heat is a factor of fertility [a] and girls become lustful at an earlier age than boys and are earlier excited to sexual activity, this fact would be no weak demonstration of their heat. A still greater and more persuasive demonstration is the fact that women easily support cold and winter weather, for most of them are less easily chilled than men and undoubtedly have need of little clothing."

3. " But the very instances you employ," said Florus, " refute your opinion, I think. In the first place, women resist cold better because often like is not easily affected by like. And, in the second place, it seems that woman's seed has never had an active part at all in generation,—the female's coldness is responsible,—but merely offers matter and nourish-

[a] *Cf. infra*, 652 D with note.

4 Pohlenz (αὐταῖς Reiske, φαίνεται Bernardakis): τὸ γόνιμον.

(651) τῷ ἀπὸ τοῦ ἄρρενος. ἔπειτα λήγουσι τίκτουσαι
πολὺ πρότερον ἢ γεννῶντες οἱ ἄνδρες. καίονται
D δὲ βέλτιον ὑπὸ πιμελῆς, ὃ δοκεῖ ψυχρότατον[1] εἶναι
τοῦ σώματος· ἥκιστα γοῦν οἱ νέοι καὶ γυμναστικοὶ
πιμελώδεις. ἡ δ' ἔμμηνος[2] κάθαρσις οὐ πλήθους
ἀλλὰ διαφθορᾶς καὶ φαυλότητός ἐστιν αἵματος· τὸ
γὰρ ἄπεπτον αὐτοῦ καὶ περιττωματικὸν οὐκ ἔχον
ἵδρυσιν οὐδὲ σύστασιν ἐν τῷ σώματι δι' ἀσθένειαν
ἐκπίπτει, παντάπασιν ἀμβλὺ καὶ θολερὸν ἀρρωστίᾳ
τοῦ θερμοῦ γιγνόμενον· δηλοῖ δὲ καὶ τὸ ῥιγοῦν καὶ
τὸ ὑποφρίττειν ὡς ἐπὶ πολὺ τὰς καθαιρομένας,
ὅτι ψυχρόν ἐστι καὶ ἄπεπτον τὸ κεκινημένον καὶ
ἀποχωροῦν ἐκ τοῦ σώματος. τὴν δὲ ψιλότητα
τίς ἂν εἴποι ὅτι[3] θερμότητος οὐχὶ μᾶλλον ψυχρό-
τητός ἐστι τὸ πάθος, ὁρῶν τὰ θερμότατα τοῦ σώ-
E ματος μέρη δασυνόμενα; πάντα γὰρ ἐξωθεῖται τὰ
τοιαῦτα τῷ θερμῷ, χαράσσοντι καὶ ἀναστομοῦντι
τὴν ἐπιφάνειαν. ἡ δὲ λειότης πυκνότητι γέγονεν
ὑπὸ ψυχρότητος· ὅτι δ' εἰσὶ πυκνότεραι τῶν
ἀνδρῶν, ὦ φίλ' Ἀθρύϊτε,[4] πυθοῦ παρὰ τῶν ἔτι
συναναπαυομένων γυναιξὶν ἢ μύρον ἀληλιμμέναις
ἢ ἔλαιον· ἀναπίμπλανται γὰρ αὐτοὶ[5] τοῦ χρίσματος
ἐν τῷ συγκαθεύδειν, κἂν μὴ θίγωσι μηδὲ προσ-
άψωνται τῶν γυναικῶν, διὰ θερμότητα καὶ μανότητα τοῦ σώματος ἕλκοντος.''[6]

---

[1] Reiske: ψυχρότερον. *Cf.* 638 B with note 2, p. 158, *supra*.
[2] Xylander: ἔμμονος.
[3] ὅτι added by Bernardakis.
[4] Hubert, Ἀουῖτε Reiske: λούϊτε. [5] Reiske: αὐτοῦ.
[6] The first sentence of Question 5 follows here in T, before
the title of that Question. Wyttenbach and ms. γ indicate a
lacuna after ἕλκοντος.

ment to the seed from the male.[a] Moreover women cease bearing children much sooner than men stop begetting them. Female corpses burn more efficiently because of fat, which seems to be the coldest constituent of the body ; at any rate, young men devoted to exercise are least fleshy. And the monthly menstruation is indicative not of a quantity of blood, but of corrupt and diseased blood ; for blood's unassimilated and excrementitious part has no position and no structure in the body and so is eliminated by its lack of vitality, its faint heat causing it to be completely dull and murky. The fact that women are apt to be seized with chills and shivering during their menstrual periods shows that the blood which has been set in motion and is now being eliminated from the body is cold and unassimilated. As for the lack of hair on a woman's body, who can say that it is a consequence of heat rather than of cold, seeing that the hottest parts of the body are hairy ? For all such growths are thrust out by heat, which furrows and holes the surface of the body. And the smoothness of women is due to the fact that their flesh is compacted by cold ; that the flesh of women is more compact than that of men you must learn, my dear Athryïtus, from those who are still going to bed with women who perfume and oil their bodies ; for the men are themselves filled with the ointment by sleeping with their women, even if they do not touch their companions or meddle with them, because a man's body by reason of its heat and open texture attracts the ointment."

[a] Cf. *Mor.* 374 f with Wyttenbach's note ; 905 b-c ; Aristotle, *De Gen. Animal.* i. 20. 1.

ΠΡΟΒΛΗΜΑ Ε

Εἰ ψυχρότερος τῇ δυνάμει ὁ οἶνος

Collocuntur Athryitus, Plutarchus, Florus

1. " Οὐ μὴν ἀλλὰ τὸ μὲν περὶ τῶν γυναικῶν,"
ἔφη,[1] " καὶ πρὸς τοὐναντίον ἀνδρικῶς ἐπικεχείρη-
ται. τὸν δ' οἶνον ἐπιθυμῶ μαθεῖν ὁπόθεν ὑπόνοιαν
ὑμῖν τοῦ[2] ψυχρὸς εἶναι παρέσχεν." " οἴει γάρ,"
652 ἔφην ἐγώ, " τοῦτον ἡμέτερον εἶναι τὸν λόγον; "
" ἀλλὰ τίνος," εἶπεν, " ἑτέρου; " " μέμνημαι μὲν
οὖν," ἔφην ἐγώ, " καὶ Ἀριστοτέλους ἐντυχὼν
οὐ νεωστὶ λόγῳ περὶ τούτου τοῦ προβλήματος
ἀλλ' ἱκανῶς πάλαι. διείλεκται δὲ καὶ Ἐπίκουρος
ἐν τῷ Συμποσίῳ πολλοὺς λόγους, ὧν τὸ κεφάλαιόν
ἐστιν ὡς ἐγῷμαι τοιόνδε. φησὶ γὰρ οὐκ εἶναι
θερμὸν αὐτοτελῶς τὸν οἶνον, ἀλλ' ἔχειν τινὰς
ἀτόμους ἐν αὐτῷ θερμασίας ἀποτελεστικὰς ἑτέρας
δ' αὖ ψυχρότητος· ὧν τὰς μὲν ἀποβάλλειν, ὅταν
εἰς τὸ σῶμα παραγένηται, τὰς δὲ προσλαμβάνειν
ἐκ τοῦ σώματος, ἕως[3] ἂν ὁπωσοῦν[4] ἔχουσι[5] κράσεως
ἡμῖν ἢ φύσεως ὁμιλήσῃ,[6] ὡς τοὺς μὲν ἐκθερμαίνε-
B σθαι τοὺς δὲ τοὐναντίον πάσχειν μεθυσκομένους."

2. " Ταῦτ'," εἶπεν[7] ὁ Φλῶρος, " ἄντικρυς εἰς
τὸν Πύρρωνα διὰ τοῦ Πρωταγόρου φέρει ἡμᾶς·
δῆλον γὰρ ὅτι καὶ περὶ ἐλαίου καὶ περὶ γάλακτος
μέλιτός τε καὶ ὁμοίως τῶν ἄλλων διεξιόντες

---

[1] Xylander : ἔφην.　　　　[2] Xylander : ἡμῖν τό.
[3] ἕως Warmington : ὡς.
[4] ὁπωσοῦν added by Warmington.
[5] Turnebus : ἔχωσι.　　　　[6] Turnebus : ὁμιλῆσαι.

QUESTION 5 [a]

Whether wine is on the cold side in its power

Speakers : Athryïtus, Plutarch, Florus

1. " Now certainly," continued Florus, " we have made a manful assault upon both sides of the discussion about women. Now for wine ! I should like to know what made you suspect that it is cold." I replied : " Do you actually think that this is my own theory ? " " Whose else ? " he said. And I answered: " I remember coming on Aristotle's discussion [b] also of this question, not recently but a long enough time ago. And Epicurus in his *Symposium* [c] has discussed the matter at great length. The sum of what he has to say, I think, is this : he holds that wine is not hot in an absolute sense, but has in it certain atoms productive of heat and others of cold ; some of these it throws off when it comes into the body and others it attracts out of the body until it adapts itself to us, whatever our constitution and nature may be. Accordingly, some men become thoroughly hot when drinking, others experience the contrary."

2. " This," said Florus, " carries us via Protagoras straight to Pyrrho [d] ; for it is clear that we shall go on about oil, about milk and honey, and other things

---

[a] Imitated by Macrobius, *Saturnalia*, vii. 6. 1 ff.

[b] Ross, *Aristotle*, xii, p. 14, frag. 12 ; *cf.* frag. 221 Rose (1886).

[c] Frag. 60 Usener ; *cf. Mor.* 1109 E ff.

[d] Pyrrhonic scepticism may be traced to Protagoras and other Sophists (de Vogel, *Gr. Philos.* iii, pp. 187, 1081) ; on Pyrrho's sceptic attitude in regard to the nature of heat or fire see Diogenes Laertius, ix. 104 f.

---

[7] Turnebus : εἰπών.

(652) ἀποδρασόμεθα τὸ λέγειν περὶ ἑκάστου, ὁποῖον τῇ
φύσει ἐστίν, μίξεσι ταῖς πρὸς ἄλληλα καὶ κράσε-
σιν ἕκαστον γίγνεσθαι φάσκοντες. ἀλλὰ σὺ πῶς
ἐπιχειρεῖς εἰς[1] τὸ ψυχρὸν εἶναι τὸν οἶνον;'' '' οὕτως,
ὡς,''[2] ἔφην, '' ὑπέδυν[3] τότε προσηναγκασμένος
αὐτοσχεδιάσαι. πρῶτον δ᾽ ἐπῄει[4] μοι τὸ γιγνόμενον ὑπὸ τῶν ἰατρῶν· τοῖς γὰρ ἐκλελυμένοις καὶ
τόνου τινὸς δεομένοις κατὰ τὰς ἀρρωστίας στομά-
χου θερμὸν μὲν οὐδὲν προσφέρουσιν οἶνον δὲ διδόντες βοηθοῦσιν. ὡς δ᾽ αὕτως καὶ τὰς ῥύσεις καὶ
C ἐφιδρώσεις οἴνῳ καταπαύουσιν, ὡς οὐδὲν ἧττον
ἀλλὰ καὶ μᾶλλον τῆς χιόνος ἱστάντι καὶ κρατύνοντι
τῷ ψύχειν καὶ περιστέλλειν φερομένην τὴν ἕξιν.
εἰ δὲ φύσιν καὶ δύναμιν εἶχεν θερμαντικήν, ὅμοιον
ἦν οἶμαι χιόνι πῦρ καὶ καρδιακοῖς ἂν[5] προσφέρειν
ἄκρατον. ἔπειτα τὸν μὲν ὕπνον οἱ πλεῖστοι περιψύξει γίγνεσθαι λέγουσι καὶ ψυκτικὰ[6] τὰ πλεῖστα
τῶν ὑπνωτικῶν φαρμάκων ἐστίν, ὡς ὁ μανδρα-
γόρας καὶ τὸ μηκώνιον· ἀλλὰ ταῦτα μὲν σφόδρα
καὶ βίᾳ πολλῇ συνωθεῖ καὶ πήγνυσιν, ὁ δ᾽ οἶνος
ἠρέμα καταψύχων ἵστησι μεθ᾽ ἡδονῆς καὶ ἀνα-
D παύει τὴν κίνησιν ἐν τῷ μᾶλλον καὶ ἧττον οὔσης
πρὸς ἐκεῖνα[7] τῆς διαφορᾶς. ἔτι δὲ τὸ μὲν θερμὸν
γόνιμον· εὔροιαν γὰρ ἡ ὑγρότης ἴσχει καὶ τόνον
τὸ πνεῦμα καὶ δύναμιν ὑπὸ τῆς θερμότητος ἐξορ-
γῶσαν· οἱ δὲ πίνοντες πολὺν ἄκρατον ἀμβλύτεροι
πρὸς τὰς συνουσίας εἰσὶν καὶ σπείρουσιν οὐδὲν εἰς
γένεσιν ἰσχυρὸν οὐδὲ κεκρατημένον, ἀλλ᾽ ἐξίτηλοι

---

[1] εἰς added by Hubert.
[2] ὡς added by Wyttenbach (after ἔφην), Hubert.
[3] Hubert : ὑπὸ δυεῖν.   [4] Bases : ὑπείμι.
[5] καρδιακοῖς ἂν P. A. C., καρδιωγμῷ Hubert : καρδίᾳ οἶνον
(Benseler deleted οἶνον).

238

in like manner and shall avoid saying about each
what its nature is by defining them in terms of their
mixtures and unions with each other. But how will
you argue on the proposition that wine is cold ? "
" In just the manner," I replied, " I slipped into
in the conversation the other day when compelled
to extemporize. A regimen used by physicians was
the first thing to occur to me ; for to ailing patients
in need of some tonic for stomach disorders they give
nothing hot, but do provide relief by giving them
wine. In like manner they stop fluxes and sweats
with wine, which, no less efficiently than snow, indeed
more so, checks (so it is claimed) and controls the
given condition by its cooling and constricting action.
And if the nature and power of wine were calorific,
administering wine to sufferers from cardiac disorder
would be, I think, like putting fire to snow. Next,
most people assert that sleep is produced by the
action of coolness, and most of the hypnotic drugs,
like belladonna and opium, are refrigerants ; but
the depressant and torporific action of these drugs is
one of very great violence, while wine cools gently,
pleasantly checking and stopping movement, the
difference between it and the hypnotics being a
matter of degree. Thirdly, heat is generative,[a] for
through the agency of heat the generative fluid has
a good flow and the spirit tension and a lusty power ;
but men who drink much wine are the duller at love-
making and the semen they emit is not at all strong
and efficient for procreation ; on the contrary, their

---

[a] Aristotle, *De Gen. Animal.* ii. 3. 11 f.

---

[6] καὶ omitted by Xylander after ψυκτικά.
[7] Xylander (translation), Meziriacus : ἐκεῖνο.

(652) καὶ ἀτελεῖς εἰσιν αἱ πρὸς τὰς γυναῖκας ὁμιλίαι
αὐτῶν διὰ φαυλότητα καὶ κατάψυξιν τοῦ σπέρματος. καὶ μὴν ὅσα πάσχουσιν ἄνθρωποι ὑπὸ
κρύους, πάντα συμβαίνει τοῖς μεθυσκομένοις, τρόμοι, βαρύτητες, ὠχριάσεις, σάλοι τοῦ περὶ τὰ
γυῖα πνεύματος, ἀσάφεια γλώττης, ἔντασις τῶν
E περὶ τοῖς ἄκροις νεύρων καὶ ἀπονάρκησις· τοῖς δὲ
πλείστοις εἰς πάρεσιν αἱ μέθαι τελευτῶσιν, ὅταν
ἐκπλήξῃ παντάπασιν καὶ κατασβέσῃ τὸ θερμὸν ὁ
ἄκρατος. ἰῶνταί γε μὴν τὰς περὶ τὸ σῶμα τῶν
μεθυσκομένων καὶ κραιπαλώντων κακώσεις εὐθὺς
μὲν ὡς ἔοικε περιστολῇ καὶ κατακλίσει συνθάλ-
ποντες, μεθ' ἡμέραν δὲ λουτρῷ καὶ ἀλείμματι καὶ
σιτίοις, ὅσα μὴ ταράττοντα τὸν ὄγκον ἅμα[1] πράως
F ἀνακαλεῖται τὸ θερμὸν ὑπὸ τοῦ οἴνου διεσπασμένον
καὶ πεφυγαδευμένον ἐκ τοῦ σώματος.

" "Ὅμως δ'," εἶπον, " ἐν τοῖς φαινομένοις καὶ
ὁμοιότητας ἀδήλους ἐξιχνεύωμεν[2] καὶ δυνάμεις.
οὐδὲν δὲ περὶ τῆς μέθης δεῖ διαπορεῖν, ὁποῖόν ποτ'
ἐστίν· ὡς γὰρ ἔοικεν ⟨μάλιστα μὲν φύσιν ἔχουσιν
οἱ πρεσβῦται ψυχράν,⟩[3] μάλιστα δ',[4] ὡς εἰρή-
καμεν, ἐοίκασι τοῖς πρεσβύταις οἱ μεθύοντες·
διὸ καὶ πρωιαίτατα γηρῶσιν οἱ φίλοινοι· τοὺς δὲ
πολλοὺς αὐτῶν καὶ φαλακρώσεις ἄωροι καὶ πολιαὶ
πρὸ ἡλικίας ἔχουσιν· πάντα δὲ ταῦτα δοκεῖ θερμότητος ἐνδείᾳ καταλαμβάνειν τὸν ἄνθρωπον. ἔτι
τοίνυν τὸ ὄξος οἴνου τινός ἐστι φύσις καὶ δύναμις·
οὐδὲν δὲ τῶν σβεστηρίων ὄξους πυρὶ μαχιμώτερον,
ἀλλὰ μάλιστα πάντων ἐπικρατεῖ καὶ συμπιέζει τὴν
φλόγα δι' ὑπερβολὴν ψυχρότητος. καὶ τῶν ἄλλων
240

intercourse with women is weak and ineffectual because their seed is worthless and cold in action. Indeed, everything men experience from cold, all of it happens to them when they get drunk : trembling, heaviness, pallor, convulsive movements in the limbs, unintelligible speech, a rigidity and numbness of the sinews at the extremities,—and for most men drunkenness ends in a paralysis, when wine has completely beaten out and quenched heat. The bodily distress of those who get drunk and have a terrible hangover is cured, it seems, by immediately putting them to bed, well covered and warmed, and the next day giving them a bath, a rub-down, and such food as does not irritate the system but restores the heat scattered and dissipated from the body by the wine.

" However," I continued, " let us track thoroughly among the phenomena of our experience obscure similarities in the properties of cold and intoxication. There need be no problem about the essential nature of intoxication ; for, as it seems, ⟨old men most certainly have a cold nature⟩ and drunkards, as I have said, especially resemble old men : wine-lovers very soon become in fact old men, and many get bald at an early age and their hair turns gray before their prime—and all this seems to afflict such men because of a deficiency of heat. Further, some wine possesses the characteristic and the property of vinegar, and there is no extinguisher more deadly to fire than vinegar ; it masters and smothers the flame best of all because of its excessive coldness. And we see

---

¹ Reiske : ἀλλά.　　² Hubert : ἐξιχνεύομεν.
³ Lacuna noted by Hubert, perhaps ⟨μάλιστα μὲν φύσιν ἔχουσιν οἱ πρεσβῦται ψυχράν,⟩ P. A. C.
⁴ δὲ omitted by Vulcobius.

(652) δὲ καρπῶν τοῖς οἰνώδεσι μᾶλλον ὡς ψυκτικοῖς
χρωμένους τοὺς ἰατροὺς ὁρῶμεν ὥσπερ ῥόαις καὶ
653 μήλοις. αὐτὴν δὲ τὴν τοῦ μέλιτος φύσιν οὐχὶ πρὸς
ὄμβριον ὕδωρ καὶ χιόνα συμμιγνύοντες οἰνοποιοῦσι,
τοῦ ψυχροῦ τὸ γλυκὺ διὰ συγγένειαν εἰς τὸ
αὐστηρόν, ὅταν κρατήσῃ, φθείροντος; οἱ παλαιοὶ
δ᾽ οὐχὶ διὰ τοῦτο τῶν ἑρπετῶν τὸν δράκοντα καὶ
τῶν φυτῶν τὸν κιττὸν ἀνέθεσαν τῷ θεῷ καὶ
καθιέρωσαν ὥς τινος ψυχρᾶς καὶ κρυώδους κυρίῳ[1]
δυνάμεως; ἐὰν δ᾽, ὅτι τὸ κώνειον ἐπιπινόμενος
ἰᾶσθαι δοκεῖ πολὺς ἄκρατος, οἴωνται τοῦτο θερμότητος εἶναι τεκμήριον, ἡμεῖς αὖ φήσομεν ἀνα-
στρέψαντες, ὅτι συγκραθὲν αὐτῷ τοῦτο φάρμακον
ἀνίατόν ἐστιν καὶ καθάπαξ ἀποκτείνει τοὺς πίνον-
B τας· ὥστε μηδὲν μᾶλλον εἶναι δοκεῖν τῷ ἀντιπράτ-
τειν θερμὸν ἢ τῷ συνεργεῖν ψυχρόν, εἴ γε δὴ[2]
ψυχρότητι τὸ κώνειον οὐκ ἄλλῃ τινὶ φύσει καὶ
δυνάμει μᾶλλον πιθανόν ἐστιν ἀναιρεῖν τοὺς πιόντας."

ΠΡΟΒΛΗΜΑ ϛ

Περὶ καιροῦ συνουσίας[3]

Collocuntur adulescentes, Zopyrus, Olympichus, Soclarus

1. Νεανίσκοι τινὲς οὐ πάλαι τοῖς παλαιοῖς λόγοις
προσπεφοιτηκότες ἐσπάραττον τὸν Ἐπίκουρον, ὡς

----

[1] κυρίῳ added by Reiske.
[2] γε δὴ Wyttenbach : δὲ μὴ.
[3] No title in T (numeral in margin).

----

[a] Honey wine or mead, 672 B, *infra*.
[b] Euripides, *Bacchae*, 101 ff. and 696 ff. with Sandys's
and Dodds's notes : Horace, *Odes*, ii. 19. 19.

physicians using vinous fruits, like pomegranates and apples, for refrigerants more than they use others. And do not people make wine *a* by mixing honey itself with rain-water and snow, since coldness because of its relationship to tartness, when it prevails, destroys the sweetness ? And did not the ancients for this reason dedicate and consecrate the snake *b* among the reptiles of the earth and the ivy *c* among plants to the god of wine as to one who is lord of a cold and chilling power ? And if it is thought to be an indication of the heat of wine that the drinking of a large quantity of it is held to be an antidote for hemlock,*d* for my part I shall deny the fact and claim that this drug is incurable when mixed with wine and kills once for all those who drink it. Accordingly, it seems to be not so much a question of wine being hot because it opposes hemlock as a question of its being cold because it reinforces the action of hemlock—if it is indeed the more probable hypothesis that the coldness of hemlock rather than some other property and power of the drug is responsible for the death of those who have drunk it."

QUESTION 6

Concerning the suitable time for coition

Speakers : Zopyrus, Olympichus, Soclarus, young men

1. CERTAIN young men with no long experience in the ancient literature were attacking Epicurus on

c Pausanias, i. 31. 6 ; *RE*, v. 1015 f.
d *Mor.* 61 B, 509 D-E ; Pliny, *Nat. Hist.* xxv. 152.

(653) οὐ καλὸν οὐδ' ἀναγκαῖον ἐμβεβληκότα λόγον περὶ
καιροῦ συνουσίας εἰς τὸ Συμπόσιον· μιμνήσκεσθαι
γὰρ ἀφροδισίων ἄνδρα πρεσβύτερον ἐν δείπνῳ
C μειρακίων παρόντων καὶ διαπορεῖν, πότερον μετὰ
δεῖπνον ἢ πρὸ δείπνου χρηστέον, ἐσχάτης ἀκο-
λασίας εἶναι. πρὸς ταῦθ' οἱ μὲν τὸν Ξενοφῶντα
παρέλαβον ὡς ἀπάγοντα τοὺς συμπότας μετὰ
δεῖπνον οὐχὶ βάδην ἀλλ'[1] ἐφ' ἵππων ἐπὶ συνουσίας
πρὸς τὰς γυναῖκας. Ζώπυρος δ' ὁ ἰατρός, εὖ
μάλα τοῖς Ἐπικούρου λόγοις ἐνωμιληχώς, οὐκ
ἔφη προσέχοντας αὐτοὺς ἀνεγνωκέναι τὸ Ἐπικούρου Συμπόσιον· οὐ γὰρ ὥσπερ ἐξ ἀρχῆς τινος
καὶ καταστάσεως τοῦτο πρόβλημα ποιησάμενον
εἶτα λόγους ἐπ' αὐτῷ περαίνειν, ἀλλὰ τοὺς νέους
ἀνιστάντα μετὰ δεῖπνον εἰς περίπατον ἐπὶ σωφρονι-
D σμῷ διαλέγεσθαι καὶ ἀνακρούειν ἀπὸ τῶν ἐπι-
θυμιῶν, ὡς ἀεὶ μὲν ἐπισφαλοῦς εἰς βλάβην τοῦ
πράγματος ὄντος, κάκιστα[2] δὲ τοὺς περὶ πότον
καὶ ἐδωδὴν[3] χρωμένους αὐτῷ διατιθέντος. " εἰ δὲ
δὴ καὶ προηγουμένως," εἶπεν, " ἐζητεῖτο περὶ
τούτου, πότερον οὐδ' ὅλως ἐσκέφθαι καλῶς εἶχε
τὸν φιλόσοφον περὶ συνουσίας καιροῦ καὶ ὥρας,
ἢ βέλτιον μὲν ἐν καιρῷ καὶ μετὰ λογισμοῦ τὰ
τοιαῦτα πράττειν, τὸν δὲ καιρὸν ἄλλως μὲν ἐπι-
σκοπεῖν οὐκ ἄωρον[4] ἐν[5] δὲ συμποσίῳ καὶ περὶ
τράπεζαν αἰσχρόν; ἐμοὶ γὰρ δοκεῖ τοὐναντίον ἂν

---

[1] βάδην ἀλλ' added by Hubert, Castiglioni : lac. 4-5.
[2] Stephanus : μάλιστα.   [3] Wyttenbach : ἡδονὴν.
[4] Doehner : ἄπορον.

the ground that he had introduced in his *Symposium* [a] an unseemly and unnecessary discussion about the proper time for coition. For an older man to talk about sex in the presence of youths at a dinner-party and weigh the pros and cons of whether one should make love before dinner or after dinner was, they claimed, the extreme of indecency. At this, some of our company brought up Xenophon, who, so to speak, took his guests home after dinner, not on foot, but on horseback, to make love to their wives.[b] And Zopyrus the physician, who was very well acquainted with the works of Epicurus, added that they had not read Epicurus's *Symposium* with attention ; for Epicurus did not propose the problem as one involving a principle or a settled procedure and then proceed with his discussion of it ; but he took the young men for a walk after dinner, conversed with them for the purpose of moral instruction, and restrained them from their lust on the ground that intercourse is always precarious and harmful, and affects worse those who engage in it when they have been eating and drinking. " Indeed," said he, " even if intercourse were the chief topic of his inquiry, would it be to the philosopher's credit to have refrained entirely from all consideration of the right time and hour for coition ? Would it not be better for him to engage, at the proper moment, in rational discussion of such matters ? And would it be to his credit that he consider this stage of his discussion not inappropriate to any occasion except drinking and dining, and there shameful ? On the contrary, indeed, one can blame, I think, a philo-

[a] Epicurus, frag. 61 Usener.
[b] Xenophon, *Symposium*, ix. 7.

⁵ ἐν added by Turnebus, Xylander.

(653) τις ἐγκαλέσαι φιλοσόφῳ μεθ' ἡμέραν ἐν τῇ διατριβῇ
E πολλῶν καὶ παντοδαπῶν ἀνθρώπων παρόντων περὶ
τούτου διαλεγομένῳ, κύλικος δὲ προκειμένης ἐν
συνήθεσι καὶ φίλοις, ἔνθα καὶ τὸ παραλέξαι μῦθον
ἀμβλὺν ὄντα[1] καὶ ψυχρὸν ἐν οἴνῳ συμφέρει, πῶς
αἰσχρὸν εἰπεῖν τι καὶ ἀκοῦσαι εἰς συνουσίας χρῆσιν
ὠφελίμως λεγόμενον; ὡς ἔγωγε, νὴ τὸν κύνα, καὶ
τοὺς Ζήνωνος ἂν ἐβουλόμην," ἔφη, " διαμηρι-
σμοὺς[2] ἐν συμποσίῳ τινὶ καὶ παιδιᾷ μᾶλλον ἢ
σπουδῆς τοσαύτης ἐχομένῳ συγγράμματι, τῇ Πολι-
τείᾳ, κατατετάχθαι."

2. Πρὸς τοῦτο πληγέντες οἱ νεανίσκοι σιωπῇ
κατέκειντο· τῶν δ' ἄλλων τὸν Ζώπυρον ἀξιούντων
τοὺς περὶ τούτου λόγους Ἐπικούρου διελθεῖν, ἔφη
F τῶν μὲν κατὰ μέρος οὐκ[3] ἀκριβῶς μνημονεύειν,
οἴεσθαι δὲ τὸν ἄνδρα τὰς ἐκ τῆς συνουσίας πληγὰς
δεδιέναι διὰ τὸν τῶν σωμάτων παλμὸν εἰς ταραχὴν
καὶ σάλον ἐν τῷ τοιούτῳ βαδιζόντων. καθόλου
μὲν γὰρ ἐξ ἕδρας τὰ σώματα μεθιστάναι πλήκτην
ὄντα καὶ κινητικὸν ταραχῆς τὸν ἄκρατον· ἂν δ'
οὕτως ἔχοντα τὸν ὄγκον ἡμῶν γαλήνη μὴ[4] παρα-
λάβῃ καὶ ὕπνος, ἀλλ' ἕτεραι διὰ τῶν ἀφροδισίων
κινήσεις, ἐκθλιβομένων καὶ μοχλευομένων τῶν
μάλιστα συνδεῖν καὶ κολλᾶν τὸ σῶμα πεφυκότων,
654 κίνδυνός ἐστιν ἀνέδραστον[5] γίγνεσθαι τὸν ὄγκον,[6]

---

[1] ἀμβλὺν ὄντα Wyttenbach : ἀμβλύνοντα.
[2] Salmasius : διαμερισμούς.
[3] οὐκ added by Vulcobius.
[4] μὴ added by Stephanus.
[5] Doehner : ἀνάδαστον.
[6] ὄγκον Xylander (translation), Stephanus : οἶκον.

sopher who talks about this matter in his day-time lecturing, when many men of all sorts are present. But among one's companions and friends, wine-cup at hand, where even the telling of a dull and silly story is suitable as wine goes round,[a] how can it be shameful to say and to hear anything useful on the subject of coition ? " And he continued : " For my part, by the Dog, I could wish that Zeno [b] had put his remarks on ' thigh-spreading ' in the playful context of some dinner-party piece and not in his *Government*, a work which aims at such great seriousness."

2. This put the young men out of countenance, and they sat in silence. The rest of the company requested Zopyrus to give them an account of what Epicurus had to say about this matter, and he replied that he did not remember the particulars accurately, but thought that the man feared the afflictions resulting from coition, due to the disturbance caused by our bodies entering into the tumult and turmoil of such activity. For wine is generally a brawler, an instigator of tumult, and unsettles our body from its base ; and if tranquillity and sleep do not take possession of our body when it is in this condition, but the new disturbances of coition supervene, the forces which naturally tie together and cement the body are crushed and dislodged, and there is danger that the body be unseated, like a house shifted from its

---

[a] The Greek has been emended to recall a phrase quoted by Philodemus, *de Musica*, iv. 12, lines 1-3 (Kemke) and attributed by Wilamowitz to Pindar (*Pindaros*, pp. 142-143, 513 ; Snell, *Pindarus*, ii [1964], p. 104, 124 d). The connection between the two fragments (if any) and the relation of either to Pindar remain doubtful: see further, Annemarie Neubecker, *Philologus*, 98 (1954), pp. 155-158, and J. Irigoin, *Gnomon*, 33 (1961), p. 265—both cited by Snell, *loc. cit.*

[b] von Arnim, *Stoic. Vet. Frag.* i. 252.

(654) ὥσπερ οἶκον¹ ἐκ θεμελίων κινούμενον²· οὐδὲ γὰρ
εὖ ῥεῖν τηνικαῦτα τὴν γονήν, σφηνώσεως διὰ τὴν
πλησμονὴν οὔσης, ἀλλὰ βίᾳ καὶ συμπεφυρμένην
ἀποσπᾶσθαι· διὸ χρῆναί φησιν ὁ ἀνήρ, ὅταν ἡσυ-
χία γένηται περὶ τὸ σῶμα καὶ λωφήσωσιν αἱ τῆς
τροφῆς ἀναδόσεις καὶ τὰ ῥεύματα διεξιούσης καὶ
φευγούσης, τὰ τοιαῦτα πράττειν, πρὶν³ ἑτέρας αὖ
πάλιν τροφῆς ἐνδεὲς γενέσθαι τὸ σῶμα. συμβάλ-
λοιτο δ᾽ ἄν τις τούτῳ⁴ τῷ Ἐπικούρου⁵ καὶ τὸν
ἰατρικὸν⁶ λόγον. ὁ⁷ γὰρ μεθ᾽ ἡμέραν καιρός, ἤδη
τῆς πέψεως⁸ κρίσιν ἐχούσης, ἀσφαλέστερός⁹ ἐστιν·
B ἡ δὲ μετὰ τὸ δεῖπνον ὁρμὴ πρὸς τὴν συνουσίαν οὐκ
ἀκίνδυνος· ἄδηλον γὰρ εἰ, τῆς τροφῆς μὴ κρατη-
θείσης, ἀπεψίᾳ δέξαιτο τὸν ἐκ τῆς συνουσίας ἄρα-
δον¹⁰ καὶ παλμόν, ὥστε διττὴν τὴν βλάβην γενέσθαι.

3. Ὑπολαβὼν δ᾽ Ὀλύμπιχος, " ἐμοὶ μέν," ἔφη,
" τὸ τοῦ Πυθαγορικοῦ Κλεινίου λίαν ἀρέσκει· λέγεται γὰρ ἐρωτηθείς, ὁπηνίκα δεῖ μάλιστα γυναι-
κὶ προσιέναι, ' ὅταν,' φάναι, ' μάλιστα τυγχάνῃς
βλαβῆναι βουλόμενος.' καὶ γὰρ ὁ Ζώπυρος εἴρηκε νῦν, ἔχει τινὰ λόγον, καὶ τὸν ἕτερον καιρὸν
ἄλλας ἀκαιρίας ἔχοντα πρὸς τὸ πρᾶγμα καὶ δυσχερείας ὁρῶ. καθάπερ οὖν Θαλῆς ὁ σοφὸς ὑπὸ
C τῆς μητρὸς ἐνοχλούμενος γῆμαι κελευούσης εὖ

¹ οἶκον added by Reiske.
² Turnebus : γινόμενον.
³ Reiske : ὑφ᾽.
⁴ Hubert : lac. 4-5. *Cf.* T. C.'s transl. : " to *this* of Epicurus." ⁵ Hubert : Ἐπικούρῳ.
⁶ Turnebus : πατρικόν.
⁷ ὁ Basel edition : οὐ.
⁸ Turnebus : ὄψεως (*sic*).
⁹ Meziriacus : ἀσθενέστερον.
¹⁰ Doehner : ἄραβον.

foundations—for the seed does not flow easily at this time, repletion blocking it, but with effort it is extracted in a clotted mass. Consequently our man says that we must engage in such activity when the body is quiet and ended are the assimilations and fluxes of the nourishment which traverses and quits the body, and must do so before the body is again in need of further nourishment. To this analysis of Epicurus one can add a physician's opinion. The fact is that the safer time for coition is during the day, when the process of digestion is now completed. Rushing on to coition after dinner is not without danger, for one does not know whether, when food has not been assimilated, an indigestion may follow the disturbance and agitation resulting from coition, and the injury thus be twice as great.

3. Olympichus took up the discussion, saying, " For my part, I very much like the retort of the Pythagorean Kleinias : in reply to the question at what time most especially ought one to have coition with a woman, he is said to have answered, ' At whatever time you happen to want most especially to suffer harm.' [a] For, on the one hand, what Zopyrus has just said is reasonable enough, and, on the other, I see that the other possible time has other disadvantages and difficulties affecting the business. Therefore, just as the wise man Thales,[b] when annoyed by his mother's pleas that he get married, avoided her im-

---

[a] Diels and Kranz, *Frag. d. Vorsokratiker*, i[10], p. 444, 54. 5 ; Diodorus Siculus, x. 9. 4, and Diogenes Laertius, viii. 9, attribute the saying to Pythagoras in different wording. On sexual restrictions imposed by the Pythagorean Society see E. R. Dodds, *The Greeks and the Irrational*, p. 154 and note 122 on p. 175, and especially Aristoxenus, frag. 39 Wehrli.

[b] Diogenes Laertius, i. 26.

(654) πως[1] ὑπεξέφυγε καὶ[2] παρήγαγε λέγων[3] πρὸς αὐτήν[4] ἐν ἀρχῇ μέν, ʼοὔπω καιρὸς ὦ μῆτερ,ʼ ὕστερον δʼ, ʼοὐκέτι καιρὸς ὦ μῆτερ,ʼ οὕτως ἄρα καὶ πρὸς ἀφροδίσια κράτιστον[5] ἔχειν ἕκαστον, ὥστε κατακλινόμενον λέγειν, ʼοὔπω καιρός,ʼ ἀνιστάμενον δʼ, ʼοὐκέτι καιρός.ʼ ʼʼ

4. ʼʼ Ἀθλητικὰ ταῦτʼ,ʼʼ εἶπεν ὁ Σώκλαρος, ʼʼ ὦ Ὀλύμπιχε, παντάπασιν ἔτι τῆς κοτταβίσεως ὄζοντα καὶ τῶν κρεοφαγιῶν ἐκείνων, οὐκ ἐν δέοντι. νέοι τε γὰρ πάρεισι γεγαμηκότες, ὑφʼ ὧν δεῖ ʼφιλοτήσια ἔργα τελεῖσθαιʼ καὶ ἡμᾶς οὔπω παντάπασιν ἡ Ἀφροδίτη πέφευγεν, ἀλλὰ καὶ προσευχόμεθα[6] δήπουθεν αὐτῇ λέγοντες ἐν τοῖς τῶν θεῶν ὕμνοις

D　　　ἀνάβαλλʼ ἄνω τὸ γῆρας,
　　　　ὦ καλὰ ʼφροδίτα.

σκοπῶμεν οὖν, εἰ δοκεῖ, πότερον ἐμμελῶς καὶ προσηκόντως ὁ Ἐπίκουρος ἢ[7] παρὰ πᾶν δίκαιον ἀφαιρεῖ τὴν Ἀφροδίτην τῆς νυκτός· ἧς[8] καὶ τὸ κράτιστον αὐτῇ θεῶν μετεῖναί φησιν ἐρωτικὸς ἀνὴρ Μένανδρος. ἐνετέθη γὰρ οἶμαι καλῶς παρακάλυμμα τῆς ἡδονῆς τὸ σκότος προθεμένοις[9] ταῦτα πράσσειν καὶ μή, διὰ φωτὸς ἐντυγχάνοντας, ἐξελαύνειν[10] τῶν ὀμμάτων τὸ αἰδούμενον καὶ τῷ ἀκολάστῳ θάρσος ἐμποιεῖν καὶ μνήμας ἐναργεῖς,

---

[1] εὖ πως Pohlenz : πῶς.
[2] καὶ added by Stephanus.
[3] Reiske : λόγῳ.　　　　[4] αὐτὴν Vulcobius : τὴν.
[5] ἔσται omitted by Bases and Castiglioni after κράτιστον.
[6] Stephanus : προσερχόμεθα.
[7] ἢ added by Turnebus.

portunities well enough and diverted her by saying to her at first, ' It is not yet the right time, mother,' and later on, ' It is no longer the right time, mother,' so the best habit for each man to have about love-making is to say, when he goes to bed, ' It is not yet the right time,' and when he gets up, ' It is no longer the right time.' "

4. "This is athletes' talk, Olympichus," said Soclarus, " still thoroughly reeking of cottabus-playing and those roast-beef dinners of theirs, and it is not opportune. For among us are young married men who must ' do love's deeds '[a] ; and, Aphroditê has not yet completely abandoned us older men, but we too are imploring her favour, I suppose, when we say in the hymns of the gods

Our old-age postpone, fair Aphroditê.[b]

Let us then consider, if you will, whether it is proper and fitting, or contrary to all justice, for Epicurus to deprive Aphroditê of night, to which she has indeed the strongest claim among the gods, as Menander, an authority on love, claims.[c] Indeed, in my opinion it was a good thing to draw a veil of darkness over the pleasure of those who engage in this activity, yet do not wish to banish modesty from their eyes by making love in daylight, or to create bold, vivid, licentious

---

[a] *Odyssey*, xi. 246.

[b] J. M. Edmonds, *Lyra Graeca* (LCL), iii, p. 510, no. 3 ; Diehl, *Anth. Lyr. Graec.* ii, p. 29. 66, following Crusius, attributes the fragment to Alcman.

[c] The reference to Menander seems to be an adaptation of frag. 789 Körte, *Menander*, ii (1959), p. 246.

---

[8] ἧς added by Doehner, who expunged καί.

[9] προθεμένοις Cherniss : προθεμένους.

[10] Basel edition : ἐξελαύνων.

(654) αἷς τὸ¹ ἐνδιατρίβειν αὖθις ἐκριπίζει² τὰς³ ἐπιθυμίας.
' ὄψις γὰρ ἡμῖν ὀξυτάτη τῶν διὰ τοῦ σώματος
E ἔρχεται ' κατὰ τὸν Πλάτωνα ' παθημάτων,' καὶ
σφόδρα ταῖς ἐγγὺς φαντασίαις⁴ τὴν ψυχὴν ἐγείρουσα
πρὸς τὰ εἴδωλα τῆς ἡδονῆς, καινὴν ἀεὶ ποιεῖ⁵ καὶ
πρόσφατον τὴν⁶ ἐπιθυμίαν. ἡ δὲ νὺξ τὰ ἄπληστα⁷
καὶ μανιωδέστατα τῶν ἔργων ἀφαιροῦσα παράγει
καὶ κατευνάζει τὴν φύσιν οὐκ ἐξοκέλλουσαν⁸ ὑπὸ
τῆς ὄψεως εἰς ὕβριν.

' "Ανευ δὲ τούτων, τίν' ἔχει λόγον ἀπὸ δείπνου
μὲν ἥκοντα γεγανωμένον, ἂν οὕτω τύχῃ, στέφανον
κομίζοντα καὶ μύρῳ κεχριμένον, ἀποστραφέντα
καὶ συγκαλυψάμενον καθεύδειν, ἡμέρας δὲ καὶ διὰ
μέσου τῶν πράξεων ἐκ τῆς γυναικωνίτιδος τὴν
γυναῖκα μεταπέμπεσθαι πρός τι τοιοῦτον ἢ πρωὶ
F δίκην ἀλεκτρυόνος συμπλέκεσθαι; τὴν γὰρ ἑσπέ-
ραν, ὦ ἑταῖρε, τῶν πόνων ἀνάπαυσιν νομιστέον,⁹ τὸν
δ' ὄρθρον ἀρχήν· καὶ τὴν μὲν ὁ Λύσιος ἐπισκοπεῖ
Διόνυσος μετὰ τῆς Τερψιχόρης καὶ Θαλείας, ὁ δὲ
πρὸς τὴν ἐργάνην Ἀθηνᾶν καὶ τὸν ἀγοραῖον Ἑρ-
μῆν ἐπανίστησιν. διὸ τὴν μὲν ᾠδαὶ κατέχουσι καὶ

---

¹ μὴ omitted after τὸ in Basel edition.
² Turnebus : ἐκριπτεῖ.
³ Aldine edition : τῆς.
⁴ εἰς omitted after φαντασίαις by Xylander, Wyttenbach.
⁵ ποιεῖ added by Doehner.
⁶ τὴν added by Hubert, Castiglioni.

memories which pre-empt attention and rekindle lust.
' For vision is the keenest of the sensations which
traverse the body,' according to Plato,[a] and it makes
very efficient use of immediate impressions to rouse
images of pleasure in the mind, constantly renewing
and refreshing desire. But night blots out the in-
satiate and wildest of the deeds of love-making and
thus diverts and calms one's constitution, which
visual stimuli do not shipwreck on the shores of
outrage.

" Apart from this, what sense does it make for a
man to come from dinner, joyful it may be, bringing
his garland and anointed with perfume, and go to
bed, turn his back on his wife, and wrap himself up
in the covers,—but during the day, in the midst of
business, send for her to come from the women's
quarters for some such activity, or, like a cock, em-
brace her the first thing in the morning ? Evening,
my friend, marks the end of the day's work, one must
suppose, and morning the beginning. Dionysus Lord
of Relaxation,[b] Terpsichorê, and Thalia take charge of
evening ; morning rouses us for our duty to Athena
Mistress of Work [c] and Hermes Lord of the Market.[d]
Thus, song, dance, and the marriage-hymn occupy

---

[a] *Phaedrus*, 250 D.   [b] *Supra*, 613 c.

[c] *Cf. Mor.* 99 A and 802 B, quoting Sophocles, frag. 844
Pearson = 760 Nauck, and inscriptions; see *RE*, *s.v.* " Er-
gane."

[d] *Cf.* Aristophanes, *Knights*, 297 with Rogers's note ;
Aristophanes elsewhere (*e.g. Acharn.* 816) has the synonym
Empolaios for Hermes. Agoraios could refer to his patronage
of public business in the Agora, where his statue was, Pausanias, i. 15. 1.

---

[7] Doehner : πλεῖστα.   [8] Benseler : ἐξοκέλλουσα.

[9] νομιστέον added by Reiske, ἔχομεν Wyttenbach.

(654) χορεῖαι καὶ ὑμέναιος

κῶμοί τ' εἰλαπίναι τε καὶ ἠχήεις θρόος αὐλῶν·

τὸν δὲ κτύποι ῥαιστήρων καὶ τρισμοὶ[1] πρίονων καὶ
655 τελωνικῶν ἐπορθρισμοὶ κεκραγμῶν καὶ κηρύγματα
καλουμένων ἐπὶ δίκας ἢ θεραπείας τινῶν βασιλέων
ἢ ἀρχόντων· ἐν ᾧ καιρῷ φροῦδα τὰ τῆς ἡδονῆς,

λήγει δὲ Κύπρις θαλίαι τε νέων,
οὐδ' ἔτι θύρσος † φῦλα Βακχίου[2]·

συντείνουσι γὰρ αἱ φροντίδες. ἔπειτα δὲ καὶ ὁ
ποιητὴς τῶν ἡρώων οὔτε γαμετῇ τινα μεθ' ἡμέραν
οὔτε παλλακίδι συγκατέκλινεν πλὴν ἢ τὸν Πάριν
δραπετεύσαντα ποιήσας καταδυόμενον εἰς τοὺς
κόλπους τῆς γυναικός, ὡς οὐκ ἀνδρὸς ἀλλὰ μοιχοῦ
λυσσῶντος οὖσαν τὴν μεθημερινὴν ἀκρασίαν. καὶ
μὴν οὐδὲ τὸ σῶμα βλάπτοιτ' ἂν ὑπὸ τῆς συνουσίας
B μᾶλλον, ὡς Ἐπίκουρος οἴεται, μετὰ τὸ δεῖπνον,
ἄν γε μὴ μεθύων τις ἢ ῥηγνύμενος ὑπὸ πλησμονῆς
ἅπτηται βεβαρημένος· ἀμέλει γὰρ οὕτως ἐπισφαλὲς
τὸ πρᾶγμα καὶ βλαβερόν. ἂν δ' ἱκανῶς ἔχων τις
αὑτοῦ καὶ μετρίως διακεχυμένος, τοῦ τε σώματος
αὑτοῦ μαλακοῦ γεγονότος καὶ τῆς ψυχῆς παρ-
εστώσης, διὰ χρόνου ποιῆται τὴν ἔντευξιν, οὔτε
ταραχὴν ἀπεργάζεται μεγάλην κατὰ[3] τὸν ὄγκον
οὔτ' αὖ τινας ἢ σφύξεις[4] ἢ μεταθέσεις[5] ἐξ ἕδρας

---

[1] Turnebus : τριμμοί.
[2] Perhaps φῦλά τε Βάκχου, which is translated. φύλλα the
Aldine edition ; Βακχείου Stephanus.
[3] Hubert, Pohlenz : διά.
[4] οὔτ' αὖ τινας ἢ σφύξεις Usener : lac. 6-8 ταγένη ψύξις
(sic) ἤ.

the evening, and

> revels
> And feasting and the piercing wail of pipes [a];

but the other is filled by the clang of hammers, the chatter of saws, the early morning cries of the tax-collectors, and the proclamations of those who summon men to court or to the service of some king or magistrate. At this time the activities of pleasure vanish :

> The deeds of the Cypriote Lady stop,
> And the joys of the young ;
> No longer the thyrsus, no longer the Bacchic troops. [b]

For the day's concerns exert their pressure. Then the Poet [c] too put none of his heroes to bed during the day either with wife or with mistress, except when he represented Paris slinking off to his wife's bosom after he had run away from his post, as much as to say that the incontinence of day-time love-making is no part of an honest husband's behaviour but a mad adulterer's. And surely the body would not suffer greater harm by coition after dinner, as Epicurus thinks it does, provided a man does not make love when he is over-burdened, drunk or stuffed full to the point of bursting. For of course, if that is the case, the thing is precarious and harmful. But if a man is sufficiently himself and moderately relaxed, his body at ease and his spirit disposed, and if then after an interval he makes love, he neither causes his body great disturbance nor does he bring on any morbid excitement or

---

[a] Placed by Otto Schneider among the " anonymous fragments " of Callimachus, *Callimachea*, ii, p. 786, no. 377.

[b] Nauck, *Trag. Gr. Frag.*, Adespoton 397.

[c] Homer, *Iliad*, iii. 441–447.

---

[5] μεταθέσεις Usener : μετάθεσις.

(655) ἀτόμων, ᾗ φησιν Ἐπίκουρος· ἀλλὰ τῇ φύσει τὸ
οἰκεῖον¹ ἀποδούς, ἑαυτὸν δέ πως ἀπογαληνίσας²
ἀναπληρώσει, νέας ἐπιρροῆς τοῖς κενώμασι γιγνομένης.

"Ἐκεῖνο δὲ μᾶλλον ἄξιον εὐλαβείας, τὸ σύνεγγυς
C ὄντα τῶν πράξεων ἀφροδισίοις χρῆσθαι, μή τι³
ἄρα μετέωρον τὸ σῶμα καὶ κεκλονημένον αἵ τε
τῆς ψυχῆς φροντίδες αἵ τε περὶ τὰς χρείας πραγ-
ματεῖαι καὶ κόποι παραλαβόντες εὐθὺς ἐκτραχύνω-
σιν, οὐχ ἱκανὸν ἐν μέσῳ διάλειμμα τῆς φύσεως εἰς
ἀνάπαυσιν λαβούσης. οὐ γὰρ πάντες, ὦ ἑταῖρε,
τὴν Ἐπικούρου σχολὴν καὶ ῥαστώνην ὑπὸ λόγου
καὶ φιλοσοφίας ἄφθονον εἰς ἀεὶ παρεσκευασμένην
ἔχουσιν, πολλοὶ δ᾽ ἕκαστον ἀγῶνες ἐκδέχονται δι᾽
ἡμέρας, γυμνάσια δ᾽ ὡς ἔπος εἰπεῖν ἅπαντας· οἷς
οὔτε καλὸν οὔτε συμφέρον οὕτω διακείμενον τὸ
D σῶμα παρέχειν λυσσώσῃ συνουσίᾳ διακεχυμένον.⁴
τὸ δὲ μακάριον καὶ ἄφθαρτον ἔστω μὲν⁵ οἷον αὐτὸ
μὴ φροντίζειν τῶν καθ᾽ ἡμᾶς· ἡμῖν δέ που νόμῳ
πόλεως συνεπομένοις⁶ ἐξευλαβητέον ἐστὶν εἰς θεοῦ
γ᾽ ἐμβάλλειν⁷ καὶ κατάρχεσθαι θυσιῶν, ὀλίγον
ἔμπροσθεν διαπεπραγμένοις τι τοιοῦτον. ὅθεν εὖ
ἔχει τὸ τὴν νύκτα καὶ τὸν ὕπνον ἐν μέσῳ θεμένους
καὶ ποιήσαντας ἱκανὸν διάλειμμα καὶ διάστημα
καθαροὺς αὖθις ὥσπερ ἐξ ὑπαρχῆς καὶ ᾽νέα⁸ ἐφ᾽
ἡμέρῃ φρονέοντας᾽ κατὰ Δημόκριτον ἀνίστασθαι.''

---

¹ ἀλλὰ τῇ φύσει τὸ οἰκεῖον added by Wyttenbach : lac. 5-6.
² ηνίσας added by Wyttenbach : ἀπογαλ lac. 5-7.
³ μή τι Turnebus : μήτε.
⁴ Doehner : δια lac. 7-8.
⁵ Stephanus : μένον.
⁶ Doehner : εὖ ἐπομένοις.

unsettling of atoms, as Epicurus claims. But if he has given nature her due and has calmed himself to some degree, he will restore his system, for a new influx will occupy the parts emptied.

" It is love-making in the midst of preoccupation with affairs that is the more deserving of caution, lest mental worries and the troubles and difficulties concerned with business take hold of the body in its state of excitement and agitation and exasperate the condition because nature has failed to receive a sufficient interval for rest in between. For all men, my friend, do not possess Epicurus's leisure and equanimity,[a] which has been provided in everlasting abundance by reason and philosophy. But each one of us is occupied with one struggle after another day after day,—the exercise-schools receive practically all of us,—and to these struggles it is neither good nor proper to bring one's body in this condition, that is, enervated by the fury of coition. Let it be granted that that blessed and immortal deity can himself disregard what concerns us ; nevertheless, I suppose we must, in obedience to our city's law, guard carefully against rushing into a god's sanctuary and beginning the sacrifices when we have been engaged in any sexual activity a short time before. Hence it is well for us to have night and sleep intervene and after a sufficient interval and period to rise pure again as before, 'with fresh thoughts,' as Democritus says, ' for the fresh day.' " [b]

[a] Epicurus, frag. 426 Usener ; *infra*, 1033 c.
[b] Democritus, frag. 158 Diels ; *infra*, 722 D and 1129 E.

[7] εἰς θεοῦ ἐμβάλλειν Headlam (*Journ. of Philology*, xxiii [1895], p. 297 ; γ' ἐμβ. Helmbold (*Class. Phil.* xxxvi [1941,] p. 87) ; *ad templa* Xylander (translation) : εἰς θέρος ἐμβαλεῖν.
[8] Reiske : νέᾳ.

(655)

ΠΡΟΒΛΗΜΑ Ζ

Διὰ τί τὸ γλεῦκος ἥκιστα μεθύσκει

Collocuntur Plutarchi pater, Hagias, Aristaenetus,
Plutarchus, alii

E   1. Τοῦ νέου οἴνου Ἀθήνησι μὲν ἑνδεκάτῃ μηνὸς
Ἀνθεστηριῶνος[1] κατάρχονται, Πιθοίγια τὴν ἡμέραν
καλοῦντες· καὶ πάλαι γ᾽ ὡς ἔοικεν εὔχοντο, τοῦ
οἴνου πρὶν ἢ πιεῖν ἀποσπένδοντες, ἀβλαβῆ καὶ
σωτήριον αὐτοῖς τοῦ φαρμάκου τὴν χρῆσιν γενέσθαι. παρ᾽ ἡμῖν δ᾽ ὁ μὲν μὴν καλεῖται Προ-
στατήριος, ἕκτῃ δ᾽ ἱσταμένου νομίζεται θύσαντας
Ἀγαθῷ Δαίμονι γεύεσθαι τοῦ οἴνου μετὰ ζέφυ-
ρον· οὗτος γὰρ μάλιστα τῶν ἀνέμων ἐξίστησιν καὶ
κινεῖ τὸν οἶνον, καὶ ὁ τοῦτον διαφυγὼν ἤδη δοκεῖ
παραμένειν βέβαιος. ἔθυσεν οὖν ὁ πατὴρ ὥσπερ
εἰώθει τὴν θυσίαν, καὶ μετὰ τὸ δεῖπνον,[2] ἐπαινου-
F μένου τοῦ οἴνου, τοῖς φιλοσοφοῦσι μειρακίοις μεθ᾽
ἡμῶν προὔβαλεν ζητεῖν λόγον, ὡς τὸ γλεῦκος ἥκιστα μεθύσκει. τοῖς μὲν οὖν πολλοῖς παράδοξον
ἐφάνη καὶ ἄπιστον· ὁ δ᾽ Ἀγίας ἔφη τὸ γλυκὺ
πανταχοῦ προσίστασθαι καὶ πλήσμιον εἶναι· διὸ

---

[1] Ἀνθεστηριῶνος added by Xylander (translation), Reiske,
Wyttenbach.
[2] τὸ δεῖπνον Turnebus : τοῦ δείπνου.

---

[a] Imitated by Macrobius, *Saturnalia*, vii. 7. 14 ff.
[b] Cf. *infra*, 735 D-E. The name means Opening of Jars,
usually interpreted as " Wine Jars " ; but P. Stenzel, *Griech.
Kultusaltertümer*, p. 238, and A. W. Persson, *Religion of
Greece in Prehistoric Times*, pp. 17 f., argue that, since an
early use of the pithos was as a receptacle for the dead, the
Pithoigia was first an All Souls' Day, though later connected
with the Wine God. See further *Kl. P.*, *s.v.* " Anthesteria."

QUESTION 7 [a]

Why sweet new wine is least intoxicating

Speakers : Plutarch's father, Hagias, Aristaenetus,
Plutarch, others

1. At Athens people consecrate the fresh wine on
the eleventh of the month Anthesterion, calling the
day Pithoigia [b] ; and long ago, it seems, they used
to pour a libation of the wine before drinking and
pray that the use of the " medicine " be harmless and
safe for them. Among us the month is called Prostaterios,[c] and on the sixth of the month it is our
custom to sacrifice to our Good Genius [d] and taste
the wine,—after a Westerly, for this wind especially
changes and alters the wine, and wine which sur-
vives it successfully seems now certain to keep good.
My father had celebrated the ritual, as was his custom,
and after dinner, while the wine was being praised,
he proposed to the young men [e] of philosophical temperament among us the examination of a saying
that sweet new wine is least intoxicating. Now this
seemed an incredible paradox to many, but Hagias [f]
remarked that sweetness everywhere was offensive
and filling, and therefore one could not easily drink a

The Attic month Anthesterion might fall as early as February
or as late as March.

[c] Doubtless connected with Apollo Prostaterios, the Protector ; cf. RE, s.v. " Apollon," col. 64, and s.v. " Prostaterios," col. 900.

[d] A chthonic spirit and guardian of the house, perhaps
originally a ghost ; cf. Rohde, Psyche[10] (1925), i, p. 254, note
2 ; RE, s.v. " Agathodaimon."

[e] Perhaps pupils ; cf. Hartman, De Plutarcho Scriptore
et Philosopho (1916), pp. 381, 384 ff. ; RE, s.v." Plutarchos,"
col. 663.

[f] Supra, 642 E, 643 E.

(655) καὶ γλεύκους[1] οὐκ ἄν τινα πιεῖν ῥᾳδίως ὅσον εἰς
μέθην ἱκανόν ἐστιν· ἀπαγορεύειν γὰρ ἀηδίᾳ τὴν
ὄρεξιν ἄχρι τοῦ μὴ διψῆν προελθοῦσαν.[2] ὅτι δὲ τοῦ
γλυκέος διαφέρει τὸ ἡδὺ καὶ τὸν ποιητὴν ἐπιστά-
μενον λέγειν

656   τυρῷ καὶ μέλιτι γλυκερῷ καὶ ἡδέι οἴνῳ·

τὸν γὰρ οἶνον ἐν ἀρχῇ μὲν εἶναι γλυκύν, γίγνεσθαι
δ' ἡδὺν ὅταν εἰς τὸ αὐστηρὸν τῇ πέψει μεταβάλῃ
παλαιούμενος.

2. Ἀρισταίνετος δ' ὁ Νικαεὺς ἔν τισιν ἐνίοις[3]
γράμμασιν ἀνεγνωκὼς ἔφη μνημονεύειν, ὅτι γλεῦκος μιχθὲν[4] οἴνῳ παύει μέθην· τῶν δ' ἰατρῶν τινας
ἔλεγεν[5] τοὺς πλέον πιόντας κελεύειν ἐμεῖν,[6] εἶθ',
ὅταν μέλλωσι καθεύδειν, ἄρτον εἰς μέλι καταβά-
ψαντας ἐμφαγεῖν.[7] εἴ τι οὖν αἱ γλυκύτητες ἀμβλύ-
νουσιν ἄκρατον, εἰκότως ὁ νέος οἶνος οὐ μεθύσκει,
πρὶν ἂν ἡ γλυκύτης μεταβάλῃ.

3. Σφόδρ' οὖν ἀπεδεξάμεθα τὴν εὑρησιλογίαν
τῶν νεανίσκων, ὅτι τοῖς ἐμποδὼν οὐκ ἐπιπεσόντες
B ἰδίων ηὐπόρησαν ἐπιχειρημάτων. ἐπεὶ τά γε πρόχειρα καὶ ῥάδια λαβεῖν ἥ τε[8] βαρύτης ἐστὶ τοῦ
γλεύκους, ὡς Ἀριστοτέλης φησίν, ἡ διακόπτουσα
τὴν κοιλίαν, καὶ τὸ πολὺ συμμεμιγμένον[9] πνευματῶδες καὶ ὑδατῶδες· ὧν τὸ μὲν εὐθὺς ἐκπίπτει

---

[1] Reiske : γλεύκος.   [2] Vulcobius : προσελθοῦσαν.
[3] So T, accepted by Doehner ; others assume corruption
and propose various solutions, among which the deletion of
ἐνίοις seems best (Bollaan, cf. Bolkestein, *Adv. Crit.* p. 80,
note 1).
[4] Amyot : γλυκὺς μιχθείς.   [5] Turnebus : λέγει.
[6] ἐμεῖν added by Wyttenbach from Macrobius, *Saturnalia*,
vii. 7. 17.

quantity of sweet new wine sufficient for intoxication, for one's appetite, once thirst was satisfied, refused more with disgust. The Poet, too (he argued), wrote

Cheese, sweet honey, and pleasant wine,[a]

recognizing that " pleasantness " differs from " sweetness " ; for wine at first is " sweet " and becomes " pleasant " when the changes due to fermentation make it " dry " as it ages.

2. Aristaenetus of Nicaea said he recollected having read in a certain number of writings that sweet new wine mixed with other wine stops intoxication.[b] And he added that some doctors recommend that those who drink too much, first vomit and then, when they are about to go to bed, soak bread in honey and eat it. If, therefore, properties of sweetness in any degree blunt the effect of wine, the fresh wine is not intoxicating, reasonably enough, until its sweetness changes.

3. Now we heartily approved the ingenuity of the young men because they did not fall upon the obvious arguments, but had a good supply of their own attempts at a solution, although the explanations lying at hand and easy to understand are the heaviness of the sweet new wine (a heaviness which, as Aristotle says,[c] breaks on through the stomach) and the large amounts of gaseous and watery elements combined with the wine ; of these last two, the one soon forces

[a] Homer, *Odyssey*, xx. 69.
[b] *Cf.* Pseudo-Aristotle, *Problems*, iii. 13, 872 b 32 ff. Aristaenetus occurs only here.
[c] Aristotle, frag. 220 Rose (1886).

---

[7] ἔδοσαν omitted by Bases after ἐμφαγεῖν.
[8] ἤ τε Stephanus : ἤ τοι.   [9] Hubert : συμμένειν.

(656) βιαζόμενον, τὸ δὲ πέφυκε[1] ἀμβλύτερον ποιεῖν τὸν οἶνον· παλαίωσις δ'[2] ἐπίτασιν[3] ποιεῖ,[4] ἐκκρινομένου τοῦ ὑδατώδους· καὶ γίγνεται μέτρῳ μὲν ἐλάττων ὁ οἶνος δυνάμει δὲ σφοδρότερος.

ΠΡΟΒΛΗΜΑ Η

Διὰ τί τῶν ἀκροθωράκων λεγομένων οἱ σφόδρα μεθύοντες ἧττον
παρακινητικοί εἰσιν

Collocuntur Plutarchi pater, Plutarchus

C 1. "Οὐκοῦν," εἶπεν ὁ πατήρ, "ἐπεὶ παρακε-κινήκαμεν τὸν Ἀριστοτέλη, καὶ περὶ τῶν ἀκροθω-ράκων τι καλουμένων ἴδιον ἐπιχειρήσομεν εἰπεῖν;[5] οὐ γὰρ ἱκανῶς μοι δοκεῖ, καίπερ ὀξύτατος ὢν ἐν τοῖς τοιούτοις ζητήμασι, διηκριβωκέναι τὴν αἰτίαν. φησὶ γὰρ οἶμαι τοῦ μὲν νήφοντος εὖ καὶ κατὰ[6] τὰ ὄντα κρίνειν τὸν λογισμόν, τοῦ δ' ἄγαν μεθύοντος ἐκλελυμένην κατέχεσθαι τὴν αἴσθησιν, τοῦ δ' ἀκροθώρακος ἔτι μὲν ἰσχύειν τὸ φανταστικόν ἤδη δὲ τετεράχθαι τὸ λογιστικόν· διὸ καὶ κρίνειν D καὶ κακῶς κρίνειν ἐπακολουθοῦντα[7] ταῖς φαντα-σίαις. ἀλλὰ πῶς," εἶπεν, "ὑμῖν δοκεῖ περὶ τού-των;"

2. "Ἐμοὶ μέν," ἔφην, "ἐπισκοποῦντι κατ' ἐμαυτὸν ἀποχρῶν οὗτος ἦν πρὸς τὴν αἰτίαν ὁ λόγος· εἰ δὲ κελεύεις ἴδιόν τι κινεῖν, ὅρα πρῶτον εἰ τὴν εἰρημένην διαφορὰν ἐπὶ τὸ σῶμα μετοιστέον

---

[1] τὸ ὑδατῶδες omitted after πέφυκε by Doehner, Hirschig.
[2] δ' added by Wyttenbach.
[3] ἐπίτασιν Stephanus : ἐπὶ τὰ lac. 5.
[4] ποιεῖ added by Wessely, ἐμποιεῖ by Wyttenbach.

its way out and escapes, the other naturally and effectively blunts the impact of the wine. But aging increases its force, the water being separated out, and the wine becomes less in measure, more powerful in strength.

QUESTION 8

Why those who are very drunk are less deranged than the so-called tipsy

Speakers: Plutarch and his father

1. " Now that we have disturbed Aristotle," said my father, " shall we attempt also to say something of our own on the subject of the ' tipsy,' so called ? For sharp indeed though Aristotle [a] was in such investigations, it seems to me that here he failed to deal adequately with causation ; for he says, I believe, that the judgement of the sober man is capable of sound and realistic distinctions, that the perception of the man who drinks too much is suppressed and destroyed, and finally that the imaginative faculty of the tipsy man is still strong but his rational faculty in disorder : he judges, and judges badly, because he follows illusory appearances. But what," he concluded, " is your opinion of the matter ? "

2. " When I examined this passage of Aristotle for myself," I replied, " I found it adequate so far as causality is concerned. But if you request me to stir up something of my own, consider first whether one must attribute to the body the variation you have

---

[a] Pseudo-Aristotle, *Problems*, iii. 2, 871 a 8 ff.

---

[5] For punctuation see Denniston, *Greek Particles*, pp. 433 ff.
[6] κατὰ added by Doehner.
[7] Xylander : ἐπακολουθοῦντας.

(656) ἐστίν. τῶν γὰρ ἀκροθωράκων ἡ διάνοια μόνον
τετάρακται, τὸ δὲ σῶμα ταῖς ὁρμαῖς ἐξυπηρετεῖν
δύναται, μήπω βεβαπτισμένον· ὅταν δὲ κατα-
σεισθῇ καὶ πιεσθῇ, προδίδωσι τὰς ὁρμὰς καὶ
παρεῖται, μέχρι γὰρ ἔργων οὐ πρόεισιν· ἐκεῖνοι δὲ
τὸ σῶμα[1] συνεξαμαρτάνον ἔχοντες οὐ τῷ μᾶλλον
ἀλογιστεῖν ἀλλὰ τῷ μᾶλλον ἰσχύειν ἐλέγχονται.

E ἀπ' ἄλλης δ'," εἶπον, "ἀρχῆς σκοποῦντι τοῦ
οἴνου τὴν δύναμιν οὐδὲν κωλύει ποικίλην εἶναι
καὶ τῇ ποσότητι συμμεταβάλλουσαν· ὥσπερ τὸ
πῦρ τὸν κέραμον, ἂν μὲν ᾖ μέτριον, συγκρατύνει
καὶ πήγνυσιν, ἂν δ' ὑπερβολῇ πλήξῃ, συνέτηξε καὶ
ῥεῖν ἐποίησεν· ἀνάπαλιν δ' ἡ ὥρα τοὺς πυρετοὺς
ἀρχομένη μὲν ἀνακινεῖ καὶ ἐκκαίει, προϊούσης δὲ
μᾶλλον καθίστανται καὶ ἀπολήγουσιν. τί οὖν
κωλύει καὶ τὴν διάνοιαν ὑπὸ τοῦ οἴνου φυσικῶς
κινουμένην, ὅταν ταραχθῇ καὶ παροξυνθῇ, πάλιν
ἀνίεσθαι καὶ καθίστασθαι πλεονάζοντος; ὁ γοῦν ἐλλέβορος ἀρχὴν τοῦ καθαίρειν ἔχει τὸ ταράττειν τὸν

F ὄγκον· ἂν οὖν[2] ἐλάττων τοῦ μετρίου δοθῇ, ταράττει
μὲν οὐδὲν δὲ καθαίρει. καὶ τῶν ὑπνωτικῶν ἔνιοι
λαβόντες ἐνδοτέρω τοῦ μετρίου θορυβωδέστερον
διατίθενται, πλέον δὲ λαβόντες[3] καθεύδουσιν. εἰκὸς
δέ που καὶ ταύτην τὴν περὶ τὸν ἀκροθώρακα
ταραχήν, ὅταν ἀκμὴν λάβῃ, μαραίνεσθαι, καὶ πρὸς
τοῦτο συνεργεῖν τὸν οἶνον· πολὺς γὰρ εἰσελθὼν τὸ

657 σῶμα συνεξέκαυσε καὶ κατανάλωσε τὸ μανιῶδες
τῆς ψυχῆς. ὥσπερ γὰρ[4] ἡ θρηνῳδία καὶ ὁ ἐπι-

---

[1] σῶμα added by Hubert after Xylander (translation).
[2] ἂν οὖν Hubert: αλοῦν (λ— or ν?— in an erasure).
[3] ἔνιοι omitted after λαβόντες by Reiske.

mentioned. Tipsy people's mind alone is disordered ; the body, not yet soaked, is still the able servant of impulse. But when the body is overthrown and oppressed by the weight of intoxication, it betrays and completely neglects its impulses, for it does not advance to the point of action. The tipsy, on the contrary, with a body which joins in error, are disgraced not by the fact that they are more irrational, but by the fact that they possess greater strength to act. And if one consider the matter," I continued, " from another point of view, there is nothing to prevent the power of wine from being variable and changing in proportion to its quantity, as fire, if it is the right amount, strengthens and hardens pottery, but if an excessive amount strikes the pottery, the fire fuses it and makes it flow. Again, the beginning of spring stirs up fevers and makes them burn, but as the hot season advances, fevers abate and cease. What, then, prevents the mind, naturally roused by wine, after it has fallen into disorder and excitement, from becoming relaxed and calm again as the wine becomes excessive ? At any rate, hellebore has the characteristic of causing the body distress as it begins its purging action ; if, then, less than the dose be given, the drug causes distress but does not purge. And some people become more excited when they take a subnormal dose of sedatives, but sleep when they take more. It is also likely, I suppose, that this disorder which characterizes the tipsy, when it attains its height, dies down and further that the wine works as a whole toward this end, for the large quantity which has come into the body joins in burning out and consuming the mind's frenzy. For, as dirge and

---

[4] γὰρ added by Wyttenbach.

(657) κήδειος αὐλὸς ἐν ἀρχῇ πάθος κινεῖ καὶ δάκρυον
ἐκβάλλει, προάγων δὲ τὴν ψυχὴν εἰς οἶκτον οὕτω
κατὰ μικρὸν ἐξαιρεῖ καὶ ἀναλίσκει τὸ λυπητικόν,
ὁμοίως ἴδοις ἂν καὶ τὸν οἶνον, ὅταν σφόδρα ταράξῃ
καὶ παροξύνῃ[1] τὸ ἀκμαῖον καὶ θυμοειδές, αὖθις
καταδύοντα καὶ καθιστάντα[2] τὴν διάνοιαν, ὡς
πορρωτέρω μέθης προϊοῦσαν ἡσυχάζειν.''

ΠΡΟΒΛΗΜΑ Θ

Περὶ τοῦ '' ἢ πέντε πίνειν ἢ τρί' ἢ μὴ τέσσαρα''

Collocuntur Aristio, Plutarchus, Plutarchi pater

B   1. Ἐμοῦ δὲ ταῦτ' εἰπόντος, Ἀριστίων ἀναβοή-
σας ὥσπερ εἰώθει, '' πέφανται,'' εἶπεν, '' εἰς τὰ
συμπόσια τῷ δικαιοτάτῳ καὶ δημοκρατικωτάτῳ
τῶν μέτρων κάθοδος, ὑπὸ δή τινος καιροῦ νήφοντος ὥσπερ τυράννου πεφυγαδευμένῳ πολὺν χρόνον.
καθάπερ γὰρ οἱ περὶ λύραν κανονικοὶ τῶν λόγων
φασὶ τὸν μὲν ἡμιόλιον τὴν διὰ πέντε συμφωνίαν
παρασχεῖν, τὸν δὲ διπλάσιον τὴν διὰ πασῶν, τὴν δὲ
διὰ τεσσάρων ἀμυδροτάτην οὖσαν ἐν ἐπιτρίτῳ συνίστασθαι, οὕτως οἱ περὶ τὸν Διόνυσον ἁρμονικοὶ
τρεῖς κατεῖδον οἴνου συμφωνίας πρὸς ὕδωρ, διὰ
C πέντε καὶ διὰ τριῶν καὶ διὰ τεσσάρων, οὕτω μὲν
λέγοντες καὶ ᾄδοντες

ἢ[3] πέντε πίνειν ἢ τρί' ἢ μὴ τέσσαρα.

πέντε γάρ ἐστιν[4] ἐν ἡμιολίῳ λόγῳ, τριῶν[5] ὕδατος

---

[1] καὶ παροξύνῃ Xylander : παροξύνει.
[2] Reiske : καταδύονται καὶ καθίστανται.
[3] ἢ added by Vulcobius.
[4] ἐστιν added by Wyttenbach : lac. 1-2.

funereal pipe at first rouse grief and cause tears to flow, and thus by leading the soul to pity little by little remove and consume distress, so in like manner you can see that wine too, when it very much harasses and excites the full vigour of passion, quiets the mind again, and calms it, and finally, as it advances farther into drunkenness, lays it peacefully to rest."

QUESTION 9

On " Drink five or three, not four "

Speakers : Aristion, Plutarch, and Plutarch's father

1. When I had said this, Aristion [a] spoke up loudly in his usual manner : " The most just and democratic of rules, one long exiled by some abstemious fashion as by a tyrant, is in sight of restitution to drinking-parties. Now just as the experts in the musical theory of the lyre assert that among ratios that of 3 : 2 gives the concord of the fifth, 2 : 1 the concord of the octave, and the concord of the fourth (which is weakest) consists in the ratio 4 : 3 ; so the musicologists of Dionysus observed three concords of wine and water, fifth, third and fourth, for in their song they say this :

Drink five or three, not four.[b]

' Five,' indeed, is in the ratio 3 : 2, three parts of

---

[a] A man learned in matters of food and wine ; cf. infra, 692 b ff., 696 e f. It is uncertain whether or not he is the same as Aristion the father of Soclarus at *Amatorius*, 749 b.

[b] Cf. The Proclan scholion on Hesiod, *Works and Days*, 591–596 (pp. 191–192 Pertusi) ; further, Athenaeus, x, 426 d.

---

[5] Basel edition : lac. 4–5 ων.

(657) κεραννυμένων[1] πρὸς δύ' οἴνου· τρία[2] δ' ἐν διπλασίῳ
πρὸς ἕνα[3] μιγνυμένων δυεῖν· τέσσαρα δ', εἰς ἕνα
τριῶν ὕδατος ἐπιχεομένων, οὗτός ἐστιν ἐπίτριτος
λόγος, ἀρχόντων τινῶν[4] ἐν πρυτανείῳ νοῦν ἐχόντων
ἢ διαλεκτικῶν τὰς ὀφρῦς ἀνεσπακότων, ὅταν τὰς
μεταπτώσεις τῶν λόγων ἀνασκοπῶσι,[5] νηφάλιος
καὶ ἀδρανὴς κρᾶσις.[6] ἐκείνων δὲ τῶν ἄλλων ἡ μὲν
δυεῖν πρὸς ἕνα τὸν ταρακτικὸν τοῦτον καὶ ἀκροθώρακα τῆς μέθης ἐπάγει τόνον

D   κινοῦντα χορδὰς τὰς ἀκινήτους φρενῶν·

οὔτε γὰρ ἐᾷ νήφειν οὔτε καταδύει[7] παντάπασι τὸν
ἀνόητον εἰς τὸν ἄκρατον· ἡ δὲ δυεῖν πρὸς τρία
μουσικωτάτη, πᾶσ' ὑπνοφόρος καὶ λαθικηδὴς καὶ
κατὰ τὴν Ἡσιόδειον ἐκείνην ‘ ἀλεξιάρην παίδων
εὐκηλήτειραν' τῶν ἐν ἡμῖν ἀγερώχων καὶ ἀκό-
σμων παθῶν διὰ βάθους ποιοῦσα γαλήνην καὶ
ἡσυχίαν.''

2. Πρὸς ταῦτα τῷ Ἀριστίωνι[8] ἀντεῖπε μὲν οὐδείς·
δῆλος γὰρ ἦν παίζων· ἐγὼ δ' ἐκέλευσα λαβόντα
ποτήριον ὥσπερ λύραν ἐντείνεσθαι τὴν ἐπαινου-
μένην κρᾶσιν καὶ ἁρμονίαν, καὶ προσελθὼν ὁ παῖς
E ὑπέχει τὸν ἄκρατον· ὁ δ' ἀνεδύετο, λέγων ἅμα
γέλωτι τῶν λογικῶν εἶναι περὶ μουσικὴν οὐ τῶν
ὀργανικῶν. ὁ μέντοι πατὴρ τοσοῦτον ἐπεῖπε τοῖς
εἰρημένοις, ὅτι δοκοῦσιν αὐτῷ καὶ οἱ παλαιοὶ τοῦ
μὲν Διὸς δύο ποιεῖν τιθήνας, τὴν Ἴδην[9] καὶ τὴν

---

[1] κεραννυμένων Turnebus, who also omitted οὐ before πρὸς:
κεραννυμένον οὐ.
[2] τρία Turnebus : τα.
[3] ἕνα added by Wyttenbach (Turnebus ἐν).
[4] Turnebus : τριῶν.
[5] Wyttenbach : ἀνασπῶσι.

water being mixed with two of wine ; ' three ' is in the ratio 2 : 1, two parts of water being mixed with one of wine ; and four,—three parts of water being poured into one of wine, this is a ratio of 4 : 3, a drink for some group of sensible magistrates in the prytaneion, or logicians their brows contracted as they meditate upon syllogistic conversions, a sober and a feeble mixture. Of the two others, the mixture with ratio 2 : 1 brings on that disturbing and half-drunk pitch of intoxication

> that plays upon
> The inviolate strings of the mind,[a]

for neither does it allow sobriety nor does it completely immerse the foolish man in strong drink. But the mixture with a ratio of 2 : 3 is most harmonious, a complete inducer of sleep and relaxer of care, a ' protecting and soothing governess,' in Hesiod's phrase,[b] because it creates a profound calm and quiet among our lordly and disordered passions."

2. No one attacked Aristion's remarks, for clearly his talk was play. And I invited him to take a cup as his lyre and tune it to the scale of the medley he praised. The servant came forward and was beginning to pour the wine, but Aristion declined, saying with a laugh that he was a theorist of music, not a performer. Then my father made the following addition to what had been said : the ancients too, it was his opinion, made Zeus's nurses two (Ida and

---

[a] Nauck, *Trag. Gr. Frag.*, Adespoton 361, quoted also in *Mor.* 43 E, 456 c, 501 A, and 502 D.
[b] *Works and Days*, 464.

---

[6] Turnebus : φασις (*sic*).   [7] Hubert : καταδύειν.
[8] 'Αρίστωνι T (*cf.* 657 B, 'Αριστίων ; 692 B, 'Αρίστωνος ; and 692 E, 'Αριστίων).   [9] Xylander : ἴτην.

(657) Ἀδράστειαν, τῆς δ' Ἥρας μίαν, τὴν Εὔβοιαν·
ἀμέλει δὲ καὶ τοῦ Ἀπόλλωνος δύο, τὴν Ἀλήθειαν
καὶ τὴν Κορυθάλειαν· τοῦ δὲ Διονύσου πλείονας,
ὅτι δεῖ τὸν θεὸν τοῦτον ἐν πλείοσι μέτροις νυμφῶν
τιθασευόμενον καὶ παιδευόμενον ἡμερώτερον ποιεῖν
καὶ φρονιμώτερον.

ΠΡΟΒΛΗΜΑ Ι

Διὰ τί τὰ κρέα σήπεται μᾶλλον ὑπὸ τὴν σελήνην ἢ τὸν ἥλιον

Collocuntur Euthydemus, Satyrus, Moschio, Plutarchus

F 1. Εὐθύδημος ὁ Σουνιεὺς ἑστιῶν ἡμᾶς σὺν ἄ-
γριον εὐμεγέθη παρέθηκεν· ἐπιθαυμασάντων δὲ
τῶν παρόντων, ἄλλον ἔφη πολὺ μείζονα κομιζό-
μονον ὑπὸ τῆς σελήνης διαφθαρῆναι καὶ σφόδρα γε
περὶ τῆς αἰτίας διαπορεῖν· οὐ γὰρ εἰκὸς εἶναι μὴ
τὸν ἥλιον μᾶλλον τὰ κρέα σήπειν θερμότερον ὄντα
658 τῆς σελήνης. ὁ δὲ Σάτυρος, " οὐ τοῦτ'," ἔφη,
" μάλιστα θαυμάσειεν ἄν τις, ἀλλὰ μᾶλλον τὸ ὑπὸ
τῶν κυνηγῶν γιγνόμενον· ὅταν γὰρ ἢ σῦν ἢ ἔλαφον
καταβαλόντες πόρρωθεν εἰς πόλιν ἀποστέλλωσι,
χαλκοῦν ἐμπηγνύουσιν ἧλον ὡς βοηθοῦντα πρὸς
τὴν σῆψιν."

2. Ὡς οὖν ἐπαυσάμεθα δειπνοῦντες καὶ πάλιν ὁ
Εὐθύδημος ἐπεμνήσθη[1] τοῦ διαπορηθέντος, Μοσχίων
ἔφησεν[2] ὁ ἰατρὸς τὴν σῆψιν τῆξιν εἶναι[3] καὶ ῥύσιν

---

[1] Stephanus : ἐπιμνησθείς.
[2] Basel edition : ἔφη.
[3] εἶναι added by Reiske.

---

[a] The Hyades (*RE*, viii. 2620) and others. *Cf. supra*, p. 13.
[b] Imitated by Macrobius, *Saturnalia*, vii. 16. 15 ff. *Cf.
De Facie in Orbe Lunae*, 939 F, with Cherniss's note *b*.

Adrastea), Hera's one (Euboea), and Apollo's of course two (Alethea and Corythalea), but gave Dionysus more, for it was necessary to make this god more gentle and prudent by giving him nymphs [a] in greater measure to tame him and civilize him.

QUESTION 10 [b]

Why meat spoils more readily in moonlight than in sunlight

Speakers: Euthydemus, Satyrus, Moschion, Plutarch

1. EUTHYDEMUS [c] of Sunium, when entertaining us at dinner, served up a wild boar of remarkable size. When the company had expressed their astonishment at the size, he said that a much larger one he had caused to be procured had been spoiled by the moon and he was very much at a loss to know the cause, for it was not likely (he thought) that the sun, being hotter than the moon, was less effective at spoiling meat. And Satyrus [d] said, "The most astonishing thing is not perhaps this, but rather the practice of hunters. When they have killed a boar or a deer and are sending it back to town, they drive a bronze nail into the carcass to preserve it against spoilage."

2. Then when we had finished dinner and Euthydemus mentioned again his perplexity, Moschion [e] the physician remarked that spoilage was a disin-

---

[c] C. Memmius Euthydamus in the list of Delphic priests, *RE*, iv. 2671; *cf. infra*, 700 E "my colleague as priest"; apparently it was to his son, Plutarch's pupil (*Mor.* 965 c), that *De Audiendis* was dedicated, *RE*, *s.v.* "Plutarchos," cols. 674 f.

[d] Apparently only here.

[e] *Mor.* 122 B, D, where his philosophic bias is lauded.

(658) σαρκὸς εἰς ὑγρὸν φθορᾷ[1] μεταβαλούσης, καὶ ὅλως
ὑγραίνεσθαι τὰ σηπόμενα· θερμασίαν δὲ πᾶσαν, ἂν
μὲν ᾖ μαλακὴ καὶ πραεῖα, κινεῖν τὰ ὑγρὰ καὶ τὴν
B ξηρότητα κωλύειν,[2] ἂν δ' ᾖ πυρώδης, τοὐναντίον
ἀπισχναίνειν τὰς σάρκας. ἐκ δὲ τούτων φανερὸν
εἶναι τὸ ζητούμενον· τὴν γὰρ σελήνην ἠρέμα
χλιαίνουσαν ἀνυγραίνειν τὰ σώματα, τὸν δ' ἥλιον
ἀναρπάζειν μᾶλλον ἐκ τῶν σωμάτων τὸ νοτερὸν
διὰ τὴν πύρωσιν· πρὸς ὃ καὶ τὸν Ἀρχίλοχον
εἰρηκέναι φυσικῶς

> ἔλπομαι, πολλοὺς μὲν αὐτῶν Σείριος καταυανεῖ[3]
> ὀξὺς ἐλλάμπων·

ἔτι δὲ σαφέστερον Ὅμηρον ἐπὶ τοῦ Ἕκτορος, ᾧ
κειμένῳ νεφέλην τινὰ σκιερὰν ὁ Ἀπόλλων ἐπήγαγεν,

> μὴ πρὶν μένος ἠελίοιο
> σκήλη ἀμφὶ περὶ χρόα ἴνεσιν ἠδὲ μέλεσσιν·

τὴν δὲ σελήνην ἀδρανεστέρας ἀφιέναι τὰς αὐγάς·

C   > μέλας γὰρ αὐταῖς οὐ πεπαίνεται βότρυς

κατὰ τὸν Ἴωνα.

3. Λεχθέντων δὲ τούτων, ἐγώ, " τἄλλα μέν,"
ἔφην, " εἴρηται καλῶς· τῇ δὲ ποσότητι καὶ τῷ
μᾶλλον καὶ ἧττον τῆς θερμασίας κρίνειν[4] τὸ
συμβὰν[5] οὐ δεῖ· καὶ[6] γὰρ ἥλιον ὁρῶμεν ἧττον ἐν[7]

---

[1] Reiske : φθορᾶς.
[2] κω erased in T. τὴν ξηρότητα added by P. A. C.
[3] Hatzidakis, Helmbold : καθαυανεῖ.
[4] τῷ μᾶλλον . . . κρίνειν Wyttenbach (Turnebus suggested
τῷ μᾶλλον, according to Hutten) : τὸ μᾶλλον κατὰ τὸν τῆς
θερμασίας καιρόν.

tegration and liquefaction of the carcass, which
changed into a fluid as it decayed, and rotted flesh
became completely liquefied. All heat (he pointed
out), if it is gentle and mild, stirs moisture and prevents dryness ; but if it is a fiery heat, it has the
opposite effect of drying out flesh. These considerations clarify the problem : the moon by its gentle
warmth humidifies carcasses ; it is rather the sun
which, because of its fiery heat, robs carcasses of
their moisture. With reference to this Archilochus
has written [a] in accord with nature

> I hope the Dog will wither lots of them
> With his keen rays !

Still clearer is what Homer said of Hector, when
Apollo brought up a cloud to shade him as he lay
dead,[b]

> Lest the strength of the sun cause the flesh
> On his muscles and limbs to dry up.

But the moon (he concluded) sends out rays which
are weaker ;

> Dark clustered grapes are not matured by them,

in Ion's phrase.[c]

3. When Moschion had finished, I said : " This is
a fine statement in almost every way, but one ought
not to judge the result by the quantity and degree of
heat. For we see that the sun heats less in winter,

---

[a] Frag. 61 Bergk, 63 Diehl (1952).
[b] Iliad, xxiii. 190 f.
[c] Nauck, *Trag. Gr. Frag.* p. 744, no. 57, quoted also at
Mor. 929 A.

---

5 συμβὰν Madvig : σύμπαν.
6 καὶ added by Wyttenbach.   7 ἐν added by Hirschig.

(658) τῷ χειμῶνι θάλποντα καὶ μᾶλλον ἐν τῷ θέρει
σήποντα τὰ σώματα· τοὐναντίον δ' ὤφειλε ποιεῖν,
εἰ μαλακότητι τῆς θερμασίας αἱ σήψεις ἐγίγνοντο·
νυνὶ δ', ὅτε μᾶλλον ἐντείνει τὸ καῦμα, θᾶσσον
διαφθείρει[1] τὰς σάρκας. οὐκοῦν οὐδ' ἡ σελήνη δι'
ἔνδειαν ἀλέας καὶ ἀσθένειαν εἰς σῆψιν ἄγει τὰ
νεκρὰ τῶν σωμάτων, ἀλλ' ἰδιότητα μᾶλλον αἰ-
D τιατέον τοῦ φερομένου ῥεύματος ἀπ' αὐτῆς. ὅτι
γὰρ οὐ μίαν ἔχει ποιότητα πᾶν τὸ θερμόν, αὐτῷ
μόνῳ τῷ μᾶλλον καὶ ἧττον διαφέρουσαν, ἀλλ'
εἰσὶ πάμπολλαι τοῦ πυρὸς δυνάμεις οὐδὲν ἀλλή-
λαις ἐοικυῖαι, δῆλον ἀπὸ τῶν προχειροτάτων. οἱ
μὲν γὰρ χρυσοχόοι διὰ τῆς ἀχυρίνης φλογὸς[2]
ἐργάζονται τὸν χρυσόν, οἱ δ' ἰατροὶ μάλιστα τῇ
κληματίνῃ τὰ συνεψόμενα τῶν φαρμάκων ὑπο-
χλιαίνουσιν· πρὸς δὲ τὴν τοῦ ὑέλου μάλαξιν καὶ
τύπωσιν εὐάρμοστον εἶναι δοκεῖ τὸ μυρίκινον· τὸ
δ' ἀπὸ τῆς ἐλαίας τὰ μὲν σώματα ταῖς πυρίαις εὖ
διατίθησι, τοῖς δὲ βαλανείοις πολέμιόν ἐστιν καὶ λυ-
E μαίνεται τὴν πινάκωσιν αὐτῶν καὶ τοὺς θεμελίους
ὑποκαιόμενον· ὅθεν οἱ χαρίεντες ἀγορανόμοι τοὺς
ἐργολαβοῦντας οὐκ ἐῶσιν ἐλαΐνοις ξύλοις χρῆσθαι,
καθάπερ οὐδ' αἴρας[3] ἐμβαλεῖν εἰς τὴν ὑπόκαυσιν, αἱ
γὰρ ἀπὸ[4] τούτων ἀναθυμιάσεις καρηβαρίας καὶ
σκοτώματα τοῖς λουομένοις ἐμποιοῦσιν. οὐδὲν
οὖν θαυμαστόν ἐστιν καὶ τὴν σελήνην τοῦ ἡλίου
διαφέρειν, τοῦ μὲν ξηραντικὰ τῆς δὲ χαλαστικὰ
καὶ κινητικὰ τῶν ἐν τοῖς[5] σώμασιν ὑγρῶν ἀφιείσης
ῥεύματα. διὸ τὰ μὲν νήπια παντάπασιν αἱ τίτθαι
δεικνύναι πρὸς[6] τὴν σελήνην φυλάττονται· πλήρη
274

yet carcasses spoil more readily in summer, and they ought to do the opposite, if spoilage were the result of gentle heat ; but actually, the more intense the heat, the faster it rots flesh. Accordingly, it is not because of a lack of heat and a weakness of heat that the moon induces spoilage in dead bodies ; on the contrary, one must claim that the cause is rather a peculiarity of the stream of heat which comes from the moon. For it is obvious from the most ordinary things that all heat is not of one kind differing in degree alone, rather that the properties of fire are indeed many with no resemblance to each other. Goldsmiths use a chaff fire for working gold, physicians use a vine-twig fire to heat by degrees decoctions of drugs, and tamarisk wood seems to be most suitable for melting and moulding glass. A fuel of olive wood for sweat baths has a beneficial effect upon people's bodies, but is injurious to bath buildings and dirties their panelling and their foundation stones as it burns underneath the building ; this is the reason why conscientious commissioners do not allow concessionaries who operate bathing establishments to use olive wood for fuel, just as they refuse to let them put darnel into their furnace fire, since the fumes of this plant give the bathers headaches and induce vertigo. It is not astonishing, then, that the moon too differs from the sun, the latter sending out withering streams of heat and the former emitting streams which loosen and set in motion the moisture in bodies. Thus nurses are exceedingly careful to avoid exposing young

---

[1] διαφθείρει Hirschig : ἐνδιαφθείρει.
[2] Basel edition : ὡς λόγος.   [3] Basel edition : ἀρᾶς.
[4] ἀπὸ Wyttenbach with E and γ : ὑπὸ.
[5] τῶν ἐν τοῖς Reiske : τοῖς ἐνίοις.
[6] πρὸς added in Basel edition.

(658) γὰρ ὑγρότητος ὄντα, καθάπερ τὰ χλωρὰ τῶν
F ξύλων, σπᾶται καὶ διαστρέφεται. τοὺς δὲ κατα-
κοιμηθέντας ἐν αὐγῇ σελήνης μόλις ἐξανιστα-
μένους οἷον ἐμπλήκτους ταῖς αἰσθήσεσι καὶ ναρ-
κώδεις ὁρῶμεν· ἡ γὰρ ὑγρότης ὑπὸ τῆς σελήνης
διαχεομένη βαρύνει τὰ σώματα. λέγεται δὲ καὶ
πρὸς εὐτοκίαν συνεργεῖν, ὅταν ᾖ διχόμηνος, ἀνέσει
τῶν ὑγρῶν μαλακωτέρας παρέχουσα τὰς ὠδῖνας.
659 ὅθεν οἶμαι καὶ τὴν Ἄρτεμιν Λοχείαν καὶ Εἰλεί-
θυιαν, οὐκ οὖσαν ἑτέραν ἢ τὴν σελήνην, ὠνομάσθαι.
Τιμόθεος δ' ἄντικρύς φησιν

διὰ κυάνεον πόλον ἄστρων,
διά τ' ὠκυτόκοιο σελάνας.

γίγνεται δὲ καὶ περὶ τὰ ἄψυχα τῶν σωμάτων
ἐπίδηλος ἡ τῆς σελήνης δύναμις· τῶν τε γὰρ
ξύλων τὰ τεμνόμενα ταῖς πανσελήνοις ἀποβάλ-
λουσιν οἱ τέκτονες ὡς ἁπαλὰ καὶ μυδῶντα ταχέως
δι' ὑγρότητα, τούς τε[1] πυροὺς οἱ γεωργοῦντες
σπεύδουσι φθίνοντος τοῦ μηνὸς ἐκ τῆς ἅλω συναί-
ρειν, ἵνα παγέντες[2] τῇ ξηρότητι μᾶλλον πρὸς τὸν
χρόνον[3] ἀντέχωσιν· οἱ δ' ἀκμῇ τῆς σελήνης δια-
κομιζόμενοι κόπτονται μάλιστα διὰ τὴν ὑγρότητα
B μαλακώτεροι γιγνόμενοι. λέγουσι δὲ καὶ τἄλευρον
ἐν ταῖς πανσελήνοις ζυμοῦσθαι βέλτιον· ἡ γὰρ
ζύμωσις ὀλίγον ἀποδεῖ σῆψις εἶναι[4]· κἂν ἀποβάλῃ
τὸ μέτρον, ἐπὶ τὴν αὐτὴν φθορὰν ἀραιοῦσα καὶ
λεπτύνουσα τὸ φύραμα προήγαγεν. αἱ δὲ σηπό-

---

[1] Ziegler : δέ.
[2] Meziriacus : πάντες.
[3] τὸν χρόνον Wyttenbach, χρόνον Turnebus : lac. 2-3 νον.

276

children to the moon, for, being full of moisture like green wood, they are thrown into spasms and convulsions. And we see that those who have gone to sleep in the light of the moon are hardly able to rise again, like men with senses stunned or doped, for the moisture poured through them by the moon makes their bodies heavy. The moon is also said to assist in easing child birth, when it occurs at full moon, by making the pains gentler by releasing moisture. For this reason, I take it, Artemis, who is none other than the moon, is called Locheia and Eileithyia. And Timotheüs says outright [a]

> Through the dark-blue vault of the stars
> And the moon who is quick to procure
> The delivery of children.

The power of the moon is also quite clear where inanimate bodies are concerned. Builders discard wood cut in the full moon as soft and quick to decay on account of its moisture. Farmers hurry to gather wheat from the threshing-floor at the end of the month so that, hardened by dryness, it may last for a longer time ; wheat in transport when the moon is full splits very easily because the moisture in it has made it softer. People say, too, that flour rises better at the time of the full moon ; indeed, leavening is much the same process as putrefaction, and if the proper time limit be ignored, leavening in making dough porous and light produces the same decomposition in the end. What happens to decomposing

---

[a] Diehl, *Anth. Lyr. Graec.* ii (1942), p. 194, frag. 12 ; *cf. Quaestiones Romanae*, no. 77, with Babbitt's note (LCL *Mor.* iv, pp. 116 f.).

---

[4] ἀποδεῖ σῆψις εἶναι Reiske, who added τοῦ before σῆψις : ἀποδεὴς εἶναι.

(659) μεναι σάρκες οὐδὲν ἄλλο πάσχουσιν ἤ, τοῦ
συνεκτικοῦ πνεύματος μεταβάλλοντος εἰς ὑγρόν,
ἐξαραιοῦνται[1] καὶ ῥέουσιν. ταὐτὸ[2] δὲ καὶ τὸν ἀέρα
πάσχοντα θεωροῦμεν· δροσοβολεῖ γὰρ ταῖς πανσελήνοις μάλιστα διατηκόμενος, ὥς που καὶ Ἀλκ-
μὰν ὁ μελοποιὸς αἰνιττόμενος τὴν δρόσον ἀέρος
θυγατέρα καὶ σελήνης

οἷα (φησί) Διὸς θυγάτηρ Ἔρσα[3] τρέφει καὶ δίας
Σελάνας.[4]

C οὕτω πανταχόθεν μαρτυρεῖται τὸ τῆς σελήνης φῶς
ἀνυγραντικὴν ἔχον[5] καὶ μαλακτικὴν δύναμιν.

" Ὁ δὲ χαλκοῦς ἧλος, εἴ γε διελαυνόμενος, ὥς
φασιν, ἀσηπτότερα διατηρεῖ τὰ κρέα, φαίνεταί τι
θεραπευτικὸν[6] ἔχων καὶ στυπτικὸν ἐν αὑτῷ· τῷ
γὰρ ἰῷ πρὸς τὰ τοιαῦτα χρῶνται τῶν φαρμάκων
ἰατροί, καὶ τούς γε διατρίβοντας ἐν τοῖς χαλκωρυ-
χείοις ἱστοροῦσιν ὠφελεῖσθαι τὰ ὄμματα καὶ
βλεφαρίδας ἐκφύειν τοὺς ἀποβεβληκότας, ἡ γὰρ
ἀπιοῦσα τῆς χαλκίτιδος ἄχνη καὶ ἐμπίπτουσα[7]
τοῖς βλεφάροις ἀδήλως ἀναστέλλει τὰ ῥεύματα καὶ
περιστύφει τὸ δάκρυον· διὸ καί φασιν ' εὐήνορα '
καὶ ' νώροπα χαλκὸν ' ὑπὸ τοῦ ποιητοῦ προσ-
D αγορεύεσθαι. Ἀριστοτέλης δὲ καὶ τὰ τραύματά
φησιν τὰ ἀπὸ τῶν χαλκῶν ἐπιδορατίδων καὶ

---

[1] Basel edition : ἐξαιροῦνται.
[2] Hubert : τοῦτο.
[3] Xylander : μέγα.
[4] δίας Σελάνας Bernardakis (but at 918 A and presumably
at 940 A the words are transposed) : ἀσελάνας.
[5] ἀνυγραντικὴν ἔχον Vulcobius : ἀνυγροντι lac. 2 κὴν.

278

flesh is simply that it becomes spongy and liquefies as the spirit which binds it together changes to moisture. The same thing happens to air, as we see ; for especially at the time of the full moon it dissolves and precipitates dew, as, I suppose, the lyrist Alcman also suggests, calling dew the daughter of air and moon when he says [a]

> Such Hersa nourishes, daughter of Zeus
> And Selenê divine.

Thus it is everywhere attested that moonlight has the property of producing moisture and softness.

"The bronze nail,—if actually, when driven into meat, it preserves the flesh in sounder condition, as people say,—obviously has some healing and astringent quality in itself. Indeed, bronze-rust is employed by physicians among their drugs for such purposes,[b] and they record that the eyes of men who pass their time in copper-mines are benefited and those who have lost their eyelashes grow them again, for the dust which comes from the copper ore and settles upon their eyes insensibly checks discharges and dries up tears. This is why the Poet, they claim, calls bronze ' man's helper ' [c] and ' eye-affector.' [d] And Aristotle [e] says that wounds from bronze spear-heads

---

[a] Frag. 48 Bergk, 43 Diehl (1942) ; cf. Mor. 918 A, 940 A, with Cherniss's notes, LCL Mor. xii, p. 175.
[b] Cf., e.g., Pliny, Nat. Hist. xxv. 42 with the legend of Achilles healing Telephus.
[c] See, e.g., Odyssey, xiii. 19.
[d] See, e.g., Iliad, ii. 578 ; the word is usually translated " flashing," " bright " (origin obscure, Boisacq, s.v.).
[e] Cf. Pseudo-Aristotle, Problems, i. 35, 863 a 25 ff.

---

[6] τι θεραπευτικὸν P. A. C., cf. 659 D τὸ στύφ. καὶ τὸ θεραπ.:
μὲν.   [7] Reiske (Macrobius incidens): πίπτουσα.

(659) μαχαιρῶν ἧττον εἶναι δυσαλγῆ καὶ ῥᾷον᾽ ἰᾶσθαι
τῶν ἀπὸ τοῦ σιδήρου διὰ τὸ φαρμακῶδες ἔχειν τι
τὸν χαλκὸν ἐν ἑαυτῷ καὶ τοῦτο ταῖς πληγαῖς
εὐθὺς ἐναπολείπειν. ὅτι δὲ¹ καὶ τῷ σήποντι τὸ
στῦφον² καὶ τὸ θεραπεῦον τῷ φθείροντι τὴν
ἐναντίαν ἔχει δύναμιν, οὐκ ἄδηλον.³ εἰ μή τις
ἄρα τῇ διελάσει φαίη τὸν ἧλον ἐφ᾽ ἑαυτὸν τὰ ὑγρὰ
συνάγειν, ἐπιφορᾶς ἀεὶ γιγνομένης πρὸς τὸ πάσχον·
διὸ καὶ περὶ αὐτὸν ἐκεῖνον τὸν τόπον οἷόν τινα⁴ μώ-
λωπα καὶ σπῖλον ὁρᾶσθαί φασιν, καὶ λόγον ἔχει⁵
τὴν ἄλλην σάρκα διαμένειν ἀπαθῆ, τῆς φθορᾶς
ἐκεῖ συντρεχούσης.''⁶

¹ δὲ added by Xylander.
² Xylander : ἄτυφον.   ³ g and Turnebus : ἄδηλος.
⁴ Aldine edition : τι.   ⁵ Reiske : ἔχειν.

and swords are less painful and heal more easily than those from an iron weapon because bronze has in itself something medicinal which it immediately leaves in wounds. It is obvious that whatever is astringent has the property of opposing what causes decay, and whatever heals has the property of opposing what destroys. Of course, someone might claim that the nail in being driven through collects moisture to itself, since there is always attraction to the hurt part. This is why people remark that in that area itself one sees something like a bruise and a stain; since the morbidness gathers there, it stands to reason that the rest of the flesh will remain sound."

---

[6] In T συντρεχούσης and decorative sigla end line 12 ; line 13, συμποσιακῶν ŷ between decorative sigla ; line 14, decorative sigla ; line 15, the heading of Book IV.

INTRODUCTION TO
BOOKS IV–VI

As in the other parts of the *Symposiacs*, the text of Books IV–VI depends mainly upon T, a Vienna codex, Vindobonensis graecus 148 (tenth or eleventh century). It suffers from a number of important lacunae, particularly in Book V from page 676 c 8 to 680 d 11 (*cf.* LCL *Mor.* ix, p. 3) ; fortunately the loss is not total, for we have copies made earlier. In addition, the exemplar from which T was copied was already defective at the end of iv. 6, where an incomplete sentence is followed by a blank in the page, and the margin has a notation to the effect that a quaternion is missing with five chapters (*sic*, the prefixed index to Book IV gives only the normal four remaining titles of Questions). I have constantly referred to a photostatic copy of T and one of E, a Paris manuscript (Parisinus 1672) of the early fourteenth century, to correct the published reports of T's readings everywhere and those of E where they become important. The text and apparatus are based mainly on Hubert (Teubner, Leipzig, 1938), who rarely, perhaps only two or three times to my knowledge, is found inaccurate. I have systematically consulted also the editions of J. G. Hutten (volume xi of his complete Plutarch, part 5 of the *Moralia*, Tübingen, 1798), whose reports of Reiske's readings I frequently adopt when Hubert fails to cite them, D. Wyttenbach (Partes 1 and 2 of Tomus III of Plutarch, *Moralia*, Oxford, 1797), and the earlier Teubner edition

in Bernardakis' *Moralia*, 1888–1896, as well as H. Bolkestein's *Adversaria Critica*. From these sources and
Hartman I have sometimes derived a fuller account of
manuscript readings or emendations than Hubert's ;
but I am aware that his judgement in omitting certain
details may have been distinctly the wiser.

For brevity I have chosen to include under the notation " Turnebus " items often labelled "exemplum
Turnebi." If this should prove inadequate to any
reader, I wish to refer him to Hubert, whose edition
is of course indispensable for scholarly purposes, rich
as it is in matter not ordinarily expected of a text
edition. Incidentally, I apply the term " after " in
the apparatus criticus to cases where the later scholar
makes a relatively slight modification of his prede-
cessor's reading, as well as to outright adoptions.

I have accepted the judgement of those who believe that Plutarch went back to the more ancient or
Attic form of Greek in using forms of γίγνεσθαι and
γιγνώσκειν, rather than γίνεσθαι or γινώσκειν. This
may be considered an inconsistent policy when I do
not alter forms, for instance, of φυλάσσειν to φυλάττειν. The evidence seems to be that our author was
himself inconsistent in presenting both θάλασσα and
θάλαττα, but it is well known that manuscript evidence is unreliable. I have altered πιπλάμενος to
πιμπλάμενος, οὐθέν to οὐδέν, but keep ἤμην at 674 E,
and with some serious doubt ἐλλέβορος for ἐλλέβορος
in vi. 693 A (the influence of Hippocrates ?).

Necessarily I have not only depended on standard
reference works, special studies such as the ones by
Volkmann, Hartman, and Ziegler, and related investigations by Hirzel, Martin, and others, but found it
useful to compare translations into Latin (Xylander

as corrected and reprinted by Wyttenbach), French (Ricard), German (Kaltwasser), and English. The English translation which I have mainly consulted was that by " T. C." at the end of the seventeenth century ; although once or twice I have looked into Philemon Holland's.

In Book IV the topics discussed include, after a proem on the relation between convivial parties and rational friendship, the question of the digestibility of an elaborate or varied diet (Question 1), that of truffles and other effects or alleged effects of thunder and lightning (Qu. 2), the reason for large wedding banquets (Qu. 3), the contributions of sea and land to our food supply, particularly the gourmet and health value of those of the sea (Qu. 4), the mystery of Jewish dietary practices and the astonishing importance of the pig (Qu. 5), and the equally astonishing identity of the God of the Hebrews with Dionysus (if we can believe it, considering the prevailing ignorance of evidence Plutarch did not consult !) (Qu. 6). The missing " Problems " of this book—according to the captions—concerned the order of the days of the week as compared to the order of the " planets " (note that Sun and Moon, but not Earth, are planets here, and of course the ancients did not know all our planets) (Qu. 7), the reason for wearing the seal-ring on a certain finger (Qu. 8), whether one ought to wear images of gods or of wise men on seal-rings (Qu. 9), and why women do not eat heart of lettuce (Qu. 10).

In Book V we find a proem of psychological nature both in the original and in our sense of " psychological," followed by discussions of the contrast in our reaction to the depiction of feeling in art and

PLUTARCH'S MORALIA

of the expression of the same emotions in real life
(Qu. 1), of the history of competitions in literature and
poetry at the Games (Qu. 2), certain facts about the
history of the crown awarded at the Isthmian Games,
with sundry learned observations (or speculations)
on the properties of the pine and celery (Qu. 3), the
meaning of a certain word used by Homer (Qu. 4),
the problem of whom or how many to invite to a
dinner party (Qu. 5), the puzzle why guests find
themselves becoming less crowded on the dining
couches during the course of a meal (Qu. 6), the " evil
eye " (Qu. 7), a couple of points of usage in Homer
and Empedocles, with some etymological considerations (Qu. 8), the paradox of a tree of bitter quality,
the fig, producing the sweetest fruit (Qu. 9), and the
proverbial " salt and bean friends " and the divine
quality of salt (Qu. 10).

Book VI begins in its proem with an anecdote
relating to Plato and his Academy : a banquet there
was wholesome and chiefly intellectual. Of the
Questions which follow, the first deals with thirst
caused by fasting, the next follows this up by raising
the matter of the physiological nature of hunger ;
similarly Question 3 ties in with this by exploring the
contradictory physical phenomenon of hunger as-
suaged by liquid food, but thirst only intensified by
solid. Question 4 investigates another not unrelated
scientific puzzle connected with this general sphere
of interest : why is the water in a vessel held sus-
pended in a well found cooler than the well-water
itself ? Question 5 asks why pebbles or bits of metal
thrown in will cool water ; Question 6 how chaff and
cloth can preserve snow ; Question 7 whether one
ought to filter wine ; Question 8 the causes of bulimy,

a kind of ravenous hunger; Question 9 another point of Homeric usage, namely calling oil liquid *par excellence*, and Question 10 the curing property of fig-trees when ἱερεῖα are hung from their limbs.

Neither the traditional captions nor this skeleton summary give even a hint of the richness of the content. Plutarch and his friends are always ready with a literary citation and a philosophical or scientific extension of the subject.

It is, as everyone knows and gladly states, a pleasant duty to acknowledge much help and friendly advice. I am indebted to the Research Council of the University of California, Los Angeles, for providing clerical help in the early stages of the project. I owe a special debt to my colleague, P. A. Clement, for his initial suggestion that I participate in this task, and for his kindness in making available books and materials. I have heavily imposed on the patience of Professors Alfred C. Andrews, Harold Cherniss, and W. C. Helmbold, and of the late Professor Ludwig Edelstein. Especially often have I called upon Professor Andrews for answers only he could provide; he has regularly responded and beyond that assisted me greatly in matters not confined to his speciality. Equally ready with acute suggestions in truly phenomenal variety has been Professor L. A. Post, *egregie cordatus homo*, whose unflagging zeal is known to countless scholars. Also far beyond what I had a right to claim I have drawn upon the various abilities and loyal co-operation of my wife. Lastly, I must record deep indebtedness to one other generous scholar, who insists on remaining anonymous.

HERBERT B. HOFFLEIT

UNIVERSITY OF CALIFORNIA
LOS ANGELES

TABLE-TALK
(QUAESTIONES CONVIVALES)
BOOK IV

ΣΥΜΠΟΣΙΑΚΩΝ

ΒΙΒΛΙΟΝ ΤΕΤΑΡΤΟΝ

Ὦ Σόσσιε Σενεκίων, τοῦ Πολυβίου Σκηπίωνι
παραινοῦντος Ἀφρικανῷ μὴ πρότερον ἐξ ἀγορᾶς
ἀπελθεῖν ἢ φίλον τινὰ ποιήσασθαι τῶν πολιτῶν
F φίλον¹ δεῖ μὴ πικρῶς μηδὲ σοφιστικῶς ἀκούειν
ἐκεῖνον τὸν ἀμετάπτωτον καὶ βέβαιον, ἀλλὰ κοινῶς
τὸν εὔνουν· ὥσπερ ᾤετο χρῆναι Δικαίαρχος εὔνους
μὲν αὑτῷ παρασκευάζειν ἅπαντας, φίλους δὲ
660 ποιεῖσθαι τοὺς ἀγαθούς. φιλία γὰρ ἐν χρόνῳ
πολλῷ καὶ δι' ἀρετῆς ἁλώσιμον· εὔνοια² δὲ καὶ
χρείᾳ καὶ ὁμιλίᾳ καὶ παιδιᾷ πολιτικῶν ἀνδρῶν
ἐπάγεται, καιρὸν λαβοῦσα πειθοῦς φιλανθρώπου
καὶ χάριτος συνεργόν.

Ἀλλ' ὅρα τὸ τῆς παραινέσεως, εἰ μὴ μόνον

---

¹ δὲ after φίλον omitted by Xylander.
² εὔνοιαν Xylander.

ᵃ Cf. Sayings of Romans, 199 F (LCL Plut. Mor. iii, pp.
184 ff.), Stobaeus 37. 35. At Rome, " friendship " was apt
to have a political sense ; see Cicero, Commentariolum Peti-
tionis, 5. 16 and L. R. Taylor, Party Politics in the Age of
Caesar, pp. 7 ff.

ᵇ See Aristotle, Eth. Nic. viii, esp. 1159 b 8, and ix, 1172 a
9 ; Cicero, De Amic. 19 and 32 ; Plutarch, De Amic. Mult.
94 A.

ᶜ Celebrated philosopher, pupil of Aristotle. See RE, v.

290

TABLE-TALK

BOOK FOUR

WHEN, dear Sossius Senecio, Polybius advises Scipio
Africanus never to return from a visit to the Forum
until he has made a new friend of one of his fellow
citizens,[a] we must not interpret " friend " with pe-
dantic strictness as referring to the celebrated ideal
type,[b] immutable and steadfast, but take it in a
broader sense as meaning any well-wisher. Just so
Dicaearchus [c] recommended securing the good will
of all and sundry, but making friends only with the
good. Friendship is an objective that can be captured
only by long effort [d] and sturdy qualities of character,[e] whereas good will is enlisted through the
ordinary associations of business, social life, and play
shared with members of the community, with the
opportunities thus afforded for the exercise of friendly
persuasion and good feeling.[f]

As to the advice of Polybius, perhaps you'll agree

546, no. 3 ; F. Wehrli, *Die Schule des Aristoteles*, Heft i, frag.
46.

[d] Aristotle, *Eth. Nic.* 1156 b 25.

[e] There is a military metaphor here, but the phrase δι'
ἀρετῆς is intended also by its other meaning to allude to
Aristotle's point in *Eth. Nic.* viii. 4 and elsewhere, that there
is a close relation between true friendship and sound character.   [f] *Cf. infra,* ix. 14, 746 A.

(660) ἔχει δεξιῶς πρὸς ἀγορὰν ἀλλὰ καὶ πρὸς συμπόσιον·
ὥστε δεῖν μὴ πρότερον ἀναλύειν ἢ κτήσασθαί τινα
τῶν συγκατακειμένων καὶ παρόντων εὔνουν ἑαυτῷ
καὶ φίλον. εἰς ἀγορὰν μὲν γὰρ ἐμβάλλουσι πραγμάτων εἴνεκεν καὶ χρειῶν ἑτέρων, εἰς δὲ συμπόσιον
οἵ γε νοῦν ἔχοντες ἀφικνοῦνται κτησόμενοι φίλους
B οὐχ ἧττον ἢ τοὺς ὄντας εὐφρανοῦντες. διότι τῶν
μὲν ἄλλων ζητεῖν ἐκφορὰν ἀνελεύθερον ἂν εἴη καὶ
φορτικόν, τὸ δὲ φίλων πλέον ἔχοντας ἀπιέναι καὶ
ἡδὺ καὶ σεμνόν ἐστιν. καὶ τοὐναντίον ὁ τούτου
παραμελῶν ἄχαριν αὐτῷ καὶ ἀτελῆ τὴν συνουσίαν
ποιεῖ καὶ ἄπεισι τῇ γαστρὶ σύνδειπνος οὐ τῇ ψυχῇ
γεγονώς· ὁ γὰρ σύνδειπνος οὐκ ὄψου καὶ οἴνου
καὶ τραγημάτων μόνον, ἀλλὰ καὶ λόγων κοινωνὸς
ἥκει καὶ παιδιᾶς[1] καὶ φιλοφροσύνης εἰς εὔνοιαν
τελευτώσης. αἱ μὲν γὰρ παλαιόντων ἐπιβολαὶ[2]
καὶ ἕλξεις κονιορτοῦ δέονται, ταῖς δὲ φιλικαῖς
λαβαῖς ὁ οἶνος ἀφὴν ἐνδίδωσι μιγνύμενος λόγῳ·
λόγος γὰρ αὐτῷ τὸ φιλάνθρωπον καὶ ἠθοποιὸν
ἐπὶ τὴν ψυχὴν ἐκ τοῦ σώματος ἐποχετεύει καὶ
C συνδιαδίδωσιν[3]· εἰ δὲ μή, πλανώμενος ἐν τῷ σώματι πλησμονῆς οὐδὲν σπουδαιότερον παρέσχεν.
ὅθεν ὥσπερ ὁ μάρμαρος, τοῦ διαπύρου σιδήρου τῷ

[1] So Xylander : παιδείας.
[2] ἐπιλαβαὶ Bases.
[3] So Hubert, ἐνδίδωσιν Wilamowitz, συνενδίδωσι Bernardakis : συνδίδωσιν.

---

[a] Cf. the interdict at sacrifices οὐκ ἐκφορά, "no removal from
the premises ! " as recorded in comedy and inscriptions ; see,
e.g., Aristophanes, Plutus, 1138, and scholia, as well as van
Leeuwen's note.
[b] Wrestlers sanded themselves after anointing with olive-
oil : RE, s.v. κόνις, and Ovid, Metamorph. ix. 55 f.

that it is well adapted not only to the market place
but also to parties. That is, we should not let a party
break up before we have made a new friend and well-
wisher among the other guests and fellow diners.
People rush to the market place on business or for
some other practical purpose ; they attend a party—
at least if they're intelligent—as much to gain new
friends as to give a good time to the old. For
though it would be low and vulgar to wish to carry
off [a] anything else, it is both a pleasure and a distinction to come away with a profitable addition to
the number of one's friends. On the other hand,
anyone who neglects to do so makes the social occasion incomplete and unrewarding to himself; he de-
parts after having partaken only with his stomach,
not his mind. A guest comes to share not only meat,
wine, and dessert, but conversation, fun, and the
amiability that leads to friendship. The grips and
tugs of wrestling require fine sand [b] ; the holds of
friendship are won by a blend of wine and conversation. For it is through conversation that wine channels from the body and distributes through the
character a generous influence that permeates the
whole man.[c] Otherwise the wine, circulating uncon-
trolled in the body, produces nothing better than
mere repletion. In consequence, just as marble [d]
eliminates excessive melting and fluidity in red-hot

[c] Or, with T, " which it contributes," *i.e.*, to the wine. On
the argument compare Plutarch's theory of music as a correc-
tive to the influence of wine, *De Musica*, 1146 e = Aristoxenus,
122 Wehrli (see Wehrli's commentary and *infra*, 713 b), and
Septem Sap. Conv. 156 d.
[d] Lime is still used as a flux in metallurgy. *Cf.* R. J.
Forbes, *Metallurgy in Antiquity* (Leyden, 1950), pp. 35 ff.
and 396.

(660) καταψύχειν τὴν ἄγαν ὑγρότητα καὶ ῥύσιν ἀφαιρῶν,
εὔτονον ποιεῖ τὸ μαλασσόμενον αὐτοῦ καὶ τυπού-
μενον, οὕτως ὁ συμποτικὸς λόγος οὐκ ἐᾷ διαφο-
ρεῖσθαι παντάπασιν ὑπὸ τοῦ οἴνου τοὺς πίνοντας,
ἀλλ᾽ ἐφίστησι καὶ ποιεῖ τῇ ἀνέσει τὸ ἱλαρὸν καὶ
φιλάνθρωπον ἐγκέραστον καὶ τὸ[1] κεχαρισμένον, ἄν
τις ἐμμελῶς ἅπτηται, καθάπερ σφραγῖδι φιλίας
εὐτυπώτων[2] καὶ ἁπαλῶν διὰ τὸν οἶνον ὄντων.

ΠΡΟΒΛΗΜΑ Α

D   Εἰ ἡ ποικίλη τροφὴ τῆς ἁπλῆς εὐπεπτοτέρα

Collocuntur Philo, Plutarchus, Philinus, Marcio

1. Τῆς οὖν τετάρτης τῶν συμποτικῶν ζητημάτων
δεκάδος ἡμῖν πρῶτον ἔσται τὸ περὶ τῆς ποικίλης
τροφῆς ζητηθέν. Ἐλαφηβολίων γὰρ ὄντων εἰς
Ὑάμπολιν ἐπὶ τὴν ἑορτὴν ἀφικνουμένους ἡμᾶς
εἱστία Φίλων ὁ ἰατρὸς ἐκ παρασκευῆς τινος, ὡς
ἐφαίνετο, νεανικῆς.[3] ἰδὼν δὲ τῶν παιδίων τῶν[4]
ἅμα τῷ Φιλίνῳ[5] τὸ νέον[6] ἄρτῳ χρώμενον ἄλλου δὲ
μηδενὸς δεόμενον, "ὦ Ἡράκλεις," ἔφη, "τοῦτ᾽

---

[1] τὸ added by Hubert.
[2] So Reiske: εὐτυπώτατον.
[3] So Reiske: νεανικῶς, defended by Hubert, cf. 686 D.
[4] τῶν παιδίων τῶν Wyttenbach: τὸ παιδίον. Perhaps τοῖν παιδίοιν.
[5] So Xylander or Amyot: φίλωνι.
[6] τὸ νεώτερον Hartman, De Avondzon des Heidendoms, i², p. 181: τὸν νέον (τὸ Reiske). τινα νέον Warmington, μόνον Post. Perhaps μόνῳ or τὸν ἕτερον.

---

[a] Imitated by Macrobius, Saturnalia, vii. 4 and 5.
[b] Dedicated to Artemis the Huntress, attested for Hyampolis in Inscriptiones Graecae, ix. 90.

iron by cooling it down, and thus gives the right tensile strength to the metal during the softening and shaping process, so table-talk prevents the complete dissipation of the drinkers' minds under the influence of the wine. Conversation steadies those who drink, adding through relaxation an element of gaiety and —yes—of kindly sociability, if people go about it in the right way, since the wine makes the company pliable and ready to take an impression, as it were, from the seal of friendship.

QUESTION 1 [a]

Whether a variety of food is more easily digested than one kind alone

Speakers : Philo, Plutarch, Philinus, and Marcion

1. THE first in our fourth decade of convivial questions shall be the discussion we had concerning variety in diet on the occasion of a banquet during the festival of the Elaphebolia,[b] for which we had gone to Hyampolis.[c] On our arrival there we were entertained at dinner by Philo [d] the physician, who, as we saw, had provided a mighty feast for us. Our host, having noticed that one of the young boys who came with Philinus [e] took bread and wanted nothing else, exclaimed," Good Lord ! So this is what the proverb

---

[c] Near Abae in Phocis.

[d] Cf. above, Table-Talk, ii. 6. 2, p. 640 D, and below, vi. 2 and viii. 9 ; RE, xx. 60, no. 61.

[e] Cf. above, Table-Talk, i. 6, and below, viii. 7 ; and De Pythiae Oraculis with Flacelière's Introduction, pp. 25 ff. See RE, xxi. 681, s.v. " Plutarchos." A later descendant of Philinus seems to be known : Hesperia xi. 71, no. 37. J. J. Hartman, De Plut. Script. et Phil. pp. 384 f., identifies τὰ παιδία as students, the μειράκια φιλοσοφοῦντα of Table-Talk, iii. 7, 655 F.

(660) ἆρ' ἦν τὸ λεγόμενον

> ἐν δὲ λίθοις ἐμάχοντο, λίθον δ' οὐκ ἦν ἀνελέ-
> σθαι."

E καὶ ἀνεπήδησεν οἰσόμενός τι τῶν χρησίμων ἐκείνοις, εἶθ' ἧκε μετὰ χρόνον συχνὸν ἰσχάδας αὐτοῖς
τινας καὶ τυρὸν κομίζων.

'Εμοῦ δ' εἰπόντος, ὅτι τοῦτο συμβαίνει τοῖς τὰ
περιττὰ καὶ πολυτελῆ παρασκευαζομένοις, ἀμελεῖν
καὶ σπανίζειν τῶν ἀναγκαίων καὶ χρησίμων, '' οὐ
γὰρ ἐμεμνήμην," εἶπεν ὁ Φίλων, '' ὅτι Σώσαστρον
ἡμῖν ὑποτρέφει¹ Φιλῖνος, ὅν φασι μήτε πότῳ χρησάμενον ἄλλῳ μήτ' ἐδέσματι πλὴν² γάλακτος διαβιῶ-
σαι πάντα τὸν βίον· ἀλλ' ἐκείνῳ μὲν ἐκ μεταβολῆς
ἀρχὴν γενέσθαι τῆς τοιαύτης διαίτης εἰκός· τὸν δ'
ἡμέτερον ἀντιστρόφως τῷ 'Αχιλλεῖ τρέφων ὁ Χεί-
ρων οὗτος εὐθὺς ἀπὸ τῆς γενέσεως ἀναιμάκτοις³ καὶ
F ἀψύχοις⁴ τροφαῖς οὐκ ἄκραν ἀπόδειξιν παρέχει⁵ ἐν
ἀέρι καὶ δρόσῳ⁶ καθάπερ οἱ τέττιγες σιτουμένου;''

¹ ὁ deleted by Benseler before Φιλῖνος.
² ἢ deleted by Bernardakis before γάλακτος.
³ So Stephanus, Wyttenbach· ἀναιμάτοις.
⁴ καὶ ἀψύχοις Wyttenbach· lac. 5-6 χοις.
⁵ παρέχει Post· ἔχει. Post would continue (ἐνδεῖ γὰρ ἔν
or ἐν μόνον?), ἀέρι, and either αὐτοῦ σιτουμένου or (with
Wyttenbach) σιτούμενον, inserting an article before ἀπόδειξιν.
Madvig proposes οὐκ εἰς μακρὰν ἀποδείξει, omitting ἔχει.
⁶ λέγουσι omitted after δρόσῳ. Bernardakis proposes ὡς
λέγουσι or καθάπερ λέγουσι τοὺς τέττιγας.

ᵃ Part of a riddle referring to shipwreck on a reef. The
riddle is quoted by Athenaeus (x, 457 в) as containing this line
along with the original of Coleridge's '' Water, water everywhere, nor any drop to drink." See Gulick on Athenaeus
(LCL), iv, pp. 572-575.
ᵇ Wyttenbach cites Amyot and the Codices Vulcobius and

means :

> Mid stones they fought, but couldn't lift a stone." [a]

With that he rushed out to get them something that they could eat. After a long time he came back with a few dried figs and some cheese for them.

" This," I remarked, " is what happens when people provide elaborate and costly fare. They're prone to be negligent and run out of the staple and essential items." To this Philo rejoined, " True enough. It had slipped my mind that Philinus has been bringing up among us a Sosaster,[b] who they say never took any food or drink but milk during his whole life. But the original Sosaster must have turned to this diet from an earlier one, whereas our young friend, unlike Achilles,[c] has been fed bloodless and vegetarian food by his Cheiron here from birth. Isn't he giving a splendid illustration of a person fed as they say cicadas [d] are on dew and air ? "

B as reading " Zoroaster," whose name is retained by Kalt-wasser and Ricard in their translations. A slight degree of support for this interpretation may be found in Pliny, xi. 97. 242, where Zoroaster is alleged to have lived on cheese for twenty years. *Cf.* Diogenes Laertius, *Lives of Ancient Philo-sophers*, Prologue, 7 and 8, with R. D. Hicks's note in Dio-genes Laertius (LCL), i, p. 8. Sosaster is unknown, but he may be identical with an obscure character in Iamblichus's *Life of Pythagoras*, 267. Sostratos (*RE*, Suppl. viii. 782) appears to have lived about a century later.

[c] Achilles was fed on meat from the start by Cheiron : Apollodorus, iii. 13. 6 ; Statius, *Achilleïd*, ii. 382 (ii. 96 ff.) ; J. D. Beazley, *Development of Attic Black-Figure*, pp. 10 f.

[d] For the belief that cicadas need no food see Plato, *Phae-drus*, 259 c, Aristophanes, *Clouds*, 1360 ; Aristotle, *Historia Animal*. 532 b ; Hesiod, *Shield*, 393. Pliny's explanation is found in *Nat. Hist.* xi. 32. 92 ff. See also *RE*, *s.v.* " Tettix," cols. 1116 f., and now E. K. Borthwick in *Class. Quart.* N.S. xvi (1966), pp. 103 ff.

(660) '' Ἡμεῖς μὲν οὖν,'' ὁ Φιλῖνος εἶπεν, '' ἠγνοοῦμεν
Ἑκατομφόνια δειπνήσοντες ὥσπερ ἐπ' Ἀριστομέ-
νους· ἐπεὶ παρῆμεν[1] ἂν ὄψα τῶν λιτῶν καὶ ὑγιαινόντων, ὥσπερ ἀλεξιφάρμακα, πρὸς οὕτω πολυτελεῖς
καὶ φλεγμαινούσας τραπέζας περιαψάμενοι· καὶ
661 ταῦτα, σοῦ[2] πολλάκις ἀκηκοότες ὅτι τῶν ποικίλων
τὰ ἁπλᾶ μᾶλλον εὔπεπτ' ἐστὶν καὶ[3] εὐπόριστα.''

Καὶ ὁ Μαρκίων πρὸς τὸν Φίλωνα, '' διαφθείρει
σου Φιλῖνος,'' ἔφη, '' τὴν παρασκευήν, ἀποτρέπων
καὶ δεδιττόμενος τοὺς δαιτυμόνας· ἀλλ' ἂν ἐμοῦ
δεηθῇς, ἐγγυήσομαι πρὸς αὐτοὺς ὑπὲρ σοῦ τὴν
ποικίλην τροφὴν εὐπεπτοτέραν εἶναι τῆς ἁπλῆς,
ὥστε θαρροῦντας ἀπολαύειν τῶν παρακειμένων.''
ὁ μὲν οὖν Φίλων ἐδεῖτο τοῦ Μαρκίωνος οὕτω
ποιεῖν.

2. Ἐπεὶ δ' ἡμεῖς παυσάμενοι τοῦ δειπνεῖν προσ-
εκαλούμεθα τὸν Φιλῖνον ἐπιθέσθαι τῇ κατηγορίᾳ
B τῆς ποικίλης τροφῆς, '' ' οὐκ ἐμός,' '' εἶπεν, '' ὁ
μῦθος' ἀλλ' οὑτοσὶ Φίλων ἑκάστοτε λέγει πρὸς
ἡμᾶς, ὅτι πρῶτον μὲν τὰ θηρία τροφαῖς μονοειδέσι
καὶ ἁπλαῖς χρώμενα μᾶλλον ὑγιαίνει τῶν ἀνθρώ-
πων· ὅσα δὲ σιτεύουσι καθείρξαντες, ἐπισφαλῆ
πρὸς τὰς νόσους ἐστὶν καὶ ῥᾳδίως ταῖς ὠμότησιν
ἁλίσκεται διὰ τὸ μικτήν τινα καὶ συνηδυσμένην
τροφὴν προσφέρεσθαι.[4] δεύτερον οὐδεὶς γέγονεν
οὕτω τῶν ἰατρῶν παράτολμος ἐν καινοτομίᾳ καὶ

[1] So Leonicus : παρ ἡμῖν.
[2] So Wyttenbach : οὐ.
[3] So Wyttenbach : ἤ. Perhaps ἔτι δὲ καὶ or καὶ δὴ καὶ, or
ἅμα καί.
[4] So Stephanus : προφέρεσθαι.

---

[a] Literally '' the slaying of a hundred enemies,'' a sacrifice

" But we," answered Philinus, " weren't aware that we had been invited to a banquet to celebrate the hekatomphonia,[a] as in Aristomenes's time. Otherwise we should have come furnished with some simple, wholesome food as with an amulet and an antidote against such luxurious and unhealthy eating. What is more, we have often heard you say that simple food is more digestible than an elaborate variety, as well as easier to obtain."

Here Marcion interposed, " Philo, Philinus is ruining all your efforts by discouraging and frightening away your guests ; but if you entreat me, I'll guarantee to them all for you that mixed food is more digestible than simple, so that your guests need have no misgivings about enjoying what is set before them here." Philo accordingly did entreat Marcion to do so.

2. So when we had finished dinner, we called upon Philinus to open the charge against variety of food ; but he answered, " ' Not mine the argument.' [b] It's Philo here who tells us on every occasion that, for one thing, animals by always sticking to simple, uniform food are generally healthier than human beings. Moreover, those that are fattened in pens are liable to disease and fall an easy prey to crude humours because the fodder that they consume is mixed and richly flavoured. In the second place, no physician has ever been so foolhardy an innovator, so courage-

<hr />

performed among the Messenians by one who had personally slain one hundred enemies in combat. Aristomenes, in the 7th century, is said to have celebrated this feat three times. See Pausanias, iv. 14 ff., 19. 3 ; Plutarch, *Life of Romulus*, xxv. 3 ; *RE*, vii. 2790 and ii. 947, no. 1.

[b] Literally " the tale " : from Euripides's *Melanippê*, frag. 484 (Nauck, *Trag. Gr. Frag.* p. 511).

(661) ἀνδρεῖος, ὥστε ποικίλην τροφὴν πυρέττοντι προσ
ενεγκεῖν· ἀλλὰ τὴν ἁπλῆν καὶ ἄκνισον ὡς ὑπήκοον
μάλιστα τῇ πέψει προσφέρουσιν. δεῖ γὰρ παθεῖν
C τὴν τροφὴν καὶ μεταβαλεῖν κρατηθεῖσαν ὑπὸ τῶν
ἐν ἡμῖν δυνάμεων· κρατεῖ δὲ καὶ βαφὴ τῶν ἁπλῶν
χρωμάτων μᾶλλον, καὶ μυρεψικοῖς φαρμάκοις τρέ
πεται τάχιστα τὸ ἀωδέστατον[1] ἔλαιον, καὶ τροφῆς
εὐπαθέστατον ὑπὸ πέψεως μεταβάλλειν[2] τὸ ἀφελὲς
καὶ μονοειδές. αἱ δὲ πολλαὶ καὶ ποικίλαι ποιότητες
ὑπεναντιώσεις ἔχουσαι καὶ δυσμαχοῦσαι φθείρονται
πρότερον προσπίπτουσαι, καθάπερ ἐν πόλει μιγά
δων καὶ συγκλύδων ἀνθρώπων πλῆθος οὐ ῥᾳδίως
μίαν οὐδ' ὁμοπαθοῦσαν ἴσχουσαι κατάστασιν, ἀλλ'
ἑκάστη πρὸς τὸ οἰκεῖον ἀντιτείνουσα καὶ δυσσύμ
βατος οὖσα πρὸς τὸ ἀλλόφυλον. ἐμφανὲς δὲ
D τεκμήριον τὸ περὶ τὸν οἶνον· αἱ γὰρ ἀλλοινίαι
λεγόμεναι τάχιστα μεθύσκουσιν, ἀπεψίᾳ δ' οἴνου
προσέοικεν ἡ μέθη· διὸ φεύγουσι τὸν μεμιγμένον
οἶνον οἱ πίνοντες, οἱ δὲ μιγνύοντες πειρῶνται
λανθάνειν ὡς ἐπιβουλεύοντες, ἐκστατικὸν γὰρ ἡ
μεταβολὴ καὶ τὸ[3] ἀνώμαλον. ὅθεν που καὶ τὰς
πολυχορδίας μετὰ πολλῆς οἱ μουσικοὶ κινοῦσιν
εὐλαβείας, αἷς[4] οὐδὲν ἄλλο κακὸν ἢ τὸ μικτόν
ἐστι καὶ ποικίλον. ἐγὼ δ' ἐκεῖν' ἔχω εἰπεῖν, ὅτι

---

[1] So Turnebus : εὐωδέστατον.
[2] So Wyttenbach : μεταβάλλει.
[3] τὸ added by Reiske.
[4] αἷς added by Xylander.

---

[a] Or " unseasoned." Cf. De Tuenda Sanitate, 123 B (LCL
Mor. ii, pp. 220-221).
[b] A relevant point is made by Plato in speaking of dyeing
in Republic, 429 D-E, with which Adam aptly compares

ous a man, as to prescribe a varied diet for fevered patients ; all give them a simple, fat-free [a] diet as the most easily digestible. For the food has to be acted upon and to suffer a change by subjection to our internal processes. In dyeing [b] also, simple colours are more likely to be fast ; and in perfumery the most scentless oil is most quickly blended ; thus simple and homogeneous nutriment is most easily converted in the process of digestion.[c] When a number of divergent qualities in food are united, essentially opposed and clashing as they are, they encounter each other prematurely and are destroyed. Like a mob of ill-assorted riffraff in a community, these elements cannot easily establish unity and harmonious order among themselves, but each pulls in its own direction, and will not come to terms with an alien kind. Wine offers a clear proof : the mixture of several wines together, the so-called *alloinia*, quickly intoxicates, and intoxication is like a kind of indigestion with respect to wine. Drinkers, for this reason, avoid a mixture of wines,[d] and those who mix wines try to conceal the wily practice. Change and irregularity are disruptive. This no doubt explains why musicians too are very cautious about striking a combination of notes together ; yet the only thing wrong about it is the combination itself and the bizarre effect. So I for my part am justified in what

Timaeus, 50 D-E, where essentially the same point is supported by an analogy from perfume-making.

[c] Or " more easily absorbed " ? With simple dyestuffs are contrasted, for instance, the prevalent *dibapha*, " double-dyed " : Pliny, *Nat. Hist*. ix. 63. 137.

[d] *Cf.* Pliny, *Nat. Hist*. xxiii. 24. 45 : " misceri plura genera [of wine] omnibus inutile," and Aristotle, *Rhetoric*, iii. 2. 4, with Cope's note : such artifice puts one on one's guard as against a plotter.

(661) μᾶλλον ἂν[1] ἐκ λόγων ὑπεναντίων γένοιτ' ἂν πίστις
καὶ συγκατάθεσις[2] ἢ πέψις ἐκ διαφόρων ποιοτήτων.
'' Εἰ δὲ δὴ[3] δοκῶ παίζειν, ταῦτ' ἐάσας ἐπὶ τὰ
E Φίλωνος ἄνειμι. πολλάκις γὰρ ἀκούομεν αὐτοῦ
λέγοντος, ὡς ἐπὶ[4] ποιότητι τροφῆς γίγνεται τὸ
δύσπεπτον καὶ εὔπεπτον,[5] ἡ δὲ[6] πολυμιγία βλαβερὸν
καὶ γόνιμον ἀλλοκότων ποιοτήτων, καὶ δεῖ τὸ
σύμφυλον ἐκ πείρας λαβόντα χρῆσθαι καὶ στέργειν.
εἰ δὲ φύσει δύσπεπτον οὐδέν, ἀλλὰ πλῆθός ἐστι τὸ
ταράσσον καὶ φθεῖρον, ἔτι μᾶλλον οἶμαι τὰ παντοδαπὰ ταῦτα καὶ ποικίλα φευκτέον, οἷς ἀρτίως
ἡμᾶς ὁ Φίλωνος ὀψοποιὸς ὥσπερ ἀντίτεχνος αὐτοῦ
κατεφάρματτεν, ἐξαλλάττων τῇ καινότητι καὶ
μεταβολῇ τὴν ὄρεξιν οὐκ ἀπαγορεύουσαν, ἀλλ'
ἀγομένην ἐπ' ἄλλα καὶ παρεκβαίνουσαν ἐν τῷ
ποικίλῳ τὸ μέτριον[7] καὶ αὔταρκες, ὥσ⟨περ ὁ τῆς
Ὑψι⟩πύλης[8] τρόφιμος ἐκεῖνος[9]

F

        ἕτερον ἐφ' ἕτερον αἰρόμενος[10]
        ἄγρευμ' ἀνθέων[11] ἡδομένα ψυχᾷ,
        τὸ νήπιον[12] ἄπληστος ἐών[13]

ἐπὶ πλεῖστον ἐξανθίζεται τοῦ λειμῶνος.
'' Ἐνταῦθα δὲ καὶ τοῦ Σωκράτους ἅμα μνημο-

---

[1] Lacuna after ἂν, perhaps ἀν⟨θρώποις⟩ Bernardakis.
[2] So Turnebus, Vulcobius : κατάθεσις.
[3] εἰ δὲ δὴ Reiske, Wyttenbach, ἵνα δὲ μὴ Xylander, Amyot:
εἰ δὲ μή.   [4] ἐπεὶ Wyttenbach, εἰ Meziriacus.
[5] καὶ εὔπεπτον added by Hubert.
[6] δὲ added by Madvig, Hubert, τε Bernardakis.
[7] τὸ μέτριον supplied by Turnebus : lac. 4.
[8] So Turnebus, cf. 93 D : ὦσ lac. 1-2 πύλης.
[9] So Kronenberg, cf. 691 D : lac. 3-4 νος.
[10] So Turnebus, Stephanus (ἐφ' ἑτέρῳ), cf. 93 D : ἐφετέρας
ἱέμενος.   [11] So Turnebus, Stephanus, cf. 93 D : ἂν συν-.

I said, because persuasion and agreement can sooner be reached by conflicting statements than good digestion by foods of divergent types.

" But if this seems frivolous, I shall drop it and get back to Philo's views. We often hear him say that good or bad digestion depends on the nature of the food consumed, and that a combination of miscellaneous viands is harmful and engenders adverse conditions. We must learn by experience what foods go together and be content to use them. But if nothing is of itself indigestible, and it is only the quantity that causes disorder and harm, then I think that we should all the more avoid the multifarious variety with which Philo's cook has just drugged us. This he does as if to set his skill in opposition to Philo's, altering our appetite by novelty and change, not letting it be appeased, but ever leading it on to something else, and causing it to exceed what is reasonable and self-sufficient by colourful variety. So our cook is like the nursling of Hypsipylê,[a] as he gathers flowers far and wide through the meadow :

> Flower after flower he plucked,
> Garnering his catch with rejoicing heart,
> Never satisfied—the child !

" In this connection we must also recall Socrates's [c]

[a] Daughter of King Thoas of Lemnos who, being enslaved, became the nurse of Opheltes, son of King Lycurgus of Nemea.

[b] Euripides, frag. 754 from the *Hypsipylê* (Nauck, *Trag. Gr. Frag.*). See now G. W. Bond's edition, Oxford, 1963, pp. 34 f. and 91 f. Opheltes is bitten by a snake and dies.

[c] Xenophon, *Memorabilia*, i. 3. 6.

---

[12] So Turnebus, Stephanus from 93 D : lac. 3-4 μηπιον.
[13] ἄπληστος ἐὼν (sic) T, ἄχρηστον ἔχων mss. at 93 D.

(661) νευτέον, παρακελευομένου φυλάττεσθαι τῶν βρωμάτων οἷα τοὺς μὴ πεινῶντας ἐσθίειν ἀναπείθει, ὡς
οὐδὲν ἀλλ᾽ ἢ τὸ παντοδαπὸν καὶ ποικίλον εὐλαβεῖσθαι καὶ δεδιέναι τῶν σιτίων παραινοῦντος. τοῦτο
662 γὰρ πορρωτέρω ἐξάγει τῆς χρείας τὴν ἀπόλαυ-
σιν ἐν θεάμασιν ἐν ἀκροάμασιν ἐν ἀφροδισίοις ἐν
παιδιαῖς ἁπάσαις καὶ διατριβαῖς, ἀναλαμβανο-
μένην ὑπὸ τοῦ περιττοῦ πολλὰς ἀρχὰς ἔχοντος· ἐν
δὲ ταῖς ἁπλαῖς καὶ μονοτρόποις ἡδοναῖς οὐ παρ-
εκβαίνει τὴν φύσιν ἡ θέλξις. ὅλως δέ μοι δοκεῖ
μᾶλλον ἄν τις ὑπομεῖναι πολυχορδίαν μουσικὸν
ἐπαινοῦντα καὶ μυραλοιφίαν ἀλείπτην ἢ πολυοψίαν
ἰατρόν· αἱ γὰρ ἐκτροπαὶ καὶ μεταβολαὶ τῆς εἰς
ὑγίειαν εὐθείας ἐκβιβάζουσιν.''[1]

3. Τοῦ δὲ Φιλίνου ταῦτ᾽ εἰπόντος, ὁ Μαρκίων
B ἔφη δοκεῖν αὐτῷ τῇ Σωκράτους ἐνέχεσθαι κατάρα
μὴ μόνον τοὺς τὸ λυσιτελὲς ἀπὸ τοῦ καλοῦ
χωρίζοντας, ἀλλὰ καὶ τοὺς ἡδονὴν διιστάντας ἀπὸ
τῆς ὑγιείας, ὡς ἀντιταττομένην αὐτῇ καὶ πολε-
μοῦσαν οὐχὶ μᾶλλον συνεργοῦσαν· '' σμικρὰ γάρ,''
ἔφη, '' καὶ ἄκοντες ὡς βιαιοτάτῳ τῶν ὀργάνων ἀλ-
γηδόνι προσχρώμεθα· τῶν δ᾽ ἄλλων οὐδεὶς ἂν οὐδὲ
βουλόμενος ἀπώσαιτο τὴν ἡδονήν, ἀλλὰ καὶ τροφαῖς
καὶ ὕπνοις καὶ περὶ λουτρὰ καὶ ἀλείμματα καὶ
κατακλίσεις ἀεὶ πάρεστιν καὶ συνεκδέχεται καὶ
συνεκτιθηνεῖται τὸν κάμνοντα, πολλῷ τῷ οἰκείῳ
C καὶ κατὰ φύσιν ἐξαμαυροῦσα[2] τὸ ἀλλότριον. ποία
γὰρ ἀλγηδών, τίς ἔνδεια, ποῖον δηλητήριον οὕτω

---

[1] So Reiske : ἐκβιάζουσιν.　　[2] So Stephanus :ἐξαμαυρουντα.

admonition to beware of those dishes that tempt
people to eat when they're not hungry ; apparently
he is simply urging us to be cautious and wary of
variety and mixing of foods. Such variety encourages
indulgence far beyond need in sights and sounds, sex,
or in any kind of sport and pastime, because it adds
certain elements which renew the pleasure by their
numerous stimuli. On the other hand, in simple,
uniform pleasures no charm or magic induces us to
overstep the bounds of nature. In general, I should
sooner expect people to tolerate a musician who finds
a jumble of mixed sounds acceptable or a gymnastic
trainer who accepts scented oils, than a physician who
commends a combination of many meats. For the
detours and changes in such a diet divert us from the
straight road to health."

3. When Philinus had ended, Marcion said that in
his view the imprecation of Socrates [a] falls not only
upon those who detach interest from honour, but
upon those who divorce pleasure from health, as if it
were an opposing and hostile force instead of a supporting one. "We have recourse to pain in treating
the sick only sparingly and reluctantly, for it is excessively violent ; from all other therapy no one could
remove pleasure, even if he wished. Eating, sleeping,
bathing, anointing and resting on a couch are all
attended by pleasure, which does its part to support
and nurse a man back to health, weakening the
abnormal and extraneous by providing abundance of
what is normal and proper. What pain, what deple-
tion, what poison [b] can so easily and simply break up

---

[a] *Stoic. Vet. Frag.* i. 558 ; Cicero, *De Officiis*, iii. 3. 11.
Socrates is said to have habitually invoked a curse upon those
who considered expediency and honour incompatible.

[b] More literally " destructive, harmful agent."

(662) ῥαδίως καὶ ἀφελῶς νόσον ἔλυσεν, ὡς λουτρὸν ἐν
καιρῷ γενόμενον καὶ οἶνος δοθεὶς δεομένοις; καὶ
τροφὴ παρελθοῦσα μεθ᾽ ἡδονῆς εὐθὺς ἔλυσε τὰ
δυσχερῆ πάντα καὶ κατέστησεν εἰς τὸ οἰκεῖον τὴν
φύσιν, ὥσπερ εὐδίας καὶ γαλήνης γενομένης. αἱ
δὲ διὰ τῶν ἐπιπόνων βοήθειαι μόγις καὶ κατὰ
μικρὸν ἀνύουσι, χαλεπῶς ἐκμοχλεύουσαι καὶ προσ-
βιαζόμεναι τὴν φύσιν. οὐκ ἂν οὖν ἡμᾶς διαβάλοι
Φιλῖνος, εἰ μὴ τὰ ἱστία ἑκάτερ᾽ ἐπαράμενοι τὴν
ἡδονὴν φεύγοιμεν, ἀλλὰ πειρῴμεθα τὸ ἡδέως καὶ
D ὑγιεινῶς ἐμμελέστερον ἢ ὡς ἔνιοι φιλόσοφοι τὸ
ἡδέως καὶ καλῶς συνοικειοῦν.

"Εὐθὺς οὖν περὶ τὸ πρῶτον, ὦ Φιλῖνε, τῶν ἐπιχειρημάτων δοκεῖς μοι διεψεῦσθαι, τὰ θηρία τῶν
ἀνθρώπων ἁπλουστέραις τροφαῖς χρῆσθαι καὶ μᾶλλον ὑγιαίνειν ὑποτιθέμενος. οὐδέτερον γὰρ ἀληθές
ἐστιν· ἀλλὰ τῷ μὲν αἱ παρ᾽ Εὐπόλιδος αἶγες ἀντι-
μαρτυροῦσιν, ὑμνοῦσαι τὴν τροφὴν ὡς παμμιγῆ καὶ
ποικίλην οὖσαν, οὕτως πως λέγουσαι

βοσκόμεθ᾽ ὕλης ἀπὸ παντοδαπῆς, ἐλάτης πρίνου
κομάρου τε
πτόρθους ἁπαλοὺς ἀποτρώγουσαι, καὶ πρὸς τού-
τοισιν ἔτ᾽ ἄλλα,[1]

---

[1] So Xylander : ἔτ lac. 3-4, T, ἐγαλλοην ms. of Macrobius,
Saturnalia, vii. 5. 9, τουτοισί γε θαλλόν Meineke, J. M.

a disease as a bath at the right time or wine provided when the patient needs it ? Nourishment taken with pleasure can quickly soothe all discomfort and set nature to rights, as when clear sky and calm sea have returned after a storm. Painful remedies work slowly and are rarely successful, harshly wrenching and doing violence to nature. Philinus, then, cannot give us a bad name [a] merely for refusing to hoist both sails and run for it to escape pleasure. Rather, we are trying to reconcile the concepts ' pleasant ' and ' healthy ' more reasonably and appropriately than some philosophers do ' pleasant ' and ' honourable.'

" Your very first argument, Philidus, is fallacious, it seems to me, when you begin by assuming that animals thrive on a simpler diet and are healthier than men. For neither point is valid. Eupolis's [b] goats testify against the first, when they chant the praises of their diet as being all-inclusive and of wondrous variety. I think the lines run as follows :

For we feed on every kind of tree [c] : silver-fir, kermes-
        oak, arbute-tree,
Chewing off the tender shoots ; and others too besides—

[a] Or " set us at variance."
[b] Eupolis, frag. 14 (Kock) and J. M. Edmonds, *Fragments of Attic Comedy*, vol. i (1957), pp. 319 ff., *The Goats.* Eupolis was a writer of Old Attic Comedy, *notus omnibus* according to Macrobius (*Saturnalia*, vii. 5. 8 with citation of the same fragment).
[c] Botanical identifications are notoriously problematic. See Sir Arthur Hort's edition of Theophrastus, *Hist. Plant.* (LCL) with its admirable index of plants. See also Edmonds's note on the fragment.

Edmonds, *Frags. of Attic Comedy*, i, p. 320 (*cf.* Athenaeus, 582 f, 587 a, Harpocration, *s.v.* Νάννιον, Plut. *Mor.* 30 c-d), τούτοις τιθύμαλλον Bergk, Eyssenhardt (" spurge "), ἀλόην τε Warmington.

(662) κύτισόν τ᾽ ἠδὲ σφάκον[1] εὐώδη καὶ σμίλακα τὴν[2]
E   πολύφυλλον,
κότινον, σχῖνον,[3] μελίαν, λεύκην,[4] ἀρίαν,[5] δρῦν,
   κιττόν, ἐρίκην,[6]
πρόμαλον, ῥάμνον, φλόμον, ἀνθέρικον, κισθόν,
   φηγόν, θύμα,[7] θύμβραν·

τὰ γὰρ κατηριθμημένα μυρίας δήπου διαφορὰς
ἔχει χυμῶν καὶ ὀδμῶν καὶ δυνάμεων· πλείονα δὲ
τῶν εἰρημένων παραλέλειπται.

" Τὸ δὲ δεύτερον Ὅμηρος ἀθετεῖ μᾶλλον ἐμπείρως, τὰ λοιμικὰ πάθη πρῶτον ἅπτεσθαι τῶν
ἀλόγων ἀποφαινόμενος. κατηγορεῖ δ᾽ αὐτῶν καὶ
ἡ βραχύτης τοῦ βίου τὸ ἐπίκηρον καὶ νοσῶδες·
οὐδὲν γὰρ ὡς εἰπεῖν πολυχρόνιόν ἐστιν, πλὴν εἰ
φαίη τις κόρακα καὶ κορώνην,[8] ἃ δὴ παμφάγα τ᾽
F ὄντα καὶ πάσης ἁπτόμενα τροφῆς ὁρῶμεν.

" Καὶ μὴν καὶ τῇ τῶν νοσούντων διαίτῃ καλῶς
ἐποίεις τὰ εὔπεπτα καὶ δύσπεπτα τεκμαιρόμενος·
καὶ γὰρ πόνος καὶ γυμνάσια καὶ[9] τὸ διαιρεῖν τὴν
663 τροφὴν εὔπεπτα[10] μέν ἐστιν, οὐχ ἁρμόζει δὲ τοῖς

---

[1] So Bodaeus Stapelius : φα lac. 5-8 T, φασ.κον ms. of
Macrobius.   [2] τὴν Macrobius : omitted in T.
[3] So in Macrobius : ἐχῖνον.
[4] So Kock : πεύκην Macrobius, omitted in T.
[5] So Lobeck : ἁλίαν Macrobius, omitted in T.
[6] So Macrobius : μυρίκην.
[7] So in Macrobius : omitted in T.
[8] κορώνην added in Basel edition to fill lac. 3-4 T ; cf.
Macrobius, Saturnalia, vii. 5. 11 " cornicibus."
[9] κατὰ Post, εἰς Hubert, διὰ Franke.
[10] συνεργὰ or πεπτικὰ Hubert, but he allows an " active "
sense to εὔπεπτα ; cf. Gulick in A.J.P. lx, pp. 493 f. on
ἄλκιμος (669 B) and λύσιμος.

---

[a] Or holm oak or yew. Smilax or milax seems to have been

308

Tree-medick and fragrant sage and leafy bindweed,[a]
Wild olive, mastic, manna ash, poplar, cork, common oak,
    ivy, and heath,
Promalus,[b] boxthorn, mullein,[c] asphodel, rock rose, va-
    lonia oak, thyme, and savory.

The plants enumerated here surely have thousands
of different flavours, fragrances, and other properties ;
and Eupolis has omitted more than he has named.

" Your second point is refuted by Homer,[d] because
of his truer observation of nature, when he represents
the plague as attacking animals first. The very short-
ness of their life-span betrays how susceptible they
are to death and disease.[e] Practically none of them
is long-lived, unless you wish to cite ravens or crows,
which we see omnivorously snapping up every kind
of food that they come upon.

" Moreover, it was kind[f] of you to distinguish
digestible from indigestible foods by reference to the
diet of the sick. For exertion, exercise and the use of
different foods[g] promote digestion, yet they are not

a name applied to two or three very different plants. *Cf.*
Theophrastus, *Hist. Plant.* iii. 16. 2 and 18. 11 ; and Pliny,
Nat. Hist. xvi. 19 and 153. The yew is a poisonous conifer
whose leaves are said to be very injurious to cattle : see Pliny,
Nat. Hist. xvi. 50 f. Hence, though leafy, the *taxi nocentes* of
Virgil, *Georgics*, ii. 257, appear unlikely as food for goats.

    [b] Perhaps a kind of willow. See Athenaeus, xv, 673 b-c,
and Apollonius Rhodius, iii. 201, with Mooney's note.

    [c] Probably " comfrey," Andrews.   [d] *Iliad*, i. 46-50.

    [e] *De Iside*, 371 B, has the same sequence of Greek words in
Xylander's emendation.

    [f] *i.e.*, to me (a way of saying " thank you for arguing on
my side.") The meaning may, however, be " it was intelligent of you."

    [g] Or " dividing the nourishment," *i.e.*, eating twice a day.
Cf. (with L. Edelstein) Celsus, i. 1. Bernardakis compares
689 D on the process of digestion. With Post's reading the
sense would be " by helping to break up the food."

(663) πυρέττουσι. τὴν δὲ μάχην καὶ τὴν διαφορὰν τῆς ποικίλης τροφῆς ἀλόγως ἐδεδίεις. εἴτε γὰρ ἐξ ὁμοίων¹ ἀναλαμβάνει τὸ οἰκεῖον ἡ φύσις καὶ² εἰς τὸν ὄγκον αὐτόθεν ἡ ποικίλη τροφὴ πολλὰς μεθιεῖσα ποιότητας ἐξ ἑαυτῆς ἑκάστῳ μέρει τὸ πρόσφορον ἀναδίδωσιν, ὥστε γίγνεσθαι τὸ τοῦ Ἐμπεδοκλέους

ὡς γλυκὺ μὲν³ γλυκὺ μάρπτε, πικρὸν δ' ἐπὶ πικρὸν
ὄρουσεν,

ὀξὺ δ' ἐπ' ὀξὺ ἔβη,⁴ δαλερὸν δαλεροῦ λάβετ' ὦκα,⁵

τῶν δὲ καὶ ἄλλων τὸ πρόσφορον ἐπιμενόντων,⁶ τῇ θερμότητι ἐν τῷ πνεύματι τοῦ μίγματος σκεδα-
B σθέντος, τὰ οἰκεῖα τοῖς συγγενέσιν ἕπεται· τὸ γὰρ οὕτως παμμιγὲς σῶμα καὶ πανηγυρικόν, ὡς τὸ ἡμέτερον, ἐκ ποικίλης ὕλης λόγον ἔχει μᾶλλον ἢ ἁπλῆς συνερανίζεσθαι καὶ ἀναπληροῦν τὴν κρᾶσιν.

" Εἴτε μὴ τοῦτ' ἐστίν, ἀλλ' ἡ καλουμένη πέψις ἀλλοιοῦν πέφυκεν καὶ μεταβάλλειν τὴν τροφήν, ἐν τῷ ποικίλῳ τοῦτο συμβήσεται θᾶττον καὶ κάλλιον· ἀπαθὲς γὰρ ὑπὸ τοῦ ὁμοίου τὸ ὅμοιον, ἡ δ' ἀντί-ταξις καὶ διαφορὰ μᾶλλον ἐξίστησι τῇ πρὸς τὸ ἐναντίον μίξει τὰς ποιότητας ἀπομαραινομένας.

" Εἰ δ' ὅλως τὸ μικτὸν ἀθετεῖς καὶ ποικίλον, ὦ Φιλῖνε, μὴ δειπνίζοντα μηδ' ὀψοποιοῦντα μόνον

---

¹ ἀνομοίων Wyttenbach, ὁμοίων καὶ ἀνομοίων Reiske, Hartman.
² Wyttenbach would delete καί.
³ ἐπὶ after μὲν deleted by Xylander with Macrobius.
⁴ ἔβη added by Xylander from Macrobius.
⁵ λάβετ' ὦκα Paton : λαβετως T, θερμὸν δ' ἐποχεύετο θερμῷ Macrobius.

310

suitable for people who have a fever. Still, you were
not justified in being afraid of conflict and disagree-
ment in a variety of foods. For it may be that the
body naturally takes its specific nutriment from the
related elements in its foods, and that a varied meal
directly transmits into the system a multiplicity of
qualities that are distributed as required to each part
of the body. What happens is the process described
by Empedocles [a]:

> Sweet seized sweet, and bitter rose to meet bitter,
> Sour went to sour, hot quickly caught up hot

—and as other elements likewise wait for their
counterparts, while the heat in the vital spirit dissolves the compound, the elements combine according to their affinities. It is right to assume that so
completely heterogeneous an assemblage of elements
as our body must draw upon many different substances rather than any single one, in order to complete the compound.

" On the other hand, if this is not so, but the
natural function of what we call ' digestion ' is
rather to alter and convert food, the alteration will
be accomplished better and more quickly with a
varied diet. For like is unaffected by like ; rather it
is opposition and contrast that, by the union of con-
traries, drive out certain qualities and make them
waste away.

" If, however, you completely reject mixture and
variety, Philinus, then you mustn't criticize Philo

[a] Frag. 90 (Diels). The language of the whole passage
also contains echoes of Empedocles, *e.g.* ὄγκος (frag. 20) and
μῖγμα (Emped. ᴀ 32 and frag. 92).

---

[6] τῶν δὲ καὶ ἄλλων τὸ πρόσφορον ἐπιμενόντων Post : (without τῶν) δὲ καὶ ἄλλου lac. 4 ἐπὶ πρόσφορον μένοντος.

(663)
C λοιδόρει Φίλωνα τοῦτον, ἀλλὰ πολὺ μᾶλλον, ὅταν
μιγνύῃ τὰς βασιλικὰς καὶ ἀλεξιφαρμάκους ἐκείνας
δυνάμεις, ἃς ' θεῶν χεῖρας ' ὠνόμαζεν Ἐρασίστρατος, διέλεγχε[1] τὴν ἀτοπίαν καὶ περιεργίαν,
ὁμοῦ μεταλλικὰ καὶ βοτανικὰ καὶ θηριακὰ καὶ τὰ
ἀπὸ γῆς καὶ θαλάττης εἰς τὸ αὐτὸ συγκεραννύντος[2]·
καλὸν γὰρ ταῦτ' ἐάσαντας ἐν πτισάνῃ καὶ σικύᾳ
καὶ ἐν ὑδρελαίῳ τὴν ἰατρικὴν ἀπολιπεῖν.

" ' Ἀλλὰ νὴ Δία τὸ ποικίλον ἐξάγει καὶ γοητεύει
τὴν ὄρεξιν οὐ κρατοῦσαν ἑαυτῆς ' · καὶ γὰρ τὸ
καθάριον,[3] ὦ δαιμόνιε, καὶ τὸ εὐστόμαχον καὶ τὸ
εὐῶδες καὶ ὅλως τὸ ἥδιον ἐφέλκεται καὶ ποιεῖ
D βρωτικωτέρους ἡμᾶς καὶ ποτικωτέρους. τί οὖν
οὐχὶ κρίμνον μὲν ἡμεῖς ἀντὶ πόλτου μάττομεν ἀντὶ
δ' ἀσπαράγου γήτεια καὶ σκολύμους παρασκευά-
ζομεν, τὸν δ' ἀνθοσμίαν ἀπωσάμενοι τουτονὶ καὶ
ἡμερίδην ἀγριώτερον πίνομεν ἐκ πίθου, κωνώπων
χορῷ περιᾳδόμενον; ὅτι φαίης ἂν οὐ φυγὴν οὐδ'
ἀπόδρασιν ἡδονῆς εἶναι τὴν ὑγιεινὴν δίαιταν, ἀλλὰ
περὶ ἡδονὰς μετριότητα καὶ τάξιν ὑπηκόῳ χρωμένην ὀρέξει τοῦ συμφέροντος.

" Ὡς δὲ λάβρον πνεῦμα κυβερνῆται πολλαῖς
μηχαναῖς ὑποφεύγουσιν, παυσάμενον δὲ καὶ μαραν-
θὲν οὐδεὶς πάλιν ἐκριπίσαι καὶ διασεῖσαι δυνατός
E ἐστιν, οὕτως πρὸς ὄρεξιν ἐνστῆναι μὲν καὶ κολοῦσαι
τὸ πλεονάζον αὐτῆς οὐ μέγ' ἔργον, ἤδη δὲ κάμ-

---

[1] So Leonicus : δ' ἐλέγχει.
[2] So Turnebus : συγκεραννῦντας.
[3] So Basel edition : κιθάριον.

---

[a] " Hands " seems here to allude to the help or the power
of the gods (see Scribonius Largus, praef. init.), although

here merely for his dinners and fine cooking. Far better instead to expose his absurdity and wasted ingenuity in compounding those kingly antidotes that Erasistratus called ' the hands of gods,' [a] and in which he combines mineral, vegetable and animal ingredients, the products of both land and sea, in one prescription. It would be a good thing to forget all that and confine medical practice to gruels, cupping, and oil-and-water.

"But you say variety encourages and bewitches appetite to such a point that it loses control of itself ; yes, but so, my dear fellow, do purity, wholesomeness and fragrances. In short, anything that is especially pleasing draws us on and makes us eat and drink more than necessary. Why is it that we never prepare a coarse barley-cake instead of porridge ? And instead of asparagus why don't we prepare horn onions [b] and golden thistles ? And why, spurning the fine bouquet of mellow wine like this, do we not drink coarse, inferior wine out of the cask—wine surrounded by a choir of singing mosquitoes ? It is because, you would answer, the healthy plan of life is not headlong flight from pleasure, but, on the contrary, moderation in the enjoyment of pleasure and an ordered pattern that makes appetite the servant of welfare.

"Navigators have many devices for escaping from a violent storm, but once it has subsided and died down, no one can fan it into fury again and renew its turmoil. Just so, it is no great task to oppose appetite and cut back its excesses, but a very grim and

later, in Oribasius and Alexander Trallianus, it refers to an ointment with five ingredients.

[b] *Getion* or *gethyon* is so translated in the Oxford *Greek-English Lexicon*, but identified as " long onion " in LCL Pliny, vol. vii, Index of Plants.

(663) νουσαν πρὸ καιροῦ καὶ μαλθακιζομένην καὶ ἀπο-
λείπουσαν τὸ οἰκεῖον ἐντεῖναι καὶ ἀναζωπυρῆσαι
παγχάλεπον, ὦ ἑταῖρε, καὶ δύσεργον. ὅθεν ἡ
ποικίλη τροφὴ βελτίων τῆς ἁπλῆς καὶ τὸ μονοειδὲς
ἐχούσης πλήσμιον,[1] ὅσῳ ῥᾷον ἱστάναι φερομένην
τὴν φύσιν ἢ κινεῖν ἀπειποῦσαν. καὶ μήν, ὅ γε
λέγουσί τινες ὡς πλησμονὴ φευκτότερον ἐνδείας,
οὐκ ἀληθές ἐστιν ἀλλὰ τοὐναντίον· εἴ γε πλησμονὴ
μέν, ὅταν εἰς φθοράν τινα τελευτήσῃ καὶ νόσον,
ἔβλαψεν, ἔνδεια δέ, κἂν ἄλλο μηδὲν ἐξεργάσηται
F κακόν, αὐτὴ καθ᾽ αὑτὴν παρὰ φύσιν ἐστίν.

"Καὶ ταῦτα μὲν ὡς ἀντίχορδα[2] κείσθω τοῖς
ὑπὸ σοῦ πεφιλοσοφημένοις. ἐκεῖνο δὲ πῶς[3] ὑμᾶς
λέληθεν 'τοὺς περὶ ἅλα καὶ κύαμον,'[4] ὅτι τὸ μὲν
ποικίλον ἥδιόν[5] ἐστι, τὸ δ᾽ ἥδιον εὐορεκτότερον,[6]
τὸ δ᾽ εὐόρεκτον ὑγιεινότερον,[7] ἂν τὴν ὑπερβολὴν
καὶ τἄγαν[8] ἀφέλῃς; προσφύεται γὰρ ὀργῶντι καὶ
δεχομένῳ τῷ σώματι, τῆς ὄψεως προοδοποιούσης·
664 τὸ δ᾽ ἀνόρεκτον πλανώμενον[9] καὶ ῥεμβόμενον ἢ
παντάπασιν ἐξέβαλεν ἡ φύσις ἢ μόλις ὑπ᾽ ἐνδείας
ἔστερξεν. ἐκεῖνό μοι μόνον φύλαττε καὶ μέμνησο,
τὸ ποικίλον ὡς οὐκ ἐν ἀβυρτάκαις καὶ κανδύλοις

[1] So Stephanus : πλησίον.
[2] So Basel edition : ἀντιχορδῆς.
[3] πῶς (T) and punctuation at end of sentence defended by
Sandbach, cf. 745 A.
[4] So Stephanus : κύμινον.
[5] ἥδιόν added by Stephanus, Amyot.
[6] So Turnebus : εὐο lac. 8 τερον.

314

difficult one indeed, my friend, to intensify it and rekindle its spark, if it has weakened prematurely,
grown soft and abandoned its proper function. For
this reason variety is better at a meal than simplicity
and monotony that is merely filling—as much better
as it is easier to halt nature in full course than to start
it moving again after it has lost momentum. Furthermore, the claim made in certain quarters, that repletion is more to be avoided than deficiency, is not true ;
quite the contrary. Granted that repletion when it
culminates in some form of impairment or disease is
harmful ; still, deficiency, even without any other ill
effect, is in and of itself contrary to nature.

" Let this be my antiphonal response, so to speak,
to your speculations. But how can you advocates of
beans and salt [a] have missed the point that variety is
more agreeable, and that the more agreeable is the
more appetizing, and the more appetizing is the more
healthful, if you prune away superfluity and excess ?
For delicious variety of foods is eagerly assimilated
by the body if it is aroused and made receptive under
the influence of the sense of sight. The unappetizing,
on the other hand, wanders aimlessly in the system,
and nature either expels it altogether, or puts up with
it reluctantly because of necessity. Only please keep
this one thing in mind without fail, that variety is not
confined to fancy sauces, like *abyrtakê*, *kandylos*,

---

[a] A play on words. The proper meaning of this proverbial
phrase seems to have been " intimate friends " ; here it has
also a loose application to advocates of a simple diet. See
below, Book V, Question 10, with note on 684 E.

---

[7] τὸ δ' εὐόρεκτον ὑγιεινότερον added by Paton.
[8] So Bernardakis : ὑπὲρ lac. 6 ἂν Τ, ὑπερβολὴν καὶ πολυ-
φαγίαν Turnebus.
[9] πλανώμενον added by Amyot, Meziriacus to fill lac. 6.

(664) καὶ καρύκαις ἐστίν· ἀλλὰ ταῦτα μὲν περίεργα καὶ
σπερμολογικά, ποικιλίαν δὲ καὶ Πλάτων παρέχει
τοῖς καλοῖς καὶ γενναίοις ἐκείνοις πολίταις, παρα-
τιθεὶς βολβούς, ἐλαίας, λάχανα, τυρόν, ἑψήματα[1]
παντοδαπά, πρὸς δὲ τούτοις οὐδὲ τραγημάτων ἀ-
μοίρους περιορᾷ δειπνοῦντας."

ΠΡΟΒΛΗΜΑ Β

Διὰ τί τὰ ὕδνα δοκεῖ τῇ βροντῇ γίνεσθαι, καὶ διὰ τί τοὺς
καθεύδοντας οἴονται μὴ κεραυνοῦσθαι

Collocuntur Agemachus, Plutarchus, Dorotheus, alii

Β 1. Ὕδνα παμμεγέθη δειπνοῦσιν ἡμῖν Ἀγέμαχος
παρέθηκεν ἐν Ἤλιδι. θαυμαζόντων δὲ τῶν παρόντων, ἔφη τις ὑπομειδιάσας, " ἄξιά γε τῶν βροντῶν
τῶν ἔναγχος γενομένων," ὡς δὴ καταγελῶν τῶν λεγόντων τὰ ὕδνα τὴν γένεσιν ἐκ βροντῆς λαμβάνειν.
ἦσαν οὖν οἱ φάσκοντες ὑπὸ βροντῆς τὴν γῆν διίστα-
σθαι καθάπερ ἥλῳ[2] τῷ ἀέρι χρωμένης,[3] εἶτα ταῖς
ῥωγμαῖς τεκμαίρεσθαι τοὺς τὰ ὕδνα μετιόντας· ἐκ
δὲ τούτου δόξαν ἐγγενέσθαι τοῖς πολλοῖς, ὅτι τὸ
C ὕδνον αἱ βρονταὶ γεννῶσιν οὐ δεικνύουσιν, ὥσπερ εἴ
τις οἴοιτο τοὺς κοχλίας ποιεῖν τὸν ὄμβρον ἀλλὰ μὴ
προάγειν μηδ' ἀναφαίνειν.

---

[1] So Turnebus from Plato, *Rep.* 372 c : ὀψίματα.
[2] So Xylander : ἡλίῳ, *cf.* 952 Λ, where the same correction
is credited to Turnebus.
[3] So Xylander : χρωμένην.

---

[a] *Abyrtakê* is a sour sauce made from leeks, cress, and
either mustard and stavesacre or pomegranate seeds : Pherecrates, 181 in *Com. Att. Frag.* i, p. 199, with Kock's note ;

karykê,[a] which are mere curiosities and frivolities. Variety is admitted even by Plato,[b] who sets before those noble citizens of the genuine state onions, olives, green vegetables, cheese and all manner of boiled viands ; he doesn't cheat them of dessert with their dinner, either."

QUESTION 2

Why truffles are thought to be produced by thunder, and why people believe that sleepers are never struck by thunder

Speakers : Agemachus, Plutarch, Dorotheüs, and others

1. At a dinner in Elis, Agemachus served us some giant truffles. Everyone present expressed admiration, and one of the guests said with a smile, " They certainly are worthy of the thunder that we've had lately," obviously laughing at those who say that truffles are produced by thunder. Several of the company held that the ground splits open when struck by thunder, the air serving as a spike, and that afterward the truffle-gatherers are guided by the cracks in the earth. This is the source, they continued, of the popular notion that thunder actually produces the truffles, instead of merely bringing them to light. It is as if someone were to imagine that rain not merely brings out snails where we can see them, but actually creates them.

Theopompus, 17 (Kock i, p. 737). *Kandylos* or *kandaulos* is a Lydian dish, of which there were several varieties, supposed to be aphrodisiac : Nicostratus, 17 (Kock ii, p. 224) ; Athenaeus, 516 c—517 a ; Menander, 462. 11 (Kock)=397. 11 (Körte). *Karykê* is another Lydian sauce, composed of blood and spices : Pherecrates, 181 (Kock i, p. 199) ; Athenaeus, 516 c.   [b] *Republic*, 372 c.

(664) Ὁ δ' Ἀγέμαχος ἰσχυρίζετο τῇ ἱστορίᾳ καὶ τὸ θαυμαστὸν ἠξίου μὴ ἄπιστον ἡγεῖσθαι. καὶ γὰρ ἄλλα πολλὰ θαυμάσια βροντῆς ἔργα καὶ κεραυνοῦ καὶ τῶν περὶ ταῦτα διοσημιῶν εἶναι, χαλεπὰς καταμαθεῖν ἢ παντελῶς ἀδυνάτους τὰς αἰτίας ἔχοντα. "καὶ γὰρ ὁ γελώμενος οὑτοσὶ καὶ παροιμιώδης,"[1] ἔφη, "βολβὸς οὐ μικρότητι δια-φεύγει τὸν κεραυνόν, ἀλλ' ἔχων δύναμιν ἀντιπαθῆ, καθάπερ ἡ συκῆ καὶ τὸ δέρμα τῆς φώκης ὥς φασι καὶ τὸ τῆς ὑαίνης, οἷς τὰ ἄκρα τῶν ἱστίων[2] οἱ
D ναύκληροι καταδιφθεροῦσιν· τὰ δ' ἀστραπαῖα τῶν ὑδάτων εὐαλδῆ καλοῦσιν οἱ γεωργοὶ καὶ νομί-ζουσιν. καὶ ὅλως εὔηθές ἐστι ταῦτα θαυμάζειν τὸ πάντων ἀπιστότατον ἐν τοῖς πάθεσι τούτοις καθορῶντας, ἐκ μὲν ὑγρῶν φλόγας ἐκ δὲ μαλακῶν νεφῶν[3] ψόφους σκληροὺς ἀναδιδομένους. ταῦτα δ'," εἶπεν, "ἀδολεσχῶ παρακαλῶν ὑμᾶς ἐπὶ τὴν ζήτησιν τῆς αἰτίας, ἵνα μὴ πικρὸς γένωμαι συμ-βολὰς τῶν ὕδνων πρασσόμενος."

2. Αὐτὸν οὖν ἔφην ἐγὼ[4] τρόπον τινὰ τῷ λόγῳ δεξιὰν ὀρέγειν τὸν Ἀγέμαχον· οὐδὲν γὰρ ἔν γε τῷ παρόντι φαίνεσθαι πιθανώτερον, ἢ[5] ὅτι ταῖς βρονταῖς πολλάκις ὕδωρ συνεκπίπτει γόνιμον.
E "αἰτία δ' ἡ τῆς θερμότητος ἀνάμιξις· τὸ μὲν

---

[1] So Basel edition : παρομοιώδης.
[2] ἱστῶν Reichardt.　　　[3] So Turnebus : lac. 3.
[4] So Benseler : ἐγὼ ἔφην.
[5] ἢ added by Xylander.

---

[a] " Signs from Zeus " (*diosemia*) usually refer to dis-suasive omens important in politics, but here Plutarch un-questionably is thinking of meteorological phenomena in the broad Greek sense of the word, including astronomy, meteor-ology in the modern sense and seismology, etc. See Aris-

Agemachus, however, upheld the popular theory, and advised us not to regard the miraculous as unworthy of belief. For indeed many other marvellous effects are, he said, produced by thunder, lightning, and other meteoric phenomena (*diosemia*),[a] though the causes of these effects are difficult or completely impossible to discover. " For instance, the much-ridiculed, proverbial tassel-hyacinth [b] here is protected against the thunderbolt not by its smallness but by a resistant property in it,[c] like the fig tree, the seal-skin,[d] they say, and the pelt of the hyena, which shipowners use to cover the mastheads. Farmers assert and believe that showers accompanied by lightning enrich the soil. In general, it is simple-minded to be surprised at such things when we observe directly the most incredible part of it all, namely, flashes of fire coming from moisture, and rough, loud crashes from soft clouds. But my chatter is meant only as an invitation to search for a theory that will explain these things ; I don't mean to be unmannerly and exact a contribution from each man to pay for the truffles."

2. Here I remarked that Agemachus himself was, after a fashion, lending a helping hand to the discussion. At the moment at least, I said, no more probable theory occurred to me than that fertile rains often accompany thunder. " The reason," I went on, " is the warmth mixed with the rain ; the in-

---

[a] totle, *Meteorologica, passim*, especially i. 1 with H. D. P. Lee's notes and his introduction to the LCL edition, p. xi.

[b] Athenaeus, ii, 64 b, has a proverb relating *bolboi* to virility, and says further that *bolboi* are hard to digest.

[c] The Pseudo-Democritean Bolos wrote a book on " antipathies " in the time of Callimachus. See *RE, s.v.* " Bolos."

[d] Compare parallel ideas and examples in Book II, 641 B above, Book V, 684 c below and Pliny, *Nat. Hist.* ii. 146.

(664) γὰρ ὀξὺ καὶ καθαρὸν τοῦ πυρὸς ἄπεισιν ἀστραπὴ
γενόμενον, τὸ δ᾽ ἐμβριθὲς καὶ πνευματῶδες ἐνει-
λούμενον τῷ νέφει καὶ συμμεταβάλλον ἐξαιρεῖ[1]
τὴν ψυχρότητα καὶ συνεκπονεῖ[2] τὸ ὑγρόν· ὥστε
μάλιστα[3] προσηνὲς ἐνδύεσθαι τοῖς βλαστάνουσι καὶ
ταχὺ παχύνειν. ἐπεὶ δὲ καὶ κράσεων ἰδιότητα καὶ
χυμοῦ διαφορὰν ἐμποιεῖ[4] τὰ τοιαῦτα τοῖς ἀρδο-
μένοις,[5] ὥσπερ αἵ τε δρόσοι γλυκυτέραν ποιοῦσι
τοῖς θρέμμασι τὴν πόαν καὶ τὰ[6] τὴν ἶριν ἐξανθοῦντα
νέφη, καθ᾽ ὧν ἂν ἐπερείσῃ ξύλων, εὐωδίας ἀναπίμπλησι (καὶ ταύτῃ γνωρίζοντες οἱ παρ᾽ ἡμῖν
F ἰρίσκηπτα[7] καλοῦσι, τὴν ἶριν ὑπολαμβάνοντες
ἐπισκήπτειν), πολλῷ[8] γε[9] μᾶλλον εἰκός ἐστι τοῖς
ἀστραπαίοις καὶ κεραυνίοις ὕδασι καὶ πνεύμασι
καὶ θερμότησιν εἰς βάθος ἐλαυνομέναις τὴν γῆν
στρέφεσθαι καὶ συστροφὰς ἴσχειν τοιαύτας καὶ
χαυνότητας, ὥσπερ ἐν τοῖς σώμασι τὰ χοιραδώδη
καὶ ἀδενώδη φύματα θερμότητές τινες καὶ ὑγρό-
τητες αἱματώδεις ἐνδημιουργοῦσιν· οὐ γὰρ ἔοικε
φυτῷ[10] τὸ ὕδνον οὐδ᾽ ἄνευ ὕδατος ἔχει τὴν γένεσιν,
665 ἀλλ᾽ ἄρριζον καὶ ἀβλαστές ἐστι[11] καὶ ἀπολελυμένον,
τῷ καθ᾽ ἑαυτὸ τὴν σύστασιν[12] ἐκ τῆς γῆς ἔχειν

---

[1] So Emperius : ἐξαίρει.
[2] So Bernardakis : συνεκπίνει.
[3] τὸ after μάλιστα deleted by Reiske.
[4] So Reiske : ἐμποιεῖν.
[5] So Stephanus : ἀρχομένοις.
[6] τὰ added by Wyttenbach.
[7] So Bernardakis : ἱερεῖς, αὐτά. There is a fragrant ἐρυσί-
σκηπτρον, apparently also called ἐρίσκηπτον, of which Pliny
has an account (*Nat. Hist.* xii. 110) closely resembling Plutarch here, except for the etymology.
[8] So Xylander : πολλῶν.
[9] So Hubert : δὲ.   [10] So Turnebus : lac. 3-4 τῳ.

tense and pure fire passes off in the form of lightning, while its heavy, vaporous element is packed in the cloud and transformed with it, drawing off the coolness and helping to discharge the moisture. This moisture in turn permeates the young shoots in a benign form, and swells them up rapidly.[a] All this imparts special characteristics and specific flavour to vegetation thus watered ; for example, dew makes grass sweeter to the cattle, and the clouds that blossom out into a rainbow fill with fragrance the trees that they rest upon. Such trees are identified by their fragrance, and in our district people call them *iriskepta* [b] in the belief that they have been struck by the rainbow. This gives us all the more reason to think that the soil is stirred, clodded, and made spongy by the deep penetration of heat, wind, and rainwater from thunderstorms ; just so, in animal bodies scrofulous and glandular growths are caused by certain kinds of heat combined with sanguinous moisture. For the truffle resembles no plant and yet does not come into being without water. It appears without roots or sprouts and unattached, because it develops in a way peculiar to itself in soil that is some-

---

[a] Parallel treatment of this subject is found in Plutarch, *Aetiae Physicae*, ii, 912 A and iv, 912 F ff., where freshness, admixture of air, heat, and some generative property in spring rains seem to be the main qualities suggested to account for the fertility of rain water or rains accompanied by lightning.

[b] The Pseudo-Aristotle tries to account for belief in fragrance attributed to rainbows as due to the moderate moisture after the rainbow, rather than to the rainbow itself : *Problems*, xii. 3 (906 a 37 ff.).

---

[11] ἀβλαστές ἐστι Vulcobius : lac. 7 τες ἔτι.
[12] τὴν σύστασιν Hubert, σύστασιν Turnebus : τὴν στάσιν.

(665) παθούσης τι καὶ μεταβαλούσης. εἰ δέ γε γλίσ-
χρος," ἔφην, " ὁ λόγος ὑμῖν δοκεῖ, τοιαῦτά τοι τὰ
πλεῖστα τῶν βρονταῖς καὶ κεραυνοῖς συνεπομένων·
διὸ καὶ μάλιστα τοῖς πάθεσι τούτοις δόξα θειότητος
πρόσεστι."

3. Παρὼν δ' ὁ ῥήτωρ Δωρόθεος, " ὀρθῶς,"
ἔφη, " λέγεις· οὐ γὰρ μόνον οἱ πολλοὶ καὶ ἰδιῶται
τοῦτο πεπόνθασιν, ἀλλὰ καὶ τῶν φιλοσόφων τινές.
ἐγὼ γοῦν οἶδα, κεραυνοῦ παρ' ἡμῖν εἰς οἰκίαν
ἐμπεσόντος καὶ πολλὰ θαυμαστὰ δράσαντος (οἶνόν
B τε γὰρ ἐκ πίθων διεφόρησε τοῦ κεράμου μηδὲν
παθόντος, ἀνθρώπου τε καθεύδοντος διαπτάμενος
οὔτ' αὐτὸν ἠδίκησεν οὔτε τῆς ἐσθῆτος ἔθιγεν,
ζώνην δὲ χαλκοῦς ἔχουσαν ὑπεζωσμένον¹ διέτηξεν
τὸ νόμισμα² πᾶν καὶ συνέχεεν) φιλοσόφῳ³ παρεπι-
δημοῦντι Πυθαγορικῷ προσελθόντα αὐτὸν⁴ καὶ
διαπυνθανόμενον· τὸν δ' ἀφοσιωσάμενον καὶ κελεύ-
σαντα τὰ⁵ καθ' ἑαυτὸν ὁρᾶν⁶ καὶ προσεύχεσθαι τοῖς
θεοῖς. ἀκούω δὲ καὶ στρατιώτου φυλάττοντος
ἱερὸν ἐν Ῥώμῃ κεραυνὸν ἐγγὺς πεσόντα διακαῦσαι
τῶν ὑποδημάτων τοὺς ἱμάντας, ἄλλο δὲ μηδὲν κακὸν ἐργάσασθαι· καὶ κυλιχνίων⁷ ἀργυρῶν ξυλίνοις
ἐγκειμένων⁸ ἐλύτροις τὸν μὲν ἄργυρον συνιζῆσαι τα-
C κέντα, τὸ δὲ ξύλον ἄθικτον καὶ ἀπαθὲς εὑρεθῆναι.

---

¹ So Turnebus : ὑπεζωσμένους.
² So Turnebus : νο lac. 3-4 μα.
³ δὲ after φιλοσόφῳ deleted by Bernardakis.
⁴ αὐτὸν " subaudiendum " Hubert. Xylander reprinted
in Wyttenbach supplies hunc hominem.
⁵ τὰ added by Meziriacus.
⁶ δρᾶν Doehner, Bernardakis " sacrifice."
⁷ So Basel edition : λυχνίων.
⁸ So Basel edition : ἐγκειμένοις.

how modified and transformed. If this seems to you but a spare account of the matter," said I, " nevertheless most of the effects of thunder and lightning are of the character that I have described. And that explains exactly why these phenomena have generally been supposed to be supernatural." [a]

3. The rhetor Dorotheüs, who was present, spoke up, saying, " You are right. For not only the general run of ordinary people but even some philosophers accept the divine theory. I at least know personally of one case in connection with a stroke of lightning in a house in our town. It produced a number of astonishing effects, such as spilling wine out of jars without damage to the vessel, and passing through a man asleep without hurting him or touching his clothes, yet completely melting and fusing the copper coins in the money belt that he was wearing.[b] He went to a Pythagorean philosopher who was staying in town and asked his opinion ; but the philosopher only made a pious gesture and told the man not to gaze higher than his own level, and to pray to the gods. I have also heard that lightning once struck close to a soldier posted before a temple in Rome and burned his shoelaces, but caused him no further harm. Another instance is that of silver cups [c] in wooden cases ; the silver was melted down completely, but the wood was later found untouched and undamaged.

[a] Pseudo-Aristotle, *Problems*, xxiv. 19, recognizes sulphur and thunderbolts as sacred.

[b] *Cf.* the story told of Mithridates, 624 B, *supra*.

[c] This interpretation is due to an emendation. The manuscript reading may be correct in referring to " lampstands " or, possibly, " lamps." Silver lamps or lampstands would be comparatively rare, though actually (*cf. RE*, xiii. 1569) silver and gold ones were known.

(665) " Καὶ ταῦτα μὲν ἔξεστι πιστεύειν καὶ μή· πάντων δὲ θαυμασιώτατον, ὃ πάντες ὡς ἔπος εἰπεῖν
ἴσμεν, ὅτι τῶν ὑπὸ κεραυνοῦ διαφθαρέντων ἄσηπτα
τὰ σώματα διαμένει· πολλοὶ γὰρ οὔτε καίουσιν οὔτε
κατορύττουσιν, ἀλλ' ἐῶσι περιφράξαντες, ὥσθ'
ὁρᾶσθαι τοὺς νεκροὺς ἀσήπτους ἀεί, τὴν Εὐριπίδου
Κλυμένην ἐλέγχοντας ἐπὶ τοῦ Φαέθοντος εἰποῦσαν·

> φίλος δέ μοι
> ἄλουτος¹ ἐν φάραγξι σήπεται νέκυς.

ὅθεν οἶμαι καὶ τὸ θεῖον ὠνομάσθαι τῇ ὁμοιότητι
τῆς ὀσμῆς, ἣν τὰ παιόμενα τοῖς κεραυνοῖς ἀφίησιν
D ἐκτριβομένην πυρώδη καὶ δριμεῖαν· ὑφ' ἧς ἐμοὶ δοκοῦσι καὶ κύνες καὶ ὄρνιθες ἀπέχεσθαι τῶν διοβλήτων σωμάτων.

" Ἀλλ'² ἐμοὶ γὰρ ἄχρι τούτου τῆς αἰτίας ὥσπερ
δάφνης παρατετρώχθω³· τὰ δὲ λοιπὰ τούτων,"
ἔφη, " παρακαλῶμεν, ἐπεὶ καὶ τοῖς ὕδνοις ἐνενυ-
μέρηκεν, ἵνα μὴ πάθωμεν τὸ τοῦ Ἀνδροκύδους·
ἐκεῖνος γὰρ ὢν ἐποίησε πάντων ἐναργέστατα⁴ καὶ
κάλλιστα⁵ τοὺς περὶ τὴν Σκύλλαν ἰχθῦς ζωγρα-
φήσας ἔδοξε τῷ πάθει μᾶλλον ἢ τέχνῃ κεχρῆσθαι,
φύσει γὰρ ἦν φίλοψος· οὕτω φήσει⁶ τις καὶ ἡμᾶς

---

¹ So Musgrave : ἀλλ' οὗτος.
² ἀλλ' added by Hubert. ³ So Reiske : παρατετάχθω.
⁴ So Anonymus : ἐνεργέστερα.
⁵ So Basel edition : μάλιστα. ⁶ So Turnebus : φησί.

ᵃ Pliny (ii. 145) says that they were buried ; cf. Lucan, ii.
607. There may be here a confusion with the *bidental*, a
place struck by lightning, never to be covered, at Rome. *Cf.
Thesaurus Ling. Lat.* and also *RE, s.v.*
ᵇ Nauck, *Trag. Gr. Frag.*, Euripides, 786.
ᶜ A highly dubious etymology.

" Now all this you may believe or not, but the most astonishing of all is what practically every one of us knows : that the bodies of those killed by lightning will not decay. For many neither cremate nor bury them,[a] but leave them undisturbed, with fences built around them, so that the bodies are seen forever in an undecayed state. Thus they prove that Clymenê in Euripides was wrong when she said of Phaëthon,

> My dear one
> Rots, unwashed, in some mountain cleft a corpse.[b]

Hence, I believe, sulphur even gets its name in Greek, *theion* [c] (divine), from the similarity of the smell to the burning, pungent odour that is forced out of objects struck by lightning. This odour, to my mind, explains why dogs and birds abstain from such Zeus-smitten carcases.

" But let this be enough of my nibbling at the problem of the explanation, as at a bay leaf.[d] For the rest, let's call upon our friend [e] here, for he has been quite successful on the topic of truffles. Let's avoid the predicament of the painter Androcydes.[f] He had a natural fondness for fish, and inasmuch as the finest and most lifelike details in any of his work were the fishes that surrounded Scylla, he was accused of having consulted his appetite rather than his art. Just so, someone will say that we too were

---

[d] The Pythian priestess is said to have chewed bay leaves to secure inspiration. *Cf.* Farnell, *Cults of the Greek States*, iv, p. 188, and Tibullus, ii. 5. 63, with note in K. F. Smith's edition. For other beliefs about the laurel and lightning see *RE*, xiii. 1439 ff.

[e] Plutarch himself. *Cf.* 665 A above.

[f] *RE*, i. 2150, no. 3 ; Athenaeus repeats the story in viii, 341 a, citing Polemon as source : *cf. RE*, *s.v.* " Polemon (Periheget)," col. 1306.

(665) ὑφ' ἡδονῆς φιλοσοφῆσαι τὰ¹ περὶ τῶν ὕδνων
ἀμφισβητήσιμον ἐχόντων τὴν γένεσιν ὡς ὁρᾷς²
E . . . ἐν δὲ τούτοις ὑποκειμένης τῷ λόγῳ τῆς
εὐπειθείας³ καὶ τὴν αἰτίαν . . . πρόδηλον⁴ εἶναι
πειθούσης.''

4. Ἐμοῦ δὲ παρακελευομένου⁵ καὶ λέγοντος και-
ρὸν⁶ εἶναι καθάπερ ἐν⁷ κωμῳδίᾳ μηχανὰς αἴροντα
καὶ βροντὰς ἐμβάλλοντα παρὰ πότον διαλέγεσθαι
περὶ κεραυνῶν, τὰ μὲν ἄλλα παρίεσαν⁸ συνομολο-
γοῦντες, περὶ δὲ τῶν ἐν ᾧ⁹ καθεύδουσιν μὴ κεραυ-
νουμένων ἀκοῦσαί τι βουλόμενοι λιπαρεῖς ἦσαν.
ἐμοὶ δὲ πλέον οὐδὲν ἐγίγνετο τῆς αἰτίας ἁψαμένῳ
κοινὸν ἐχούσης τὸν λόγον· ὅμως δ' οὖν ἔφην ὡς τὸ
κεραύνιον πῦρ ἀκριβείᾳ καὶ λεπτότητι θαυμαστόν
ἐστιν, αὐτόθεν τε¹⁰ τὴν γένεσιν ἐκ καθαρᾶς καὶ ἀγ-
F νῆς ἔχον οὐσίας, καὶ πᾶν εἴ τι συμμίγνυται νοτερὸν ἢ γεῶδες αὐτῷ τῆς περὶ τὴν κίνησιν ὀξύτητος
ἀποσειομένης καὶ διακαθαιρούσης.

'' Διόβλητον μὲν οὐδέν,'' ὥς φησι Δημόκριτος,
'' γήινον οἷον τὸ¹¹ παρ'¹² αἰθρίης στέγειν εὐαγὲς¹³ σέ-
λας.'' τὰ μὲν οὖν πυκνὰ τῶν σωμάτων, σίδηρος,¹⁴

---

¹ So Wyttenbach : φιλοσοφήσαντας.
² ὡς θρασύτατ' Hubert, [ὡς] ῥᾳστωνεύειν δ' ἐν τούτοις Paton,
ἱστορίας παραδέχεσθαι ῥᾳδίως Pohlenz, ὡς ῥᾷστ' ἐνδοῦναι, οὐδὲν
δὲ τούτοις . . . νεῖμαι Post. Pohlenz also suggests ἐλλείπειν or
ἀπαγορεύειν after ἐν δὲ τούτοις. The dots in these lines mark
the letter spaces left in T.
³ εὐπαθείας Turnebus.
⁴ So Bernardakis, Paton : προδήλῳ τῷ.
⁵ παραιτουμένου Wyttenbach '' begging to be excused.''
⁶ ἄκαιρον '' unseasonable, improper '' Wyttenbach.
⁷ So Stephanus : εἰ.
⁸ So Stephanus : πάρεισι.
⁹ So Emperius : τοῖς. Perhaps ἐν τῷ καθεύδειν Kronenberg.
¹⁰ So Diels : περί.

guided by our own pleasure when we philosophized about truffles and their obviously so controversial origin. In cases like this, the discussion is affected by an underlying willingness to be convinced, which persuades us that the explanation is obvious." [a]

4. I urged that we should pursue the topic, and said that it was time, as in a comedy, to hoist the stage machinery and hurl some thunderbolts [b] in our after-dinner discussion of thunder and lightning. The others, however, while agreeing to omit other phases of the subject, were insistent in their determination to hear something on the topic why sleeping persons are immune to strokes of lightning. But when I attempted an explanation of this immunity, which is an open question, I found that I could make no headway. Still, I ventured to say that the thunderbolt is fire of a marvellous purity and fineness, because it originates directly in a pure and uncontaminated substance. The speed with which it moves dislodges and eliminates any watery or earthy matter that is mixed in it.

"No earthen object that is struck by lightning," according to Democritus,[c] "can support the bright flash that comes from the sky." The dense substances

---

[a] The translation reflects the sense of the extant words, as amended, in the text, but the ms. has gaps : see critical note.

[b] On the *bronteion*, "thunder machine," see Haigh, *Attic Theatre*, p. 218, where Pollux, iv. 130 and a scholion to Aristophanes, *Clouds*, 292, are cited.

[c] Frag. 152. Diels adopts from Bernardakis a reading which he interprets, "No Zeus-sent lightning fails to carry the pure radiance of the aether."

---

11 γήινον οἷον τὸ added by Pohlenz, Gulick : lac. 5-6.
12 So Aldine edition : περ. ¹³ So Diels : lac. 4-5.
14 So Turnebus : lac. 6.

(665) χαλκός, ἄργυρος, χρυσός,[1] ἀποστέγει καὶ φθείρεται
καὶ τήκεται, πάσχοντα τῷ προσμάχεσθαι καὶ
ἀντερείδειν[2]· τῶν δ᾽ ἀραιῶν καὶ πολυπόρων καὶ
666 χαλώντων ὑπὸ μανότητος ἄψαυστὶ διεκθεῖ, καθάπερ[3] ἱματίων καὶ ξύλων αὔων· τὰ δὲ χλωρὰ καίει,
τῆς ὑγρότητος ἀντιλαμβανομένης καὶ συνεξαπτο-
μένης. εἴπερ οὖν τὸ τοὺς καθεύδοντας μὴ ἀπο-
θνήσκειν ὑπὸ κεραυνῶν ἀληθές ἐστιν, ἐνταῦθα
δεῖ ζητεῖν οὐκ ἀλλαχόθι τὴν αἰτίαν. μᾶλλον γὰρ
ἔρρωται καὶ συνέστηκεν καὶ ἀντερείδει τὰ σώματα
τῶν ἐγρηγορότων, ἅτε δὴ πᾶσι τοῖς μέρεσι
πεπληρωμένα πνεύματος· ὑφ᾽ οὗ καὶ τὰς αἰσθήσεις
ἐπιστρέφοντος ὥσπερ ἐν ὀργάνῳ καὶ σφίγγοντος
εὔτονον γέγονε καὶ συνεχὲς αὐτῷ καὶ πυκνὸν τὸ
ζῷον. ἐν δὲ τοῖς ὕπνοις ἐξανεῖται καὶ μανὸν[4] καὶ
ἀνώμαλον καὶ ἄτονον καὶ διακεχυμένον, καὶ πόρους
B ἔσχηκε πολλούς, τοῦ πνεύματος ἐνδιδόντος καὶ
ἀπολείποντος, δι᾽ ὧν φωναί τε καὶ ὀσμαὶ διεκ-
θέουσιν μηδεμίαν αἴσθησιν ἑαυτῶν παρέχουσαι. τὸ
γὰρ ἀντερεῖδον καὶ τῷ[5] ἀντερείδειν πάσχον οὐκ
ἀπαντᾷ τοῖς προσφερομένοις, ἥκιστα δὲ τοῖς ὑπὸ
λεπτότητος καὶ ὠκύτητος τοιαύτης ὥσπερ ὁ κεραυνὸς διϊπταμένοις[6]· τὰ μὲν γὰρ ἧττον ἰσχυρὰ
δυσπαθείαις ἡ φύσις ἀμύνεται, σκληρότητας προ-
βαλλομένη καὶ πυκνότητας· ὧν δ᾽ ἄμαχος ἡ
δύναμίς ἐστιν, ὑπὸ τούτων ἧττον ἀδικεῖται τὰ
εἴκοντα τῶν ἀνθισταμένων.

---

[1] So Turnebus : lac. 4-5.
[2] So Basel edition : .. τερείδειν.
[3] So Xylander : καθαρ.
[4] Reiske would add ἐστι, Bernardakis, Hartman ὄν, Ziegler γέγονεν.   [5] So Basel edition : τό.
[6] So Turnebus : διισταμένοις.

like iron, copper, silver, or gold, which block the path
of lightning, are broken down and melted in consequence of their opposition and resistance. But the
lightning passes without contact through loose-
textured and porous substances, which are slack and
open, like clothing and dry timber. It burns green
wood because the moisture, by intercepting the
lightning, catches fire. If, then, it is true that sleeping persons are never killed by lightning, we must
look for the reason here rather than elsewhere. The
body of those awake is firmer, compacter, and more
resistant, because it is filled in all its parts with vital
spirit. This vital spirit [a] tightens up and attunes the
organs of sense like strings in a musical instrument,
and gives the whole animal its proper tension, solidity,
and compactness. In sleep, on the other hand, the
body relaxes, becomes loose-textured and uneven in
its consistency, and is left untensed and diffuse. The
result is that many passages are opened as the vital
spirit weakens and is lost. Through these, sounds
and smells pass unperceived. For there is no resistance to encounter onrushing particles and to receive
an impression from them, especially when the
particles that speed through are as fine and swift as
those of lightning. Nature defends itself against
weaker assault by various degrees of imperviousness,
throwing up a shield of hardness and density ; but
where the destructive force is irresistible, less damage
is suffered by soft, yielding substances than by those
that stand firm.

[a] This seems to be an echo of the theory held by Erasistratus, the famous physician of the 3rd century B.C. *Cf.* Well-
mann in *RE*, *s.v.* " Erasistratos," col. 341. See also *supra*, i.
7, 625 B-C.

(666)　"Πρόσλαβε[1] δὲ τούτοις," ἔφην, "οὔτι[2] μικρὰν
ἔκπληξιν πρὸς τὰ τοιαῦτα καὶ φόβον καὶ τάρβος,
ὑφ' ὧν πολλοὶ μηδὲν ἄλλο παθόντες αὐτῷ τῷ δεῖσαι
τὸ[3] ἀποθανεῖν ἀπέθανον. καὶ γὰρ τὰ θρέμματα
C διδάσκουσι βροντῆς γενομένης οἱ ποιμένες εἰς
ταὐτὸ συνθεῖν καὶ συννεύειν· τὰ γὰρ σποράδην
ἀπολειφθέντα διὰ τὸν φόβον ἐκτιτρώσκει. καὶ
μυρίους ἤδη τεθνηκότας ἰδεῖν ἔστιν ὑπὸ βροντῆς,
οὐδὲν οὔτε πληγῆς ἴχνος οὔτε καύσεως ἔχοντας,
ἀλλ' ὑπὸ φόβου τῆς ψυχῆς ' ὡς ἔοικεν ὄρνιθος δίκην
ἀποπταμένης τοῦ σώματος'· 'πολλοὺς' γάρ (ὡς ὁ
Εὐριπίδης φησί), 'βροντῆς πνεῦμ'[4] ἄναιμον ὤλεσε.'
καὶ γὰρ ἄλλως[5] τῶν αἰσθητηρίων ἡ ἀκοὴ παθητι-
κώτατόν ἐστιν, καὶ μεγίστας οἱ διὰ ψόφου θόρυβοι
καὶ φόβοι ταραχὰς ἐπιφέρουσιν· ὧν τῷ καθεύδοντι
πρόβλημα τὸ ἀναίσθητόν ἐστιν. οἱ δ' ἐγρηγορότες
D καὶ ταῖς προπαθείαις ἀναλίσκονται καί, τοῦ δέους
τὸ σῶμα συνδέοντος ὡς ἀληθῶς καὶ συνάγοντος
καὶ πυκνοῦντος, ἰσχυρὰν ποιοῦσι τὴν πληγὴν τῷ
ἀντερείδειν."

ΠΡΟΒΔΗΜΑ Γ

Διὰ τί πλείστους ἐν γάμοις ἐπὶ δεῖπνον καλοῦσιν

Collocuntur Sossius Senecio, Theo, alii

1. Ἐν τοῖς Αὐτοβούλου τοῦ υἱοῦ γάμοις συν-
εώρταζεν ἡμῖν παρὼν ἐν Χαιρωνείᾳ[6] Σόσσιος

---

[1] So Stephanus : προσέλαβε.
[2] So Bernardakis : ἔτι.
[3] τὸ added by Benseler, Stegmann, Castiglioni.
[4] τραῦμα Theon of Smyrna, Wilamowitz.

" Add to that," I said, " the not inconsiderable
effect of surprise, fear, and panic ; such things cause
emotions that have caused the death of many simply
by fear of death. Shepherds in fact train their sheep,
at the sound of thunder, to run to one place and huddle
together, because thunder causes miscarriage through
fright in any that are left isolated. What is more, the
evidence is plain that countless thousands of people
have been killed by thunder and lightning without a
trace of wound or burn ; ' apparently the life in panic
took flight from the body like a bird.' For, as Euripides [a] says,

Many the bloodless breath of thunder has destroyed.

In general, our hearing is of all our senses the most
liable to shock, and therefore the upset and terror
produced by a noise cause the greatest disorders.
Now the sleeper is protected against these by being
unconscious ; whereas people in a waking state are
not only doomed by their imagination but also add
force to the actual blow by opposing it, because fear
(*deos*) really does bind (*dein*), contract, and solidify
the body."

QUESTION 3

Why it is customary to invite the most guests to wedding
suppers

Speakers : Sossius Senecio, Theon, and others

1. At the wedding of my son Autobulus, Sossius
Senecio was present in Chaeronea as one of our

---

[a] Nauck, *Trag. Gr. Frag.*, Euripides, 982 : πολλοὺς δὲ κτλ.

[5] So Basel edition : ἄλλους.
[6] So Volkmann, Hartman : ἐκ χαιρωνείας ὁ.

(666) Σενεκίων, καὶ πολλῶν λόγων[1] ἄλλων τε τῇ τόθ'
ἑορτῇ μάλα πρεπόντων παρέσχεν[2] ἀφορμὰς καὶ
περὶ τῆς αἰτίας,[3] δι' ἣν πλεῖστοι τῶν ἄλλων[4] ἐπὶ
E τὰ γαμικὰ δεῖπνα παραλαμβάνονται, διηπόρησε·
καὶ γὰρ τῶν νομοθετῶν τοὺς τῇ πολυτελείᾳ κατὰ
κράτος πολεμήσαντας ὁρίσαι μάλιστα τῶν εἰς
τοὺς γάμους καλουμένων τὸ πλῆθος. " ὁ γὰρ
εἰπών," ἔφη, " περὶ τῆς αἰτίας αὐτῆς τῶν παλαιῶν
φιλοσόφων οὐδέν, ἐμοὶ γοῦν κριτῇ, πιθανὸν εἴρηκεν,
Ἑκαταῖος ὁ Ἀβδηρίτης[5]· λέγει δὲ τοὺς ἀγομένους
γυναῖκας πολλοὺς παρακαλεῖν ἐπὶ τὴν ἑστίασιν,
ἵνα πολλοὶ συνειδῶσι καὶ μαρτυρῶσιν ἐλευθέροις
οὖσι καὶ παρ' ἐλευθέρων γαμοῦσι. τοὐναντίον γὰρ
οἱ κωμικοὶ τοὺς πολυτελῶς καὶ σοβαρῶς λαμπρό-
τητι δείπνων καὶ παρασκευῆς[6] γαμοῦντας ὡς οὐ
βεβαίως οὐδὲ θαρραλέως[7] ἐπισυνάπτουσιν· ὡς
F Μένανδρος πρὸς τὸν κελεύοντα ταῖς λοπάσι περι-
φράττειν τὸν γάμον[8]·

δεινῶς ἀσώτου φράγμα κοὐ νύμφης λέγεις.[9]

2. " Ἀλλ' ὅπως[10] μή, τὸ ῥᾷστον,[11] ἐγκαλεῖν ἑτέροις δοκῶμεν αὐτοὶ μηδὲν λέγοντες, ἀποφαίνο-
μαι[12] πρῶτος," εἶπεν, " ἐγώ, οὐδεμίαν ἑστιάσεως

---

[1] So Wyttenbach, προβλημάτων Meziriacus : lac. 3.
[2] So Stephanus, παρεῖχεν Turnebus, προεῖτ' Bolkestein :
lac. 3-4.   [3] τῆς αἰτίας Stephanus : τῃ lac. 4 ασ.
[4] ἀνθρώπων Reiske, ἀλλοτρίων or φίλων Wyttenbach.
[5] So Xylander : ἀβαρρήτης.
[6] So Reiske : παρασκευῇ.
[7] Reiske suspects a lacuna here, βεβαίους οὐδὲ θαρραλέους
Amyot, Meziriacus.   [8] τὸν γάμον added by Post.
[9] So Paton, but δεινῆς : lac. 4-5 ωπον δεινῶς lac. 3-5 οὐ
πραγμα ν. λ.   [10] So Reiske : ὅμως.
[11] So Reiske : μὴ lac. 4-5 ιστον.

guests. Among many subjects that he brought forward which were particularly appropriate to the occasion, he raised the question why people invite more guests to wedding dinners than to other parties. For it is true, he observed, that those lawgivers who have campaigned most vigorously against extravagance have particularly sought to limit the number of guests at weddings. " But as to the reason itself for these large numbers," said Senecio, " the only ancient philosopher who had anything to offer was Hecataeus [a] of Abdera, who, in my judgement, said nothing convincing. His point was this : At their marriage men invite a crowd to the banquet so that there may be many witnesses to testify that the hosts themselves are of good family and that their brides come from good families. On the other hand, the comic poets attack those who celebrate a wedding in a prodigal and ostentatious style, with splendid dinners and great outlay, as not putting down a secure foundation or looking courageously to the future. Menander,[b] for instance, said with reference to someone who ordered that his marriage should be fenced around with dishes,

> This fencing-in you talk about
> Befits a frightful debauchee,
> But not a bride.

2. " But to avoid what is all too easy, the appearance of accusing others when I myself have nothing to offer, I shall be the first," he said, " to state my

---

[a] *RE*, vii. 2750, no. 4 ; Diels, *Vorsokratiker*, Hekataios von Abdera, A 5.

[b] Menander, frag. 865 (Kock), frag. 747 (Körte).

---

[12] So Reiske : ἀποφαῖνεν ἀποφανῶ. Warmington.

(666) πρόφασιν οὕτως ἔκδηλον εἶναι καὶ περιβόητον ὡς
τὴν τῶν γαμούντων· καὶ γὰρ θύοντας θεοῖς καὶ
προπέμποντας φίλον καὶ ξενίζοντας ἔστι πολλοὺς
διαλαθεῖν τῶν ἐπιτηδείων, ἡ δὲ γαμήλιος τράπεζα
667 κατήγορον ἔχει τὸν ὑμέναιον μέγα βοῶντα καὶ
τὴν δᾷδα καὶ τὸν αὐλόν, ἅ φησιν Ὅμηρος καὶ τὰς
γυναῖκας ἱσταμένας ἐπὶ ταῖς θύραις θαυμάζειν καὶ
θεᾶσθαι. διὸ μηδενὸς ἀγνοοῦντος τὴν ὑποδοχὴν
καὶ τὴν κλῆσιν, αἰσχυνόμενοι παραλιπεῖν πάντας
τοὺς συνήθεις καὶ οἰκείους καὶ ἁμωσγέπως προσ-
ήκοντας αὐτοῖς παραλαμβάνουσιν."

3. Ἀποδεξαμένων δ' ἡμῶν ὑπολαβὼν ὁ Θέων,
" καὶ τοῦτ'," ἔφη, " κείσθω, οὐκ ἀπίθανον γάρ
ἐστι, κἀκεῖνο πρόσθες, εἰ βούλει, τὰς τοιαύτας
ἑστιάσεις μὴ μόνον φιλικὰς ἀλλὰ καὶ συγγενικὰς
B εἶναι, καταμιγνυμένης εἰς τὸ γένος ἑτέρας οἰκειό-
τητος. ὃ δὲ τούτου μεῖζόν ἐστιν, οἴκων εἰς τὸ
αὐτὸ συνιόντων δυοῖν ὅ τε λαμβάνων τοὺς τοῦ
διδόντος οἰκείους καὶ φίλους ὅ τε διδοὺς τοὺς τοῦ
λαμβάνοντος οἰόμενοι δεῖν φιλοφρονεῖσθαι διπλα-
σιάζουσιν τὴν ὑποδοχήν. ἔτι[1] πολλὰ τῶν γαμι-
κῶν ἢ τὰ πλεῖστα δρᾶται διὰ γυναικῶν· ὅπου δὲ
γυναῖκες πάρεισι, καὶ τοὺς ἄνδρας ἀναγκαῖόν ἐστι
παραλαμβάνεσθαι."

---

[1] So Turnebus, Anonymus : ἐπεί.

view. It is that of all the occasions for a banquet, none is more conspicuous or talked about than a wedding. When we offer sacrifice to the gods, or honour a friend on the eve of a journey, or entertain guests from abroad, it is possible to do so unnoticed by many of our intimates and relatives; but a wedding-feast betrays us by the loud marriage cry, the torch, and the shrill pipe, things which according to Homer [a] even the women stand at their doors to watch and admire. Consequently, since no one is unaware that we are receiving guests and must have invited them, we include all our relatives, acquaintances, and connections of any degree, because we are afraid to leave anyone out."

3. When we had applauded this, Theon took up the thread with these words : " Let us adopt this theory, for it is quite probable. But add, if you will, a further point, that these particular banquets are not merely friendly entertainments but important family occasions, which solemnize the incorporation of a new set of relatives into the family. What is more important than this, at the union of two houses, each father-in-law regards it as a duty to demonstrate good will to the friends and relatives of the other, and so the guest-list is doubled. Besides, many or most of the activities relating to a wedding are in the hands of women, and where women are present it is necessary that their husbands also should be included."

[a] *Iliad*, xviii. 495 f.

(667)

ΠΡΟΒΛΗΜΑ Δ

Εἰ ἡ θάλασσα τῆς γῆς εὐοψοτέρα

Collocuntur Polycrates, Symmachus, Lamprias, alii

C 1. Τῆς Εὐβοίας ὁ Αἰδηψός,[1] οὗ τὰ Θερμὰ
χωρίον ἐστὶν αὐτοφυῆ[2] πολλὰ πρὸς ἡδονὰς ἔχον
ἐλευθερίους καὶ κατεσκευασμένον οἰκήσεσι καὶ
διαίταις, κοινὸν οἰκητήριον ἀποδέδεικται τῆς Ἑλ-
λάδος· πολλῶν δὲ καὶ πτηνῶν καὶ χερσαίων
ἁλισκομένων, οὐχ ἧττον ἡ θάλαττα παρέχει τὴν
ἀγορὰν εὐτράπεζον, ἐν τόποις καθαροῖς καὶ ἀγχιβα-
θέσι γενναῖον ἰχθὺν καὶ πολὺν ἐκτρέφουσα. μάλιστα δ' ἀνθεῖ τὸ χωρίον ἀκμάζοντος ἔαρος· πολλοὶ
γὰρ ἀφικνοῦνται τὴν ὥραν αὐτόθι[3] καὶ συνουσίας
ποιοῦνται μετ' ἀλλήλων ἐν ἀφθόνοις πᾶσι καὶ πλεί-
D στας περὶ λόγους ὑπὸ σχολῆς διατριβὰς ἔχουσι.
Καλλιστράτου δὲ τοῦ σοφιστοῦ παρόντος ἔργον
ἦν ἀλλαχόθι δειπνεῖν· ἄμαχος γὰρ ἡ φιλοφροσύνη,
καὶ τὸ πάντας εἰς τὸ αὐτὸ συνάγειν ἐπιεικῶς τοὺς
χαρίεντας ἥδιστον[4] παρεῖχε· πολλάκις μὲν γὰρ
ἐμιμεῖτο τῶν παλαιῶν τὸν Κίμωνα πολλοὺς καὶ
παντοδαποὺς ἑστιῶν ἡδέως, ἀεὶ δ'[5] ὡς ἔπος εἰπεῖν

---

[1] So Turnebus, Xylander : γαληψός.
[2] So Reiske : αὐτοφυές.
[3] Franke adds διατρίψοντες here.
[4] Post suggests τὸ δεῖπνον after ἥδιστον.
[5] δ' added by Xylander.

---

[a] See J. J. Hartman, *De Plutarcho Scriptore et Philosopho*,
pp. 382 ff., *De Avondzon des Heidendoms*, i², p. 173.
[b] *Infra*, vii. 5. 1 and 3, 704 ε and 705 в ; *De Defect. Orac.*
410 ᴀ with Flacelière's note 4 ; *RE*, *s.v.* " Plutarchos ", col.

QUESTION 4

Whether the sea is richer in delicacies than the land

Speakers : Polycrates, Symmachus, Lamprias, and others

1. AEDEPSUS [a] in Euboea has become a popular resort
for people from all over Greece, particularly because
of the place called Hot Springs, which possesses many
natural resources for the worthy enjoyment of leisure,
and is further embellished by villas and elegant apart-
ment houses. Game and fowl are caught there in
abundance, and the sea no less lavishly supplies the
market with provisions for the table, producing many
a fine, noble fish in the deep, clear waters close to
shore. This resort flourishes especially when spring
is at its height, for many continue to come there all
that season. They gather together, exempt from
every want, and, having the leisure, engage endlessly
in conversation. When Callistratus [b] the sophist was
there, it was difficult to dine at anyone else's house,
for his graciousness was irresistible, and made the
occasion very pleasant [c] when he brought practically
all the choicer spirits together in one group. For he
often copied Cimon [d] among the ancients in giving
delightful banquets for a large and miscellaneous
company ; he virtually always imitated Celeus,[e] who

676. An official of Delphi, no doubt one of the Callistrati
attested in inscriptions as holding several offices there.

[c] Or " made him very popular," following Wyttenbach's
interpretation in his *Index Verb. in Plut.*

[d] Cimon was, according to Theopompus in Athenaeus, xii,
533 a-b, exceedingly generous to the poor of Athens, for
whom he kept open house and an open purse. He was the
celebrated general, the son of Miltiades.

[e] Legendary king of Eleusis in the Homeric *Hymn to
Demeter*, 473, and elsewhere.

(667) τὸν Κελεόν, ὃν πρῶτον ἱστοροῦσιν εὐδοκίμων καὶ
ἀγαθῶν ἀνδρῶν κατασκευάσαντα σύνοδον καθη-
μερινὴν ὀνομάσαι πρυτανεῖον.

2. Ἐγίγνοντο δὴ λόγοι τοιαύτῃ συνουσίᾳ πρέ-
ποντες ἑκάστοτε· καί ποτε παρέσχον αἱ τράπεζαι
E ποικιλώταται γιγνόμεναι ζήτησιν ὑπὲρ ὄψων,
πότερον τὰ ἐκ γῆς ἢ τὰ ἐκ θαλάττης ἐπιτηδειότερα·
καὶ τῶν ἄλλων σχεδὸν ἁπάντων ὑμνούντων τὰ ἐκ
γῆς πολλὰ καὶ παντοδαπὰ καὶ δυσεξαρίθμητα τοῖς
γένεσι καὶ ταῖς διαφοραῖς, τὸν Σύμμαχον[1] ὁ Πολυκράτης προσαγορεύσας, " σὺ δ᾽," εἶπεν, " ἀμφίαλον
ὢν ζῷον καὶ τοσαύταις ἐντεθραμμένος θαλάτταις,
αἳ τὴν ἱερὰν πέριξ[2] ὑμῶν ἑλίττουσι Νικόπολιν, οὐκ
ἀμύνεις τῷ Ποσειδῶνι; " " βούλομαί γε νὴ Δί᾽,"
ὁ Σύμμαχος εἶπεν, " καὶ σὲ παραλαμβάνω καὶ
παρακαλῶ, τὰ ἥδιστα τῆς Ἀχαϊκῆς καρπούμενον
θαλάττης." " οὐκοῦν," ἔφη, " πρῶτον," ὁ Πολυκράτης, " ἴωμεν ἐπὶ τὴν συνήθειαν. ὡς γὰρ
F πολλῶν ὄντων ποιητῶν ἕνα τὸν κράτιστον ἐξαι-
ρέτως ποιητὴν καλοῦμεν, οὕτως πολλῶν ὄντων
ὄψων ἐκνενίκηκεν ὁ ἰχθὺς μόνος[3] ἢ μάλιστά γ᾽
ὄψον καλεῖσθαι διὰ τὸ πολὺ πάντων ἀρετῇ κρατεῖν.

---

[1] So Aldine edition : σίμαχον (and immediately below
σίμαχος) T, σύμαχον E (σύμαχος below).
[2] So Stephanus : περί.
[3] So Bernardakis from Athenaeus, 276 e : μόνον.

---

[a] This is to be distinguished from the better known use of
the term for a political administrative unit during the Athenian democracy.

[b] Polycrates of Sicyon in Achaïa, descendant of Aratus ;
cf. Plutarch, Aratus, i. 3 ; the Life of Aratus is dedicated to
him.

first, according to the record, established a diurnal council of excellent and respected citizens, which he called a *prytaneum*.[a]

2. Hence there was always conversation worthy of such an assemblage. At one such dinner, the elaborate fare gave rise to a discussion whether food produced by the soil or food from the sea is preferable. Most of the company sang the praises of the products of the land, citing their abundance, variety, and almost infinite diversity of qualities and types. But Polycrates,[b] turning to Symmachus,[c] said, "You're a seagirt specimen, raised as you were amid all those seas that course around your sacred Nicopolis.[d] Aren't you going to rise to the defence of Poseidon ? " "Yes, I certainly want to," answered Symmachus, "and I call upon you to back me up, since you reap a harvest of the most delicious sea food that the Achaean [e] waters have to offer." "All right," said Polycrates. "First let us consider word usage. Though there are many poets, we call the best one pre-eminently ' the poet [f] ' ; and so, though there are many delicacies, fish has won the title, either exclusively or pre-eminently, of ' delicacy ' (*opson*),[g] because it far excels all others in quality. In fact, we

[c] According to Ricard, the physician mentioned by Martial, v. 9, etc. ; but according to Ziegler, in *RE*, *s.v.* " Plutarchos," he is a member of the Amphictyonic Council from Nicopolis.

[d] City founded by Augustus on a peninsula near Actium, in honour of his victory there.

[e] Because Polycrates comes from the region Achaïa on the Gulf of Corinth.

[f] Homer.

[g] *Opson* varies in meaning from any prepared food to an especial delicacy. It is sometimes defined as anything eaten with bread (as in Plut. *Mor.* 99 D). *Cf.* Gulick's note on Athenaeus, 276 e (LCL).

(667) καὶ γὰρ ὀψοφάγους καὶ φιλόψους[1] λέγομεν οὐχὶ
668 τοὺς βοείοις χαίροντας ὥσπερ Ἡρακλῆς ὃς ' τοῖς
κρέασι χλωρὰ σῦκ' ἐπήσθιεν,'[2] οὐδὲ τὸν φιλόσυ-
κον[3] οἷος ἦν Πλάτων, οὐ φιλόβοτρυν οἷος Ἀρκεσίλαος, ἀλλὰ τοὺς περὶ τὴν ἰχθυοπωλίαν ἀναδιδόν-
τας ἑκάστοτε καὶ τοῦ κώδονος[4] ὀξέως ἀκούοντας.
καὶ ὁ Δημοσθένης τὸν Φιλοκράτην φησὶν ἐκ τοῦ
προδοτικοῦ χρυσίου ' πόρνας καὶ ἰχθῦς ἀγοράζειν,'
ἐπ' ὀψοφαγίᾳ καὶ ἀσελγείᾳ τὸν ἄνδρα λοιδορῶν.
ὁ δὲ Κτησιφῶν οὐ κακῶς, ὀψοφάγου τινὸς ἐν τῇ
βουλῇ βοῶντος ῥαγήσεσθαι, ' μηδαμῶς,' εἶπεν,
' ὦ ἄνθρωπε, ποιήσῃς ἡμᾶς ἰχθυοβρώτους.' ὁ δὲ
τὸ στιχίδιον τοῦτο ποιήσας

> πρὸς καππάριον ζῇς δυνάμενος πρὸς ἀνθίαν

B τί ποτε βούλεται; τί δ' οἱ πολλοὶ βούλονται, πρὸς
θεῶν, ὅταν ἡδέως γενέσθαι παρακαλοῦντες ἀλλήλους λέγωσι ' σήμερον ἀκτάσωμεν '; οὐχὶ τὸ
παρ' ἀκτῇ δεῖπνον ἥδιστον ἀποφαίνουσιν ὥσπερ
ἔστιν; οὐ διὰ τὰ κύματα καὶ τὰς ψηφῖδας (τί γάρ;
ἐπ' ἀκτῆς τις λέκιθον ὀψᾶται καὶ κάππαριν;),

---

[1] So Basel edition : ὀλοψύχους.
[2] So Xylander from Athenaeus, 276 f : ἔχων ἤσθιεν.
[3] So Basel edition from Athenaeus, 276 f : φιλόσοφον.
[4] So Basel edition : κόνωνος.

---

[a] Euripides, frag. 907 (Nauck, *Trag. Gr. Frag.*). Athenaeus, who has this whole passage almost verbatim in vii,
276 f, adds *boeia* (" of beef ") to " meat."
[b] Founder of the Middle Academy.
[c] Strabo, xiv. 2. 21, p. 658, has an amusing story about
people's quick response to the bell that announced the sale of
opsa from the sea.
[d] *On the False Legation*, xix. 229. Philocrates was the
340

describe as ' eaters of delicacies ' and ' lovers of
delicacies ' not those who enjoy their beef, like
Heracles—' he downed green figs after his meat ' [a]
—nor any lover of figs like Plato, or of the grape like
Arcesilaüs,[b] but those who always show up when fish
are sold and who have a keen ear for the bell.[c]
Demosthenes,[d] too, by way of an accusation for gluttony and licentiousness, says that Philocrates [d] used
money gained by treason to buy harlots and fish.
Again, Ctesiphon [e] wittily answered a devoted eater
of delicacies who shouted in the Council that he was
about to burst with anger : ' My dear fellow, please
don't ! You'd get us all eaten alive by fish.' But
what is the poet getting at who wrote the neat line,

> You live on capers,[f] when you could have *anthias* ? [g]

Or what, in heaven's name, do people mean when
they say, inviting each other to have a good time,
' Let's have a shore party to-day ' ? Aren't they de-
claring what is certainly true, that a dinner by the
shore is the most delicious ? This isn't because of the
waves and the pebbles—does anyone ever make a
meal of porridge and capers at the beach ?—it is

sponsor of the peace of 346 B.C. between Athens and Philip of
Macedon, and was accused by Demosthenes of treason
against Athens.

[e] A minor public figure at Athens, known chiefly because
of his proposal that a gold crown should be bestowed upon
Demosthenes.

[f] Starvation rations, as Philemon, frag. 98 (Kock), shows.

[g] Probably the Mediterranean barbier, according to Andrews's Zoological Index to *De Sollertia Animalium* in LCL
Mor. xii, p. 484. For further extensive lore on this fish see
A. W. Mair in Oppian (LCL), pp. iii ff., and D'Arcy Thompson, *Glossary of Greek Fishes*, pp. 14 ff., and note *a* on p. 426
of LCL Plut. *Mor.* xii, 977 c.

(668) ἀλλ᾽ ὡς ἰχθύος ἀφθόνου καὶ νεαροῦ τὴν παράλιον
τράπεζαν εὐπορῦσαν.

" Καὶ μέντοι καὶ πιπράσκεται παρὰ[1] λόγον
ἁπάντων τιμιώτατον τὸ θαλάττιον ὄψον· ὁ γοῦν
Κάτων οὐχ ὑπερβολικῶς ἀλλ᾽ ἀληθῶς πρὸς τὴν
τρυφὴν καὶ πολυτέλειαν τῆς πόλεως δημηγορῶν
C εἶπεν, ὅτι πλείονος πιπράσκεται ἐν Ῥώμῃ ἰχθὺς
ἢ βοῦς κεράμιόν τε ταρίχους[2] πωλοῦσι τιμῆς, ὅσην
οὐκ ἂν ἑκατόμβη βούπρωρος ἄλφοι κατακοπεῖσα.

" Καίτοι φαρμάκων δυνάμεως ὁ ἰατρικώτατος
ἄριστος κριτὴς καὶ μελῶν ἀρετῆς ὁ φιλομουσό-
τατος, οὐκοῦν καὶ ἀρετῆς ὄψων ὁ φιλοψότατος.
οὐ γὰρ Πυθαγόρᾳ γε τούτων οὐδὲ Ξενοκράτει
διαιτητῇ χρηστέον, Ἀνταγόρᾳ δὲ τῷ ποιητῇ καὶ
Φιλοξένῳ τῷ Ἐρύξιδος καὶ τῷ ζωγράφῳ Ἀνδρο-
κύδῃ, ὅν φασι τὴν Σκύλλαν ζωγραφοῦντα τοὺς περὶ
αὐτὴν ἰχθῦς ἐμπαθέστατα καὶ ζωτικώτατα δι᾽
ὀψοφαγίαν ἐξεργάσασθαι. Ἀνταγόρᾳ δ᾽ ὁ βασιλεὺς Ἀντίγονος ἐν τῷ στρατοπέδῳ λοπάδα γόγ-
D γρων ἕψοντι περιεζωσμένῳ παραστάς, ' ἆρά γ᾽,'
εἶπε, ' τὸν Ὅμηρον οἴει τὰς τοῦ Ἀγαμέμνονος
πράξεις ἀναγράφειν γόγγρους ἕψοντα; ' κἀκεῖνος
οὐ φαύλως, ' σὺ δ᾽ οἴει,' ἔφησε, ' τὸν Ἀγαμέμνονα
τὰς πράξεις ἐκείνας ἐργάσασθαι πολυπραγμο-
νοῦντα, τίς ἐν τῷ στρατοπέδῳ γόγγρον ἕψει ; '

---

[1] So Basel edition : περί.
[2] So Reiske from Athenaeus, 275 a : γάρ.

---

[a] The Censor, 234–149 B.C. *Cf.* Athenaeus, vi, 274 f.
[b] Head of the Academy from 339 to 314 B.C.

because at the seashore there is abundance of fresh fish for the table.

"Furthermore, sea food is out of all proportion the most expensive. Cato [a] assuredly wasn't exaggerating but speaking plain truth in his harangue against the luxury and extravagance of the capital, when he said that a fish sells for more at Rome than a cow, and they sell a cask of smoked fish for a price that a hundred sheep plus one ox in the lead wouldn't bring, cut in pieces.

"Again it is certainly true that as the most competent physician is the best judge of the effect of a drug, and as the most ardent lover of music is the best qualified to appraise a tune, so the best critic of the excellence of a dish must be the greatest gourmet. Obviously, we cannot appeal to Pythagoras or Xenocrates [b] to arbitrate such matters; but only to such as Antagoras [c] the poet, Philoxenus [d] the son of Eryxis, or the painter Androcydes.[e] Androcydes, they say, in a painting of Scylla, elaborately rendered the fishes swimming in the water around her in a most enthusiastic and lifelike manner because of his appetite for fish. As for Antagoras, King Antigonus once found him in the camp girt like a cook and boiling a dish of conger-eels, and asked him, 'Do you think Homer has recorded the deeds of Agamemnon while cooking eels?' Antagoras's apt reply was, 'Do you imagine Agamemnon performed those deeds while busying himself with finding out who was boiling a conger-eel in the camp?' That is what I have

[c] *RE*, i. 2338, no. 4. Epic poet of the 3rd century B.C. Intimate of King Antigonus Gonatas of Macedonia.

[d] *RE*, xx. 190, no. 5. Notorious roué, ridiculed by Aristophanes.

[e] See *supra*, 665 D with note. *Cf.* Athenaeus, viii, 340 f.

(668) ταῦτ'," εἶπεν ὁ Πολυκράτης, "ἔγωγε συμβάλλομαι
καὶ ὑμῖν¹ καὶ νὴ Δία τοῖς ἰχθυοπώλαις ἀπὸ τῶν
μαρτύρων καὶ τῆς συνηθείας."

3. "Ἐγὼ δ'," ὁ Σύμμαχος² ἔφη, "τῷ πράγ-
ματι μετὰ σπουδῆς πρόσειμι καὶ διαλεκτικώτερον.
εἰ γὰρ ὄψον ἐστὶ τὸ τὴν τροφὴν ἐφηδῦνον, ἄριστον
ἂν ὄψον εἴη τὸ μάλιστα³ τὴν ὄρεξιν ἐπὶ τῷ σίτῳ
E κατασχεῖν δυνάμενον. ὥσπερ οὖν οἱ προσαγορευ-
θέντες Ἐλπιστικοὶ φιλόσοφοι συνεκτικώτατον εἶναι
τοῦ βίου τὸ ἐλπίζειν ἀποφαίνονται⁴ τῷ ἀπούσης⁵
ἐλπίδος οὐδ'⁶ ἡδυνούσης οὐκ ἀνεκτὸν⁷ εἶναι τὸν
βίον, οὕτω καὶ τῆς ἐπὶ τὴν τροφὴν ὀρέξεως
συνεκτικὸν θετέον οὗ μὴ παρόντος⁸ ἄχαρις γίγνεται
τροφὴ πᾶσα καὶ δυσπρόσφορος.⁹ τῶν μὲν οὖν ἐκ
γῆς τοιοῦτον οὐδὲν εὑρήσεις, τῶν δὲ θαλαττίων
τὸν ἅλα πρῶτον, οὗ χωρὶς¹⁰ οὐδὲν ὡς ἔπος εἰπεῖν
ἐστιν ἐδώδιμον· ἀλλὰ καὶ τὸν ἄρτον οὗτος ἐμ-
μιγνύμενος συνηδύνει (διὸ καὶ Δήμητρος σύνναος ὁ
F Ποσειδῶν) καὶ τῶν ἄλλων ὄψων οἱ ἅλες ἥδιον
ὄψον εἰσίν.

"Οἱ γοῦν ἥρωες εὐτελοῦς καὶ λιτῆς ἐθάδες ὥσπερ ἀσκηταὶ διαίτης ὄντες καὶ τῆς τροφῆς πᾶσαν
ἡδονὴν ἐπίθετον καὶ περίεργον ἀφελόντες, ὡς μηδ'
ἰχθύσι χρῆσθαι παρὰ τὸν Ἑλλήσποντον στρατοπε-

---

¹ καὶ added by Madvig, ὑμῖν by Wyttenbach.
² σίμαχος T, σύμαχος E.
³ τὸ after μάλιστα deleted in Basel edition.
⁴ So Turnebus : ἀποφαι lac. 4-5.
⁵ ἀπούσης Xylander : .πάσης.
⁶ So Reiske : οὐχ.
⁷ οὐκ ἀνεκτὸν Turnebus : lac. 4-5 νεκτον.
⁸ So Stephanus : παντὸς.
⁹ So Xylander, δυσπρόσοιστος Turnebus : δυσπρο lac. 1-2.
¹⁰ οὗ χωρὶς added by Stephanus.

to offer to you—and, by George, to the fish-peddlers,"
said Polycrates, " from the testimony of history and
from usage."

3. " Well," said Symmachus, " for my part I shall
attack the subject in a serious and rather more logical
vein. If a relish (*opson*) is something that makes a
dish palatable, then the best relish would be the one
that does most to attract our appetite. The philosophers called Elpistics [a] declare that hope is the
strongest bond of life, pointing out that in the absence
of hope and without its seasoning life is unendurable.
Correspondingly we may assert that the means to
sustain appetite is something without which all food
is tasteless and unpalatable. You will find nothing of
the sort in foods produced on land [b]; whereas from
the sea you will. First there is salt, without which
practically nothing is eatable. Salt is added even to
bread and enriches its flavour ; this explains why
Poseidon shares a temple with Demeter. Salt is also
the best relish to season other relishes.

" The heroes of old, at any rate, who were accustomed to a modest, simple diet, and who acted as if
they were in training, excluding all superfluous
elaborations and condiments, even did without fish,
though they were camping by the Hellespont [c]; yet

---

[a] From *elpis*, " hope."

[b] Obviously Plutarch is thinking of salt as derived only
from the sea, although Herodotus shows that salt mines and
rock salt were known (Herod. iv. 185). See now A. S. Pease
on Cicero, *De Natura Deorum*, ii. 53. 132 "salinae"; *RE, s.v.*
" Salz."

[c] Plato in *Republic*, 404 B-C, defends the frugality of the
original citizens of his simple state on exactly this basis, that
Homer did not indulge his heroes in fish from the near-by
Hellespont.

(668) δεύοντες, οὐχ ὑπέμενον τὰ κρέα χωρὶς ἁλῶν προσφέρεσθαι, μαρτυροῦντες ὅτι τοῦτο τῶν ὄψων μόνον
ἀπαραίτητόν ἐστιν. ὡς γὰρ τὰ χρώματα τοῦ[1] φωτός,
οὕτως οἱ χυμοὶ τοῦ[2] ἁλὸς δέονται πρὸς τὸ κινῆσαι[3]
669 τὴν αἴσθησιν· εἰ δὲ μή,[4] βαρεῖς τῇ γεύσει προσ-
πίπτουσι καὶ ναυτιώδεις. ' νέκυες γὰρ κοπρίων ἐκ-
βλητότεροι,' καθ' Ἡράκλειτον, κρέας δὲ πᾶν νεκρόν
ἐστιν καὶ νεκροῦ μέρος· ἡ δὲ τῶν ἁλῶν δύναμις,
ὥσπερ ψυχὴ παραγενομένη, χάριν αὐτῷ καὶ ἡδονὴν
προστίθησι. διὸ καὶ προλαμβάνουσι τῆς ἄλλης
τροφῆς τὰ δριμέα καὶ τὰ ἁλμυρά, καὶ ὅλως ὅσα μάλιστα τῶν ἁλῶν μετέσχηκε· γίγνεται γὰρ φίλτρα
ταῦτα τῇ ὀρέξει πρὸς τὰ ἄλλ' ὄψα, καὶ δελεασθεῖσα
διὰ τούτων ἐπ' ἐκεῖνα πρόσεισιν νεαλὴς καὶ πρόθυ-
μος· ἐὰν δ' ἀπ' ἐκείνων ἄρξηται, ταχέως ἀπαγο-
ρεύει.

B   " Οὐ μόνον τοίνυν πρὸς τὴν τροφὴν ἀλλὰ καὶ
πρὸς τὸ[5] ποτὸν ὄψον εἰσὶν οἱ ἅλες. τὸ μὲν γὰρ
Ὁμηρικὸν ἐκεῖνο, ' κρόμυον ποτῷ ὄψον,' ναύταις
καὶ κωπηλάταις μᾶλλον ἢ βασιλεῦσιν ἐπιτήδειον
ἦν· τὰ δ' ὑφαλμυρίζοντα μετρίως τῶν σιτίων δι'
εὐστομίαν πᾶν μὲν οἴνου γένος ἡδὺ τῇ γεύσει καὶ
λεῖον ἐπάγει, πᾶν δ' ὕδωρ προσφιλὲς παρέχει καὶ[6]
ἄλκιμον[7]· ἀηδίας δὲ καὶ δυσχερείας, ἣν ἐμποιεῖ

---

[1] τοῦ φωτός Benseler (φωτός Turnebus) : lac. 6-7 τος.
[2] τοῦ ἁλὸς Benseler (ἁλὸς Turnebus) : lac. 2-3 λος.
[3] So Turnebus : lac. 4-5 σαι.
[4] εἰ δὲ μή Stephanus : εμη.
[5] τὸ added by Bernardakis.
[6] So Bollaan, cf. Helmbold, Class. Philol. xxxvi, p. 85 : παρέχεσθαι.   [7] δόκιμον Post, ἄλυπον Bernardakis.

---

[a] Diels, frag. 96 (Diels-Kranz[8], p. 172) ; Strabo, xvi. 4. 26, p. 784.

they could not endure to eat meat without salt. They testify that salt is the only relish that cannot be dispensed with. Just as colour requires light, so flavour requires salt to stimulate the sense ; otherwise flavours are disagreeable and nauseous to the taste. The bodies of the dead, according to Heracleitus,[a] are fitter to be cast out than dung, and all meat is either a dead body or part of one. But the effect of salt upon meat, like the addition of a veritable soul,[b] is to lend flavour and an agreeable quality to it. This is why it is conventional before a main course to take appetizers that are sharp or briny, and in general anything that has a highly salty character. For these relishes act as charms to entice the appetite towards the other delicacies ; and appetite, caught by this magic, attacks the other viands with youthful[c] vigour. If, however, these other viands are the first food presented to the appetite, it quickly wearies.

" Nor is salt a seasoning only for food ; it also seasons drinks. The Homeric phrase, ' the onion, a relish to a drink,'[d] would be better suited to sailors and oarsmen than to princes ; but moderately salty foods, on account of their pleasant taste, bring out the sweetness and smoothness of any kind of wine, and also make any water agreeable and tonic,[e] without a trace of the disagreeable and objectionable effect that

[b] Cf. Cicero, De Natura Deorum, ii. 64. 160, " animam ipsam pro sale datum " (to the sow), with Pease's note.

[c] Combined perhaps with another meaning, " newly salted."

[d] Iliad, xi. 630.

[e] With Gulick in A.J.P. lx (1939), pp. 493 f. ; or " fortifying " (so Oxford Greek-English Lexicon, s.v. ἄλκιμος ii) ; with Post's emendation the meaning would be " acceptable."

(669) τὸ κρόμμυον, οὐδ' ὀλίγον μετέσχηκεν· ἀλλὰ καὶ
διαφορεῖ τὴν ἄλλην τροφὴν καὶ παραδίδωσιν εὐ-
πειθῆ καὶ μαλακωτέραν τῇ πέψει,[1] χάριν[2] μὲν[3]
ὄψου δύναμιν δὲ φαρμάκου τῷ σώματι τῶν ἁλῶν[4]
C προσφερομένων. καὶ μὴν τά γ' ἄλλα θαλάττης ὄψα
πρὸς τῷ ἡδίστῳ καὶ τὸ ἀβλαβέστατον ἔχει· κρεώδη
μὲν γάρ ἐστιν, οὐ βαρύνει δ' ὁμοίως ἀλλὰ κατα-
πέττεται καὶ διαφορεῖται ῥᾳδίως. μαρτυρήσει δ'
οὑτοσὶ Ζήνων καὶ νὴ Δία Κράτων, οἳ τοὺς ἀσθε-
νοῦντας πρὸ τῶν ἄλλων ἁπάντων ἐπὶ τὸν ἰχθὺν
ἄγουσιν ὡς κουφότατον ὄψων. καὶ λόγον ἔχει
τὴν θάλατταν ὑγιεινὰ καὶ διαπεπονημένα τοῖς
σώμασιν ἐκτρέφειν, εἴ γε καὶ ἡμῖν ἀέρα λεπτότητι
καὶ καθαρότητι πρόσφορον ἀναδίδωσιν.''

4. '' Ὀρθῶς,'' ἔφη, '' λέγεις,'' ὁ Λαμπρίας,
'' ἀλλ' ἔτι τῷ λόγῳ προσφιλοσοφήσωμεν. ὁ γὰρ
ἐμὸς πάππος εἰώθει λέγειν ἑκάστοτε τοὺς Ἰουδαίους ἐπισκώπτων, ὅτι τὸ δικαιότατον κρέας
D οὐκ ἐσθίουσιν· ἡμεῖς δὲ φήσομεν δικαιότατον ὄψον
εἶναι τὸ ἐκ θαλάττης. πρὸς μὲν γὰρ[5] ταυτὶ τὰ
χερσαῖα κἂν ἄλλο μηδὲν ἡμῖν ᾖ δίκαιον, ἀλλὰ
τρέφεταί γε τοῖς αὐτοῖς καὶ λαμβάνει τὸν αὐτὸν
ἀέρα, καὶ λουτρὰ καὶ ποτὸν αὐτοῖς ἅπερ ἡμῖν
ἔστιν· ᾗ καὶ[6] σφάττοντες ἐδυσωποῦντο φωνὴν

---

[1] So Turnebus : ὄψει.
[2] χάριν Post : εὔχαριν. εἰς χάριν Turnebus, ὡς χάριν Wyttenbach, εὔχαριν μὲν χάριν Bernardakis, cf. 685 A.
[3] γὰρ after μὲν deleted by Turnebus.
[4] So Basel edition : ἄλλων.
[5] So Bernardakis : γε.
[6] ᾗ καὶ Wyttenbach, ἃ καὶ Stephanus, καὶ Basel edition :
νίκαι.

your onion produces. Beyond that, salty food aids
digestion of any other [a]; it makes any food tender
and more susceptible to concoction; the salt contributes at once the savour of a relish and the good
effect of a medicine. Moreover, the other delicacies
of the sea, in addition to being most gratifying to the
taste, are also the safest to eat; for they have the
character of meat without its heaviness, and are easily
digested and assimilated. Here is Zeno [b] to testify,
and yes, so help me, Crato,[c] too! Both prescribe
fish for invalids, because it is the lightest meat,
before allowing them any other. One more point:
it is logical that what the sea brings forth should be
wholesome and well-perfected, since the sea sends us
air that is healthful because of its lightness and
purity."

4. "You are right," said Lamprias, "but let us add
a little to our speculations. My grandfather used to
say on every occasion, in derision of the Jews, that
what they abstained from was precisely the most
legitimate meat. But we shall say that of all delicacies
the most legitimate kind is that from the sea. As
far as the land animals whose meat is here before us
are concerned, we must admit at least this if nothing
else, that they consume the same food and breathe
the same air as we do, and drink and bathe in water
no different from ours. This has in times past made
men ashamed when they butchered them in spite of
their pitiful cries and in spite of having made com-

[a] Cf. infra, 688 B.
[b] Occurs only here, according to RE, s.v. "Plutarchos,"
col. 686.
[c] A relative of Plutarch's by marriage, supra, i. 4, 620 A.
There is a physician of this name from Athens in the early
Roman Empire in Inscriptiones Graecae, iii. 1327.

(669) ἀφιέντα γοερὰν καὶ τὰ πλεῖστα πεποιημένοι συνήθη καὶ σύντροφα ταῖς διαίταις. τὸ δὲ τῶν
ἐναλίων γένος ἔκφυλον ὅλως καὶ ἄποικον ἡμῶν,
ὥσπερ ἐν ἄλλῳ τινὶ κόσμῳ γεγονότων καὶ ζώντων,
οὔτ᾽ ὄψις οὔτε φωνή τις οὔθ᾽ ὑπουργία παραιτεῖται
τῆς προσφορᾶς[1] (οὐδὲν γὰρ αὐτοῖς ἔχει χρήσασθαι
E ζῷον, ὃ μηδ᾽ ὅλως ζῇ παρ᾽ ἡμῖν), οὐδὲ δεῖ τινος
ἐπ᾽ αὐτὰ στοργῆς, ἀλλ᾽ ὥσπερ ῞Αιδης αὐτοῖς ἐστιν
οὗτος ὁ παρ᾽ ἡμῖν τόπος· ἐλθόντα γὰρ εἰς αὐτὸν
εὐθέως τέθνηκεν."

ΠΡΟΒΛΗΜΑ Ε

Πότερον οἱ Ἰουδαῖοι σεβόμενοι τὴν ὗν ἢ δυσχεραίνοντες
ἀπέχονται τῶν κρεῶν

Collocuntur Callistratus, Polycrates, Lamprias

1. Ἐπεὶ δὲ ταῦτ᾽ ἐρρήθη, βουλομένων τινῶν
ἀντικατατείνειν τὸν ἕτερον λόγον ἐκκρούων ὁ
Καλλίστρατος ἔφη, " πῶς ὑμῖν δοκεῖ λελέχθαι τὸ
F πρὸς τοὺς Ἰουδαίους, ὅτι τὸ δικαιότατον κρέας
οὐκ ἐσθίουσιν; " " ὑπερφυῶς," ἔφη ὁ Πολυκράτης,
" ἐγὼ δὲ καὶ προσδιαπορῶ, πότερον οἱ ἄνδρες τιμῇ
τινι τῶν ὑῶν ἢ μυσαττόμενοι τὸ ζῷον ἀπέχονται
τῆς βρώσεως αὐτοῦ· τὰ γὰρ παρ᾽ ἐκείνοις λεγό-
μενα μύθοις ἔοικεν, εἰ μή τινας ἄρα λόγους σπουδαί-
ους ἔχοντες οὐκ ἐκφέρουσιν."
2. " Ἐγὼ μὲν τοίνυν," εἶπεν ὁ Καλλίστρατος,

[1] So Anonymus : προσ lac. ας.

---

[a] The same argument is advanced, on the contrary, in
viii. 8, 729 A *infra*, as the genuine reason for abstention from
all products of the sea by the Egyptians. In 729 D *ibid.* that
attitude is ascribed to the Pythagoreans.

panions of most of them and shared their store of food with them. Sea animals, on the other hand, are a species entirely alien and remote from us,[a] as if they had sprung up and were living in some different world.[b] Neither look nor voice nor service rendered pleads with us not to eat them, for no animal can employ these pleas that has no life at all among us ; nor need we feel any affection for them. Our world is equivalent to Hades for them, since to come here is instant death."

QUESTION 5

Whether the Jews abstain from pork because of reverence or aversion for the pig

Speakers : Callistratus, Polycrates, Lamprias

1. When he had finished, and some of those present would have made an extended reply to his arguments, Callistratus headed them off by saying, " What do you think of the assertion that it is precisely the most proper type of meat that the Jews avoid eating ? " [c] " I heartily agree with it," replied Polycrates, " but I have another question : do they abstain from eating pork by reason of some special respect for hogs or from abhorrence of the creature ? Their own accounts sound like pure myth, but perhaps they have some serious reasons which they do not publish."

2. " My impression," said Callistratus, " is that the

[b] For this obvious point cf. the simpler statement in 729 c infra : air is destructive to fishes.

[c] These questions and the whole theme of the bias and misconceptions revealed here in Plutarch as well as elsewhere in ancient pagan literature are discussed in detail by Heinemann in RE, Suppl. v. 19-35.

(669)   " οἶμαί τινα τιμὴν τὸ ζῷον ἔχειν παρὰ τοῖς ἀν-
670 δράσιν· εἰ δὲ δύσμορφον ἡ ὗς καὶ θολερόν, ἀλλ'
οὐ¹ κανθάρου καὶ μυγαλῆς² καὶ³ κροκοδείλου καὶ
αἰλούρου⁴ τὴν ὄψιν ἀτοπώτερον⁵ ἢ τὴν φύσιν
ἀμουσότερον⁶· οἷς ὡς ἁγιωτάτοις ἱερεῖς Αἰγυπτίων
ἄλλοις⁷ ἄλλοι προσφέρονται. τὴν δ' ὗν ἀπὸ χρηστῆς αἰτίας⁸ τιμᾶσθαι λέγουσι· πρώτη γὰρ σχί-
σασα τῷ προΰχοντι τοῦ ῥύγχους,⁹ ὥς φασι, τὴν
γῆν ἴχνος ἀρόσεως ἔθηκε καὶ τὸ τῆς ὕνεως
ὑφηγήσατ' ἔργον· ὅθεν καὶ τοὔνομα γενέσθαι τῷ
ἐργαλείῳ λέγουσιν ἀπὸ τῆς ὑός. οἱ δὲ τὰ μαλθακὰ
καὶ κοῖλα τῆς χώρας Αἰγύπτιοι γεωργοῦντες οὐδ'
B ἀρότου δέονται τὸ παράπαν· ἀλλ' ὅταν ὁ Νεῖλος
ἀπορρέῃ καταβρέξας τὰς ἀρούρας, ἐπακολουθοῦντες
τὰς ὗς κατέβαλον, αἱ δὲ χρησάμεναι πάτῳ καὶ
ὀρυχῇ ταχὺ τὴν γῆν ἔτρεψαν ἐκ βάθους καὶ τὸν
σπόρον ἀπέκρυψαν. οὐ δεῖ δὲ θαυμάζειν, εἰ διὰ
τοῦτό τινες ὗς οὐκ ἐσθίουσιν, ἑτέρων ζῴων μείζονας ἐπ' αἰτίαις γλίσχραις, ἐνίων δὲ καὶ πάνυ
γελοίαις, τιμὰς ἐχόντων παρὰ τοῖς βαρβάροις. τὴν
μὲν γὰρ μυγαλῆν ἐκτεθειάσθαι λέγουσιν ὑπ' Αἰγυπτίων τυφλὴν οὖσαν, ὅτι τὸ σκότος τοῦ φωτὸς
ἡγοῦντο πρεσβύτερον· τίκτεσθαι δ' αὐτὴν ἐκ μυῶν
πέμπτῃ γενεᾷ νουμηνίας οὔσης· ἔτι δὲ μειοῦσθαι τὸ
ἧπαρ ἐν τοῖς ἀφανισμοῖς τῆς σελήνης.

¹ ἀλλ' οὐ Turnebus : lac. 5.
² μυγαλῆς Xylander, cf. 670 B : γρυ lac. 3.
³ So Aldine or Basel edition : ἐκ.
⁴ So Basel edition : lac. 5-7 υρου.
⁵ So Basel edition : ἀτοπωτάτην.

352

beast enjoys a certain respect among that folk [a];
granted that he is ugly and dirty, still he is no more
absurd in appearance or crude in disposition than
dung-beetle, field-mouse, crocodile, or cat, each of
which is treated as sacred by a different group of
Egyptian priests. They say, however, that the pig
is honoured for a good reason : according to the story,
it was the first to cut the soil with its projecting snout,
thus producing a furrow and teaching man the function of a ploughshare. Incidentally, this is the origin,
they say, of the word *hynis* (from *hys*, ' swine ') for that
implement. The Egyptians who cultivate the soft
soil of their low-lying areas have no use for plough-
ing at all. After the Nile overflows and soaks their
acres, they follow the receding water and unload the
pigs, which by trampling and rooting quickly turn
over the deep soil and cover the seed. We need not
be surprised if some people do not eat pork for this
reason. Other animals receive even greater honours
among the barbarians for slight and in some cases
utterly ridiculous reasons. The field-mouse is said to
have been deified among the Egyptians because of
its blindness, since they regarded darkness as superior
to light ; and they thought that the field-mouse was
born of ordinary mice every fifth generation at the
new moon, and also that its liver was reduced in size
at the dark of the moon.

[a] This suggestion is even more forcibly made in an epigram attributed to Petronius (Bücheler, *Petronii reliquiae*,
1862, with preface, p. xxxvi), fragment 47, line 1 : " Iudaeus
licet ut porcinum numen adoret."

───────────────────

[6] μυσαρώτερον Hirschig, " dirtier, more loathsome."
[7] ἄλλοις added in Basel edition.
[8] ἀπὸ χρηστῆς αἰτίας Madvig : ἀποχρηστῆσαι καὶ καὶ (*sic*).
[9] τοῦ ῥύγχους Reiske : τῆς ὀρυχῆς, which may be right.

(670)
C

" Τὸν δὲ¹ λέοντα τῷ ἡλίῳ συνοικειοῦσιν, ὅτι
τῶν γαμψωνύχων τετραπόδων βλέπονon τίκτει
μόνος, κοιμᾶται δ' ἀκαρὲς χρόνου καὶ ὑπολάμπει
τὰ ὄμματα καθεύδοντος· κρῆναι δὲ κατὰ χασμάτων²
λεοντείων ἐξιᾶσι κρουνούς, ὅτι Νεῖλος ἐπάγει νέον
ὕδωρ ταῖς Αἰγυπτίων ἀρούραις ἡλίου τὸν λέοντα
παροδεύοντος. τὴν δ' ἶβίν φασιν ἐκκολαφθεῖσαν
εὐθὺς ἕλκειν δύο δραχμάς, ὅσον ἄρτι παιδίου
γεγονότος καρδίαν³· ποιεῖν δὲ τῇ τῶν ποδῶν⁴
ἀποστάσει⁵ πρὸς ἀλλήλους⁶ καὶ πρὸς τὸ ῥύγχος
ἰσόπλευρον τρίγωνον. καὶ τί ἄν τις Αἰγυπτίους
αἰτιῷτο τῆς τοσαύτης ἀλογίας, ὅπου καὶ τοὺς
D Πυθαγορικοὺς ἱστοροῦσιν καὶ ἀλεκτρυόνα λευκὸν
σέβεσθαι καὶ τῶν θαλαττίων μάλιστα τρίγλης καὶ
ἀκαλήφης ἀπέχεσθαι, τοὺς δ' ἀπὸ Ζωροάστρου
μάγους τιμᾶν μὲν ἐν τοῖς μάλιστα τὸν χερσαῖον
ἐχῖνον, ἐχθαίρειν δὲ τοὺς ἐνύδρους μῦς καὶ τὸν
ἀποκτείνοντα πλείστους θεοφιλῆ καὶ μακάριον
νομίζειν; οἶμαι δὲ καὶ τοὺς Ἰουδαίους, εἴπερ
ἐβδελύττοντο τὴν ὗν, ἀποκτείνειν ἄν, ὥσπερ οἱ
μάγοι τοὺς μῦς ἀποκτείνουσι· νῦν δ' ὁμοίως τῷ
φαγεῖν τὸ ἀνελεῖν ἀπόρρητόν ἐστιν αὐτοῖς. καὶ
ἴσως ἔχει λόγον, ὡς τὸν ὄνον⁷ ἀναφήναντα πηγὴν

---

¹ δὲ added by Reiske.
² δὲ κατὰ χασμάτων Turnebus, cf. Mor. 366 A : δὲ καὶ κατα-
σχάμματα.
³ So Aldine edition : καρδία.
⁴ So Basel edition : πόνων.
⁵ So Hubert, cf. διαστάσει 381 D : ἀποτάσει.
⁶ So Basel edition : ἄλλους.
⁷ δὲ after ὄνον deleted in Basel edition.

ᵃ In Plutarch's time a drachm was equivalent to ⅛ oz. or
c. 3·4 grams (Hultsch in *RE*, *s.v.* " Drachme," col. 1629).

" They associate the lion with the sun because it, alone of quadrupeds that have claws, bears young that can see at birth, sleeps only for a moment, and has eyes that gleam in sleep. Egyptian fountains pour forth their water through lion mouths, because the Nile brings new water to the fields of Egypt when the sun passes through Leo. They say that the ibis when hatched weighs two drachms,[a] as much as the heart of a new-born infant, and forms an equilateral triangle by the position of its outspread feet and bill. How could anyone blame the Egyptians for such irrationality when it is recorded that the Pythagoreans respect even a white cock,[b] and that they abstain particularly from the red mullet and the sea anemone among marine animals ?[c] Or when we remember that the Magi, followers of Zoroaster, especially esteem the hedgehog and abominate water mice,[d] regarding the person who kills the greatest number of the latter as blest and dear to the gods ? So I think the Jews would kill pigs if they hated them, as the Magi kill water mice ; but in fact it is just as unlawful for Jews to destroy pigs as to eat them. Perhaps it is consistent that they should revere the

[b] Diogenes Laertius, viii. 34, has fuller arguments and analogies in support of this Pythagorean precept or practice.

[c] Aulus Gellius, iv. 11. 11 ff., quotes this passage, identifying ἀκαλήφη with sea-nettle (urtica), and citing from a lost work of Plutarch on Homer.

[d] Or " sea voles," " sea shrews," or " sea rats." These were not adequately differentiated. See De Lacy and Einarson's comments on 537 A above (LCL Mor. vii, p. 97, note f). Another possibility, attractive because it explains the abhorrence, is the highly poisonous globe-fish : see A. C. Andrews in Trans. Am. Phil. Assoc. lxxix (1948), pp. 232 ff. Prof. Warmington suggests " water-shrews " or " water-voles " or both, because the Magi were of an inland race.

(670) αὐτοῖς ὕδατος τιμῶσιν, οὕτως καὶ τὴν ὗν σέβεσθαι
σπόρου καὶ ἀρότου διδάσκαλον γενομένην· εἰ μή,[1]
E νὴ Δία, καὶ τοῦ λαγωοῦ φήσει[2] τις ἀπέχεσθαι τοὺς
ἄνδρας ὡς μυσερὸν καὶ ἀκάθαρτον δυσχεραίνοντας
τὸ ζῷον."

3. "Οὐ δῆτ'," ἔφη[3] ὁ Λαμπρίας ὑπολαβών,[4]
"ἀλλὰ τοῦ μὲν λαγωοῦ φείδονται[5] διὰ τὴν πρὸς τὸν
ὄνον τιμώμενον[6] ὑπ' αὐτῶν μάλιστα[7] θηρίον ἐμφέ-
ρειαν.[8] ὁ γὰρ λαγὼς μεγέθους ἔοικε καὶ πάχους
ἐνδεὴς ὄνος[9] εἶναι· καὶ γὰρ ἡ χρόα καὶ τὰ ὦτα καὶ
τῶν ὀμμάτων ἡ λιπαρότης καὶ τὸ λαμυρὸν[10] ἔοικε
θαυμασίως· ὥστε μηδὲν οὕτω[11] μικρὸν μεγάλῳ τὴν
μορφὴν ὅμοιον γεγονέναι. εἰ μὴ νὴ Δία καὶ πρὸς
τὰς ποιότητας[12] αἰγυπτιάζοντες τὴν ὠκύτητα τοῦ
ζῴου θεῖον ἡγοῦνται καὶ τὴν ἀκρίβειαν τῶν
F αἰσθητηρίων· ὅ τε γὰρ ὀφθαλμὸς ἄτρυτός ἐστιν
αὐτῶν, ὥστε καὶ καθεύδειν ἀναπεπταμένοις τοῖς
ὄμμασιν, ὀξυηκοΐᾳ τε δοκεῖ διαφέρειν, ἣν Αἰγύπτιοι
θαυμάσαντες ἐν τοῖς ἱεροῖς γράμμασιν ἀκοὴν ση-
μαίνουσιν οὓς λαγωοῦ[13] γράφοντες.

"Τὸ δ' ὕειον κρέας οἱ ἄνδρες ἀφοσιοῦσθαι

---

[1] εἰ μή added by Xylander. [2] So Reiske : φησί.
[3] δῆτ' ἔφη Reiske, δῆτ' εἶπεν Hubert : δ lac. 7-8.
[4] So Aldine edition : ὑπολ lac. 4-6.
[5] So Doehner : lac. 2-3 ται. Stephanus ἀπέχονται.
[6] ὄνον τιμώμενον Franke, ὄνον, ὑπ' αὐτῶν μυσαχθέντα
("loathed") Scaliger, ὄνον" e veteribus codicibus" : μενον
ὑπ' ἀυτῶνμ lac. 4-5 στα.
[7] μάλιστα Reiske, cf. preceding note.
[8] So Scaliger, Franke : ἐμφερέστατον.
[9] πάχους ἐνδεὴς ὄνος Doehner : τάχους ἐν δεινοῖς.
[10] So Reiske : ἀλμυρὸν.
[11] μηδὲ after οὕτω deleted by Doehner.

pig who taught them sowing and plowing, inasmuch as they honour the ass [a] who first led them to a spring of water. Otherwise, so help me, someone will say that the Jews abstain from the hare because they can't stomach anything so filthy and unclean."

3. "No indeed," countered Lamprias, "they abstain from the hare because of its very close resemblance to the ass which they prize so highly. The hare appears to be simply an ass inferior in bulk and size; for its coat, ears, bright eyes, and salacity are amazingly similar, so much so that nothing small ever so closely resembled something large. Perhaps, to be sure, following the Egyptians even in their conception of traits of animals, they regard the swiftness of the creature and the keenness of its senses as something divine. For its eye is untiring: the hare even sleeps with its eyes wide open. In acuteness of hearing it is found to be unrivalled; the Egyptians admire this so much that in their hieroglyphics they draw a hare's ear to represent the idea of hearing.

"The Jews apparently abominate pork because

---

[a] Tacitus (*Histories*, v. 3 ff.) has an ampler version of this, naming Moses and apparently misrepresenting Exodus, xv. 23 ff. Josephus (*Contra Apionem*, ii. 7. 86) denies that the Jews honour the ass as the Egyptians do crocodiles. See B. Latzarus, *Les Idées religieuses de Plutarque* (Paris, 1920), p. 164. Plutarch himself rejects (*De Iside*, 363 c) a connection between the Jews and Typhon (Set), who both rode an ass and was otherwise identified with the animal. Latzarus adduces a number of Old Testament passages to which Plutarch may be indirectly indebted, which show that, the ass was given a favoured place by the Hebrews. ? Jesus's entry into Jerusalem.

---

[12] So Reiske : ὁμοιότητας.
[13] οὖς λαγωοῦ Reiske : τοὺς λαγωούς.

(670) δοκοῦσιν,[1] ὅτι μάλιστα πάντων[2] οἱ βάρβαροι τὰς
ἐπὶ χρωτὸς λεύκας[3] καὶ λέπρας δυσχεραίνουσι καὶ
τῇ προσβολῇ τὰ τοιαῦτα καταβόσκεσθαι πάθη
671 τοὺς ἀνθρώπους οἴονται, πᾶσαν[4] δ᾽ ὗν ὑπὸ τὴν
γαστέρα λέπρας ἀνάπλεων καὶ ψωρικῶν ἐξανθη-
μάτων[5] ὁρῶμεν, ἃ δή, καχεξίας τινὸς ἐγγενομένης[6]
τῷ σώματι καὶ φθορᾶς, ἐπιτρέχειν δοκεῖ τοῖς
σώμασιν.[7] οὐ μὴν ἀλλὰ καὶ τὸ θολερὸν περὶ τὴν
δίαιταν τοῦ θρέμματος ἔχει τινὰ πονηρίαν· οὐδὲν
γὰρ ἄλλο βορβόρῳ χαῖρον οὕτω καὶ τόποις ῥυπα-
ροῖς καὶ ἀκαθάρτοις ὁρῶμεν, ἔξω λόγου τιθέμενοι
τὰ[8] τὴν γένεσιν καὶ τὴν φύσιν ἐν αὐτοῖς ἔχοντα τούτοις. λέγουσι δὲ καὶ τὰ ὄμματα τῶν ὑῶν οὕτως
ἐγκεκλάσθαι καὶ κατεσπάσθαι ταῖς ὄψεσιν, ὥστε
B μηδενὸς ἀντιλαμβάνεσθαι μηδέποτε τῶν ἄνω μηδὲ
προσορᾶν τὸν οὐρανόν, ἂν μὴ φερομένων ὑπτίων
ἀναστροφήν τινα παρὰ φύσιν αἱ κόραι λάβωσιν·
διὸ καὶ μάλιστα κραυγῇ χρώμενον τὸ ζῷον
ἡσυχάζειν, ὅταν οὕτω φέρηται, καὶ σιωπᾶν κατα-
τεθαμβημένον ἀηθείᾳ τὰ οὐράνια καὶ κρείττονι
φόβῳ τοῦ βοᾶν συνεχόμενον. εἰ δὲ δεῖ καὶ τὰ
μυθικὰ προσλαβεῖν, λέγεται μὲν ὁ Ἄδωνις ὑπὸ
τοῦ συὸς διαφθαρῆναι, τὸν δ᾽ Ἄδωνιν οὐχ ἕτερον
ἀλλὰ Διόνυσον εἶναι νομίζουσιν, καὶ πολλὰ τῶν
τελουμένων ἑκατέρῳ περὶ τὰς ἑορτὰς βεβαιοῖ τὸν
λόγον· οἱ δὲ παιδικὰ τοῦ Διονύσου γεγονέναι·

---

[1] So Stephanus : lac. 4-5 κοῦσιν.
[2] πάντων Bernardakis : lac. 2-3.
[3] ἐπὶ χρωτὸς λεύκας Hubert : ἐπὶ lac. 2 + lac. 4 λευκίας.
[4] πᾶσαν Stephanus : ἐς ἄν.
[5] So Stephanus : ἐξανθησάντων.   [6] So Reiske : ἐκγενομένης.
[7] τοῖς ἔξω μέρεσιν Paton.   [8] So Reiske : μετα.

barbarians especially abhor skin diseases like lepra[a] and white scale, and believe that human beings are ravaged by such maladies through contagion. Now we observe that every pig is covered on the under side by lepra and scaly eruptions, which, if there is general weakness and emaciation,[b] are thought to spread rapidly over the body. What is more, the the very filthiness of their habits produces an inferior quality of meat. We observe no other creature so fond of mud and of dirty, unclean places, if we leave out of account those animals that have their origin and natural habitat there. People say also that the eyes of swine are so twisted and drawn down that they can never catch sight of anything above them or see the sky unless they are carried upside down so that their eyes are given an unnatural tilt upward. Wherefore the animal, which usually squeals immoderately, holds still when it is carried in this position, and remains silent because it is astonished at the unfamiliar sight of the heavenly expanse and restrained from squealing by an over-powering fear. If it is legitimate to bring in mythology too, Adonis is said to have been slain by the boar. People hold Adonis to be none other than Dionysus,[c] a belief supported by many of the rites at the festivals of both ; though others have it that he was the favourite of Dionysus. Phanocles,[d] an erotic

[a] Lepra : any scaly condition, *cf.* psoriasis.

[b] Or, with Kronenberg's reading αἵματι for σώματι, " since a morbidity is engendered in the blood." The body referred to may be that of the pig or that of a human being who touches him.

[c] See *infra*, Question 6, notes on Adonis, etc.

[d] Elegiac poet, perhaps of the 3rd century B.C.

(671) καὶ Φανοκλῆς, ἐρωτικὸς ἀνήρ, οὐκ εἰκῇ[1] δήπου
πεποίηκεν·

C   ἠδ' ὡς θεῖον Ἄδωνιν ὀρειφοίτης Διόνυσος
     ἥρπασεν, ἠγαθέην Κύπρον[2] ἐποιχόμενος.''

ΠΡΟΒΛΗΜΑ ς[3]

Τίς ὁ παρ' Ἰουδαίοις θεός

Collocuntur Symmachus, Moeragenes, alii

1. Θαυμάσας οὖν τὸ ἐπὶ πᾶσι[4] ῥηθὲν ὁ Σύμμαχος,[5] '' ἆρ','' ἔφη, '' σὺ τὸν πατριώτην θεόν, ὦ Λαμ-
πρία, 'εὔιον ὀρσιγύναικα μαινομέναις ἀνθέοντα
τιμαῖσι Διόνυσον' ἐγγράφεις καὶ ὑποποιεῖς τοῖς
Ἑβραίων ἀπορρήτοις; ἢ τῷ ὄντι λόγος ἔστι τις
ὁ τοῦτον ἐκείνῳ τὸν αὐτὸν ἀποφαίνων;'' ὁ δὲ
Μοιραγένης ὑπολαβών, '' ἔα τοῦτον,'' εἶπεν· '' ἐγὼ
γὰρ Ἀθηναῖος ὢν ἀποκρίνομαί σοι καὶ λέγω μηδέν' ἄλλον εἶναι· καὶ τὰ μὲν πολλὰ τῶν εἰς τοῦτο
D τεκμηρίων μόνοις ἐστὶ ῥητὰ καὶ διδακτὰ τοῖς μυου-
μένοις παρ' ἡμῖν εἰς τὴν τριετηρικὴν παντέλειαν· ἃ

---

[1] οὐκ εἰκῇ Hubert : ου lac. 2 T.
[2] So Xylander : κύπριν.
[3] There is no heading in T or E, the text being continuous,
but the title is listed in the index prefixed to the Book.
[4] So Reiske : πᾶν.
[5] σίμακος T, σύμαχος E.

---

[a] On this entire question see B. Latzarus, *Les Idées religieuses de Plutarque* (Paris, 1920), chap. xiv, and Heinemann
in *RE*, Suppl. v. 18-35.   [b] *Supra*, 667 E.
[c] Dionysus in many accounts is the son of Semelê of
Thebes, and so a Boeotian compatriot of Plutarch and his
brother Lamprias.   [d] *Lyrici Adesp.* 131.

poet, surely knew whereof he spoke when he wrote the following lines :

> And how mountain-coursing Dionysus
> Seized the divine Adonis,
> As the god did visit holy Cyprus."

QUESTION 6

Who the god of the Jews is[a]

Speakers : Symmachus, Moeragenes, and others

1. SYMMACHUS,[b] surprised at this last statement, asked, " Lamprias, are you enrolling your national god [c] in the calendar of the Hebrews and insinuating into their secret rites ' him of the orgiastic cry, exciter of women, Dionysus, glorified with mad honours ' ?[d] Is there actually some tradition that demonstrates identity between him and Adonis ? "[e] Moeragenes[f] interposed, " Never mind him. I as an Athenian can answer you and say that the god is no other. Most of the relevant proofs can lawfully be pronounced or divulged only to[g] those of us who have been initiated into the Perfect Mysteries[h] celebrated every other year, but what I am going to

[e] Adonis (probably from Semitic adon " Lord ") of Cyprus, Byblos, and other Semitic or near-Semitic places, was a god or demigod in many respects comparable to Dionysus.

[f] Unknown unless identical with the Moeragenes cited by Philostratus as one of his authorities in his Life of Apollonius of Tyana, i. 3.   [g] Or " by."

[h] See RE, s.v. " Panteleia." It is a controversial question whether the Panteleia belonged to Bacchus or to Demeter, and whether it refers to Perfection or Consummation, as the etymology would suggest, or, as Müller-Graupa (in RE) insists, rather to the simpler concept of " great mysteries." On the significance of the two-year periods see RE, vii A, 122-124, and Farnell, Cults of the Greek States, v, chaps. 4, 5.

(671) δὲ λόγῳ διελθεῖν οὐ κεκώλυται πρὸς φίλους ἄνδρας,
ἄλλως τε καὶ παρ' οἶνον ἐπὶ τοῖς τοῦ θεοῦ δώροις,
ἂν οὗτοι κελεύωσι, λέγειν ἕτοιμος.''

2. Πάντων οὖν κελευόντων καὶ δεομένων, '' πρῶτον μέν,'' ἔφη, '' τῆς μεγίστης καὶ τελειοτάτης
ἑορτῆς παρ' αὐτοῖς ὁ καιρός ἐστιν καὶ ὁ τρόπος
Διονύσῳ προσήκων. τὴν γὰρ λεγομένην νηστείαν
ἄγοντες[1] ἀκμάζοντι τρυγητῷ τραπέζας τε προτίθεν-
ται παντοδαπῆς ὀπώρας ὑπὸ σκηναῖς καὶ καλιάσιν[2]
ἐκ κλημάτων μάλιστα καὶ κιττοῦ διαπεπλεγμέναις·
καὶ τὴν προτέραν τῆς ἑορτῆς σκηνὴν ὀνομάζουσιν.
Ε ὀλίγαις δ' ὕστερον ἡμέραις ἄλλην ἑορτήν, οὐκέτι[3]
δι' αἰνιγμάτων ἀλλ' ἄντικρυς Βάκχου καλουμένην,[4]
τελοῦσιν. ἔστι δὲ καὶ κραδηφορία[5] τις ἑορτὴ καὶ
θυρσοφορία παρ' αὐτοῖς, ἐν ᾗ θύρσους ἔχοντες εἰς
τὸ ἱερὸν εἰσίασιν· εἰσελθόντες δ' ὅ τι δρῶσιν, οὐκ
ἴσμεν, εἰκὸς δὲ βακχείαν εἶναι τὰ ποιούμενα· καὶ
γὰρ σάλπιγξι μικραῖς, ὥσπερ Ἀργεῖοι τοῖς Διο-
νυσίοις, ἀνακαλούμενοι τὸν θεὸν χρῶνται, καὶ
κιθαρίζοντες ἕτεροι προίασιν,[6] οὓς αὐτοὶ Λευίτας
προσονομάζουσιν, εἴτε παρὰ τὸν Λύσιον εἴτε μᾶλλον παρὰ τὸν Εὔιον τῆς ἐπικλήσεως γεγενημένης.

---

[1] ἄγοντες added by Madvig.   [2] So Scaliger : καθιᾶσιν.
[3] οὐκέτι Bollaan, οὐκ αὖ Reiske : οὐκ ἂν.
[4] So Reiske : καλουμένου.
[5] So Turnebus : κρατηροφορία.   [6] So Reiske : προσιᾶσιν.

---

[a] Evidently an allusion to *skenopegia*, " Feast [not " Fast "]
of Tabernacles " ; *cf.* the scholiast in T.

[b] See below, the note on Sabaoth. A scholium in T identifies the reference " in my opinion " with τὸ παρ' αὐτοῖς φάσκα
i.e. πάσχα " Passover," but see below, note *d*.

[c] Josephus, *Jewish War*, v. 210 and *Jewish Antiquities*, xv.
11. 395, in his description of the gate of the Temple, speaks
of golden vines with huge clusters of grapes. *Cf.* Tacitus, *His-*

speak of is not forbidden in conversation with friends, especially over after-dinner wine, while we are enjoying the god's own bounty. I am ready to speak if these gentlemen urge me."

2. At this, all did urge him and beg him to go on. "First," he said, "the time and character of the greatest, most sacred holiday of the Jews clearly befit Dionysus. When they celebrate their so-called Fast, at the height of the vintage, they set out tables of all sorts of fruit under tents and huts plaited for the most part of vines and ivy. They call the first of the two days Tabernacles.[a] A few days later they celebrate another festival, this time identified with Bacchus not through obscure hints but plainly called by his name,[b] a festival that is a sort of ' Procession of Branches ' or ' Thyrsus Procession,' in which they enter the temple each carrying a thyrsus.[c] What they do after entering we do not know, but it is probable that the rite is a Bacchic revelry, for in fact they use little trumpets [d] to invoke their god as do the Argives at their Dionysia. Others of them advance playing harps ; these players are called in their language *Levites*, either from *Lysios* (Releaser) or, better, from *Evius* (God of the Cry).[e]

<hr>

tories, v. 5. Latzarus, p. 165, note 6, quotes a commentator on Luke, xiv. 1-6 on the disregard of the Jews for their abstemious principles in respect to wine and food on the Sabbath.

[d] Deubner, *Attische Feste*, p. 96, note 4 ; Aristophanes, *Acharn*. 1000 ; Grove, *Dict. of Music*, article on Hebrew Music ; Sachs, *Hist. of Mus. Instruments*, p. 112 ; Leviticus, xxiii. 24 ; Numbers, x. 1 ff. ; a scholium in T possibly identifies Plutarch's reference as being to *phaska* (shofar ?). *Cf.* 1 Chronicles xv. 16 and 28.

[e] One of the few scholia in T scornfully expostulates against this nonsense. The names Lysios (*supra*, 613 c) and Evius are epithets of Bacchus.

(671) " Οἶμαι δὲ καὶ τὴν τῶν σαββάτων ἑορτὴν μὴ
F παντάπασιν ἀπροσδιόνυσον εἶναι· Σάβους γὰρ καὶ
νῦν ἔτι[1] πολλοὶ τοὺς Βάκχους καλοῦσιν καὶ ταύτην
ἀφιᾶσι τὴν φωνὴν ὅταν ὀργιάζωσι τῷ θεῷ, οὗ
πίστωσιν[2] ἔστι δήπου καὶ παρὰ Δημοσθένους λαβεῖν καὶ παρὰ Μενάνδρου, καὶ οὐκ ἀπὸ τρόπου[3]
τις ἂν φαίη τοὔνομα[4] πεποιῆσθαι πρός τινα[5] σό-
672 βησιν,[6] ἢ κατέχει τοὺς βακχεύοντας. αὐτοὶ δὲ
τῷ λόγῳ μαρτυροῦσιν, ὅταν σάββατα τελῶσι,[7]
μάλιστα μὲν πίνειν καὶ οἰνοῦσθαι παρακαλοῦντες
ἀλλήλους, ὅταν δὲ κωλύῃ τι μεῖζον, ἀπογεύεσθαί
γε πάντως ἀκράτου νομίζοντες. καὶ ταῦτα μὲν
εἰκότα φαίη τις ἂν εἶναι· κατὰ κράτος δὲ τοὺς
ἐναντίους[8] πρῶτον μὲν ὁ ἀρχιερεὺς ἐλέγχει, μιτρη-
φόρος τε προϊὼν ἐν ταῖς ἑορταῖς καὶ νεβρίδα
χρυσόπαστον ἐνημμένος, χιτῶνα δὲ ποδήρη φορῶν
καὶ κοθόρνους, κώδωνες δὲ πολλοὶ κατακρέμανται
τῆς ἐσθῆτος, ὑποκομποῦντες ἐν τῷ βαδίζειν, ὡς
καὶ παρ' ἡμῖν· ψόφοις δὲ χρῶνται περὶ τὰ νυκτέ-

---

[1] So Stephanus : ὅτι.
[2] οὗ πίστωσιν Hubert, ὧν πίστιν Scaliger, βεβαίωσιν Bernardakis : lac. 8-10 σιν.
[3] So Stephanus : lac. 4-5 που.
[4] So Turnebus : τοῦ ἅμα.
[5] So Stephanus : τήν.   [6] So Reiske : ἀσέβησιν.
[7] σάββατα τελῶσι Hubert, σάββατα already in g γ acc. to
Wyttenbach : σάμβα τιμῶσι T.
[8] δὲ τοὺς ἐναντίους Madvig, δὲ τοὺς ἐναντιουμένους Wyttenbach : ἐν αὑτοῖς.

---

[a] When the Hebrews spoke of *Sabaoth* (" armies," heavenly
or earthly : *cf.* Romans, ix. 29 ; Isaiah, i. 9) they would seem
to a Greek to be referring to *Sabazios* or *Sabos*, who was
identified with Dionysus. The Romans in 139 B.C. put themselves on record officially as guilty of the same confusion by

" I believe that even the feast of the Sabbath[a] is not completely unrelated to Dionysus. Many even now call the Bacchants *Sabi* and utter that cry when celebrating the god. Testimony to this can be found in Demosthenes[b] and Menander.[c] You would not be far off the track if you attributed the use of this name *Sabi*[d] to the strange excitement (*sobesis*) that possesses the celebrants. The Jews themselves testify to a connection with Dionysus when they keep the Sabbath by inviting each other to drink and to enjoy wine ; when more important business interferes with this custom, they regularly take at least a sip of neat wine.[e] Now thus far one might call the argument only probable ; but the opposition is quite demolished, in the first place by the High Priest, who leads the procession at their festival wearing a mitre and clad in a gold-embroidered fawnskin, a robe reaching to the ankles, and buskins, with many bells attached to his clothes and ringing below him as he walks.[f] All this corresponds to our custom. In the second place, they also have noise as an element in

---

expelling the Jews for allegedly introducing Sabazios to Rome. See Wissowa as quoted in *RE*, *s.v.* " Sabazios," col. 1547, and Valerius Maximus, i. 3. 3. The cry *euoi saboi* (εὐοῖ σαβοῖ), derisively quoted by Demosthenes, is referred to Dionysus Sabazius by various Greek authorities.

[b] *De Corona*, 260. *Cf.* preceding note.

[c] Menander, fr. 905 (Körte) = 1060 (Kock).

[d] Plutarch is playing with variants on the root *sab*. A different reading would make the meaning " reverence " or " awe."

[e] Ricard and Kaltwasser cite Leviticus, x. 9, which completely refutes this ; however, see Judges, ix. 13 ; xix. 19 ; Psalms, civ. 15 ; which give very weak support to Plutarch.

[f] Much of this reproduces Exodus, xxviii ; but whence are the fawnskin and buskins derived ? Helmbold compares Josephus, *Jewish Antiquities*, iii. 159 ff.

(672)

B λια,[1] καὶ χαλκοκρότους τὰς[2] τοῦ θεοῦ τιθήνας
προσαγορεύουσιν· καὶ ὁ δεικνύμενος ἐν τοῖς ἀετοῖς[3]
τοῦ νεὼ θύρσος ἐντετυπωμένος καὶ τύμπανα· ταῦτα
γὰρ οὐδενὶ δήπουθεν ἄλλῳ θεῶν[4] ἢ Διονύσῳ προσ-
ῆκεν.

" Ἔτι τοίνυν μέλι μὲν οὐ προσφέρουσι ταῖς
ἱερουργίαις, ὅτι δοκεῖ φθείρειν τὸν οἶνον κεραν-
νύμενον καὶ τοῦτ᾽ ἦν σπονδὴ καὶ μέθυ, πρὶν ἄμπελον φανῆναι· καὶ μέχρι νῦν τῶν τε βαρβάρων
οἱ μὴ ποιοῦντες οἶνον μελίτειον πίνουσιν, ὑποφαρ-
μάσσοντες τὴν γλυκύτητα οἰνώδεσι ῥίζαις καὶ
αὐστηραῖς, Ἕλληνές τε νηφάλια ταὐτὰ καὶ μελί-
σπονδα θύουσιν, ὡς ἀντίθετον φύσιν μάλιστα τοῦ
μέλιτος πρὸς τὸν οἶνον ἔχοντος. ὅτι δὲ τοῦτο
C νομίζουσι, κἀκεῖνο σημεῖον οὐ μικρόν ἐστι, τὸ
πολλῶν τιμωριῶν οὐσῶν παρ᾽ αὐτοῖς μίαν εἶναι
μάλιστα διαβεβλημένην, τὴν οἴνου τοὺς κολα-
ζομένους ἀπείργουσαν, ὅσον ἂν τάξῃ χρόνον ὁ
κύριος τῆς κολάσεως· τοὺς δ᾽ οὕτω κολα . . ."[5]

---

[1] So Turnebus : νῦν τελεια.
[2] χαλκοκρότους τὰς Corais : χαλκοκροδυστας.
[3] So Doehner : ἐναντίοις.
[4] So Bernardakis : θεῷ.
[5] The rest of the page in T is blank, with a notation in the
margin in a smaller hand to say that a quaternion containing
five headings is missing. Only four, however, are lost, the
miscount being due to the inclusion of Qu. 6 with 5, see note
on 671 c.

---

[a] As emended by Corais, an epithet of Demeter, associated

their nocturnal festivals, and call the nurses of the
god ' bronze rattlers.' [a] The carved thyrsus in the
relief on the pediment of the Temple and the drums
(provide other parallels).[b] All this surely befits (they
might say) no divinity but Dionysus.

" Further, the Jews use no honey [c] in their religious services because they believe that honey spoils
the wine with which it is mixed ; and they used
honey as libation and in place of wine before the vine
was discovered. Even up to the present time those
of the barbarians who do not make wine drink mead,
counteracting the sweetness somewhat by the use of
winelike bitter roots. The Greeks, on the other hand,
offer the same libations as ' sober libations ' and *meli-
sponda* [d] on the principle that there is a particular
opposition between honey and wine. To show that
what I have said is the practice of the Jews we may
find no slight confirmation in the fact that among
many penalties employed among them the one most
disliked is the exclusion of a convicted offender from
the use of wine for such a period as the sentencing
judge may prescribe. Those thus punished . . ." [e]

in Pindar with Dionysus : *Isth.* vii (vi). 3, where Fennell in his
edition says that it was originally an epithet of Rhea.

[b] The words in parentheses here give the sense implied by
the context. There is at least a verb missing.

[c] Correct for once, except for the reason alleged. See Leviticus, ii. 11.

[d] See Helmbold on 464 c (LCL *Mor.* vi, p. 159) : such
" honey-offerings " or wine-less libations were made to the
Eumenides.

[e] The text of Book IV breaks off here. Titles of Questions
7-10 are derived from the table of contents at the beginning
of the MS.

(672)

ΠΡΟΒΛΗΜΑ Ζ

Διὰ τί τὰς ὁμωνύμους τοῖς πλάνησιν ἡμέρας οὐ κατὰ τὴν ἐκείνων τάξιν ἀλλ' ἐνηλλαγμένως ἀριθμοῦσιν· ἐν ᾧ καὶ περὶ ἡλίου τάξεως

ΠΡΟΒΛΗΜΑ Η

Διὰ τί τῶν δακτύλων μάλιστα τῷ παραμέσῳ σφραγῖδας φοροῦσιν

ΠΡΟΒΛΗΜΑ Θ

Εἰ δεῖ θεῶν εἰκόνας ἐν ταῖς σφραγῖσιν ἢ σοφῶν ἀνδρῶν φορεῖν

ΠΡΟΒΛΗΜΑ Ι

Διὰ τί τὸ μέσον τῆς θρίδακος αἱ γυναῖκες οὐ τρώγουσιν

---

a The answer to this question may partly be recovered from the two in Dio Cassius, xxxvii. 18. The positions of the known planets, sun, and moon, and their orbits were believed to be in the order : (1) Saturn, (2) Jupiter, (3) Mars, (4) Sun, (5) Venus, (6) Mercury, (7) Moon. The hours of the day were named each after a planet, in the order given. Each day was named after the planet of its first hour ; then, if the first day was named for the first planet, the second day, beginning 24 hours later, would be named for the fourth planet, the third day for the seventh planet, and so on through third, sixth, second, and fifth. The alternative explanation in Dio Cassius, which is described as based on " the principle of the tetrachord," amounts, in simple terms, to the following : if the degrees of the musical scale are numbered from one through seven, and these are grouped in terms of tetrachords (as the Greeks had practical reasons for doing), the same series 1-4-7-3-6-2-5 is again arrived at as by the astronomical approach. The identification between music and mathematical astronomy would be to Greeks like Pythagoras, Plato, and Plutarch almost automatic. Our weekdays are still named after Teutonic equivalents, as those of the Romance languages are

QUESTION 7

Why days named after the planets are arranged in a different order from the planetary positions [a]; also on the
position of the sun

QUESTION 8

Why seal rings are worn on the finger next the middle
finger [b]

QUESTION 9

Whether it is more proper to wear images of the gods [c]
or of wise men on seal rings

QUESTION 10

Why women do not eat the heart of lettuce [d]

derived from the Latin names of the planets, sun, and moon,
in the sequence established in antiquity. Note, however, that
in languages derived from Latin the first day of the week is
the Lord's day rather than Sunday. The Welsh term, however, comes from *dies solis*.

[b] See Macrobius, *Saturnalia*, vii. 13. 7 ff., where two
reasons are suggested. One, called the Egyptian, is to the
effect that a nerve from this finger leads to the heart; the
other, called Etruscan, is quoted from Ateius Capito, and is
based on more practical reasons connected with the use of
signet rings, such as not wearing one on the right hand,
where it would be more easily damaged.

[c] Pythagoras (see Porphyry, *Life of Pythag.* 42, in Diels-
Kranz, *Vorsokratiker*[8], vol. i, p. 466, lines 5 f.) and Ateius
Capito (in Macrobius, *Saturnalia*, vii. 13. 11) forbade images
of gods on rings. Under the emperor Claudius courtiers wore
his image on a ring (Pliny, *Nat. Hist.* xxxiii. 12. 41).

[d] Lettuce was considered antiaphrodisiac. See Pliny, *Nat.
Hist.* xix. 127, and especially Dioscorides, *Materia Medica*, ii.
136.

TABLE-TALK
(QUAESTIONES CONVIVALES)
BOOK V

ΣΥΜΠΟΣΙΑΚΩΝ

ΒΙΒΛΙΟΝ ΠΕΜΠΤΟΝ

Περὶ τῶν τῆς ψυχῆς καὶ σώματος ἡδονῶν, ὦ
Σόσσιε Σενεκίων, ἣν σὺ νῦν ἔχεις γνώμην, ἐμοὶ
γοῦν ἄδηλόν ἐστιν,

ἐπεὶ μάλα πολλὰ μεταξὺ
οὔρεά τε σκιόεντα θάλασσά τε ἠχήεσσα·

πάλαι γε μὴν ἐδόκεις μὴ πάνυ τι συμφέρεσθαι μηδ᾽
ἐπαινεῖν τοὺς οὐδὲν ἴδιον τῇ ψυχῇ τερπνὸν οὐδὲ
χαρτὸν οὐδ᾽ αἱρετὸν ὅλως προσνέμοντας[1] ἀλλ᾽
E ἀτεχνῶς τῷ σώματι παραζῶσαν αὐτὴν οἰομένους
τοῖς ἐκείνου συνεπιμειδιᾶν πάθεσι καὶ πάλιν αὖ
συνεπισκυθρωπάζειν, ὥσπερ ἐκμαγεῖον ἢ κάτ-
οπτρον εἰκόνας καὶ εἴδωλα τῶν ἐν σαρκὶ γιγνομένων αἰσθήσεων ἀναδεχομένην. ἄλλοις τε γὰρ
πολλοῖς ἁλίσκεται ψεύδους[2] τὸ ἀφιλόκαλον τοῦ
δόγματος, ἔν τε τοῖς πότοις[3] οἱ ἀστεῖοι καὶ χαρίεντες εὐθὺς μετὰ τὸ δεῖπνον ἐπὶ τοὺς λόγους ὥσπερ
δευτέρας τραπέζας φερόμενοι καὶ διὰ λόγων εὐφραί-
νοντες ἀλλήλους, ὧν σώματι μέτεστιν οὐδὲν ἢ

---

[1] προσνέμοντας or παραχωροῦντας added by Hubert, *qui con-cedebant* Xylander, εἶναι or ὑπάρχειν Turnebus.
[2] So Meziriacus : ψεῦδος.
[3] So Basel edition : νότοις.

TABLE-TALK

BOOK FIVE

WHAT you now think, Sossius Senecio, about the pleasures of the body and the mind I am not in a position to know,

> For between us lie
> Full many a shadowy mountain and resounding sea [a];

but certainly we used to think that you had no great sympathy or esteem for the opinion of those [b] who suppose that the soul is without any special pleasure or delight or predilection of its own. According to them the soul is simply the body's partner in life, whose aspect is smiling or gloomy only as the body rejoices or suffers. In other words, the soul is merely a sort of stamp [c] or mirror, receiving the impressions and images of the sensations that occur in the flesh. This philistine view is refuted by many facts. For instance, at parties men of wit and taste hurry at once after dinner to ideas as if to dessert,[d] finding their entertainment in conversation that has little or nothing to do with the concerns of the body; and so

---

[a] Homer, *Iliad*, i. 156f.
[b] Epicureans: see H. Usener, *Epicurea*, frags. 410 and 429; Plutarch, *Non Posse Suaviter Vivi*, 1088 E, 1092 D, 1096 C.
[c] Impression of a matrix.
[d] Or, as at *Mor.* 133 E, " a second repast " (F. C. Babbitt).

(672) βραχὺ παντάπασιν, ἴδιόν τι τοῦτο τῇ ψυχῇ ταμι-
εῖον εὐπαθειῶν ἀποκεῖσθαι μαρτυροῦσι καὶ ταύ-
F τας[1] ἡδονὰς μόνας εἶναι τῆς ψυχῆς, ἐκείνας δ' ἀλ-
λοτρίας, προσαναχρωννυμένας τῷ σώματι.

Ὥσπερ οὖν[2] αἱ τὰ βρέφη ψωμίζουσαι τροφοὶ μικρὰ μετέχουσι τῆς ἡδονῆς, ὅταν δ' ἐκεῖνα κορέσωσι[3]
καὶ κοιμίσωσι παυσάμενα κλαυθμυρισμῶν, τηνικαῦτα καθ' ἑαυτὰς γιγνόμεναι τὰ πρόσφορα σιτία
673 καὶ ποτὰ λαμβάνουσι καὶ ἀπολαύουσιν, οὕτως ἡ
ψυχὴ τῶν περὶ πόσιν καὶ βρῶσιν ἡδονῶν μετέχει
ταῖς τοῦ σώματος ὀρέξεσι δίκην τίτθης ὑπηρετοῦσα
καὶ χαριζομένη δεομένῳ καὶ πραΰνουσα τὰς ἐπιθυμίας, ὅταν δ' ἐκεῖνο μετρίως ἔχῃ καὶ ἡσυχάσῃ,
πραγμάτων ἀπαλλαγεῖσα καὶ λατρείας ἤδη τὸ λοι-
πὸν ἐπὶ τὰς αὐτῆς ἡδονὰς τρέπεται, λόγοις εὐω-
χουμένη καὶ μαθήμασι καὶ ἱστορίαις καὶ τῷ ζητεῖν
τι[4] τῶν περιττῶν. καὶ τί ἄν τις λέγοι περὶ τούτων,
ὁρῶν ὅτι καὶ οἱ φορτικοὶ καὶ ἀφιλόλογοι μετὰ τὸ
δεῖπνον ἐφ' ἡδονὰς ἑτέρας τοῦ σώματος ἀπωτάτω
τὴν διάνοιαν ἀπαίρουσιν, αἰνίγματα καὶ γρίφους
B καὶ θέσεις ὀνομάτων ἐν ἀριθμοῖς ὑποσυμβόλοις[5]
προβάλλοντες; ἐκ τούτου δὲ καὶ μίμοις καὶ ἠθολόγοις[6] καὶ τοῖς Μένανδρον ὑποκρινομένοις τὰ συμ-

---

[1] So Wyttenbach, ταύτας τὰς Turnebus : τὰς.
[2] So Turnebus : νῦν.
[3] So Turnebus : κορεσθῶσι.
[4] ἀκούειν deleted after τι by Bases after Xylander.
[5] So R. Foerster cited in *RE* i A, col. 111, ἢ ὑπὸ συμβόλου
Franke : ὑποσύμβολα.
[6] καὶ Μενάνδρῳ deleted after ἠθολόγοις by Pohlenz.

---

[a] Plutarch says much the same thing about the arts in
705 A, below.
[b] Or " inquiries."

374

they make it clear that there is a private store of delights set aside for the soul, and that these are its only true pleasures,[a] the others being alien and derived from the body through contact.

Nurses feeding babies by hand get little pleasure from it at the time ; only when the children are fed, put to sleep, and their crying quieted, do the nurses, being left alone, help themselves to the food and drink they want and enjoy them. In the same way our soul partakes of the pleasures of eating and drinking while attending, like a nurse, to the appetites of the body, complying with its demands and calming its passions ; but when the body is comfortable and at peace, then at last the soul, released from care and servitude, can devote itself to its own pleasures and feast on ideas, learning, tales of the past,[b] and speculation about unusual questions. Actually, what need is there to go into this, in view of the fact that after dinner even common, unliterary people allow their thoughts to wander to other pleasures, as far away as possible from the concerns of the body ? They take up conundrums and riddles,[c] or the Names and Numbers game.[d] Hence also, drinking parties have provided occasion for the performance of mimes, impersonations, and scenes from Menander,[e] not because such

[c] See *RE*, *s.v.* " Rätsel." Athenaeus, x, 448 b, has a discussion with many examples of various types of riddles.

[d] The letters of the alphabet were regularly used as numerals, *alpha* being 1, *beta* being 2, etc. In a game called *isopsepha* the sum of the values of the letters of a name was equated with the sum comprised in another name. Examples in verse are to be found in *Anth. Pal.* vi. 321 ff.

[e] Readings of Menander and other poets of the New Comedy at banquets are mentioned also by Plutarch in vii. 8, 712 B *infra*, and in *Aristophanes and Menander*, 854 B.

(673) πόσια χώραν ἔδωκεν, οὐδεμίαν " ἀλγηδόνα τοῦ σώ-
ματος¹ ὑπεξαιρουμένοις " οὐδὲ ποιοῦσι² " λείαν ἐν
σαρκὶ καὶ προσηνῆ κίνησιν," ἀλλ' ὅτι τὸ φύσει φιλο-
θέαμον³ ἐν ἑκάστῳ καὶ φιλόσοφον τῆς ψυχῆς ἰδίαν
χάριν ζητεῖ καὶ τέρψιν, ὅταν τῆς περὶ τὸ σῶμα
θεραπείας καὶ ἀσχολίας ἀπαλλαγῶμεν.

C   ΠΡΟΒΛΗΜΑ Α

Διὰ τί τῶν μιμουμένων τοὺς ὀργιζομένους καὶ λυπουμένους ἡδέως
ἀκούομεν, αὐτῶν δὲ τῶν ἐν τοῖς πάθεσιν ὄντων ἀηδῶς

Collocuntur Plutarchus, Epicurei

1. Περὶ ὧν ἐγένοντο λόγοι καὶ σοῦ παρόντος ἐν
Ἀθήναις ἡμῖν, ὅτε Στράτων ὁ κωμῳδὸς εὐημέ-
ρησεν (ἦν γὰρ αὐτοῦ πολὺς λόγος), ἑστιωμένων
ἡμῶν παρὰ Βοήθῳ τῷ Ἐπικουρείῳ· συνεδείπνουν
δ' οὐκ ὀλίγοι τῶν ἀπὸ τῆς αἱρέσεως.⁴ εἶθ' οἷον ἐν⁵
φιλολόγοις περιέστησεν ἡ τῆς κωμῳδίας μνήμη τὸν
λόγον εἰς ζήτησιν αἰτίας δι' ἣν ὀργιζομένων ἢ
D λυπουμένων ἢ δεδιότων φωνὰς ἀκούοντες ἀχθόμεθα
καὶ δυσκολαίνομεν, οἱ δ' ὑποκρινόμενοι ταῦτα τὰ πάθη καὶ μιμούμενοι τὰς φωνὰς αὐτῶν καὶ τὰς διαθέσεις
εὐφραίνουσιν ἡμᾶς.

¹ So Turnebus : ὄμματος.
² So Aldine edition : οὐδ' επιοῦσι.
³ So Xylander, Anonymus : φιλόθεσμον.
⁴ ἀπὸ τῆς αἱρέσεως αὐτῆς Xylander : ἀποδιαιρέσεως.
⁵ οἷον ἐν Bernardakis : οἱονεί.

ᵃ According to Epicurus, *Kyriae Doxae*, no. 3 (Usener,
Epicurea, p. 72 ; Diogenes Laertius, x. 139), pleasure is
measured and consummated by complete removal of pain.
Cf. Cicero, *De Finibus*, i. 11. 37, with Reid's note.
ᵇ A definition (or mode) of pleasure according to Aristippus and Epicurus. *Cf.* Usener, *Epicurea*, frag. 411, and Plu-

performances " remove any physical pain "[a] or produce " smooth and gentle motions[b] in the body,"
but because in each person a natural fondness for
spectacle[c] and thirst for knowledge in the soul seek
their own gratification and delight whenever we are
relieved of the endless task of taking care of our
bodies.

QUESTION 1

Why we take pleasure in hearing actors represent anger and
pain but not in seeing people actually experience these
emotions[d]

Speakers : Plutarch, Epicurean friends of Plutarch

1. The views that I have mentioned were the subject
of discussion once when you were yourself with us at
Athens. It was at the time when the comedian
Strato[e] won his victory, for I recall that everybody
was talking about him. We were at dinner at the
house of Boëthus[f] the Epicurean with many others
of his persuasion. As was natural among people of an
inquiring turn of mind, the mention of comedy led us
into a discussion : why is it that, although we are
distressed and annoyed to hear the voices of people
in anger, pain or fear, we yet are greatly entertained
when mimics reproduce these emotions and copy the
tones and attitudes of the sufferers ?

tarch, *Adversus Colotem*, 1122 e. See R. Westmann, *Acta
Philosophica Fennica*, vii (1955), p. 179.

   [c] Or " speculation," Post.
   [d] This question is also raised in Plutarch, *Quomodo Adu-
lescens Poetas Audire Debeat*, 17 f—18 c, and is suggested by
Plato (*Republic*, 605 c ff.) and Aristotle (*Rhetoric*, 1371 b 7,
and *Poetics*, 1448 b 10).   [e] Apparently unknown.
   [f] An Epicurean friend of Plutarch's, according to several
of his essays. *RE*, *s.v.* " Plutarchos," col. 669.

(673)   Ἐκείνων μὲν οὖν ἁπάντων σχεδὸν εἷς ἦν λόγος·
ἔφασαν γάρ, ἐπειδὴ κρείττων ὁ μιμούμενός ἐστι
τοῦ πάσχοντος ἀληθῶς καὶ τῷ μὴ πεπονθέναι διαφέρει, συνιέντας ἡμᾶς τοῦτο[1] τέρπεσθαι καὶ χαίρειν.
(2) ἐγὼ δέ, καίπερ ἐν ἀλλοτρίῳ χορῷ[2] πόδα τιθείς,
εἶπον ὅτι φύσει λογικοὶ καὶ φιλότεχνοι γεγονότες
πρὸς τὸ λογικῶς καὶ τεχνικῶς πραττόμενον οἰκείως διακείμεθα καὶ θαυμάζομεν, ἂν ἐπιτυγχάνηται.
E   " καθάπερ γὰρ ἡ μέλιττα τῷ φιλόγλυκυς εἶναι πᾶσαν ὕλην ᾗ τι[3] μελιτῶδες ἐγκέκραται περιέπει καὶ
διώκει, οὕτως ὁ ἄνθρωπος, γεγονὼς φιλότεχνος καὶ
φιλόκαλος, πᾶν ἀποτέλεσμα καὶ πρᾶγμα νοῦ καὶ
λόγου μετέχον ἀσπάζεσθαι καὶ ἀγαπᾶν πέφυκεν.

" Εἰ γοῦν παιδίῳ μικρῷ προθείη τις ὁμοῦ[4] μὲν ἄρτον, ὁμοῦ δὲ πεπλασμένον ἐκ τῶν ἀλεύρων κυνί-
διον ἢ βοΐδιον, ἐπὶ τοῦτ' ἂν ἴδοις φερόμενον· καὶ
ὁμοίως εἴ τις[5] ἀργύριον ἄσημον, ἕτερος δὲ ζῴδιον
ἀργυροῦν ἢ ἔκπωμα παραστάι διδούς, τοῦτ' ἂν
λάβοι μᾶλλον, ᾧ τὸ τεχνικὸν καὶ λογικὸν ἐνορᾷ
F   καταμεμιγμένον. ὅθεν καὶ τῶν λόγων τοῖς ἠνιγ-
μένοις χαίρουσι μᾶλλον οἱ τηλικοῦτοι καὶ τῶν
παιδιῶν ταῖς περιπλοκήν τινα καὶ δυσκολίαν ἐχού-
σαις· ἕλκει γὰρ ὡς οἰκεῖον ἀδιδάκτως τὴν φύσιν

---

[1] So Xylander, τούτου (" listening to *him* ") Stephanus :
τοῦ.
[2] So Aldine edition : χωρῷ.
[3] So Xylander : τινι.
[4] μικρὸν after ὁμοῦ deleted by Reiske.
[5] εἴ τις added by Turnebus.

---

[a] In *De Se Ipsum Laudando*, 540 b this proverb is explained : anyone who set foot in another's chorus was a fool
and a meddler (De Lacy and Einarson's translation). *Cf.*
Leutsch and Schneidewin, *Paroemiogr. Graec.* ii, p. 690.

The other guests were practically unanimous in saying that, inasmuch as the imitator enjoys a superiority and advantage over the actual sufferer by not having suffered himself, awareness of that fact gives us pleasure and delight. (2) But I spoke up, " setting foot in another's chorus." [a] I said that, since we are naturally endowed with reason and love of art,[b] we have an affinity for any performance that exhibits reason or artistry, and admire success therein. " Just as the bee, loving sweetness, seeks out and busies itself with any object that contains a suggestion of honey, so a human being, born with a love of art and beauty, is by nature disposed to welcome and cherish every product or action that bears the stamp of mind and reason.

" Certainly, if someone were to place in front of a small child both a loaf of bread and a little dog or a cow made of the dough, you would see the child irresistibly drawn to the miniature figure. Likewise, if one person presents to him a shapeless lump of silver, while another brings him a little silver animal or cup, the child will take by preference the second, in which he perceives art and meaning. This explains why children like stories better that involve riddles, and games that offer some complication or difficulty. People require no instruction [c] to be at-

---

[b] " Art " (*technē*) includes " artifice " or " ingenuity." Similarly, *panurgia*, translated " cunning " below, basically means " knavery."

[c] An effective point, because the Epicureans taught that one test of value is untutored instinct. *Cf. Adversus Coloten*, 1122 E (Usener, *Epicurea*, frag. 411), and Sextus Empiricus, *Adversus Dogmaticos*, v. 96 in Usener, *Epicurea*, p. 274. In both passages language similar to that of the above passage is used (" untaught," " without a tutor ").

(673) τὸ γλαφυρὸν καὶ πανοῦργον. ἐπεὶ τοίνυν ὁ μὲν
ἀληθῶς ὀργιζόμενος ἢ λυπούμενος ἔν τισι κοινοῖς
πάθεσι καὶ κινήμασιν[1] ὁρᾶται, τῇ δὲ μιμήσει παν-
ουργία τις ἐμφαίνεται καὶ πιθανότης ἅπερ ἐπι-
674 τυγχάνεται, τούτοις μὲν ἥδεσθαι πεφύκαμεν ἐκείνοις δ' ἀχθόμεθα.

"Καὶ γὰρ ἐπὶ τῶν θεαμάτων ὅμοια πεπόνθαμεν·
ἀνθρώπους μὲν γὰρ ἀποθνήσκοντας καὶ νοσοῦντας
ἀνιαρῶς ὁρῶμεν· τὸν δὲ γεγραμμένον Φιλοκτήτην
καὶ τὴν πεπλασμένην Ἰοκάστην, ἧς φασιν εἰς τὸ
πρόσωπον ἀργύρου τι συμμῖξαι τὸν τεχνίτην, ὅπως
ἐκλείποντος[2] ἀνθρώπου καὶ μαραινομένου λάβῃ
περιφάνειαν ὁ χαλκός, ἰδόντες[3] ἡδόμεθα καὶ θαυμάζομεν.

"Τοῦτο δ'," εἶπον, "ἄνδρες Ἐπικούρειοι, καὶ
τεκμήριόν ἐστι μέγα τοῖς Κυρηναϊκοῖς πρὸς ὑμᾶς
τοῦ μὴ περὶ τὴν ὄψιν εἶναι μηδὲ περὶ τὴν ἀκοὴν
B ἀλλὰ περὶ τὴν διάνοιαν ἡμῶν τὸ[4] ἡδόμενον[5] ἐπὶ
τοῖς ἀκούσμασι καὶ θεάμασιν. ἀλεκτορὶς γὰρ βο-
ῶσα συνεχῶς καὶ κορώνη λυπηρὸν ἄκουσμα καὶ
ἀηδές ἐστιν, ὁ δὲ μιμούμενος ἀλεκτορίδα βοῶσαν
καὶ κορώνην εὐφραίνει· καὶ φθισικοὺς μὲν ὁρῶντες
δυσχεραίνομεν, ἀνδριάντας δὲ καὶ γραφὰς φθισικῶν

---

[1] So Salmasius : μιμήμασιν.
[2] So Bernardakis : ἐκλιπόντος.
[3] ἰδόντες added by Hubert from *Mor.* 18 A, ὁρῶντες after
ἡδόμεθα Vulcobius ; Wyttenbach and Wilamowitz reject any
addition here.   [4] So Stephanus : τόν.
[5] So Aldine (according to Hutten), Basel editions: δεόμενον.

---

[a] Philoctetes suffered extremely from a festering wound in
his leg, as in Sophocles's celebrated play. According to Plu-

tracted, as by some natural kinship, to subtlety and cleverness. Under the influence of genuine anger or pain a man always displays certain universal emotions and gestures, whereas a successful imitation manifests a cunning and authority of its own, so that we take a natural delight in the performance, but are distressed by the reality.

" We have a similar experience in relation to the plastic arts. We feel acute pain at the sight of the sick or the dying ; but a painting of Philoctetes [a] or a statue of Jocasta [b] gives us pleasure and elicits our admiration. They say that the artist added silver [c] to Jocasta's face in order to give his bronze statue the appearance of a person on the verge of death.

" This, my Epicurean friends," I said, " is really good evidence in favour of the Cyrenaics,[d] who contend in their dispute with you that it is not in our sight or our hearing but in our minds that we receive pleasure from sights and sounds. A hen that cackles ceaselessly or a cawing crow is unpleasant and painful to hear, but the imitator of noisy hens and crows delights us. We are shocked to see consumptives, but we contemplate statues and paintings of them

tarch, *De Audiendis Poetis*, 18 c, Philoctetes was the subject of a painting by Aristophon in the 6th century B.C.

[b] Mother of Oedipus, who hanged herself, or, according to Euripides, stabbed herself to death. She was sculptured by Silanion in the 4th century B.C. *Cf.* Plutarch, *ibid.* 18 c ; *RE*, *s.v.* " Silanion," col. 3.

[c] That the Greeks did succeed in adding silver to bronze is now known from the bronze head discussed by Homer A. Thompson in the article " A Golden Nike from the Agora," *Harvard Studies in Classical Philology*, Supplementary volume i (1940), pp. 183 ff.

[d] Cyrenê, in Africa, was the home of the hedonistic philosopher Aristippus and his school.

(674) ἡδέως θεώμεθα τῷ τὴν διάνοιαν ὑπὸ τῶν μιμημά-
των ἄγεσθαι[1] κατὰ τὸ οἰκεῖον.

" Ἐπεὶ τί πάσχοντες ἢ τίνος ἔξωθεν γενομένου
πάθους τὴν ὗν τὴν[2] Παρμένοντος οὕτως ἐθαύμασαν,
ὥστε παροιμιώδη γενέσθαι; καίτοι φασὶ τοῦ
Παρμένοντος εὐδοκιμοῦντος ἐπὶ τῇ μιμήσει, ζη-
λοῦντας ἑτέρους ἀντεπιδείκνυσθαι· προκατειλημ-
C μένων δὲ τῶν ἀνθρώπων καὶ λεγόντων, ' εὖ μὲν
ἀλλ' οὐδὲν πρὸς τὴν Παρμένοντος ὗν,' ἕνα λαβόντα
δελφάκιον ὑπὸ μάλης προσελθεῖν· ἐπεὶ δὲ καὶ τῆς
ἀληθινῆς φωνῆς ἀκούοντες ὑπεφθέγγοντο, ' τί οὖν
αὕτη πρὸς τὴν Παρμένοντος ὗν;' ἀφεῖναι[3] τὸ δελφάκιον εἰς τὸ μέσον, ἐξελέγχοντα τῆς κρίσεως
τὸ πρὸς δόξαν οὐ πρὸς ἀλήθειαν. ᾧ[4] μάλιστα δῆλόν
ἐστιν, ὅτι τὸ αὐτὸ τῆς αἰσθήσεως πάθος οὐχ ὁμοίως διατίθησι τὴν ψυχὴν ὅταν μὴ προσῇ δόξα τοῦ
λογικῶς ἢ φιλοτίμως περαίνεσθαι τὸ γιγνόμενον."[5]

D ΠΡΟΒΛΗΜΑ Β

Ὅτι παλαιὸν ἦν ἀγώνισμα τὸ τῆς ποιητικῆς

Collocuntur Plutarchus, alii

Ἐν Πυθίοις ἐγίγνοντο λόγοι περὶ τῶν ἐπιθέτων
ἀγωνισμάτων, ὡς ἀναιρετέα. παραδεξάμενοι γὰρ

---

[1] καὶ after ἄγεσθαι deleted by Wyttenbach.
[2] ὗν τὴν added by Bernardakis, τὴν Παρμένοντος ὗν Basel
edition.
[3] ὗν, ἀφεῖναι Basel edition : συναφεῖναι.
[4] ᾧ Basel edition : ὅ.   [5] So Bernardakis : γενόμενον.

---

[a] Or, " because of a fellow-feeling," E. H. W.
[b] F. C. Babbitt's Index to Plut. Mor. i (LCL) identifies
Parmeno as a famous comic actor of the latter part of the 4th

with pleasure, because the mind, by its own[a] nature, is attracted to imitations.

" What emotion or what external happening made people admire Parmeno's pig so much that it has become proverbial ? You know the story : one time when Parmeno was already famous for his mimicry, some competitors put on a rival show, but the populace, being prejudiced in favour of Parmeno, said, ' Good enough !—but nothing, compared with Parmeno's sow.' [b] Then one of the performers stepped forward with a sucking pig concealed under his arm ; but the people, even when they heard the genuine squeal, murmured, ' Well, what's this compared to Parmeno's pig ? ' Thereupon the fellow let the pig go in the crowd to prove that their judgement was based on prejudice instead of truth. This plainly demonstrates that the very same sensation will not produce a corresponding effect a second time in people's minds unless they believe that intelligence or conscious striving is involved in the performance."

QUESTION 2

That the poetry competition was ancient

Speakers : Plutarch and others

AT the Pythian Games [c] there was a discussion whether the newer competitions ought to be elimi-

century B.C., but the *Paroemiogr. Graec.* i, p. 412, surprisingly makes him a painter and the pig a painted one so realistic that everyone thought that his squeal could be heard.

[c] Plutarch was long an official at Delphi. *Cf. An Seni Res Publica Gerenda Sit*, 792 F, and J. J. Hartman, *De Avondzon des Heidendoms*, i, pp. 17 f, and now R. H. Barrow, *Plutarch and his Times*, p. 31.

(674) ἐπὶ τρισὶ τοῖς καθεστῶσιν ἐξ ἀρχῆς, αὐλητῇ Πυ-
θικῷ καὶ κιθαριστῇ καὶ κιθαρῳδῷ, τὸν τραγῳδόν,
ὥσπερ πύλης ἀνοιχθείσης οὐκ ἀντέσχον ἀθρόοις συν-
επιτιθεμένοις καὶ συνεισιοῦσι παντοδαποῖς ἀκροά-
μασιν· ὑφ' ὧν ποικιλίαν μὲν ἔσχεν οὐκ ἀηδῆ καὶ
πανηγυρισμὸν ὁ ἀγών, τὸ δ' αὐστηρὸν καὶ μου-
E σικὸν οὐ διεφύλαξεν, ἀλλὰ καὶ πράγματα τοῖς κρί-
νουσιν παρέσχεν καὶ πολλὰς ὡς εἰκὸς ἡττωμένων
πολλῶν ἀπεχθείας.

Οὐχ ἥκιστα δὲ τὸ τῶν λογογράφων καὶ ποιητῶν
ἔθνος ᾤοντο δεῖν ἀποσκευάσασθαι τοῦ ἀγῶνος, οὐχ
ὑπὸ μισολογίας, ἀλλὰ πολὺ πάντων τῶν ἀγωνι-
στῶν γνωριμωτάτους ὄντας ἐδυσωποῦντο τούτους
καὶ ἤχθοντο, πάντας ἡγούμενοι χαρίεντας, οὐ πάντων δὲ νικᾶν δυναμένων. ἡμεῖς οὖν ἐν τῷ συν-
εδρίῳ παρεμυθούμεθα τοὺς τὰ[1] καθεστῶτα κινεῖν
βουλομένους καὶ τῷ ἀγῶνι καθάπερ ὀργάνῳ πολυχορδίαν καὶ πολυφωνίαν ἐπικαλοῦντας. καὶ παρὰ
F τὸ δεῖπνον, ἑστιῶντος ἡμᾶς Πετραίου τοῦ ἀγωνο-
θέτου, πάλιν ὁμοίως[2] λόγων προσπεσόντων, ἠμύνο-
μεν τῇ μουσικῇ· τήν τε ποιητικὴν ἀπεφαίνομεν
οὐκ ὄψιμον οὐδὲ νεαρὰν ἐπὶ τοὺς ἱεροὺς ἀγῶνας
ἀφιγμένην, ἀλλὰ πρόπαλαι στεφάνων ἐπινικίων
τυγχάνουσαν. ἐνίοις μὲν οὖν ἐπίδοξος ἤμην ἕωλα
παραθήσειν πράγματα, τὰς Οἰολύκου τοῦ Θεττα-

---

[1] τὰ added by Reiske.
[2] So Turnebus : ὁμοίως.

---

[a] Originally Apollo was said to be opposed to the *aulos*
(pipe), but from 586 B.C. on the *aulos* was introduced at Delphi
and gradually became so popular that the " Pythian nome "
came to mean exclusively an auletic melody. See von Jan in
RE, *s.v.* " Auletik," cols. 2404 f. A Pythian *auletes* (piper)
occurs in *Inscript. Graec.* vii. 1776.

nated. For, once having accepted the tragic competitor as an addition to the original three (the Pythian piper,[a] the lyricist, and the singer to the lyre), the authorities found that as if the gate had been opened, they could no longer withstand the massed attack and incursion of all manner of entertainments addressed to the ear. This gave a pleasing variety and popular appeal to the festival at the cost of its severe and strictly musical character ; it also made trouble for the judges and naturally created much animosity because the defeated in the competitions were many.

Some of our company thought that particularly the tribe of prose writers and poets ought to be withdrawn. This was not because of any bias against literature, but because we were embarrassed before those most celebrated of all the contestants and vexed that not all of them could win a victory, though they all seemed to us accomplished. During the Council meeting I attempted to dissuade those who wished to change established practices and who found fault with the festival as if it were a musical instrument with too many strings and too many notes. Later, when this general subject came up again at a dinner given us by Petraeus,[b] the Director of the Games, I once more defended the cause of the arts. I made the point that poetry was not a late arrival nor a novelty at the religious festivals, but had in fact received the crown of victory in very ancient times. Some of my friends expected me to cite well-worn examples like the funeral ceremonies of Oeolycus [c]

[b] Lucius Cassius Petraeus. *RE*, xix. 1179 ; *De Pythiae Orac.* 409 c.

[c] Unknown. Not among the Oeolyci in *RE*.

675 λοῦ ταφὰς καὶ τὰς Ἀμφιδάμαντος τοῦ Χαλκιδέως
ἐν αἷς Ὅμηρον καὶ Ἡσίοδον ἱστοροῦσιν ἔπεσι
διαγωνίσασθαι. καταβαλὼν δὲ ταῦτα τῷ διατε-
θρυλῆσθαι πάνθ' ὑπὸ τῶν γραμματικῶν, καὶ τοὺς
ἐπὶ ταῖς Πατρόκλου ταφαῖς ἀναγιγνωσκομένους ὑπό
τινων οὐχ "ἤμονας" ἀλλὰ "ῥήμονας," ὡς δὴ καὶ
λόγων ἆθλα τοῦ Ἀχιλλέως προθέντος, ἀφείς, εἶπον
ὅτι καὶ Πελίαν θάπτων Ἄκαστος ὁ υἱὸς ἀγῶνα
ποιήματος παράσχοι καὶ Σίβυλλα νικήσειεν. ἐπιφυομένων δὲ πολλῶν καὶ τὸν βεβαιωτὴν ὡς ἀπίστου
καὶ[1] παραλόγου τῆς ἱστορίας ἀπαιτούντων, ἐπιτυ-
χῶς ἀναμνησθεὶς ἀπέφαινον Ἀκέσανδρον ἐν τῷ περὶ
B Λιβύης ταῦθ' ἱστοροῦντα. "καὶ τοῦτο μέν,"
ἔφην, "τὸ ἀνάγνωσμα τῶν οὐκ ἐν μέσῳ ἐστίν·
τοῖς δὲ Πολέμωνος τοῦ Ἀθηναίου περὶ τῶν ἐν
Δελφοῖς θησαυρῶν οἶμαι πολλοῖς[2] ὑμῶν ἐντυγχάνειν ἐπιμελές ἐστι καὶ χρή, πολυμαθοῦς καὶ οὐ νυ-
στάζοντος ἐν τοῖς Ἑλληνικοῖς πράγμασιν ἀνδρός·
ἐκεῖ τοίνυν εὑρήσετε γεγραμμένον, ὡς ἐν τῷ

---

[1] καί added by Stephanus.
[2] οἶμαι πολλοῖς E, οἶμαι ὅτι πολλοῖς T.

---

[a] Hesiod (*Works and Days*, 654 ff.) mentions the contest
but not Homer. *The Contest of Homer and Hesiod* (Hesiod,
LCL, pp. 570 ff.) elaborates the story, and Plutarch, *Septem
Sapientium Convivium*, 153 F ff., gives further details.

[b] *Iliad*, xxiii. 886.

[c] King of Iolcus in Thessaly, whom Medea killed under
pretence of rejuvenating him in a boiling cauldron.

[d] Apparently some one of the large number of ecstatic
prophetesses known by this name. Possibly the "Thessalian
Sibyl," Manto, best suits the context here.

of Thessaly and those of Amphidamas *[a]* of Chalcis, at which it is said that Homer and Hesiod contended in epic verse. But I scorned all this hackneyed lore of the schoolroom, dismissing also the " speakers " (*rhemones*) in Homer, as read by some for " throwers " (*hemones*) *[b]* at the funeral of Patroclus, as if Achilles had awarded a prize in speaking in addition to the other prizes. I merely mentioned that even Acastus at the funeral of his father Pelias *[c]* held a contest of poetry at which the Sibyl *[d]* won. I was immediately fastened on by many, who demanded my authority for so incredible and paradoxical a statement; luckily I remembered and told them that Acesander *[e]* in his *Libya* has the tale. " This reference," I went on, " is not generally accessible,*[f]* but I know that many of you will be interested, as you ought to be, in consulting the account of the Treasuries *[g]* at Delphi by Polemon *[h]* of Athens, a man of wide learning, tireless and accurate in his study of Greek history. In that book you will find that in the Treasury of the Sicyo-

---

[e] Historian of the 3rd or 2nd century B.C.: *Frag. Hist. Graec.* (C. Müller), iv. 285; *Frag. Griech. Historiker* (F. Jacoby), iii B, 469 F 7. There was some connection between Libya and the Sibyls. According to Varro, one of the Sibyls was Libyan; and Pausanias (x. 12. 1) cites " the Libyans " as being somehow authorities on Sibyls. See *RE*, *s.v.* " Sibyllen," col. 2096, no. 16.

[f] Or " this book is not widely known."

[g] Buildings erected by many cities as repositories for archives and other treasures at shrines like Delphi, where two of them have been restored. On the Treasury of the Sicyonians and its remains see P. de la Coste-Messelière, *Au Musée de Delphes* (Paris, 1936), pp. 56 ff.

[h] Famous antiquary, commonly called Polemon of Ilium or of Pergamum. See Athenaeus, vi, 234 d, Sandys, *Hist. Class. Scholarship*, vol. i, p. 154, and Esther V. Hansen, *The Attalids of Pergamon*, p. 363.

(675) Σικυωνίων[1] θησαυρῷ χρυσοῦν ἀνέκειτο βιβλίον
Ἀριστομάχης ἀνάθημα τῆς Ἐρυθραίας ἐπικῷ[2] ποι-
ήματι δὶς[3] Ἴσθμια νενικηκυίας.
"Οὐ μὴν οὐδὲ τὴν Ὀλυμπίαν," ἔφην, "ἄξιόν
ἐστιν ὥσπερ εἱμαρμένην ἀμετάστατον καὶ ἀμετά-
θετον ἐν τοῖς ἀθλήμασιν ἐκπεπλῆχθαι. τὰ μὲν γὰρ[4]
C Πύθια τῶν μουσικῶν ἔσχε τρεῖς ἢ τέτταρας ἐπεισο-
δίους ἀγῶνας, ὁ δὲ γυμνικὸς ἀπ' ἀρχῆς ὡς ἐπὶ τὸ
πλεῖστον οὕτως κατέστη, τοῖς δ' Ὀλυμπίοις πάντα
προσθήκη πλὴν τοῦ δρόμου γέγονεν· πολλὰ δὲ καὶ
θέντες ἔπειτ' ἀνεῖλον, ὥσπερ τὸν τῆς κάλπης ἀγῶνα
καὶ τὸν τῆς ἀπήνης· ἀνῃρέθη δὲ καὶ παισὶ πεντάθ-
λοις στέφανος τεθείς· καὶ ὅλως πολλὰ περὶ τὴν
πανήγυριν νενεωτέρισται. δέδια δ' εἰπεῖν[5] ὅτι πάλαι καὶ μονομαχίας ἀγὼν περὶ Πῖσαν ἤγετο μέχρι
φόνου καὶ σφαγῆς τῶν ἡττωμένων καὶ ὑποπιπτόν-
των, μή με πάλιν ἀπαιτῆτε[6] τῆς ἱστορίας βεβαι-
D ωτὴν κἂν διαφύγῃ τὴν μνήμην ἐν οἴνῳ τὸ ὄνομα
καταγέλαστος γένωμαι."

ΠΡΟΒΛΗΜΑ Γ

Τίς αἰτία δι' ἣν ἡ πίτυς ἱερὰ Ποσειδῶνος ἐνομίσθη καὶ Διονύσου·
καὶ ὅτι τὸ πρῶτον ἐστεφάνουν τῇ πίτυι τοὺς Ἴσθμια νικῶντας,
ἔπειτα σελίνῳ, νυνὶ δὲ πάλιν τῇ πίτυι

Collocuntur Praxiteles, Lucanius, Plutarchus, rhetor, alii

1. Ἡ πίτυς ἐζητεῖτο καθ' ὃν λόγον ἐν Ἰσθμίοις[7]

---

[1] So Preller, Herwerden : σικυωνίῳ.
[2] ἐπίκω or ἐπίκω lac. 2 T.
[3] π. δὶς Bernardakis : ποιηματίαις.
[4] So Meziriacus : γε.
[5] So Reiske : εἶπεν.
[6] So Xylander : ἀπατᾶτε.   [7] So Xylander : ἰσθμοῖς.

nians was deposited a golden tablet dedicated by Aristomachê [a] of Erythrae, twice victor in epic verse at the Isthmia.

" Nor should we," I continued, " be overawed by Olympia, as if its policies with respect to types of competition were as undeviating and immutable as fate. The Pythia acquired only three or four musical contests as additions to the athletic competition, which was established from the beginning largely as it is now ; whereas at Olympia only the footrace is original, everything else being in addition. Many events were added and then dropped, for instance the trotting race [b] and the four-wheeler.[c] They abolished also the award for the boys' pentathlon. In general, many innovations have been made in the festival. I hesitate to say that in older times the duels at Pisa [d] were carried to the point of manslaughter for the defeated as they fell, for fear that you may again demand authority for my statement and that, if the name escapes my memory because of the wine, I shall become an object of ridicule."

QUESTION 3

Why the pine was held sacred to Poseidon and Dionysus ; originally the victor's crown at the Isthmia was of pine, later of celery, but now again is of pine

Speakers : Praxiteles, Lucanius, Plutarch, a professor of rhetoric and others

1. The pine, and why it was used for the crown at the

[a] Either a Sibyl or simply a poetess. It is not clear which Erythrae is meant. The greatest of all Sibyls, Herophilê, came apparently from the great city of Erythrae in Ionia, though this was disputed (see Pausanias, x. 12).

[b] See Pausanias, v. 9. 1.   [c] See Pausanias, *ibid.*

[d] District in which the shrine of Olympia lay.

(675) στέμμα γέγονε· καὶ γὰρ ἦν τὸ δεῖπνον ἐν Κορίνθῳ,
Ἰσθμίων ἀγομένων ἑστιῶντος ἡμᾶς[1] Λουκανίου τοῦ
E ἀρχιερέως. Πραξιτέλης μὲν οὖν ὁ περιηγητὴς τὸ
μυθῶδες ἐπῆγεν, ὡς λεγόμενον εὑρεθῆναι τὸ σῶμα
τοῦ Μελικέρτου πίτυι προσβεβρασμένον ὑπὸ τῆς
θαλάττης· καὶ γὰρ οὐ πρόσω Μεγάρων εἶναι
τόπον, ὃς " Καλῆς δρόμος " ἐπονομάζεται, δι᾽ οὗ
φάναι Μεγαρεῖς τὴν Ἰνὼ τὸ παιδίον ἔχουσαν δρα-
μεῖν ἐπὶ τὴν θάλατταν. κοινῶς δ᾽ ὑπὸ πολλῶν
λεγομένου ὡς ἴδιόν ἐστι στέμμα Ποσειδῶνος ἡ
πίτυς, Λουκανίου δὲ προστιθέντος ὅτι καὶ τῷ Διονύσῳ καθωσιωμένον τὸ φυτὸν οὐκ ἀπὸ τρόπου
ταῖς περὶ τὸν Μελικέρτην συνῳκείωται τιμαῖς, αὐτὸ
τοῦτο ζήτησιν παρεῖχεν, ᾧτινι λόγῳ Ποσειδῶνι
F καὶ Διονύσῳ τὴν πίτυν οἱ παλαιοὶ καθωσίωσαν.

Ἐδόκει δ᾽ ἡμῖν[2] μηδὲν εἶναι παράλογον· ἀμφό-
τεροι γὰρ οἱ θεοὶ τῆς ὑγρᾶς καὶ γονίμου κύριοι
δοκοῦσιν ἀρχῆς εἶναι· καὶ Ποσειδῶνί γε Φυταλμίῳ
Διονύσῳ δὲ Δενδρίτῃ πάντες ὡς ἔπος εἰπεῖν
Ἕλληνες θύουσιν. οὐ μὴν ἀλλὰ κατ᾽ ἰδίαν τῷ
676 Ποσειδῶνι φαίη τις ἂν τὴν πίτυν προσήκειν, οὐχ
ὡς Ἀπολλόδωρος οἴεται παράλιον φυτὸν οὖσαν
οὐδ᾽ ὅτι φιλήνεμός ἐστιν ὥσπερ ἡ θάλασσα (καὶ

---

[1] So Turnebus : ἡμῖν.
[2] δ᾽ ἡμῖν Bernardakis, δέ μοι Xylander : δέμιν.

---

[a] Praxiteles is again introduced later, Book VIII, Question 4, 723 f ff., in another discussion on the crowns awarded
at the Games.
[b] Or " interpreter." Cf. Parke and Wormell, The Delphic
Oracle, ii, pp. xiii ff. Minar in the LCL translation at 723 f
takes the word in its other sense of " geographer."
[c] The young son of Ino, who was driven to leap with him

390

Isthmia, was the subject of a discussion at a dinner given us in Corinth itself during the Games by Lucanius, the chief priest. Praxiteles,[a] the official guide,[b] appealed to mythology, citing the legend that the body of Melicertes [c] was found cast up by the sea at the foot of a pine. Not far from Megara there is, he pointed out, a place named " The Beauty's Flight," along which, according to the Megarians, Ino rushed down to the sea with her child in her arms. Many of the company stated that according to common belief the crown of pine belonged specifically to Poseidon ; but Lucanius added that, because the tree was dedicated also to Dionysus, it had quite appropriately become a part of the cult of Melicertes. It was this last remark that prompted our inquiry how the ancients came to dedicate the pine to Poseidon and Dionysus.

To us there seemed nothing illogical in this, because both gods are by common acceptance sovereign over the domains of the moist and the generative. Practically all Greeks sacrifice to Poseidon the Life-Giver [d] and to Dionysus the Tree-god.[e] Still, one might well say that the pine is especially connected with Poseidon, not, as Apollodorus [f] believes, because it grows by the sea, nor because it, like the

into the sea. He became the sea god Palaemon, to whom according to some the Isthmian Games were originally dedicated. Ino was an aunt, and one of the nurses, of Dionysus.

[d] For Poseidon Phytalmios see *Inscr. Graec.* ii². 5051, xii (1). 905 ; Farnell, *Cults of the Greek States*, iv, p. 6.

[e] For Dionysus Dendrites see Farnell, *op. cit.* v, p. 118. Dionysus was a vegetation divinity, not merely a wine god.

[f] Apollodorus of Athens, born *c.* 180 B.C., author of many scholarly works including a mythological *Bibliothekê* and a work *On the Gods. Frag. Griech. Historiker* (F. Jacoby), 244 F 123.

(676) γὰρ τοῦτό τινες λέγουσιν), ἀλλὰ διὰ τὰς ναυπηγίας
μάλιστα. καὶ γὰρ αὐτὴ καὶ τὰ ἀδελφὰ δένδρα,
πεῦκαι καὶ στρόβιλοι, τῶν τε ξύλων παρέχει τὰ
πλοϊμώτατα πίττης τε καὶ ῥητίνης ἀλοιφήν, ἧς
ἄνευ τῶν συμπαγέντων ὄφελος οὐδὲν ἐν τῇ θαλάττῃ.

Τῷ δὲ Διονύσῳ τὴν πίτυν ἀνιέρωσαν ὡς ἐφηδύ-
νουσαν τὸν οἶνον· τὰ γὰρ πιτυώδη χωρία λέγουσιν
ἡδύοινον τὴν ἄμπελον φέρειν. καὶ τὴν θερμότητα
τῆς γῆς Θεόφραστος αἰτιᾶται· καθόλου γὰρ ἐν
B ἀργιλώδεσι τόποις φύεσθαι τὴν πίτυν, εἶναι δὲ τὴν
ἄργιλον θερμήν, διὸ καὶ συνεκπέττειν τὸν οἶνον,
ὥσπερ καὶ τὸ ὕδωρ ἐλαφρότατον καὶ ἥδιστον ἡ
ἄργιλος ἀναδίδωσιν, ἔτι δὲ καὶ καταμιγνυμένη πρὸς
σῖτον ἐπίμετρον ποιεῖ δαψιλές, ἁδρύνουσα καὶ δι-
ογκοῦσα τῇ θερμότητι τὸν πυρόν.

Οὐ μὴν ἀλλὰ καὶ τῆς πίτυος αὐτῆς εἰκὸς ἀπολαύειν τὴν ἄμπελον, ἐχούσης ἐπιτηδειότητα πολλὴν
πρὸς σωτηρίαν οἴνου καὶ διαμονήν· τῇ τε γὰρ
πίττῃ πάντες ἐξαλείφουσι τὰ ἀγγεῖα, καὶ τῆς ῥητίνης ὑπομιγνύουσι πολλοὶ τῷ οἴνῳ καθάπερ Εὐβο-
εῖς τῶν Ἑλλαδικῶν καὶ τῶν Ἰταλικῶν οἱ περὶ τὸν
C Πάδον οἰκοῦντες, ἐκ δὲ τῆς περὶ Βίενναν Γαλατίας
ὁ πισσίτης οἶνος κατακομίζεται, διαφερόντως τι-
μώμενος ὑπὸ Ῥωμαίων. οὐ γὰρ μόνον εὐωδίαν τινὰ
τὰ τοιαῦτα προσδίδωσιν, ἀλλὰ καὶ τὸν οἶνον[1] παρ-
ίστησι ταχέως ἐξαιροῦντα[2] τῇ θερμότητι τοῦ οἴνου
τὸ νεαρὸν καὶ ὑδατῶδες.

---

[1] ἐμποιεῖ after οἶνον deleted by Hubert, εὐφυῆ Basel edition·
εὔποτον Wyttenbach.   [2] So Madvig : ἐξαίρων.

---

[a] Hubert calls attention to the totally different theory also
attributed to Theophrastus at 648 D *supra* ; the present reference has not been traced in the extant works of Theophrastus.

sea, loves the wind (for some argue to this effect) ;
but above all because of its use in shipbuilding. The
pine and kindred trees, like fir and stone-pine, produce the woods most suitable for shipbuilding, as well
as pitch and resin for waterproofing, without which
no hull is seaworthy.

On the other hand, the pine has been dedicated to
Dionysus because it is thought to sweeten wine ; for
they say that country abounding in pines produces
sweet-wine grapes. Theophrastus attributes this
effect to the heat in the soil,[a] saying that in general
the pine grows in clayey soil, and clay, being hot,
matures the wine, even as it also yields the lightest
and sweetest spring-water. Incidentally, if clay is
mixed with wheat, its heat considerably increases the
bulk by distending and thickening the kernels.

It is also probable, however, that the pine itself
contributes to the growth of the grapevine, since this
tree is rich in substances efficacious in preserving
wine and guaranteeing its quality ; pitch is always
used to seal wine-vessels, and many people mix wine
with resin. For instance, in Greece the Euboeans do
so, and in Italy those who live near the Po ; pitch-
flavoured wine [b] is imported from the region about
Vienna [c] in Gaul and is highly esteemed by the
Romans. These uses of pitch not only give the wine
a certain bouquet but add body [d] to it, because they
quickly remove by heat the insipidity of the new wine.

[b] For further discussion of the use of pitch in connection
with wine see Pliny, *Nat. Hist.* xiv. 124 ff., xvi. 22.53 ff. Compare the modern *retsinato*.

[c] The modern Vienne in France. *Cf.* Pliny, *Nat. Hist.*
xxiii. 24.47, on the near-by Helvian district.

[d] Or " potency " (*vigorem*), after Hubert, who cites Theophrastus, *De Causis Plant.* vi. 16. 5-6. (Hubert's "v" is a slip.)

(676)   2. Ὡς δὲ ταῦτ' ἐρρήθη, τῶν ῥητόρων ὁ μάλιστα
δοκῶν ἀναγνώσμασιν ἐντυγχάνειν ἐλευθερίοις,[1] " ὦ
πρὸς θεῶν," εἶπεν, " οὐ γὰρ ἐχθὲς ἡ πίτυς ἐνταῦθα καὶ πρῴην[2] στέμμα γέγονε τῶν Ἰσθμίων, πρότερον δὲ τοῖς[3] σελίνοις ἐστέφοντο; καὶ τοῦτ' ἔστι
μὲν ἐν τῇ κωμῳδίᾳ φιλαργύρου τινὸς ἀκοῦσαι λέ-
γοντος·

τὰ δ' Ἴσθμι' ἀποδοίμην ἂν ἡδέως ὅσου
D   ὁ τῶν σελίνων στέφανός ἐστιν ὤνιος.

ἱστορεῖ δὲ καὶ Τίμαιος ὁ συγγραφεύς, ὅτι Κοριν-
θίοις,[4] ὁπηνίκα μαχούμενοι πρὸς Καρχηδονίους
ἐβάδιζον ὑπὲρ τῆς Σικελίας, ἐνέβαλόν τινες ὄνοι[5]
σέλινα κομίζοντες· οἰωνισαμένων δὲ τῶν πολλῶν
τὸ σύμβολον ὡς οὐ χρηστόν, ὅτι δοκεῖ τὸ σέλινον
ἐπικήδειον[6] εἶναι καὶ τοὺς[7] ἐπισφαλῶς νοσοῦντας
δεῖσθαι τοῦ σελίνου φαμέν, ἄλλως θ'[8] ὁ Τιμολέων
ἐθάρρυνεν αὐτοὺς καὶ ἀνεμίμνησκε τῶν Ἰσθμοῖ σελίνων, οἷς ἀναστέφουσι Κορίνθιοι τοὺς νικῶντας.

" Ἔτι τοίνυν ἡ Ἀντιγόνου ναυαρχὶς ἀναφύσασα
περὶ πρύμναν αὐτομάτως σέλινον Ἰσθμία ἐπωνο-

---

[1] Ἐλευθέριος (usually a divine epithet) Reiske.

[2] After this word a quaternion of T is lost, to 680 D ἱστορεῖται δέ, but copies are preserved, which we cite from Hubert,
checked against the photostat of E.

[3] δὲ τοῖς Stephanus, γὰρ τοῖς Turnebus according to Hutten: αὐτοῖς.

[4] So Xylander, Hubert: Κορίνθιοι.

[5] So Reiske: οὐ (οὐ οὐ E), which Wyttenbach and Hutten
delete. In the Life of Timoleon, xxvi, ἡμίονοι.

[6] So Faehse (Bolkestein, Adv. Crit. p. 78, see also Pliny,
Nat. Hist. xx. 113): ἀνεπιτήδειον.

[7] So Basel edition: τό.

[8] ἄλλως θ' Bases (cf. Life of Timoleon, xxvi): ὡς.

2. On hearing these remarks, a professor of rhetoric, who was reputed to have a wider acquaintance with polite literature than anyone else, said, " In heaven's name ! Wasn't it only yesterday or the day before that the pine became the garland of victory at the Isthmia ? Formerly it was celery.[a] This is evident from the comedy where a miser says :

> I'd gladly sell the entire Isthmian show
> For the price at which the celery crown will go.[b]

The historian Timaeus [c] records the following anecdote. During their campaign against the Carthaginians in the war for Sicily, the Corinthians suddenly saw some asses carrying celery. Most of the troops interpreted the encounter as a bad omen, because celery is regarded as a symbol of mourning,[d] and we say of those who are critically ill that ' a sprig of celery is all you can give them now.' Timoleon,[e] however, restored the spirits of his men precisely by reminding them of the celery used as the crown of victory at the Isthmus.

" And then there is the flagship of Antigonus,[f] which was given the name ' Isthmia ' because celery

---

[a] Unblanched celery was more serviceable for garlands than our modern table variety. See A. C. Andrews in *Class. Phil.* xliv (1949), pp. 91 ff.

[b] *Com. adesp.* 153 (Kock, *Com. Att. Frag.* iii, p. 438).

[c] Celebrated historian of Sicily, *c.* 356–260 B.C. See Truesdell S. Brown, *Timaeus of Tauromenium* (Univ. of California Press, 1958), especially p. 87.

[d] So also Pliny, *Nat. Hist.* xx. 113. *Cf.* A. C. Andrews, *loc. cit.* p. 98.

[e] Timoleon, a Corinthian general fighting for Syracuse, defeated the Carthaginians at the Crimisus near Segesta in 341 or 339 B.C. See Plutarch, *Life of Timoleon,* xxvi.

[f] King Antigonus Gonatas of Macedon, 283–240 B.C., or Antigonus Doson, 227–221 B.C.

(676)
E μάσθη. καὶ τοῦτο δὴ τὸ σκολιὸν ἐπίγραμμα δηλοῖ[1]
κεραμεᾶν[2] ἀμύστιδα βεβυσμένην[3] σελίνῳ· σύγκειται
δ' οὕτω[4]·

ἡ Κωλιὰς γῆ[5] πυρὶ κατηθαλωμένη
κεύθει κελαινὸν αἷμα Διονύσου θοοῦ,[6]
ἔχουσα κλῶνας Ἰσθμικοὺς ἀνὰ στόμα.

ἦ ταῦτ'," εἶπεν, " οὐκ ἀνεγνώκαθ' ὑμεῖς οἱ[7] τὴν
πίτυν ὡς οὐκ ἐπείσακτον οὐδὲ νέον ἀλλὰ πάτριον
καὶ παλαιὸν δὴ στέμμα τῶν Ἰσθμίων σεμνύνοντες;"
ἐκίνησεν οὖν τοὺς[8] νέους ὡς ἂν πολυμαθὴς ἀνὴρ
καὶ πολυγράμματος.

3. Ὁ μέντοι Λουκάνιος εἰς ἐμὲ βλέψας ἅμα καὶ
μειδιῶν, " ὦ Πόσειδον," ἔφη, " τοῦ πλήθους τῶν
γραμμάτων· ἕτεροι δ' ἡμῶν τῆς ἀμαθίας ὡς ἔοικε
F καὶ τῆς ἀνηκοΐας ἀπέλαυον ἀναπείθοντες τοὔν-
αντίον, ὡς ἡ μὲν πίτυς ἦν στέμμα τῶν ἀγώνων
πάτριον, ἐκ δὲ Νεμέας κατὰ ζῆλον ὁ[9] τοῦ σελίνου
ξένος ὢν ἐπεισῆλθε δι' Ἡρακλέα καὶ κρατήσας ἠ-
μαύρωσεν ἐκεῖνον[10] ὡς ἱερὸν ἐπιτήδειον.[11] εἶτα μέντοι χρόνῳ πάλιν ἀνακτησαμένη τὸ πάτριον γέρας ἡ
πίτυς ἀνθεῖ τῇ τιμῇ."

----

[1] So Wyttenbach, Madvig: δῆλον.
[2] So Bernardakis, κεραμέαν Reiske, κεραμίαν Madvig: κε-
ραμέα.
[3] ἀμύστιδα βεβυσμένην Madvig: νομίζει διαβεβυσμένην.
[4] οὕτω Madvig, οὕτως ἔχον Wyttenbach: οὕτω χθών.
[5] ἡ Κωλιὰς γῆ Winckelmann, Madvig (who cites " iam
interpretatio Latina "), (χθὼν) ἥδε πλαστή " this fashioned
earth " Wyttenbach, ἡ Παλλάδος γῆ A. Junius, (χθὼν) ἡ
Πελασγὴ Stephanus: ἡ παλὰς γῆ.
[6] Warmington suggests θεοῦ (god) for θοοῦ (rushing).
[7] ἀνεγνώκαθ' ὑμεῖς οἱ Franke: ἀνέγνωκατευμαι σοι (and
slight variations).

sprouted spontaneously on its stern. I can cite also
a scolion which mentions an earthen vessel closed with
celery. The words run as follows :

> The Attic potter's clay,[a] baked in the fire,
> Conceals the rushing wine-god's dark red blood,
> And bears the Isthmian sprigs inside its mouth.

Have you not read this, that you exalt the pine as
ancient crown of the Isthmia, and consider it not as a
new importation but as a heritage from our fathers ? "
The rhetorician, you may be sure, impressed the
younger men by his great learning and wide reading.

3. But Lucanius looked at me with a smile, and said,
" Poseidon ! What a parade of quotations ! It looks
as if other people have taken advantage of our untutored ignorance to convince us, on the contrary,
that the pine was the traditional garland at these
games, and that the crown of celery was imported
more recently from Nemea because of rivalry with
Heracles.[b] According to them, although the celery
prevailed as a fitting sacred symbol and caused the
pine to be forgotten, nevertheless in the course of
time the pine recovered its original prerogative, to
flourish now in high honour."

---

[a] From Colias, the promontory where fine clay was dug.

[b] According to Plutarch, *Life of Theseus*, xxv. 4, the Isthmian Games were established by Theseus in emulation of
Heracles's foundation of the Olympic Games. *Cf. infra*, 677
B, in the quotation from Callimachus, where we further note
the mention of Nemea, which is also connected with Heracles.

---

[8] οὖν τοὺς Bryan according to Bernardakis, Reiske : οὐ.

[9] Stephanus added στέφανος, but that may be simply implied, *cf.* Hubert.   [10] ἐκείνην Wyttenbach.

[11] ἱεροῖς ἐπιτήδειος Stephanus, ἥρωϊ ἀνεπιτήδειον Wyttenbach,
ἡρῷον ἐπινίκιον " an emblem of Heracles's victory " Kronenberg.

677 Ἐγὼ γοῦν ἀνεπειθόμην καὶ προσεῖχον, ὥστε καὶ
τῶν μαρτυρίων ἐκμαθεῖν πολλὰ καὶ μνημονεύειν, Εὐ-
φορίωνα μὲν οὕτω πως περὶ Μελικέρτου λέγοντα·

κλαίοντες δέ τε κοῦρον ἐπ᾽ ἀγχιάλοις[1] πιτύεσσι
κάτθεσαν, ὀκκότε[2] δὴ στεφάνωμ᾽[3] ἄθλοις φορέον-
ται.[4]
οὐ γάρ πω τρηχεῖα λαβὴ κατεμήσατο χειρῶν
Μήνης[5] παῖδα χάρωνα παρ᾽ Ἀσωποῦ γενετείρῃ,
ἐξότε πυκνὰ σέλινα κατὰ κροτάφων ἐβάλοντο,

Καλλίμαχον δὲ μᾶλλον διασαφοῦντα· λέγει δ᾽ ὁ
Ἡρακλῆς αὐτῷ[6] περὶ τοῦ σελίνου·

B   καί μιν Ἀλητιάδαι, πουλὺ γεγειότερον
τοῦδε παρ᾽ Αἰγαίωνι θεῷ τελέοντες ἀγῶνα,
θήσουσιν νίκης σύμβολον Ἰσθμιάδος,
ζήλῳ τῶν Νεμέηθε· πίτυν δ᾽ ἀποτιμήσουσιν,
ἣ πρὶν ἀγωνιστὰς ἔστεφε τοὺς Ἐφύρῃ.

Ἔτι δ᾽ οἶμαι Προκλέους[7] ἐντετυχηκέναι γραφῇ
περὶ τῶν Ἰσθμίων ἱστοροῦντος, ὅτι τὸν πρῶτον
ἀγῶν᾽ ἔθεσαν περὶ στεφάνου πιτυΐνου· ὕστερον δέ,

---

[1] So Meineke, Powell, αἰγιαλοῦ Schneider : αἰλίσι.
[2] ὀκκόθε " of which " Reiske, Powell.
[3] So Bernardakis : στεφάνων.   [4] φορέοντο Scheidweiler.
[5] So Meineke : μήμης (μίμης E).
[6] Perhaps παρ᾽ αὐτῷ Post.
[7] So Turnebus : πατροκλέους or περικλέους mss. except Paris
2074.

---

[a] Probably Euphorion of Chalcis, born c. 276 B.C., a poet
proverbially obscure in style and deviousness of mythological
reference. (See Powell, *Collectanea Alexandrina*, Euph. 84.)
[b] The Nemean lion, son of the Moon (Menê or Selenê),
according to Hyginus and Epimenides (Diels, *Frag. d. Vorsokratiker*, Epimenides, frag. 2).

I for one was persuaded and gave the matter my attention and have committed to memory many authorities that go to prove Lucanius right. Euphorion,[a] for instance, wrote about Melicertes somewhat to this effect :

> Weeping they laid the youth by the shore on boughs of pine,
> When still they bore them as the victor's crown.
> Not yet had savage grip of hands brought down
> Menê's fierce-eyed son [b] by Asopus' daughter's side. [c]
> But ever since they've put full wreaths of celery on their brows.

I remember Callimachus also,[d] who makes the point clearer. In his poem Heracles says of celery :

> The sons of Aletes,[e] keeping festival more ancient far than this,
> By god Aegaeon's shore this crown shall make the badge of Isthmic victory ;
> In rivalry with Nemea, but the pine they shall misprise
> Which erstwhile crowned each champion there at Ephyra.[f]

It seems to me that I have also read a passage on the Isthmia by Procles,[g] in which the author records that the first contest was held for a crown of pine, but

---

[c] The stream Nemea named after the daughter (*geneteira*) of Asopus, god of the river near the seat of the Nemean Games. See Pausanias, v. 22. 6.

[d] This passage is from *Aetia*, iii, frag. 59 Pfeiffer (ed. Trypanis, LCL, 1958 and 1968, pp. 44 f.), lines 5-9.

[e] National hero of Dorian Corinth. Pindar, *Olympian* xiii. 14 (17) and *Isthmian* ii. 15 (22), with the scholia.

[f] Said to be the old name of Corinth, but the authenticity of this very ancient identification is challenged by Lenschau in *RE*, Suppl. iv. 1009. 3.

[g] *Frag. Hist. Graec.* (C. Müller), ii. 342 in a note to frag. 2 of Menecrates the Academic, whose pupil Procles was. The title of his work seems to have been *On Festivals*.

(677) τοῦ ἀγῶνος ἱεροῦ γενομένου, ἐκ τῆς Νεμεακῆς
πανηγύρεως μετήνεγκαν ἐνταῦθα τὸν τοῦ σελίνου
στέφανον. ὁ δὲ Προκλῆς[1] οὗτος ἦν εἷς τῶν ἐν
Ἀκαδημίᾳ Ξενοκράτει συσχολασάντων.

C ΠΡΟΒΛΗΜΑ Δ

Περὶ τοῦ " ζωρότερον δὲ κέραιε "[2]

Collocuntur Niceratus, Sosicles, Antipater, Plutarchus

1. Γελοῖος ἐδόκει τισὶ τῶν συνδειπνούντων ὁ
Ἀχιλλεὺς ἀκρατότερον ἐγχεῖν τὸν Πάτροκλον κελεύων, εἶτ' αἰτίαν τοιαύτην ἐπιλέγων·

οἱ γὰρ φίλτατοι ἄνδρες ἐμῷ ὑπέασι μελάθρῳ.

Νικήρατος μὲν οὖν ὁ ἑταῖρος ἡμῶν ὁ Μακεδὼν
ἄντικρυς ἀπισχυρίζετο[3] μὴ ἄκρατον ἀλλὰ θερμὸν
εἰρῆσθαι τὸ " ζωρὸν " ἀπὸ τοῦ ζωτικοῦ καὶ τῆς
ζέσεως, ὃ δὴ καὶ λόγον ἔχειν, ἀνδρῶν ἑταίρων
παρόντων νέον ἐξ ὑπαρχῆς κεράννυσθαι κρατῆρα·
D καὶ γὰρ ἡμᾶς, ὅταν τοῖς θεοῖς ἀποσπένδειν μέλ-
λωμεν, νεοκρᾶτα ποιεῖν. Σωσικλῆς δ' ὁ ποιητὴς
τοῦ Ἐμπεδοκλέους ἐπιμνησθεὶς εἰρηκότος ἐν τῇ
καθόλου μεταβολῇ γίγνεσθαι " ζωρά τε τὰ πρὶν
ἄκρητα " μᾶλλον ἔφη τὸ εὔκρατον ἢ τὸ ἄκρατον
ὑπὸ τοῦ ἀνδρὸς ζωρὸν λέγεσθαι καὶ μηδέν γε
κωλύειν ἐπικελεύεσθαι τῷ Πατρόκλῳ τὸν Ἀχιλλέα

_____

[1] So Paris 2074 : πατροκλῆς (πρόκλης E).
[2] κέραιρε Vaticanus 1676, Athenaeus, x, 423 e, κέρερε E.
[3] So Reiske : ἐπισχυρίζεται.

_____

[a] Head of the Academy 339–314 B.C.
[b] Athenaeus, 423 e, appears to be derived from this Question or its source, cf. Bolkestein, Adv. Crit. pp. 26 ff.

that later, when the contest was made sacred, they adopted the celery crown from the Nemean Games. The Procles I refer to was a fellow student of Xenocrates [a] in the Academy.

QUESTION 4 [b]

On Homer's " Mix the wine stronger "

Speakers : Niceratus, Sosicles, Antipater, Plutarch

1. At a dinner, some of the guests said that they thought Achilles ridiculous in urging Patroclus to pour stronger [c] wine and then adding as a reason,

These friends most dear are under my roof. [d]

Niceratus, our friend from Macedonia, went so far as to maintain flatly that Homer's word *zōros* means not " unmixed " but " hot," deriving it from *zōtikos* (life-giving) and *zesis* (boiling). In his opinion it was right to mix a new bowl when friends come, even as we mix fresh wine when about to pour libations to the gods. But Sosicles the poet, recalling that Empedocles [e] had said that in the universal evolution " what was until then *akrêtos* (unmixed) became *zôros*," argued that *zôros* was used by the poet in the sense of " well-mixed " (*eukratos*) rather than " unmixed " (*akratos*). Nothing hindered Achilles from urging Patroclus to prepare well-mixed wine for drink-

[c] The guests here use *akratoteron* as a synonym for Homer's *zōroteron* (*Iliad*, ix. 203). See now *Class. Rev.* xvi, N.S. (1966), pp. 135 f. M. L. West); xvii (1967), pp 245 f. (F. Solmsen).

[d] *Iliad*, ix. 204.

[e] Empedocles, frag. 35, line 15, in Diels's *Vorsokratiker* : Aristotle's reading of the fragment (*Poetics*, 1461 a 23), if the ms. is sound, would have robbed Sosicles of his argument.

(677) παρασκευάζειν εὔκρατον εἰς πόσιν τὸν οἶνον· εἰ δ᾽
ἀντὶ τοῦ ζωροῦ " ζωρότερον " εἶπεν, ὥσπερ " δεξι-
τερὸν " ἀντὶ τοῦ δεξιοῦ καὶ " θηλύτερον " ἀντὶ τοῦ
θήλεος, οὐκ ἄτοπον εἶναι· χρῆσθαι γὰρ ἐπιεικῶς
ἀντὶ τῶν ἁπλῶν τοῖς συγκριτικοῖς. Ἀντίπατρος δ᾽
ὁ ἑταῖρος ἔφη τοὺς μὲν ἐνιαυτοὺς ἀρχαϊκῶς
E " ὥρους " λέγεσθαι, τὸ δὲ¹ ζα μέγεθος εἰωθέναι²
σημαίνειν· ὅθεν τὸν πολυετῆ³ καὶ παλαιὸν οἶνον
ὑπὸ τοῦ Ἀχιλλέως ζωρὸν ὠνομάσθαι.⁴

2. Ἐγὼ δ᾽ ἀνεμίμνησκον αὐτούς, ὅτι τῷ⁵ " ζωρότερον " τὸ θερμὸν⁶ ἔνιοι⁷ σημαίνεσθαι λέγουσι τῷ δὲ
θερμοτέρῳ τὸ τάχιον· ὥσπερ ἡμεῖς ἐγκελευόμεθα
πολλάκις τοῖς διακονοῦσι θερμότερον ἅπτεσθαι τῆς
διακονίας. ἀλλὰ μειρακιώδη τὴν φιλοτιμίαν αὐτῶν
ἀπέφαινον, δεδιότων ὁμολογεῖν ἀκρατότερον εἰρῆσθαι τὸ ζωρότερον, ὡς ἐν ἀτόπῳ τινὶ τοῦ Ἀχιλλέως ἐσομένου· καθάπερ ὁ Ἀμφιπολίτης Ζωΐλος⁸
ὑπελάμβανεν, ἀγνοῶν ὅτι πρῶτον μὲν ὁ Ἀχιλλεὺς
τὸν Φοίνικα καὶ τὸν Ὀδυσσέα πρεσβυτέρους ὄν-
F τας εἰδὼς οὐχ ὑδαρεῖ χαίροντας ἀλλ᾽ ἀκρατοτέρῳ,
καθάπερ οἱ ἄλλοι γέροντες, ἐπιτεῖναι κελεύει τὴν
κρᾶσιν.

Ἔπειτα Χείρωνος ὢν μαθητὴς καὶ τῆς περὶ τὸ
σῶμα διαίτης οὐκ ἄπειρος ἐλογίζετο δήπουθεν, ὅτι
τοῖς ἀργοῦσι καὶ σχολάζουσι παρὰ τὸ εἰωθὸς σώμα-
678 σιν ἀνειμένη καὶ μαλακωτέρα κρᾶσις ἁρμόζει· καὶ
γὰρ τοῖς ἵπποις ἐμβάλλει μετὰ τῶν ἄλλων χορτα-

---

¹ δὲ added by Turnebus.
² So Reiske : εἴωθεν.
³ πολυετῆ Stephanus : πολυτελῆ, which might be right.
⁴ ὀνομάζεσθαι E.
⁵ So Stephanus : τὸ.
⁶ θερμότερον Hubert. See Aristotle, *Poetics*, 1461 a 14-16.

ing, nor was it strange for him to use the comparative form *zôroteros* for *zôros* just as he uses *dexiteros* for *dexios* ("right hand") and *thêlyteros* for *thêlys* ("female"), because Homer is apt to use the comparative forms interchangeably with the positive. Our friend Antipater, however, said that in ancient times the year was called *hôros*, and that customarily the prefix *za* had intensive force ; this explains why Achilles calls wine that is many years old and aged *zôros*.

2. But I reminded them that some maintain that the term *zôroteros* signifies " hot " (*thermos*) and that *thermoteros* (hotter) signifies " faster," as when we urge our helpers and servants to apply themselves " more warmly " (*thermoteron*) to their work. On the other hand, I pointed out, their own gallant effort was schoolboyish because they were afraid to admit that *zôroteron* means " stronger " (*akratoteron*), as if this would put Achilles in an awkward position. Zoïlus of Amphipolis [a] made just this mistake, not realizing that, in the first place, Achilles told Patroclus to strengthen the mixture because he knew that older men like Phoenix and Odysseus prefer their wine strong rather than watery.

Secondly, Achilles, the pupil of Cheiron and therefore not ignorant of the principles of diet, must have reflected that a weaker, milder mixture was suitable for those (like himself and Patroclus) who were enjoying unaccustomed leisure and idleness. For just this reason he feeds the horses celery [b] along with

---

[a] Cynic philosopher and critic, famous as the " Scourge of Homer," 4th century B.C. See Sandys, *Hist. Class. Schol.* i, pp. 108 ff. [b] *Iliad*, ii. 775 ff.

---

[7] So Stephanus : ἐνίοις or ἐνίους.
[8] Ζώιλος Basel edition : ζῆλος.

(678) σμάτων τὸ σέλινον οὐκ ἀλόγως, ἀλλ' ὅτι βλάπ-
τονται μὲν οἱ[1] σχολάζοντες ἀσυνήθως ἵπποι τοὺς
πόδας, ἔστι δὲ τούτου μάλιστ' ἴαμα τὸ σέλινον·
ἄλλοις γοῦν οὐκ ἂν εὕροις παραβαλλόμενον ἵπποις
ἐν Ἰλιάδι σέλινον ἤ τινα τοιοῦτον χιλόν· ἀλλ'
ἰατρὸς ὢν ὁ Ἀχιλλεὺς τῶν θ' ἵππων πρὸς τὸν
καιρὸν οἰκείως ἐπεμελεῖτο καὶ τῷ σώματι τὴν ἐλα-
φροτάτην δίαιταν, ὡς ὑγιεινοτάτην ἐν τῷ σχολά-
ζειν, παρεσκεύαζεν· ἄνδρας δ' ἐν μάχῃ καὶ ἀγῶνι
δι' ἡμέρας γεγενημένους οὐχ ὁμοίως ἀξιῶν διαιτᾶν
B τοῖς ἀργοῦσιν ἐπιτεῖναι τὴν κρᾶσιν ἐκέλευσε. καὶ
μὴν οὐδὲ φύσει φαίνεται φίλοινος ἀλλ' ἀπηνὴς ὁ
Ἀχιλλεύς·

οὐ γάρ τι γλυκύθυμος ἀνὴρ ἦν οὐδ' ἀγανόφρων,
ἀλλὰ μάλ' ἐμμεμαώς·

καί που παρρησιαζόμενος ὑπὲρ αὐτοῦ, " πολλάς,"
φησίν, " ἀύπνους νύκτας ἰαῦσαι"· βραχὺς δ'
ὕπνος οὐκ ἐξαρκεῖ τοῖς χρωμένοις ἀκράτῳ. λοι-
δορούμενος δὲ τῷ Ἀγαμέμνονι πρῶτον αὐτὸν
" οἰνοβαρῆ " προσείρηκεν, ὡς μάλιστα τῶν νοση-
μάτων τὴν οἰνοφλυγίαν προβαλλόμενος. διὰ ταῦτα
δὴ πάντα λόγον εἶχεν αὐτὸν ἐννοῆσαι, τῶν ἀνδρῶν
ἐπιφανέντων, μή ποθ' ἡ συνήθης κρᾶσις αὐτῷ τοῦ
οἴνου πρὸς ἐκείνους ἀνειμένη καὶ ἀνάρμοστός ἐστιν.

---

[1] οἱ Palatinus 170, Basel edition : οἷς.

other fodder—quite rightly, because celery is the specific remedy for horses that are lame from unaccustomed idleness. At least there is no other case where we find celery or any such green forage thrown to horses in the *Iliad*. But like the good doctor he was, Achilles gave exactly that care to the horses which was proper to the circumstances, by providing the lightest diet as the most healthful during idleness. He did not see fit to treat alike those men who had spent the day in combat and struggle and those who had been idle ; so he ordered a strengthening of the mixture. In fact, it is evident that Achilles by temperament is no lover of wine but a rough, unsocial character :

> Not sweet of spirit was the man, nor gentle,
> But in a passion . . .[a]

He somewhere says, when talking freely about himself, that he " spent many sleepless nights "[b]; but a brief sleep will not satisfy a drinker of neat wine. When he jeers at Agamemnon, the first epithet that he hurls at him is " wine-sodden," [c] as if casting up to him winebibbing above all other weaknesses. There was every reason, therefore, why Achilles should think, when Odysseus and Phoenix appeared, that perhaps his usual mixture would be mild and inadequate for them.

[a] *Iliad*, xx. 467 f.   [b] *Iliad*, ix. 325.
[c] *Iliad*, i. 225.

ΠΡΟΒΛΗΜΑ Ε

C

Περὶ τῶν πολλοὺς ἐπὶ δεῖπνον καλούντων

Collocuntur Plutarchus, Lamprias avus

1. Τὸ περὶ τὰς κατακλίσεις φαινόμενον ἄτοπον πλείονα λόγον παρέσχεν ἐν ταῖς ὑποδοχαῖς, ἃς ἐποιεῖτο τῶν φίλων ἕκαστος ἑστιῶν ἡμᾶς ἥκοντας ἀπὸ τῆς Ἀλεξανδρείας· ἐκαλοῦντο γὰρ ἀεὶ πολλοὶ τῶν ὁπωσοῦν προσήκειν δοκούντων, καὶ τὰ συμπόσια θορυβώδεις εἶχε τὰς συμπεριφορὰς καὶ τὰς δια-λύσεις ταχείας. ἐπειδὴ δ' Ὀνησικράτης ὁ ἰατρὸς

D οὐ πολλοὺς ἀλλὰ τοὺς σφόδρα συνήθεις καὶ οἰκειο-τάτους παρέλαβεν ἐπὶ τὸ δεῖπνον, ἐφάνη μοι τὸ λεγόμενον ὑπὸ Πλάτωνος, " αὐξομένην πόλιν πό-λεις,[1] οὐ πόλιν," συμποσίῳ δεδόσθαι.[2] " καὶ γὰρ συμποσίου μέγεθος ἱκανόν ἐστιν, ἄχρι οὗ συμπόσιον ἐθέλει μένειν· ἐὰν δ' ὑπερβάλῃ διὰ πλῆθος, ὡς μηκέτι προσήγορον ἑαυτῷ μηδὲ συμπαθὲς εἶναι ταῖς φιλοφροσύναις μηδὲ γνώριμον, οὐδὲ συμπόσιόν ἐστι. δεῖ γὰρ οὐχ ὥσπερ ἐν στρατοπέδῳ διαγγέλοις οὐδ' ὥσπερ ἐν τριήρει χρῆσθαι κελευσταῖς, αὐτοὺς δὲ δι' ἑαυτῶν ἐντυγχάνειν ἀλλήλοις, ὥσπερ χοροῦ τοῦ συμποσίου τὸν κρασπεδίτην τῷ κορυφαίῳ συνήκοον ἔχοντος."

2. Ἐμοῦ δὲ ταῦτ' εἰπόντος, εἰς μέσον ἤδη φθεγ-

E ξάμενος ὁ πάππος ἡμῶν Λαμπρίας, " ἆρ' οὖν," εἶπεν,[3] " οὐ περὶ τὰ δεῖπνα μόνον, ἀλλὰ καὶ περὶ

---

[1] αὐξομένην πόλιν πόλεις Hubert, αὐξομένην πόλιν Reiske, αὐξανομένην πόλιν τελευτῶσαν Turnebus, ἐπ' αὐξομένῃ πόλει Wyttenbach: αὐξομένη πόλει.

[2] οὐκ ἐπὶ πόλει μᾶλλον ἢ συμποσίῳ λελέχθαι Wyttenbach, κἀπὶ συμπ. λελέχθαι Hartman, εἰς συμπόσια ἀποδεδόσθαι Mad-

QUESTION 5

On those who invite large numbers to dinner

Speakers : Plutarch and his grandfather Lamprias

1. THE awkward problem that turns up of finding places for guests at table was the subject of considerable discussion at the parties that each of my friends gave me on my return from Alexandria. For on every occasion many were included who had even the slightest apparent claim to an invitation, and consequently the gatherings were turbulent and broke up early. But when Onesicrates the physician invited, not a large crowd, but only some very dear friends and close relatives, it struck me that you could apply to parties the words of Plato [a] : " An augmented state is not one state but several." " For the size of a party also," I said, " is right so long as it easily remains one party. If it gets too large, so that the guests can no longer talk to each other or enjoy the hospitality together or even know one another, then it ceases to be a party at all. For at a social gathering there should be no need for aides-de-camp, as in an army, or boatswains to set the stroke, as in a trireme, but people should converse directly with one another ; even as in a chorus the end man is within earshot of the leader."

2. When I had said this, my grandfather Lamprias, raising his voice so that everyone could hear, said, " Do I understand that we must observe moderation then, not only in eating, but in the number of

[a] *Republic*, 422 E—423 D.

vig, συμποσίῳ καλῶς ἀποδεδόσθαι Pohlenz, συμποσίῳ κανὼν δ. Kronenberg. [3] ἆρ' οὖν εἶπεν Xylander : ἄρα συνεῖπεν.

(678) τὰς κλήσεις[1] δεόμεθα τῆς ἐγκρατείας; ἔστι γάρ
τις οἶμαι καὶ φιλανθρωπίας ἀκρασία, μηδένα παρ-
ερχομένης τῶν συμποτῶν ἀλλὰ πάντας ἑλκούσης ὡς
ἐπὶ θέαν ἢ ἀκρόασιν. ἔμοιγ' οὖν οὔτ' ἄρτος οὔτ'
οἶνος ἐπιλείπων τοῖς κεκλημένοις οὕτω δοκεῖ τὸν κε-
κληκότα ποιεῖν γελοῖον ὡς χώρα καὶ τόπος· ὧν καὶ
μὴ κεκλημένοις ἀλλ' ἐπελθοῦσιν αὐτομάτως ξένοις
καὶ ἀλλοτρίοις ἀεὶ παρεσκευασμένην ἀφθονίαν ὑπάρχειν δεῖ. ἔτι δ' ἄρτου μὲν καὶ οἴνου ἐπιλειπόν-
F των ἔστι καὶ τοὺς οἰκέτας ὡς κλέπτοντας αἰτιᾶσθαι,
τόπου δὲ πενία καὶ κατανάλωσις εἰς πλῆθος ὀλιγωρία
τίς ἐστι τοῦ καλοῦντος. εὐδοκιμεῖ δὲ θαυμαστῶς
καὶ Ἡσίοδος εἰπών·

> ἤτοι μὲν πρώτιστα χάος γένετ'·

χώραν γὰρ ἔδει καὶ τόπον προϋποκεῖσθαι τοῖς γιγ-
679 νομένοις, οὐχ ὡς χθὲς οὑμὸς υἱός," ἔφη, " τὸ
Ἀναξαγόρειον, ' ἦν ὁμοῦ πάντα χρήματα,' τὸ σύνδειπνον ἐποίησεν.

" Οὐ μὴν ἀλλὰ κἂν τόπος ὑπάρχῃ καὶ παρα-
σκευή, τὸ πλῆθος αὐτὸ φυλακτέον ὡς ἄμικτον τὴν
συνουσίαν ποιοῦν καὶ ἀπροσήγορον· οἴνου γὰρ ἀνελεῖν ἧττόν ἐστι κακὸν ἢ λόγου κοινωνίαν ἐκ δείπ-
νου· διὸ καὶ Θεόφραστος ἄοινα συμπόσια παίζων
ἐκάλει τὰ κουρεῖα διὰ τὴν λαλιὰν τῶν προσκαθιζ-
όντων. λόγων δὲ κοινωνίαν ἀναιροῦσιν οἱ πολλοὺς

---

[1] So Palatinus 170, Xylander : κλίσεις.

---

[a] See below, Book VII, Question 6, and particularly
Plato's *Symposium*, 174 A-B, which Plutarch cites there, on

guests that we invite ? It seems to me that there is such a thing as going too far even in hospitality, when you omit no possible guest but drag everybody in, as if to some show or public recitation. The host who runs out of bread or wine is not so ridiculous, to my way of thinking, as the one who fails to provide room and place for his guests. There ought at all times to be ample provision even for uninvited guests,[a] including total strangers who come of their own accord. Besides, if bread and wine give out, it is possible to lay the blame on thieving servants, but if space gives out because it has been spent on too great a crowd, then the host himself is guilty of a kind of insult to his guests. Incidentally, this line of Hesiod is amazingly popular :

Before all else in the world, void came into existence,[b]

simply because room and place were prerequisite to all subsequent creation. Contrast that with the way in which my son yesterday[c] converted the banquet into the famous Anaxagorean plenum : ' All things were one solid mass.'[d]

"However, if both space and the provisions are ample, we must still avoid great numbers, because they in themselves interfere with sociability and conversation. It is worse to take away the pleasure of conversation at table than to run out of wine. Theophrastus[e] in jest calls barbershops " wineless drinking parties " just because of the chatter of those who come to sit there. People who bring together too

these " shadows " as they were called, who were often brought to the banquet by some invited guest.
  [b] *Theogony*, 116.   [c] *Table-Talk*, ii. 10, 644 c.
  [d] Diels, *Frag. d. Vorsokratiker*, Anaxagoras, frag. 1.
  [e] Wimmer, Theophrastus, frag. 76.

(679) εἰς ταὐτὸ συμφοροῦντες, μᾶλλον δ' ὀλίγους ποιοῦσιν
ἀλλήλοις συνεῖναι[1]· κατὰ δύο γὰρ ἢ τρεῖς ἀπολαμ-
B βάνοντες ἐντυγχάνουσι καὶ προσδιαλέγονται, τοὺς
δὲ πόρρω κατακειμένους οὐδ' ἴσασιν οὐδὲ προσορῶ-
σιν ἵππου δρόμον ἀπέχοντας

> ἠμὲν ἐπ' Αἴαντος κλισίας Τελαμωνιάδαο
> ἠδ' ἐπ' Ἀχιλλῆος.

ὅθεν οὐκ ὀρθῶς οἱ πλούσιοι νεανιεύονται κατασκευ-
άζοντες οἴκους τριακοντακλίνους καὶ μείζους· ἀμί-
κτων γὰρ αὕτη καὶ ἀφίλων δείπνων ἡ παρασκευὴ
καὶ πανηγυριάρχου μᾶλλον ἢ συμποσιάρχου δεομένων. ἀλλ' ἐκείνοις μὲν ταῦτα συγγνώμη ποιεῖν·
ἄπλουτον γὰρ οἴονται τὸν πλοῦτον καὶ τυφλὸν
ἀληθῶς καὶ ἀνέξοδον,[2] ἂν μὴ μάρτυρας ἔχῃ καὶ[3]
καθάπερ τραγῳδία θεατάς· ἡμῖν δ' ἂν ἵαμα γένοιτο
C τοῦ πολλοὺς ὁμοῦ συνάγειν τὸ πολλάκις κατ'
ὀλίγους παραλαμβάνειν. οἱ γὰρ σπανίως καὶ ' δι'
Ἅρματος,' ὥς φασιν, ἐστιῶντες ἀναγκάζονται τὸν
ὁπωσοῦν ἐπιτήδειον ἢ γνώριμον καταγράφειν· οἱ δὲ
συνεχέστερον κατὰ τρεῖς ἢ τέτταρας ἀναλαμβάνοντες
ὥσπερ πορθμεῖα τὰ συμπόσια κουφότερα[4] ποιοῦσι.

" Ποιεῖ δέ τινα τοῦ πολλοῦ τῶν φίλων πλήθους
διάκρισιν καὶ ὁ τῆς αἰτίας διηνεκὴς ἐπιλογισμός·

---

[1] καὶ after συνεῖναι deleted by Bases.
[2] So Herwerden : ἀδιέξοδον.
[3] καὶ added by Wilamowitz.
[4] So Herwerden : κοῦφά τε.

---

[a] *Iliad*, xi. 7 f.
[b] *Cf. De Cupid. Divit.* 528 A-B. Wealth has been " blind "
since Hipponax : see frag. 29 Diehl.
[c] See Strabo, ix. 2. 11, p. 404. Certain Pythaïstae watched
the sky three days in each of three months during the year

many guests to one place do prevent general conversation ; they allow only a few to enjoy each other's society, for the guests separate into groups of two or three in order to meet and converse, completely unconscious of those whose place on the couches is remote and not looking their way because they are separated from them by practically the length of a race course. The distance is like that from the centre

> Both ways, to the tents of Telamonian Ajax
> And to those of Achilles . . .[a]

So it is a mistake for the wealthy to build showy dining-rooms that hold thirty couches or more. Such magnificence makes for unsociable and unfriendly banquets where the manager of a fair is needed more than a toastmaster. However, in their case we must forgive this display, for they consider wealth, unless it has witnesses and, like a tragedy, spectators, no wealth but something blind indeed [b] and cut off from the world. But the rest of us can protect ourselves against the risk of gathering too large a crowd by entertaining frequently in small groups. Those who give dinner parties as seldom as ' the lightning flashes over Harma,' [c] as the saying goes, are forced to include in the guest list every acquaintance and relative, however distant. People, on the other hand, who entertain more frequently, three or four guests at a time, keep their parties light and manageable as a ferryman keeps his boat.

" A way to select among many friends which to invite is to bear constantly in mind the purpose of

for lightning from this direction, to determine when to " send the offering to Delphi." Harma is a rock near Phylê in the Parnes range in northern Attica. *Cf.* R. E. Wycherley in *Am. Jour. Arch.* lxiii (1959), p. lxiii.

(679) ὡς γὰρ ἐπὶ τὰς χρείας οὐ πάντας ἀλλὰ τοὺς ἁρμότ-
τοντας ἑκάστῃ παρακαλοῦμεν, βουλευόμενοι μὲν
τοὺς φρονίμους δικαζόμενοι δὲ τοὺς λέγοντας ἀπο-
δημοῦντες δὲ τοὺς ἐλαφροὺς μάλιστα τοῖς βιωτικοῖς
καὶ σχολὴν ἄγοντας, οὕτως ἐν ταῖς ὑποδοχαῖς ἑκάστοτε τοὺς ἐπιτηδείους παραληπτέον. ἐπιτήδειοι
δὲ τῷ μὲν ἡγεμόνα[1] δειπνίζοντι συνδειπνεῖν οἵ τ᾽
ἄρχοντες, ἐὰν ὦσι φίλοι, καὶ οἱ πρῶτοι τῆς πό-
λεως· ἐν δὲ γάμοις ἢ[2] γενεθλίοις οἱ κατὰ γένος
D προσήκοντες καὶ Διὸς ὁμογνίου κοινωνοῦντες· ἐν
δὲ ταῖς τοιαύταις ὑποδοχαῖς ἢ προπομπαῖς τοὺς[3]
ἐκείνοις[4] μάλιστα κεχαρισμένους εἰς ταὐτὸ συν-
ακτέον.

"Οὐδὲ γὰρ θεῷ θύοντες πᾶσι τοῖς ἄλλοις θεοῖς,
ἀλλὰ[5] μάλιστα[6] συννάοις καὶ συμβώμοις κατευχόμε-
θα, καὶ[7] τριῶν κρατήρων κιρναμένων τοῖς μὲν ἀπὸ
τοῦ πρώτου σπένδομεν τοῖς δ᾽ ἀπὸ τοῦ δευτέρου τοῖς
E δ᾽ ἀπὸ τοῦ τελευταίου· ' φθόνος γὰρ ἔξω θείου χοροῦ
ἵσταται '· θεῖος δέ που καὶ ὁ τῶν φίλων χορὸς εὐ-
γνωμόνως διανεμόμενος ἐν ταῖς συμπεριφοραῖς."

---

[1] So Franke : ἡγεμόνι.
[2] καὶ after ἢ deleted by Hubert.
[3] So Vaticanus 1676 : ταῖς.
[4] So Bernardakis : ἐκείνων.
[5] ἀλλὰ added by Hubert, δὲ after μάλιστα Reiske.
[6] καὶ after μάλιστα deleted by Hubert, Reiske, Hutten.
[7] καὶ Hartman, καὶ ἅμα Reiske : ἀλλά.

the gathering. For assistance in practical matters we appeal, not to all our friends, but only to those who are particularly competent to help. For instance, when we desire advice, we call upon the wise ; when we go to law, we summon pleaders ; and for companionship on a journey we look to those who are at leisure and unburdened by daily cares. It is equally true that for our parties we must always be careful to choose the right guests. The right guests for a banquet in honour of a political leader are public officials and civic leaders, if they are friends. At weddings and birthday parties, it is relatives, those who share in the worship of Zeus, Protector of the Family.[a] In parties like the present one to welcome home a friend, or else to bid him farewell, the host should gather together the persons most likely to please the guest of honour.

" When we sacrifice to a god we do not offer prayers to all the other gods but to those especially who share the same temple or altar : having mixed three bowls of wine,[b] we offer a libation out of the first to some gods, out of the second to others, and out of the last to still others ; for ' Jealousy has no place in the choir of the gods.' [c] Surely the choir of friends, too, is divine, and can be divided wisely [d] into successive social gatherings."

---

[a] A. B. Cook, *Zeus*, Zeus, iii. 963 ; Farnell, *Cults of the Greek States*, i, p. 53 with note 95, p. 156.

[b] Roscher, *Lexikon der griech. und röm. Mythologie, s.v.* " Heros," col. 2509.

[c] Plato, *Phaedrus*, 247 A.

[d] Or " in a spirit of kindness."

(679)

ΠΡΟΒΛΗΜΑ ς

Τίς αἰτία τῆς ἐν ἀρχῇ στενοχωρίας τῶν δειπνούντων
εἶθ᾽ ὕστερον εὐρυχωρίας

Collocuntur Lamprias avus, alii

Ῥηθέντων δὲ τούτων, εὐθὺς ἐζητεῖτο περὶ τῆς ἐν
ἀρχῇ στενοχωρίας τῶν κατακειμένων εἶτ᾽ ἀνέσεως·
οὗ τοὐναντίον εἰκὸς ἦν συμβαίνειν διὰ τὴν ἐπὶ τοῦ
δείπνου πλήρωσιν. ἔνιοι μὲν οὖν ἡμῶν τὸ σχῆμα
F τῆς κατακλίσεως ᾐτιῶντο· πλατεῖς γὰρ ὡς ἐπίπαν
κατακειμένους δειπνεῖν, ἅτε δὴ τὴν δεξιὰν προτεί-
νοντας ἐπὶ τὰς τραπέζας· δειπνήσαντας δ᾽ ἀναστρέ-
φειν αὑτοὺς μᾶλλον ἐπὶ πλευράν, ὀξὺ τὸ σχῆμα
ποιοῦντας τοῦ σώματος καὶ οὐκέθ᾽ ὡς εἰπεῖν κατ᾽
ἐπίπεδον, ἀλλὰ κατὰ γραμμὴν τῆς χώρας ἁπτο-
680 μένους· ὥσπερ οὖν οἱ ἀστράγαλοι τόπον ἐλάττω
κατέχουσιν ὀρθοὶ πίπτοντες ἢ πρηνεῖς, οὕτως ἡμῶν
ἕκαστον ἐν ἀρχῇ μὲν ἐπὶ στόμα προνεύειν ἀπο-
βλέποντα[1] πρὸς τὴν τράπεζαν ὕστερον δὲ μετασχη-
ματίζειν ἐπὶ βάθος ἐκ πλάτους τὴν κατάκλισιν.

Οἱ δὲ πολλοὶ τὴν συνένδοσιν τῆς στρωμνῆς
προεφέροντο· θλιβομένην γὰρ ἐν τῇ κατακλίσει
πλατύνεσθαι καὶ διαχωρεῖν, ὥσπερ τῶν ὑποδημάτων τὰ τριβόμενα, κατὰ μικρὸν ἐπιδιδόντα[2] καὶ
χαλῶντα τοῖς πόροις, εὐρυχωρίαν τῷ ποδὶ καὶ
ἀναστροφὴν παρέχει. ὁ δὲ πρεσβύτης ἅμα παίζων
B δύ᾽ ἔφη τὸ αὐτὸ συμπόσιον ἀνομοίους ἔχειν ἐπιστά-
τας τε καὶ ἡγεμόνας, ἐν ἀρχῇ μὲν τὸν λιμὸν ᾧ τῶν

---

[1] So Stephanus : ἀποβλέποντας.
[2] ἐνδιδόντα Hirschig (" yielding, giving, softening ").

QUESTION 6

Why there is lack of space for the diners at the beginning
of a meal and ample space later

Speakers : Grandfather Lamprias and others

IMMEDIATELY after this discussion, we raised the
question why the space for the diners seems inadequate at the beginning of a meal, but later seems
comfortably ample. The very opposite would be expected because of the effect of the intake of food.
Some of the company sought the explanation in the
position of the diners on the couches ; in general,
each guest, while eating, assumes a posture [a] almost
flat, since he must stretch his right hand forward to
the table ; but after eating he turns back more upon
his side, forming a sharper angle with the couch and
occupying no longer a flat surface, but merely, one
might say, a line. Just as knucklebones occupy less
space if they come to rest on end instead of flat on
one side, so each of us takes up space at the beginning
of a meal by leaning forward to face the table but
later changes position on the couch so as to occupy
more space vertically than horizontally.

Most of our company, however, found the answer
to the question in the settling of the cushions as they
are crushed by the weight of the diners ; they flatten
and spread like old shoes that by gradually widening
and becoming roomy because of the porousness of the
material provide space and play for the foot. But
the old gentleman playfully said that one identical
feast has two dissimilar presidents and directors : at
the beginning Hunger, who has nothing to do with

[a] Resting on the left elbow.

(680) τακτικῶν οὐδὲν μέτεστιν, ὕστερον δὲ τὸν Διόνυσον
ὃν πάντες ἄριστον γεγονέναι στρατηγὸν ὁμολογοῦ-
σιν· ὥσπερ οὖν ὁ Ἐπαμεινώνδας, εἴς τινα δυσχω-
ρίαν τῶν στρατηγῶν ὑπ' ἀπειρίας εἰσβαλλόντων[1] τὴν
φάλαγγα περιπίπτουσαν ἑαυτῇ καὶ ταρασσομένην[2]
ὑπολαβών, ἐξέλυσε[3] καὶ κατέστησεν εἰς τάξιν, οὕτως ἡμᾶς ἐν ἀρχῇ συμπεφορημένους ὑπὸ τοῦ λιμοῦ
κυνηδὸν ἄρτι παραλαμβάνων ὁ Λυαῖος θεὸς καὶ
Χορεῖος εἰς τάξιν ἱλαρὰν καὶ φιλάνθρωπον καθίστησιν.

ΠΡΟΒΛΗΜΑ Ζ

Περὶ τῶν καταβασκαίνειν λεγομένων

Collocuntur Mestrius Florus, Plutarchus, Patrocleas,
Soclarus, Caius

C   1. Περὶ τῶν καταβασκαίνειν λεγομένων καὶ βάσκανον ἔχειν ὀφθαλμὸν ἐμπεσόντος λόγου παρὰ δεῖπνον οἱ μὲν ἄλλοι παντάπασιν ἐξεφλαύριζον[4] τὸ
πρᾶγμα καὶ κατεγέλων· ὁ δ' ἑστιῶν ἡμᾶς Μέστριος
Φλῶρος ἔφη τὰ μὲν γιγνόμενα τῇ φήμῃ θαυμαστῶς
βοηθεῖν, τῷ δ' αἰτίας ἀπορεῖν ἀπιστεῖσθαι τὴν ἱστο-
ρίαν, οὐ δικαίως, ὅπου μυρίων ἐμφανῆ τὴν οὐσίαν
ἐχόντων ὁ τῆς αἰτίας λόγος ἡμᾶς διαπέφευγεν.

---

[1] εἰσβαλόντων Palatinus 170, Turnebus.
[2] So Palatinus, Vulcobius : καταρασσομένην "broken."
[3] ἐξέλευσε most mss. including E, " stoned " (?).
[4] So Turnebus : ἐξεφλυάριζον.

---

[a] Dionysus's military expeditions " all over the world " are
cited in Diodorus Siculus, iii. 64. 6.
[b] For details of the expedition against Alexander of Phe-
rae, which is probably referred to here, see Diodorus Siculus,
xv. 71. 5 ff. During a battle on level ground the losing and
desperate troops made Epaminondas general.

military tactics, but later Dionysus, whom all admit
to be an excellent general.[a] Epaminondas once
found that the generals had because of inexperience
led the army into a difficult [b] position where it was
thrown into complete confusion and disorder ; he
took charge, disentangled it, and reformed the ranks.
Just so, we who at the beginning of dinner were all
demoralized by hunger like a pack of yelping hounds,
have now been taken in hand by Dionysus, the
Releaser and Choral Leader, and reduced to a cheerful and sociable co-ordination.

QUESTION 7

On those who are said to cast an evil eye [c]

Speakers : Mestrius Florus, Plutarch, Patrocleas,
Soclarus, Gaius

1. ONCE at dinner a discussion arose about people who
are said to cast a spell and to have an evil eye. While
everybody else pronounced the matter completely
silly and scoffed at it, Mestrius Florus,[d] our host,
declared that actual facts lend astonishing support to
the common belief. Yet the reports of such facts are
commonly rejected because of the want of an explanation ; but this is not right, in view of the thousands
of other cases of indisputable fact in which the logical
explanation escapes us.[e]

[c] On the whole subject see *RE*, *s.v.* " Fascinum."

[d] See above, i. 9, 626 E, and iii. 3, 650 A ; the prominent
Roman to whom Plutarch seems to have owed his Roman
citizenship and his Roman name.

[e] Similarly Themistocles at 626 F and Agemachus at
664 c defend acceptance of unexplained facts. *Cf. Septem
Sapientium Convivium*, 20 (LCL *Mor.* ii, 163 D).

(680) "Ὅλως δ'," εἶπεν, "ὁ ζητῶν ἐν ἑκάστῳ τὸ εὔλογον ἐκ πάντων ἀναιρεῖ τὸ θαυμάσιον· ὅπου γὰρ
D ὁ τῆς αἰτίας ἐπιλείπει λόγος, ἐκεῖθεν ἄρχεται τὸ
ἀπορεῖν, τουτέστι τὸ φιλοσοφεῖν· ὥστε τρόπον τινὰ
φιλοσοφίαν ἀναιροῦσιν οἱ τοῖς θαυμασίοις ἀπι-
στοῦντες. δεῖ δ'," ἔφη, "τὸ μὲν διὰ τί γίγνεται τῷ
λόγῳ μετιέναι,[1] τὸ δ' ὅτι γίγνεται παρὰ τῆς ἱστορίας λαμβάνειν. ἱστορεῖται δὲ πολλὰ[2] τοιαῦτα·
γιγνώσκομεν γὰρ ἀνθρώπους τῷ καταβλέπειν τὰ
παιδία μάλιστα βλάπτοντας, ὑγρότητι τῆς ἕξεως
καὶ ἀσθενείᾳ τρεπομένης ὑπ' αὐτῶν καὶ κινουμένης
ἐπὶ τὸ χεῖρον, ἧττον δὲ τῶν στερεῶν καὶ πεπηγότων
ἤδη τοῦτο πασχόντων. καίτοι τούς γε περὶ τὸν
Πόντον οἰκοῦντας πάλαι Θιβεῖς[3] προσαγορευο-
μένους ἱστορεῖ Φύλαρχος οὐ παιδίοις μόνον ἀλλὰ
καὶ τελείοις ὀλεθρίους εἶναι· καὶ γὰρ τὸ βλέμμα
E καὶ τὴν ἀναπνοὴν καὶ τὴν διάλεκτον αὐτῶν παρα-
δεχομένους τήκεσθαι καὶ νοσεῖν· ᾔσθοντο δ' ὡς
ἔοικε τὸ γιγνόμενον οἱ μιγάδες[4] οἰκέτας ἐκεῖθεν
ὠνίους ἐξάγοντες. ἀλλὰ τούτων τὸ μὲν ἴσως
ἧττόν ἐστι θαυμαστόν· ἡ γὰρ ἐπαφὴ καὶ συνανά-
χρωσις ἔχει τινὰ φαινομένην πάθους ἀρχήν, καὶ
καθάπερ τὰ τῶν ἄλλων ὀρνέων πτερὰ τοῖς τοῦ
ἀετοῦ συντεθέντα διόλλυται ψηχόμενα[5] καὶ ἀπανθεῖ

---

[1] So Anonymus, Reiske : μετεῖναι.
[2] T begins again with this word.
[3] Θιβεῖς or Θιβίους Xylander, Salmasius, cf. Hesychius,
Stephanus of Byzantium, Pliny the Elder : Θηβεῖς.
[4] μιγάδας Valesius : "by those who brought half-Greek
slaves . . ."
[5] So Doehner : ψυχόμενα.

---

[a] Wonder is the origin of philosophy, according to Plato,

" In general," he went on, " the man who demands
to see the logic of each and every thing destroys the
wonder in all things. Whenever the logical explanation for anything eludes us, we begin to be puzzled,
and therefore to be philosophers.[a] Consequently, in
a way, those who reject marvels destroy philosophy.
The right method," he maintained, " is to search out
the reason for facts by means of logic, but to take the
facts themselves as they are recorded. Now, many
instances of such unexplained phenomena as the evil
eye are on record. We know, for instance, of persons
who seriously hurt children by looking at them, in-
fluencing and impairing their susceptible, vulnerable
constitutions, but who are less able to affect in this
way the firm and established health of older persons.
And yet the so-called Thibaeans,[b] who anciently
lived near the Pontus, were, according to Phylarchus,[c]
deadly not only to children but to adults. He says
that those who were subjected to the glance, breath,
or speech of these people, fell ill and wasted away, a
phenomenon apparently observed by the half-Greeks
who brought slaves for sale from there. Now, one
element in this story will hardly surprise anyone, for
obviously enough an attack of illness may be due to
contact and infection. When the feathers of other
birds are put together with those of eagles, they rub
against them and are destroyed through putre-

Theaetetus, 155 D ; *cf.* especially Aristotle, *Metaphysics*, 982
b 12, in a discussion of the relation between causation (*aitia*)
or logical explanation and knowledge.

[b] Phylarchus in Jacoby, *Frag. Griech. Historiker*, 81 F 79
a ; for more about this mythical people see Stephanus of
Byzantium, *s.v.* " Thibaïs," and Pliny, *Nat. Hist.* vii. 2. 17.

[c] Historian of the 3rd century B.C. See *RE*, Suppl. viii,
cols. 471-489.

(680) τῶν πτίλων μυδώντων, οὕτως οὐδὲν ἀπέχει καὶ
ἀνθρώπου ψαῦσιν τὴν μὲν ὠφέλιμον εἶναι τὴν δ'
F ἀπηνῆ καὶ βλαβεράν· τὸ δὲ καὶ προσβλεφθέντας
ἀδικεῖσθαι συμβαίνει μὲν ὥσπερ εἴρηκα, τῷ δὲ τὴν
αἰτίαν ἔχειν δυσθήρατον ἀπιστεῖται."

2. " Καὶ μήν," ἔφην ἐγώ, " τρόπον τινὰ τῆς
αἰτίας αὐτὸς¹ ἴχνος τι καὶ τρίβον ἀνεύρηκας, ἐπὶ
τὰς ἀπορροίας τῶν σωμάτων ἀφικόμενος· καὶ γὰρ
ἡ ὀσμὴ καὶ ἡ φωνὴ καὶ τὸ ῥεῦμα τῆς ἀναπνοῆς
ἀποφοραί τινές εἰσι τῶν ζῴων καὶ μέρη κινοῦντα
τὰς αἰσθήσεις, ὅταν ὑπ' αὐτῶν προσπεσόντων πά-
681 θωσι. πολὺ δὲ μᾶλλον εἰκός ἐστι τῶν ζῴων ἀπο-
φέρεσθαι τὰ τοιαῦτα διὰ τὴν θερμότητα καὶ τὴν
κίνησιν, οἱονεί τινα σφυγμὸν καὶ κλόνον ἔχοντος
τοῦ πνεύματος, ὑφ' οὗ τὸ σῶμα κρουόμενον ἐνδε-
λεχῶς ἐκπέμπει τινὰς ἀπορροίας. μάλιστα δὲ τοῦτο
γίγνεσθαι διὰ τῶν ὀφθαλμῶν εἰκός ἐστι· πολυκίνη-
τος γὰρ ἡ ὄψις οὖσα μετὰ πνεύματος αὐγὴν² ἀφι-
έντος πυρώδη θαυμαστήν τινα διασπείρει δύναμιν,
ὥστε πολλὰ καὶ πάσχειν καὶ ποιεῖν δι' αὐτῆς τὸν
ἄνθρωπον. ἡδοναῖς τε γὰρ συμμέτροις καὶ ἀηδίαις
ὑπὸ τῶν ὁρατῶν τρεπόμενος συνέχεται.

" Καὶ τῶν ἐρωτικῶν, ἃ δὴ μέγιστα καὶ σφοδρό-

¹ So Xylander : αὐτοῖς.   ² So Turnebus : αὐτὴν.

───────

ᵃ The Greek here seems pleonastic, unless πτίλα can
refer to the barbs or vane of a feather.

ᵇ A similar device for building up a discussion is used
above in iv. 2. 2, 664 D.

ᶜ Empedocles, frag. 89 (Diels) : there are effluences from
all things. *Cf.* Democritus's εἴδωλα below at 682 F f. The
present reference is to 680 E, above.

ᵈ For emanations and the circumstances which favour their
reception see below, viii, 734 F ff. (=Democritus, A 77 Diels,
and Epicurus, 326 Usener). *Cf.* also Lucretius's example of

faction.[a] Just so, there is no reason to doubt that contact between human beings may prove in some cases beneficial and in others rough and harmful. It also does happen sometimes, as I have said, that people are injured by a mere look ; but because the reason is hard to track down, the fact is not believed."

2. " Indeed," I answered, " in a way you yourself have found the track and trail of the reason [b] at the point where you came to effluences [c] from bodies. For odour, voice, and breathing are all emanations of some kind, streams of particles from living bodies, that produce sensation whenever our organs of sense are stimulated by their impact. Living bodies are, because of their warmth and motion,[d] far more likely in reason to give off these particles than are inanimate bodies, inasmuch as breathing produces a certain pulsation and turmoil whereby the body is struck and emits a continuous stream of emanations. In all probability the most active stream of such emanations is that which passes out through the eye. For vision, being of an enormous swiftness and carried by an essence [e] that gives off a flame-like brilliance, diffuses a wondrous influence. In consequence, man both experiences and produces many effects through his eyes. He is possessed and governed by either pleasure or displeasure exactly in proportion to what he sees.

" Vision provides access to the first impulse to love,

the lion terrified by the emanations from the cock, *De Rer. Nat.* iv. 712 ff.

[e] *Pneuma* : " Something midway between the material and the spiritual " (Parke and Wormell, *Delphic Oracle*, i, p. 23). *Cf.* the prophetic *pneuma* and other effluences in Plutarch, *De Defectu Orac.* 432 D ff.; and Milton's " bright effluence of bright essence increate " in *Paradise Lost*, iii. 6.

(681)

B τατα παθήματα τῆς ψυχῆς ἐστιν, ἀρχὴν ἡ ὄψις
ἐνδίδωσιν, ὥστε ῥεῖν καὶ λείβεσθαι τὸν ἐρωτικόν,
ὅταν ἐμβλέπῃ τοῖς καλοῖς, οἷον ἐκχεόμενον[1] εἰς
αὑτούς. διὸ καὶ θαυμάσειεν ἄν τις οἶμαι μάλιστα
τῶν πάσχειν[2] μὲν καὶ κακοῦσθαι τὸν ἄνθρωπον διὰ
τῆς ὄψεως οἰομένων, οὐκέτι δὲ δρᾶν καὶ βλάπτειν.
αἱ γὰρ ἀντιβλέψεις τῶν ἐν ὥρᾳ καὶ τὸ διὰ τῶν
ὀμμάτων ἐκπῖπτον, εἴτ' ἄρα φῶς εἴτε ῥεῦμα, τοὺς
ἐρῶντας ἐκτήκει[3] καὶ ἀπόλλυσι μεθ' ἡδονῆς ἀλγη-
δόνι μεμιγμένης, ἣν αὐτοὶ γλυκύπικρον ὀνομάζου-
σιν· οὔτε γὰρ ἁπτομένοις οὔτ' ἀκούουσιν οὕτω
C τιτρώσκεσθαι συμβαίνει καὶ πάσχειν, ὡς προσβλε-
πομένοις καὶ προσβλέπουσι. τοιαύτη γὰρ γίγνεται
διάδοσις καὶ ἀνάφλεξις ἀπὸ τῆς ὄψεως, ὥστε παντελῶς ἀπειράτους ἔρωτος ἡγεῖσθαι τοὺς τὸν Μηδικὸν
νάφθαν θαυμάζοντας ἐκ διαστήματος ὑπὸ τοῦ πυρὸς
ἀναφλεγόμενον· αἱ γὰρ τῶν καλῶν ὄψεις, κἂν πάνυ
πόρρωθεν ἀντιβλέπωσι,[4] πῦρ ἐν ταῖς τῶν ἐρωτικῶν
ψυχαῖς ἀνάπτουσιν.

"Καὶ μὴν τό γε τῶν ἰκτερικῶν βοήθημα πολλάκις ἱστοροῦμεν· ἐμβλέποντες γὰρ τῷ χαραδριῷ
θεραπεύονται· τοιαύτην ἔοικε τὸ ζῷον φύσιν καὶ

---

[1] So Wyttenbach : ἐρχόμενον.
[2] So Stephanus : στοίχειν.
[3] So Reiske, cf. Psellus : ἐντήκει.
[4] So Reiske, cf. Psellus : ἀντιβλέψωσι.

---

[a] Sappho, frag. 81 (LCL *Lyra Graeca*, vol. i, p. 238).
[b] Strabo cites Eratosthenes as saying that naphtha is found
in Susis (xvi. 1. 15, p. 743); see also *RE, s.v.* " Asphalt," col.
1729. Plutarch describes a test of " naphtha " which cruelly
burned a lad who accompanied Alexander to Babylon, in
Life of Alexander, xxxv. 1-5. This is reported also by Strabo.
[c] *Cf.* the scholium on Plato's *Gorgias*, 494 B, quoting

that most powerful and violent experience of the soul, and causes the lover to melt and be dissolved when he looks at those who are beautiful, as if he were pouring forth his whole being towards them. For this reason, we are entitled, I think, to be most surprised at anyone who believes that, while men are passively influenced and suffer harm through their eyes, they yet should not be able to influence others and inflict injury in the same way. The answering glances of the young and the beautiful and the stream of influence from their eyes, whether it be light or a current of particles, melts the lovers and destroys them, amid pleasure commingled with pain, a pleasure that they themselves call ' bittersweet.' [a] Neither by touch nor by hearing do they suffer so deep a wound as by seeing and being seen. Such are the diffusion of effluences and the kindling of passion through eyesight that only those unacquainted with love itself could, in my judgement, be astonished at the natural phenomenon that takes place when Median naphtha [b] catches fire at a distance from a flame. The glances of the beautiful kindle fire, even when returned from a great distance, in the souls of the amorous.

" Then again, we are often told about the remedy used to help sufferers from jaundice, who are cured by looking at a plover.[c] The nature and bodily temperament of this bird is apparently such that it draws

---

Hipponax 48 (Diehl) : plovers were sold with their heads covered to prevent loss of their commercial value. " Plover " is now the common identification of the *charadrios*, but others have been suggested, *e.g.*, the golden oriole ; some yellow or partly yellow bird would seem natural in the context. See Pliny, *Nat. Hist.* xxx. 28. 94 on the " jaundice-bird." See also Additional Note, on p. 516.

(681) κρᾶσιν ἔχειν, ὥσθ᾽ ἕλκειν καὶ δέχεσθαι τὸ πάθος
ἐκπῖπτον,[1] ὥσπερ ῥεῦμα, διὰ τῆς ὄψεως· ὅθεν οὐ
προσβλέπουσιν οἱ χαραδριοὶ τοὺς τὸν ἴκτερον ἔχον-
D τας οὐδὲ καρτεροῦσιν, ἀλλ᾽ ἀποστρέφονται καὶ τὰ
ὄμματα συγκλείσαντες ἔχουσιν, οὐ φθονοῦντες, ὡς
ἔνιοι νομίζουσι, τῆς ἀπ᾽ αὐτῶν ἰάσεως ἀλλ᾽ ὥσπερ
ὑπὸ πληγῆς τιτρωσκόμενοι. τῶν δ᾽ ἄλλων νοσημά-
των μάλιστα καὶ τάχιστα τὰς ὀφθαλμίας ἀναλαμβάνουσιν οἱ συνόντες· οὕτω δύναμιν ἔχει ὀξεῖαν ἡ
ὄψις ἐνδοῦναι καὶ προσβαλεῖν ἑτέρῳ πάθους ἀρχήν."

3. " Καὶ μάλ᾽," ἔφη, " λέγεις ὀρθῶς," ὁ Πατροκλέας, " ἐπί γε τῶν σωματικῶν· τὰ δὲ τῆς ψυχῆς,
ὧν ἐστι καὶ τὸ βασκαίνειν, τίνα τρόπον καὶ πῶς
διὰ τῆς ὄψεως τὴν βλάβην εἰς τοὺς ὁρωμένους
διαδίδωσιν;" " οὐκ οἶσθ᾽," ἔφην, " ὅτι πάσχουσ᾽
ἡ ψυχὴ τὸ σῶμα συνδιατίθησιν; ἐπίνοιαι γὰρ
ἀφροδισίων ἐγείρουσιν αἰδοῖα, καὶ θυμοὶ κυνῶν ἐν
E ταῖς πρὸς τὰ θηρία γιγνομέναις ἁμίλλαις ἀποσβεν-
νύουσι τὰς ὁράσεις πολλάκις καὶ τυφλοῦσι, λῦπαι
δὲ καὶ φιλαργυρίαι καὶ ζηλοτυπίαι τὰ χρώματα
τρέπουσιν καὶ καταξαίνουσι τὰς ἕξεις· ὧν οὐδενὸς
ὁ φθόνος ἧττον ἐνδύεσθαι τῇ ψυχῇ πεφυκὼς ἀναπίμπλησι καὶ τὸ σῶμα πονηρίας, ἣν οἱ ζωγράφοι
καλῶς ἐπιχειροῦσιν ἀπομιμεῖσθαι τὸ τοῦ φθόνου
πρόσωπον ὑπογράφοντες. ὅταν οὖν οὕτως ὑπὸ τοῦ
φθονεῖν διατεθέντες[2] ἀπερείδωσι τὰς ὄψεις, αἱ δ᾽
ἔγγιστα τεταγμέναι τῆς ψυχῆς σπάσασαι[3] τὴν
κακίαν ὥσπερ πεφαρμαγμένα βέλη προσπίπτωσιν,
F οὐδὲν οἶμαι συμβαίνει παράλογον οὐδ᾽ ἄπιστον, εἰ

---

[1] So Xylander : ἔκλιπτον. Bernardakis ἔκλειπτον with E
(" shed," from λείβω).
424

out and takes to itself the affliction, which passes like a stream through the eyes of the patient. Consequently, plovers cannot bear to face people who are afflicted with jaundice, but turn away and keep their eyes closed, not because they begrudge the effect of their healing power, as some think, but because they are wounded thereby, as if by a blow. Finally, diseases of the eye are more contagious to those exposed and more instantaneously so than other diseases, so penetrating and swift is the power of the eye to admit or communicate disease."

3. " You are indeed right," said Patrocleas, " so far as the physiological effects go. But as regards the psychical, including the casting of spells, how precisely can harm spread to others by a mere glance of the eye ? " I answered : " Don't you know that the body is sympathetically affected when the mind is subjected to any influence ? Amorous thoughts will excite the sexual organs ; the frenzy of hounds in their struggle with their prey often dims their sight and even blinds them ; and pain, greed for gold, or jealousy will cause a man to change colour, and wear away his health. Envy, which naturally roots itself more deeply in the mind than any other passion, contaminates the body too with evil. This is the morbid condition that artists well attempt to render when painting the face of envy. When those possessed by envy to this degree let their glance fall upon a person, their eyes, which are close to the mind and draw from it the evil influence of the passion, then assail that person as if with poisoned arrows ; hence, I conclude, it is not paradoxical or incredible

---

² So Aldine edition : διατιθέντες.

³ So Meziriacus : σπάσωσι.

(681) κινοῦσι[1] τοὺς προσορωμένους· καὶ γὰρ τὰ δήγματα
τῶν κυνῶν χαλεπώτερα γίγνεται μετ' ὀργῆς δακνόν-
των, καὶ τὰ σπέρματα τῶν ἀνθρώπων μᾶλλον ἅπτε-
σθαί φασιν ὅταν ἐρῶντες πλησιάζωσι, καὶ ὅλως τὰ
πάθη τὰ τῆς ψυχῆς ἐπιρρώννυσι καὶ ποιεῖ σφοδροτέρας τὰς τοῦ σώματος δυνάμεις. διὸ καὶ τὸ τῶν
λεγομένων προβασκανίων γένος οἴονται πρὸς τὸν
682 φθόνον ὠφελεῖν ἑλκομένης διὰ τὴν ἀτοπίαν τῆς
ὄψεως, ὥσθ' ἧττον ἐπερείδειν τοῖς πάσχουσιν. αὐ-
ταί σοι," εἶπον, "ὦ Φλῶρε, συμβολαὶ τῆς εὐωχίας
ἀπηριθμήσθωσαν."

4. Καὶ ὁ Σώκλαρος, " ἄν γ'," ἔφη, " πρότερον
ἡμεῖς αὐτὰ[2] δοκιμάσωμεν· ἔστι γὰρ ὅ τι τοῦ λόγου
καταφαίνεται κίβδηλον. εἰ γὰρ ἃ λέγουσι πολλοὶ
περὶ τῶν βασκαινομένων ὡς ἀληθῆ τίθεμεν, οὐκ
ἀγνοεῖς δήπουθεν ὅτι καὶ φίλους καὶ οἰκείους, ἔνιοι
δὲ καὶ πατέρας ἔχειν ὀφθαλμὸν βάσκανον ὑπολαμβάνουσιν, ὥστε μὴ δεικνύναι τὰς γυναῖκας αὐτοῖς
B τὰ παιδία μηδὲ πολὺν ἐᾶν χρόνον ὑπὸ τῶν τοιούτων
καταβλέπεσθαι· πῶς οὖν ἔτι δόξει φθόνου τὸ πάθος
εἶναι; τί δ', ὦ πρὸς τοῦ Διός, ἐρεῖς περὶ τῶν ἑαυτοὺς καταβασκαίνειν λεγομένων; καὶ γὰρ τοῦτ'
ἀκήκοας· εἰ δὲ μή, πάντως ταῦτ' ἀνέγνωκας·

---

[1] εἰ κινοῦσι Meziriacus : ἐκείνους δ.
[2] αὐτὰς Vulcobius, Reiske.

---

[a] Here again, a device comparable to iv. 2, 664 D : " I do

426

that they should have an effect on the persons who encounter their gaze. The bite of dogs too is more dangerous when they are angry ; and it is said that in human beings the sperm is more likely to lay hold and cause conception when union is accompanied by love. In general, the emotions of the mind increase the violence and energy of the body's powers. What I have said shows why the so-called amulets are thought to be a protection against malice. The strange look of them attracts the gaze, so that it exerts less pressure upon its victim. Count this, Florus, as my contribution toward the expense of the entertainment." [a]

4. " Very well," Soclarus replied, " if and when we accept it as good coin, for I detect something counterfeit in the argument. If we do set down as true what many say about victims of the evil eye, surely you are not ignorant that some people believe that friends and relatives, and in some cases even fathers, have the evil eye, so that their wives will not show them their children nor allow the children to be gazed upon by them for very long.[b] How under those circumstances can we still believe that this affliction derives from envy ? And in Heaven's name what will you say about those who are alleged to bewitch themselves ? You must have heard of that. If not, at any rate you have read these lines [c] :

not wish to make you pay for the truffles " ; and to iv. 4, 668
D : " this is my contribution to you and the fishmongers."
See also iii. 1. 2, 646 E.

[b] Compare the Polish father who blinded himself to protect his children against his evil eye, and other examples from Ireland, Naples, and Egypt in *Encyc. Brit.*, 11th ed., *s.v.* " Evil Eye," pp. 21 f.

[c] Euphorion, frag. 175 (Powell, *Collectanea Alexandrina*).

(682)   καλαὶ μέν ποτ' ἔσαν, καλαὶ¹ φόβαι Εὐτελίδαο·
ἀλλ' αὐτὸν² βάσκαινεν³ ἰδὼν ὀλοφώιος ἀνὴρ
δίνῃ ἐν ποταμοῦ⁴· τὸν δ' αὐτίκα νοῦσος ἀεικής—

ὁ γὰρ Εὐτελίδας λέγεται, καλὸς ἑαυτῷ φανεὶς καὶ
παθών τι⁵ πρὸς τὴν ὄψιν, ἐκ τούτου νοσῆσαι καὶ
τὴν εὐεξίαν μετὰ τῆς ὥρας ἀποβαλεῖν. ἀλλ' ὅρα
πῶς ἔχεις εὑρησιλογίας πρὸς τὰς τοιαύτας ἀτο-
πίας."

5. "'Ἄλλως μέν," ἔφην,⁶ " οὔ⁷ μάλ' ἱκανῶς· πί-
C νων δ' ὡς ὁρᾷς ἐκ τῆς τηλικαύτης κύλικος, οὐκ
ἀτόλμως λέγω διότι τὰ μὲν πάθη πάντα, ταῖς
ψυχαῖς ἐμμείναντα πολὺν χρόνον, ἕξεις ἐνεργάζεται
πονηράς· αὗται δ', ὅταν ἰσχὺν φύσεως λάβωσιν,
ὑπὸ τῆς τυχούσης κινούμεναι προφάσεως, πολλάκις καὶ ἄκοντας ἐπὶ τὰ οἰκεῖα καὶ συνήθη κατα-
φέρουσι πάθη. σκόπει δὲ τοὺς δειλοὺς ὅτι καὶ τὰ
σῴζοντα φοβοῦνται, καὶ τοὺς ὀργίλους ὅτι καὶ τοῖς
φιλτάτοις δυσκολαίνουσι, καὶ τοὺς ἐρωτικοὺς καὶ
ἀκολάστους ὅτι τελευτῶντες οὐδὲ τῶν ἁγιωτάτων
ἀπέχεσθαι δύνανται σωμάτων. ἡ γὰρ συνήθεια
δεινὴ πρὸς τὸ οἰκεῖον ἐξάγειν τὴν διάθεσιν, καὶ τὸν
D ἀκροσφαλῶς ἔχοντα πᾶσι προσπταίειν ἀνάγκη τοῖς
ὑποπίπτουσιν. ὥστ' οὐκ ἄξιον θαυμάζειν τοὺς
τὴν φθονητικὴν καὶ βασκαντικὴν ἀπειργασμένους
ἐν ἑαυτοῖς ἕξιν, εἰ καὶ πρὸς τὰ οἰκεῖα κατὰ τὴν τοῦ
πάθους ἰδιότητα κινοῦνται· κινούμενοι δ' οὕτως ὃ
πεφύκασιν οὐχ ὃ βούλονται ποιοῦσιν. ὡς γὰρ ἡ

¹ καλαὶ Meineke, Emperius : καὶ.
² So Xylander : αὐτὸν.
³ So Turnebus : βασκαίνειν.
⁴ δίνῃ ἐν ποταμοῦ Xylander, δινήεντι ῥόῳ Reiske, δινῆντ' ἐν
ποταμῷ Powell : δινήεντι ποταμῷ.

Fair once were, fair indeed the tresses of Eutelidas ;
But he cast an evil spell on himself, that baneful man,
Beholding self in river's eddy ; and straight the fell di-
    sease . . .

The legend is that Eutelidas, beautiful in his own
estimation, being affected by what he saw, fell sick
and lost his beauty with his health. See if you have
the ingenuity to account for extraordinary phenomena
like that."

5. " Well," I replied, " I haven't enough otherwise ; but since I'm drinking out of this big cup, as
you see, I have the boldness to say that all emotions,
after having been a long time in the mind, produce
evil conditions. These evil conditions, when they
acquire the force of second nature, will under any
chance stimulus cause a relapse, even against the
person's will, into the habitual and familiar emotion.
Consider how the cowardly are afraid even of things
that would save their lives, and how the irascible are
peevish towards even their dearest friends, and how
the lustful and licentious end by being unable to
refrain from assaulting the most sacred persons.
Habit is powerful to influence disposition according
to a set pattern, and it is inevitable that a man prone
to lapse will trip over every temptation that falls in
his way. Accordingly there is no reason for surprise
if those who have brought themselves into a state of
envy and malignity are activated even against their
near and dear as befits their special pathological
condition. In these circumstances they are acting as
their nature but not as their will directs. As a

---

[5] παθών τι Basel edition : παθόν τι(?) T, παθόντι E.
[6] So Vulcobius, Xylander : ἔφη.
[7] οὐ Wyttenbach : καί.

(682) σφαῖρα κινεῖσθαι σφαιρικῶς καὶ κυλινδρικῶς ὁ
κύλινδρος ἀναγκάζεται κατὰ τὴν τοῦ σχήματος
διαφοράν, οὕτως τὸν¹ φθονερὸν ἡ διάθεσις φθο-
νητικῶς πρὸς ἅπαντα κινεῖ. οὐ μὴν ἀλλὰ καὶ
καταβλέπειν² εἰκός ἐστιν αὐτοὺς τὰ οἰκεῖα καὶ
ποθούμενα μᾶλλον· διὸ καὶ βλάπτουσι μᾶλλον.

" Ὁ δὲ βέλτιστος Εὐτελίδας³ καὶ ὅσοι λέγονται
Ε καταβασκαίνειν ἑαυτοὺς οὐκ ἀλόγως μοι δοκοῦσι
τοῦτο πάσχειν. σφαλερὸν γὰρ ἡ ἐπ᾽ ἄκρον εὐεξία
κατὰ τὸν Ἱπποκράτην, καὶ τὰ σώματα προελ-
θόντα μέχρι τῆς ἄκρας ἀκμῆς οὐχ ἕστηκεν, ἀλλὰ
ῥέπει καὶ ταλαντεύεται πρὸς τοὐναντίον· ὅταν οὖν
ἐπίδοσιν ἀθρόαν λάβωσι καὶ⁴ βέλτιον ἢ προσε-
δόκων ἔχοντας ἑαυτοὺς ἐπιβλέπωσιν, ὥστε θαυμάζειν καὶ κατασκοπεῖν τὸ σῶμα, τῆς μεταβολῆς
ἐγγύς εἰσι καὶ φερόμενοι ταῖς ἕξεσι πρὸς τὸ χεῖρον
ἑαυτοὺς δοκοῦσι⁵ καταβασκαίνειν. τοῦτο δὲ γίγνεται μᾶλλον ἀπὸ τῶν πρὸς ὕδασιν ἤ τισιν ἄλλοις
ἐσόπτροις ὑφισταμένων ῥευμάτων· ἀναπνεῖ γὰρ
Ϝ ἐπ᾽ αὐτοὺς τοὺς ὁρῶντας, ὥσθ᾽ οἷς ἑτέρους ἔβλαπ-
τον, αὐτοὺς κακοῦσθαι. τοῦτο δ᾽ ἴσως καὶ περὶ τὰ
παιδία γιγνόμενον καταψεύδεται πολλάκις τὴν
αἰτίαν τῶν ἐνορώντων."

6. Ἐμοῦ δὲ παυσαμένου, Γάιος ὁ Φλώρου
γαμβρός, " τῶν δὲ Δημοκρίτου," ἔφη, " εἰδώλων,
ὥσπερ Αἰγιέων ἢ Μεγαρέων, ἀριθμὸς οὐδεὶς οὐδὲ

---

¹ οὕτω after τὸν deleted by Reiske.
² So Wyttenbach : καταβλάπτειν Ε, καταβλ(ά)π(τ)ειν Τ with
erasures. Ε lacks the last clause διὸ . . . μᾶλλον.
³ ὁ before καὶ deleted by Meziriacus.
⁴ καὶ added by Turnebus, Vulcobius.
⁵ δοκοῦσι added by Xylander, Wyttenbach.

sphere by its distinctive shape is forced to roll like a
sphere, and a cylinder like a cylinder, so a man whose
disposition is envious has to act in an envious manner
in all things. Besides, it is natural for him to cast his
gaze oftener on those near and dear to him and
consequently to hurt them more than he does others.

" To my mind it seems reasonable enough that the
excellent Eutelidas and all others who are said to
have cast a spell on themselves should have encoun-
tered such a misfortune. For supreme good health is,
according to Hippocrates,[a] precarious. When the
body reaches the pinnacle of health, it does not
remain there, but wavers and sinks towards the opposite condition. Therefore, when people experience a
complete improvement in health and find themselves
better off than they had expected, they marvel and
look closely at themselves; but actually they are now
near a reversal, and when their condition takes a sudden turn for the worse, they are thought to have put
themselves under a spell. Self-bewitchment is most
frequently brought about by the streams of particles
reflected from sheets of water or other mirror-like
surfaces ; these reflections rise like vapour and
return to the beholder, so that he is himself injured
by the same means by which he has been injuring
others. And perhaps when this happens in the case
of children, the blame is often wrongly fastened upon
those who gaze at them."

6. When I had finished, Florus's son-in-law Gaius
asked, " What, do we completely despise and leave
out of account the *simulacra* or shapes of Democritus,[b]
as the oracle of old left out the people of Aegium or

---

[a] *Aphorisms*, i. 3 ; and Celsus, ii. 2.
[b] Democritus, A 77 (Diels).

(682) λόγος; ἅ φησιν ἐκεῖνος ἐξιέναι τοὺς φθονοῦντας,
683 οὔτ' αἰσθήσεως ἄμοιρα παντάπασιν οὔθ' ὁρμῆς,
ἀνάπλεά τε τῆς ἀπὸ τῶν προϊεμένων μοχθηρίας
καὶ βασκανίας, μεθ' ἧς ἐμπλασσόμενα καὶ παρα-
μένοντα καὶ συνοικοῦντα τοῖς βασκαινομένοις ἐπι-
ταράττειν καὶ κακοῦν αὐτῶν τό τε σῶμα καὶ τὴν
διάνοιαν· οὕτως γὰρ οἶμαί πως τὸν ἄνδρα τῇ δόξῃ,
τῇ δὲ λέξει δαιμονίως λέγειν καὶ μεγαλοπρεπῶς."

" Πάνυ μὲν οὖν," ἔφην, " ἀλλὰ θαυμάζω, πῶς
ἔλαθον ὑμᾶς οὐδὲν ἄλλο τῶν ῥευμάτων τούτων ἢ
τὸ ἔμψυχον ἀφελὼν καὶ προαιρετικόν· ἵνα μή με
δόξητε πόρρω νυκτῶν οὖσιν[1] ὑμῖν ἐπάγοντα φάσ-
ματα καὶ εἴδωλα πεπνυμένα καὶ φρονοῦντα μορ-
B μολύττεσθαι καὶ διαταράττειν. ἕωθεν οὖν, ἐὰν
δοκῇ, περὶ τούτων σκεψώμεθα."

ΠΡΟΒΛΗΜΑ Η

Διὰ τί τὴν μηλέαν " ἀγλαόκαρπον" ὁ ποιητὴς εἶπεν, Ἐμπεδοκλῆς
δ' "ὑπέρφλοια"[2] τὰ μῆλα

Collo*cuntur* Trypho, Plutarchus, grammatici, Lamprias avus

1. Ἑστιωμένων ἡμῶν ποτ' ἐν Χαιρωνείᾳ καὶ
παρατεθείσης παντοδαπῆς ὀπώρας, ἐπῆλθέ τινι τῶν
κατακειμένων ἀναφθέγξασθαι τὸν στίχον ἐκεῖνον

C συκέαι τε γλυκεραὶ καὶ μηλέαι ἀγλαόκαρποι

───────────
[1] So Reiske : οὐσῶν.
[2] So Basel edition : ὑπερφυᾶ.

───────────

[a] This is proverbial (Leutsch und Schneidewin, *Paroemiogr. Graec.* i, p. 19), based on an oracle delivered either to
Megara or to Aegium, informing them that they were no-
where in the reckoning. Aegium is a city of Achaïa on the

Megara ? [a] Democritus says that these *simulacra* are emanations emitted not altogether unconsciously or unintentionally by the malevolent, and are charged with their wickedness and envy. According to him, these *simulacra* with their burden of evil, adhering to their victims and in fact permanently lodged in them, confound and injure both their bodies and their minds. So, I believe, runs his text and his intention, expressed in language both lofty and inspired."

I answered, " Quite true, but I wonder how it escaped you that the only things that I denied to the emanations were life and free will. Don't think that I want to make your flesh creep and throw you into a panic late at night like this by bringing on sentient, purposeful shapes and apparitions. Let's talk about such things in the morning, if you like." [b]

QUESTION 8

Why Homer speaks of the apple tree as " splendid in its fruit " and Empedocles calls apples *hyperphloia*

Speakers : Tryphon, Plutarch, scholars, Grandfather Lamprias

1. ONCE when we were banqueting at Chaeronea, autumn fruit of every sort had been set before us, and it occurred to one of the company to recite that famous line,[c]

Both sweet fig trees and apple trees splendid in their fruit,

Corinthian Gulf. (See Parke and Wormell, *Delphic Oracle*, ii, p. 1.)

 [b] To such scholars as Hubert and Hartman this last statement would seem more appropriate if placed next to the *rheumata* associated with mirrors on the preceding page.

 [c] A combination of parts of *Odyssey*, vii, lines 115 and 116.

(683) καὶ " ἐλαῖαι τηλεθόωσαι." ζήτησις οὖν ἦν, διὰ
τί τὰς μηλέας ὁ ποιητὴς " ἀγλαοκάρπους " ἐξ-
αιρέτως προσεῖπεν. καὶ Τρύφων μὲν ὁ ἰατρὸς ἔ-
λεγε κατὰ τὴν πρὸς τὸ δένδρον εἰρῆσθαι σύγκρισιν,
ὅτι μικρὸν ὂν κομιδῇ καὶ τὴν ὄψιν εὐτελὲς καλὸν
καὶ μέγαν ἐκφέρει τὸν καρπόν. ἄλλος δέ τις ἔφη
τὸ καλὸν ἐκ πάντων συντεθὲν[1] μόνῳ τούτῳ τῶν
ἀκροδρύων ὁρᾶν ὑπάρχον· καὶ γὰρ τὴν ψαῦσιν ἔχει
καθάριον,[2] ὥστε μὴ μολύνειν ἀλλ' εὐωδίας ἀνα-
πιμπλάναι τὸν ἁπτόμενον, καὶ τὴν γεῦσιν ἡδεῖαν,
ὀσφραίνεσθαί τε καὶ ἰδεῖν ἐπιτερπέστατόν ἐστι·
D διὸ καὶ πάσας ὁμοῦ τι τὰς αἰσθήσεις προσαγόμενον
εἰκότως ἐπαινεῖσθαι.

2. Ταῦτα μὲν οὖν ἔφαμεν ἡμεῖς μετρίως λέγε-
σθαι· τοῦ δ' Ἐμπεδοκλέους εἰρηκότος

οὕνεκεν ὀψίγονοί τε σίδαι καὶ ὑπέρφλοια μῆλα,

τὸ μὲν τῶν σιδῶν ἐπίθετον νοεῖν ὅτι τοῦ φθινο-
πώρου λήγοντος ἤδη καὶ τῶν καυμάτων μαραινο-
μένων ἐκπέττουσι τὸν καρπόν· ἀσθενῆ γὰρ αὐτῶν
τὴν ὑγρότητα καὶ γλίσχραν οὖσαν οὐκ ἐᾷ λαβεῖν
σύστασιν ὁ ἥλιος, ἂν μὴ μεταβάλλειν ὁ ἀὴρ ἐπὶ τὸ
ψυχρότερον ἄρχηται· διὸ καὶ μόνον τοῦτό φησιν
Θεόφραστος τὸ δένδρον ἐν τῇ σκιᾷ βέλτιον ἐκπέτ-
τειν τὸν καρπὸν καὶ τάχιον. τὰ δὲ μῆλα καθ'
ἥντινα διάνοιαν ὁ σοφὸς " ὑπέρφλοια " προσειρήκοι,
E διαπορεῖν, καὶ μάλιστα τοῦ ἀνδρὸς οὐ καλλιγραφίας
ἕνεκα τοῖς εὐπροσωποτάτοις τῶν ἐπιθέτων, ὥσπερ

---

[1] So Turnebus : συντιθέντα.
[2] So Reiske : καθάπερ ἰόν.

---

[a] These words are found in *Odyssey*, vii. 116.

adding the words [a] " flourishing olive trees." This made us wonder why Homer singled out the apple tree as bearing splendid fruit. Tryphon,[b] the physician, said that this expression was intended to contrast the fruit with the tree, which, though indeed quite small and insignificant in appearance, produces fine, big fruit. Someone else rejoined that, so far as he could see, no other fruit unites the fine qualities of all fruits as does the apple. For one thing, its skin is so clean when you touch it that instead of staining the hands it perfumes them. Its taste is sweet and it is extremely delightful both to smell and to look at. Thus, by charming all our senses at once, it deserves the praise that it receives.

2. I remarked that this was a fair statement ; but that I was puzzled by a line of Empedocles,[c]

Because late-grown pomegranates and succulent apples.

The epithet that he applies to pomegranates is clear : it signifies that they ripen when the late harvest season is coming to an end and the heat is becoming less intense. The hot sun will not allow the weak and meagre sap of the pomegranate to develop to a proper consistency until the air begins to change and grow cooler. That is why, according to Theophrastus,[d] this is the only tree that allows its fruit to mature better and more quickly in the shade. But what puzzled me, I confessed, was what the philosopher meant by calling apples " succulent " (hyperphloia) ; especially since he was not in the habit of tricking out facts for the sake of elegant writing by using

[b] Trypho(n) is one of the speakers above in Table-Talk, iii. 1 and 2.
[c] Fragment 80 (Diels).
[d] Apparently not in Theophrastus.

(683) ἀνθηροῖς χρώμασι, τὰ πράγματα γανοῦν εἰωθότος, ἀλλ' ἕκαστον οὐσίας τινὸς ἢ δυνάμεως δήλωμα ποιοῦντος, οἷον " ἀμφιβρότην χθόνα " τὸ τῇ ψυχῇ[1] περικείμενον σῶμα, καὶ " νεφεληγερέτην " τὸν ἀέρα καὶ " πολυαίματον " τὸ ἧπαρ.

3. Εἰπόντος οὖν ἐμοῦ ταῦτα, γραμματικοί τινες ἔφασαν " ὑπέρφλοια " λελέχθαι τὰ μῆλα διὰ τὴν ἀκμήν· τὸ γὰρ ἄγαν ἀκμάζειν καὶ τεθηλέναι " φλύειν " ὑπὸ τῶν ποιητῶν λέγεσθαι. καὶ τὸν Ἀντίμαχον οὕτω πως " φλείουσαν[2] ὀπώραις " F εἰρηκέναι τὴν τῶν Καδμείων πόλιν· ὁμοίως τὸν Ἄρατον ἐπὶ τοῦ Σειρίου λέγοντα

καὶ τὰ μὲν ἔρρωσεν, τῶν[3] δὲ φλόον ὤλεσε πάντα

τὴν χλωρότητα καὶ τὸ ἄνθος τῶν καρπῶν " φλόον " προσαγορεύειν[4]· εἶναι δὲ καὶ τῶν Ἑλλήνων τινάς, οἱ Φλείῳ Διονύσῳ θύουσιν. ἐπεὶ τοίνυν μάλιστα τῶν καρπῶν ἡ χλωρότης καὶ τὸ τεθηλέναι τῷ μήλῳ παραμένει, " ὑπέρφλοιον " αὐτὸ τὸν φιλόσοφον προσαγορεῦσαι.

684 Λαμπρίας δ' ὁ πάππος ἡμῶν ἔφη τὴν " ὑπὲρ " φωνὴν οὐ μόνον τὸ ἄγαν καὶ τὸ σφοδρὸν δηλοῦν, ἀλλὰ καὶ τὸ ἔξωθεν καὶ τὸ ἄνωθεν· οὕτω γὰρ " ὑπέρθυρον " καὶ " ὑπερῷον " καλεῖν ἡμᾶς, τὸν δὲ

---

[1] τῇ ψυχῇ Turnebus : τὴν ψυχὴν.
[2] So Hubert, φλοίουσαν previous editors : φλιουσαν (at 735 D φλειοῦσαν). [3] So Salmasius, cf. Aratus : τὸν.
[4] So Basel edition : προσαγορεύων.

---

[a] Fragments 148-150 (Diels).
[b] Or according to the variant reading *phloiein*, "to swell."
[c] Thebes. Antimachus, born c. 444 B.C., wrote an epic *Thebaïd*, of which this is Fragment 40 (Wyss, *Antimachus*) or Fragment 36, *Epic. Graec. Frag.* (Kinkel).

grandiose epithets, as if he were laying on gaudy colours, but in every case aimed at simple description of an essential fact or property. For instance, he applies [a] the expression " earth that envelops a mortal " to the body that clothes us, and " cloud-gatherer " to the air, and " rich in blood " to the liver.

3. When I finished, some scholars who were present said that the apples were described as " succulent " (*hyperphloia*) because they were at their prime. For the poets use the term " to bubble " (*phlyein*) [b] to mean " be at the height and flourish." Antimachus also, they argued, in very much the same way, described the city of the Cadmeians [c] as " teeming with fruit " (*phleiousan*). Likewise Aratus,[d] speaking of Sirius in the line,

To some he gives strength but of others he blights the bark (*phloon*) utterly,

was calling the freshness and bloom of fruit " bark " (*phloos*). Then, the argument went on, there are some Greeks [e] who sacrifice to Dionysus Phleios. Therefore, since apples more than any other fruit retain their freshness and bloom, the philosopher called them *hyperphloia* (" abnormally luxuriant ").

But my grandfather Lamprias said that *hyper* meant not merely " excessively " or " violently " but also " outside " or " on top." In this way we use the expression *hyperthyron* (" over the door ") for " lintel," and *hyperôon* for " upper story." Homer has the

[a] *Phaenomena*, 335. The translation is that of G. R. Mair (LCL).

[e] Specifically, those of Prienê, Erythrae, Ephesus. See Wilamowitz, *Glaube der Hellenen*, ii, p. 373, note 1. See also Farnell's *Cults of the Greek States*, v, pp. 118 ff., 281 ff., note 11, where the reading *Phloios* instead of *Phleios* is adopted.

(684) ποιητὴν καὶ " κρέ' ὑπέρτερα " τὰ ἔξω τοῦ ἱερείου,
ὥσπερ " ἔγκατα " τὰ ἐντός. " ὅρα τοίνυν," ἔφη,
" μὴ πρὸς τοῦτο μᾶλλον ὁ Ἐμπεδοκλῆς πεποίηκε
τὸ ἐπίθετον, ὅτι, τῶν ἄλλων καρπῶν τὸ ἔξωθεν ὑπὸ
τοῦ φλοιοῦ περιεχομένων καὶ τὰ καλούμενα λεπύ-
χανα καὶ κελύφη καὶ ὑμένας καὶ λοβοὺς ἐπιπολῆς
ἐχόντων, ὁ τοῦ μήλου φλοιὸς ἐντός ἐστι κολλώδης
B χιτὼν καὶ λιπαρός, ᾧ προσίσχεται τὸ σπέρμα· τὸ
δ' ἐδώδιμον, ἔξωθεν αὐτῷ περικείμενον, εἰκότως
' ὑπέρφλοιον ' ὠνόμασται."[1]

ΠΡΟΒΛΗΜΑ Θ

Τίς ἡ[2] αἰτία, δι' ἣν ἡ συκῆ δριμύτατον οὖσα δένδρον
γλυκύτατον παρέχει τὸν καρπόν

Collocuntur Lamprias avus, alii

Μετὰ δὲ ταῦτα περὶ τῶν σύκων διηπορήθη, τί
δήποτε πίων καὶ γλυκὺς οὕτως καρπὸς ἀπὸ δέν-
δρου φύεται πικροτάτου· τῆς γὰρ συκῆς καὶ τὸ
φύλλον διὰ τὴν τραχύτητα θρῖον ὠνόμασται, καὶ
τὸ ξύλον ὀπῶδές ἐστιν, ὥστε καιόμενον μὲν ἐκδι-
C δόναι δριμύτατον καπνὸν κατακαυθὲν[3] δὲ τὴν ἐκ
τῆς τέφρας κονίαν ῥυπτικωτάτην παρέχειν ὑπὸ
δριμύτητος. ὃ δ' ἐστὶ θαυμασιώτατον, ἀνθούντων
ἁπάντων ὅσα βεβλάστηκε καὶ καρπογονεῖ, μόνον
ἀνανθές ἐστι τὸ τῆς συκῆς φυτόν· εἰ δ', ὥς φασιν,
οὐ κεραυνοῦνται, καὶ τοῦτ' ἄν τις ἀναθείη τῇ
πικρότητι καὶ καχεξίᾳ τοῦ στελέχους· τῶν γὰρ
τοιούτων οὐ δοκοῦσιν ἐπιθιγγάνειν οἱ κεραυνοί,

---

[1] So Turnebus : ὠνόμάσθαι.   [2] ἡ added in Aldine edition.
[3] So Turnebus : κατακαυθεῖσαν.

---

[a] See, e.g., Odyssey, iii. 65.   [b] See, e.g., Iliad, xi. 176.

expression *kre' hypertera* [a] (" outside pieces ") in speaking of the sacrificial animal, just as he uses *enkata* [b] (" inwards ") for the inside pieces. " So," he went on, " consider whether Empedocles did not employ the term rather with this intention : whereas other fruits are encased by a *phloios* ('husk') on the outside (that is, they have what is called a rind, pod, capsule, or shell on the surface), apples have their *phloios* inside as a shiny, glutinous coat to which the seed is attached, so that the edible part surrounding all this on the outside is with good reason called *hyperphloion* (' outside the rind ')."

QUESTION 9

Why the fig tree though extremely bitter produces
extremely sweet fruit

Speakers : Grandfather Lamprias and others

NEXT the question was raised why so mellow and sweet a fruit as the fig grows on the bitterest of trees. The leaf of this tree is even called from its roughness *thrion* [c]; the wood is full of an acid sap and produces a very acrid smoke when burned,[d] and the powder derived from its ash is most detergent because of its causticity. But what is most astonishing is that, though all plants bud and produce fruit, the fig alone is without flowers. If, as they say, a fig is never struck by lightning, this too could be attributed to the bitterness and poorness of its trunk. For it is held that lightning never strikes objects of that

[c] *Thrion* and *trachys* (" rough ") are here evidently con‾sidered cognate.

[d] The bitterness of the tree is again pointed out at *Table-Talk*, vi. 10, 696 F ff. below.

καθάπερ οὐδὲ τῆς φώκης τοῦ δέρματος οὐδὲ τῆς
ὑαίνης.

Ὑπολαβὼν οὖν ὁ πρεσβύτης ἔφη, ὅσον ἂν ἐνῇ[1]
τῷ φυτῷ γλυκύτητος, ἅπαν τοῦτο συνθλιβόμενον
εἰς τὸν καρπὸν εἰκότως δριμὺ ποιεῖν[2] καὶ ἄκρατον τὸ
D λειπόμενον· ὥσπερ γὰρ τὸ ἧπαρ, εἰς ἕνα τόπον τοῦ
χολώδους ἀποκριθέντος, αὐτὸ γίγνεται γλυκύτατον,
οὕτω τὴν συκῆν εἰς τὸ σῦκον ἅπαν τὸ λιπαρὸν καὶ
νόστιμον ἀφιεῖσαν αὐτὴν ἄμοιρον εἶναι γλυκύτητος.
" ἐπεί, ὅτι γε μετέχει τινὸς εὐχυμίας τὸ ξύλον,
ἐκεῖν'," ἔφη,[3] " ποιοῦμαι σημεῖον, ὃ λέγουσιν οἱ
κηπουροί· λέγουσι δὲ τοῦ πηγάνου τὸ φυόμενον
ὑπ' αὐτῇ καὶ παραφυτευόμενον ἥδιον εἶναι καὶ τῷ
χυμῷ μαλακώτερον, ὡς ἂν ἀπολαῦόν[4] τινος γλυκύτητος, ᾗ κατασβέννυται τὸ ἄγαν βαρὺ καὶ
κατάκορον, εἰ μὴ νὴ Δία τοὐναντίον ἡ συκῆ
περισπῶσα τὴν τροφὴν ἐξαιρεῖ τι[5] τῆς δριμύτητος."

ΠΡΟΒΛΗΜΑ Ι

E   Τίνες οἱ περὶ ἅλα καὶ κύαμον[6]· ἐν ᾧ καὶ διὰ τί τὸν ἅλα "θεῖον"
ὁ ποιητὴς εἶπεν

Collocuntur Florus, Apollophanes, Plutarchus, Philinus

1. Ἐζήτει Φλῶρος, ἑστιωμένων ἡμῶν παρ' αὐτῷ, τίνες ἂν εἶεν " οἱ περὶ ἅλα καὶ κύαμον "[6] ἐν τῇ

---

[1] ὅσον ἂν ἐνῇ added by Bernardakis, cf. Psellus, De Omnifaria Doctrina, 152.
[2] So Turnebus : ποιεῖ.   [3] So Vulcobius : ἔφην.
[4] ἂν ἀπολαῦόν Vulcobius : ἀναπαῦόν.
[5] τι Meziriacus : τό.
[6] So Vulcobius : κύμινον " cumminseed."

description, just as it never strikes sealskins or hyena pelts.[a]

The old gentleman, however, countered that since whatever sweetness is in the plant is concentrated entirely in the fruit, it naturally leaves the rest bitter and undiluted. As the liver itself is sweet to the taste when the bile has been drawn off into its proper place, so the fig tree, discharging all its oily and succulent matter into the fruit, is itself robbed of all sweetness. " For," he said, " I base my belief that the wood partakes of some latent sweetness on what the gardeners say about rue. According to them, rue has a sweeter and milder taste if it grows under or is planted [b] beside a fig tree, as if it derived from that a certain sweetness that counteracts its strong, heavy flavour ;—unless, on the contrary, bless my soul, the fig reduces the bitterness by drawing off the nourishment in the soil."

QUESTION 10

Who " salt and bean friends " are ; and, incidentally, why Homer calls salt divine

Speakers : Florus, Apollophanes, Plutarch, Philinus

1. DURING a dinner given us by Florus, he asked who are meant by " salt and bean friends " [c] in the pro-

[a] For the relation between lightning and biology cf. above, iv. 2, especially 664 c.

[b] Or " grafted " ? Cf. Pseudo-Aristotle, Problems, 924 b 35 ff. See also Theophrastus, De Causis Plant. v. 6. 10 and Dioscorides, iii. 45. 1.

[c] See above, iv. 1, 663 F, and Paroemiogr. Graec. i, pp. 8 and 188, where the explanation is offered that priestly hospitality to consultants of oracles consisted of salt and beans. Compare the different proverb on salt, ibid. p. 24, no. 62.

(684) παροιμίᾳ λεγόμενοι. καὶ τοῦτο μὲν ἐκ προχείρου
διέλυσεν Ἀπολλοφάνης ὁ γραμματικός· " οἱ γὰρ
οὕτω συνήθεις," ἔφη, " τῶν φίλων, ὥστε καὶ πρὸς
F ἅλα δειπνεῖν[1] καὶ κύαμον,[2] ὑπὸ τῆς παροιμίας
προβάλλονται." τὴν δὲ τῶν ἁλῶν τιμὴν ἀφ' ὅτου
γένοιτο διηποροῦμεν, Ὁμήρου μὲν ἄντικρυς λέ-
γοντος·

πάσσε δ' ἁλὸς θείοιο,

Πλάτωνος δὲ[3] τῶν ἁλῶν σῶμα κατὰ νόμον ἀνθρώπων θεοφιλέστατον[4] εἶναι φάσκοντος· ἐπέτεινε δὲ
τὴν ἀπορίαν τὸ τοὺς Αἰγυπτίους ἱερέας ἁγνεύοντας[5]
ἀπέχεσθαι τὸ πάμπαν ἁλῶν, ὥστε καὶ τὸν ἄρτον
ἄναλον προσφέρεσθαι· πῶς γάρ, εἰ θεοφιλὲς καὶ
θεῖον, ἀφωσιώσαντο;[6]

2. Φλῶρος μὲν οὖν ἐὰν ἐκέλευε τοὺς Αἰγυπτίους,
685 Ἑλληνιστὶ δ' αὐτοὺς εἰπεῖν τι πρὸς τὸ ὑποκεί-
μενον. ἐγὼ δ' ἔφην οὐδὲ τοὺς Αἰγυπτίους μάχεσθαι τοῖς Ἕλλησιν· αἱ γὰρ ἁγνεῖαι καὶ παιδοποιίαν
καὶ γέλωτα καὶ οἶνον καὶ πολλὰ τῶν ἄλλως ἀξίων
σπουδῆς ἀφαιροῦσι· τοὺς δ' ἅλας τάχα μὲν ὡς ἐπὶ
συνουσίαν ἄγοντας ὑπὸ θερμότητος, ὡς ἔνιοι λέγουσι, φυλάττονται καθαρεύοντες· εἰκὸς δὲ καὶ ὡς
ὄψον ἥδιστον παραιτεῖσθαι· κινδυνεύουσι γὰρ οἱ ἅλες

---

[1] συνδειπνεῖν Reiske, Hubert.
[2] So Vulcobius: κύμινον "cumminseed."
[3] δὲ τὸ Meziriacus.   [4] θεοφιλὲς Plato, *Timaeus*, 60 E.
[5] So Wyttenbach: ἀγνοὺς ὄντας.
[6] So Reiske: ἀφωσίωσαν.

---

[a] To take potluck : either to take a meal of salt and a bean
or to take a meal that costs only the value of salt and a bean.
Cheapness is connoted by the phrase πρὸς ἅλα (" for the price
of salt ") in Menander, 805 (Körte), according to Zenobius

verb. The scholar Apollophanes had a ready answer for this, saying, " The proverb refers to friends who are so close to us as to be content to dine with us on salt and a bean." [a] Then we raised the question why salt is so highly esteemed.[b] For Homer goes so far as to say,

> He sprinkled with salt divine,[c]

and Plato [d] says that by the custom of mankind salt is regarded as of all substances the one most favoured by the gods. The question was complicated by the fact that the Egyptian priests made it a point of religion to abstain completely from salt,[e] even eating their bread unsalted ; how, if it is god-favoured and divine, did they come to avoid its use on religious grounds ?

2. Florus then told us to leave the Egyptians out of it, and to find a good Greek answer to our own question. But I said that actually the Egyptians were not here in conflict with the Greeks. Strict religious observances prohibit, at certain times, pro- creation, laughter, wine, and many other things which usually deserve approval. So perhaps the Egyptians from motives of purity avoid salt on account of the aphrodisiac properties sometimes attributed to it because of its heat.[f] But it is just as probable that they protest against salt because it is delicious as a

and Diogenianus, who give us this fragment, and Pollux, among others cited by Körte.

[b] *Cf.* above, iv. 4. 3, 668 E ff.   [c] *Iliad*, ix. 214.

[d] *Timaeus*, 60 E, but Plato uses only the positive degree : " a god-favoured substance."

[e] *Cf.* below, viii. 8. 2, 729 A, and *De Iside*, 352 F (LCL *Mor.* v). These passages speak of the priests only " during their periods of holy living."

[f] *Cf.* below, 697 B and above, 651 B.

(685) τῶν ἄλλων ὄψων ὄψον εἶναι καὶ ἤδυσμα, διὸ καὶ
" χάριτας " ἔνιοι προσαγορεύουσιν αὐτούς, ὅτι τῆς
τροφῆς τὸ ἀναγκαῖον ἡδὺ ποιοῦσιν.

3. " Ἆρ' οὖν," ὁ Φλῶρος ἔφη, " διὰ τοῦτο
B θεῖον εἰρῆσθαι τὸν ἅλα φῶμεν; " " ἔστι μὲν δή,"
εἶπον,[1] " οὐδὲ τοῦτ' ἐλάχιστον. οἱ γὰρ ἄνθρωποι
τὰ κοινὰ καὶ διήκοντα ταῖς χρείαις ἐπὶ τὸ πλεῖστον
ἐκθειάζουσιν, ὡς τὸ ὕδωρ, τὸ φῶς, τὰς ὥρας·
τὴν δὲ γῆν οὐ μόνον θεῖον, ἀλλὰ καὶ θεὸν ὑπολαμ-
βάνουσιν· ὧν οὐδενὸς λείπεται χρείᾳ τὸ τῶν ἁλῶν,
θρίγκωμα τῆς τροφῆς γιγνόμενον εἰς τὸ σῶμα[2]
καὶ παρέχον εὐαρμοστίαν αὐτῇ πρὸς τὴν ὄρεξιν.

" Οὐ μὴν ἀλλὰ καὶ σκόπει, μὴ κἀκεῖνο θεῖον
αὐτῷ συμβέβηκεν, ὅτι τῶν σωμάτων τὰ νεκρὰ
διατηροῦν ἄσηπτα καὶ μόνιμα πολὺν χρόνον ἀντι-
τάττεται τῷ θανάτῳ καὶ οὐκ ἐᾷ παντελῶς ἐξολέ-
C σθαι καὶ ἀφανισθῆναι τὸ θνητόν· ἀλλ' ὥσπερ ἡ
ψυχή, θειότατον οὖσα τῶν ἡμετέρων, τὰ ζῷα
συνέχει καὶ ῥεῖν οὐκ ἐᾷ τὸν ὄγκον, οὕτως ἡ τῶν
ἁλῶν φύσις τὰ νεκρὰ παραλαμβάνουσα καὶ μιμου-
μένη τὸ τῆς ψυχῆς ἔργον ἀντιλαμβάνεται φερομένων ἐπὶ τὴν φθορὰν καὶ κρατεῖ[3] καὶ ἵστησιν,
ἁρμονίαν παρέχουσα καὶ φιλίαν πρὸς ἄλληλα τοῖς
μέρεσι. διὸ καὶ τῶν Στωικῶν ἔνιοι τὴν ὗν[4] σάρκα
νεκρὰν[5] γεγονέναι λέγουσι, τῆς ψυχῆς, ὥσπερ
ἁλῶν, παρεσπαρμένης ὑπὲρ τοῦ διαμένειν. ὁρᾷς
δ' ὅτι καὶ τὸ κεραύνιον πῦρ ἱερὸν ἡγούμεθα καὶ
θεῖον, ὅτι τὰ σώματα τῶν διοβλήτων ἄσηπτα πρὸς
πολὺν ἀντέχοντα χρόνον ὁρῶμεν. τί οὖν θαυ-

---

[1] δὴ εἶπον Xylander : δεῖπνον.
[2] εἰς τὸ σῶμα] εὐστομίᾳ Kronenberg.   [3] κρατύνει Hubert.
[4] So Xylander : νῦν.   [5] So Doehner, cf. 669 A : κρέα.

seasoning, for salt is very nearly a seasoning and condiment to other seasoning ; some even call it *charites* (joys), because it makes needful food enjoyable.

3. " Shall we say then," asked Florus, " that this is a reason why salt has been termed divine ? " " Indeed it is," I answered, " and not the least important one, either. For men consider divine the common things which most completely supply their practical needs, like water, light, and the seasons, and they conceive of the earth as not merely ' divine ' but as actually a goddess. Salt is inferior to none of these in usefulness. It serves as a kind of finishing touch or coping to the meal for the body, and adapts the food to our appetite.

" Consider also whether this other property of salt is not divine too : preserving bodies uncorrupted for a long time, it is the opponent of death, and does not allow the dead to decay completely and vanish. As the soul, our most divine element, preserves life by preventing dissolution of the body, just so salt, when bodies are laid in it, closely parallel in its effect, intervenes, controls and checks the process of decay, by harmonizing and reconciling the constituent parts.[a] That is why some of the Stoics say that the sow at birth is dead flesh,[b] but that the soul is implanted in it later, like salt, to preserve it. You observe also that we consider the fire of lightning as sacred and divine because we find the bodies of those struck by it preserved for a long time against decay.[c]

[a] Macrobius (*Saturnalia*, vii. 12. 3 ff.) rephrases the passage.
[b] Von Arnim, *Stoic. Vet. Frag.* i. 516 ; ii. 722, 723 and 1154. *Cf.* Pliny, *Nat. Hist.* viii. 207, and Chrysippus in Cicero, *De Natura Deorum*, ii. 64. 160 with Pease's note.
[c] *Cf.* above, iv. 2, 665 c.

(685)

D μαστόν, εἰ καὶ τὸν ἅλα, τὴν αὐτὴν ἔχοντα τῷ θείῳ
δύναμιν πυρί, θεῖον ὑπέλαβον οἱ παλαιοί;"

4. Σιωπήσαντος δ' ἐμοῦ, Φιλῖνος ὑπολαβών, " τὸ
δὲ γόνιμον οὐ δοκεῖ σοι," ἔφη, " θεῖον εἶναι,
εἴπερ ἀρχὴ¹ θεὸς πάντων;" ὁμολογήσαντος δ'
ἐμοῦ, " καὶ μήν," ἔφη, " τὸν ἅλ' οὐκ ὀλίγον πρὸς
γένεσιν συνεργεῖν οἴονται, καθάπερ αὐτὸς ἐμνήσθης
τῶν² Αἰγυπτίων. οἱ γοῦν τὰς κύνας φιλοτρο-
φοῦντες, ὅταν ἀργότεραι πρὸς συνουσίαν ὦσιν, ἄλλοις τε βρώμασιν ἁλμυροῖς καὶ ταριχευτοῖς κρέασι
κινοῦσι καὶ παροξύνουσιν τὸ σπερματικὸν αὐτῶν
ἡσυχάζον. τὰ δ' ἁληγὰ πλοῖα πλῆθος ἐκφύει μυῶν
ἄπλετον, ὡς μὲν ἔνιοι λέγουσι, τῶν θηλειῶν καὶ
E δίχα συνουσίας κυουσῶν, ὅταν τὸν ἅλα λείχωσιν·
εἰκὸς δὲ μᾶλλον ἐμποιεῖν τὴν ἁλμυρίδα τοῖς μορίοις³
ὀδαξησμοὺς καὶ συνεξορμᾶν τὰ ζῷα πρὸς τοὺς συν-
δυασμούς. διὰ τοῦτο δ' ἴσως καὶ κάλλος⁴ γυναικὸς
τὸ μήτ' ἀργὸν μήτ' ἀπίθανον, ἀλλὰ μεμιγμένον
χάριτι καὶ κινητικόν, ἁλμυρὸν καὶ δριμὺ καλοῦσιν.
οἶμαι δὲ καὶ τὴν Ἀφροδίτην ἁλιγενῆ τοὺς ποιητὰς
προσαγορεύειν καὶ μῦθον ἐπ' αὐτῇ πεπλασμένον
ἐξενεγκεῖν, ὡς ἀπὸ θαλάσσης ἐχούσῃ⁵ τὴν γένεσιν,
εἰς τὸ τῶν ἁλῶν γόνιμον αἰνιττομένους. καὶ γὰρ
αὐτὸν τὸν Ποσειδῶνα⁶ καὶ ὅλως τοὺς πελαγίους⁷
F θεοὺς πολυτέκνους καὶ πολυγόνους ἀποφαίνουσιν·
αὐτῶν δὲ τῶν ζῴων οὐδὲν ἂν χερσαῖον ἢ πτηνὸν

446

What wonder, then, that the ancients considered salt to be divine also, since it has the same property as the divine fire ? "

4. When I stopped speaking, Philinus took up the thread : " Don't you think that generation is divine, since the beginning of anything is always a god ? " I said yes, and he went on : " Well, people hold that salt contributes not a little to generation, even as you yourself have said in talking about the Egyptians. Dog-fanciers, at any rate, whenever their dogs are sluggish towards copulation stimulate and intensify the seminal power dormant in the animals by feeding them salty meat and other briny food. Ships carrying salt breed an infinite number of rats, because, according to some authorities, the females conceive without coition by licking the salt. But it is more likely that the saltiness imparts a sting to the sexual members and serves to stimulate copulation. For this reason, perhaps, womanly beauty is called ' salty ' and ' piquant ' when it is not passive nor unyielding, but has charm and provocativeness. I imagine that the poets called Aphroditê " born of the brine " and have spread the fiction of her origin in the sea by way of alluding to the generative property of salt. For they also represent Poseidon himself and the sea gods in general as fertile and prolific. Even among the animals you cannot find one species of land or air that is so proliferous as are

---

[1] So Amyot : ἄρχει. ὁ after it deleted by Hubert.
[2] ἐπὶ τῶν Reiske, Hartman.
[3] So Leonicus : μυρίοις.
[4] καλῆς Stegmann.
[5] So Hubert : ἐχούσης.
[6] ἀλλὰ before καὶ deleted by Wyttenbach.
[7] So Reiske, πελαγικοὺς Basel edition : πελασγικοὺς.

(685) εἰπεῖν ἔχοις οὕτω γόνιμον, ὡς πάντα τὰ[1] θαλάττια·
πρὸς ὃ καὶ πεποίηκεν ὁ Ἐμπεδοκλῆς·

φῦλον ἄμουσον ἄγουσα πολυσπερέων καμασήνων."

[1] τὰ added by Faehse.

----

[a] Frag. 74 (Diels); *agousa* (leading) may refer perhaps to
Aphroditê.

all the creatures of the sea. This is the point of Empedocles's [a] line :

> Leading the mute tribe of fruitful [b] fish."

[b] The translation here is in accordance with Plutarch's context, but elsewhere the word is applied to men and means simply " multitudinous."

TABLE-TALK
(QUAESTIONES CONVIVALES)
BOOK VI

ΣΥΜΠΟΣΙΑΚΩΝ

ΒΙΒΛΙΟΝ ΕΚΤΟΝ

Τιμόθεον τὸν Κόνωνος, ὦ Σόσσιε Σενεκίων,
ὡς ἐκ τῶν πολυτελῶν καὶ στρατηγικῶν[1] δείπνων
B ἀναλαβὼν ὁ Πλάτων ἐδείπνισεν ἐν ᾿Ακαδημίᾳ
μουσικῶς καὶ ἀφελῶς " ταῖς ἀφλεγμάντοις," ὥς
φησιν ὁ ῎Ιων, " τραπέζαις," αἷς ὕπνοι τε καθαροὶ
καὶ βραχυόνειροι φαντασίαι, τοῦ σώματος εὐδίαν
καὶ γαλήνην ἔχοντος,[2] ἕπονται, μεθ᾽ ἡμέραν[3] ὁ
Τιμόθεος αἰσθόμενος τῆς διαφορᾶς ἔφη τοὺς παρὰ
Πλάτωνι δειπνήσαντας[4] καὶ τῇ ὑστεραίᾳ καλῶς
γίγνεσθαι. μέγα γὰρ ὡς ἀληθῶς εὐημερίας ἐφόδιον εὐκρασία σώματος ἀβαπτίστου καὶ ἐλαφροῦ
καὶ παρεστῶτος ἀνυπόπτως ἐπὶ πᾶσαν ἐνέργειαν.
ἀλλ᾽ ἕτερον οὐκ ἔλαττον ὑπῆρχε τοῦτο τοῖς παρὰ
C Πλάτωνι δειπνήσασιν, ἡ τῶν λαληθέντων παρὰ
πότον ἀναθεώρησις· αἱ μὲν γὰρ τῶν ποθέντων[5]
ἢ βρωθέντων[6] ἡδοναὶ τὴν ἀνάμνησιν ἀνελεύθερον

---

[1] So Turnebus, cf. Athenaeus, 419 c, Aelian, *Varia Hist.* ii.
18 : στρατιωτικῶν.
[2] So Xylander : ἔχοντες.
[3] οὖν after ἡμέραν deleted by Bernardakis.
[4] τοῖς ... δειπνήσασι Turnebus, Vulcobius. But cf. Athenaeus, 419 c.
[5] ποθέντων Wyttenbach, καταποθέντων Reiske : ποθούντων.
[6] ἢ βρωθέντων added by Doehner ; cf. Xylander.

TABLE-TALK

BOOK SIX

PLATO, dear Sossius Senecio, once got Timotheüs,[a] the son of Conon,[a] away from the sumptuous officers' messes he frequented, and entertained him at dinner in the Academy with simplicity and respect for the Muses. It was the sort of table that Ion [b] called " unfevered," [c] a table that is followed by undisturbed sleep and only light dreams, because the body is in a state of calm and tranquillity. In the morning Timotheüs was conscious of the difference and observed that Plato's dinner guests felt well even on the day after. It is truly a great contribution to our health and happiness to have our bodies in a good state of balance, not sodden with wine, but light and ready unhesitatingly for any activity. Another and not less valuable privilege guaranteed to Plato's guests was that of recalling afterwards what had been said over the drinks. Remembering past delights in food and drink is an ignoble kind of pleasure and one

---

[a] Both celebrated Athenian generals of the 5th and 4th centuries B.C., whose lives are to be found in Nepos.

[b] Ion of Chios, historian and poet, c. 490–c. 421 B.C., acquaintance of many of the prominent Athenians of the period. Bergk, Poet. Lyr. Graec. ii, p. 257.

[c] Or " not heating," " not inflaming," even " not filling." For the anecdote see also Cicero, Tusc. Disp. v. 100, with Dougan and Henry's note ; Athenaeus, x, 419 c-d ; Aelian, Varia Hist. ii. 18. Hegesander is quoted as source by Athenaeus (as on the opsophagi) : RE, vii. 2600, no. 4.

(686) ἔχουσιν καὶ ἄλλως ἐξίτηλον, ὥσπερ ὀσμὴν ἕωλον
ἢ κνῖσαν ἐναπολειπομένην, προβλημάτων δὲ καὶ
λόγων φιλοσόφων ὑποθέσεις αὐτούς τε[1] τοὺς μεμνη-
μένους εὐφραίνουσιν, ἀεὶ πρόσφατοι παροῦσαι, καὶ
τοὺς ἀπολειφθέντας οὐχ ἧττον ἑστιᾶν[2] παρέχουσι
τοῖς αὐτοῖς, ἀκούοντας καὶ μεταλαμβάνοντας· ὅπου
καὶ νῦν τῶν Σωκρατικῶν συμποσίων μετουσία καὶ
ἀπόλαυσίς ἐστι τοῖς φιλολόγοις, ὥσπερ αὐτοῖς
D ἐκείνοις τοῖς τότε δειπνοῦσι. καίτοι, εἰ[3] τὰ
σωματικὰ τὰς ἡδονὰς παρεῖχεν, ἔδει καὶ Ξενοφῶντα καὶ Πλάτωνα μὴ τῶν λαληθέντων ἀλλὰ
τῶν παρατεθέντων ἐν Καλλίου καὶ Ἀγάθωνος
ὄψων καὶ πεμμάτων καὶ τραγημάτων ἀπογραφὴν
ἀπολιπεῖν· νῦν δ' ἐκεῖνα μὲν οὐδέποτε, καίπερ ὡς
εἰκὸς ἐκ παρασκευῆς γενόμενα[4] καὶ δαπάνης, λόγου
τινὸς ἠξιώθη, τὰ δὲ φιλοσοφηθέντα μετὰ παιδιᾶς
σπουδάζοντες εἰς γραφὴν ἀπετίθεντο, καὶ κατέ-
λιπον παραδείγματα τοῦ μὴ μόνον συνεῖναι διὰ
λόγων ἀλλήλοις παρὰ πότον ἀλλὰ καὶ μεμνῆσθαι
τῶν λαληθέντων.

ΠΡΟΒΛΗΜΑ Α

E   Τίς ἡ αἰτία, δι' ἣν οἱ νηστεύοντες διψῶσι μᾶλλον ἢ πεινῶσιν

Collocuntur Plutarchus, alii

Ἕκτον οὖν τοῦτό σοι πέμπω τῶν Συμποσιακῶν,

---

[1] τε added by Reiske.   [2] ἑστιᾶν Wyttenbach : εἰς αἰτίαν.
[3] καίτοι εἰ Basel edition : καὶ τοῖσι.
[4] So Reiske : γιγνόμενα.

---

[a] The wealthy Callias and Agathon the poet were the
hosts in Xenophon's and Plato's *Symposium*, respectively.
[b] Plato speaks of his writing and speculation as παιδιά
454

that is, besides, as unsubstantial as yesterday's perfume or the lingering smell of cooking. On the other hand, the topics of philosophical inquiry and discussion not only give pleasure by remaining ever present and fresh to those who actually recall them, but they also provide just as good a feast on the same food to those who, having been left out, partake of them through oral report. In this way, it is even to-day open to men of literary taste to enjoy and share in the Socratic banquets as much as did the original diners. Yet if pleasure were purely physical, the proper thing would have been for both Xenophon and Plato to leave us a record, not of the conversation, but of the relishes, cakes, and sweets served at Callias's house and Agathon's.[a] As it is, they never deign to mention such matters, for all the expense and effort these presumably involved ; but they preserve in writing only the philosophical discussions, combining fun [b] with serious effort. Thus they have left precedents to be followed not only in meeting together for good conversation over wine, but in recording the conversation afterward.

QUESTION 1[c]

Why those who fast are more thirsty than hungry

Speakers : Plutarch and others

HERE, then, is the sixth book of my *Table-Talk*, in

" play " in *Phaedrus*, 265 c, *Timaeus*, 59 c. Xenophon, *Symp.* viii. 41, implies that serious discourse must be restricted at symposiums. Plutarch in his extensive discussion of humour at banquets in *Table-Talk*, ii. 1, especially 634 E-F, quotes Plato's *Laws* to much the same effect.

[c] The discussion is closely imitated by Macrobius, *Saturnalia*, vii. 13. 1-5.

(686) ἐν ᾧ πρῶτόν ἐστι τὸ περὶ τοῦ διψῆν μᾶλλον ἢ πεινῆν τοὺς νηστεύοντας.

Ἄλογον γὰρ ἐφαίνετο διψῆν μᾶλλον ἢ πεινῆν τοὺς ἐκνηστεύσαντας· ἡ γὰρ ἔνδεια τῆς ξηρᾶς τροφῆς ἀναπλήρωσιν οἰκείαν ἐδόκει καὶ[1] κατὰ φύσιν ἐπιζητεῖν. ἔλεγον οὖν ἐγὼ τοῖς παροῦσιν, ὅτι τῶν ἐν ἡμῖν ἢ μόνον ἢ μάλιστα δεῖται τροφῆς

F τὸ θερμόν[2]· "ὥσπερ ἀμέλει βλέπομεν ἔξω[3] μήτ' ἀέρα μήθ' ὕδωρ μήτε γῆν ἐφιέμενα τοῦ τρέφεσθαι μηδ' ἀναλίσκοντα τὸ πλησιάζον, ἀλλὰ μόνον τὸ πῦρ. ᾗ καὶ τὰ νέα βρωτικώτερα τῶν πρεσβυτέρων ὑπὸ θερμότητος· καὶ τοὐναντίον οἱ γέροντες ῥᾷστα νηστείαν φέρουσιν, ἀμβλὺ γὰρ ἐν αὐτοῖς καὶ μικρὸν ἤδη τὸ θερμόν ἐστιν, ὥσπερ ἐν τοῖς ἀναίμοις τῶν ζῴων, ἃ δὴ καὶ τροφῆς ἥκιστα προσδεῖται δι'

687 ἔνδειαν θερμότητος· αὐτόν θ' ἕκαστον αὐτοῦ[4] γυμνάσια καὶ κραυγαὶ καὶ ὅσα τῷ κινεῖν αὔξει τὸ θερμὸν ἥδιον φαγεῖν ποιεῖ καὶ προθυμότερον. τροφὴ δὲ τῷ θερμῷ, καθάπερ νομίζω, ὃ πρῶτον[5] κατὰ φύσιν μάλιστα, τὸ ὑγρόν ἐστιν, ὡς αἵ τε φλόγες αὐξανόμεναι τῷ ἐλαίῳ δηλοῦσιν καὶ τὸ πάντων ξηρότατον εἶναι τέφραν· ἐκκέκαυται γὰρ τὸ νοτερόν, τὸ δὲ γεῶδες ἔρημον ἰκμάδος λέλειπται· καὶ ὁμοίως[6] διίστησι[7] καὶ διαιρεῖ τὰ σώματα τὸ

---

[1] καὶ added by Bernardakis.
[2] For punctuation see Bolkestein, *Adv. Crit.* p. 118 on 635 D.
[3] ἔξω Psellus, Stephanus (Turnebus according to Wyttenbach) : ἐξ ὦν.
[4] So Bernardakis : αὐτοῦ. [5] πρῶτον τῶν Reiske.
[6] So Stephanus : ὅμως. [7] So Stephanus : δὲ ἴστησι.

which the first subject of discussion is why those who fast suffer thirst more than hunger. It appeared illogical that those who have starved themselves should suffer thirst more than hunger, because we thought that according to nature the want of dry food would call for a corresponding kind of replenishment. I therefore argued to those present that, in our bodies, it is solely or chiefly the hot element [a] that demands nourishment; "just as we see in fact that outside ourselves it is not air nor water nor earth, but only fire, that requires to be fed and consumes anything within reach. Thus, young animals are more ravenous than adults because of the heat in their bodies; conversely, aged men endure fasting most easily, for the fire in them is by now blunted and reduced, like that of bloodless animals which require less food than all other animals precisely because of their lack of heat. Exercise, shouting, or anything that by motion increases heat will always cause a man to eat with greater pleasure and a better will. Moisture, probably the most primary substance in nature, in my opinion, is the element that provides nourishment for heat.[b] This is proved by the fact that flames increase whenever oil is added, and that ashes are the driest of all substances, because the dampness has been burned away and the earthy residue is left without a trace of moisture. Similarly, fire opens and tears

---

[a] A reference to the theory of four elements (fire, air, water and earth) as applied to physiology. See Hippocrates (LCL), i, p. xlix. *Cf.*, for instance, *Table-Talk*, ii. 2, 635 c.

[b] Or, as T. C. (in the edition by Several Hands, London, 1684–1694): "The most natural and principal nourishment of heat is moisture." There is perhaps an allusion to Thales, for whose theory Aristotle tries to account in language that seems reflected here. See *Metaphysics*, 983 b 22 ff. Plutarch returns to the point below, in *Table-Talk*, vi. 9. 2, 696 B.

(687) πῦρ τῷ ἐξαιρεῖν[1] τὴν κολλῶσαν ὑγρότητα καὶ
συνδέουσαν. ὅταν οὖν νηστεύσωμεν, ἐκ τῶν ὑπο-
λειμμάτων τῆς ἐν τῷ σώματι τροφῆς ἀποσπᾶται
B βίᾳ τὸ ὑγρὸν ὑπὸ τοῦ θερμοῦ τὸ πρῶτον, εἶτ' ἐπ'
αὐτὴν βαδίζει τὴν σύμφυτον λιβάδα τῆς σαρκὸς
ἡ πύρωσις διώκουσα τὸ νοτερόν[2]· γενομένης οὖν
ὥσπερ ἐν πηλῷ ξηρότητος, ποτοῦ μᾶλλον τὸ σῶμα
δεῖσθαι πέφυκεν, ἄχρι οὗ πιόντων ἀναρρωσθὲν καὶ
ἰσχῦσαν τὸ θερμὸν ἐμβριθοῦς τροφῆς ὄρεξιν ἐργά-
σηται."

ΠΡΟΒΛΗΜΑ Β

Πότερον ἔνδεια ποιεῖ τὸ πεινῆν καὶ διψῆν ἢ πόρων
μετασχηματισμός

Collocuntur Philo, Plutarchus, alii medici

1. Λεχθέντων δὲ τούτων οἱ περὶ Φίλων' ἰατροὶ
τὴν πρώτην θέσιν ἐκίνουν· ἐνδείᾳ γὰρ οὐ γίγνεσθαι
C τὸ δίψος, ἀλλὰ πόρων τινῶν μετασχηματισμῷ.
τοῦτο μὲν γὰρ οἱ νύκτωρ διψῶντες, ἂν ἐπικατα-
δάρθωσι, παύονται τοῦ διψῆν μὴ πιόντες· τοῦτο
δ' οἱ πυρέττοντες, ἐνδόσεως γενομένης ἢ παντάπασι
τοῦ πυρετοῦ λωφήσαντος, ἅμα καὶ[3] τοῦ διψῆν
ἀπαλλάττονται· πολλοῖς δὲ λουσαμένοις καὶ νὴ Δί'
ἐμέσασιν ἑτέροις λήγει τὸ δίψος. ὧν ὑπ' οὐδενὸς
αὔξεται τὸ ὑγρόν, ἀλλὰ μόνον οἱ πόροι παρέχουσι,
πάσχοντές[4] τι τῷ μετασχηματίζεσθαι, τάξιν ἑτέραν
καὶ διάθεσιν.

[1] So Madvig : ἐξαίρειν.
[2] τὸ νοτερόν Basel edition, cf. Psellus : τὸν ἔτερον.
[3] ἅμα καὶ Bernardakis : καὶ ἅμα.
[4] παρέχουσι, πάσχοντες Hutten ; πάσχοντες Turnebus, Stephanus ; παρέσχον, πάσχοντες Wyttenbach : παρασχόντες.

apart any solids by drawing off the moisture that
cements and holds them together. So, when we fast,
the moisture is first abstracted forcibly by the heat
from any remnants of food left in the body. Then
the burning process, seeking moisture, goes on to the
natural juices of the body. Accordingly, since this
produces dryness (compare how mud dries in the
heat), it is natural for the body to want drink more
until, reinvigorated and fortified by our drinking, the
hot element arouses an appetite for solid food."

QUESTION 2

Whether hunger and thirst are caused by deficiency
or by a change in shape of the passages

Speakers : Plutarch, Philo and other physicians

1. AT this point in the discussion, Philo and the other
physicians attacked the original premise, saying that
thirst arises, not from a deficiency, but from a change
of shape *a* in certain channels in the body. For one
thing, those who suffer from thirst at night lose their
thirst without drinking, if they fall asleep ; for
another, those who have a fever are also freed of thirst
as soon as the fever subsides or entirely ceases. Many
are relieved of thirst after a bath, others, surprisingly,
after vomiting. In these cases the moisture in their
bodies is not increased by anything ; it is only that
the channels, being subjected to a change of shape,
exhibit a new posture and condition.

a There is a discussion of shapes or " structures " in
Pseudo-Hippocrates, *On Ancient Medicine*, 22. 1. *Cf.* 649
D, *supra*, where the word *poroi*, here translated " passages "
or " channels," is used to refer to " vessels of the vascular
system " in plants. See now Sandbach in LCL Plut. *Mor.*
xi, p. 141.

(687) Ἐκδηλότερον δὲ τοῦτο γίγνεται περὶ τὴν πεῖναν. ἐνδεεῖς γὰρ ἅμα πολλοὶ[1] γίγνονται καὶ ἀνόρεκτοι τῶν νοσούντων· ἐνίοις δ' ἐμπιπλαμένοις οὐδὲ ἓν αἱ D ὀρέξεις χαλῶσιν, ἀλλὰ καὶ κατατείνουσι καὶ παραμένουσιν. ἤδη δὲ πολλοὶ τῶν ἀποσίτων, ἐλαίαν ἁλμάδα λαμβάνοντες ἢ κάππαριν, γευσάμενοι ταχέως ἀνέλαβον καὶ παρεστήσαντο τὴν ὄρεξιν. ᾧ καὶ μάλιστα δῆλόν ἐστιν, ὅτι πάθει τινὶ πόρων οὐχ ὑπ' ἐνδείας ἐγγίγνεται τὸ πεινῆν ἡμῖν· τὰ γὰρ τοιαῦτα βρώματα τὴν μὲν ἔνδειαν ἐλαττοῖ προστιθεμένης τροφῆς, * *[2] ποιοῦσιν, οὕτως αἱ τῶν ἐφάλμων βρωμάτων εὐστομίαι καὶ δριμύτητες ἐπιστρέφουσαι καὶ πυκνοῦσαι τὸν στόμαχον ἢ πάλιν ἀνοίγουσαι καὶ χαλῶσαι δεκτικήν τινα τροφῆς εὐαρμοστίαν περιειργάσαντο περὶ αὐτόν, ἣν ὄρεξιν καλοῦμεν.

2. Ἐδόκει δή μοι ταῦτα πιθανῶς μὲν ἐγκεχειρῆσθαι, πρὸς δὲ τὸ μέγιστον ἐναντιοῦσθαι τῆς E φύσεως τέλος, ἐφ' ὃ πᾶν ἄγει ζῷον ὄρεξις, ἀναπλήρωσιν τοῦ ἐνδεοῦς ποθοῦσα καὶ τὸ[3] ἐκλεῖπον ἀεὶ τοῦ οἰκείου διώκουσα· "τὸ γὰρ ᾧ διαφέρει μάλιστα τὸ ζῷον τοῦ ἀψύχου, τοῦτο μὴ φάναι πρὸς σωτηρίαν καὶ διαμονὴν ὑπάρχειν ἡμῖν, ὥσπερ ὄμμα, τῶν[4] οἰκείων τῷ σώματι καὶ δεητῶν[5] ἐγγεγενημένον,[6] ἀλλὰ πάθος εἶναι καὶ τροπήν τινα

---

[1] So Xylander : πολύ.
[2] Turnebus indicated a lacuna and supplied ⟨τὸ δὲ πεινῆν⟩, changing the following ποιοῦσι to ποιεῖ. Hubert believes that more is lost, suggesting ⟨πεῖναν δὲ ποιεῖ· ὡς γὰρ αἱ στύψεις

This is more obvious in the case of hunger. Many of the sick are in need of food and yet lack appetite; whereas some eat their fill, yet have appetites not only unabated but actually intensified and persistent. In fact, there have been many cases of loss of appetite when a taste of pickled olive or caper has brought prompt recovery and restored the appetite. This proves conclusively that our hunger springs from some modification of the passages and is not caused by deficiency; for this kind of food diminishes the want since nourishment is added, yet causes hunger. So the sharpness and pungency of salted food either twists and contracts the stomach or, conversely, by opening and relaxing it again, produces a kind of adjusted receptivity in it to nourishment, which we call appetite.

2. This seemed to me a plausible theory, but one that contradicts the most insistent purpose of nature, toward which appetite leads every creature; for appetite craves to fill every need and always pursues whatever is lacking to its own proper satisfaction. " Not to admit," I went on, " that appetite, one of the things that particularly differentiate the animate from the inanimate, is a means provided us for our protection and survival, one of the things that are implanted in us as needful and proper to our body, like an eye, but instead to imagine that appetite is some peculiar condition or modification of the chan-

---

τὰς ὀθόνας δεκτικωτέρας τῆς βαφῆς⟩ ποιοῦσιν, from the last sentence of the Question and the immediate context here.

[3] καὶ τὸ Xylander : αὐτό.

[4] ὄμμα τῶν Reiske, ὄχημα Faehse : ὀμμάτων.

[5] δεητῶν suspect since Stephanus, who preferred δεκτῶν, defended by Reiske, δεόντων Madvig : δέη τῶν.

[6] So Doehner, ἐγγενόμενον Reiske : ἐγγεγενημένων.

(687) πόρων οἴεσθαι μεγέθεσι καὶ μικρότησι συμβαί-
νουσαν εἰς οὐδέν' ἦν λόγον ἁπλῶς τιθεμένων τὴν
φύσιν.

"Ἔπειτα ῥιγοῦν μὲν[1] ἐνδείᾳ θερμότητος οἰκείας
τὸ σῶμα, μηκέτι δὲ[2] διψῆν μηδὲ πεινῆν ὑγρότητος
ἐνδείᾳ τῆς[3] κατὰ φύσιν καὶ τροφῆς, ἄλογόν ἐστι·
F τούτου δ' ἀλογώτερον, εἰ κενώσεως μὲν ἐφίεται
διὰ πλήρωσιν ἡ φύσις, πληρώσεως δ' οὐ διὰ
κένωσιν, ἀλλ' ἑτέρου τινὸς πάθους ἐγγενομένου.
καὶ μὴν αἵ γε τοιαῦται περὶ τὰ ζῷα χρεῖαι καὶ
ἀναπληρώσεις οὐδέν τι τῶν περὶ τὰς γεωργίας
γιγνομένων διαφέρουσιν· πολλὰ γὰρ ὅμοια πάσχει
καὶ βοηθεῖται· πρὸς μὲν γὰρ τὰς ξηρότητας
688 ἀρδείαις ποτίζομεν,[4] καὶ ψύχομεν[5] μετρίως ὅταν
φλέγηται, ῥιγοῦντα δ' αὐτὰ θάλπειν πειρώμεθα καὶ
σκέπειν πόλλ' ἄττα[6] περιβάλλοντες· καὶ ὅσα μὴ
παρ' ἡμᾶς ἐστιν, εὐχόμεθα τὸν θεὸν διδόναι, δρό-
σους μαλακὰς καὶ εἰλήσεις ἐν πνεύμασι μετρίοις,[7]
ὡς ἀεὶ τοῦ ἀπολείποντος ἀναπλήρωσιν ἡ φύσις
ἔχοι,[8] διατηροῦσα τὴν κρᾶσιν. οὕτω γὰρ οἶμαι
καὶ τροφὴν ὠνομάσθαι τὸ τηροῦν τὴν φύσιν·
τηρεῖται δὲ τοῖς μὲν φυτοῖς ἀναισθήτως ἐκ τοῦ
περιέχοντος, ὥς φησιν Ἐμπεδοκλῆς, ὑδρευομένοις
τὸ πρόσφορον· ἡμᾶς δ' ἡ ὄρεξις ζητεῖν διδάσκει
καὶ διώκειν τὸ ἐκλεῖπον τῆς κρᾶσεως.

---

[1] μὲν added by Hirschig, Hartman, μὲν φάναι Reiske.
[2] δὲ added by Xylander.
[3] τῆς Anonymus : τῆι.
[4] So Xylander, Madvig : ποτιζόμενα.
[5] So Xylander, Madvig : ψυχόμενα.
[6] πόλλ' ἄττα Turnebus : πολλοστὰ (πολλαστὰ Venetus).

nels brought about by differences in size—that, I say, is worthy of someone who simply leaves nature out of account.

" Further, it is illogical to hold, on the one hand, that the body is cold through a deficiency of proper heat, and, on the other hand, to refuse to say that it suffers thirst or hunger through a deficiency of natural moisture or nutriment. Still more illogical than this is the notion that although nature seeks evacuation because there is repletion, it seeks replenishment not because there is an emptiness, but on account of some other condition that supervenes. Moreover, these needs of animal life with their satisfactions differ in no respect from those that occur in agriculture ; many of the conditions and their remedies are similar. For instance, in the case of drought we irrigate ; when anything is scorched, we make it moderately cool, and when the plants are cold, we try to warm and protect them by many sorts of covering. What is not in our power to provide we pray the god to grant, such as gentle dews or sunshine with mild breezes, so that nature may always have a replenishment of what is lost and thus preserve the balance of elements. I think that this is how the word *trophê* (nurture) originated ; it is that which preserves nature (*têrei physin*). Plants preserve nature unconsciously, because, according to Empedocles,[a] they draw as much water from the atmosphere as is needful. But in our case, it is appetite that teaches us to seek and pursue any element wanting in our balance.

[a] Fragment 70 (Diels).

---

[7] So Wyttenbach, μετρίας Reiske : μετρίως.
[8] ἔχῃ Hubert after Bernardakis, who also adds ἂν after ὡς.

(688) " Οὐ μὴν ἀλλὰ καὶ τῶν εἰρημένων ἕκαστον
B ἴδωμεν ὡς οὐκ ἀληθές ἐστι. τὰ μὲν γὰρ εὐστομίαν ἔχοντα καὶ δριμύτητα τάχα μὲν οὐκ ὄρεξιν,
ἀλλὰ δηγμὸν ἐμποιεῖ τοῖς δεκτικοῖς[1] μέρεσι τῆς
τροφῆς, οἷον κνησμοὶ[2] κατὰ θίξιν ἐνίων ἀμυσ-
σόντων· εἰ δὲ καὶ τοῦτο τὸ πάθος ὀρεκτικόν
ἐστιν, εἰκός ἐστιν ὑπὸ τῶν τοιούτων βρωμάτων
λεπτυνόμενα διακρίνεσθαι τὰ προϋπόντα,[3] καὶ
ποιεῖν μὲν ἔνδειαν, οὐ μεταρρυθμιζομένων δὲ[4] τῶν
πόρων ἀλλὰ κενουμένων καὶ καθαιρομένων· τὰ
γὰρ ὀξέα καὶ δριμέα καὶ ἁλμυρὰ θρύπτοντα τὴν
ὕλην διαφορεῖ[5] καὶ σκίδνησιν, ὥστε νεαρὰν ποιεῖν
τὴν ὄρεξιν ἐκθλιβομένων[6] τῶν ἑώλων καὶ χθιζῶν.
τῶν δὲ λουομένων οὐ μετασχηματιζόμενοι παύου-
C σιν οἱ πόροι τὸ δίψος, ἀλλ' ἰκμάδα διὰ[7] τῆς
σαρκὸς ἀναλαμβάνοντες καὶ ἀναπιμπλάμενοι νοτε-
ρᾶς ἀτμίδος.

" Οἱ δ' ἔμετοι τὸ ἀλλότριον ἐκβάλλοντες ἀπό-
λαυσιν τῇ φύσει τοῦ οἰκείου παρέσχον. οὐ γὰρ
ἁπλῶς τοῦ[8] ὑγροῦ τὸ δίψος, ἀλλὰ τοῦ κατὰ φύσιν
καὶ οἰκείου· διό, κἂν πολὺ παρῇ τὸ ἀλλόφυλον,
ἐνδεὴς ὁ ἄνθρωπός ἐστιν· ἐνίσταται[9] γὰρ τοῖς κατὰ
φύσιν ὑγροῖς, ὦν ἡ ὄρεξίς ἐστι, καὶ οὐ δίδωσιν
ἀνάμιξιν οὐδὲ κατάκρασιν, ἄχρι ἂν ἐκστῇ καὶ
ἀποχωρήσῃ· τότε δ' οἱ πόροι τὸ σύμφυλον ἀναλαμβάνουσιν. οἱ δὲ πυρετοὶ τὸ ὑγρὸν εἰς βάθος

---

[1] So Aldine edition : δηκτικοῖς.
[2] κνησμῷ Hubert, κνησμὸν Emperius, κνησμὸν καὶ (for κατὰ)
Reiske.
[3] So Doehner : πρέποντα " the proper constituents."
[4] δὲ added by Meziriacus.
[5] So Stephanus, cf. 669 B : διαφέρει.
[6] So Reiske : εἰσθλιβομένων.

" Not only that, but let us see in detail how false is
each of the arguments offered. First, sharp and pungent foods perhaps produce not appetite but a sting-
ing effect on the members which receive them, an
effect much like the irritation caused by touching
certain prickly things. Now if this is actually what
excites appetite, it is probably because the eating of
such things causes the comminution and disintegration of food already present in the system, and creates
a deficiency, not because the passages are forced to
adopt new shapes, but because they are emptied and
purged. Sour, pungent, or salty foods break up, dis-
tribute, and disperse the crude stuff, and thus renew
appetite because in the process the previous day's
stale residue is squeezed out. Secondly, in the case
of the bathers, thirst is abated, not through the re-
shaping of the channels, but by their absorption of
liquid through the flesh and by their being thus re-
filled with moist steam.

" Next, vomiting, by expelling foreign matter, enables nature to benefit by its proper food. Thirst is
not merely desire for liquid without qualification ; it
is desire for drink that is natural and suitable. Accordingly, even if there is an abundance of the wrong
kind of nourishment, a man is still in want. Such
abundance blocks the natural liquids craved by thirst,
and permits no mixing or blending of food and drink
until it is removed and passes off ; then only can the
channels receive their kindred [a] food. Fevers force

----

[a] On " kindred " food *cf. Table-Talk*, iv. i. 2, 661 E.

----

[7] διὰ added by Faehse (Bolkestein, *Adv. Crit.* p. 78), Doehner.

[8] ἁπλῶς τοῦ Meziriacus : ἀπλήστου.

[9] So Reiske : ἐφίσταται.

(688) ἀπωθοῦσιν, καὶ τῶν μέσων φλεγομένων ἐκεῖ πᾶν
D ἀποκεχώρηκεν καὶ κρατεῖται πεπιεσμένον· ὅθεν
ἐμεῖν τε πολλοὺς ἅμα συμβαίνει, πυκνότητι τῶν
ἐντὸς ἀναθλιβόντων[1] τὰ ὑγρά, καὶ διψῆν[2] δι' ἔνδειαν
καὶ ξηρότητα τοῦ λοιποῦ σώματος. ὅταν οὖν
ἄνεσις γένηται καὶ τὸ θερμὸν ἐκ τῶν μέσων ἀπίῃ,
σκιδνάμενον αὖθις ὑπονοστεῖ[3] καὶ διὸν,[4] ὡς πέφυκε,
πάντῃ τὸ νοτερὸν[5] ἅμα τοῖς τε μέσοις ῥᾳστώνην
παρέσχεν καὶ τὴν σάρκα λείαν καὶ ἁπαλὴν ἀντὶ
τραχείας καὶ αὐχμώδους γενομένην ἐμάλαξεν, πολλάκις δὲ καὶ ἱδρῶτας ἐπήγαγεν· ὅθεν ἡ ποιοῦσα
διψῆν ἔνδεια λήγει καὶ παύεται, τῆς ὑγρότητος
E ἀπὸ τοῦ βαρυνομένου καὶ δυσαναβλυστοῦντος[6] ἐπὶ
τὸν δεόμενον καὶ ποθοῦντα μεθισταμένης τόπον.
ὡς γὰρ ἐν κήπῳ, φρέατος ἄφθονον ὕδωρ ἔχοντος,
εἰ μή τις ἐπαντλοῖ καὶ ἄρδοι τὰ φυτά,[7] διψῆν καὶ
ἀτροφεῖν ἀναγκαῖόν ἐστι, οὕτως ἐν σώματι, τῶν
ὑγρῶν εἰς ἕνα κατασπωμένων τόπον, οὐ θαυμαστὸν ἔνδειαν εἶναι περὶ τὰ λοιπὰ καὶ ξηρότητα,
μέχρι οὗ πάλιν ἐπιρροὴ καὶ διάχυσις γένηται·
καθάπερ καὶ ἐπὶ τῶν πυρεττόντων, ὅταν ἀνεθῶσι,
συμβαίνει καὶ τῶν ἐγκαταδαρθανόντων τῷ διψῆν·
καὶ γὰρ τούτοις ὁ ὕπνος ἐκ μέσων ἐπανάγων τὰ
ὑγρὰ καὶ διανέμων πάντῃ τοῖς μέρεσιν ὁμαλισμὸν
ἐμποιεῖ καὶ ἀναπλήρωσιν.

" Ὁ γὰρ δὴ λεγόμενος τῶν πόρων μετασχη-

---

[1] So Meziriacus : ἀναθλιβέντων.
[2] So Basel edition : δύψαν.
[3] So Basel edition, Turnebus : ὑπονοστεῖν.
[4] So Turnebus : ἴδιον.
[5] τὸ νοτερὸν Basel edition : τὸν ἕτερον.

moisture downward, so that as the middle area is in-
flamed, the moisture withdraws to that one place and
is subjected to violent pressure. In consequence, it
is true that many men both vomit, because the con-
densation of matter inside by its pressure forces all
liquids upward, and at the same time are thirsty
because of deficiency and drought elsewhere in the
body. Therefore, when the fever subsides and the
heat leaves the central parts of the body, the moisture,
as it spreads, returns to its level, and permeates the
whole body, in keeping with its nature. At the same
time, it provides relief to those central parts, and
softens the flesh which has now become smooth and
tender instead of rough and parched. This often even
brings on sweating. Thus the deficiency that has
caused thirst ends, and its effect is lost, as moisture
shifts its position from the region where it causes
distress and stoppage of the flow to the region where
it is needed and missed. In a garden, even if there is
an excellent well, the plants inevitably wither from
thirst unless someone draws the water and irrigates ;
so, in our body, if all the liquid is drawn off to one
spot, it is no wonder that there is deficiency and
drought in the rest of the system until the flow and
diffusion of moisture are restored. Similar also is the
experience of patients after a fever and of those who
fall asleep while thirsty. In those cases, too, sleep
draws up the liquids from the central area and passes
them on, thus bringing about a uniform distribution
and a proper supply to all parts of the body.

" What sort of change of shape in the passages is it

---

[6] So Hubert after Duebner and Doehner : δυσαναβλαστοῦν-
τος " growing with difficulty."

[7] τὰ φυτὰ Xylander : αὐτά.

(688)

F ματισμὸς οὗτος,[1] ᾧ τὸ πεινῆν ἢ τὸ διψῆν ἐγγίγνεται,[2] ποῖός τίς ἐστιν; ἐγὼ μὲν γὰρ οὐχ ὁρῶ
περὶ πόρους[3] διαφορὰς ἄλλας[4] κατὰ πάθος[5] ἢ τὸ
συμπίπτειν καὶ τὸ διίστασθαι· καὶ συμπίπτοντες[6]
μὲν οὔτε ποτὸν οὔτε τροφὴν δέχεσθαι δύνανται, δι-
ιστάμενοι δὲ κενότητα καὶ χώραν ποιοῦσιν, ἔνδειαν
οὖσαν τοῦ κατὰ φύσιν καὶ οἰκείου. καὶ γὰρ αἱ
στύψεις, ὦ βέλτιστε, τῶν βαπτομένων," ἔφη,
689 " πόκων[7] ἔχουσι τὸ δριμὺ καὶ ῥυπτικόν, ᾧ τῶν
περισσῶν ἐκκρινομένων καὶ ἀποτηκομένων οἱ πόροι
δέχονται μᾶλλον καὶ στέγουσι[8] δεξάμενοι τὴν βαφὴν ὑπ' ἐνδείας καὶ κενότητος."

ΠΡΟΒΛΗΜΑ Γ

Διὰ τί πεινῶντες μέν, ἐὰν πίωσι, παύονται, διψῶντες δ', ἐὰν
φάγωσιν, ἐπιτείνονται

Collocuntur convivator, Plutarchus

1. Ῥηθέντων δὲ τούτων ὁ ἑστιῶν ἡμᾶς καὶ
ταῦτ' ἔφη μετρίως λέγεσθαι καὶ πρὸς ἄλλην ἀπο-
B ρίαν τὰς τῶν πόρων κενώσεις καὶ ἀναπληρώσεις
βοηθεῖν, διὰ τί τοῖς μὲν πεινῶσιν, ἐὰν πίωσι,
παύεται τὸ πεινῆν[9] ἐν τῷ παραυτίκα, τοῖς δὲ διψῶσι τοὐναντίον,[10] ἐὰν ἐμφάγωσιν, ἐπιτείνειν συμβαίνει τὸ δίψος. " τοῦτο δὴ[11] τὸ πάθος οἱ τοὺς

---

[1] So Basel edition : οὕτως.
[2] So Reiske : ἐγγένηται.
[3] πόρους Bernardakis, τοὺς πόρους Doehner : πόρου ἢ πόρων,
where the scribe was in doubt, cf. Gulick in Am. Journ.
Philol. lx (1939), p. 493.
[4] So Basel edition : ἀλλά.
[5] πάθος Bernardakis, τὸ πάθος Doehner : πλῆθος.
[6] So Basel edition : συμπίπτοντος.

to which you refer, by which hunger and thirst are occasioned ? *I* cannot conceive any kind of contrast brought about by change in the condition of the channels, except contraction and expansion. When they contract, they cannot receive either food or drink ; when they expand, they create emptiness and space, which is simply the want of some natural and proper substance. Observe also, my friend," I said, " that the steeping in astringent solution of fabric to be dyed involves the use of penetrating detergents to remove and dissolve extraneous matter in the channels or pores of the fabric, that they may better receive and hold the dye in the spaces thus provided and requiring to be filled."

QUESTION 3 [a]

Why hunger is appeased by drinking, but thirst increased by eating

Speakers : Plutarch, his host

1. At this point in the discussion our host said that this was a fair statement, and besides, the theory of the emptying and filling of passages might help us to answer another question : why does hunger cease immediately upon drinking while, on the contrary, those who thirst actually become thirstier on eating ? " This strange effect is," he went on, " accounted for

---

[a] *Cf.* Macrobius, *Saturnalia*, vii. 12. 18 f.

[7] πόκων Bernardakis : τόπον.
[8] So Meziriacus : στέργουσι.
[9] βοηθεῖν, . . . πεινῆν added by Hubert after Madvig.
[10] So Emperius : ἐναντίον.
[11] δὴ Wyttenbach : δέ.

(689) πόρους ὑποτιθέμενοι[1] ῥᾷστα καὶ πιθανώτατά μοι
δοκοῦσιν, εἰ καὶ μὴ πολλὰ μόνον πιθανῶς, αἰ-
τιολογεῖν. πᾶσι γὰρ ὄντων πόρων, ἄλλας πρὸς
ἄλλα[2] συμμετρίας ἐχόντων,[3] οἱ μὲν εὐρύτεροι τὴν
ξηρὰν ἅμα καὶ τὴν ὑγρὰν τροφὴν ἀναλαμβάνουσιν,
οἱ δ' ἰσχνότεροι τὸ μὲν[4] ποτὸν παραδέχονται, τὸ
δὲ σιτίον οὐ παραδέχονται.[5] ποιεῖ δὲ τὴν μὲν
δίψαν ἡ τούτων κένωσις, ἡ δ' ἐκείνων τὴν πεῖναν.
C ὅθεν, ἐὰν μὲν φάγωσιν οἱ διψῶντες, οἱ μὲν οὐ
βοηθοῦνται, τῶν πόρων διὰ λεπτότητα τὴν ξηρὰν
τροφὴν μὴ δεχομένων ἀλλ' ἐπιδεῶς τοῦ οἰκείου
διαμενόντων· οἱ δὲ πεινῶντες ἐὰν πίνωσιν, ἐνδυό-
μενα τὰ ὑγρὰ τοῖς μείζοσι πόροις καὶ ἀναπληροῦντα
τὰς κενότητας αὐτῶν ἀνίησι τὸ σφοδρὸν ἄγαν τῆς
πείνης.''

2. Ἐμοὶ δὲ τὸ μὲν συμβαῖνον ἀληθὲς ἐφαίνετο,
τῇ δ' ὑποθέσει τῆς αἰτίας οὐ προσεῖχον. '' καὶ
γὰρ εἰ τοῖς πόροις τούτοις,'' ἔφην, '' ὧν ἔνιοι
περιέχονται καὶ ἀγαπῶσι, κατατρήσειέ τις τὴν
σάρκα, πλαδαρὰν καὶ τρομώδη[6] καὶ σαθρὰν ἂν[7]
ποιήσειε[8]· τό τε μὴ ταὐτὰ τοῦ σώματος μόρια τὸ
ποτὸν προσδέχεσθαι καὶ τὸ σιτίον ἀλλ' ὥσπερ ἠθ-
μοῖς καταρρεῖσθαι καὶ ἀποκρίνεσθαι κομιδῇ πλα-
D σματῶδες καὶ ἀλλόκοτον. αὕτη γὰρ ἡ πρὸς τὸ
ὑγρὸν ἀνάμιξις, θρύπτουσα τὰ σιτία καὶ συνεργὰ
λαμβάνουσα τὸ θερμὸν τὸ ἐντὸς καὶ τὸ πνεῦμα,
πάντων ὀργάνων ἀκριβέστατα πάσαις τομαῖς καὶ
διαιρέσεσι λεπτύνει τὴν τροφήν, ὥστε πᾶν μόριον
αὐτῆς παντὶ μορίῳ γίγνεσθαι φίλον καὶ οἰκεῖον,

---

[1] So Turnebus : ἐπιτιθέμενοι.
[2] ἄλλας πρὸς ἄλλα Kronenberg : ἄλλος πόρος ἄλλας.

most easily and most convincingly, in my opinion, by
the advocates of this theory of passages, although it
isn't often that they are even so much as plausible.
There are channels for everything, varying in capacity
according to their purpose ; the wider passages
receive both solid and liquid matter, but the narrower
only the liquid. Emptiness in these latter causes
thirst ; in the former it causes hunger. Hence, if
those who are thirsty eat, they do not benefit, because
the channels, being narrow, do not admit the dry
food, and continue to miss what they require. On
the other hand, if people who are hungry take a drink,
the liquid does enter the larger passages, fills them,
and alleviates the more violent pangs of hunger."

2. To my mind, the fact was clearly true, but I did
not agree with the reason suggested for it. " For if
you were to perforate the flesh," I said, " with these
passages that certain people so fondly cling to, you
would make it weak, quivering and unsound ; to
believe that both wet and dry food are not received
into the same parts, but are filtered and separated
as if through a strainer—that is unrealistic and absurd. The blending in our bodies of solid food with
liquid, breaking it up with the help of the internal
heat and vital spirit, reduces the food by every process of division and dissection in more accurate fashion
than any instrument. This renders every particle
adaptable and homogeneous to every other, not as

---

³ ἔχει Stephanus, ἔχει· ὧν Duebner.

⁴ τὸ μὲν MS., μόνον τὸ Wyttenbach.

⁵ τὸ δὲ σιτίον οὐ παραδέχονται added by Madvig, τὸν δὲ
σῖτον οὔ Reiske.

⁶ σπογγώδη Herwerden.

⁷ ἄν added by Herwerden.

⁸ So Herwerden after Basel edition and Reiske : ποιήσας.

(689) οὐκ ἐναρμόττον ὥσπερ ἀγγείοις[1] καὶ τρήμασιν ἀλλ'
ἐνούμενον καὶ προσφυόμενον. ἄνευ δὲ τούτων
οὐδὲ λέλυται τῆς ἀπορίας τὸ μέγιστον· οἱ γὰρ
ἐμφαγόντες, ἂν μὴ πίωσιν, οὐ μόνον οὐ λύουσιν
ἀλλὰ καὶ προσεπιτείνουσι τὸ δίψος· πρὸς τοῦτο δ'
οὐδὲν εἴρηται.

E   " Σκόπει δὲ καὶ τὰ παρ' ἡμῶν," ἔφην, " εἰ
φαινομένας ὑποθέσεις λαμβάνομεν, πρῶτον μὲν
λαμβάνοντες τὸ ὑγρὸν ὑπὸ[2] τοῦ ξηροῦ διαφθείρεσθαι
δαπανώμενον, τῷ δ' ὑγρῷ τὸ ξηρὸν βρεχόμενον
καὶ μαλασσόμενον διαχύσεις ἴσχειν καὶ ἀναθυμιά-
σεις· δεύτερον δὲ μὴ νομίζοντες ἔκθλιψιν εἶναι
παντάπασιν μήτε τῆς ξηρᾶς τροφῆς τὴν[3] πεῖναν
μήτε τῆς ὑγρᾶς τὴν δίψαν, ἀλλὰ τοῦ μετρίου καὶ
ἀρκοῦντος ἔνδειαν· οἷς γὰρ ὅλως ἂν ἐλλίπῃ θάτερον, οὔτε πεινῶσιν οὔτε διψῶσιν ἀλλ' εὐθὺς ἀπο-
θνῄσκουσιν. ὑποκειμένων δὲ τούτων οὐ χαλεπὸν
ἤδη τὴν[4] αἰτίαν συνιδεῖν. ἡ μὲν γὰρ δίψα τοῖς φα-
γοῦσιν ἐπιτείνεται τῶν σιτίων τῇ ξηρότητι, εἴ
τι[5] διεσπαρμένον ὑγρὸν καὶ ἀπολειπόμενον ἀσθενὲς
F καὶ ὀλίγον ἐν τῷ σώματι, συλλεγόντων καὶ προσ-
εξικμαζόντων· ὥσπερ ἔξω γῆν ὁρῶμεν καὶ κόνιν
καὶ ψάμμον[6] τὰ μιγνύμενα τῶν ὑγρῶν ἀναλαμ-
βάνουσαν εἰς ἑαυτὴν καὶ ἀφανίζουσαν. τὴν δὲ
πεῖναν αὖ πάλιν ἀναγκαίως τὸ ποτὸν ἀνίησιν· ἡ
γὰρ ὑγρότης τὰ ὑπόντα σιτία περισκελῆ καὶ
γλίσχρα βρέξασα καὶ διαχέασα, χυμῶν ἐγγενο-
690 μένων καὶ ἀτμῶν, ἀναφέρει τούτοις[7] εἰς τὸ σῶμα
καὶ προστίθησι τοῖς δεομένοις· ὅθεν οὐ κακῶς

---

[1] So Stephanus : ἀστείοις.
[2] So Stephanus : ἀπό.
[3] τὴν added by Reiske.

fitting into vessels and apertures, but as being amalgamated and brought into organic agreement. Otherwise, the most difficult part of the problem isn't actually solved, the fact that those who take food without drinking anything actually increase instead of relieving their thirst ; nothing has been said to explain that.

" Consider also," I went on, " whether we accept as evident two points which I have to make. The first is that moisture is consumed and destroyed by dryness, while dryness is saturated and softened by moisture so that it is dissolved and vaporized. My second point is that hunger and thirst result not from the total expulsion of dry or wet food, but from a lack of the proper and sufficient amount of either ; because those who are totally deprived of either do not suffer hunger or thirst, but simply die. These premises granted, it is already easy to perceive the explanation that we seek. When we have eaten, thirst is aggravated because solid food, by its dryness, concentrates and draws off such scant and feeble moisture as is left scattered in the body. So outside the body we see earth, dust, and sand absorb any moisture that is mixed with them and make it disappear. However, on the other hand, drinking does necessarily relieve hunger. For the liquid drenches and dissolves such hard, tough remnants of food as are present in the system, and by means of the juices and vapours that are generated conveys them through the body and delivers them to those parts that need

----

4 ἤδη τὴν Basel edition : ἤδημεν.
5 εἴ τι added by Reiske.
6 ψάμμον or μαλλόν " wool " Wyttenbach : μᾶλλον.
7 So Kronenberg : τούτους.

(690) ὄχημα τῆς τροφῆς τὸ ὑγρὸν ὁ Ἐρασίστρατος
προσεῖπεν· τὰ γὰρ ὑπὸ ξηρότητος ἢ πάχους[1] ἀργὰ
καὶ βαρέα μιγνύμενον ἀναπέμπει καὶ συνεξαίρει.
πολλοὶ δὲ καὶ μὴ πιόντες ἀλλὰ λουσάμενοι μόνον
ἐπαύσαντο συντόμως[2] σφόδρα πεινῶντες· ἐνδυο-
μένη γὰρ ἔξωθεν ἡ ὑγρότης εὐχυμότερα ποιεῖ καὶ
τροφιμώτερα τῷ ἐγχαλᾶσθαι τὰ ἐντός, ὥστε τῆς
πείνης τὸ σφόδρα πικρὸν καὶ θηριῶδες ἐνδιδόναι
καὶ παρηγορεῖσθαι. διὸ καὶ πολὺν ζῶσιν ἔνιοι
τῶν ἀποκαρτερούντων χρόνον, ἂν ὕδωρ μόνον
B λαμβάνωσιν, ἄχρι ἂν οὗ[3] πᾶν ἐξικμασθῇ τὸ τρέφειν
καὶ προστίθεσθαι τῷ σώματι δυνάμενον.''

ΠΡΟΒΛΗΜΑ Δ

Διὰ τίν' αἰτίαν τὸ φρεατιαῖον[4] ὕδωρ ἀρυσθέν, ἐὰν ἐν αὐτῷ τῷ
τοῦ φρέατος ἀέρι νυκτερεύσῃ, ψυχρότερον γίνεται

Collocuntur hospes, Plutarchus, alii

1. Ψυχροπότῃ ξένῳ τρυφῶντι παρεσκεύασαν οἱ
θεράποντες τοῦ ἐκ[5] φρέατος ὕδωρ ψυχρότερον·
ἀρυσάμενοι γὰρ ἀγγείῳ καὶ κρεμάσαντες τὸ ἀγ-
C γεῖον ἐν τῷ φρέατι τῆς πηγῆς[6] μὴ ἀπτόμενον[7]
εἴασαν ἐπινυκτερεῦσαι, καὶ πρὸς τὸ δεῖπνον ἐκο-
μίζετο τοῦ προσφάτου ψυχρότερον. ἦν δ' ὁ ξένος φιλόλογος ἐπιεικῶς, καὶ τοῦτ' ἔφη λαβεῖν ἐκ
τῶν Ἀριστοτέλους μετὰ λόγου κείμενον· εἶναι δὲ
τοιόνδε τὸν λόγον. πᾶν ὕδωρ προθερμανθὲν ψύ-

---

[1] So Reiske, Madvig : πάθους.
[2] So Reiske : συντόνως. [3] οὐ Xylander : οὐ.
[4] φρεατιαῖον Stephanus, Lex., cf. Helmbold, Class. Philol.
xxxvi (1941), p. 85 : φρεατίδιον Τ.
[5] τοῦ ἐκ Reiske : ἐκ τοῦ. [6] So Leonicus : γῆς.
[7] μὴ ἀπτόμενον Leonicus : μαλαττόμενον Τ.

them. Therefore Erasistratus appropriately called water the vehicle of nourishment, since it combines with the food that is heavy and inert because of dryness or bulk and helps lift and carry it away. There are even many cases where, without drinking, but merely by bathing, men have found quick relief from extreme hunger. For the external moisture penetrates to the inward parts and, by causing relaxation, makes the food that is there more nourishing and more productive of healthy humours. The effect of this is to overcome and soothe the savage, bitter pangs of hunger. Therefore, some who are starving themselves to death survive even for a long time, if they merely keep on drinking water until everything is absorbed that can nourish and be added to the body."

QUESTION 4

Why water drawn from a well becomes cooler if it is kept overnight in the very air of the well[a]

Speakers : a guest, Plutarch and others

1. For a guest who indulged in the luxury of cold drinks the servants procured water which was colder than that which came from the well by drawing it in a vessel and suspending the vessel all night long in the shaft of the well, but not in contact with the water below ; thus it was brought to dinner cooler than newly drawn water. The guest, who was a fairly well-read man, said that he had found this in the writings of Aristotle,[b] where the reason was explained. The explanation was as follows : all water will get

---

[a] *Cf.* Plut. *De Primo Frigido*, 12, 949 c-f.

[b] Frag. 216 Rose (1886).

(690) χεται μᾶλλον, ὥσπερ τὸ τοῖς βασιλεῦσι παρα-
σκευαζόμενον· ὅταν γὰρ ἑψηθῇ μέχρι ζέσεως,
περισωρεύουσι τῷ ἀγγείῳ χιόνα πολλὴν καὶ γίγνεται ψυχρότερον· ὥσπερ ἀμέλει καὶ τὰ ἡμέτερα
σώματα λουσαμένων περιψύχεται μᾶλλον· ἡ γὰρ
ὑπὸ τῆς θερμότητος ἄνεσις πολύπορον τὸ σῶμα[1]
D καὶ μανὸν ἀπειργασμένη πολὺν δέχεται τὸν ἔξωθεν
ἀέρα καὶ βιαιοτέραν ποιεῖ τὴν μεταβολήν· ὅταν
οὖν ἀποσπασθῇ[2] τῆς πηγῆς[3] τὸ ὕδωρ, ἐν τῷ ἀέρι,
προθερμανθέν, περιψύχεται ταχέως.

2. Τὸν μὲν οὖν ξένον ἐπηνέσαμεν ὡς ἀνδρικῶς
καταμνημονεύσαντα[4]· περὶ δὲ τοῦ λόγου διηποροῦμεν. ὁ γὰρ ἀήρ, ἐν ᾧ κρέμαται τὸ ἀγγεῖον, εἰ
μὲν ψυχρός ἐστι, πῶς θερμαίνει τὸ ὕδωρ; εἰ δὲ
θερμός, πῶς περιψύχει πάλιν; ἄλογον γὰρ ὑπὸ
τοῦ αὐτοῦ τὸ αὐτὸ πάσχειν τὰ ἐναντία, μηδεμιᾶς
διαφορᾶς γενομένης. σιωπῶντος δ' αὐτοῦ καὶ
διαποροῦντος, οὐδὲν ἔφην[5] δεῖν περὶ τοῦ ἀέρος
διαπορεῖν· ἡ γὰρ αἴσθησις λέγει ὅτι ψυχρός ἐστι,
E καὶ μάλιστά γ' ὁ[6] ἐν βάθει φρεάτων· ὥστ' ἀμήχα-
νον ὑπ' ἀέρος ψυχροῦ θερμαίνεσθαι τὸ ὕδωρ· ἀλλὰ
μᾶλλον ὁ ψυχρὸς οὗτος ἀὴρ τὴν μὲν πηγὴν διὰ
πλῆθος οὐ δύναται μεταβάλλειν, ἂν δέ τις ἀφαιρῇ
κατ' ὀλίγον, μᾶλλον κρατῶν[7] περιψύξει.

---

[1] τὸ σῶμα Stephanus : τὰ σώματα.
[2] So Meziriacus, cf. 949 c : ὑποπλασθῇ ὑπὸ (ὑπὸ deleted by Benseler).
[3] So Frankfurt edition : πληγῆς.
[4] So Reiske : καὶ μνημονεύσαντα.
[5] So Turnebus : ἔφη.

cooler if it is preheated, like that provided for royalty[a]; it is the practice, after the water is heated to the boiling point, to pack snow abundantly around the container, and the result is cooler water. Analogously, as is well known, our bodies too cool off more completely after a warm bath, because the relaxation caused by heat opens pores all over the body and makes it loose-textured, so that it lets in a flood of air from outside and causes a more drastic change from hot to cold. So, then, water withdrawn from the well cools quickly in the air, if preheated.

2. We applauded the stranger for his valiant feat of memory, but continued to puzzle over this theory. For how can the air in which the vessel hangs, if cold, heat the water ? On the other hand, if it is hot, how can it cool the water ? It is illogical for opposite effects to be produced in the same object by the same cause, if no difference has been introduced. When our friend was silent and puzzled at this, I said that there was no need to worry about the air, for our senses tell us that air is cold, especially deep in a well. It is, then, impossible to think that water is heated by cold air. Rather, this cold air cannot change the temperature of the well-water because there is too much of it ; but if you draw off a little water at a time, the air gains the advantage and will cool it.[a]

[a] Or " the Emperors " Warmington.
[b] Plutarch says (*De Primo Frigido, loc. cit.*) that air is the cause of coldness. He fails to identify the effect of evaporation, which is multiplied by the use of porous jars. *Cf.* Helmbold's note b in LCL *Mor.* xii, p. 251.

---

[6] γ' ὁ Hubert, ὁ τῶν Reiske : τῶν.
[7] So Basel edition : ἐρᾶτῶν.

(690)

ΠΡΟΒΛΗΜΑ Ε

Διὰ τίν' αἰτίαν οἱ χάλικες καὶ αἱ μολιβδίδες ἐμβαλλόμεναι
ψυχρότερον τὸ ὕδωρ ποιοῦσιν

Collocuntur Plutarchus, hospes

F " 'Αλλὰ μὴν περὶ τῶν χαλίκων," ἔφην, " ἢ τῶν
ἀκμόνων,[1] οὓς ἐμβάλλοντες εἰς τὸ ὕδωρ ψύχειν
αὐτὸ καὶ στομοῦν δοκοῦσιν, εἰρημένον 'Αριστοτέλει
μνημονεύεις; " " αὐτὸ τοῦτ'," ἔφη, " μόνον ἐν
προβλήμασιν εἴρηκε τὸ γιγνόμενον· εἰς δὲ τὴν αἰτίαν ἐπιχειρήσομεν[2] ἡμεῖς· ἔστι γὰρ μάλιστα δυσ-
θεώρητος."

" Πάνυ μὲν οὖν," ἔφην,[3] " καὶ θαυμάσαιμ' ἄν,
εἰ μὴ διαφύγοι ὁ λόγος ἡμᾶς· ὅρα δ'[4] ὅμως.[5] πρῶτον οὐ δοκεῖ σοι περιψύχεσθαι[6] μὲν ὑπὸ τοῦ ἀέρος
691 τὸ ὕδωρ ἔξωθεν ἐμπίπτοντος,[7] ὁ δ' ἀὴρ μᾶλλον
ἰσχύειν[8] πρὸς τοὺς λίθους καὶ τοὺς ἄκμονας[9] ἀπε-
ρειδόμενος; οὐ γὰρ ἐῶσιν αὐτὸν ὥσπερ τὰ χαλκᾶ
καὶ τὰ κεραμεᾶ τῶν ἀγγείων, διεκπίπτειν, ἀλλὰ τῇ
πυκνότητι στέγοντες ἀνακλῶσιν[10] εἰς τὸ ὕδωρ ἀπ'
αὐτῶν, ὥστε δι' ὅλου καὶ ἰσχυρὰν[11] γίγνεσθαι[12] τὴν
περίψυξιν. διὸ καὶ χειμῶνος οἱ ποταμοὶ ψυχρότεροι
γίγνονται τῆς θαλάττης· ἰσχύει γὰρ ἐν αὐτοῖς ὁ
ψυχρὸς ἀὴρ ἀνακλώμενος,[13] ἐν δὲ τῇ θαλάττῃ διὰ
βάθος ἐκλύεται πρὸς μηδὲν ἀντερείδων.

---

[1] ἀκόνων Junius, Stephanus.
[2] ἐπιχειρήσωμεν Stephanus.   [3] ἔφη E, perhaps rightly.
[4] ὅρα δ' Wyttenbach: ὁρᾶτε.   [5] So Reiske: ὅλως.
[6] So Reiske: προψύχεσθαι.
[7] So Anonymus: ἐκπίπτοντος.
[8] So Wyttenbach: ἰσχύει.
[9] τὰς ἀκόνας Stephanus.
[10] So Doehner from Psellus: ἀναλοῦσιν.

QUESTION 5 [a]

Why pebbles and lumps of lead thrown into water
serve to make it cooler

Speakers : Plutarch and a guest

" Yes, and do you remember," I said, " a statement
by Aristotle [b] about pebbles or lumps of metal,[c]
which people are said to drop into water to cool and
temper it ? " "About that," he answered, " he mentioned only the phenomenon itself as you've stated
it, as one of a number of problems. It is up to us to
try to explain the cause, which is extremely hard to
discover."

" Quite so," said I, " I should really be surprised
if it did not elude us ; but look into it, anyway.
First of all, don't you think that the water is cooled
by the outside air that assails it, and that the air has
more effect if it comes down against stones and lumps
of metal ? For these objects do not allow it to escape,
as the bronze or clay vessels do, but by their density
keep it and reflect it back into the water, so that the
cooling pervades the whole and becomes thorough.
That is why in fact rivers in winter are colder than
the ocean ; in them the cold air is effective because
it is reflected from the bottom, whereas in the ocean
it is dissipated, since because of the depth it comes
against nothing solid to stop it.

[a] Excerpted by Psellus, *De Omnifaria Doctrina*, 154.
[b] Frag. 213.
[c] *akmones* : the common meaning of this word, " anvils,"
seems unsuited here. *Cf.* below on " whetstones."

---

[11] So Basel edition : $\iota\sigma\chi\upsilon\sigma\alpha\nu$.
[12] So Bernardakis from Psellus : $\gamma\epsilon\nu\acute{\epsilon}\sigma\theta\alpha\iota$.
[13] So Doehner from Psellus : $\dot{\alpha}\nu\alpha\lambda\acute{\omega}\mu\epsilon\nu\sigma\varsigma$.

(691)   " Κατ' ἄλλον δὲ τρόπον εἰκός ἐστι τὰ λεπτότερα
τῶν ὑδάτων περιψύχεσθαι μᾶλλον¹ ὑπὸ τοῦ ψυχροῦ·
B κρατεῖται γὰρ δι' ἀσθένειαν. αἱ δ' ἀκόναι καὶ οἱ
χάλικες λεπτύνουσι τὸ ὕδωρ, ὅ τι θολερὸν καὶ
γεῶδες ἀναμέμικται, τοῦτο συνάγοντες καὶ κατα-
σπῶντες ἀπ' αὐτοῦ, ὥστε λεπτότερον καὶ ἀσθενέστερον τὸ ὕδωρ γενόμενον μᾶλλον ὑπὸ περιψύξεως
κρατεῖσθαι. καὶ μὴν ὅ τε μόλιβδος τῶν φύσει ψυχρῶν ἐστιν, ὅς γε τριβόμενος ὄζει τὸ ψυκτικώτα-
τον τῶν θανασίμων φαρμάκων ἐξανίησι ψιμύθιον·
οἵ τε χάλικες πυκνότητι τὸ ψυχρὸν διὰ βάθους
ποιοῦσιν· πᾶς μὲν γὰρ λίθος κατεψυγμένης καὶ
πεπιλημένης ὑπὸ κρύους γῆς πάγος ἐστίν, μᾶλλον
δ' ὁ μᾶλλον πεπυκνωμένος· ὥστ' οὐκ ἄτοπον, εἰ
τὴν ψυχρότητα τοῦ ὕδατος ἀντερείδων συνεπιτείνει
C καὶ ὁ λίθος καὶ ὁ μόλιβδος."

ΠΡΟΒΛΗΜΑ ϛ

Διὰ τίν' αἰτίαν ἀχύροις καὶ ἱματίοις τὴν χιόνα διαφυλάττουσι

Collocuntur hospes, Plutarchus

1. Μικρὸν οὖν ὁ ξένος διαλιπών, " οἱ ἐρῶντες,"
ἔφη, " μάλιστα μὲν αὐτοῖς τοῖς παιδικοῖς, εἰ δὲ
μή, περὶ αὐτῶν ἐπιθυμοῦσι διαλέγεσθαι· τοῦτο²
πέπονθα περὶ τῆς χιόνος. ἐπεὶ γὰρ οὐ πάρεστιν
οὐδ' ἔχομεν,³ ἐπιθυμῶ⁴ μαθεῖν, τίς αἰτία δι' ἣν

---

¹ ἢ after μᾶλλον deleted by Basel edition.
² τοῦτο Basel edition, τούτοις ταὐτὸ Doehner : τούτοις.
³ οὐδὲ λαμβάνειν ποθὲν ἔχομεν Reiske : οὐδὲ ἔχομεν.
⁴ So Leonicus : ἐπιθυμίαν.

" In another way also it is probable that thinner water is more easily refrigerated ; it is overpowered by cold because of its own weakness. Whetstones [a] and pebbles thin the water ; they collect and precipitate any mud and solid matter that is carried in it. This makes the water thinner and weaker, and consequently more subject to cooling. Moreover, lead is a naturally cold substance. For if triturated with vinegar, it gives off the most refrigerant of deadly drugs, lead acetate.[b] Pebbles too are dense enough to cool water all through, for any stone is a compact solid of earth, chilled and compressed by icy cold, the denser the colder. It is not surprising, then, if both stone and lead by their solidity help to increase the coldness of the water."

QUESTION 6 [c]

Why snow is covered with straw and cloth to preserve it

Speakers : Plutarch and a guest

1. AFTER a pause the guest said, " Lovers desire above all to talk directly to the boys that they're fond of ; if they cannot, they desire at least to talk about them. That is my case now with reference to snow. Since there is no snow here and we can supply none, I have a desire to be informed why it is pre-

---

[a] Or " pigs of lead " : Aristotle apparently, according to Plutarch, uses the term similarly. Cf. De Primo Frigido, 11, 949 c (LCL Mor. xii, pp. 248 ff., and notice particularly note a on p. 250).

[b] See Pliny, Nat. Hist. xxxiv. 175 with Warmington's note (LCL vol. ix), where the process of manufacture is described.

[c] Excerpted by Psellus, De Omnifaria Doctrina, 155.

(691) ὑπὸ τῶν θερμοτάτων φυλάσσεται. καὶ γὰρ ἀχύροις
D σπαργανοῦντες αὐτὴν καὶ περιστέλλοντες ἱματίοις
ἀγνάπτοις ἐπὶ πολὺν χρόνον ἄπταιστον διατηροῦ-
σιν. θαυμαστὸν οὖν, εἰ συνεκτικὰ τὰ θερμότατα
τῶν ψυχροτάτων ἐστί."

2. '' Κομιδῇ γ','' ἔφην, '' εἴπερ ἀληθές ἐστιν· οὐκ
ἔχει δ' οὕτως, ἀλλ' αὐτοὺς παραλογιζόμεθα, θερμὸν εὐθὺς[1] εἶναι τὸ θερμαῖνον ὑπολαμβάνοντες· καὶ
ταῦθ' ὁρῶντες ὅτι ταὐτὸν ἱμάτιον ἐν χειμῶνι θερ-
μαίνειν[2] ἐν δ' ἡλίῳ ψύχειν γέγονεν[3]· ὥσπερ ἡ τρα-
γικὴ τροφὸς ἐκείνη τὰ τῆς Νιόβης τέκνα τιθηνεῖ-
ται·

λεπτοσπαθήτων[4] χλανιδίων ἐρειπίοις
θάλπουσα καὶ ψύχουσα.

Γερμανοὶ μὲν οὖν κρύους πρόβλημα ποιοῦνται τὴν
E ἐσθῆτα μόνον, Αἰθίοπες δὲ θάλπους μόνον, ἡμεῖς
δ' ἀμφοῖν. ὥστε τί μᾶλλον, εἰ θάλπει, θερμὴν
ἢ ψυχρὰν ἀπὸ τοῦ περιψύχειν λεκτέον; εἰ δὲ δεῖ
τῇ αἰσθήσει τεκμαίρεσθαι, μᾶλλον ἂν ψυχρὰ γέ-
νοιτο· καὶ γὰρ ὁ χιτὼν ψυχρὸς ἡμῖν προσπίπτει
τὸ πρῶτον ἐνδυσαμένοις καὶ τὰ στρώματα κατα-
κλινεῖσιν· εἶτα μέντοι συναλεαίνει τῆς ἀφ'[5] ἡμῶν
πιμπλάμενα θερμασίας καὶ ἅμα μὲν περιστέλλοντα
καὶ κατέχοντα τὸ θερμὸν ἅμα δ' ἀπείργοντα τὸ
κρύος καὶ τὸν ἔξωθεν[6] ἀέρα τοῦ σώματος. οἱ μὲν
οὖν πυρέττοντες ἢ καυματιζόμενοι συνεχῶς ἀλ-
λάττουσι τὰ ἱμάτια τῷ[7] ψυχρὸν εἶναι τὸ ἐπιβαλ-

---

[1] So Stephanus : εὐθὺ.
[2] So Basel edition : θερμαίνει.
[3] So Duebner : λέγομεν.
[4] So Turnebus, Vulcobius, and, according to Wyttenbach,
γ, Anonymus : λεπτὸς πάθη τῶν.

served by the hottest of materials. People swathe it like an infant in straw, and wrap it in cloth of un-fulled wool to keep it for a long time intact. It is certainly astonishing that the warmest things should be capable of preserving the coldest."

2. " Very much so, indeed," I answered, " if it is true. But it isn't so, and we mislead ourselves if we assume that anything that warms is by the same to-ken hot, especially when we see that the same gar-ment can keep us warm in winter and yet cool in the sun. Witness in tragedy the way the celebrated nurse takes care of Niobê's children,[a]

> With fragments of fine-woven little garments,
> Both warming and cooling them.

The German tribes use clothes for protection only against cold, the Ethiopians against heat, and we against both. So why must we say that clothing is " hot " if it warms, rather than " cold " because it cools ? If we are to judge by sense-impression, it would rather be proved cool, for when we first put on our undergarments, or lie down in the blankets, their touch is cool. Afterwards, to be sure, they help to warm us, after they have absorbed our body heat, not only by enclosing and retaining the warmth, but also by excluding the outer air with its chill. Sufferers from fever or heat continually change their clothes because of the momentary coolness of a fresh garment

---

[a] Author unknown; Nauck, *Trag. Gr. Frag.*, p. 839, frag. 7. Quoted more fully in *Mor.* 496 E ; but note that the emen-dation in LCL *Mor.* vi, p. 350, is inconsistent with the present passage.

---

[5] So Psellus, Doehner : ὑφ.
[6] So Benseler : ἔξω.
[7] So Basel edition : τὸ.

(691)
F λόμενον, ἂν δ' ἐπιβληθῇ, παραχρῆμα γίγνεσθαι[1]
θερμὸν ὑπὸ τοῦ σώματος. ὥσπερ οὖν ἡμᾶς θερ-
μαινόμενον θερμαίνει τὸ ἱμάτιον, οὕτως τὴν χιόνα
ψυχόμενον ἀντιπεριψύχει· ψύχεται δ' ὑπ' αὐτῆς
ἀφιείσης[2] πνεῦμα λεπτόν· τοῦτο γὰρ συνέχει τὴν
πῆξιν αὐτῆς ἐγκατακεκλεισμένον[3]· ἀπελθόντος δὲ
τοῦ πνεύματος, ὕδωρ οὖσα ῥεῖ καὶ διατήκεται, καὶ
ἀπανθεῖ τὸ λευκὸν ὅπερ ἡ τοῦ πνεύματος πρὸς τὸ
ὑγρὸν ἀνάμιξις ἀφρώδης γενομένη παρεῖχεν· ἅμα
τ' οὖν τὸ ψυχρὸν ἐγκατέχεται περιστεγόμενον τῷ
692 ἱματίῳ, καὶ ὁ ἔξωθεν ἀὴρ ἀπειργόμενος οὐ τέμνει
τὸν πάγον οὐδ' ἀνίησιν. ἀγνάπτοις δὲ τούτοις
χρῶνται τοῖς ἱματίοις[4] πρὸς τοῦτο διὰ τὴν τραχύτητα καὶ ξηρότητα τῆς κροκύδος οὐκ ἐώσης
ἐπιπεσεῖν βαρὺ τὸ ἱμάτιον οὐδὲ συνθλῖψαι τὴν
χαυνότητα τῆς χιόνος· ὥσπερ καὶ τὸ ἄχυρον διὰ
κουφότητα μαλακῶς περιπῖπτον οὐ θρύπτει τὸν
πάγον, ἄλλως δὲ πυκνόν ἐστι καὶ στεγανόν, ὥστε[5]
καὶ τὴν[6] θερμότητα τοῦ ἀέρος ἀπείργειν καὶ τὴν
ψυχρότητα κωλύειν ἀπιέναι τῆς χιόνος. ὅτι δ' ἡ
τοῦ πνεύματος διάκρισις ἐμποιεῖ τὴν τῆξιν, ἐμφα-
νές ἐστι τῇ αἰσθήσει· τηκομένη γὰρ ἡ χιὼν πνεῦμα
ποιεῖ."

---

[1] γίνεσθαι Hubert : γίνεται.
[2] So Psellus, Doehner : ἀφείσης.
[3] So Psellus, Doehner : ἐγκατακείμενον.

as it is first put on, though it immediately becomes hot from the body.[a] Accordingly, a garment or piece of cloth, just as it warms us while being warmed by us, will likewise cool snow, while being cooled by it. The cooling by the snow is due to a fine vapour that is given off. This vapour, while locked in, maintains the frozen condition of the snow, but as soon as it has departed, the snow, being only water, becomes fluid and melts away, losing the whiteness produced by the frothy effect of the vapour mixed with water. When snow is wrapped in cloth, the cold is held in by the insulating effect of the cloth, which at the same time excludes the outer air and prevents it from breaking up and melting the frost. Unfulled material is used for this because the roughness and dryness of the nap keeps the weight of the cloth from bearing down and compressing the loose structure of the snow. Likewise, the straw, having no weight, makes a light covering which does not crush the ice, yet is packed close and tight enough to exclude the heat of the air and prevent the escape of cold from the snow. That the escape of vapour is the cause of melting is obvious to the senses, for snow as it melts gives off steam."

[a] *Cf. Mor.* 100 B.

---

[4] χρῶνται τοῖς ἱματίοις added by Xylander.
[5] So Basel edition : ὥσπερ.
[6] τὴν added by Leonicus.

ΠΡΟΒΛΗΜΑ Ζ

Εἰ δεῖ τὸν οἶνον ἐνδιηθεῖν

Collocuntur Niger, Aristio

1. Νίγρος[1] ὁ πολίτης ἡμῶν ἀπὸ σχολῆς ἀφῖκτο
συγγεγονὼς ἐνδόξῳ φιλοσόφῳ χρόνον οὐ πολύν,
ἀλλ᾽ ἐν ὅσῳ τὰ τοῦ ἀνδρὸς οὐ καταλαμβάνοντες[2]
ἀνεπίμπλαντο τῶν ἐπαχθῶν ἀπ᾽ αὐτοῦ μιμούμενοι[3]
τὸ ἐπιτιμητικὸν καὶ ἐλέγχοντες[4] ἐπὶ παντὶ πράγ-
ματι τοὺς συνόντας. ἑστιῶντος οὖν ἡμᾶς Ἀριστίωνος,[5] τήν τ᾽ ἄλλην χορηγίαν ὡς πολυτελῆ καὶ
περίεργον ἐμέμφετο καὶ τὸν οἶνον οὐκ ἔφη δεῖν
ἐγχεῖσθαι[6] διηθημένον,[7] ἀλλ᾽, ὥσπερ Ἡσίοδος
C ἐκέλευσεν, ἀπὸ τοῦ πίθου πίνεσθαι τὴν σύμφυτον
ἔχοντα ῥώμην καὶ δύναμιν. '' ἡ δὲ τοιαύτη κάθαρσις αὐτοῦ πρῶτον μὲν ἐκτέμνει τὰ νεῦρα καὶ τὴν
θερμότητα κατασβέννυσιν· ἐξανθεῖ γὰρ καὶ ἀποπνεῖ
διερωμένου[8] πολλάκις.

'' Ἔπειτα περιεργίαν καὶ καλλωπισμὸν ἐμφαίνει
καὶ τρυφὴν εἰς τὸ ἡδὺ καταναλίσκουσα τὸ χρήσιμον.
ὥσπερ γὰρ τὸ τοὺς ἀλεκτρυόνας ἐκτέμνειν[9] καὶ
τοὺς χοίρους, ἁπαλὴν αὐτῶν παρὰ φύσιν τὴν σάρκα
ποιοῦντας καὶ θήλειαν, οὐχ ὑγιαινόντων ἐστὶν
ἀνθρώπων ἀλλὰ διεφθαρμένων ὑπὸ λιχνείας, οὕτως,
εἰ δεῖ μεταφορᾷ χρησάμενον λέγειν,[10] ἐξευνουχί-

---

[1] So Xylander from *Mor.* 131 A : Νίκρος.
[2] So Reiske : καταλαμβάνοντος.
[3] So Basel edition : μιμουμένου.
[4] So Basel edition : λέγοντος.
[5] So Xylander : Ἀρίστωνος.   [6] So Turnebus : ἐλέγχεσθαι.
[7] So Doehner : ἠθημένον.   [8] So Xylander : διεωρωμένου.
[9] So Bernardakis : ἐκτεμεῖν.
[10] So Xylander, ἐλέγχειν Budaeus, Turnebus : ἔχειν.

QUESTION 7

Whether it is right to strain wine

Speakers: Niger, Aristion

1. My fellow-townsman Niger [a] had returned from a brief course of instruction under a noted philosopher. The time had been long enough, however, for students, though they might not take hold of the man's teaching, to catch some of his annoying habits. They would reproduce his censorious manner and take the company to task on every possible occasion; so, when we were entertained at dinner by Aristion, Niger began to find everything too costly and elaborate. Specifically, he told us that wine ought not to be filtered, but ought to be drunk straight from the winejar, according to Hesiod's prescription,[b] with all its natural power and strength. "Purifying it like this," said he, "cuts out its sinew and quenches its fire. There is a loss of bloom and a dissipation of the bouquet from the repeated straining.

"In the second place, this practice reflects a tendency to over-refinement, vainglory, and luxury, and sacrifices the useful in favour of the pleasurable. To castrate pigs and cocks, making their flesh unnaturally soft and effeminate, is typical of men whose health and character are ruined by gluttony. Just so, if I may use the metaphor, do people caponize

---

[a] Niger or Nigros is known only from this passage and the *De Tuenda Sanitate* (LCL *Mor.* ii, pp. 260-261) where there is an account of his death in Galatia on a lecture tour. The present passage seems to prove that he came from Chaeronea, as Ziegler thinks (*op. cit.* 679).

[b] *Works and Days*, 368: "when the jar is first opened." But this is far from close.

(692) ζουσι[1] τὸν ἄκρατον καὶ ἀποθηλύνουσιν οἱ διη-
D θοῦντες, οὔτ' ἄφθονον[2] ὑπ' ἀσθενείας οὔτε πίνειν[3]
μέτριον δυνάμενοι διὰ τὴν ἀκρασίαν· ἀλλὰ σόφισμα
τοῦτ' ἐστὶν αὐτοῖς καὶ μηχάνημα πολυποσίας·
ἐξαιροῦσι[4] δὲ τοῦ οἴνου τὸ ἐμβριθές, τὸ λεῖον[5]
ἀπολιπόντες, ὥσπερ οἱ τοῖς ἀκράτως ἔχουσι πρὸς
ψυχροποσίαν ἀρρώστοις ἀφεψημένον[6] διδόντες· ὅ τι
γὰρ στόμωμα τοῦ οἴνου καὶ κράτος[7] ἐστίν, τοῦτ'
ἐν τῷ διυλίζειν ἐξαιροῦσι[8] καὶ ἀποκρίνουσι. μέγα
δὲ[9] τεκμήριον νὴ Δία φθορᾶς[10] τὸ μὴ διαμένειν ἀλλ'
ἐξίστασθαι καὶ μαραίνεσθαι, καθάπερ ἀπὸ ῥίζης
κοπέντα τῆς τρυγός· οἱ δὲ παλαιοὶ καὶ τρύγα τὸν
οἶνον ἄντικρυς ἐκάλουν, ὥσπερ ψυχὴν καὶ κεφαλὴν
E τὸν ἄνθρωπον εἰώθαμεν ἀπὸ τῶν κυριωτάτων
ὑποκορίζεσθαι, καὶ τρυγᾶν λέγομεν τοὺς δρεπο-
μένους τὴν ἀμπελίνην ὀπώραν, καὶ ' διατρύγιόν '
που Ὅμηρος εἴρηκεν, αὐτὸν δὲ τὸν οἶνον ' αἴθοπα '
καὶ ' ἐρυθρὸν ' εἴωθε καλεῖν· οὐχ ὡς Ἀριστίων
ἡμῖν ὠχριῶντα καὶ χλωρὸν ὑπὸ τῆς πολλῆς καθ-
άρσεως παρέχεται.''

2. Καὶ ὁ Ἀριστίων γελάσας, '' οὐκ ὠχριῶντ',''
εἶπεν, '' ὦ τᾶν, οὐδ' ἀναίμον', ἀλλὰ μειλίχιον καὶ
ἡμερίδην, ἀπὸ τῆς ὄψεως αὐτῆς πρῶτον. σὺ δ'
ἀξιοῖς τοῦ νυκτερινοῦ καὶ μελαναίγιδος ἐμφορεῖσθαι,

---

[1] So Leonicus : ἐξονυχίζουσι.
[2] So Hubert, φέρειν Wilamowitz, φορεῖν Xylander : φρονεῖν.
[3] τὸν after πίνειν deleted by Hubert.
[4] So Duebner : ἐξαίρουσι.
[5] τὸ λεῖον Stephanus : τέλειον.
[6] So Basel edition : ἀφηψαμένον.
[7] So Basel edition : ἄκρατός.
[8] So Duebner : ἐξαίρουσι.   [9] δὲ added by Basel edition.
[10] νὴ Δία φθορᾶς Reiske, τῆς διαφθορᾶς Basel edition : ἡ δια-
φθορά· καὶ.

and emasculate wine, filtering it because they are too poor in health to drink hard and too intemperate to drink in moderation. Why, this is nothing but a trick, a contrivance that enables them to drink on and on, since it takes the heaviness out of wine and leaves it smooth. It reminds me of the way that water is boiled for patients unable to control their thirst for cold liquids. Some substance that constitutes the edge and power of the wine is removed and lost in the process of filtering. Now a positive indication of the destructive power of this process is that filtered wine does not keep its quality, but weakens and fades as if cut off from its root, that is, the lees. The ancients even went so far as to call wine ' lees,' [a] just as we affectionately call a person ' soul ' or ' head ' from his ruling part. So we use *trygân* [b] of those who gather the harvest of the vine, and Homer somewhere has the expression *diatrygios*, ' yielding *trygê* throughout the season,' and is accustomed to apply to wine itself the adjectives ' fiery-looking ' (*aithops*) and ' red,' and not—as Aristion serves it—' pale ' and ' bilious-looking ' from excessive purification."

2. Aristion laughed and said, " Not bilious-looking, my dear fellow, nor bloodless, but mellow and sunny,[c] as appears first of all in its face. But you want us to fill up on wine dark as night and sable-palled,[d] and

[a] The same word (*tryx*) is used for " lees " and " fresh wine " or " must."

[b] Plutarch takes this as meaning " to gather lees," but τρύγη, the immediate source of the verb, is used of harvested grain as well as of vintage, not specifically of must.

[c] From ἥμερος (tame, cultivated) ; the form used signifies a cultivated vine, but is taken here as the opposite of " nocturnal," as if from ἡμέρα (day).

[d] Used by Aesch. *Sept.* 699, of an Erinys ; literally " of dark aegis."

(692) καὶ ψέγεις τὴν κάθαρσιν ὥσπερ χολημεσίαν δι'
F ἧς[1] τὸ βαρὺ καὶ μεθυστικὸν ἀφιεὶς[2] καὶ νοσῶδες
ἐλαφρὸς καὶ ἄνευ ὀργῆς ἀναμίγνυται ἡμῖν, οἷον
Ὅμηρός φησι πίνειν τοὺς ἥρωας· αἴθοπα γὰρ οὐ
καλεῖ τὸν ζοφερόν, ἀλλὰ τὸν διαυγῆ καὶ λαμπρόν·
οὐ γὰρ ἄν, ὦ φίλε, τὸν[3] ' εὐήνορα ' καὶ ' νώροπα
χαλκόν ' ' αἴθοπα ' προσηγόρευεν.

" Ὥσπερ οὖν ὁ σοφὸς Ἀνάχαρσις ἄλλ' ἄττα
693 τῶν Ἑλλήνων μεμφόμενος ἐπήνει τὴν ἀνθρακείαν[4] ὅτι τὸν καπνὸν ἔξω καταλιπόντες οἴκαδε πῦρ
κομίζουσιν, οὕτως ἡμᾶς ἐφ' ἑτέροις ἂν ψέγοιτε
μᾶλλον οἱ σοφοὶ ὑμεῖς· εἰ δὲ τοῦ οἴνου τὸ ταρακτικὸν καὶ ὀχλῶδες ἐξωθούμενοι καὶ ἀποσκεδάσαν-
τες, αὐτὸν δὲ φαιδρύνοντες[5] οὐ καλλωπίσαντες, οὐδ'
ὥσπερ σιδήρου στόμωμα καὶ ἀκμὴν ἀποκόψαντες,
ἀλλὰ μᾶλλον ὥσπερ ἰὸν ἢ ῥύπον ἀποκαθάραντες
προσφερόμεθα, τί πλημμελοῦμεν; ' ὅτι νὴ Δία
πλέον ἰσχύει μὴ διηθούμενος '· καὶ γὰρ ἄνθρωπος,
ὦ φίλε, φρενετίζων καὶ μαινόμενος· ἀλλ' ὅταν
ἐλλεβόρῳ χρησάμενος ἢ διαίτῃ καταστῇ, τὸ μὲν
B σφοδρὸν ἐκεῖνο καὶ σύντονον οἴχεται καὶ γέγονεν
ἐξίτηλον, ἡ δ' ἀληθινὴ δύναμις καὶ σωφροσύνη

---

[1] δι' ἧς Meziriacus : εἰς (ς in erasure).
[2] So Stephanus, ἀφεὶς Basel edition : ἀφιει.
[3] ἄν, ὦ φίλε, τὸν Pohlenz, ἂν ὁ λέγων Wyttenbach : ανω-
φλεγων.
[4] ἀνθρακείαν Hubert : ἀνθρακιάν.
[5] δὲ φαιδρύνοντες Reiske, -αντες Wyttenbach : δ' εὐφραίνον-
τες.

you find fault with purification in terms that suggest the purging of bile ; actually, it is a means to rid the wine of heavy, intoxicating, morbid elements and make it light in the mixture and free from anger, as Homer [a] says the heroes drank. For *aithops* in Homer doesn't mean 'murky'[b] but 'translucent' and 'gleaming'; otherwise, my dear friend, he wouldn't have called bronze *aithops* as well as 'manly' and 'flashing.'

'Wise Anacharsis,[c] while objecting to other traits and customs of the Greeks, praised their use of charcoal, by which they left the smoke out of doors and brought only the fire into the house. Similarly, you learned people might better find fault with us on other grounds. No, even if we do extract and banish from wine its disturbing and offensive element, brightening without bedizening it,[d] not taking off the fine temper of its edge as from steel or iron, but rather cleaning away corrosion and dirt before we partake of it, why are we wrong in doing that ? ' Why, because,' you say, ' wine is stronger unfiltered.' Yes, my friend, so is a madman stronger in his frenzy. But when he recovers, after a dose of hellebore or some curative regimen, his violence and tension are eradicated and disappear, while genuine strength and soundness of mind return to his sys-

[a] See below, *Table-Talk*, ix, 736 D : an interpretation of Achilles's invitation to the single combatants at the funeral feast of Patroclus as implying that Achilles desired them to lay aside any anger or ill will that might have arisen between them (*Iliad*, xxiii. 810). Another possibility is that in *Iliad* ix. 224 (*cf.* 260) the drinking symbolizes the attempt to reconcile Achilles and Agamemnon.

[b] In some late authors *aithops* means " black."

[c] A Scythian wise man who travelled in Greece *c.* 630 B.C.

[d] Or, " removing the dirt without adding rouge," Post.

491

(693) παραγίνεται τῷ σώματι· οὕτω δὴ καὶ ἡ κάθαρσις
τοῦ οἴνου τὸ πληκτικὸν ἀφαιροῦσα καὶ μανικόν,
εἰς πραεῖαν ἕξιν καὶ ὑγιαίνουσαν καθίστησι.

" Περιεργίαν δ᾽ οἶμαι πάμπολυ διαφέρειν καθα-
ριότητος[1]· καὶ γὰρ αἱ γυναῖκες φυκούμεναι καὶ
μυριζόμεναι καὶ χρυσὸν φοροῦσαι καὶ πορφύραν
περίεργοι δοκοῦσιν, λουτρὸν δὲ καὶ ἄλειμμα καὶ
κόμης ῥύψιν[2] οὐδεὶς αἰτιᾶται. χαριέντως δὲ τὴν
διαφορὰν ὁ ποιητὴς ἐπιδείκνυσιν ἐπὶ τῆς κοσ-
μουμένης Ἥρας,

<blockquote>
ἀμβροσίῃ μὲν πρῶτον ἀπὸ χροὸς ἀθανάτοιο[3]
C λύματα πάντα κάθηρεν, ἀλείψατο δὲ λίπ᾽ ἐλαίῳ·
</blockquote>

μέχρι τούτων ἐπιμέλεια[4] καθαριότητός ἐστιν· ὅταν
δὲ τὰς χρυσᾶς περόνας ἀναλαμβάνῃ καὶ τὰ διηκρι-
βωμένα τέχνῃ ἐλλόβια καὶ τελευτῶσα τῆς περὶ
τὸν κεστὸν ἅπτηται γοητείας, περιεργία τὸ χρῆμα
καὶ λαμυρία μὴ πρέπουσα γαμετῇ γέγονεν. οὐκοῦν
καὶ τὸν οἶνον οἱ μὲν ἀλόαις χρωτίζοντες ἢ κιν-
ναμώμοις καὶ κρόκοις ἐφηδύνοντες ὥσπερ γυναῖκα
καλλωπίζουσιν εἰς τὰ συμπόσια καὶ προαγωγεύ-
ουσιν· οἱ δ᾽ ἀφαιροῦντες τὸ ῥυπαρὸν καὶ ἄχρηστον[5]
ἐξ αὐτοῦ θεραπεύουσι καὶ καθαίρουσιν. ἐπεὶ πάντ᾽
D ἂν εἴποις ταῦτα περιεργίαν, ἀρξάμενος ἀπὸ τοῦ
οἴκου· τί γὰρ οὕτως κεκονίαται; τί δ᾽ ἀνέῳγε τοῦ
περιέχοντος ὅθεν ἂν μάλιστα πνεῦμα λαμβάνοι καθαρὸν καὶ τοῦ φωτὸς ἀπολαύοι περιόντος[6] ἐπὶ τὰς
δύσεις; τί δὲ τῶν ἐκπωμάτων ἕκαστον ἐκτέτριπται
καὶ διέσμηκται πανταχόθεν ὥστε λάμπειν καὶ περι-
στίλβειν; ἢ τὸ μὲν ἔκπωμ᾽ ἔδει μὴ ῥύπου μηδὲ

---

[1] So Reiske : καθαρότητος.   [2] So Doehner : θρύψιν.

tem. Just so, clarifying removes the violent, insane element and brings the wine into a gentle, wholesome state.

"Being finical is to me a far cry from being clean. When women wear rouge, perfume, and gold and purple, they are considered too showily dressed ; but no one takes exception to bathing, the use of oil, or shampooing. Homer brings out the difference very neatly in his lines on Hera adorning herself [a] :

> First with ambrosia she cleaned all soil from her person.
> Then with sleek oil she anointed herself.

So far she is showing concern for cleanliness, but when she picks up those gold brooches and finely wrought earrings, and, lastly, turns to the witchery of Aphrodité's magic band, it is plainly a case of overdoing things and of wanton conduct unbecoming to a wife. Even so, those who colour wine with aloes or sweeten it with cinnamon or saffron are adorning it like a woman's face in preparation for a gay party, and are acting as a kind of pander ; those who draw off the impurities and unpalatable elements are simply tending and cleaning it. You might speak of everything we have here as overelaboration, beginning with the house. For why is it stuccoed as it is ? And why is it open to catch the pure air of heaven and enjoy the light as the sun moves round to its setting ? Why is each cup scoured and polished so as to gleam and glitter all over ? Must the cup be free of fusty, vile

[a] *Iliad*, xiv. 170.

---

[3] ἱμερόεντος Homer.

[4] καὶ after ἐπιμέλεια deleted by Hubert.

[5] So Basel edition, E, and a corrector of T : ἄχριστον.

[6] So Reiske : περιόντος, which may stand, as from the compound of εἶμι, see LSJ.

(693) μοχθηρίας ὁδωδὸς εἶναι, τὸ δ' ἐξ αὐτοῦ πινόμενον
εὐρῶτος ἢ κηλίδων ἀναπεπλῆσθαι;

"Καὶ τί δεῖ τὰ ἄλλα λέγειν; ἡ γὰρ αὐτοῦ τοῦ
πυροῦ διαπόνησις[1] εἰς τὸν ἄρτον, οὐδὲν ἕτερον ἢ
κάθαρσις οὖσα, θέασαι μεθ' ὅσης γίγνεται πραγμα-
τείας· οὐ γὰρ μόνον ὑποσκαφισμοὶ καὶ διαττήσεις[2]
E καὶ ἀποκρίσεις[3] καὶ διακρίσεις εἰσὶ τῶν σιτίων
καὶ τῶν ἀλλοτρίων[4] ἀλλ' ἡ τρῖψις ἐκθλίβουσα τοῦ
φυράματος τὸ τραχὺ καὶ ἡ πέψις ἐξικμάζουσα τὸ
ὑγρόν[5] καθαίρουσι καὶ συστέλλουσι τὴν ὕλην εἰς
αὐτὸ τὸ ἐδώδιμον. τί οὖν ἄτοπον, εἰ καὶ τοῦ οἴνου
τὸ τρυγῶδες ὡς κρίμνον ἢ σκύβαλον ἡ διήθησις
ἐξαιρεῖ[6] μήτε δαπάνης τινὸς τῇ καθάρσει μήτ'
ἀσχολίας πολλῆς προσούσης;"

ΠΡΟΒΛΗΜΑ Η

Τίς αἰτία βουλίμου

Collocuntur Plutarchus, Soclarus, Cleomenes, alii

1. Θυσία τις ἔστι πάτριος, ἣν ὁ μὲν ἄρχων ἐπὶ
τῆς κοινῆς ἑστίας δρᾷ τῶν δ' ἄλλων ἕκαστος ἐπ'
οἴκου· καλεῖται δὲ "βουλίμου ἐξέλασις"· καὶ τῶν
F οἰκετῶν ἕνα τύπτοντες ἀγνίναις ῥάβδοις διὰ θυρῶν

---

[1] So Basel edition : διαπνόησις.
[2] So Anonymus, Stephanus : διαιτήσεις.
[3] So Stephanus : ἀποκρούσεις.
[4] So Turnebus, ἀχύρων Pohlenz : ἀλετρίων.
[5] καὶ after ὑγρὸν omitted in g.
[6] So Duebner : ἐξαίρει.

---

[a] Excerpted by Psellus, De Omnifaria Doctrina, 156. Plutarch seems to refer to our discussion in Life of Brutus, xxv
fin.

odours, while the drink that we take from it is contaminated with scum and filth ?

" What need to go on with the list ? Observe how much activity is required merely to make wheat into bread, though the process is nothing but one of purification ; it involves more than merely the winnowing and sifting, the extraction and separation of the grain from the foreign matter. The grinding which crushes out the bran, and the baking which dries out the moisture further purify and reduce the material to its proper edible form. What wonder then if the lees of wine are removed too by filtering, like any sediment or refuse, especially since the process involves neither extra expense nor any great trouble ? "

QUESTION 8 [a]

The cause of bulimy [b]

Speakers : Plutarch, Soclarus, Cleomenes and others

1. THERE is a traditional rite of sacrifice, which the archon performs at the public hearth but everyone else at home, called the driving out of bulimy. They strike one of the servants with wands of *agnus castus*

---

[b] βούλιμος, βουλιμία : often translated " ox-hunger " or " voracious appetite " ; cf. Paulus ex Festo, De Significatu Verbor. 32 M " bulimam Graeci magnam famem dicunt." From the present passage we see that the meaning is not altogether clear, and Wilhelm Schulze (*Kuhns Zeitschrift*, xxxiii (1895), p. 243), has shown that the etymology from *bous* " ox " is doubtful. Cf. " vim quandam famis non tolerabilem " in Aulus Gellius, xvi. 3. 9 f., where a quotation from Erasistratus on the subject is introduced. On flagellation and evil geniuses cf. G. Soury, La Démonologie de Plutarque, p. 53.

(693) ἐξελαύνουσιν, ἐπιλέγοντες " ἔξω Βούλιμον[1] ἔσω δὲ
Πλοῦτον καὶ Ὑγίειαν." ἄρχοντος οὖν ἐμοῦ
694 πλείονες ἐκοινώνουν τῆς θυσίας· κᾆθ' ὡς ἐποιήσα-
μεν τὰ νενομισμένα καὶ πάλιν κατεκλίνημεν, ἐζητεῖτο πρῶτον ὑπὲρ αὐτοῦ τοῦ ὀνόματος, ἔπειτα
τῆς φωνῆς ἣν ἐπιλέγουσι τῷ διωκομένῳ, μάλιστα
δ' ὑπὲρ τοῦ πάθους καὶ τῶν κατ' αὐτὸ γιγνομένων.
τὸ μὲν οὖν λιμὸν ἐδόκει μέγαν ἢ δημόσιον ἀπο-
σημαίνειν, καὶ μάλιστα παρ' ἡμῖν τοῖς Αἰολεῦσιν
ἀντὶ τοῦ β τῷ π χρωμένοις· οὐ γὰρ βούλιμον, ἀλλὰ
πούλιμον,[2] οἷον πολὺν ὄντα λιμόν,[3] ὀνομάζομεν.
ἐδόκει δ' ἡ βούβρωστις ἕτερον[4] εἶναι· τὸ δὲ
τεκμήριον ἐλαμβάνομεν ἐκ τῶν Μητροδώρου Ἰω-
νικῶν· ἱστορεῖ γάρ, ὅτι Σμυρναῖοι τὸ παλαιὸν
B Αἰολεῖς ὄντες θύουσι Βουβρώστει ταῦρον μέλανα
καὶ κατακόψαντες αὐτόδορον ὁλοκαυτοῦσιν. ἐπεὶ
δὲ πᾶς μὲν ἔοικεν[5] λιμὸς νόσῳ, μάλιστα δ' ὁ
βούλιμος, ὅτι γίγνεται[6] παθόντος παρὰ φύσιν τοῦ
σώματος, εἰκότως ἀντιτάττουσιν ὡς μὲν ἐνδείᾳ
τὸν πλοῦτον ὡς δὲ νόσῳ τὴν ὑγίειαν· ὡς δὲ ναυτιᾶν
ὠνομάσθη μὲν ἐπὶ τῶν ἐν νηὶ κατὰ πλοῦν τὸν στόμαχον ἐκλυομένων, ἔθει δ' ἴσχυκεν ἤδη καὶ κατὰ
τῶν ὁπωσοῦν τοῦτο πασχόντων ὄνομα τοῦ πάθους
εἶναι, οὕτως ἄρα καὶ τὸ βουλιμιᾶν ἐκεῖθεν ἀρξά-

[1] Capitals due to Wilamowitz.
[2] So Turnebus, Xylander, cf. Psellus : πολύλιμον.
[3] πολὺν ὄντα λιμόν Reiske, πολὺν ὄντα πάλιν g : πολυνον πάλιν T.
[4] οὐχ ἕτερον Madvig, Hartman, ἕτερον τοιοῦτον Pohlenz.

and drive him out of doors, chanting, " Out with
Bulimy, in with Wealth and Health." When I was
archon,[a] a larger number than usual participated in
the public rite. After we had completed the ritual
acts and returned to our places at table we discussed
first the term bulimy (*bulimos*), then the formula
which they repeat as the servant is driven out, and
especially the affliction itself and the particulars of a
case of it. The name, we thought, signified a great
or general famine, especially among us Aeolians who,
in our dialect, use *p* for *b* ; we pronounce not *bulimos*
but *pulimos* as if to say *polys limos* (famine multiplied).
We decided that *bubrostis* (ravenous appetite) is different, on the evidence of Metrodorus's [b] *History of
Ionia.*[c] Metrodorus records that the people of
Smyrna, originally Aeolians, sacrifice to Bubrostis a
black bull, which they cut up and burn entirely, hide
and all, on the altar. Now, since any kind of starvation, and particularly bulimy, resembles a disease, inasmuch as it occurs when the body has been affected
by an unnatural condition, people quite reasonably
contrast it with the normal state, as they do want
with wealth and disease with health. Nausea got its
name with reference to those whose stomachs are
upset on a ship (*naus*) at sea, but by dint of usage the
term is now applied to any similar case of upset, no
matter how it comes about. Just so, the term bulimy,
originating as I have said, has developed to its present

---

[a] *Table-Talk*, ii. 10. 1, 642 F.
[b] Probably Metrodorus of Chios, *RE*, *s.v.* (no. 14), cols.
1475 f.
[c] *Frag. Griech. Historiker* (Jacoby), 43 F 3.

---

5 ὁ before λιμὸς deleted by Herwerden, Hubert.
6 ὅτι γίνεται Hubert, ἐπιγίνεται Turnebus : ἐπιγίνεσθαι.

(694) μενον ἐνταῦθα διέτεινεν. ταῦτα μὲν οὖν ἔρανον
κοινὸν ἐκ πάντων συνεπληροῦμεν[1] λόγων.[2]

2. Ἐπειδὴ δ᾽[3] ἡπτόμεθα τῆς αἰτίας τοῦ πάθους,
C πρῶτον μὲν ἠπορήθη τὸ μάλιστα βουλιμιᾶν τοὺς
διὰ χιόνος πολλῆς βαδίζοντας, ὥσπερ καὶ Βροῦτος
ἐκ Δυρραχίου πρὸς Ἀπολλωνίαν ἰὼν[4] ἐκινδύνευσεν
ὑπὸ τοῦ πάθους· ἦν δὲ νιφετὸς πολὺς καὶ τῶν τὰ
σιτία κομιζόντων οὐδεὶς ἐξηκολούθει· λιποθυμοῦν-
τος οὖν αὐτοῦ καὶ ἀπολιπόντος, ἠναγκάσθησαν οἱ
στρατιῶται προσδραμόντες τοῖς τείχεσιν ἄρτον
αἰτῆσαι παρὰ τῶν τειχοφυλάκων πολεμίων ὄντων[5]·
καὶ λαβόντες εὐθὺς ἀνεκτήσαντο τὸν Βροῦτον· διὸ
καὶ φιλανθρώπως ἐχρήσατο πᾶσι κύριος τῆς πόλεως γενόμενος. πάσχουσι δὲ τοῦτο καὶ ἵπποι καὶ
ὄνοι,[6] καὶ μάλισθ᾽ ὅταν[7] ἰσχάδας ἢ μῆλα κομί-
D ζωσιν. ὃ δὲ θαυμασιώτατόν ἐστιν, οὐκ ἀνθρώπους
μόνον ἀλλὰ καὶ κτήνη μάλιστα πάντων ἐδωδίμων
ἀναρρώννυσιν ἄρτος· ὥστε, κἂν ἐλάχιστον ἐμφάγωσιν,[8] ἵστανται[9] καὶ βαδίζουσι.

3. Γενομένης δὲ σιωπῆς, ἐγὼ συννοῶν ὅτι τὰ
τῶν πρεσβυτέρων ἐπιχειρήματα τοὺς μὲν ἀργοὺς
καὶ ἀφυεῖς οἷον ἀναπαύει καὶ ἀναπίμπλησι, τοῖς δὲ
φιλοτίμοις καὶ φιλολόγοις ἀρχὴν ἐνδίδωσιν οἰκείαν

---

[1] So Amyot, συνεπλήρουν Meziriacus : συνεπλήρου.
[2] So Turnebus, Xylander : λέγων.
[3] ἐπειδὴ δ᾽ Benseler : ἐπεὶ δὲ δή.
[4] ἰὼν added by Madvig.
[5] ὄντων added by Paton, Castiglioni.
[6] ἡμίονοι Psellus (Migne, *Patrol.*, but καὶ ὄνοι καὶ ἡμ. acc.
to Hubert).   [7] ἢ after ὅταν deleted by Psellus, Doehner.
[8] So Stephanus : ἐὰν φάγωσιν.
[9] ἵστανται Doehner (εὐθὺς ἵστανται Psellus) : ἰῶνται.

---

[a] *Cf.* the stylistic device at iv. 4. 2, 668 D, *supra*.

meaning. This was the picnic of argument to which we all brought our share.[a]

2. But when we undertook to account for the cause of the affliction, the first question we considered was why bulimy attacks especially those who walk through heavy snow,[b] like Brutus[c] on the way from Dyrrachium to Apollonia, when his life was endangered by this affliction. There was a heavy snow, and none of the provision train kept up with him, so that when he grew faint and lost consciousness, the troops were forced to run up to the walls and beg bread from the guards on the enemy side. When they got it, they immediately succeeded in reviving Brutus.[d] This explains why he treated all the inhabitants humanely when he gained possession of the town. Horses and donkeys also suffer from bulimy, especially when transporting dried figs and apples. The most astonishing thing of all is that bread restores strength not only to man but to beast better than any other food ; so much so that if sufferers take even a morsel of it they get on their feet and go on.

3. There was a silence during which I reflected that to the idle and dull the solutions of their predecessors[e] to such questions provide only a chance to imbibe and be content ; to an eager scholar, however, they present an opening and incentive for

[b] *Cf.* the quotation from Erasistratus referred to in the note on *bulimos* above : the affliction is commoner in cold weather.

[c] See *The Life of Brutus*, xxv f. (LCL vol. vi, pp. 180-183).

[d] This experience closely resembles that of Xenophon's men who suffered from bulimy as reported in *Anabasis*, iv. 5. 7-8.

[e] The reference may be to " the older men " who participated in the discussions at Plutarch's school. *RE*, *s.v.* " Plutarchos," col. 663, ll. 50 f.

(694) καὶ τόλμαν ἐπὶ τὸ ζητεῖν καὶ ἀνιχνεύειν τὴν ἀλήθειαν, ἐμνήσθην τῶν Ἀριστοτελικῶν, ἐν οἷς λέγεται, ὅτι, πολλῆς περιψύξεως γενομένης ἔξωθεν,
ἐκθερμαίνεται σφόδρα τὰ ἐντὸς καὶ πολὺ σύντηγμα
E ποιεῖ· τοῦτο δ᾽, ἐὰν μὲν ἐπὶ τὰ σκέλη ῥυῇ, κόπους
ἀπεργάζεται καὶ βαρύτητας, ἐὰν δ᾽ ἐπὶ τὰς τῆς κινήσεως καὶ τῆς ἀναπνοῆς ἀρχάς, ἀψυχίαν[1] καὶ
ἀσθένειαν.

Ὅπερ οὖν εἰκός, τοῦ λόγου λεχθέντος ἐπεραίνετο,
τῶν μὲν ἐπιφυομένων τῷ δόγματι τῶν δ᾽ ὑπερδι-
κούντων. (4) Σώκλαρος δὲ τὴν ἀρχὴν ἔφη τοῦ
λόγου κάλλιστα κεῖσθαι· περιψύχεσθαι γὰρ ἱκανῶς[2]
καὶ πυκνοῦσθαι τὰ σώματα τῶν βαδιζόντων διὰ
χιόνος· τὸ δὲ σύντηγμα τὴν θερμότητα ποιεῖν καὶ
τοῦτο καταλαμβάνειν τὰς ἀρχὰς τῆς ἀναπνοῆς
αἰτηματῶδες εἶναι· μᾶλλον οὖν δοκεῖν αὐτῷ τὴν
θερμότητα συστελλομένην καὶ πλεονάζουσαν ἐντὸς ἀναλίσκειν τὴν τροφήν, εἶτ᾽ ἐπιλειπούσης καὶ
F αὐτὴν[3] ὥσπερ πῦρ ἀπομαραίνεσθαι· διὸ πεινῶσι
σφόδρα καὶ βραχὺ παντελῶς ἐμφαγόντες εὐθὺς
ἀναλάμπουσι· γίγνεται γὰρ ὥσπερ ὑπέκκαυμα[4] τῆς
θερμότητος τὸ προσφερόμενον.

5. Κλεομένης δ᾽ ὁ ἰατρὸς ἄλλως ἔφη τῷ ὀνόματι
τὸν λιμὸν συντετάχθαι δίχα τοῦ πράγματος, ὥσπερ
695 τῷ[5] καταπίνειν τὸ πίνειν καὶ τῷ[6] ἀνακύπτειν τὸ[6]
κύπτειν· οὐ γὰρ εἶναι λιμόν, ὥσπερ δοκεῖ, τὴν

---

[1] ἢ before καὶ deleted by Reiske.
[2] ἰσχυρῶς Psellus, Doehner.   [3] So Bases, Capelle : αὐτῆς.
[4] So Xylander, Junius : ὑπέκλυμα.
[5] τῷ Basel edition : τοι.
[6] τῷ . . . τὸ Turnebus : τὸ . . . τῷ.

---

[a] Pseudo-Aristotle, *Problems*, 888 a 1 ff. *Cf.* 884 a 13 and

500

boldly seeking and tracking down the truth, on his own. Then I brought up the Aristotelian passage [a] in which it is stated that when there is great cold outside the body the inward parts become exceedingly heated and produce a great deal of morbid liquefaction. Now if the liquefied matter collects in the legs it causes fatigue and heaviness ; if it gathers at the roots of motor energy or of respiration, it causes fainting and weakness.

Naturally enough, when I had said that, the discussion continued, some attacking and others defending Aristotle's theory. (4) Soclarus said that the first part of the argument was sound. It was true that the bodies of those who travel through snow are quite chilled and congealed ; but to argue that heat produces abnormal liquefaction which clogs the centres of respiration was to beg the question, according to him. He preferred the view that the heat is contracted and too much concentrated internally, so that it uses up the supply of food ; and then, like fire when the fuel gives out, the heat itself dies down. This explains both why, in the cold, people suffer severe hunger, and why, when they eat the slightest morsel of food, they have a quick flare-up of energy. The food consumed acts as a kind of fuel to rekindle the heat.

5. Cleomenes the physician, however, said that the word *limos* (hunger) in the compound signifies nothing as to the facts, just as the word *katapinein* (to swallow) differs from the simple verb *pinein* (to drink), or *anakyptein* (to bob up) differs from *kyptein* (to lean forward). Bulimy is not, as people think, hunger

889 a 36. Below at 696 D Plutarch seems to consider this work authentic.

(695) βουλιμίαν, ἀλλὰ πάθος ἐν τῷ[1] στομάχῳ διὰ συν-
δρομὴν θερμοῦ[2] λιποψυχίαν ποιοῦν. ὥσπερ οὖν
τὰ ὀσφραντὰ πρὸς τὰς λιποθυμίας βοηθεῖν, καὶ
τὸν ἄρτον[3] ἀναλαμβάνειν[4] τοὺς βουλιμιῶντας, οὐχ
ὅτι τροφῆς ἐνδεεῖς εἰσι (μικρὸν γοῦν παντάπασιν
λαβόντες[5] ἀναζωπυροῦσιν), ἀλλ' ὅτι τὸ πνεῦμα καὶ
τὴν δύναμιν ἀνακαλεῖται καταφερομένην. ὅτι δ'
ἔστι λιποθυμία καὶ οὐ πεῖνα, μηνύει τὸ τῶν ὑπο-
ζυγίων· ἡ γὰρ[6] τῶν ἰσχάδων ἀποφορὰ καὶ ἡ τῶν
μήλων ἔνδειαν μὲν οὐ ποιεῖ, καρδιωγμὸν δέ τινα
μᾶλλον καὶ νὴ Δί' εἴλιγγον.[7]

B   6. Ἡμῖν δὲ καὶ ταῦτα μετρίως ἐδόκει λέγεσθαι,
καὶ[8] ἀπὸ τῆς ἐναντίας ἀρχῆς δυνατὸν εἶναι, μὴ
πύκνωσιν ἀλλ' ἀραίωσιν ὑποθεμένοις, διασῶσαι τὸ
πιθανόν. τὸ γὰρ ἀπορρέον πνεῦμα τῆς χιόνος ἐστὶ
μὲν οἷον αἰθὴρ τοῦ πάγου καὶ ψῆγμα λεπτομερέ-
στατον, ἔχει δέ τι τομὸν καὶ διαιρετικὸν οὐ σαρκὸς
μόνον ἀλλὰ καὶ ἀργυρῶν καὶ χαλκῶν ἀγγείων·
ὁρῶμεν γὰρ ταῦτα μὴ στέγοντα τὴν χιόνα· πνεο-
μένη γὰρ ἀναλίσκεται καὶ τὴν ἐκτὸς ἐπιφάνειαν
τοῦ ἀγγείου νοτίδος ἀναπίμπλησι λεπτῆς καὶ κρυ-
σταλλοειδοῦς, ἣν[9] ἀπολείπει τὸ πνεῦμα διὰ τῶν
πόρων ἀδήλως ἀπερχόμενον. τοῦτο δὴ τοῖς βαδί-
C   ζουσι διὰ χιόνος ὀξὺ καὶ φλογοειδὲς προσπῖπτον
ἐπικαίειν δοκεῖ τὰ ἄκρα τῷ τέμνειν καὶ παρελθεῖν[10]
τῇ σαρκί, καθάπερ τὸ πῦρ· ὅθεν[11] ἀραίωσις γίγνεται
περὶ τὸ σῶμα πολλὴ καὶ ῥεῖ τὸ θερμὸν ἔξω καὶ
διὰ[12] τὴν ψυχρότητα τοῦ πνεύματος περὶ τὴν ἐπι-

---

[1] τῷ added by Doehner from Psellus.
[2] So Psellus, Doehner : λιμοῦ.
[3] So Basel edition : αὐτόν.
[4] καὶ before τοὺς deleted in Basel edition.
[5] λαβόντες Wyttenbach : ἀναλαβόντες.

(*limos*), but a pathological state of the stomach that causes fainting by concentration of heat. Just as smelling-salts are useful in cases of fainting, so bread revives those suffering from bulimy ; not because they are starved (for the very slightest morsel re-kindles the spark of life), but because the bread summons back the sinking energy and vital breath. That it is a fainting weakness, not hunger, is indicated by the case of draught animals ; the exhalations from dried figs and apples do not produce a deficiency but rather a sort of heartburn, yes, and dizziness.

6. We found this reasonable enough, yet felt that it was possible to make out a good case on the contrary hypothesis that what occurs is not condensa-tion but dilation. The vapour emitted by snow is, as it were, an aura of frost or a very fine dust. It has a piercing, separative effect not only on flesh but on vessels of silver and bronze ; we know by observa-tion that these vessels are not impermeable to snow, which exudes and evaporates, covering the exterior surface with a fine, icy dew that is deposited by the vapour as it passes impeceptibly through the vessel's pores. When people travel through snow, this vapour, with its sharp and flamelike touch, seems to burn the extremities, cutting and biting [a] into the flesh like fire. Hence considerable dilation occurs in the body ; its heat escapes and, because of the cold

[a] The ms. has " entering." See textual note.

---

[6] So Meziriacus : τα.

[7] νὴ Δι' εἰλιγγον Reiske, ἰλιγγον Meziriacus : διειλιγμόν.

[8] καὶ added by Reiske.   [9] ἦν Basel edition : ἦ.

[10] παρεσθίειν τῆς σαρκός Hubert, perhaps παρεισελθεῖν " penetrate."   [11] πῦρ· ὅθεν Turnebus : πυρωθέν.

[12] διὰ for καὶ Anonymous, καὶ διὰ Turnebus : καὶ.

(695) φάνειαν σβεννύμενον ἱδρῶτα δροσώδη διατμίζει
καὶ λεπτόν, ὥστε τήκεσθαι καὶ ἀναλίσκεσθαι[1] τὴν
δύναμιν. ἐὰν μὲν οὖν ἡσυχάζῃ τις, οὐ πολλὴ τοῦ
σώματος ἀπέρχεται θερμότης· ὅταν δὲ τὴν μὲν
τροφὴν τοῦ σώματος ἡ κίνησις εἰς τὸ θερμὸν
ὀξέως μεταβάλλῃ τὸ δὲ θερμὸν ἔξω φέρηται,
διακρινομένης τῆς σαρκός, ἀθρόαν ἀνάγκη τῆς
D δυνάμεως ἐπίλειψιν γενέσθαι.

Ὅτι δὲ τὸ ἐκψύχεσθαι οὐ πήγνυσιν μόνον ἀλλὰ
καὶ τήκει τὰ σώματα, δῆλόν ἐστιν· ἐν μὲν γὰρ τοῖς
μεγάλοις χειμῶσιν ἀκόναι μολίβδου διατηκόμεναι
τό τε τῆς ἀφιδρώσεως καὶ τὸ πολλοῖς μὴ πεινῶσι
συμπίπτειν τὴν βουλιμίασιν ἀραίωσιν[2] κατηγορεῖ
μᾶλλον καὶ ῥύσιν ἢ πύκνωσιν τοῦ σώματος.
ἀραιοῦνται δὲ χειμῶνος μέν, ὥσπερ εἴρηται, τῇ
τοῦ πνεύματος[3] λεπτότητι, ἄλλως δὲ τοῦ κόπου
καὶ τῆς κινήσεως ἀποξυνούσης τὴν[4] ἐν τῷ σώματι
θερμότητα[4]· λεπτὴ γὰρ γενομένη καὶ κοπιῶσα ῥεῖ
πολλὴ καὶ διασπείρεται διὰ τοῦ σώματος. τὰ δὲ
μῆλα καὶ τὰς ἰσχάδας εἰκὸς ἀποπνεῖν τι τοιοῦτον,
E ὥστε τῶν ὑποζυγίων τὸ θερμὸν ἀπολεπτύνειν καὶ
κατακερματίζειν· ἄλλα γὰρ ἄλλοις ὥσπερ ἀναλαμβάνειν καὶ καταλύεσθαι πέφυκεν.

---

[1] καὶ before τὴν deleted by Meziriacus, who added καὶ before περὶ τὴν ἐπιφάνειαν above.
[2] ἀραίωσιν added by Reiske here, read below in place of καὶ
ῥύσιν by Meziriacus.

vapour from the snow, is diminished at the surface and gives off a fine, dewy sweat, so that energy is dissolved and expended. If a man is inactive, not much is lost of the body's heat; but when the movement of the body causes quick conversion of food into heat, and the heat flows off as the flesh opens, then it is inevitable that a complete collapse of strength should occur.

That chilling may not only freeze but melt bodies is manifest: the melting of lead whetstones [a] in severe winters, the phenomenon of sweating, and the fact that bulimy attacks many when they are not hungry indicate porosity and liquefaction rather than compression in our bodies. During winter, as has been said, bodies are made porous by the fineness of the cold vapour, especially when fatigue and motion make the heat in the body more intense; attenuated and weakened,[b] it overflows and is dispersed through the body. It is probable that dried figs and apples give off an exhalation of a sort that causes extreme attenuation and fragmentation of heat in pack animals. For by nature different creatures are so to speak revived or collapse from different causes.

[a] Cf. Helmbold in Plut. Mor. xii (LCL), note on p. 250: " Tin [rather than lead] is reduced to powder by severe cold."
[b] More literally " fatigued."

---

[3] τοῦ πνεύματος added by Meziriacus.
[4] τὴν . . . θερμότητα Basel edition: τῆς . . . θερμότητος.

(695)

ΠΡΟΒΛΗΜΑ Θ

Διὰ τί ὁ ποιητὴς ἐπὶ μὲν τῶν ἄλλων ὑγρῶν τοῖς ἰδίοις ἐπιθέτοις
χρῆται, μόνον δὲ τὸ ἔλαιον ὑγρὸν καλεῖ

Collocuntur Plutarchus, alii

1. Ἠπορήθη ποτὲ καὶ διὰ τί πολλῶν ὑγρῶν
ὄντων τὰ μὲν ἄλλα τοῖς ἰδίοις ἐπιθέτοις ὁ ποιητὴς
εἴωθε[1] κοσμεῖν, τὸ γάλα τε λευκὸν καὶ τὸ μέλι
χλωρὸν καὶ τὸν οἶνον ἐρυθρὸν καλῶν, τὸ δ' ἔλαιον
ἀπὸ[2] κοινοῦ[3] τοῦ πᾶσι συμβεβηκότος μόνον ἐπιεικῶς
F ὑγρὸν προσαγορεύει. εἰς τοῦτ' ἐλέχθη, ὅτι ὡς[4]
γλυκύτατόν ἐστι τὸ δι' ὅλου γλυκὺ καὶ λευκότατον
τὸ δι' ὅλου λευκόν, δι' ὅλου δὲ τοιοῦτόν[5] ἐστιν, ᾧ
μηδὲν ἐμμέμικται τῆς ἐναντίας φύσεως, οὕτω δὴ[6]
καὶ[7] ὑγρὸν μάλιστα ῥητέον, οὗ μηδὲν μέρος ξηρόν
ἐστι· τοῦτο δὲ τῷ ἐλαίῳ συμβέβηκεν.

2. Πρῶτον μὲν ἡ λειότης αὐτοῦ τὴν ὁμαλότητα
696 τῶν μορίων ἐπιδείκνυται· δι' ὅλου γὰρ αὐτῷ συμ-
παθεῖ πρὸς τὴν ψαῦσιν.[8] ἔπειτα τῇ ὄψει παρέχει
καθαρώτατον ἐνοπτρίσασθαι· τραχὺ γὰρ οὐδὲν ἔν-
εστιν[9] ὥστε διασπᾶν τὴν ἀνταύγειαν, ἀλλ' ἀπὸ
παντὸς μέρους δι' ὑγρότητα καὶ σμικρότατον ἀνα-
κλᾷ τὸ φῶς ἐπὶ τὴν ὄψιν· ὥσπερ αὖ τοὐναντίον
τὸ γάλα τῶν ὑγρῶν μόνον οὐκ ἐσοπτρίζει,[10] πολλῆς
ἀναμεμιγμένης αὐτῷ γεώδους οὐσίας.[11] ἔτι δὲ κι-
νούμενον ἥκιστα ψοφεῖ τῶν ὑγρῶν· ὑγρὸν γάρ ἐστι
δι' ὅλου· τῶν δ'[12] ἄλλων ἐν τῷ ῥεῖν καὶ φέρεσθαι τὰ

---

[1] So Hubert : εἰώθει.　　　　　　　　[2] So Reiske : ὑπό.
[3] Hartman would delete κοινοῦ.　　　[4] So Reiske : καί.
[5] So Xylander : τοιουτός.　　　　　　[6] So Reiske : δέ.
[7] τό after καί deleted by Hubert.　　[8] So Xylander : ψύξιν.
[9] So Hubert : ἐστιν.　　[10] So Basel edition : ἐσοπτρίζειν.
[11] οὐσίας added by Turnebus, συστάσεως Stephanus.

QUESTION 9

Why Homer uses special adjectives for other liquids
but calls only olive oil " liquid "

Speakers : Plutarch and others

1. ONCE the question was raised why, when there
are many liquids, Homer is accustomed to embellish
most with specific adjectives, calling milk " white,'
honey " yellow," and wine " ruddy," but to use of oil
alone the adjective " liquid," [a] which properly refers
to the quality common to them all. To this the
answer was given that, just as the sweetest substance
is one that is sweet through and through, the whitest
one that is white through and through—and " through
and through " means that there is no admixture of
the opposite quality—just so the expression " liquid "
should be used particularly of anything which has no
ingredient of dryness in it ; and that is the case
with oil.

2. In the first place, its smoothness demonstrates
the uniformity of its parts ; it is at all points consistently the same to the touch. Further, visually it is the
clearest reflector, having no unevenness to distort the
reflection. From every part of itself, on account of
its liquidity, it reflects even the minutest light to the
eye. Just so, on the contrary, milk is the only liquid
that does not mirror objects, because there is in it a
great admixture of the earthy.[b] Besides, oil, when
stirred, is the most silent of all liquids because it is
liquid throughout ; whereas, when other liquids flow

---

[a] e.g., Odyssey, vi. 79, 215 ; Iliad, xxiii. 281.
[b] See Aristotle, Meteorologica, 383 a 14, 22.

---

[12] δ' added by Turnebus.

(696) σκληρὰ καὶ γεώδη μέρη[1] προσκρούσεις λαμβάνοντα
καὶ πληγὰς ψοφεῖ διὰ τραχύτητα.[2] καὶ μὴν μόνον
B ἄκρατον[3] διαμένει καὶ ἄμικτον· ἔστι γὰρ πυκνότα-
τον· οὐ γὰρ ἔχει μεταξὺ τῶν ξηρῶν καὶ γεωδῶν ἐν
αὑτῷ μερῶν κενώματα καὶ πόρους, οἷς δέξεται τὸ
παρεμπῖπτον, ἀλλὰ[4] δι᾿ ὁμοιότητα τῶν μερῶν εὐ-
άρμοστόν[5] ἐστιν καὶ συνεχές.

"Οταν δ᾿ ἀφρίζῃ τὸ ἔλαιον, οὐ δέχεται τὸ πνεῦμα
διὰ λεπτότητα καὶ συνέχειαν. τοῦτο δ᾿ αἴτιον καὶ
τοῦ τρέφεσθαι τὸ πῦρ ὑπ᾿ αὐτοῦ· τρέφεται μὲν
γὰρ οὐδενὶ πλὴν ὑγρῷ, καὶ τοῦτο μόνον καυστόν
ἐστιν· ἐκ γοῦν τῶν ξύλων ὁ μὲν ἀὴρ ἄπεισι καπνὸς
γενόμενος, τὸ δὲ γεῶδες ἐκτεφρωθὲν ὑπολείπεται,
μόνον δ᾿ ὑπὸ τοῦ πυρὸς τὸ νοτερὸν ἀναλοῦται,
τούτῳ γὰρ τρέφεσθαι πέφυκεν· ὕδωρ μὲν οὖν καὶ
C οἶνος καὶ τὰ λοιπά, πολλοῦ μετέχοντα τοῦ θολεροῦ
καὶ γεώδους, ἐμπίπτοντα τὴν φλόγα διασπᾷ καὶ
τῇ τραχύτητι καὶ τῷ βάρει θλίβει καὶ κατασβέννυσι,
τὸ δ᾿ ἔλαιον, ὅτι μάλιστ᾿ εἰλικρινῶς ὑγρόν ἐστι, διὰ
λεπτότητα μεταβάλλει καὶ κρατούμενον ἐκπυροῦται.

3. Μέγιστον δ᾿ αὐτοῦ τῆς ὑγρότητος τεκμήριον
ἤ[6] ἐπὶ πλεῖστον ἐξ ὀλιγίστου διανομὴ καὶ χύσις·
οὔτε γὰρ μέλιτος οὔθ᾿ ὕδατος οὔτ᾿ ἄλλου τινὸς
ὑγροῦ βραχὺς οὕτως ὄγκος[7] ἐπίδοσιν λαμβάνει
τοσαύτην,[8] ἀλλ᾿ εὐθὺς ἐπιλείπων[9] καταναλίσκεται[10]

---

[1] So Basel edition, Turnebus : μέτρα.
[2] So Turnebus : βραχύτητα.
[3] ἄκρατον Basel edition, ἀκρότατον E : ἀκράτητον.
[4] So Anonymus, Turnebus : ἄμα.
[5] So Stephanus : ἀνάρμοστόν.
[6] ἤ added by Meziriacus.
[7] So Wyttenbach : ὁπὸς " juice."
[8] So Bernardakis : τοιαύτην.

and rush along, their hard, earthy parts suffer blows and collisions that produce sound because of the irregularity of their shapes. Moreover, oil alone remains pure and undiluted, for it is the most compact and has no empty spaces or passages between dry, earthy particles to which it could admit intrusive elements. The uniformity of its particles produces smoothness and coherence in it.

When oil foams, it does not admit air, because of its fine texture and coherence. This accounts also for the fact that fire is fed by it. Fire is fed only by moisture, and moisture alone is combustible.[a] At any rate, when wood is burned as fuel, the air is given off as smoke and the earthy element is left reduced to ash ; only the moisture is consumed by fire, for fire naturally feeds on liquid. Now when water, wine, and the other liquids with their high proportion of muddy, earthy matter encounter fire, they rend it apart and by their roughness and weight crush and extinguish it ; while oil, because it is a superlatively pure liquid, has such minute particles that it suffers change and is overpowered and reduced to flames.

3. A supreme proof of its liquidity is the fact that the least quantity of it spreads and flows over the most space. Neither honey nor water nor any other liquid in such slight mass spreads so far ; instead, they immediately disappear, being consumed on ac-

[a] This theory is found in Aristotle in his discussion of earlier philosophers. See *Metaphysics*, i. 3, 983 b 23, and *Meteorologica*, ii. 2, 354 b 33 ff. ; W. Jaeger, *Aristoteles*, p. 153, n. 2 ; Plut. *De Primo Frigido*, 954 E (LCL *Mor.* xii, pp. 280 f.). *Cf. supra*, p. 457, note *b*.

[9] So Bernardakis, ἐπιλείπει Stephanus, ἐπιπολάζων Paton : ἐπιπλεῖστον. [10] So Bernardakis : καὶ ἀναλίσκεται.

(696)

D διὰ ξηρότητα· τὸ δ' ἔλαιον, ὅλκιμον πανταχῆ καὶ
μαλακόν, ἄγεται περὶ τὸ σῶμα χριομένοις καὶ
συνεπιρρεῖ πορρωτάτω δι' ὑγρότητα τῶν μερῶν
μηκυνομένων, ὥστε καὶ παραμένειν δυσεξίτηλον.
ὕδατι μὲν γὰρ[1] βρεχθὲν ἱμάτιον ἀποξηραίνεται
ῥᾳδίως, ἐλαίου δὲ κηλῖδας οὐ τῆς τυχούσης ἐστὶ
πραγματείας[2] ἐκκαθᾶραι· μάλιστα γὰρ ἐνδύεται τῷ
μάλιστα λεπτὸν καὶ ὑγρὸν εἶναι· καὶ γὰρ οἶνον
κεκραμένον δυσχερέστερον ἐξαιροῦσι[3] τῶν ἱματίων,
ὡς Ἀριστοτέλης φησίν, ὅτι λεπτότερός[4] ἐστι καὶ
μᾶλλον ἐνδύεται τοῖς πόροις.

ΠΡΟΒΛΗΜΑ Ι

E   Τίς αἰτία, δι' ἣν ψαθυρὰ γίνεται ταχὺ τὰ ἐκ συκῆς κρεμαν-
νύμενα τῶν ἱερείων

Collocuntur Aristio, Plutarchus, alii

Ὁ[5] Ἀριστίωνος εὐημερεῖ[6] παρὰ τοῖς δειπνοῦσι
μάγειρος, ὡς τά τ' ἄλλα χαριέντως ὀψοποιήσας
καὶ τὸν ἄρτι[7] τῷ Ἡρακλεῖ τεθυμένον ἀλεκτρυόνα
παραθεὶς ἁπαλὸν ὥσπερ χθιζόν,[8] νεαρὸν ὄντα καὶ
πρόσφατον. εἰπόντος οὖν τοῦ Ἀριστίωνος, ὅτι
τοῦτο γίγνεται ταχέως, εἰ σφαγεὶς εὐθὺς ἀπὸ
συκῆς κρεμασθείη, τὴν αἰτίαν ἐζητοῦμεν. ὅτι μὲν
δὴ πνεῦμα τῆς συκῆς ἄπεισιν ἰσχυρὸν καὶ σφοδρόν,

----

[1] So Reiske : γε.
[2] So Leonicus : γραμματείας.
[3] So Duebner : ἐξαίρουσι.
[4] So Meziriacus : λεπτοτερόν.
[5] ὁ added in g, according to Wyttenbach.
[6] So Turnebus : εὐημερεῖ.
[7] So Doehner, τὸν νεωστὶ Basel edition : τὸν ὅτι.

count of their own dryness. But olive oil, which is soft and ductile to any extent, is spread over the body when we anoint ourselves, and is carried farther than any other liquid as its particles grow longer on account of their liquidity. Accordingly, it also resists evaporation and does not easily disappear. When a garment happens to be soaked with water, it dries easily, but an oil stain requires more than ordinary effort to remove. Oil stains enter deepest into the fabric because the refinement and liquidity of oil is greatest. As Aristotle [a] says, wine is also more difficult to remove from cloth when mixed, because it is then of finer grain and settles more deeply into the pores.

QUESTION 10 [b]

Why sacrificial meat when hung from a fig tree quickly becomes tender

Speakers : Aristion, Plutarch and others

ARISTION's cook made a hit with the dinner guests not only because of his general skill, but because the cock that he set before the diners, though it had just been slaughtered as a sacrifice to Heracles, was as tender as if it had been a day old. Aristion said that meat cures rapidly if, immediately upon killing, it is hung on a fig tree ; and we went on to discuss why this should be so. Two things indicate that a strong, intense exhalation [c] is given off by the fig tree ; first,

---

[a] *Problems*, 874 a 30.

[b] Excerpted by Psellus, *De Omnifaria Doctrina*, 157.

[c] G. Soury connects this with Stoic theory (*pneuma* is the word used) in *Revue Ét. Gr.* lxi (1949), pp. 322 f. *Cf. supra*, 642 c.

---

[8] χθιζόν E : χιζὸν T.

(696)

F ἣ τ᾽ ὄσφρησις[1] ἐκμαρτυρεῖ καὶ τὸ περὶ τῶν ταύρων
λεγόμενον, ὡς ἄρα συκῇ προσδεθεὶς ὁ χαλεπώτατος
ἡσυχίαν ἄγει καὶ ψαύσεως ἀνέχεται καὶ ὅλως ἀφί-
ησι τὸν θυμὸν ὥσπερ ἀπομαραινόμενον. τὴν δὲ
πλείστην αἰτίαν καὶ δύναμιν ἡ δριμύτης εἶχεν· τὸ
γὰρ φυτὸν ἁπάντων ὀπωδέστατον, ὥστε καὶ τὸ
σῦκον αὐτὸ καὶ τὸ ξύλον καὶ τὸ θρῖον[2] ἀναπεπλῆσ-
697 θαι· διὸ καιόμενόν τε τῷ καπνῷ δάκνει μάλιστα
καὶ κατακαυθέντος ἡ τέφρα ῥυπτικωτάτην παρέχει
κονίαν.[3]

Ταῦτα[4] δὲ πάντα θερμότητος· καὶ τὴν πῆξιν
ἐμποιεῖν τῷ γάλακτι τὸν ὀπὸν οἴονταί τινες οὐ
σκαληνίᾳ σχημάτων περιπλέκοντα καὶ κολλῶντα
τὰ τραχέα[5] μέρη τοῦ γάλακτος, ἐκθλιβομένων ἐπιπολῆς τῶν λείων καὶ περιφερῶν, ἀλλὰ[6] ὑπὸ θερμότητος ἐκτήκοντα τοῦ ὑγροῦ τὸ ἀσύστατον καὶ
ὑδατῶδες. τεκμήριον δὲ καὶ τὸ ἄχρηστον[7] γλυκὺν[8]
εἶναι τὸν ὀρόν,[9] ἀλλὰ πομάτων φαυλότατον· οὐ
γὰρ τὸ λεῖον ὑπὸ τῶν σκαληνῶν, ἀλλὰ τὸ ψυχρὸν
B ἐξανέστη[10] καὶ ἄπεπτον ὑπὸ τῆς θερμότητος· καὶ
πρὸς τοῦτο συνεργοῦσιν οἱ ἅλες, θερμοὶ γάρ εἰσι,
πρὸς δὲ τὴν λεγομένην περιπλοκὴν καὶ σύνδεσιν
ἀντιπράττουσι,[11] διαλύειν γὰρ μάλιστα πεφύκασι.

Θερμὸν οὖν πνεῦμα καὶ δριμὺ καὶ τμητικὸν ἀφ-

---

[1] So Wyttenbach : ὄψις.
[2] So Amyot : ἔργον.
[3] So Xylander : κόνιν.
[4] So Hubert : ταῦτα.
[5] τραχέα added by Hubert.
[6] καὶ after ἀλλὰ deleted by Xylander, Wyttenbach.
[7] οὐ χρηστὸν Reiske, Bernardakis.
[8] So Reiske, Doehner, Paton (all with other changes that
conflict with our interpretation) : γλυκύ.
[9] So Doehner : ὀπὸν.   [10] So Hubert : ἔστη.

our sense of smell, and second, the alleged fact that the fiercest of bulls, if tied to a fig tree, becomes quiet, lets people touch him, and completely abandons his rage, as if the spirit were withering within him. This effect is mainly due to the bitterness of the plant, for the fig is the richest in sap of all plants, not only the fruit but the wood and the leaf too being full of it. Wherefore, too, the smoke of burning figwood is especially acrid and the ash from it provides a most detergent lye.

Yet the very same effects all come from heat. Therefore, some think that fig juice curdles milk through heat, not because the rough particles, owing to their irregular shape, combine and stick to each other, while smooth,[a] round particles are forced to the surface ; but because the particles under the influence of heat melt out the uncohesive, watery element in the moist compound. A proof is that sweet whey is unusable, in fact is the vilest of drinks. Evidently it is not a case of smooth particles being expelled by rough,[b] but of cold and unconcocted elements being dislodged by heat. Salt will also contribute to this process, for it is hot and counteracts the so called interlocking and binding together of particles, since it is a powerful natural solvent.

So we infer that the fig gives off a hot, bitter, in-

---

[a] Lucretius, iv. 622 ff., explains the effect of smooth atoms in producing sweetness to the taste, while rough atoms produce pungency and the like. This theory is derived from Democritus (Diels, *Frag. d. Vorsokratiker*, Democritus, A 135) as reported in Theophrastus, *De Sensu*, 65. For the alternative theory here cited Aristotle, *Meteorologica*, 384 a 22 and Pseudo-Aristotle, *Problems*, 924 b 39 lend some support.

[b] Or " irregular," *cf.* σκαληνιᾷ above.

---

[11] διάλυσιν before διαλύειν deleted by Xylander.

(697) ἴησιν ἡ συκῆ, καὶ τοῦτο θρύπτει καὶ πεπαίνει τὴν
σάρκα τοῦ ὄρνιθος. τὸ αὐτὸ δὲ πάσχει καὶ πυρῶν
ἐντεθεὶς[1] σωρῷ[2] καὶ νίτρῳ συνημμένος,[3] ὑπὸ θερμότητος. ὅτι δ' ὁ πυρὸς ἔχει τι θερμόν, τεκμαί-
ρονται τοῖς ἀμφορεῦσιν, ὧν ἐντιθεμένων εἰς σιρὸν[4]
ἐξαναλίσκεται ταχέως ὁ οἶνος.

[1] ἐντεθεὶς defended by Hartman as referring to τοῦ ὄρνιθος
rather than τὴν σάρκα.
[2] σιρῷ Doehner. Note also συνημμένος in same line.
[3] So g, Stephanus, σμηχόμενος Reiske, συμπεπασμένος Doeh-

cisive vapour which cures the flesh of the bird by making it friable. The same effect is produced by heat if you store the bird in a pile of wheat-grains with[a] sodium carbonate. That wheat is by nature somewhat hot is attested by the fact that when wine jars are placed in the wheat pits, their wine is quickly evaporated.

[a] Or, "when it has been treated (laced) with" S. Warmington.

ner : συνημένος (η in erasure with space on each side) T, συνειμένος E.

[4] So Doehner : σῖτον " grain."

ADDITIONAL NOTE

(EDITORIAL)

P. 422, 681 c : χαραδιός. I had suggested grey wagtail, which haunts gullies and hill-streams and has a yellow breast. But more likely is the stone-curlew, which, though in Britain it inhabits heaths, brecks and downs, has large eyes with yellow " irises." See the scholars cited by E. R. Dodds, *Plato : Gorgias*, p. 306, on *Gorgias*, 494 в 6.—E. H. Warmington.

INDEX

INDEX

diet of, 299, 307 f., 403 f., 457; —, skins of seals and hyenas, 319; — and thunder, 331, 353 f., 357; *see also* "anthias," ass, bark-beetles, bees, boar, butterfly, caterpillar, "charadrius," cicadas, cock, conger-eel, crane, crocodile, daws, deer, dogs, echeneïs, eel, elephant, field-mouse, fish, fox, frogs, goats, hare, hedgehog, hen, herald-fish, horses, ibis, lice, lion, lizards, locusts, mice, mullet, mussels, pigs, purple-mollusc, scorpion, sheep, shrews, snakes, sucking-fish, turtles, viper, vole, wolves, woodworms

Antagoras, 343; epic poet, third century B.C.

Anthesterion, 259

"anthias" fish, 341

Antigonus I, 131, 133; Alexander's general, one of the "Successors" of Alexander; prob. 382–301 B.C.

Antigonus Gonatas, 343, 395; king of Macedon

Antilochus, 37; Nestor's son

Antimachus, 437; of Colophon, epic and elegiac poet

Antipater, 403; friend of Plutarch

antipathies, 319; resistant properties

Antisthenes, 13, 127; friend of Socrates and founder of the Cynics, *circa* 455–*circa* 360 B.C.

Aphidna, 99

Aphroditê, 251, 255, 447, 448, 493

Apollo, 271, 273

Apollodorus, 391; of Athens

Apollonia, 499; in Illyria, 40 miles south of Dyrrachium

Apollonides, 231; *taktikos*, friend of Plutarch

Apollophanes, 443; a scholar

apple(s), 169, 243, 433 ff.

Aratus, 437; of Soli, author of an extant poem on astronomy and meteorology translated by Cicero and others

Arcesilaüs, 135, 137, 341; Academic philosopher, *circa* 315–241 B.C.

Archias, 47; Theban polemarch

Archilochus, quoted, 273; lyric poet, probably of the seventh century B.C.

Archippus, 131, 133; Athenian politician

Argives, 363

Argos, 119

Aridices, 137; pupil of Arcesilaüs

Aristaenetus, 259, 261; of Nicaea, a friend of Plutarch

Aristides, 127; Athenian statesman and soldier, *circa* 520–468 B.C.

Aristion, 267, 269, 487 f., 511; friend of Plutarch

Aristodemus, 205; friend of Socrates

Aristomachê, 389; a "Sibyl," or a poetess

Aristomenes, 299; of Messenia, seventh century B.C.

Ariston, 9; friend of Plutarch

Aristotle, 7, 31, 89 ff., 141, 227 f., 235 ff., 261, 263, 279, 475, 479, 501. 511; the philosopher, 384–322 B.C.

Arsinoê, 138; wife of Lysimachus, later of Ptolemy Keraunos (her half-brother) and finally of Ptolemy II Philadelphus (her full brother), *circa* 316–270 B.C.

art and artists, 325, 381, 425

Artemis, 277

Asclepius, 71

Asopus, 399; river near Nemea

asparagus, 313

ass, 357

Assyrians, 61

astronomy, 111

Athena, 35, 253

Athenian(s), 53, 101, 131, 361

Athenodorus Cordylion, 139; librarian at Pergamon, first century B.C.

Athens and Attica, 9, 95, 203, 259, 337 ff., 377, 397

Athletics, 159 ff., 163 ff.; *see* Games

Athrÿtus, 231, 235, 237; physician friend of Plutarch

Atreus, 119; father of Agamemnon

Attica, *see* Athens

INDEX

Aufidius Modestus, 43, 123 ; friend of Plutarch
Autobulus, 25, 179, 259, 263, 267 ; father of Plutarch
Autobulus, 331 ; son of Plutarch

Babylon, 219, 225
Bacchants, Bacchi, 365 ; Bacchic, 69, 255
Bacchus, 363 ; *see also* Bacchants, Dionysus
banquets, symposia, feasts, 9 ff., 25 ff., 49 ff., 183 ff., 203 ff., 267 ff., 295, 331 ff., 337 ff., 373 ff., 407 f., 415, 453, 455 ; *see* Plato, *Table-Talk*, Xenophon
bark-beetles, 149
basil, 175
beans, 137, 145
beer, 221
bees, 171
belladonna, 239
berries, 217, 221
Bias, 29 ; of Prienê, one of the seven wise men
biology, 317, 447 ; *see* animals, plants
birds, *see* animals
blood, 77, 155, 233 ff.
boar, 271
Boeotian, 141, 255
Boëthus, 377 ; the Epicurean
Bolus, 175
boxing, 73, 159 ff., 163 ff.
bread, 143, 185 ff., 261, 499
Brutus, Marcus Junius the "Liberator," 499
bulimy, bubrostis, ravenous appetite or famine, 497
butterfly, 149
Byzantium, 131

Cabiri, 129 ; the deities
Cadmeians=Thebans, 437
cakes, 191
calendar, 368 f.
Callias, 13, 107, 455 ; wealthy Athenian, friend of Socrates
Callimachus, 101 ; polemarch at Marathon
Callimachus, quoted, 255, 399 ; of Cyrenê; Alexandrian scholar and poet

Callisthenes, 71 ; of Olynthus, historian
Callistratus, 337, 351 ; a sophist, friend of Plutarch
Candaules, 65 ; Lydian king
Caria, 145
Carthage, Carthaginians, 395
Cassander, 131 ; son of Antipater, *circa* 358–297 B.C.
cassia, 71
caterpillar, 145, 149
Cato the Elder, 343
celery, 395, 397 ff., 403 f.
Celeus, 337 ; king of Eleusis
Cephissus River, 169
Chaeremon or Chaeremonianus, 175 ; of Tralles ; a friend of Plutarch
Chaeronea, 433 ; birthplace of Plutarch and site of battle of 338 B.C.
"charadrius," 423 ; commonly translated "plover"
Charmides, 13 ; Plato's uncle
chaste tree, 177
cheese, 261
Cheiron, 211, 297, 403 ; the centaur, one of the first two practitioners of medicine
Chrysippus, quoted, 89 ; Stoic philosopher, *circa* 280–207 B.C.
Chthonic Goddesses, 211
cicadas, 153, 297
Cicero, 121 ; the Roman orator, 106–43 B.C.
cider, 221
Cimon, 337 ; Athenian general
Cithaeron, 101
Clearchus, 53 ; Spartan officer with Xenophon's Ten Thousand, lived *circa* 450–401 B.C.
Cleinias, 249 ; Pythagorean
Cleomenes, 501 ; physician, friend of Plutarch
Clymenê, 325
Clytomedeus, 165 ; Nestor's opponent in boxing
cock, 43, 65, 253, 355
coition, 71, 239 ff., 243 ff.
Colias, 397 ; promontory in Attica
comedy, 327, 333, 377, 395
Concerning Drunkenness, 227 ; work by Aristotle
conger eel, 343

519

INDEX

INDEX

Eileithyia, 277 ; epithet of Artemis

elephant, 175

Eleusis, 141

Elis, 317

Elpistics, 345 ; philosophers of hope

emanations (effluences), 421 f., 425, 431, 433 ; rheumata

Empedocles, 225 ; quoted, 39, 209, 223, 311, 401, 435, 439, 449, 463 ; philosopher, fifth century B.C.

envy, 425 ff.

Epaminondas, 41, 133, 417 ; Theban statesman and general, *circa* 420–362 B.C.

Ephemerides, 71 ; royal *Journal* of Alexander the Great

Ephyra, 399 ; identified with Corinth

Epicurean, 141, 145 ; — philosophers, 373, 377, 379, 381

Epicurus, 7, 141, 237, 243 ff., 255, 257 ; the philosopher of Samos and Athens, 342–271 B.C.

epithymides, 215

Erasistratus, 313, 329, 475 ; of Ceos, eminent physician and scientific researcher, third century B.C.

Erato, 203, 207, 217, 221 ; young musical friend of Plutarch

Eryximachus, 13 ; a friend of Socrates

Eryxis, 343

Ethiopians, 207, 483

etymology and linguistic usage, 23, 159 ff., 179, 211 ff., 217, 229, 301, 321, 325, 331, 339, 353, 363, 365, 387, 401 ff., 433 ff., 437 f., 439, 445, 447, 463, 489, 491, 497, 501 f., 507 ff.

Euboea, 271 ; Hera's nurse

Euboea, Euboeans, 337, 393

eulogies, 65

Eumelus, 37 ; the Homeric hero

Euphorion, 399, 427 f. (quoted) ; the poet

Eupolis, quoted, 307 f.

Euripides, 15 ; quoted, 7, 25, 61, 63, 113, 115, 189, 193, 299, 303, 325, 331 ; Athenian playwright, *circa* 484–406 B.C.

Eutelidas, 429, 431

Euthydemus, C. Memmius, 271 ; a friend of Plutarch

evil eye, 417, 421 ff.

Evius, 363 ; god of the cry = Dionysus

fast(ing) or "feast" : — of the Jews, 363 f.

fennel, 5

Festivals, *see* Games ; *cf.* 363, 365

field-mouse, 353

figs, 13, 169, 175, 341, 439, 511 f.

fine arts, 325, 381 f., 425

fir, 169 ff., 219

fire, 329

Firmus, 145, 147, 151 ; friend of Plutarch

fish, 89, 174, 175, 189, 337 ff. ; *see* animals

Florus, Mestrius, 87, 227, 231, 233, 237, 417, 427, 431, 441 ff. ; influential Roman friend of Plutarch

flour, 277

flowers, *see* plants

food, *see* diet

foot-race, 161, 163 ff.

Forum Romanum, 291

fox, 19, 21, 77

frankincense, 71

friendship, 291

frogs, 153

fruit(s), 141, 143, 173, 207, 243 ; *see also* plants

fuels, 275

Gaius, 431 ; son-in-law of Mestrius Florus

Games (*see also* Isthmian, Nemean, Olympia, Pythian) : 375 (entertainment at table, etc.), 379 (for children), 383 ff., 387 (funeral games)

garlands, 203 ff.

garlic, 175

Gaul, 393

Genius, 259

German tribes, 483

Glaucias, 95, 99, 101, 141 ; Athenian rhetor and friend of Plutarch

goats, 217, 307

Gobryas, 109, 111 ; friend and relative by marriage to Cyrus the Elder

INDEX

523

INDEX

Mithridates, 72, 73 ; the Great, king of Pontus

Mitylenê, 129

Moeragenes, 361 ; of Athens

moonlight, 271 ff.

Moschion, 271, 273 ; friend of Plutarch

mulberries, 169

mullet, 355

Muses, 13, 139, 203, 209, 453

music, musical instruments, musicians, 9, 67, 95 ff., 107, 129, 137, 199, 203, 267 ff., 293, 301, 305, 329, 335, 343, 363, 365, 368, 385 ; *see also* singing

mussels, 39

Myconos, 29 ; Aegean island

myrtle, 23, 169, 223

Mysoi, 203 ; play by Agathon

Mysteries, 5 (at Ephesus) ; 57 (at Eleusis) ; 361 (Panteleia)

Mytilenê, 129

naphtha, 422-423

narcissus, 211

narthex, 5 ; fennel-stalk

Nausicaä, 89, 93 ; Phaeacian princess

Neanthes, 97, 99 ; of Cyzicus ; a historian of third century B.C.

Neleus, 119 ; father of Nestor

Nemea, 397, 399 ; in Argolis, seat of Games

Nemean Games, 399, 401

Nestor, 113, 119, 163 ; king of Pylos

Nicaea, 261

Niceratus, 401 ; of Macedon ; friend of Plutarch

Nicopolis, 339 ; near Actium

Niger (Nigros), 487 ; friend of Plutarch

Nile, the, 353, 355

Niobê, 483

nurses, 375

Nymphs, 13, 101

oaks, 169, 175

Octavius, 121 ; of Libya; acquaintance of Cicero

Odysseus, 17, 93, 113, 115, 165, 181, 403, 405

Odyssey, see Homer

Oedipus, 115, 127 ; son of Laïus ; king of Thebes

Oenops, 165

Oeolycus, 385 ; of Thessaly

oil, 171, 175, 219, 237

old men, 55, 77 ff., 81 ff., 165, 227 ff., 241, 457

olive, 169, 219, 275, 317

Olympia, 163 ; Games, 389

Olympichus, 243, 249, 251 ; friend of Plutarch

Olynthian, 71

Onesicrates, 407 ; physician

onion, 313, 317

Opening of Jars, 258 ; Pithoigia so interpreted

opson, 339, 343, 345

Orestes, 11, 185 ; son of Agamemnon and Clytemnestra

Orphic(s), 145, 149

Palaemon (Melicertes), 391, 399

Pammenes, 41 ; of Thebes

pancratiasts, 161, 163

Panteleia, 361 (Perfect Mysteries)

Paris, 255 ; prince of Troy

Parmeno, 383 ; the mimic

parties (symposia), 293, 373 ; *see also* banquets, etc.

Pasiades, 131

passages, or pores, 213, 215, 221, 225, 459, 471, 477, 505, 509

Patras, 111

Patrocleas, 181, 425 ; Plutarch's relative by marriage

Patroclus, 163, 387, 401, 403 ; Achilles' friend

Paullus, Aemilius, 27 ; victor in Third Macedonian War, 168 B.C.

Pausanias, 13 ; friend of Socrates

pears, 169

Pelias, king of Iolcus, 387

Periander, 24 ; tyrant of Corinth

Pericles, 51, 53 ; Athenian statesman, 495-429 B.C.

Peripatetic(s), 7, 84, 141

Perseus, 27 ; king of Macedon, ruled 179-168 B.C.

Persians, 9, 45, 109, 111

Petraeus, L. Cassius, 385

Phaeacians, 165

Phaedrus, 19 ; Roman fabulist, *circa* 15 B.C.-*circa* A.D. 50

Phaedrus, 13 ; Socratic philosopher, *circa* 450-400 B.C.

Phaëthon, 325

Phanocles, 359 ; elegiac poet

INDEX

INDEX

INDEX

527

INDEX

Printed in Great Britain by R. & R. Clark, Limited, *Edinburgh*